Roman Alcester Series

Volume 1

ROMAN ALCESTER: SOUTHERN EXTRAMURAL AREA
1964–1966 Excavations

PART 2: FINDS AND DISCUSSION

Roman Alcester Series

Volume 1

ROMAN ALCESTER: SOUTHERN EXTRAMURAL AREA
1964–1966 Excavations

PART 2: FINDS AND DISCUSSION

edited by Stephen Cracknell and Christine Mahany

with contributions by
Don Bailey, Justine Bayley, Paul Booth, Richard Brickstock, P J Casey, P W Clogg, Sally Cottam, John Crossling, C B Denston, Brenda Dickinson, Jeremy Evans, Rowan Ferguson, Pedro Funari, A J Gouldwell, B R Hartley, K F Hartley, Martin Henig, Frances Lee, Gerda Lindquist, Joan Liversidge, G Lloyd-Morgan, Gerry McDonnell, D F Mackreth, Quita Mould, P J Osborne, Hedley Pengelly, Jennifer Price, Stephanie Ratkai, Val Rigby, V Snetterton-Lewis, A H V Smith, J H Thornton, Roberta Tomber, and D F Williams

CBA Research Report 97
Council for British Archaeology
1994

Published 1994 by the Council for British Archaeology
Bowes Morrell House, 111 Walmgate, York YO1 2UA

British Library Cataloguing in Publication Data
A catalogue for this book is available from the British Library

ISSN 0141 7819

ISBN 1 872414 42 7

Typeset from authors' discs by Archetype, Stow-on-the-Wold

Printed in Great Britain at Adpower, Halifax

The publishers acknowledge with gratitude a grant from
English Heritage towards the publication of this report.

Front cover *Caravsivs et fratres svi* coin
Back cover Headstud brooch from site E

Contents

List of illustrations

Text

Microfiche

List of tables

Text

Microfiche

List of Plates

Text

List of microfiche

Summary

The 1964–6 excavations at the Roman small town of Alcester, Warwickshire (NGR SP090575), were directed by Christine Mahany for the Ministry of Public Buildings and Works. The work was concentrated on the southern extramural area at Birch Abbey, where a housing estate was due to be constructed. There were also investigations of the town defences (sites K and M) and one excavation in the northern extramural area (site L). The results are reported in two monographs, Parts 1 and 2.

Part 1 describes the background to the excavations and the stratigraphy and structures found on the sites. It contains a discussion of the structures and their layout, and includes a review of work in the town up to December 1989.

The earliest 1st-century structures were located in the northern part of the site and there was an extensive enclosure system to the south. Subsequently, occupation was most intensive on either side of the main east–west through route. From the late 2nd or early 3rd century onwards a large area in the central part of the site was used for gravel quarrying with the dumping of rubbish in the worked-out pits. In the late 2nd to mid-3rd century a substantial east–west ditch was dug along the base of the river terrace but it was backfilled before the end of the 3rd century. During the 4th century, developments on all parts of the site were complex.

A wide variety of structures was recovered, including native-type huts and enclosures, timber buildings, and buildings incorporating stone foundations. A total of 56 human burials was represented on the site.

The settlement at Alcester may have originated in the context of early Roman military activity although there was no evidence for this from the Birch Abbey sites. The street pattern was irregular. The defences, investigated on site M, only enclosed about one-fifth of the built-up area. There was a large store building and a possible market place outside the defences.

This volume, Part 2, reports on the finds recovered and brings together all the information from the excavations to interpret the economy of the site and its context. The pottery report is based on the type series laid down whilst the excavations were in progress. The printed part of the report consists of an illustrated corpus of vessel types divided into broad fabric groups, separate sections on the samian, *amphorae*, graffiti, and *mortaria*, and a discussion. The microfiche contains a table showing which features contained pottery similar to the illustrated examples; an illustrated corpus of four significant pit groups; and short notes on the petrography of Severn Valley ware and the capacity of Severn Valley tankards.

Of the **coarse pottery** types, the Black-Burnished ware seems fairly typical of a site with continuous occupation from the 2nd century. Reduced coarse wares as a whole comprise 50% of the recorded pottery, with oxidized wares making up 33%, largely comprising Severn Valley ware. Despite this relatively high percentage, Alcester lies near to the edge of the Severn Valley ware distribution. The Oxfordshire industry seems to have been the predominant fine ware supplier at Alcester throughout its fine ware production period whereas Nene Valley wares are not well represented, despite the lack of any major fine ware competition between AD 170 and 240.

The **graffiti** on the pottery exhibit a number of strikingly unusual features being mainly confined to coarse wares and concentrated on one site, G. One pot had a dedication to the goddess Epona.

The site **samian** list suggests that the town was founded in the AD 60s. In terms of annual losses, the Central Gaulish peak is much stronger than the South Gaulish one which agrees with the structural evidence showing that the development of the site was more intensive in the Hadrianic–Antonine period than in the 1st century. One pit group contained 69 vessels, many complete. However, samian supply seems to have declined early, from AD 170, despite the ample evidence for continued occupation.

In the 1st and 2nd centuries ***mortaria*** reached Alcester from a wide variety of sources. The principal early suppliers, North-East Gaul and the *Verulamium* region began to be replaced by Mancetter/Hartshill towards the middle of the 2nd century with the Oxfordshire region becoming important slightly later.

As might be expected in a site so remote from the coast, few ***amphorae*** fragments were recovered but one is worth special note. Found in a mid-2nd-century pit group, along with a large collection of complete samian bowls and several glass vessels, this *amphora* was inscribed before firing and painted at two points in a cursive script. One of the *tituli picti* might be a number; the other was originally published as 'prime extract of mackerel' but this reading is now disputed.

Other reported ceramics include three Iron Age sherds from site M, medieval pottery associated with the drying kiln, and a parchment ware lamp.

Metal artefacts include coins, brooches, copper alloy, iron, lead, and **pewter**, and there was also evidence for metalworking in the form of hearths, tools, iron slag, and crucibles. The 458 Roman and five 'Dobunnic' **coins** from the 1964–6 excavations are compared with the accumulated total of 1525 coins from the town as a whole. The coin loss pattern suggests inception of the Birch Abbey site about AD 60. It follows the well-established pattern for developing Romano-British towns apart from in the mid-4th century when there are more Constantinian III coins (period 24) and fewer Valentinianic (period 25 coins) than expected, a phenomenon which has been observed on other urban sites (Ravetz 1964). There are enough coins of the Theodosian II period to confirm occupation through to the end of the Roman era. One coin of Caurausius is of particular interest, having been made from a previously unrecorded die. (The microfiche contains XRF analysis of the Dobunnic coins and a complete list.)

The **brooches** are typical of west Midlands sites apart from the presence of the iron brooches including a *Kragenfibel*. The **copper alloy** objects include a wide range of bracelet types whilst the **iron** objects include stylii from site G and metalworking tools associated with the **slag** and smithy on site D. The presence of **crucibles** (analysed by XRF) confirms limited bronze-working and brass-working perhaps by itinerant workers on sites D and G. **Lead** scrap was found on several sites.

Bone was represented by animal bone, **worked bone**, and human bone. The **animal bone** from several pits was examined on site, with cow dominating the assemblage, followed by sheep/goat. The **human bone** consisted of 31 adult inhumations, 24 non-adult inhumations, and one cremation, an adult male buried with parts of a sheep/goat and a bird. The inhumations in this small sample showed most deaths at before 18 months and between 30 and 45 years.

Some **ecological remains** were studied. The **charred plant remains** associated with the medieval corn dryer were not particularly enlightening but the **insect remains** from the Roman pit F, the 'Leather Pit', included species indicating various lifestyles. The majority were insects which live in decaying organic refuse including those with a predeliction for the dung of grazing animals and grass cuttings. There were also indigenous and Mediterranean furniture beetles (the latter presumably arriving in imported wood), pests of stored grain, and possible bed bugs.

Building materials comprised burnt daub, wall plaster, **mortar** (not studied), tile, *tesserae*, wood, and stone (see stone objects). The bulk of the **burnt daub** came from site D and probably related to building DC. Decorated **wall plaster** was recovered from sites C, D, and G with buildings CEA, CEB, DB, GC, and GE being the most likely sources. Both hexagonal limestone and fired clay **tiles** are known from Alcester. One was stamped NI[, a stamp peculiar to the town. Hypocaust tile was found *in situ* on site L and there were also three fragments on site F; there was no indication of a hypocaust in the vicinity of the latter site. Eight white limestone ***tesserae*** were recovered. Preserved **wood** was found in several low-lying features but failed to survive.

Other finds consist of coal, **intaglios**, glass, leather, **jet**, **shale**, and stone. The **coal** originated in the north Warwickshire coalfield. The **glass** included a wide range of table wares and household wares but only two fragments of window glass. Most of the fragments were 1st or 2nd century in date, including the six or more vessels in the mid-2nd-century pit group D II 29A. A square bottle from this group incorporated the letters SAI on the base. Nearly one-tenth of the glass was melted bottles, much of it found in a context associated with metalworking debris but glassworking is not suspected. The **leather** comprised cutting scrap and parts of shoes.

The **stone** objects included a Constantinian milestone which had been reused in the wall of a building, two altars from a well on site B, whetstones, hones, a few fragments of tufa suggesting a hypocaust, and a number of grinding stones and quern stones. There were two notable groups of grinding/quern stones, one in the north-west corner of site D I and the other on A XIV. The latter group included a heavy millstone giving rise to one possible interpretation of the major east–west ditch (ditch A) as a mill leet.

A few of the post-Roman artefacts are reported (principally those connected with the drying kiln) but most were unstratified; information on these finds can be obtained from the site archive.

Tantalizing glimpses of the **economy and social activities** are afforded by some of the finds assemblages but most of the buildings are likely to have combined the functions of house/farm, shop, workshop, and warehouse. On **sites AA and C** the only substantial building, AA, was a complex structure of more than one build. There was a pit containing leather scraps, and it may be that building AA was a leather workshop. The main feature of the **site A trial trenches** was the millstone found on A XIV. **Site D** was initially occupied by enclosures (along with sites A, B, C, and H) and only intermittently occupied by buildings. The mid-2nd-century pit group, D II 29A, might be interpreted as a shopkeeper's stock. In the 4th century the site housed a smithy with copper alloy working and hand milling being secondary activities.

Sites E, F, J, and P, at the junction of streets A and C, contained a series of enigmatic structures, although the first (round) houses fall into the standard British pattern. An early double-quadrilateral enclosure was replaced by a series of dispersed booths and rectilinear buildings but there is nothing in the finds assemblage to confirm that these might have been associated with a postulated market place to the north. During the 4th century they were replaced by another cluster of buildings of uncertain use. It was not until after these buildings had themselves been demolished that significant numbers of finds, particularly coins, began to appear on the site.

The most interesting feature of **sites H, B I and B IA** was a well which contained two uninscribed altars and a variety of other rubbish which may be religious, iconoclastic, or merely domestic in nature. The **site B trial trenches** were twice as extensive as those on site A, yet fewer indications of occupation were recovered, showing that the south-west corner of the town was less densely populated than elsewhere.

Three of the five Dobunnic coins and four of the nine early iron brooches were found on **site G**, a reflection of probable 1st-century settlement to its north. Site G contained remarkable structures and an unusual collection of finds. Building GC was constructed with one wall supported on multiple posts — some in common pits — and the others supported on stone foundations. It was plastered. The structure was demolished and subsequently rebuilt on the same plan (building GE) incorporating the milestone of Constantine. Finds from the site included storage jars with graffiti, many coins, *amphorae*, stylii, and seal boxes. Although not all of these can be linked directly with buildings GC and GE the site seems to have been used at times for storage and perhaps trade and was also a 'focus' of literacy.

The main feature of the **site L trial trenches** was a building containing a hypocaust, with finds of *tesserae* and *opus signinum* indicating a substantial structure.

Discussion of the significance of the defences on **site M** is reserved for a future volume in the Alcester series although the finds are reported here.

Most of the finds from the Birch Abbey sites date to the first two centuries AD although many of the structures are later. There were twelve objects with military associations but these were distributed over the whole site and do not indicate any military focus. The town had economic connections with a wide area although it lay near the western edge of the more Romanized 'lowland' Britain. The origins of some of the artefacts and their parallels may indicate a Dobunnic influence but the case is not yet proven.

Acknowledgements

The excavations and post-excavation work to 1986 were directed by Christine Mahany. Stephen Cracknell took on the co-ordination of the project on behalf of the Warwickshire Museum in 1989.

The excavations were funded by the Ministry of Public Buildings and Works, with the post-excavation funded by the Department of the Environment, the Manpower Services Commission, and English Heritage.

A J Gouldwell would like to record his thanks to Mr Russell Heath for assistance in the laboratory, and to Mr G C Morgan of the Department of Archaeology, University of Leicester for advice on some of the charcoal samples. Don Mackreth is grateful to Mrs M E Snape for giving permission to use her M Phil thesis on the brooches from the Stangate forts. Frances Lee and Gerda Lindquist wish to thank Alastair and Anne Anderson, Paul Booth, Cherry Goudge, Rob Perrin, Helen Rees, John Samuels, Roberta Tomber, Graham Webster, and Chris Young for their advice and encouragement. Jeremy Evans wishes to thank Paul Booth for his advice in connection with the pottery discussion and Elizabeth Wright for her generous comments on the draft of the stone report. Richard Brickstock and John Casey are very grateful to Mr W Seaby for his kind permission to use his unpublished Alcester coin records in this study.

The illustrations were drawn by Richard Langley, Christine Mahany, Stephen Taylor, and Steve Rigby. The photographs were taken by Trevor Woods and Robert Wilkins.

Introduction to Part 2

This part of the report on the 1964–6 excavations at Alcester discusses the finds and the significance of the excavations as a whole. It is divided into major sections dealing with the ceramics, metal artefacts, bone and bone products, ecological remains, building materials, other finds, and a general discussion. The illustrations, descriptions of the illustrated items, and discussions of the assemblages appear in print; the complete catalogues and detailed tables appear in microfiche. In some cases, where nearly all the objects are illustrated (eg brooches), the whole catalogue appears in print. There are several pit groups containing large quantities of coarse pottery. These pots are illustrated in the pottery corpus in print and for convenience are brought together in a special microfiche section. Tables and figures prefixed 'M' are to be found in the microfiche.

A single series of catalogue numbers has been used for both the printed and microfiche reports with the result that not all catalogue numbers appear in the printed section. The origin of the object on site is indicated in parentheses, for example (FE 278, G V 46, phase III?, 3rd/4th century) meaning (small find number, site trench context number, phase number (if allocated to a phase), date of phase).

The figures in square brackets, for example [M1:B7] or [p 178], at the beginning of each section indicate the location of supplementary material.

The report is the product of work undertaken in four separate decades and the individual sections reflect the changes in collection policy and reporting over that time. For example, in the 1960s it was common practice to study pottery on site and not retain the duplicated sherds afterwards. The sherds which *were* kept were re-examined in the early 1980s and again — to a lesser extent — in the early 1990s. The animal bone was the subject of a limited study on site but it was not retained. Details of the quantities of finds recovered and reported here can be found in table 1. The dating evidence is summarized in tables M1 and M8. Where the reports are more than about five years old this is noted in the text.

Most of the post-Roman objects were unstratified and, with the exception of those associated with the medieval drying kiln, are not reported here. Further details of these are available in the site archive which together with most of the finds is stored in Warwickshire Museum. The human bone is stored by the Department of Anthropology, Cambridge University.

Table 1 Summary table of finds excavated and reported

Type of material	No of items excavated	No of items reported	Print	Micro	Figs	Comments
Pottery						
Roman coarse pottery	*c* 70,000? *c* 5,000 'min vessels'	1172 types	3	M1:A6	1–43, 56–60	'Min vessels' — see definition in report. Mostly discarded on site
Samian	–	2918+ vessels	93		44–53	latest decorated vessel in context/pieces of intrinsic interest: *c* 300. Potters' stamps: 48.
Amphorae	*c* 34 'min vessels'	19 sherds	120		54, 55	Includes *tituli picti*
Mortaria		565 sherds	132	M2:C4	61–5	
Pottery and ceramic small finds	–	82	150	M2:C13	68, 69	
Iron Age pottery	–	3 sherds	153		70	From site M
Post-Roman pottery	–	183 sherds	154		71	Presumably sampled only
Metal artefacts						
Coins	488 small finds	463 Roman plus 22 later	157	M2:F5	72–4, plate 1	
Brooches		95	163		75–81	Includes 9 iron brooches
Copper alloy (ex brooches)	418	356	177	M3:D12	82–92	'Missing' objects probably mostly unidentifiable fragments.
Iron objects	415 small finds	550+	195	M4:A4	93–7	
Iron nails	–	2065	195	M4:A4	–	Presumably sampled only
Iron slag	–	27.5kg	206	M4:C12	–	Sample only retained
Crucibles		5	206		98	
Lead objects	31 small finds	8 Roman	206	M4:D1	99, 100	0.9kg scrap
Bone and bone products						
Animal bone	–	–	211		–	Discarded on site; summary report of limited samples
Worked bone	100 small finds	98	211	M4:D4	101–2	
Human bone	56 individuals	56 individuals	215	M4:E3	–	Stored at Dept of Anthropology, Cambridge
Ecology						
Botanical remains	131 soil samples	5	217	M4:G12	–	Only samples associated with drying kiln studied
Insects	1 sample	1 sample	217		–	
Building materials						
Daub	–	from 18 contexts	221		–	
Decorated wall plaster	–	from 69 contexts	221	M5:A3	–	No longer extant
Mortar	58 samples				–	Not studied; largest group (19) from G
Tile	–	9	222		103	Sample only retained; includes IN[stamp
Tesserae	–	3	222		–	white limestone
Wood	33	33	222	M5:A7	–	No longer extant, described from site notes
Other finds						
Coal	63 samples	5	223	M5:A9	–	?North Warwickshire coalfield
Intaglios	3	3	223		plate 2	
Glass	296 small finds	198 small finds	224	M5:A13	104–5	42+ vessels reported; some missing
Leather	7	7	229		106	
Jet and shale	12	10	229		107	
Stone objects	*c* 95 small finds	88	231	M5:B11	108–19	

(Note: where possible the 'number of items excavated' is derived from site records)

Romano-British coarse pottery

Frances Lee and Gerda Lindquist, with Jeremy Evans

Introduction

[M1:A6] The pottery report for Birch Abbey was written during 1982/3, and while some dates and parallels have been updated the majority of the report stands as it was originally written.

The Alcester type series was originally laid down by Trevor Miles while the excavations were in progress, and has needed some alteration in the light of more recent research. Due to the method of recording it was not possible to make any radical change but the series as set down here incorporates all the differentiations that could be made through visual inspection.

The cataloguing system for the Birch Abbey pottery was organized in the following manner. As each sherd of pottery came from the site it was given a letter-and-number code, the letters indicating the fabric types, the numbers indicating different forms within the fabric (hence BC 26 indicated a jar, form 26, in a hard, grey, sandy fabric, BC). The first or most complete specimen of each kind became the type sherd. Other examples of the same vessel type and fabric were recorded using the type number and then discarded.

In addition a catalogue was made of all the contexts in which a particular type was found. With this system it was theoretically possible to see all the types found in a specific context. Conversely all contexts in which a given form was found were available. By grouping sets of type-series or context cards it was also possible to consider all the relationships of any individual sherd or context on the site, as a check on the residuality of sherds or on unreliable contexts.

Clearly the authors were not able to verify the fabrics for the discarded material where subdivisions were made. There is therefore an implicit assumption that the absent sherds were the same as the type series.

Nor was it possible to attempt any valid statistical analysis in the absence of much of the pottery. However some indication of the relative proportions of fabric groups was deemed useful. Therefore *tentative*, or approximate, percentages are given based on the total number of sherds recorded for specific fabric groups. Tables illustrating the distribution of forms and fabrics across the sites are available in the site archive. All of these statistics provide no more than a general indication of frequency and should not be used in comparison with more reliably quantified data.

All the pottery within the type series has been illustrated, except in cases where the sherd is so small as to render the illustration less useful than the description. In addition selected groups have been discussed and illustrated separately (microfiche M2:A1).

The dating of the Birch Abbey pottery has been taken from two sources, first from the kiln sources and other sites, and second from the internal evidence. Where parallels have been taken from other sites the date is given for the parallel, copy, or imitation of the well-dated form. This date does not, however, refer to the date of the sherd's introduction or termination from the site. Other established dates are derived from the samian, *mortaria*, inscriptions, brooches, and numismatic evidence.

The internal evidence relies on dating from the contexts and phase associations on the site, and is aided by several pit groups which are well sealed, offering *terminus ante quem* dates. In some cases, dates have been arrived at for the group as a whole, enabling the group forms to be used for dating when found in other contexts.

Classification of Romano-British coarse pottery

The main classification of the pottery is based on variations in fabric. A binocular microscope with a magnification of 20× was used, taking into account the proportion and type of temper, the colour and conditions of firing, and the specialist treatment. The corpus is thus divided into three major groups: reduced, red oxidized, and white wares. Within these are the subcategories reduced Black-Burnished wares, red oxidized colour-coated wares, and white colour-coated wares. The type series is described in detail in the corpus of pottery. Within each class the individual fabric types are noted, with the number of vessels expressed as a percentage of the total pottery assemblage.

Where a directly equivalent Warwickshire Museum fabric class exists this has been noted at the end of the fabric descriptions.

Classification of local wares

Coarse wares, probably local in origin and produced for the home market, represent the bulk of the pottery assemblage at Alcester, with approximately 73% of the vessels on the site in this group. These are presumed to have been produced within a 40–50km radius.

The main clays which would have been available to the local potters were the iron-rich clays of the Severn and Avon valleys, which were used to produce the grey ware and coarse oxidized Severn Valley vessels. The finer, white, iron-free clays came from further afield, with identified vessels from the Oxfordshire and Mancetter/Hartshill areas.

The reduced wares are all utilitarian vessels and are limited in their distribution.

The Severn Valley wares, on the other hand, have a common family of forms and decorative techniques, and were produced in a number of kilns throughout the Severn basin. At present it is not possible to establish exactly where the Alcester vessels were manufactured.

Cross-references to the illustrated sherds can be found under each group heading. In addition, a list at the end of the catalogue of illustrated vessels tabulates the same information, but in catalogue number order, thus enabling the reader to work back from the illustrations to the appropriate fabric groups.

Local coarse wares

Group 1: sandy wares

These occur in the reduced fabrics BC, BD, BE, BH, BU, BX, CJ, CS, CT and DY, and as the oxidized fabrics BJ, CK, CM, DEA, DIA, DJ, DR, DS, DU, DX, DZ, DZA, and FB representing c 41% of the assemblage (for fabric descriptions see 'Corpus', p 12). (Illustration nos R.11–R.22, R.27–R.31, R.115–R.150, R.164, R.173–R.220, R.230–R.240, R.245–R.252, R.254–R.268, R.271, R.280–R.282, R.292–R.296, R.299–R.300, R.304, R.307–R.310, R.320, R.322–R.326, R.330, R.332–R.336, R.343–R.347, R.350, R.352–R.353, R.356, R.358–R.375, R.377–R.379, R.382–R.385, R.395–R.398, R.406–R.418, R.422–R.423, R.428–R.434, R.440–R.443, R.445–R.446, R.449, R.452–R.454, R.458–R.461, R.465–R.479, R.482, R.484–R.488, O.10–O.20, O.25–O.33, O.40–O.42, O.46, O.63–O.73, O.76, O.79–O.81, O.125–O.129, O.136–O.141, O.148–O.149, O.153–O.154, O.157, O.159–O.160, O.164–O.171, O.175–O.176, O.182–O.192, O.201–O.209, O.215–O.216, O.225–O.226, O.229–O.235, O.239, O.241–O.244, O.249, O.252, O.255, O.257, O.272–O.285, O.288–O.290, O.293, O.307–O.313, O.316–O.318, O.320, O.323–O.331, O.333–O.339, O.342–O.344, O.354–O.355, O.376–O.378, O.382–O.384, O.386–O.387, O.392–O.393, O.395, O.400–O.401, O.406–O.407, O.409, O.429–O.431, O.433, O.437–O.438, O.440–O.443, O.448, O.452, O.454, O.459–O.460.)

This group of vessels is moderately hard-fired and characterized by its use of sand temper, predominantly in the form of inclusions of quartz and quartzite. They are all wheel-made, and occur in both oxidized and reduced fabrics, with the colour range varying from the grey BC and black CT fabrics to the orange and reddish-brown Severn Valley wares, fabrics DEA, DIA, and DZ.

There is a great variety of forms, all of which are utilitarian although the Severn Valley potters also produced characteristic Roman types, for example flagons, while the grey wares were produced exclusively in traditional forms. This group shows many common decorative features, with the strongest influences coming from the Severn Valley and Black-Burnished ware potters. The vessels from group 1 are those regarded as likely to have been made from clay resources found within 50km of Alcester. Unfortunately there is little evidence for the location of kilns in the area.

Group 1a: white sandy wares

This is a subdivision of group 1 based on the use of the iron-free clays (as opposed to the iron-rich clay) and includes fabrics AB and ED, accounting for a very small proportion of the assemblage, approximately 0.5%. (Illustration nos W.1, W.5–W.7, W.12–W.13, W.16, W.24–W.25, W.43–W.46.)

These are hard, sandy wares tempered with abundant inclusions of quartz and with red and black grits occurring frequently. All of the vessels are wheel-made and are usually white to cream in colour, although fabric AB is generally fired to a pink core. The vessel types are limited to the coarser table wares including flagons, jugs, beakers, and bowls. These vessels are thought to have originated from the iron-free clays found in the Mancetter/Hartshill area, 45km to the north of Alcester. (Warwickshire Museum fabric W12.)

Group 2: vessels with a fine clay matrix and no visible inclusions

Reduced fabrics BA, BF, BG, BK, BN, BR, and the oxidized fabrics CH, DG, DI, DK, DV, EC, EJ, EH, FA, and FD, representing c 10% of the total pottery assemblage. (Illustration nos R.1, R.4–R.10, R.23–R.24, R.26, R.32–R.35, R.113–R.114, R.151–R.163, R.165–R.172, R.221–R.223, R.228–R.229, R.241–R.244, R.253, R.269–R.270, R.272–R.277, R.279, R.283–R.290, R.297–R.298, R.301, R.303, R.305, R.311–R.314, R.327–R.328, R.331, R.337, R.348–R.349, R.354–R.355, R.357, R.376, R.381, R.394, R.399–R.405, R.419–R.421, R.424–R.425, R.438–R.439, R.444, R.447–R.448, R.451, R.455–R.457, R.462, R.489, O.35–O.36, O.74–O.75, O.82, O.152, O.155, O.158, O.195–O.196, O.210, O.217–O.224, O.227–O.228, O.236, O.250–O.251, O.256, O.286, O.291–O.292, O.314–O.315, O.319, O.332, O.356, O.363, O.379, O.385, O.390–O.391, O.402, O.404, O.408, O.432, O.444, O.450, O.457, O.458.)

Preliminary macroscopic examination showed that although the clay matrix for these vessels was essentially similar to that in group 1, the use of temper was quite different, with few or no identifiable inclusions, compared with the abundant usage of subangular quartzite in group 1. All of the vessels are wheel-made, with the colour range spanning light to dark grey and buff to a reddish-brown. The texture varies from hard to soft and soapy. The vessel types are similar to group 1, with the main utilitarian grey ware and a few of the Severn Valley forms present including jars, tankards, and bowls with rough-cast jars in fabric FA in addition. The clays are thought to have been found in the proximity of Alcester and were probably used to fabricate vessels for the local market.

Group 3: metamorphic rock-tempered wares

Reduced fabrics CCC and CCF, representing c 3.1% of the total assemblage. (Illustration nos R.36–R.37, R.41, R.69–R.95, R.386–R.393, R.480–R.481.)

This group is characterized by the use of angular metamorphic rock fragments as a method of tempering. All of these vessels are hand-made in reduced fabrics which are black to a warm brown in colour. Typologically these vessels are heavily influenced by the Black-Burnished tradition both in form and decorative techniques employed. The most common forms are the cooking vessels, in particular the tubby cooking pots, coarse bowls, and dishes with decoration in the form of burnished lines and lattices.

The metamorphic inclusions are consistent with those identified from the narrow ridge of the Malvern Hills or in their immediate vicinity, 40km to the west of Alcester (Peacock 1968a). (Warwickshire Museum fabric G44.)

Group 4: angular limestone-tempered wares

Fabric CCE accounting for c 0.4% of the total assemblage. (Illustration nos R.38–R.40, R.96–R.102.)

The vessels are similar to those in group 3 excepting that they are tempered with angular limestone fragments rather than metamorphic rock. The vessels, with two exceptions (illustrations nos R.39 and R.101), are all hand-made. The fabric is moderately hard and extremely crumbly, with a fairly open matrix. The colour ranges from black to a warm brown. Typologically these vessels are identical to group 3. They are well finished with a smooth surface disguising the coarse nature of their matrix and temper. Tubby cooking pots, coarse bowls, and pie dishes are the most common forms, imitating the Black-Burnished tradition in vessel form and decoration. The distinctive vessel form and fabric suggests an origin in the immediate vicinity of the Malvern Hills, with an Antonine date for their production (Peacock 1968a).

Group 5: fine limestone-tempered wares

Fabric DE accounting for c 11.4% of the total pottery assemblage. (Illustration nos O.2–O.9, O.21–O.24, O.34, O.44–O.45, O.51–O.62, O.119–O.124, O.130–O.135, O.142–O.147, O.150–O.151, O.161–O.163, O.177–O.181, O.197–O.200, O.213–O.214, O.237–O.238, O.248, O.254, O.258, O.264–O.271, O.297–O.306, O.322, O.341, O.347–O.353, O.357–O.362, O.365–O.375, O.380–O.381, O.396–O.398, O.405, O.428, O.436, O.447, O.451, O.453, O.456.)

This group consists of the fine-textured Severn Valley ware (fabric DE) which has a clay matrix containing mica and moderate quantities of small subangular and angular quartz (approximately 0.005mm in size). The diagnostic features of this group are the abundant inclusions of subangular and rounded limestone (see Tomber below, p 131). All of the vessels are wheel-made in oxidized fabrics with the colour range varying from orange to red and with the vessel forms and decorative techniques common to the Severn Valley, including flagons, narrow-necked and wide-mouthed jars, tankards, beakers, and bowls. The presence of limestone suggests a source in Warwickshire with a number of outcrops known in the vicinity of Alcester. Chronologically these vessels appear to have been produced over a wide period of time spanning the Roman period. (Probably equivalent to Warwickshire Museum fabrics O25, O27, and O33.)

Group 6: shell-tempered wares

Fabric GA accounting for c 1.35% of the total pottery assemblage. (Illustration nos R.42–R.43, R.103–R.112, R.380, R.435–R.437.)

These vessels are wheel-made and distinguishable by the abundant use of shell temper. The fabric is friable with a relatively open matrix which is ideal for cooking purposes, having a high tolerance to thermal shock. The sherds are grey to a grey-brown in colour with frequent soot encrustation on the exterior and with a rough surface texture.

All of the vessel types were probably used for cooking, with the cooking pot and deep coarse bowl predominant. Generally these vessels appear in late Roman contexts at Alcester. (Warwickshire Museum fabric C11.)

Group 7: vesicular wares

Fabrics DA and GC accounting for c 5.5% of the total assemblage. (Illustration nos R.25, R.51–R.68, R.450, O.1, O.43, O.47–O.50, O.83–O.118, O.211–O.212, O.245–O.247, O.253, O.261–O.263, O.294–O.296, O.321, O.340, O.345–O.346, O.364, O.388–O.389, O.426–O.427, O.445–O.446, O.455.)

Vesicular wares originally contained carbonized organic fragments, and calcitic inclusions which have dissolved away. They contain a high proportion of fine quartz silt and mica with the occasional clay pellet or inclusion of grog. All of the vessels are wheel-made and hard-fired, with a range of oxidized and reduced states existing. The reduced examples are grey throughout while the oxidized ones are a light orange to buff with a heavy grey core. The most common form is the storage jar with fabric GC composed entirely of this form, while fabric DA also has examples of tankards, cups, and bowls. Parallels for the forms are to be found at Gloucester (Rawes 1972), but the inclusions of calcite suggest a more local source. The dating of group 7 is problematic as a result of the predominance of storage jars; the robust nature of these vessels results in their use over a significantly longer period than the other pottery types, indeed they may have been in constant use for anything up to a century after production. Their innate conservatism and long life-span make it difficult to assign definite starting and finishing dates for their production, but the contexts in which they are found would suggest that they were in use throughout the Roman period. (At least partly equivalent to Warwickshire Museum fabric R31, which ceases to be used after the 2nd century at Alcester.)

Group 8: grog-tempered ware

Fabrics GB and BW. This is a small group of only sixteen samples. (Illustration nos R.44–R.50, R.483.)

All the vessels are wheel-made. The fabric is reduced and moderately soft, fired to a grey core and frequently has an oxidized interior and exterior. The surface is rough in texture. A number of decorative techniques were employed including burnishing, incised comb lines and finger scallop decoration. All of the forms are storage vessels; their origins are unknown but they are probably local.

Group 9: coarse sandy colour-coated wares

Fabrics CI and DTA. This is a small group with only fifteen examples. (Illustration nos C.8–C.9, C.29, C.41–C.42, C.67, C.75–C.77.)

The fabrics are hard, coarse, and micaceous with abundant inclusions of quartz. There are two types of colour-coat represented, CI is black, while DTA is dark brown in colour. The vessel forms include jars, beakers, cups, and bowls with decorative techniques including burnishing, rouletting, and white paint. The exact origin of these vessels is unknown but probably they are the products of local colour-coated industries imitating the major late colour-coated producers. The vessels in fabric DTA would appear to have strong parallels in form to those from the Oxfordshire industry and are probably a coarse local imitation.

Local fine wares

Group 10: London-type ware

Fabrics BB, BBA, and CE, accounting for c 0.8% of the total pottery assemblage and c 15% of the fine wares. (Illustration nos R.224–R.227, R.278, R.291, R.302, R.306, R.315–R.319, R.321, R.338–R.342, R.351, R.426–R.427, R.463–R.464.)

Note: Fabric BB is *not* Black-Burnished ware, for which see fabric CB.

The vessels are wheel-made with a hard fabric containing varying amounts of small uniform quartz inclusions (fabric BB is almost sandless). The colour is essentially grey with darker surfaces burnished to a fine exterior. The vessels are characterized by their form, with incised lines, compass-drawn designs, rouletting, and clay slip. The forms include beakers, cups, carinated, and samian-derived bowls and dishes.

London ware itself is unlikely to have travelled so far from its production centre and a local manifestation of this type is thought to be responsible for the fine grey wares occurring at Alcester. The origins of London and London-type ware are not the result of a single influence, but are derived from a number of vessel types, the most influential of these being the samian forms and the Belgic potters' use of incised decoration and fine black fabrics (Marsh 1978). In date, London ware is limited to the early 2nd century, enjoying only a temporary success, possibly because there was not a sufficient market for fine grey wares, with the potters reverting to the production of more traditional forms by the end of the 2nd century. (Warwickshire Museum fabric R80.)

Group 11: fine oxidized wares

Fabric DW accounting for c 1.25% of the total pottery assemblage and 21% of the fine wares. (Illustration nos O.37–O.39, O.77–O.78, O.156, O.172–O.174, O.193–O.194, O.240, O.259–O.260, O.287, O.394, O.399, O.403, O.410–O.425, O.434–O.435, O.439, O.449, O.461.)

The vessels are all wheel-made with a hard, very fine sandy micaceous fabric. The colour ranges from light orange to red, frequently with a thin slip on the exterior and fired to a brown surface. The vessels are finely made and are all table wares. They include jars, bowls, cups, and dishes with the bowls originally derived either from samian or London ware types. The decorative techniques include the extensive use of burnishing and white paint. The precise origin of these vessels is unknown. The forms have their strongest parallels in the Oxfordshire industry, but the fabric is too coarse to suggest that these potters were the producers (C Young pers comm). This is probably a fine Severn Valley ware, possibly the product of a migrant potter from the Oxfordshire kilns.

Classification of non-local and imported wares

The term non-local refers to vessels which were produced outside the Alcester region and which would have travelled a distance of over 50km. The imported vessels are those originating on the Continent.

Non-local and imported wares account for approximately a quarter of the pottery assemblage at Alcester with around 74% of these accounted for by the coarse Black-Burnished vessels originating in Dorset. The fine table wares on the other hand form only a small proportion of the assemblage, approximately 6% including the local fine wares.

Non-local coarse ware

Group 12: Black-Burnished ware

Fabric CB accounting for c 18% of the total pottery assemblage. (Illustration nos B.1–B.75.)

This is essentially a hard, close-grained fabric with a high tourmaline content, heavily tempered with medium-grained quartz and chalky calcitic inclusions. All the vessels are hand-made with the colour varying from dark grey to black, although a reddish-grey layer is common beneath the black surface. The range of vessel types is limited; all are basic utilitarian forms with the majority composed of cooking pots, bowls, and dishes.

Heavy mineral analysis indicated that the Black-Burnished 1 from Birch Abbey was probably produced around Poole Harbour, with the tertiary sands being the source of the tourmaline (Peacock 1967). This is one of the largest fabric groups represented at Alcester accounting for 18% of the assemblage. The vessels date from *c* AD 120 to the later 4th century.

Non-local fine wares (excluding samian)

The term fine ware is used to define table wares and includes all the vessels which are free from visible added temper (especially when compared with the coarse utilitarian vessels). The majority of fine wares have all-over colour-coats, sometimes with additional barbotine, painted motifs, and impressed decoration. A simple classification is laid out here based on the macroscopic divisions. A distinctive source cannot be given for every class, but general areas of production are suggested, based on significant parallels. Where the fabrics are not distinguishable the division is made on the basis of form, but the general fabric group still applies.

The primary aim of this classification is to attempt to define as many regional sources as possible. Where applicable these classes have been dealt with chronologically and therefore illustrate the influences at work on the Romano-British potters.

Group 13: North Gaulish fabric 1 and British copies

Fabric DT. There are only twelve examples of this group. (Illustration nos C.12–C.21.)

The fabric is extremely hard, fine, with no visible inclusions, and covered by a blue-black colour-coat, frequently with wipe marks on the rim interior. All the vessels are wheel-made with the bag-shaped beaker, and its characteristic grooved cornice rim, the predominant form. A shoulder groove defines the upper extent of clay rough-cast decoration with the particle size dependent on the dimensions of the individual vessel. Their restricted repertoire is reflected in their short life-span, appearing on military and civilian sites in Britain during the late 1st and 2nd century. The definition of North Gaulish pottery has now been seriously questioned (Symmonds 1990) and it is not certain that there is a meaningful separation between this group and group 16, 'Colchester-type ware'.

Group 14: Rhenish ware

Fabric DO, with twenty examples from Alcester. (Illustration nos C.24–C.28, C.43–C.44.)

This fabric includes groups of vessels manufactured in central Gaul and Trier. Most types of Rhenish ware were made in both centres and it is frequently difficult to distinguish between the two. The Rhenish wares appearing in Britain are dated to the mid-2nd to mid-3rd century with central Gaulish wares possibly appearing earlier than those from Trier, which persisted until the 3rd century.

Central Gaul

Illustration nos C.26 and 28, 43 and 44.

Very fine wheel-made vessels in an orange fabric with inclusions of mica. The colour coat is a fine glossy black, frequently with a metallic lustre. The vessel types are dominated by beakers and cups with decoration in the form of fine rouletted lines and barbotine decoration.

Trier

Illustration nos C.24, C.25, C.27.

All the vessels are wheel-made with a very hard, fine, dark red fabric and a grey core. The colour coat is a fine glossy black with a high lustre. The predominant form is the beaker, with rouletted lines and indentations as typical forms of decoration.

Group 15: Cologne ware

This is represented by only one sherd at Birch Abbey, in fabric DN. (Illustration no CW.20.)

The fabric is fine, white, with no visible inclusions and covered with a black colour-coat. The main form in this ware is the beaker. The Birch Abbey sherd is a barbotine decorated body sherd with leaves and tendrils, and is presumably from a hunt cup. The plant motif was extensively used in the lower Rhineland, with a date for the Birch Abbey sherd in the late 2nd to 3rd century.

In Britain the distribution of this fabric is essentially eastern, its presence at Birch Abbey indicating a trading network from the east to the west of the country (Anderson 1980).

Group 16: Colchester-type ware

Fabric FE, represented by two type sherds. (Illustration nos C.22 and C.23.)

The vessels are wheel-made with a hard, fine, reddish-brown fabric and are covered with a self-coloured colour-coat, frequently with a metallic lustre. The forms are bag-shaped beakers with a cornice rim and clay particle rough-cast decoration. These vessels are related to the industries of eastern Gaul and the Rhineland and are probably the result of migrant potters from the samian workshops arriving in Britain.

These vessels have an Antonine date range at Birch Abbey.

It is no longer certain that this group can be separated from group 13 'North Gaulish fabric 1' (see Symonds 1990).

Group 17: Nene Valley ware

Fabric DM, representing 0.5% of the total pottery assemblage and 10% of the fine wares. (Illustration nos CW.1–CW.19.)

All of the vessels are wheel-made with a hard, white to off-white fabric. The range of colour-coats varies from a reddish-brown to black, invariably matt in texture. The forms include beakers (hunt cups and long elongated-necked vessels), samian-derived bowls, and Castor boxes. Typical decorative techniques are rouletting, barbotine, and white paint.

The origins of the Nene Valley potters are debatable. However, the diversified nature of their repertoire would seem to suggest a varied source of inspiration. Production in the Nene Valley began in the Antonine period but it was not until the decline in samian imports to Roman Britain that the potters began to expand their range of vessel forms for export, producing a range of table wares (Howe *et al* 1980). The earliest Nene Valley forms at Alcester are dated to the late 2nd century. During the 3rd and 4th centuries Nene Valley ware had a much wider distribution which is reflected in the increase in the number of vessels reaching the site.

Group 18: Oxfordshire and Oxfordshire-type wares

These vessels are in fabric DF and DHA, and possibly DQ, accounting for c 1% of the total pottery assemblage and c 18% of the fine wares. (Illustration nos C.3–C.7, C.10–C.11, C.30–C.33, C.38–C.40, C.45–C.64, C.68–C.69, C.72–C.73.)

The fabric is hard, sandy, and frequently micaceous, often with small red and black inclusions. The colour range is orange to reddish-brown, frequently with a grey core and with a colour-coat varying from an orange-red (DF) to a reddish-brown (DHA). The vessel forms are all wheel-made and limited but include flagons, beakers, and samian-derived bowls. The enclosed forms (for example flagons and beakers) have a high incidence of the use of brown colour-coat, while the open vessels, such as bowls, generally have an orange to red colour-coat; this is so consistent that it must have been a deliberate practice. The techniques employed by the Oxfordshire potters include the use of barbotine, rouletted, impressed, and white paint decoration.

By AD 240 the kilns were producing colour-coated vessels and they continued to do so throughout the 4th century (Young 1977). The earliest example from Birch Abbey is dated to the late 3rd century.

Group 19: fine white ware

Fabrics EB and BL accounting for c 1% of the total pottery assemblage and c 15% of the fine wares. (Illustration nos W.2–W.4, W.8–W.11, W.14–W.15, W.17–W.23, W.26–W.42, W.47–W.50.)

The vessels are all wheel-made with a hard, fine, white to off-white fabric, occasionally with a pinkish core. The matrix is tempered with fine sand and frequent small red and black inclusions. The exteriors of the vessels are generally well finished, with rouletting and red paint as typical forms of decoration. The vessels are typical table wares and include flagons, beakers, cups, bowls, and one example of a candlestick. These vessels originate from an iron-free clay source and parallels have been identified from both Oxfordshire and Mancetter, with both of these industries producing vessels which were reaching Alcester.

Group 20: South-Western brown slipped ware

Fabric DH. (Illustration nos C.1–C.2, C.34–C.37, C.65–C.66, C.70–C.71.)

The fabric is hard, micaceous, and has sand tempering. It is red in colour with a grey core and a colour-coat which varies from a reddish to a dark brown. The vessel types include flagons, beakers, and bowls with forms and decorative techniques paralleled in the Oxfordshire industry. In fact the types are so typical of the Oxfordshire potters that a migration may have been involved, with an enterprising potter producing within the Oxfordshire area of distribution. The fabrics identified as South-Western brown slip have parallels at Cirencester, dating to the 4th century. Cirencester Excavation Committee fabric 105B (J Richardson pers comm; Keeley 1986).

Typology: vessel form and function

The Alcester pottery is further classified into vessel forms based on the criteria of shape, form, and decorative techniques employed. As far as possible these follow the standardization of forms as outlined in the CBA guide to Romano-British coarse pottery (Webster 1969).

A number of 'seconds' were found at Birch Abbey, although there were no true wasters. These 'seconds' are so called because the vessels are misshapen rather than badly fired, but would still have been serviceable.

Reduced ware 'seconds' predominate, with conical rusticated jars (which are early in date) accounting for approximately 50% of the vessels. The few oxidized wares represented are in Severn Valley ware; the presence of both the reduced and oxidized wares would seem to suggest that although the 'seconds' may have travelled, they were probably produced in the vicinity of Alcester.

There are fifteen major typological groups with an additional category covering miscellaneous types. Whenever possible or applicable the volume and range of volumes of the pots has been calculated. The vessels are illustrated in figs 1–43.

Vessel types

Flagons

These occur in reduced fabrics BA, BC, BE, oxidized fabrics DA, DE, DEA, DK, and DW, colour-coated wares DH and DHA, and white fabrics AB, EB, and ED. (Illustration nos R.1–R.3, O.1–O.39, C.1–C.3, W.1–W.13.)

There are 115 examples of flagons with three broad categories: grooved rim, cupped mouth, and ring-necked flagons, with a further category for miscellaneous types. Approximately 90% of the Birch Abbey flagons are in Severn Valley fabrics, most of which are characterized by a chalky white slip on the exterior and a single-, double- or triple-ribbed handle. The volume of these vessels ranges from 0.96 litres (illustration no O.10) to 3.6 litres (illustration no O.22).

The larger flagons were most probably used as an intermediary vessel for decanting liquids from, for example, *amphorae*, rather than as table wares. They are also a convenient shape for the transport of liquids and may have held water for washing and cooking purposes. The smaller finer flagons, including the colour-coated vessels, were probably used as table wares for serving liquids such as water, wine, and oil. Flagons appear to be more popular than pottery jugs during the Roman period despite their handicap in pouring.

Jugs

These occur in Black-Burnished ware fabric CB, Severn Valley ware fabric DEA, and white wares fabrics EB and ED. (Illustration nos B.1, O.41–O.42, W.14–W.16.)

Pottery jugs are uncommon in Roman Britain, with only nine examples identified in this collection. From the two complete vessels an attempt was made to estimate the range of volume, with the bottom of the scale at 0.65 litres (illustration no O.41) ranging up to the top at 1.9 litres (illustration no B.1), although visually illustration W.16 would appear to have had a greater capacity. These vessels are produced in coarser fabrics than the flagons, but are essentially table wares.

Storage vessels

These occur in reduced fabrics BA, BC, BE, BF, BG, BM, CCC, CCE, CCF, GA, and GC, and in oxidized fabrics DA, DE, DEA, and DIA. (Illustration nos R.26–R.68, O.47–O.157.)

This is a broad general category incorporating the smaller narrow-necked and wide-mouthed containers, as well as the large coarse storage vessels. This is a functionally grouped category with 606 examples in total. There would appear to be some continuity in form and decorative techniques employed by the potters producing the reduced and Severn Valley narrow-necked jars and the large coarse storage vessels.

The use of pottery storage jars would have provided more protection from rodents than barrels, cloth sacks, and baskets. The narrow-necked vessels are in general smaller and finer than the other storage jars. Illustration R.16 is encrusted with soot suggesting that this form may also have been used for cooking purposes.

Some type of cover, possibly in cloth, leather, or wood, placed over the mouth of the vessels might have served as a lid. The wide-mouthed jars produced in the Severn Valley with their everted hooked rims would have been ideally suited for securing a cover.

Cooking pots

These occur in fabrics CCC, CCE, GA, and Black-Burnished ware CB. (Illustration nos R.69–R.112, B.2–B.29.)

These are fabrics with a fairly open matrix, which has a higher tolerance to heat than the denser grey wares. There are three major fabrics in which cooking pots predominate, with only a handful of vessels appearing in other fabrics. The majority of these vessels occur in Black-Burnished ware with 383 examples typologically classed as cooking pots, although only 116 have signs of having been used as such. The second group of cooking pots are those which are influenced by the Black-Burnished tradition, and comprise the Malvernian wares, with 152 examples. Finally there are the shell-tempered cooking pots with approximately 80 examples.

Where decoration occurs on these vessels it follows the Black-Burnished tradition with burnished rims and shoulders, and with the frequent use of acute or obtuse burnished lattices on the exterior.

Jars

These occur in most reduced and oxidized fabrics, as well as colour-coated fabrics CI, DF, and DN. (Illustration nos R.169–R.310, O.158–O.224, C.8–C.11, and CW.1–CW.2.)

This is the largest category and comprises a number of well-defined groups. All are utilitarian vessels with the only subdivision here being rusticated vessels, which predominate. Nevertheless there is a variety of other forms illustrated in the corpus of pottery, spanning the Roman period. Jars were primarily used as containers with their importance lying not so much in function, but in the substances they contained and the trade which this indicates.

Rusticated jars

These occur in fabrics BA, BC, BD, BE, BG, and BR. (Illustration nos R.113–R.168.)

These vessels are important in that they can be closely dated and show regional variations (as discussed in the corpus of reduced wares). There are two main vessel types: first, the conical rusticated jar and second, the globular or pear-shaped jar. The conical jars appear to be fairly consistent in size, with the radii in the region of 80mm and the heights approximately 160mm, with only a few deviating from this median. The capacity or volume is estimated to be between 1.42 and 1.53 litres, with one exception, an unusually small vessel with a capacity of 0.71 litres.

Rusticated jars are considered to have been used as cooking pots, although relatively few of the corpus show evidence of burning, with the rustication having both a decorative and practical function as the provider of a firm handhold.

Beakers

These occur in reduced fabrics BA, BB, and BC, in oxidized fabrics CM, DE, DEA, DI, DIA, DJ, DW, DZ, and DZA, colour-coated wares DF, DH, DHA, DO, DT, and FE, and in white wares BL, EB, ED, DM, and DN. (Illustration nos R.311–R.320, O.229–O.244, C.12–C.39, W.17–W.25, and CW.3–CW.13.)

There are approximately 100 examples, with the largest group of beakers occurring in the finer wares, in particular as colour-coated vessels, although coarse examples do occur in the reduced grey wares and Severn Valley fabrics.

In terms of fabric and form, beakers are the most diverse and easily identifiable table ware category and encompass the highest incidence of non-local vessels. The term beaker is used to define drinking vessels of a suitable size to hold in the hands. However, many of the forms described would not have been practical for this purpose and an alternative function is more probable.

Cups

These occur in reduced fabrics BB, BC, BD, BE, BG, BR, BU, and CJ, in oxidized fabrics DA, DE, DEA, DI, and DIA, in colour-coated fabrics CI and DO, and in white fabrics represented by fabric EB. (Illustration nos R.321–R.330, O.245–O.252, C.42–C.44, and W.26–W.27.)

There are 49 examples of cups with the majority occurring in oxidized fabrics. The main forms are the carinated and curved-wall vessels.

Tankards

These occur in reduced fabrics BA, BC, and BN, and in oxidized fabrics DA, DE, DEA, DIA, DK, DW, and DZ. (Illustration nos R.331–R.337, O.261–R.290.)

There are 443 examples of which over *c* 97% are in Severn Valley oxidized wares. The most common form is the straight-sided vessel with an incised groove immediately beneath the rim and with a double-ribbed handle. These vessels can be divided on the basis of volume, with the smaller vessels having a range of 0.28–0.62 litres and the larger vessels having a consistent range of 1.19–1.59 litres.

The larger tankards are unlikely to have been used for drinking, but were used more probably for household purposes; their consistency in size and their carrying capacity would seem to suggest that they were used as a form of measure for substances such as corn. In Roman metrology the range of these vessels is between 2.2 *sextarii* (the Roman equivalent to the pint) and 2.9 *sextarii*. An attempt was made to correlate the rim radii and the volume of the complete or quantifiable vessels. Unfortunately there were insufficient examples to illustrate a high correlation (and to draw accurate and reliable regression lines), but the results give a general outline of the values of the incomplete vessels (see tables M6 and M7).

The smaller tankards are by comparison infrequent.

Bowls

These occur in most reduced and oxidized fabrics. The colour-coated vessels are represented by fabrics DF, DH and DTA, and in white colour-coated fabric DM. The white wares are represented by fabrics EB and ED. (Illustration nos R.338–R.461, B.38–B.57, O.291–O.425, C.45–C.67, W.28–W.45, and CW.12–CW.13.)

This is the second largest category with over 1100 examples. There are many well-defined groups within the category which are outlined in the corpus of pottery. However, a distinction must be made between the coarse vessels and the fine table wares. The coarser bowls are utilitarian vessels and were presumably used predominantly for the preparation and mixing of food, with the deeper vessels possibly serving a similar function to casseroles. The shallower bowls and dishes may have been used for low-temperature heating. Evidence for this comes from a number of bowl forms with soot encrustation on the exterior, particularly those in the sandy fabrics BC and BE. The fine table wares were mostly produced in colour-coated wares with a few examples of London-type ware and fine Severn Valley vessels imitating samian forms.

Dishes

These occur in reduced fabrics BA, BB, BC, BD, BU, CS, and CT, in Black-Burnished ware fabric CB, and in oxidized fabrics DA, DE, DEA, DI, DIA, and DW. (Illustration nos R.462–R.471, B.58–B.75, O.426–O.435.)

There are 292 examples of dishes of which 272 are in Black-Burnished wares and are decorated accordingly.

Lids

These occur in reduced fabrics BC, BD, BE, CCC, and CT, oxidized fabrics CH, DA, DE, DIA, and DW, and colour-coated fabric DF. (Illustration nos R.472–R.482, O.444–O.450.)

There are 107 examples from Birch Abbey, almost all of which occur in the coarse grey and Severn Valley wares, with a few examples in Black-Burnished 1 and Malvernian ware. The dearth of compatible lids to vessels would seem to suggest that they may have been fabricated in another material (for example wood). They would have served as well as their ceramic counterparts and were possibly easier to produce.

Miscellaneous vessels

(Illustration nos R.483, O.436–O.443, W.46–W.47, and CW.14–CW.17.)

These examples include tazzas produced in Severn Valley fabric DEA and a coarse white ware example in fabric AB, triple vases (fabrics BW and DX), and a candlestick (fabric EB). There is also a 'skillet' (illustration no O.443), although there is no evidence that it was used as such. In the white colour-coated Nene Valley fabric (DM) there are a number of Castor boxes.

Discussion

The material examined covers a large period of time spanning the 1st to 4th centuries, with evidence for a variety of fabrics and vessel types suggesting that the site was using the products of a number of manufacturing centres.

The most important and the commonest vessels which are positively dated to this early period are the grey rusticated jars and the Severn Valley flagons with the flagons in particular illustrating the capacity of British potters to adopt specialist Roman forms. There are also a number of jar and bowl forms which were in use throughout the period of occupation, and undoubtedly some of these date to the earliest period at Alcester.

Unfortunately there is no evidence for kilns in the vicinity of Alcester, but the quantity of material in similar fabrics and forms, in particular grey rusticated jars, might suggest that these vessels were produced fairly locally, perhaps within a day's journey, *c* 16km radius of the site.

During the later 1st and early 2nd century, fine wares were traded alongside the samian, and were reaching Birch Abbey in the form of rough-cast colour-coated beakers.

In essence the 1st-century coarse pottery is seen to be local in origin, with vessels produced for the civilian settlement which had grown up in association with the established military fort, while the fine wares were supplied from the Continent.

The 2nd century was the period of greatest expansion of the town; indeed the fully developed road system probably dates to this time. During the earlier part of the century the demand for most of the fine wares continued to be met by the Continent, with samian and fine colour-coated vessels capturing most of the market. However, there was an attempt by one group of British potters to imitate these designs. This was initiated by the London ware potters manufacturing fine grey wares in and around London, with manifestations in other areas imitating the London ware forms, and probably being produced during a similar period. There is a notable quantity in this corpus, with the most plausible location for a production centre being the west Midlands. London and London-type ware probably filled a temporary gap in the samian supply, with the potters returning to their traditional forms when the supply of samian resumed (Marsh 1981).

The latter half of this century saw a broadening of fine ware types with imported fine, black, colour-coated beakers and cups produced in Central Gaul and the Rhineland appearing at Alcester. British colour-coated vessels were produced at Colchester, with forms heavily influenced by migrant potters from the samian factories. The Nene Valley industries also began producing a limited range of colour-coated vessels in this period. The earliest forms appearing on the site are the beakers and hunt cups which started to be manufactured in the late 2nd century.

Coarse pottery vessels in Black-Burnished fabric 1 appear in increasing numbers during the 2nd century and continue to feature in the pottery assemblage throughout the 4th century. The Black-Burnished 1 potters were producing on a much larger scale than the local potters with the production centre for the Alcester vessels based in Dorset close to Poole Harbour (Peacock 1967). BB1 may possibly have reached Alcester and the west Midlands by travelling up the navigable part of the river Severn.

Pottery production in the Malvern Hills, 40km to the west of Alcester, is known from the Iron Age, with Romano-British potters continuing the production of hand-made cooking vessels for both the civilian and military markets (Peacock 1968a). During the late 2nd century their repertoire widened to include Black-Burnished imitations with cooking pots, bowls, and dishes appearing in considerable quantities at Alcester.

The general picture for local wares during this period is one of growth and prosperity sufficient to establish the local industries and with an adequate market for them to have survived. This development is a reflection of the increasing demand from the civilian population for inexpensive cooking and kitchen wares. The late 2nd and early 3rd century was a period of general decline in Britain, with a fall in demand for fine wares and a decrease in buildings and coins dating to this period. This period also illustrates the sensitivity of the fine wares to fluctuations within the economy, with a notable absence of table wares at Alcester dating to this period. The major producers with a wide distribution in the 1st and 2nd centuries must have been extremely sensitive to both the decline in demand and the increase in transport costs. Factories such as Colchester were severely affected, while those producing on a smaller scale or for a more stable market (for instance a predominantly military market) survived with only a minor reduction in output and area of distribution. Examples of these producers are the Nene Valley, Mancetter, and possibly the Black-Burnished 1 potteries.

This placed the local producers supplying the community with pottery as a staple commodity in an even stronger position, with a relatively stable market and minimal transport costs compared to the imported products. It is not surprising, therefore, to find that the main fabrics represented at Alcester during this period are the local utilitarian wares, with substantial although reduced amounts of Black-Burnished ware.

The later 3rd century and the 4th century marked a period of resurgence. The town appears to have prospered, with new construction tending towards buildings with stone cills and with added expenditure on the strengthening of defences with the addition of a stone wall.

By the late 3rd century Romano-British pottery was independent of the continental suppliers. The British fine ware industries, although slow to start, had begun to develop as a result of native markets adopting Roman habits and culinary practices, and the prosperity of later Roman Britain is reflected in the emergence of these major industries. Illustrated in the late pottery assemblage from this corpus is a sudden introduction of new fine wares and an increase in the number of existing wares such as Nene Valley. These industries were employing specialist potters who were producing forms derived from their continental predecessors, but in local materials and for a much more regionalized market. The location of these major kilns was predominantly rural and results from a change in both social and economic considerations. First, the new locations would have been less restrictive in terms of access to raw materials, and second, a central rural location on a good communications network would have provided a greater range of established markets.

The development of the Oxfordshire industry from a moderate producer to one of the great fine ware industries of late Roman Britain is a direct response to the commercial and economic opportunities which presented themselves during this period (Young 1977). The potters began to produce for a widespread market after AD 240. They were ideally located for a western distribution along Akeman Street to Cirencester and the lower Severn Valley. It is here that a denser pattern of finds occurs in the 4th century when production was at its height (*ibid*).

At Alcester the predominant table ware for this period was the Oxfordshire or Oxfordshire-type ware, representing 40% of the total colour-coated vessels. The manufacturing dates for these vessels are AD 240–400 presumably reaching Alcester during this period, although a date after AD 270 is most probable. Fine white wares from Oxfordshire were traded alongside the colour-coated vessels with examples of these wares found on the site. There is also an increase in the quantity of Nene Valley ware, with a wider range of forms in the late 3rd and 4th century than previously. These are represented by elongated necked beakers, bowls, and Castor boxes.

During the 4th century, fine wares appear to undergo a change in social status, with an apparently lower standing in the later period. There are a number of imitations of fine wares from major industries. The potters producing these vessels were essentially local, but with close associations with the Oxfordshire industry, producing within its area of distribution. The vessels represented are in fabric DH, South-Western brown slip and fabric DTA, considered to be a coarse locally produced ware.

South-Western brown slip is similar both in style and decoration to Oxfordshire ware with the fabrics at times difficult to differentiate, although South-Western brown slip may have added sand temper. Its close parallels with the Oxfordshire industry imply that a migrant potter was involved, producing locally and probably undercutting the Oxfordshire market.

Fabric DTA on the other hand is a coarse sandy colour-coated ware imitating the fine ware types. It is of low quality and is rough in execution, suggesting a local production centre and possibly reflecting the eventual demise of the Roman pottery industry.

Black-Burnished ware continued in importance throughout this period and its presence is presumably a reflection of the inability of the local potters to compete with the popularity of these vessels.

The Severn Valley forms continued to flourish, producing for the local market. However by the late 4th century the production of Severn Valley wares was coming to an end, with no known sites in the area containing examples of it in their late 4th-century contexts.

The exact date for the end of Roman Alcester is unknown but the general collapse of the Roman material culture in Britain is thought to have occurred at the end of the 4th century or early in the 5th. One suggestion for this decline is that it was caused not so much by the collapse of the manufacturers as by the collapse of the market systems with the major industries unable to survive as a result.

It would appear that the imported pottery arriving during the first two centuries at Alcester is an expression of a cultural phenomenon with the rate of Romanization initially heavily influenced by the demand of the army, while the local industries quickly established themselves to deal with the increased demand for utilitarian vessels. However, during the later period a different pattern emerges governed by economic considerations with the main industries changing to a more rural location.

Corpus

The pottery is illustrated under the three major divisions based on the clay types and conditions of firing. These are the reduced, oxidized, and white oxidized wares. Every type of sherd has been illustrated except where it offers no further information as to the type of vessel and decorative techniques employed (for example BC 19, a rusticated body sherd is not illustrated as it is a typical rusticated body sherd). The layout of the illustrations is based on the division of vessel forms as discussed above. Because of the inevitable changes within the type series it was not feasible to illustrate under the manufacturing centres, and rather than place the pots under small misleading headings it was thought preferable to keep them within large universal groups, where possible giving references for kiln parallels and manufacturing dates.

In the corpus below, the parentheses at the end of each entry contain information about the context from which the type sherd originated, viz: (area, trench, context number, phase, date of phase). This date is not necessarily the date of manufacture of the vessel. In some cases the context has not been assigned to a particular phase. In rare cases the context from which the vessel originated can no longer be identified. (Note: each site was divided into phases individually so that phases may not be the same date on different sites — see Part 1 for details.)

Reduced wares (figs 1–17)

Reduced wares account for the majority of the vessels on the sites at Alcester, representing over *c* 50% of the total ceramic assemblage. The potters were principally concerned with utilitarian vessels and the pots were in use throughout the occupation of the site. Unfortunately the conservative nature of these vessels makes the dating of these pots difficult and only one or two vessel types are datable to within a short time span. For example, rusticated jars date to the late 1st and 2nd centuries, London-type ware dates to the early 2nd century.

Fabrics

There is a wide range of reduced fabrics at Alcester with 31 different types (excluding Black-Burnished ware which is listed separately). Most of these fall into very small categories with only a handful of sherds in each group, leaving only 14 major fabrics. These all fit into the classification of local wares, groups 1, 2, 4, 5, 6, and 7, with London-type ware as the only example of fine table ware. The individual fabric descriptions are listed below.

BA: Hard smooth vessels with a homogeneous grey colour and few to no visible inclusions. The vessels are all wheel-made and the forms include jars, beakers, and bowls. Date: 1st–4th century. Fabric Group 2.

BB: Hard smooth sandless London-type ware, but locally produced. The colour is essentially grey with darker surfaces and burnished to a fine exterior. All the vessels are wheel-made and include jars, beakers, bowls, and dishes. Date: early 2nd century. Fabric Group 10.

BBA: Hard fine vessels similar to fabric BB but with sandy rod-like quartz and abundant small black inclusions. All the vessels are wheel-made and the forms include jars and bowls. Date: 2nd century. Fabric Group 10.

BC: Hard, sandy vessels tempered with abundant inclusions of quartz. The colour is essentially grey and the vessels have all been either highly fired or overfired. All are wheel-made and include storage jars, jars, tankards, beakers, bowls, and dishes. Date: 1st–4th century. Fabric Group 1.

BD: Vesiculated grey vessels with a corky appearance. All the vessels are wheel-made with vessel forms including jars, cooking pots, beakers, cups, and bowls. Date: 1st–4th century. Fabric Group 1.

BE: Very sandy grey fabric with a rough surface texture. All the vessels are wheel-made with forms including jars, cooking pots, beakers, cups, and bowls. Date: 1st–4th century. Fabric Group 1.

BF: Hard, fine vessels with few or no visible inclusions. The fabric is fired grey with reddish-brown margins and is frequently covered by a grey slip. All the vessels are wheel-made and include storage jars, jars, and bowls. Fabric Group 2.

BG: Fairly soft grey vessels with few inclusions, wheel-made, with vessel forms including storage jars, jars, bowls, and lids. Date: 1st–4th century. Fabric Group 2.

BH: Fairly soft, fine, sandy fabric with abundant inclusions of quartz. The colour is a greyish buff, and the vessel form is a wheel-made jar. Date: 2nd–3rd century. Fabric Group 1.

BI: Hard, fine fabric. The vessel form is a jar. Date: 2nd–3rd century. Fabric Group 2.

BK: Micaceous grey fabric with a pimply texture and covered by a thin slip. All the vessels are wheel-made and the forms include storage jars, jars, and bowls. Date: 2nd–4th century. Fabric Group 2.

BN: Grey reduced Severn Valley fabric. Tankard. Date: 2nd century. Fabric Group 2.

BR: Fairly soft vessels with few inclusions. The colour is essentially a dark grey often covered with black slip. All the vessels are wheel-made and include jars, beakers, and bowls. Date: 1st–4th century. Fabric Group 2.

BU: Fairly soft, with a very sandy fabric. The vessels have a black surface which is frequently the result of a slip. All the vessels are wheel-made with forms including jars, beakers, bowls, and lids. Date: 1st–3rd century. Fabric Group 1.

BW: Hard, grey buff fabric tempered with grog. The surface is covered with a cream slip. Vessel form is a triple vase. Fabric Group 8.

BX: A hard, sandy fabric heavily tempered with quartz. The vessels are generally well burnished on the exterior. All the vessels are wheel-made and include jars and bowls. Date: 1st–4th century. Fabric Group 1.

CA: Very sandy fabric fired to a stable grey core with brown margins and covered by a black slip. Wheel-made, jars. Date: 2nd–4th century. Fabric Group 1.

CCC: Malvern ware. A moderately hard fabric, usually fired to a warm brown or black and tempered with crushed igneous metamorphic rock. All the vessels are hand-made with forms including jars, cooking pots, dishes, bowls, and lids. Date: 1st century onwards. Fabric Group 3.

CCE: Malvern ware. A moderately hard fabric fired to a warm brown or black, and tempered with abundant inclusions of angular limestone. All the vessels are hand-made with forms including jars, cooking pots, and bowls. Date: 1st century onwards. Fabric Group 4.

CCF: A very coarse fabric tempered with large inclusions of metamorphic rock. Storage jar. Fabric Group 3.

CE: Very thin-walled, fine, smooth black vessels. All are wheel-made and include bowls and beakers. Date: 2nd century. Fabric Group 9.

CJ: Hard, fine micaceous, black and red-gritted fabric with a dark buff core and black interior and exterior. Hand-made, cup. Fabric Group 1.

CR: Fairly soft coarse mottled ware. Crucibles and moulds. Hand-made. Date: from mid-3rd century. Fabric Group 2.

CS: Wheel-made black-burnished type fabric. Close-grained and heavily tempered with medium-sized quartz. The forms include jars and dishes. All the vessels are decorated in the black-burnished tradition. Date: after AD 120. Fabric Group 1 (but see also Group 12).

CT: Hard, sandy fabric with abundant inclusions of quartz. These vessels are often fired to a red core and are either slipped or fired to a black surface. All the vessels are wheel-made and the forms include jars, bowls, and dishes. Date: 1st–4th century. Fabric Group 1.

DL: Hard, micaceous vessels with a grey core and covered by a thin orange slip. Wheel-made base sherd. Fabric Group 2.

DY: Hard, fine micaceous sandy fabric, fired to a red core with a dark grey interior and exterior. All the vessels are wheel-made and the forms are jars. Fabric Group 1.

GA: Coarse shell-tempered ware. The colour is a grey-brown. All the vessels are wheel-made and the vessel forms include storage jars, jars, and bowls. Date: 4th century. Fabric Group 6.

GB: Grey coarse vessels tempered with dark grey grits and grog. Wheel-made storage jars, probably late in date. Fabric Group 8.

GC: Sandy, vesiculated grey fabric, which was originally vegetable and perhaps calcareously-tempered although the grits have long since been dissolved out. Wheel-made storage jars which are similar in type to those produced in the oxidized fabric DA. Date: 1st–2nd century. Fabric Group 7.

Range of vessel types

The range of vessel types found at Alcester in the reduced fabrics is wide but can be misleading, as a number of the forms represented in the type series are not at all common. These types tend to be copies of forms common in the oxidized wares and which are specialist Roman forms, for example, flagons, jugs, and tankards. The major groupings in the reduced wares are:

(i) Narrow-necked jars in fabrics BA and BC (illustration nos R.4–R.25)
(ii) Storage jars in fabrics BK, CCC, CCE, GA, GB, and GC (R.26–R.68)
(iii) Cooking pots in fabrics CCC, CCE, and GA (illustration nos R.69–R.112)
(iv) Rusticated jars in fabrics BA, BC, BE, BG, and BR (illustration nos R.113–R.168)
(v) Other jars in most fabrics (illustration nos R.169–R.310)
(vi) Beakers in finer grey fabrics BA and BB (illustration nos R.311–R.330)
(vii) Tankards mostly in sandy grey fabrics which could be reduced equivalent of Severn Valley wares. Fabrics BC and BN (illustration nos R.331–R.337)
(viii) Bowls in most fabrics (illustration nos R.338–R.461). The major distinction is between the fine table wares in fabric BB and the coarser utilitarian vessels.

All of these types are basically utilitarian with the exception of London-type ware which was produced in the early 2nd century. The London-type ware appears to have been an attempt to produce a fine grey table ware and comprises mostly beakers and samian-derived forms.

Decorative techniques

The range of decorative techniques employed on the reduced wares is fairly catholic with some showing chronological and typological differentiation. Grooves, cordons, and carination are found in most of the categories and are present in all periods of manufacture. Rustication is a very common feature on the Alcester grey ware jars. The rustication is nearly always linear and is considered to be late 1st/mid-2nd century in date. Slashing and stabbing is not a common method of decoration at Alcester with the only known example being a narrow-necked jar (illustration R.17). Rouletting is also uncommon except on the fine London-type ware vessels, especially beakers. Compass and inscribed lines are exclusively a feature of London-type ware and date to the early 2nd century. Incised lines occur on a number of jar forms as wavy lines and combed decoration. Burnishing is by far the most common form of decoration on reduced ware at Alcester. Burnishing is not limited to any particular form, but is found on most vessel types. It is most common on the rim, neck, and shoulder of these vessels, with burnished patterns, in particular lattices, occurring on the body of the pot.

Distribution

The majority of the reduced wares (fabrics BA, BB, and BC) are thought to have been produced in the vicinity of Alcester with a purely local distribution, unlikely to have penetrated further than 16km from the site of production, or one day's march. However, as there have been no kilns found near the site this is only put forward as a hypothesis based on the evidence from other areas which show that grey wares rarely travel far.

Illustrated vessels

In this section the first number is the illustration number, followed by the type fabric series number. WMFC in the vessel description indicates the Warwickshire Museum form class. ABA indicates vessel found on adjacent site excavated by Hughes or Tomlinson. (The comment 'residual' after the phase date indicates that the drawn example was probably residual in that context. Earlier occurrences of the type may be found, however; see table M1.)

Flagons

Flagons in grey wares are uncommon, with only four examples from Birch Abbey. These vessels are stylistically copies of oxidized forms.

R.1 BA 93 Flagon or bottle with upright rim and two incised lines near rim, burnished exterior. (D I 145, phase I, 1st century to early Antonine). WMFC 13.
R.2 BC 251 Flagon, with burnished ext. (H II 2). WMFC 13.
R.3 BE 102 Ring-necked flagon with handle scar. (AA II 78, phase II, late 2nd century to early 3rd century — residual). Late 1st to early 2nd century. WMFC 11.

Narrow-necked jars

These vessels are similar in form to those produced in the Severn Valley ware fabrics.

R.4 BA 37 Narrow-necked jar with everted rim, cordon on shoulder, derived from a Belgic form. Shoulder is burnished with band of diagonal lines between cordon and a line on body. (D I 196). WMFC 21.
R.5 BA 45 Narrow-necked jar with deep collared rim. Between rim and shoulder, ext. decorated by burnished zig-zag line. Face mask, probably female, luted onto side of rim. Burnished body and handle scar. Probably 3rd–4th century. (F V 3). WMFC 18.
R.6 BA 99 Narrow-necked jar with everted rim. Dark grey slip covers ext. with burnished line on rim int. Two burnished lines at base of neck. 1st–4th century. (D I 246, phase II, later 2nd to early 3rd century?). WMFC 20.
R.7 BA 102 Narrow-necked jar with slightly everted, curved rim and flange. Ext. decorated with burnished lines. (AA III 4, phase VI, late 3rd to early 4th century). WMFC 20.
R.8 BA 86 Narrow-necked jar with upright rim and burnished ext. (C VI 4, phase IX, mid-4th century on). WMFC 20.
R.9 BA 68 Narrow-necked jar with everted rim and well-burnished rim int. and ext. (A IX 1A). WMFC 20.
R.10 BA 81 Narrow-necked jar with upright rim and two incised lines beneath lip, and filled flange. Ext. highly burnished. (AA I 65B). WMFC 20.
R.11 BC 381 Narrow-necked jar with collared rim. (D II 29A). WMFC 20.
R.12 BC 150 Narrow-necked jar with slightly everted rim. Core fired red with a grey int. and ext. 1st–4th century (C VI 55, phase IV, later 3rd century on). WMFC 20.
R.13 BC 379 Narrow-necked jar with everted rim and beaded lip. A cordon at base of neck and acute lattice burnished lines decorating a band beneath the cordon. (AA I 30, phase VI, late 3rd to early 4th century — probably residual). WMFC 20.
R.14 BC 104 Narrow-necked jar with slightly everted rim and well-burnished int. and ext. (AA II 8A). WMFC 20.
R.15 BC 405 Narrow-necked jar with everted rim. At base of neck is a thin incised line. The core is fired red with a grey int. and ext. 1st–4th century (AA II 85, phase III, 3rd century). WMFC 20.

R.16 BC 176 Narrow-necked jar with everted rim. Two incised lines beneath neck form a double cordon. On body ext. are two incised lines, between them a band of burnished X decoration with horizontal bands beneath, and a solid burnished area above the base. The ext. of jar is soot-encrusted. 1st–4th century. (D I 229, phase II, later 2nd to early 3rd century?). WMFC 20.
R.17 BC 389 Narrow-necked jar with everted rim and row of stab marks immediately beneath. (F V 14A). WMFC 20.
R.18 BC 191 Fine narrow-necked jar with everted rim and well-burnished neck. At base of neck is an incised line with another two incised lines on shoulder, between which an area of burnishing. A band decorated by a zig-zag line and bordered by an incised groove occurs beneath. Beneath all the above are three burnished lines. (B I 3, phase II, Antonine to 3rd century). WMFC 20.
R.19 BC 89 Narrow-necked jar with dished moulded rim. Burnished ext. (AA II 78, phase II, late 2nd to early 3rd century). WMFC 17.
R.20 BC 403 Narrow-necked jar with dished moulded rim and handle scar. (A XVI 6). WMFC 17.
R.21 BC 179 Narrow-necked spheroid jar with everted frilled rim and well-burnished neck and rim. Shoulder and upper part of body burnished, with two incised lines on upper part of body defining the area of burnishing. Badly weathered. (G IV 12, phase V, later 4th century). WMFC 20.
R.22 BE 53 Narrow-necked jar with everted rim and handle. (A IX 1A). WMFC 20.
R.23 BG 137 Closed mouth jar with everted rim. Core red with grey int. and ext. At base of neck is a double cordon below which are burnished vertical lines and a shallow incised groove. 1st–4th century (AA II 91, phase II, late 2nd to early 3rd century). WMFC 20.
R.24 BG 30 Narrow-necked jar with upright rim and slightly everted bead lip. At base of neck is a cordon. (AA III 57, phase III, later 3rd century — probably residual). WMFC 20.
R.25 GC 16 Constricted necked jar with beaded rim and cordon on shoulders. WMFC 20.

Storage jars

Storage jars account for approximately 5% of the reduced ware assemblage. The main groups are in fabrics GB and GC with a few others in Malvern wares (CCC, CCE, and CCF) and a handful of examples in fabrics BC, BD, BF, BK, and GA. Many of these are decorated, burnishing being especially common. Storage jars in fabrics CCC and CCE have decorative features strongly influenced by Black-Burnished ware, lattice and line burnishing being the most common. Incised line, comb, and scallop decoration are the main features of fabric GB. Storage jars in fabric GC are decorated similarly to their oxidized counterparts (fabric DA) with burnished hatched decoration between two areas of solid burnishing. A high proportion of the GC storage jars have graffiti on the rim or body. The design of these varies from simple lines or crosses to more complicated motifs, and is thought to be indicative of the quantity or content of the vessels (see 'Vessels with incised graffiti' below, p 124).

R.26 BA 83 Wide-mouth storage jar. Burnished ext. except for a band 12mm wide on shoulder. (A IX 24). WMFC 39.
R.27 BC 409 Fine storage jar with everted rim and pronounced shoulder with shallow groove where neck joins body. Red core with grey int. and ext. Covered by a brown slip. (G II 28). WMFC 35.
R.28 BC 197 Storage jar with everted rim and burnished ext. (J II 21). WMFC 35.
R.29 BC 304 Storage jar with everted rim and beaded lip. The int. and ext. of rim are burnished. At base of neck is a shallow incised line. Shoulder decorated by burnished zig-zag decoration, with a burnished band on either side. (G V 103, phase VI, late 4th century). WMFC 35.
R.30 BC 188 Storage jar with everted rim and a cordon at the base of neck. On the cordon a wavy line and below this a burnished lattice. (G II 31, phase III?, 3rd/4th century?). WMFC 21.
R.31 BD 17 Storage jar with everted rim. (A IX 3, phase VI, late 3rd to early 4th century). WMFC 35.
R.32 BF 97 Storage jar with everted rim and groove underneath the lip. At base of neck are two incised horizontal bands. Highly burnished ext. (D I 176). WMFC 35.
R.33 BG 39 Storage jar with short everted neck and tapering lip. Two incised horizontal lines on shoulder. (H II 7C, phase III, Antonine to 3rd century on). WMFC 35.
R.34 BG 144 Storage jar with upright neck and slightly everted lip. (C VI 32). WMFC 21.
R.35 BK 22 Storage jar with short everted neck. Pimply surface, covered with black slip on int. Parallel: Wroxeter, 2nd century. (AA III 7A). WMFC 35.
R.36 CCC 61 Storage jar with short everted neck, hand-made. (Cf Peacock 1968a). 1st to early 2nd century (G I 59, phase IV, early to mid-4th century — residual). WMFC 35.
R.37 CCC 59 Storage jar, hand-made. Burnished ext. (Cf Peacock 1968a.) After AD 120. (C I 17). WMFC 35.
R.38 CCE 6 Storage jar, hand-made, with burnished ext. and rim int. After AD 120. (D II 21). WMFC 35.
R.39 CCE 9 Storage jar, wheel-made, buff int. and ext., burnished rim and lightly burnished ext. (A XVI 6). WMFC 35.
R.40 CCE 4 Storage jar with short everted neck, triangular-shaped rim, hand-made, lightly burnished ext. (A XVII 3). WMFC 35.
R.41 CCF 1 Very large storage vessel, with sharply everted rim and tapering lip, hand-made. (AA II 51B). WMFC 39.
R.42 GA 6 Grey storage jar with everted rim, hand-made. (D I 36, phase VI, mid- to late 4th century?). WMFC 35.
R.43 GA 14 Grey storage jar with everted rim and overturned lip. Distinctive fine horizontal ridges cover ext. (F I 5, phase XIII, after AD 353). WMFC 26.
R.44 GB 3 Large wide-necked storage jar, sharply everted rim with two large parallel grooves. Diameter approximately 700mm. (Cf Webster 1976, no 55). 2nd–3rd century. (G V 46, phase III?, 3rd/4th century). WMFC 39.
R.45 GB 1 Large narrow-necked storage jar with everted rim and cordon at base of neck. Neck and shoulder burnished with large wavy combed lines beneath the burnished area. (D II 47). WMFC 21.
R.46 GB 5 Storage jar with sharply everted rim flattened on the top and with groove on lip. (A IV 29). WMFC 35.
R.47 GB 2 Storage jar with gently everted rim and beaded lip. Burnished rim; two incised grooves on shoulder between which are two scalloped lines. (L I 16, phase II, late 2nd century on). WMFC 35.
R.48 GB 7 Small storage jar with an upright rim with lid-seating. Soot-encrusted ext. (D II 28). WMFC 25.
R.49 GB 4 Storage jar with everted rim and burnished ext. (H II 16, phase III, Antonine to 3rd century on). WMFC 35.
R.50 GB 8 Large storage jar 500mm in diameter. Everted rim with shallow grooves on ext. The rim and neck are burnished, with a burnished hatched decoration on shoulder. (D I 87, phase V, early to mid-4th century?). WMFC 35.
R.51 GC 4 Storage jar with everted rim and overturned lip. Burnished ext. with finger-impressed decoration below shoulder. (C IXA 12). WMFC 35.
R.52 GC 5 Storage jar with everted rim and tapering lip. Burnished ext. with burnished line hatching on shoulder. (A XVI 6). WMFC 35.
R.53 GC 36 Storage jar with everted rim. Burnished ext. and rim. Graffito: see Graffiti no 12. (G IA 85A). WMFC 21.
R.54 GC 9 Grey storage jar with sharply everted rim. The surface is rough, like goose-flesh. (D II 1). WMFC 35.
R.55 GC 34 Grey storage jar with everted rim. Burnished rim and shoulder. Graffito: no 1. (G I 168, phase IV, early to mid-4th century — probably residual). WMFC 21.
R.56 GC 6 Storage jar with everted rim and beaded lip. Burnished ext. (A XVI 6). WMFC 35.
R.57 GC 3 Large storage jar with short neck and upright rim. Burnished rim and ext. (A IX 21). WMFC 35.
R.58 GC 44 Grey storage jar with everted rim. Burnished rim with graffito, no 9. (D I 28). WMFC 21.
R.59 GC 22 Grey storage jar with everted rim and well-burnished rim and body. Shoulder decorated with a zone of right-hatched

lines. Graffito, no 3. (G IA 70, phase IV, early to mid-4th century — probably residual). WMFC 21.
R.60 GC 31 Grey storage jar with everted rim and downward-turning lip. Rim and shoulder burnished with bands of left- and right-hatched lines. Graffito, no 11. (G IA 63, phase V, later 4th century — probably residual). WMFC 35.
R.61 GC 21 Grey storage jar with everted rim. Burnished rim and body. Graffito, no 6. (G IA 68, phase IV, early to mid-4th century — probably residual). WMFC 21.
R.62 GC 29 Grey storage jar with burnished rim and shoulder. Below shoulder a band of right-hatched lines. Graffito, no 5. (D II 83, phase IX, late 4th century — probably residual). WMFC 35.
R.63 GC 1 Storage jar with everted rim and burnished shoulder. A band of right-hatched burnished lines decorate the shoulder. Graffito, no 13. (G IA 63, phase V, later 4th century — probably residual). WMFC 35.
R.64 GC 20 Grey storage jar with everted rim. Burnished rim and shoulder. Graffito, no 7. (G IA 68, phase IV, early to mid-4th century — probably residual). WMFC 35.
R.65 GC 45 Storage jar with upright rim and graffito no 8. Ext. of vessel covered by buffish-cream slip. (G IV 26, phase VI, late 4th century — probably residual). WMFC 21.
R.66 GC 8 Storage jar with everted rim and a downward-sloping lip. Burnished ext. (B IA 23). WMFC 35.
R.67 GC 15 Storage jar with upright rim and thickened lip. The rim int. and ext. are burnished. (E I 36B). WMFC 35.
R.68 GC 49 Storage jar with everted rim and beaded downward-turning lip. Burnished ext. (B I 15, phase II, Antonine to 3rd century). WMFC 35.

Cooking pots

These occur in shell-tempered and Malvern wares. The latter are hand-made with smooth surfaces concealing the coarse temper, and are derived from Black-Burnished forms. The majority of this pottery is concentrated in Herefordshire and Worcestershire, thinning out into Warwickshire. The tubby cooking pots which are the most common form are found on Hadrianic sites, but mostly occur in Antonine contexts. The vessels with inward-turning rims are 1st to early 2nd century in date.

R.69 CCC 12 Cooking pot with inward-turned beaded rim, with acute burnished lattice decoration on the ext. Malvern ware (Peacock 1968a, fig 1, no 9), 1st to early 2nd century. (C VI 32). WMFC 27.
R.70 CCC 34 Cooking pot with an inturned beaded rim. The rim and shoulder are burnished with horizontal lines, below which is an acute burnished lattice decoration. Malvern ware. 1st to early 2nd century. (B I 3, phase II, Antonine to 3rd century — residual). WMFC 27.
R.71 CCC 10 Cooking pot with short slightly everted rim and burnished horizontal lines on ext. Malvern ware. 1st to early 2nd century. (C VI 105). WMFC 27.
R.72 CCC 54 Cooking pot with inturned bead-rim. Malvern ware. 1st to early 2nd century. (C V 5). WMFC 27.
R.73 CCC 1 Cooking pot with inward-turning rim and horizontal lines beneath, and an acute burnished lattice on body ext. Malvern ware. 1st to early 2nd century. (A VIII 10). WMFC 27.
R.74 CCC 28 Cooking pot with inturned bead-rim and acute burnished lattice on body ext. Malvern ware (Peacock 1968a, no 9). 1st to early 2nd century. (B VIII U/S). WMFC 27.
R.75 CCC 25 Tubby cooking pot with beaded rim. Haphazard horizontal burnishing below rim, and vertical lines on ext. Malvern ware (Peacock 1968a, no 16). 1st to early 2nd century. (A XII 18, phase III, later 3rd century — residual). WMFC 27.
R.76 CCC 30 Tubby cooking pots with burnished lines on ext. Malvern ware (Peacock 1968a, no 10). 1st to early 2nd century. (J II 21A). WMFC 27.
R.77 CCC 32 Cooking pot with closed mouth and burnished lines on ext. Malvern ware (Peacock 1968a, no 10). 1st to early 2nd century. (J II 22). WMFC 27.
R.78 CCC 3 Cooking pot with inward-turning bead-rim. An acute lattice burnished on ext. Malvern ware (Peacock 1968a, no 10). 1st to early 2nd century (AA II 87, phase III, 3rd century — residual). WMFC 27.
R.79 CCC 51 Tubby cooking pot with burnished horizontal lines beneath rim and vertical lines on body ext. Malvern ware (Peacock 1968a, no 3). Antonine. (L VI 1). WMFC 27.
R.80 CCC 50 Cooking pot with inward-turning rim. Malvern ware (Peacock 1968a, no 11). 1st to early 2nd century. (AA I 65, phase II. late 2nd to mid-3rd century — residual). WMFC 27.
R.81 CCC 36 Cooking pot with inward-turned beaded rim and burnished rim and shoulder. Malvern ware (Peacock 1968a, no 11). 1st to early 2nd century. (J II 21). WMFC 27.
R.82 CCC 41 Cooking pot with inturned beaded rim with burnished line. Malvern ware (Peacock 1968a, no 11). 1st to early 2nd century. (E II 31A, phase V, late 2nd century? — residual). WMFC 27.
R.83 CCC 47 Cooking pot with burnished lattice on body. Malvern ware (Peacock 1968a, no 11). 1st to early 2nd century. (AA II 29, phase V, later 3rd century on — residual). WMFC 27.
R.84 CCC 38 Tubby cooking pot with burnished rim and ext. Malvern ware (Peacock 1968a, no 7). Antonine. (E II 34, phase V, late 2nd century?). WMFC 27.
R.85 CCC 49 Tubby cooking pot with slightly left-hatched burnished lines on ext. Malvern ware (Peacock 1968a, no 4). Antonine. (G IA 72A). WMFC 28.
R.86 CCC 26 Tubby cooking pot with burnished band under rim on ext. and vertical burnished lines on int. and ext. Malvern ware (Peacock 1968a, no 1). Antonine. (G V 68). WMFC 28.
R.87 CCC 37 Tubby cooking pot with burnished thickened rim. Burnished left to right hatching on the ext. Malvern ware. Antonine. (E V 38). WMFC 27.
R.88 CCC 7 Tubby cooking pot with burnished vertical lines on the ext. Malvern ware (Peacock 1968a, no 4). Antonine. (A XVII T/S). WMFC 27.
R.89 CCC 15 Tubby cooking pot with lightly burnished int. and ext. Antonine. (D I 33, phase IV, late 3rd century? — residual). WMFC 27.
R.90 CCC 4 Tubby cooking pot with burnished latticing on ext. Malvern ware (Peacock 1968a, no 6/7). Antonine. (AA III 2). WMFC 27.
R.91 CCC 22 Tubby cooking pot with vestigial beaded lip. Ext. burnished with vertical lines. Malvern ware (Peacock 1968a, no 1). Antonine. (H II 80, phase II, Antonine to 3rd century). WMFC 28.
R.92 CCC 6 Cooking pot with pushed-down rim, wheel-made. (A XVIII T/S). WMFC 50.
R.93 CCC 21 Cooking pot with everted rim. Rim and shoulder burnished with acute lattice. Immediately above the base a burnished area. This is a Black-Burnished copy, Hadrianic–Antonine. (H II 74, phase II, Antonine to 3rd century). WMFC 26.
R.94 CCC 14 Cooking pot with everted rim and beaded lip. Black-Burnished copy. Hadrianic–Antonine. (AA II 8). WMFC 26.
R.95 CCC 19 Cooking pot with slightly everted rim, copy of Black-Burnished form. Hadrianic–Antonine. (D II 22). WMFC 26.
R.96 CCE 5 Cooking pot with a short neck and everted rim. Beneath the rim a burnished acute lattice. Malvern ware. Antonine. (H II 94, phase III, Antonine to 3rd century on). WMFC 34.
R.97 CCE 3 Cooking pot with slightly everted rim. A burnished band beneath the rim with burnished vertical lines on body ext. Malvern ware. Antonine. (D II 49). WMFC 34.
R.98 CCE 1 Tubby cooking pot with burnished vertical lines on body ext. Malvern ware. Antonine. (G VI 1). WMFC 34.
R.99 CCE 2 Tubby cooking pot with burnished vertical lines on body ext. Malvern ware (Peacock 1968a, no 3). Antonine. (G IV 38, phase I?, late 2nd/3rd century?). WMFC 34.
R.100 CCE 7 Cooking pot with slightly everted rim, and lightly burnished ext. (AA I 2). WMFC 34.
R.101 CCE 11 Cooking pot with everted rim. (E II 92, phase III, Neronian/Trajanic). WMFC 23.
R.102 CCE 8 Cooking pot. Perhaps a copy of a Black-Burnished form. (G IA 14). WMFC 32.
R.103 GA 26 Cooking pot/jar with everted rim and overhanging lip. After AD 340 (Plouviez 1976, 91). (K I 27). WMFC 26.
R.104 GA 3 Cooking pot with everted rim. 4th century. (C IIIC 1). WMFC 26.
R.105 GA 15 Cooking pot/jar with everted rim and frilled lip. (AA II 2). WMFC 26.

R.106 GA 30 Cooking pot with everted rim and overhanging lip. Burnished rim. After AD 340 (Plouviez 1976, 91). (G IA 21, phase X, late 4th century). WMFC 26.
R.107 GA 2 Cooking pot with everted rim and lightly burnished int. and ext. After AD 340. (A IX 21). WMFC 26.
R.108 GA 23 Cooking pot with sharply everted rim. 4th century. (A XIV 26). WMFC 26.
R.109 GA 4 Cooking pot with everted rim. Regular thumb impressions beneath rim on the ext. (C IIID 1). WMFC 26.
R.110 GA 24 Large cooking pot with everted neck and thickened rim. 4th century. (G V 100, phase VI, late 4th century). WMFC 26.
R.111 GA 5 Cooking pot with everted rim. (D I 2A, phase VIII, late 4th century). WMFC 26,
R.112 GA 19 Deep flanged bowl/wide-mouthed jar (F I 5, phase XIII, after AD 353). WMFC 37.

Rusticated and closely related jars

Rusticated jars have regional variations and can be dated to within a short time span. The rustication itself may serve two purposes, first as a method of decoration and second as a means of providing a secure way to hold the vessel. These vessels occur in a variety of fabrics (BA, BC, BD, BE, BG, and BR). All are in the utilitarian grey wares which are thought to have been produced in the vicinity of Alcester. The range of types is narrow; all are either conical, globular, or pear-shaped.

There are features common to all of these vessels. The rims are straight and sharply everted, forming a marked angle with the neck of the jar; the shoulder is distinguished by a groove defining the upper limit of rustication with one of two types of rustication beneath. Linear rustication is most common although there are examples of nodular rustication. The foot of the jar is frequently moulded.

Rusticated vessels demonstrate both geographic and chronological characteristics. A clear regional division occurs between the nodular and linear types of rustication, with a geographical dividing line for these from the head of the Severn estuary to East Anglia. Alcester lies to the north of this line, where the form of rustication is linear. This is reflected in the Alcester pottery assemblage by the predominant use of this form.

Chronologically, these vessels appear to have had a relatively short life, belonging to the early part of the Roman occupation. There are no similar jar types known from the Iron Age, but they have known continental affinities, with the origin of the form suggested to have been in the Rhineland. A useful distinction can be made between jars with a globular profile which are dated to the pre-Flavian to Flavian period (AD 50–80), compared to the pear- and conical-shaped jars dated to the Flavian–Trajanic period (AD 70–120) (Thompson 1958).

R.113 BA 97 Conical jar with linear rustication. AD 70–120. (B IA 7). WMFC 24.
R.114 BA 34 Globular jar with upright rim. Rustication is all over. (D I 40, phase V, early to mid-4th century — residual). WMFC 23.
R.115 BC 400 Conical jar with regularly spaced linear rustication. AD 70–120. (C IA 11). WMFC 24.
R.116 BC 171 Conical jar with regularly spaced linear rustication. Moulded base. AD 70–120. (D I 196). WMFC 24.
R.117 BC 376 Conical jar with periodically spaced linear rustication. AD 70–120. (AA I 36, phase III, later 3rd century — residual). WMFC 24.
R.118 BC 170 Conical jar with regularly spaced linear rustication. Moulded and burnished base. AD 70–120. (D I 196). WMFC 24.
R.119 BC 239 Pear-shaped jar. Int. of rim decorated by burnished lines, and rim and shoulder also burnished. AD 70–120. (D I 29, phase IV, late 3rd century? — residual). WMFC 24.
R.120 BC 229 Conical jar with regularly spaced linear rustication. Moulded base with hole punched through the bottom of it after firing. AD 70–120. (D I 246, phase II, later 2nd to early 3rd century? — residual). WMFC 24.
R.121 BC 232 Conical jar, with regularly spaced linear rustication. Moulded base. AD 70–120. (D I 246, phase II, later 2nd to early 3rd century? — residual). WMFC 24.
R.122 BC 206 Conical jar with regularly spaced linear rustication. Moulded base. AD 70–120. (C VI 32). WMFC 24.
R.123 BC 123 Conical jar with burnished lines on rim and shoulder; regularly spaced linear rustication. AD 70–120. (A XVI 12). WMFC 24.
R.124 BC 231 Conical jar with burnished rim and shoulder. Groove on shoulder defines upper limit of decoration in the form of a burnished 'V' design, the lower body to the base is burnished. Similar in form to the rusticated jars. (B I 2, phase II, Antonine to 3rd century). WMFC 24.
R.125 BC 192 Conical jar with regularly spaced vertical lines on ext. Similar in form to rusticated jars, and probably Flavian. (D I 246, phase II, later 2nd to early 3rd century?). WMFC 24.
R.126 BC 212 Conical jar. Broadly Flavian. (B I 14). WMFC 24.
R.127 BC 213 Conical jar with burnished line on rim, and burnished on ext. up to shoulder groove. AD 70–120. (B I 14). WMFC 24.
R.128 BC 407 Conical jar. AD 70–120. (A XII 17). WMFC 24.
R.129 BC 38 Conical jar. AD 70–120. (A IX 6). WMFC 24.
R.130 BC 372 Conical jar. AD 70–120. (AA II 128). WMFC 24.
R.131 BC 412 Globular jar, burnished on rim and neck. Dense area of irregular rustication beneath the shoulder groove. AD 50–80. (G IV 39, phase IV, early to mid-4th century — residual). WMFC 23.
R.132 BC 149 Globular jar with everted rim and nodular rustication. AD 50–80. (H I 14). WMFC 23.
R.133 BC 285 Small globular jar with short everted rim. Rustication regularly spaced and nodular. AD 50–80. (C VIA 85, phase III, 3rd century — residual). WMFC 24.
R.134 BC 189 Globular jar with linear rustication, and burnished rim and shoulder. AD 50–80. (C I 110). WMFC 23.
R.135 BC 187 Pear-shaped jar with burnished neck and rim, and regularly spaced linear rustication. AD 70–120. (C V 48). WMFC 24.
R.136 BC 354 Globular jar with two incised lines on shoulder, above rustication. AD 50–80. (L I 16, phase II, late 2nd century on — residual). WMFC 23.
R.137 BC 148 Pear-shaped jar with irregular rustication. AD 70–120. (C VIA 107, phase V, later 3rd century on — residual). WMFC 24.
R.138 BC 380 Pear-shaped jar with upright rim, rusticated. AD 70–120. (A IX 5). WMFC 24.
R.139 BC 302 Pear-shaped jar with lid-seating. Probably rusticated. AD 70–120. (J II 22A). WMFC24.
R.140 BC 198 Moulded base with two burnished lines on ext. Int. covered with a black slip. The form is similar to rusticated jars. (D I 246, phase II, late 2nd to early 3rd century? — probably residual).
R.141 BC 264 Pear-shaped jar. AD 70–120. (D II 76). WMFC 24.
R.142 BC 374 Pear-shaped jar. Overfired and with bubbled surface. On shoulder is a groove above nodular rustication. AD 70–120. (C VIA 42B). WMFC 24.
R.143 BC 185 Pear-shaped jar. AD 70–120. (C VIA 21). WMFC 24.
R.144 BD 22 Pear-shaped jar with linear rustication. AD 70–120. (C IV 3). WMFC 24.
R.145 BE 42 Conical-necked jar with a bead-rim. Moulded base. The rustication is nodular and regularly spaced. (E IV 23, phase III, Neronian/Trajanic). WMFC 37.
R.146 BE 46 Conical-shaped jar with three incised wavy lines on body ext. The form is similar to the rusticated jars. (D I 229, phase II, later 2nd to early 3rd century?). WMFC 24.
R.147 BE 73 Large conical jar. AD 70–120. (J II 21). WMFC 24.
R.148 BE 83 Conical jar with two rows of incised wavy lines on body of the jar. In form this is similar to rusticated jars. (D I 246, phase II, later 2nd to early 3rd century?). WMFC 24.

R.149 BE 36 Globular jar with nodular rustication. AD 50–80. (C VI 74, phase II, late 2nd century — residual). WMFC 23.
R.150 BE 60 Pear-shaped jar with moulded base and long linear rustication. AD 70–120. (D I 47, phase VI, mid- to late 4th century? — residual). WMFC 24.
R.151 BG 145 Conical jar with regularly spaced linear rustication. AD 70–120. (E II 28). WMFC 24.
R.152 BG 129 Conical jar, probably rusticated. AD 70–120. (A IX 3, phase VI, late 3rd to early 4th century — residual). WMFC 24.
R.153 BG 29 Large conical jar with linear rustication. AD 70–120. (A II 120). WMFC 23.
R.154 BG 18 Conical or pear-shaped jar with burnished ext. AD 70–120. (A IX 2, phase VII, late 3rd to early 4th century — residual). WMFC 24.
R.155 BG 132 Conical jar with regularly spaced linear rustication. AD 70–120. (D I 246, phase II, later 2nd to early 3rd century? — residual). WMFC 24.
R.156 BG 32 Conical jar with regularly spaced rustication. Moulded base. AD 70–120. (C VI 32). WMFC 24.
R.157 BG 110 Conical jar with regularly spaced linear rustication. AD 70–120. (D I 126A, phase II, later 2nd to early 3rd century? — residual). WMFC 24.
R.158 BG 136 Small conical jar with regularly spaced rustication. AD 70–120. (D I 246, phase II, later 2nd to early 3rd century — residual). WMFC 24.
R.159 BG 149 Black conical jar with regularly spaced linear rustication. AD 70–120. (D I 31, phase I, 1st century to early Antonine). WMFC 24.
R.160 BG 152 Conical jar with burnished lines on rim and neck, probably rusticated. AD 70–120. (C I 85). WMFC 24.
R.161 BG 7 Conical jar. AD 70–120. (AA II 100, phase I, late 1st to 2nd century). WMFC 24.
R.162 BG 28 Conical jar. The form is similar to rusticated vessels. (A IX U/S). WMFC 24.
R.163 BG 126 Body sherd from a linear-rusticated jar. A leaf design branches off from the main rusticated ridge. Flavian. (D I 126A, phase II, later 2nd to early 3rd century? — residual).
R.164 BH 1 Conical jar with regularly spaced burnished vertical lines on ext. beneath shoulder groove. The base moulded with a scalloped line on foot of jar. The form is similar to the rusticated jars but with a different method of decoration. (A IX 28). WMFC 24.
R.165 BR 14 Globular jar with irregular rustication which is continuous all over the body. Near the base the jar is burnished. Flavian. (D I 110). WMFC 23.
R.166 BR 1 Coarse globular jar with burnished neck and shoulder, and with regularly spaced nodular rustication. AD 50–80. (D I 169, phase VI, mid- to late 4th century — residual). WMFC 23.
R.167 BR 10 Pear-shaped jar with everted rim and pronounced shoulder defining limit of rustication, which is linear and regularly spaced. Burnished neck and shoulder. AD 70–120. (C VI 32). WMFC 32.
R.168 BR 9 Globular jar with burnished area above nodular rustication. AD 50–80. (G V 1). WMFC 23.

Wheel-made Black-Burnished ware copies

These wheel-made jars were produced in local grey wares imitating the Black-Burnished tradition in both form and decorative techniques. They are likely to be Hadrianic or later.

R.169 BA 61 Jar with obliquely everted rim and well-emphasized shoulder. Burnished rim and shoulder. Burnished design on body ext. Probably 2nd century. (A IX 1A). WMFC 26.
R.170 BA 59 Jar with obliquely everted rim. A ledge marks junction between neck and body of jar. (C VI 11, phase VI, early to mid-4th century — probably residual). WMFC 26.
R.171 BA 14 Jar with everted rim and pronounced shoulder. Hadrianic–Antonine. (AA II 91, phase II, late 2nd to early 3rd century). WMFC 26.
R.172 BA 17 Jar with everted rim and beaded lip. Burnished lines on the neck and shoulder. Hadrianic–Antonine. (AA II 91, phase II, late 2nd to early 3rd century). WMFC 26.
R.173 BC 52 Jar with short everted rim and horizontal burnished lines over whole body with band of solid burnishing above the base. (AA II 86, phase III, 3rd century, probably residual). WMFC 26.
R.174 BC 346 Jar with obliquely everted rim. Rim and shoulder burnished with an acute burnished lattice on ext. Copy of a Black-Burnished form. Hadrianic–Antonine. (C VI 32). WMFC 26.
R.175 BC 395 Jar with short everted rim and burnished horizontal lines on body ext. Burnished rim. Hadrianic–Antonine. (AA II 87, phase III, 3rd century — residual). WMFC 26.
R.176 BC 365 Jar with everted rim ending in slight bead. Burnished rim and shoulder above an acute lattice. Hadrianic–Antonine. (AA IIA 9). WMFC 26.
R.177 BC 373 Jar with curved everted rim. Ext. decorated with burnished horizontal lines. (AA II 87, phase III, 3rd century — probably residual). WMFC 26.
R.178 BC 226 Jar with wide everted rim and burnished horizontal lines on ext. 2nd to early 3rd century. (D I 64, phase IV, late 3rd century? — residual). WMFC 26.
R.179 BC 394 Jar with everted rim and pronounced shoulder. Both rim and shoulder burnished, acute lattice decoration on body ext. Copy of a Black-Burnished jar. Hadrianic–Antonine. (A IX 8, phase VI, late 3rd to early 4th century — residual). WMFC 26.
R.180 BC 322 Fine jar with everted rim. (B I 14). WMFC 26.
R.181 BC 134 Jar with everted, outcurving rim. Burnished rim and shoulder. Body ext. decorated with burnished vertical lines. (C I 89). WMFC 26.
R.182 BC 204 Jar with obliquely everted rim and slightly beaded lip. Burnished rim, neck, and shoulder. Below shoulder a burnished acute lattice. Hadrianic–Antonine. (D I 246, phase II, later 2nd to early 3rd century?). WMFC 26.
R.183 BC 399 Jar with obliquely everted rim ending in a slight bead. A burnished line on body ext. (C V 56). WMFC 26.
R.184 BC 72 Jar with everted rim. At base of rim is an incised line where it joins the body. (C I 72, phase III, 3rd century — probably residual). WMFC 26.
R.185 BC 370 Jar/cooking pot with curved everted rim and incised line where neck meets shoulder. Burnished rim and shoulder, above an acute burnished lattice. Antonine. (AA II 87 (Pit F), phase III, 3rd century — residual). WMFC 26.
R.186 BC 347 Neckless jar with everted rim and beaded lip. Burnished shoulder above an acute burnished lattice. Hadrianic–Antonine. (B I 3, phase II, Antonine to 3rd century). WMFC 26.
R.187 BC 327 Jar with everted rim and beaded lip. At base of neck an incised groove. Ext. highly burnished. (B I 36). WMFC 26.
R.188 BC 381 Cavetto-rimmed jar with burnished rim and shoulder. On body ext. is burnished acute lattice. Between lattice and base, the jar is burnished. (D II 29A). WMFC 26.
R.189 BC 98 Jar with everted rim and slight beading of the lip. (AA II 100, phase I, late 1st to 2nd century). WMFC 26.
R.190 BD 29 Jar with everted rim and slight beading of the lip. On body ext. are two burnished horizontal lines. (J II 21). WMFC 26.
R.191 BD 65 Small jar with upright rim and well-defined shoulder. Ext. decorated with burnished horizontal lines (cf Gillam 1976, 19). Early to mid-2nd century. (D II 5). WMFC 63.
R.192 BD 64 Jar with everted rim and beaded lip, burnished rim and ext. Hadrianic–Antonine. (B IA 9). WMFC 26.
R.193 BE 74 Jar with oblique everted rim and beaded lip. Hadrianic–Antonine. (C VI 32). WMFC 26.
R.194 BE 64 Jar with everted rim. A groove runs along base of rim. (AA I 66, phase VI, late 3rd to early 4th century — probably residual). WMFC 26.
R.195 BE 92 Jar with everted rim. Hadrianic–Antonine. (AA II 102, phase III, 3rd century — residual). WMFC 26.
R.196 BE 107 Jar with everted rim. Body decorated by parallel diagonal lines at regular intervals. Tooling marks on rim int. (AA III 84, phase III, later 3rd century). WMFC 26.
R.197 BE 51 Neckless jar with oblique everted rim and beaded lip. On rim ext. a burnished line, the shoulder is also burnished. Hadrianic–Antonine. (C VIA 85, phase III, 3rd century — residual). WMFC 26.
R.198 BE 15 Jar with an upright slightly curved rim. Pronounced shoulder. (A IX 10). WMFC 26.
R.199 BE 62 Cavetto-rimmed jar with pronounced shoulder. Body decorated with burnished acute lattice. A Black-Burnished form. Hadrianic–Antonine. (AA II 100, phase I, late 1st to 2nd century). WMFC 26.

R.200 BE 63 Jar with everted rim. Burnished rim and shoulder. Body decorated with regular diagonal burnished lines. Hadrianic–Antonine. (AA II 65B). WMFC 26.
R.201 BE 66 Jar with short everted rim and burnished acute lattice on body ext. Hadrianic–Antonine. (A V 19, phase VI, late 3rd to early 4th century — residual). WMFC 26.
R.202 BE 68 Neckless jar with oblique everted rim and prominent shoulder. Body decorated with burnished vertical lines on ext. Hadrianic–Antonine. (ABA L I 17). WMFC 26.
R.203 CT 1 Neckless jar with everted rim. A ridge at base of rim defines the shoulder. Burnished rim int. Horizontal burnished lines decorate body ext. (D I 19, phase VI, mid- to late 4th century?). WMFC 26.
R.204 CT 38 Black-Burnished copy with everted rim. Burnished rim. Shoulder decorated with burnished horizontal lines. An acute burnished lattice decorates the body ext. Between lattice and base is another area of burnishing. Hadrianic–Antonine. (D II 60). WMFC 26.
R.205 CT 21 Black-Burnished jar copy with obliquely everted rim. Burnished rim and shoulder. On body ext. is an acute burnished lattice. Hadrianic–Antonine. (L III 8, phase I). WMFC 26.
R.206 CT 51 Jar with everted rim and acute burnished lattice decoration. Hadrianic–Antonine. (B I 5, phase II, Antonine to 3rd century). WMFC 26.

Bead-rim jars

This is a well-known pre-Roman form. However, those decorated with burnished designs do not appear until well into the 2nd century on most sites. The bead-rim jar is a very common Antonine form with a few examples continuing into the 3rd century.

R.207 BC 335 Bead-rim jar with well-burnished ext. and rim. (AA I 30, phase VI, late 3rd to early 4th century — residual). WMFC 27.
R.208 BC 350 Bead-rim jar covered with black iridescent slip and with burnished rim and ext. (AA II 87, phase III, 3rd century — residual). WMFC 27.
R.209 BC 49 Bead-rim jar with faint lattice decoration on girth. (D II 20). WMFC 27.
R.210 BC 334 Thick bead-rim jar with burnished horizontal lines on rim and ext. On ext. at regular intervals are pairs of faintly burnished parallel diagonal lines. (C IXA 11). WMFC 27.
R.211 BC 383 Bead-rim jar. (AA III 60, phase II, late 2nd to mid-3rd century). WMFC 27.
R.212 BC 57 Bead-rim jar. (AA II 78, phase II, late 2nd to early 3rd century). WMFC 27.
R.213 BC 326 Bead-rim jar. (C VI 32B). WMFC 27.
R.214 BC 339 Neckless jar with short, sharply everted rim. Burnished rim. A burnished line on body ext. (G V 46, phase III?, 3rd/4th century — possibly residual). WMFC 27.
R.215 BD 28 Bead-rim jar with burnished shoulder and acute burnished lattice. (J II 21). WMFC 27.
R.216 BE 29 Bead-rim jar. (AA II 100, phase I, late 1st to 2nd century). WMFC 27.
R.217 BE 50 Bead-rim jar. (B I 36). WMFC 27.
R.218 CS 28 Bead-rim jar. On body are two grooves with a band of burnished zig-zag decoration between them. Burnished rim and ext. (G I 106A, phase V, later 4th century — residual). WMFC 58.
R.219 CT 13 Bead-rim jar with a groove on the shoulder and a burnished ext. A few metamorphic inclusions within the normal fabric. (A X 15). WMFC 27?
R.220 CT 18 Globular jar with bead-rim. On body ext. is a randomly burnished acute lattice. Hadrianic–Antonine. (H II 5, phase III, Antonine to 3rd century on). WMFC 34.

Globular jars

R.221 BA 33 Fine globular jar with short neck and beaded rim. Burnished rim and shoulder. On body ext. are regularly spaced vertical stripes made from an applied grey slip (cf Gillam 1970, no 99). AD 110–30. (AA III 26, phase III, later 3rd century — residual). WMFC 23.
R.222 BA 105 Fine globular jar with short neck and bead-rim. Burnished rim. On shoulder an incised line defining an upper area of regularly spaced vertical stripes, made from an applied clay slip. (Cf Gillam 1970, no 99). AD 110–30. (A IX 20). WMFC 23.

Jars with small oblique rim, similar in date to bead-rim jars

R.223 BA 57 Globular jar with short everted rim and a pair of incised grooves on shoulder above an area of rouletted decoration. Burnished ext. (C IXA 12). WMFC 23.
R.224 BB 48 Fine, bulbous jar/beaker with everted rim and a cordon on the shoulder. Below the cordon in triangular zones are rows of barbotine dots. Ext. covered by pink/brown slip. Burnished ext. and rim. Neronian to early Flavian. (D II 2, phase IX, late 4th century — residual). WMFC 23.
R.225 BB 10 Small globular jar/beaker with everted rim and slipped dot decoration on ext. (C VI 46A, phase IV, later 3rd century on — residual). WMFC 23.
R.226 BB 9 Neckless globular jar with short everted rim. Burnished rim and shoulder. On shoulder, two incised grooves with rouletted decoration between them. (D I 176). WMFC 23.
R.227 BB 44 Plain globular jar with short everted rim and highly burnished ext. London-type ware (cf Marsh 1978, no 22). Early 2nd century (D I 173, phase II, later 2nd to early 3rd century? — residual). WMFC 42?
R.228 BBA 25 Small globular jar/beaker with everted rim. London-type ware (cf Marsh 1978, no 22). First half of 2nd century. (AA I 36, phase III, later 3rd century — residual). WMFC 23.
R.229 BBA 17 Jar with oblique rim. Burnished rim and ext. London-type ware. (AA I 18, phase VII, late 3rd to early 4th century — residual). WMFC 42.
R.230 BC 113 Closed-mouth jar with short obliquely everted rim and high shoulder. Burnished ext. (AA I 74). WMFC 23.
R.231 BC 15 Small-oblique rimmed jar with burnished ext. (A VII 1A). WMFC 42.
R.232 BC 272 Closed-mouth jar with short oblique rim. Burnished rim and ext. (A IX 8, phase VI, late 3rd to early 4th century — probably residual). WMFC 42.
R.233 BC 38 Globular jar with short everted rim and burnished shoulder above an acute burnished lattice. Decoration influenced by Black-Burnished ware. After AD 120. (AA II 90). WMFC 63.
R.234 BC 44 Jar with short everted rim and downward-turning lip. (A IX 10). WMFC 23?
R.235 BC 411 Neckless jar with everted rim and prominent shoulder. Burnished rim and ext. (D I 173, phase II, later 2nd to early 3rd century?). WMFC 33.
R.236 BC 64 Jar with everted rim. (AA II 79, phase II, late 2nd to early 3rd century). WMFC 23.
R.237 BC 69 Jar with everted rim. An incised line on rim int. for lid-seating. Grooved shoulder. (C I 66). WMFC 25.
R.238 BC 117 Globular jar with small oblique rim. Rim int. ridged to seat a lid. Ext. decorated with burnished pairs of diagonal lines at regularly spaced intervals. Below is a shallow groove. (C I 110). WMFC 25.
R.239 BC 40 Small pear-shaped jar with everted rim. Grooved shoulder. Burnished ext. (A IX 4, phase III, later 3rd century — probably residual). WMFC 23.
R.240 BE 104 Jar with short oblique rim. (B I 15, phase II, Antonine to 3rd century). WMFC 23?
R.241 BF 109 Jar/beaker with short oblique rim. The ext. decorated with rouletted vertical lines cut by incised horizontal lines. (D I 109, phase II, later 2nd to early 3rd century?). WMFC 42.
R.242 BG 6 Jar with oblique rim. (D I 47, phase VI, mid- to late 4th century? — probably residual). WMFC 23.
R.243 BG 12 Jar with everted rim. Two shallow grooves on shoulder. Burnished lines decorate ext. (AA I 33, phase VI, late 3rd to early 4th century — probably residual). WMFC 22.
R.244 BG 108 Jar with everted rim. An incised groove on rim int. and ext. The shoulder is grooved. Burnished body ext. (A IX 14, phase V, later 3rd century on — probably residual). WMFC 22.
R.245 BU 15 Black jar with short oblique rim. On body ext. are wide vertical incised grooves. Burnished rim and body ext. (D I 148, phase VI, mid- to late 4th century — probably residual). WMFC 23.

Romano-British coarse pottery

R.246 CT 28 Jar with small oblique rim. Highly burnished rim and int. (D I 47, phase VI, mid- to late 4th century). WMFC 23.

Jars with well-turned-out rim and high shoulders

R.247 BC 352 Jar with sharply everted rim, the int. ledged for a lid. (B I 15). WMFC 25.
R.248 BC 167 Jar with everted rim and high shoulder. (G IA 60, phase V, later 4th century). WMFC 26.
R.249 BC 402 Jar with thick rim, thinning out where it joins body. On the shoulder are two incised grooves. (cf Kenyon 1948, fig 27, no 29). AD 80–120. (C I 110). WMFC 23.
R.250 BD 21 Jar with short everted rim. A pair of incised grooves on the girth. Burnished ext. (Cf Kenyon 1948, fig 27, no 29). AD 80–120. (D I 2, phase VIII, late 4th century — residual). WMFC 23.
R.251 BD 11 Jar with everted rim and high shoulder. (A IX 20). WMFC 23.
R.252 BE 12 Jar with everted rim and groove where rim joins body. (A IX 4, phase III, later 3rd century). WMFC 23.
R.253 BG 128 Jar with short everted rim thickened at the lip. High shoulder. (A XVI 15). WMFC 25.

Jars with thickened rims frequently ridged to seat lids

R.254 BC 101 Jar with everted rim. The rim int. has lid-seating. (A IX 5). WMFC 25.
R.255 BU 2 Short-necked jar with everted rim with lid-seating. Ext. covered by black slip. (G I 153, phase I?, late 2nd to 3rd century?). WMFC 25.
R.256 BU 12 Jar with everted thickened rim. (G V 36). WMFC 23.
R.257 BX 1 Jar with everted rim ridged for lid-seating. At base of neck is a burnished line. (D I 164, phase I, 1st century to early Antonine). WMFC 25.
R.258 BX 3 Jar with everted rim, very coarse in execution. (G I 110, phase IV, early to mid-4th century — possibly residual). WMFC 25

Jars with high shoulder

R.259 BC 124 Coarse jar with everted tapering rim and high shoulder. Lightly burnished ext. with oblique scoring. (B IA 14, phase IV, mid- to late 4th century — possibly residual). WMFC 23.
R.260 BC 349 Jar with everted rim and high shoulder. Well-burnished rim and ext. (D I 48, phase VI, mid- to late 4th century — probably residual). WMFC 26.
R.261 BE 33 Short-necked jar with everted rim and high shoulder. (AA II 12). WMFC 23.
R.262 BU 9 Short-necked jar with everted rim and high shoulder. (H I 14). WMFC 26.

Jars with rolled-over rims

R.263 BC 415 Necked jar with rolled-over everted rim and high shoulder. The core is red/brown, fired to a grey int. and ext. (Cf Kenyon 1948, fig 27, no 53). AD 130–200. (D I 173, phase II, later 2nd to early 3rd century?). WMFC 32.
R.264 BC 71 Jar with everted rolled-over rim. Iridescent grey slip. (C I 72, phase III, 3rd century). WMFC 26?
R.265 BD 14 Jar with rolled-over thick beaded rim and high shoulder. (G IV 39, phase IV, early to mid-4th century). WMFC 38?
R.266 BD 24 Jar with rolled-over rim and high shoulder. Black ext. (G IV 55). WMFC 38.
R.267 BE 49 Jar with rolled-over beaded rim. (C V 5). WMFC 38.
R.268 BE 40 Jar with everted thickened rim. (G I 110, phase IV, early to mid-4th century — probably residual). WMFC 23?
R.269 BG 95 Jar with short neck and rim that begins to roll over. Beaded lip. Dark grey slip. (AA III 89, phase III, later 3rd century — probably residual). WMFC 26.
R.270 BK 8 Necked jar with rolled-over rim and beaded lip. (AA II 83, phase II, late 2nd to early 3rd century). WMFC 32.
R.271 BX 4 Necked jar with everted thickened rim and high shoulder. Well-burnished ext. (G I 90). WMFC 32.

Necked jars

R.272 BA 78 Fine narrow-necked jar with long curving neck, and slightly beaded lip. Well-burnished rim and ext. (A XIV 26). WMFC 20.
R.273 BA 5 Very fine narrow-necked jar with everted rim and burnished ext. (A IX 1A). WMFC 20.
R.274 BA 91 Fine narrow-necked jar with slight beading of the rim. Burnished rim and ext. (A IX 4, phase III, later 3rd century). WMFC 20.
R.275 BA 74 Necked jar with slightly everted rim. On the shoulder a groove. Burnished line on ext. immediately beneath the rim. (C VIA 131). WMFC 32.
R.276 BA 82 Carinated jar with wide everted rim and beaded lip. Neck forms a sharp angle with body. Well-burnished rim and ext. (L I 7). WMFC 53.
R.277 BA 51 Necked jar with everted rim. Burnished rim and ext. (AA I 11). WMFC 32.
R.278 BB 54 Fine-necked jar with beaded lip. The shoulder is grooved, making junction of neck and body prominent. Below shoulder an incised groove. (L XI 2). WMFC 32.
R.279 BBA 55 Fine necked jar covered with a black slip. Burnished ext. Burnished horizontal line on neck. (AA II 19, phase V or later, later 3rd century on). WMFC 32.
R.280 BC 345 Wide-necked jar with a beaded lip and tapering body. Burnished rim and ext. (A IX 21). WMFC 37.
R.281 BE 91 Necked jar with beaded rim. A pair of incised grooves on neck. (C I 23). WMFC 32.
R.282 BE 113 Wide-necked jar with an everted rim. (A I 3). WMFC 33.
R.283 BG 118 Necked jar. (C VIA 53/36, phase IX, mid-4th century on). WMFC 33.
R.284 BG 124 Necked jar. (A VIII 1). WMFC 32.
R.285 BG 117 Fine wide-necked jar with flattened rim and pronounced shoulder. Covered with grey slip. Burnished ext. (C VIA 34, phase VI, early to mid-4th century — probably residual). WMFC 32.
R.286 BG 46 Base sherd of jar with moulded foot. Covered by black slip. (D I 246, phase II, later 2nd to early 3rd century?).
R.287 BG 114 Fine base sherd of jar. Burnished ext. (B I 14).
R.288 BG 109 Base sherd of a jar. Int. and ext. are covered by black slip. (D I 246, phase II, later 2nd to early 3rd century?).

Miscellaneous jars

R.289 BA 48 Wide-mouthed jar. Burnished rim int. and ext. A pair of incised lines on shoulder. (L V 9). WMFC 38?
R.290 BA 63 Jar with everted rim. On neck there are burnished thin horizontal lines. Near base of jar are wide burnished lines. (C VIA 34, phase VI, early to mid-4th century). WMFC 38.
R.291 BB 29 Fine necked jar with beaded rim. Above shoulder are two incised grooves. Well-burnished ext. (C X 40). WMFC 20.
R.292 BC 369 Necked jar with beaded lip and irregular rim. A pair of incised grooves on neck with another pair beneath the shoulder. Burnished rim and ext. (C I 36). WMFC 32.
R.293 BC 155 Necked jar with everted rim. Burnished rim int. and ext. Prominent and high shoulder. (AA I 3). WMFC 32.
R.294 BD 35 Necked jar with beaded rim. Pair of incised wavy lines on the shoulder. (G I 123, phase IV, early to mid-4th century — probably residual). WMFC 32.
R.295 BE 32 Jar/bowl with everted rim. (B IA 11). WMFC 38.
R.296 BE 103 Short-necked jar with beaded rim. Parallel incised lines on shoulder. (C I 67). WMFC 32.
R.297 BG 130 Jar with a flat everted rim and slightly burnished ext. (A IX 13, phase IV, later 3rd century on — probably residual). WMFC 24?.
R.298 BR 7 Thick-walled jar/beaker with incised line on ext. (AA III 69, phase II, late 2nd to mid-3rd century). WMFC 20.
R.299 BU 6 Small jar with everted rim and slightly burnished ext. (A XVI 6). WMFC 22.
R.300 CT 26 Jar with a bead-rim. Black slip. (G I 89, phase IV, early to mid-4th century). WMFC 32.

Small miscellaneous jars

R.301 BA 80 Tiny jar with a bead rim and burnished ext. On the rim int. there is a wood mark. (L XII 1). WMFC 63.
R.302 BB 52 Small jar with short everted rim. Beneath rim an incised line. Well-burnished rim and ext. (H II 74, phase II, Antonine to 3rd century). WMFC 63.
R.303 BBA 50 Small jar with a cavetto rim and beaded lip. Pronounced shoulder with burnished horizontal lines and an acute lattice beneath. Burnished rim. A Black-Burnished ware copy, Hadrianic–Antonine. (D IV 4, phase V, early to mid-4th century — residual). WMFC 26.
R.304 BC 190 Small jar with beaded rim. Body decorated with burnished horizontal and diagonal lines at irregular intervals. (B I 24). WMFC 63.
R.305 BR 4 Tiny jar with beaded rim. (B IA 1). WMFC 66.
R.306 CE 6 Small jar with a high shoulder and small everted rim. On the upper body are three incised lines. The lower body of the jar is burnished. (J I 31, phase VIII, 3rd century? — probably residual). WMFC 63.

Narrow-necked jars / beakers with prominent shoulders

R.307 BU 1 Narrow-necked jar/beaker with prominent shoulder; the ext. is black, iridescent, and highly burnished. (D I 175, phase I, 1st century to Antonine). WMFC 44?
R.308 BU 8 Carinated jar/beaker with groove around base of neck. Well-burnished ext. (G IV 38B). WMFC 47.
R.309 BU 7 Necked jar. Below the rim a small ridge. Cordon on neck. (G IA 70, phase IV, early to mid-4th century). WMFC 54.
R.310 CT 12 Poppy-necked (?) jar with a bead-rim and cordon on neck. Highly burnished ext. (AA III 32, phase II, late 2nd to mid-3rd century). WMFC 54.

Beakers

R.311 BA 64 Beaker with burnished zig-zag design on neck. (A XVI 6). WMFC 41.
R.312 BA 43 Beaker with curving upper wall and horizontal burnished lines on ext. (A XII 17). WMFC 41.
R.313 BA 96 Base sherd of beaker. Rouletting on body ext. Fabric is fired grey but covered on int. and ext. by an orange slip. (AA I 44, phase V, later 3rd century on).
R.314 BA 84 Base sherd of beaker with moulded foot. Body ext. decorated with three lines of rouletting. (D II 29A).
R.315 BB 24 Beaker with short everted rim. Beneath rim is an incised groove. Prominent high shoulder. 2nd century. (B IA 25, phase III, Antonine to 3rd century on). WMFC 63.
R.316 BB 41 Poppy-headed beaker with well-burnished ext. and rim. Body decorated with applied barbotine dots. Poppy-headed beakers are rare until the 2nd century. (H II 76, phase III, Antonine to 3rd century on — residual). WMFC 40.
R.317 BB 51 Beaker with curving upper wall and small beaded rim. Incised line beneath rim. Highly burnished rim and ext. London-type ware (Marsh 1978, no 17). Early 2nd century. (H II 61). WMFC 44.
R.318 BB 30 Body sherd of beaker, decorated with incised groove dividing upper area of herring-bone type decoration. (D I 87, phase V, early to mid-4th century — residual).
R.319 BB 32 Body sherd from a beaker. Burnished ext. Body decorated with barbotine dots. Neronian–Hadrianic. (A XVI 3).
R.320 BC 116 Beaker with plain rim. On neck ext. are three incised lines with another three horizontal lines above carination. Between these is a band of burnished vertical lines. (C IC 24). WMFC 51.

Cups

R.321 BB 47 Campanulate cup with beaded rim, imitating Dr 27. London-type ware (Marsh 1978, no 12). Early 2nd century. (C VI 27, phase VII, early to mid-4th century — residual). WMFC 59.
R.322 BC 134 Carinated cup with burnished ext. Below rim are two incised lines, and above the carination a further two, forming burnished cordons. Between these two sets of incised lines are vertical burnished lines. (C I 89). WMFC 51?
R.323 BC 236 Cup with cordon and two burnished lines on body. (C IXA 11). WMFC 54.
R.324 BD 8 Carinated cup with bead-rim and straight sides. Ext. decorated with thin burnished horizontal lines. (F III 13). WMFC 54.
R.325 BD 19 Small beaded cup, very vesiculated. (G IA 60, phase V, later 4th century). WMFC 34.
R.326 BE 26 Cup with incised horizontal line beneath rim. Another on the ext. (C I 59A). WMFC 54.
R.327 BG 135 Cup with everted rim. A groove on body ext. (B I 14). WMFC 54.
R.328 BR 11 Cup with everted rim, carinated, with cordons on waist and girth. Burnished ext. (H I 14). WMFC 54.
R.329 BU 4 Cup with a plain rim and groove on neck. Possibly carinated. Burnished ext. (A XVI 16). WMFC 47.
R.330 CJ 1 Cup or small mug? Int. and ext. burnished. (F I 5, phase XIII, after AD 353). WMFC 60.

Tankards

These forms are common in red oxidized Severn Valley ware fabrics, but comparatively rare in reduced grey wares. The examples here are possibly reduced Severn Valley wares (Webster 1976).

R.331 BA 88 Tankard with incised line beneath rim. Well-burnished ext. 2nd to 3rd century. (D I 246, phase II, later 2nd to early 3rd century?). WMFC 61.
R.332 BC 177 Tankard with two incised lines beneath rim. Possibly Severn Valley ware (cf Webster 1976, no 38). Mid- to late 1st century. (D II 22). WMFC 61.
R.333 BC 277 Tankard with incised groove beneath rim. Handle scar. Burnished rim and ext. (Cf Webster 1976, no 43). Later 2nd to 3rd century. (A X 18). WMFC 62.
R.334 BC 324 Tankard with incised groove beneath rim. Well-burnished rim and ext. (Cf Webster 1976, no 43). Later 2nd to 3rd century. (C I 24). WMFC 62.
R.335 BC 340 Tankard with incised groove beneath rim. Handle scar, around which are burnished vertical lines. 2nd–3rd century. (B I 3, phase II, Antonine to 3rd century). WMFC 62.
R.336 BC 288 Body sherd with handle. Burnished ext. and handle. (K I 26).
R.337 BN 1 Small tankard with groove immediately beneath rim. Body decorated by groups of burnished vertical lines on ext. (Cf Webster 1976, no 38). Mid- to late 1st century. (AA I 65, phase II, late 2nd to mid-3rd century residual). WMFC 61.

Carinated bowls and jars

Five vessel types, R.338–R.342, are carinated bowls in fabric BB, London-type ware, imitating Dr. 30. These vessels are straight-sided bowls with vertical walls and with decorative techniques typical of London ware.

True London ware is unlikely to have had an area of distribution greater than thirty miles from its production centre. However the pattern of distribution suggests that there were a number of local manifestations with a producer in the west Midlands supplying Alcester. These fine grey table wares are attributed to the 2nd century.

R.338 BB 14 Straight-sided bowl with vertical walls. Form based on Dr. 30, and the decoration typical of London-type ware. The decoration occurs beneath rim and is bounded by two incised grooves, below which are regularly spaced, triple concentric semi-circles, compass-drawn with central point visible. From each semi-circle vertical lines descend to another pair of incised grooves, below which is another band of rouletting. (Cf Marsh 1978, type 48). Early 2nd century. (D II 3). WMFC 66.
R.339 BB 20 Carinated bowl copying Dr. 30. Local manifestation of London-type ware. On body is a pair of incised lines below which is area of semi-circles made from trailed slip. Early 2nd century. (AA II 8). WMFC 51.

R.340 BB 37 Body sherd, well-burnished with applied dots in rows. (D II 29A).
R.341 BB 7 Straight-sided bowl with vertical walls, based on Dr. 30. Local manifestation of London-type ware. Below rim a band of rouletting, bordered by incised grooves and the bowl is decorated by grey slip rings. (Cf Marsh 1978, type 48). Early 2nd century. (D I 47, phase VI, mid- to late 4th century? — residual). WMFC 51.
R.342 BB 16 Carinated bowl copying Dr. 30. Local manifestation of London ware. Decoration on body occurs beneath two incised grooves and is in form of regularly spaced hairpins made from slip, with barbotine dots bordering them. (Cf Marsh 1978, type 48). Early 2nd century. (C VI 98). WMFC 51.
R.343 BC 315 Fine carinated bowl with everted bead-rim. On body is pair of incised grooves with another groove beneath. Highly burnished ext. (C VI 42B). WMFC 53.
R.344 BC 175 Bowl with rolled-over rim and pair of incised grooves on body. Burnishing occurs on the rim and above and below the incised lines. (D II 20). WMFC 66.
R.345 BC 145 Carinated bowl with out-turned rim and incised lines on body. Burnished ext. (Cf Young 1977, no R.58). AD 100–200. (H I 1). WMFC 53.
R.346 BC 161 Carinated bowl with incised line on rim and two wide grooves on body ext. (AA II 73, phase V, later 3rd century on — residual). WMFC 53.
R.347 BC 368 Carinated bowl with cordon beneath rim. (C VIA 68, phase IV, later 3rd century on — residual). WMFC 54.
R.348 BF 42 Carinated bowl with wide shallow depressions forming an almost corrugated wall. Highly burnished ext. (A XVI 12). WMFC 53.
R.349 BR 15 Carinated jar with outward-curving neck. Groove below rim. Neck decorated with thin burnished horizontal lines. (G IV 39, phase IV, early to mid-4th century — residual). WMFC 53.
R.350 BU 13 Carinated jar with rolled-over rim. Body decorated with burnished horizontal lines. Above carination an incised line. Ring groove on base ext. (D I 115, phase VI, mid- to late 4th century — residual). WMFC 51.
R.351 CE 1 Very fine hemispherical bowl. Copy of Dr. 37. On body a pair of incised grooves. Very highly polished. (Cf Marsh 1978, type 42.11). Early 2nd century. (D II 48). WMFC 66.
R.352 CT 53 Straight-sided bowl with incised line beneath rim decorated by fine wavy line. Int. and ext. covered by black slip. (AA I 48, phase I, late 1st to early 2nd century). WMFC 50.
R.353 CT 17 Carinated bowl with straight sides. Body decorated by incised horizontal grooves intersected by thin vertical incisions. Burnished ext. (D I 142). WMFC 53.

Bag-shaped bowls

R.354 BA 50 Bowl with burnished rim with incision directly beneath. Body decorated with regularly spaced vertical lines. (A XVIII T/S). WMFC 66.
R.355 BA 67 Bowl with three burnished horizontal lines beneath rim. Regularly spaced vertical lines decorate the ext. Int. of neck also decorated by three burnished lines. (C IIIB I). WMFC 66.
R.356 BC 97 Bowl, the body decorated with regularly spaced burnished vertical lines. (AA II 100, phase I, late 1st to 2nd century). WMFC 34.

Straight-sided bowls with everted rims

The rim form is flat or curved. The sides of the bowl are straight with a carinated or chamfered base. This form is a common 2nd-century one derived from Black-Burnished 1.

R.357 BA 71 Straight-sided bowl with everted rim and chamfered base. Burnished rim. Burnished horizontal lines occur on ext. 2nd century. (B I 2, phase II, Antonine to 3rd century). WMFC 68.
R.358 BC 127 Straight-sided bowl with rolled-over rim. 2nd century. (C VI 37, phase VII, early to mid-4th century — residual). WMFC 68.
R.359 BC 328 Flat everted rim with incised line under rim. Straight-sided bowl with chamfered base. The ext. is covered with burnished lines. 2nd century. (D II 49). WMFC 68.
R.360 BC 319 Straight-sided bowl with everted rim and chamfered base. Body decorated with burnished horizontal lines. 2nd century. (B I 3, phase II, Antonine to 3rd century). WMFC 68.
R.361 BC 408 Small straight-sided bowl with everted rim and carination. 2nd century. (AA II 8A). WMFC 68.
R.362 BC 163 Carinated bowl with everted flat rim turning downwards. Body decorated with horizontal lines, two above carination and three beneath. (H II 49B, phase II, Antonine to 3rd century). WMFC 52.
R.363 BC 414 Straight-sided dish/bowl with slightly everted rim and chamfered base. (A IX 17, phase II, late 2nd to mid-3rd century). WMFC 82.
R.364 BC 233 Bowl with everted rounded rim. Well-burnished ext. (Cf Webster 1976, no 52). 2nd–3rd century. (C IXA 11). WMFC 66.
R.365 BC 410 Straight-sided bowl/dish with everted rim and flat base. On ext. are horizontal burnished lines. Black-Burnished copy. 2nd century. (A IX 25, phase VI, late 3rd to early 4th century — residual). WMFC 68.
R.366 BC 401 Straight-sided bowl/dish with everted rim with lip curved over. Flat base. Ext. decorated with burnished lines. 2nd century. (A IIIA 12). WMFC 68.
R.367 BC 139 Straight-sided bowl/dish with rounded everted rim and flat base. 2nd century. (C VI 79, phase IV, later 3rd century on — residual). WMFC 68.
R.368 BC 41 Straight-sided dish/bowl with rounded everted rim and flat base. Burnished rim. A band of thin horizontal lines decorates body ext. (A IX 5). WMFC 68.
R.369 BC 183 Straight-sided bowl with flat base and flanged rim. Copy of later Roman Black-Burnished form. Later 3rd to 4th century. (A X 5). WMFC 68.
R.370 BD 18 Straight-sided bowl with everted rim and carinated base with an incised line above the carination. (G I 60D). WMFC 51.
R.371 BE 101 Straight-sided bowl with everted rim. 2nd century. (AA II 100, phase I, late 1st to 2nd century). WMFC 68.
R.372 BE 72 Straight-sided deep bowl with everted rim. 2nd century. (C VI 32). WMFC 68.
R.373 BE 78 Bowl with everted flat-topped rim and curved wall. 2nd century. (B I 14). WMFC 68.
R.374 BE 90 Straight-sided bowl with everted rim with lip curving over. Flat base. Ext. decorated with burnished horizontal lines. 2nd century. (B VIIIA 6). WMFC 68.
R.375 BE 16 Straight-sided bowl with everted rim. Burnished rim and ext. 2nd century. (A IX 11). WMFC 68.
R.376 BG 8 Straight-sided bowl with out-turned rim. Derived from a Black-Burnished form. 2nd century. (C II 1). WMFC 68.
R.377 BX 6 Bowl with everted rim and gently curved sides. 2nd century. (E II 55, phase IV, Hadrianic–Antonine). WMFC 68.
R.378 CS 16 Very fine straight-sided bowl with sharply everted rim. Copy of Black-Burnished ware tradition. Very well-burnished with acute lattice on int. and ext. Hadrianic–Antonine. (B I 2, phase II, Antonine to 3rd century). WMFC 68.
R.379 CT 9 Straight-sided bowl with out-turned rim and chamfered base. Ext. decorated by horizontal burnished lines. Form derived from a Black-Burnished type. 2nd century. (B I 3, phase II, Antonine to 3rd century). WMFC 68.
R.380 GA 31 Bowl with everted flat rim, and curved walls. (G IA 49, phase IX, late 4th century — residual). WMFC 56.

Reeded-rim bowls with carination

R.381 BA 94 Carinated bowl with reeded rim; above the carination an incised line. 1st to early 2nd century. (D II 2, phase IX, late 4th century — residual). WMFC 52.
R.382 BC 151 Carinated bowl with reeded rim and burnished ext. 1st to early 2nd century. (C VIA 107, phase V, later 3rd century on — residual). WMFC 56.
R.383 BD 37 Carinated bowl with reeded rim. Ext. is burnished with horizontal lines and fired black. 1st to early 2nd century. (D I 70, phase IV, late 3rd century? — residual). WMFC 52.
R.384 BE 48 Carinated bowl with reeded rim. 1st to early 2nd century. (D II 97, phase III, later 2nd to early 3rd century on — residual). WMFC 56.
R.385 BU 16 Reeded-rim bowl with straight sides. 1st to early 2nd century. (G II 2). WMFC 56.

Malvern ware dishes

These are derived from Black-Burnished ware types and consequently date to after AD 120. The vessels are hand-made and tempered with angular metamorphic rock. Parallels are to be found in Peacock (1968a).

R.386 CCC 45 Hand-made dish copying a Black-Burnished form. Int. burnished with ext. decorated by oblique lattice. AD 120+. (AA II 90). WMFC 82.
R.387 CCC 44 Hand-made dish copying Black-Burnished ware. Burnished parallel lines and lattice on ext. AD 120+. (C VI 22, phase VIII, early to mid-4th century on). WMFC 82.
R.388 CCC 39 Hand-made dish copying Black-Burnished ware. Ext. and base have an obtuse lattice. 3rd century or later. (E III 31, phase VIII, 3rd century?). WMFC 82.
R.389 CCC 55 Hand-made dish. Black-Burnished copy. Ext. burnished. Obtuse lattice on ext. and base. 3rd century or later. (B I 20). WMFC 82.
R.390 CCC 56 Hand-made dish with bead-rim copying Black-Burnished forms. Base int. decorated by burnished lines radiating from centre. Ext. and base decorated by an acute burnished lattice. AD 120+. (AA III 19, phase IV, later 3rd century on — residual). WMFC 82.
R.391 CCC 2 Hand-made dish with acute burnished lattice on int. and ext. After AD 120+. (A IX 1A). WMFC 82.
R.392 CCC 9 Hand-made dish or lid with straight sides, very coarse. Burnished int. (C XIX 1). WMFC 86.
R.393 CCC 16 Hand-made dish or lid. Black-Burnished copy. Int. is burnished. Acute burnished lattice on ext. After AD 120+. (H II 91, phase III, Antonine to 3rd century on). WMFC 88.

Wide-mouthed bowls with flat rims and curving sides

R.394 BA 55 Bowl with flat everted rim and curved walls. Burnished rim and ext. (A XV 1). WMFC 65.
R.395 BC 63 Bowl with flat out-turned rim and curved walls. (AA II 91, phase II, late 2nd to early 3rd century). WMFC 65.
R.396 BD 27 Wide-mouthed bowl with flat out-turned rim, curved walls, and high shoulder. Ext. covered by dark grey slip, and decorated by horizontal burnished lines. (J II 21). WMFC 65.
R.397 BE 65 Bowl with flat out-turned rim and walls curving inwards. (A I 2A). WMFC 65.
R.398 BE 48 Necked bowl with rolled-over rim. Derived from Belgic necked jars. Around girth are incised grooves. Burnished rim. (D II 97, phase III, later 2nd to early 3rd century on — residual). WMFC 65.
R.399 BG 106 Bowl with flat out-turned rim and curved sides. (C I 59). WMFC 65.
R.400 BG 24 Bowl with out-turned rim and curved sides. (AA II 91, phase II, late 2nd to early 3rd century). WMFC 65.
R.401 BG 37 Bowl with out-turned flat rim, curved walls, and high shoulder. Ext. decorated by horizontal burnished lines. (C I 59). WMFC 65.
R.402 BG 102 Necked bowl with corrugated upper wall. Burnished ext. (B I 14). WMFC 65.
R.403 BG 25 Shallow, necked bowl with out-turned rim. (A XII 12). WMFC 65.

Shouldered bowls

R.404 BR 2 Small, shouldered bowl with flaring rim. Slight neck, high shoulder, and curving sides. (D I 173, phase II, later 2nd to early 3rd century?). WMFC 65.
R.405 BR 3 Bowl with flaring rim, slight neck, and high shoulder. Burnished ext. (B IA 1). WMFC 69.
R.406 BU 11 Flat everted-rim bowl with high shoulder and curved furrowed walls. Black int. and ext. (G II 28). WMFC 65.
R.407 BX 2 Upright bowl with slightly everted rim and faint, wide, rounded, girth grooves. Cordon on body. Well-burnished ext. (D II 49). WMFC 65.
R.408 BX 5 Carinated bowl with incised groove on rim int. and at base of neck. On shoulder a cordon-like protrusion, below which is an incised groove with another beneath the carination. Black and highly burnished ext. (G IA 68, phase IV, early to mid-4th century — probably residual). WMFC 69.

Straight-sided bowls with upright rims

R.409 BC 313 Hard, fine bowl with straight oblique walls. Well-burnished with two parallel incised grooves on ext. (D II 60). WMFC 52.
R.410 BC 159 Large straight-sided bowl with bead-rim and rouletted decoration on body ext. (AA I 50, phase IV, later 3rd century on — probably residual). WMFC 53.
R.411 BC 74 Bowl with upright rim and ridged upper wall. (AA II 78, phase II, late 2nd to early 3rd century). WMFC 66.
R.412 BC 278 Straight-sided bowl with bead-rim. Burnished acute lattice on ext. Black-Burnished copy. Hadrianic–Antonine. (D I 143, phase VI, mid- to late 4th century? — residual). WMFC 82.
R.413 BC 312 Straight-sided bowl with carination. Ext. has three shallow incised grooves. Between second and third is a band of regularly spaced diagonal lines. Immediately beneath third groove is the carination. Both int. and ext. highly burnished. (G I 60D). WMFC 56.
R.414 BE 59 Straight-sided bowl with lipless rim. Immediately beneath is an external groove. (AA II 78, phase II, late 2nd to early 3rd century). WMFC 66?
R.415 BE 52 Straight-sided bowl with two pairs of parallel incised grooves, one pair beneath rim and another on body. (A V 18, phase VI, late 3rd to early 4th century — probably residual). WMFC 66.
R.416 BE 57 Straight-sided bowl with groove directly beneath lip. Chamfered base. (AA II 23). WMFC 56.
R.417 BE 24 Bead-rim bowl with steep-sided straight walls. (AA II 91, phase II, late 2nd to early 3rd century). WMFC 66.
R.418 BE 109 Bowl with bead-rim. Int. has two incised horizontal grooves, one beneath rim and another on body int. (D I 110). WMFC 54.
R.419 BG 50 Hemispherical bowl with pair of parallel incised lines beneath rim. Another line on body ext. denotes area of regularly spaced diagonal lines. (AA II 78, phase II, late 2nd to early 3rd century). WMFC 66.
R.420 BG 121 Straight-sided bowl with pair of parallel lines immediately beneath rim. (AA II 83, phase II, late 2nd to early 3rd century). WMFC 66.
R.421 BG 151 Straight-sided tankard?, with two incised grooves beneath rim. Int. and ext. burnished, with an acute burnished lattice on ext. (Cf Webster 1976, no 39). 2nd century. (A IX 8, phase VI, late 3rd to early 4th century — residual). WMFC 61.
R.422 CT 2 Straight-sided bowl/dish with two horizontal incised grooves. Well-burnished int. and ext. (A IX 1A). WMFC 82.
R.423 CT 24 Hand-made bowl with carination. Rim slightly outward-turning. Int. and ext. highly burnished. (D I 27, phase IV, late 3rd century?). WMFC 52.

Bowls with flanged rims

R.424 BA 104 Small bowl with flanged and burnished rim. (G IA 9). WMFC 67.
R.425 BA 18 Small bowl with flange. Int. and ext. covered with a tan-coloured slip. (AA IIIA 4). WMFC 67.
R.426 BB 45 Bowl with curved flanged rim, possibly a copy of Curle 11 or Dr. 35. Early 2nd century. London-type ware. (Cf Marsh 1978, no 34). (D I 47, phase VI, mid- to late 4th century? — residual). WMFC 67.
R.427 BB 13 Bowl with curved flanged rim with internal beading. Copy of Curle 11 or Dr. 35. (Cf Marsh 1978, no 34: 11). Early 2nd century. (C VI 60, phase IV, later 3rd century on — residual). WMFC 67.
R.428 BC 183 Bowl with flanged curved-over rim. On rim int. is incised line. Burnished int. and ext. (A X 5). WMFC 67.
R.429 BC 256 Bowl with flanged rim with internal beading. Int. and ext. burnished. (H II 52). WMFC 67.
R.430 BC 283 Bowl with curved flanged rim, and traces of black slip on the int. (AA III 60, phase II, late 2nd to mid-3rd century). WMFC 65.
R.431 BC 297 Shallow flanged bowl with black int. and ext. Slipped. (AA I 48, phase I, late 1st to early 2nd century). WMFC 69.

Romano-British coarse pottery

R.432 BC 250 Straight-sided bowl with flanged rim. Copy of late Roman Black-Burnished form, from the late 3rd century onwards. (AA III 9). WMFC 68.
R.433 BC 169 Flange-rimmed bowl with burnished rim and burnished horizontal lines on ext. Form similar to Severn Valley types. (D I 176). WMFC 65.
R.434 BD 16 Bowl with bead-rim and flange curving over. Int. and ext. burnished with two burnished lines on the body int. (A XVIII T/S). WMFC 67.
R.435 GA 13 Large coarse bowl with flanged rim. Mid- to late 4th century. (C IIIA 14). WMFC 67.
R.436 GA 28 Large bowl with flanged rim with burnished int. and ext. Mid- to late 4th century. (Context unknown). WMFC 67.
R.437 GA 18 Large coarse bowl with flanged rim. Mid- to late 4th century. (F I 5, phase XIII, after AD 353). WMFC 67.

Miscellaneous wide-mouthed bowls/jars

R.438 BA 110 Jar with everted rim. (A IX 12, phase V, later 3rd century on). WMFC 23.
R.439 BBA 33 Wide-necked jar with a wide incised line on rim ext. creating a small flange. Int. and ext. covered by black slip. (AA I 19, phase VIII, late 3rd to early 4th century). WMFC 38.
R.440 BC 166 Wide-mouthed jar with sharply everted reeded rim. Ext. burnished. (G I 92). WMFC 38.
R.441 BC 181 Wide-mouthed jar with rolled-over rim. Well-burnished rim. (G V 7, phase V, later 4th century). WMFC 38.
R.442 BC 396 Wide-mouthed jar with everted rolled-over rim. On body a shallow incised groove with pair of burnished lines on ext. (C VIA 98, phase V, later 3rd century on). WMFC 38.
R.443 BE 47 Squat fine jar with everted rim. On shoulder are five incised horizontal lines. Black int. and ext. (D II 106, phase III, later 2nd to early 3rd century on). WMFC 24.
R.444 BG 10 Jar with everted rim and well-burnished ext. (C VI 37, phase VII, early to mid-4th century). WMFC 23.
R.445 CT 29 Jar with an everted rim, well-burnished. (A IX 3, phase VI, late 3rd to early 4th century). WMFC 22.
R.446 CT 3 Wide-mouthed jar with everted rim and an incised groove on shoulder. Rim and ext. burnished. (D I 143, phase VI, mid- to late 4th century?). WMFC 38.

Bowls with cordons beneath the rim

R.447 BA 49 Bowl with grooved rim and cordon on body ext. (Hughes' excavations, ABA L6 2). WMFC 68.
R.448 BA 35 Bowl with flanged rim and burnished ext. (E I 10, phase III, Neronian–Trajanic). WMFC 68.
R.449 BC 55 Bowl with cordon immediately beneath rim and burnished loop decoration on body ext. (AA II 94, phase I, late 1st to 2nd century). WMFC 68.
R.450 GC 14 Bowl or constricted-necked jar with a cordon beneath the rim. Burnished int. and ext. (G I 105, phase IV, early to mid-4th century — probably residual). WMFC 53.

Bowls and jars with straight sides and everted rims

R.451 BA 181 Necked squat jar with high shoulder. (A IX 8, phase VI, late 3rd to early 4th century). WMFC 31.
R.452 BC 400 Bowl with straight sides and everted rim. (AA I 74). WMFC 51.
R.453 BC 255 Bowl with everted rim. Ext. decorated by burnished horizontal lines. Int. and ext. burnished. (A IX 5). WMFC 51.
R.454 BC 147 Straight-sided bowl with everted rim. Burnished horizontal lines on the ext. (C VIA 94, phase V, later 3rd century on). WMFC 22.
R.455 BG 20 Bowl with a sharply everted rim. Burnished rim and burnished horizontal lines on the ext. (A IX 3, phase VI, later 3rd to early 4th century — probably residual). WMFC 53.
R.456 BG 101 Bowl with sharply everted rim. Burnished int. and burnished horizontal lines on ext. (A IX 3, phase VI, late 3rd to early 4th century — probably residual). WMFC 51.

Miscellaneous

R.457 BA 62 Large base sherd of carinated bowl. Pair of incised lines and burnished lattice. On base is a ring groove. (C VIA 85, phase III, 3rd century — probably residual).
R.458 BC 172 Carinated bowl with inward-turning rim, and cordon immediately beneath. Rim and area beneath the cordon burnished. (D I 126A, phase II, later 2nd to early 3rd century?). WMFC 59.
R.459 BE 106 Bowl with flat inward-turning rim and wavy incised line on body ext. Dark grey core with red/brown int. and ext. (E I 3, phase XIII, after AD 353). WMFC 68.
R.460 BE 99 Body sherd of bowl. Ext. decorated by two bands of rouletted decoration with large girth groove between. (G I 105, phase IV, early to mid-4th century).
R.461 CT 33 Large body sherd with pie-crust cordon. Burnished triple zig-zag on body ext. (A XVIIA 5).

Dishes

R.462 BA 53 Straight-sided dish with flat base and well-burnished int. and ext. (D I 107, phase I, 1st century to early Antonine). WMFC 82.
R.463 BB 49 Simple dish with flat base. Groove internally at junction between body wall and base. Form is of Belgic derivation or possibly copying Pompeian red-ware forms. London-type ware (Marsh 1978, type 24). Early 2nd century. (D I 2A, phase VIII, late 4th century — residual). WMFC 82.
R.464 BB 53 Simple platter with curved wall slightly turned in at top. On ext. a feather mark. Copy of a Pompeian red-ware form. London-type ware (Marsh 1978, type 24). Early 2nd century. (D I 210). WMFC 81.
R.465 BC 265 Gallo-Belgic derived dish with foot ring. Burnished int. and ext. (A IX 3, phase VI, late 3rd to early 4th century — residual). WMFC 81.
R.466 BC 132 Dish with chamfered base and flattened rim. (C VIA 24, phase IX, mid-4th century on). WMFC 82.
R.467 BC 358 Dish with rim internally stepped. Chamfered base. On int. where walls meet base are two incised grooves. Int. black and highly burnished, ext. grey and burnished. (A XVI 8). WMFC 81.
R.468 BD 54 Coarse dish with flat rim thickened towards the centre. Ext. crudely burnished. (G IV 39, phase IV, early to mid-4th century). WMFC 81.
R.469 BU 3 Very fine carinated dish with cordon on carination. Well-burnished black int. and ext. (A XVIIIB 11). WMFC 80.
R.470 CS 18 Dish. Terra Nigra copy (Camulodunum form 24). Carinated with flat base and foot rim. Int. and ext. burnished with rouletted decoration on base ext. Claudian–Neronian. (B VIII 1). WMFC 80.
R.471 CT 19 Thick-walled dish with flat base. Burnished int. and ext. Camulodunum form 28, Claudian–Neronian. (C VIA 107, phase V, later 3rd century on). WMFC 82.

Lids

R.472 BC 136 Lid. (A XVI 4). WMFC 86.
R.473 BC 138 Lid with burnished horizontal lines on ext. (C VIA 42B). WMFC 86.
R.474 BC 311 Lid with three burnished horizontal lines. (B I 3, phase II, Antonine to 3rd century). WMFC 86.
R.475 BC 156 Lid. (AA I 33, phase VI, late 3rd to early 4th century). WMFC 88.
R.476 BD 46 Lid with burnished horizontal lines on ext. (B I 3, phase II, Antonine to 3rd century). WMFC 86.
R.477 BD 43 Lid with three burnished lines on ext. Covered with a black slip on int. and ext. (B I 3, phase II, Antonine to 3rd century).
R.478 BE 100 Black lid with hole drilled through top. (C V 5).
R.479 BE 28 Lid with flattened everted rim. Fired to a red ext. (AA II 100, phase I, late 1st to 2nd century). WMFC 88.
R.480 CCC 60 Hand-made lid with pie-crust finger decoration, burnished. (D I T/S). WMFC 88.
R.481 CCC 8 Hand-made rim of lid with lightly burnished int. Probably Antonine (Peacock 1968b). (A XVI T/S). WMFC 86.
R.482 CT 37 Lid with horizontal bands burnished concentrically on ext. (C VI 32). WMFC 86.

Triple vase

R.483 BW 1 Triple vase. (C III 1). WMFC 94.

Handles etc

R.484 BC 196 Handle, cylindrical in form. (J II 21).
R.485 BC 353 Animal handle with dark grey slip on int. and ext. (C VIA 58, phase VIII, early to mid-4th century on).
R.486 BC 215 Handle with black slip. (D I 246, phase II, later 2nd to early 3rd century?).
R.487 BC 195 Handle. (D I 246, phase II, later 2nd to early 3rd century?).
R.488 BE 61 Large body sherd, with four feet (paws) of an animal — ?handle; toes are incised. Pair of incised lines runs horizontally from lower feet around girth of vessel. (AA III 98, phase I, late 1st to early 2nd century).
R.489 BA 95 Body sherd, decorated with roller stamp/rouletting. (Hughes' excavations, ABA L6 2).

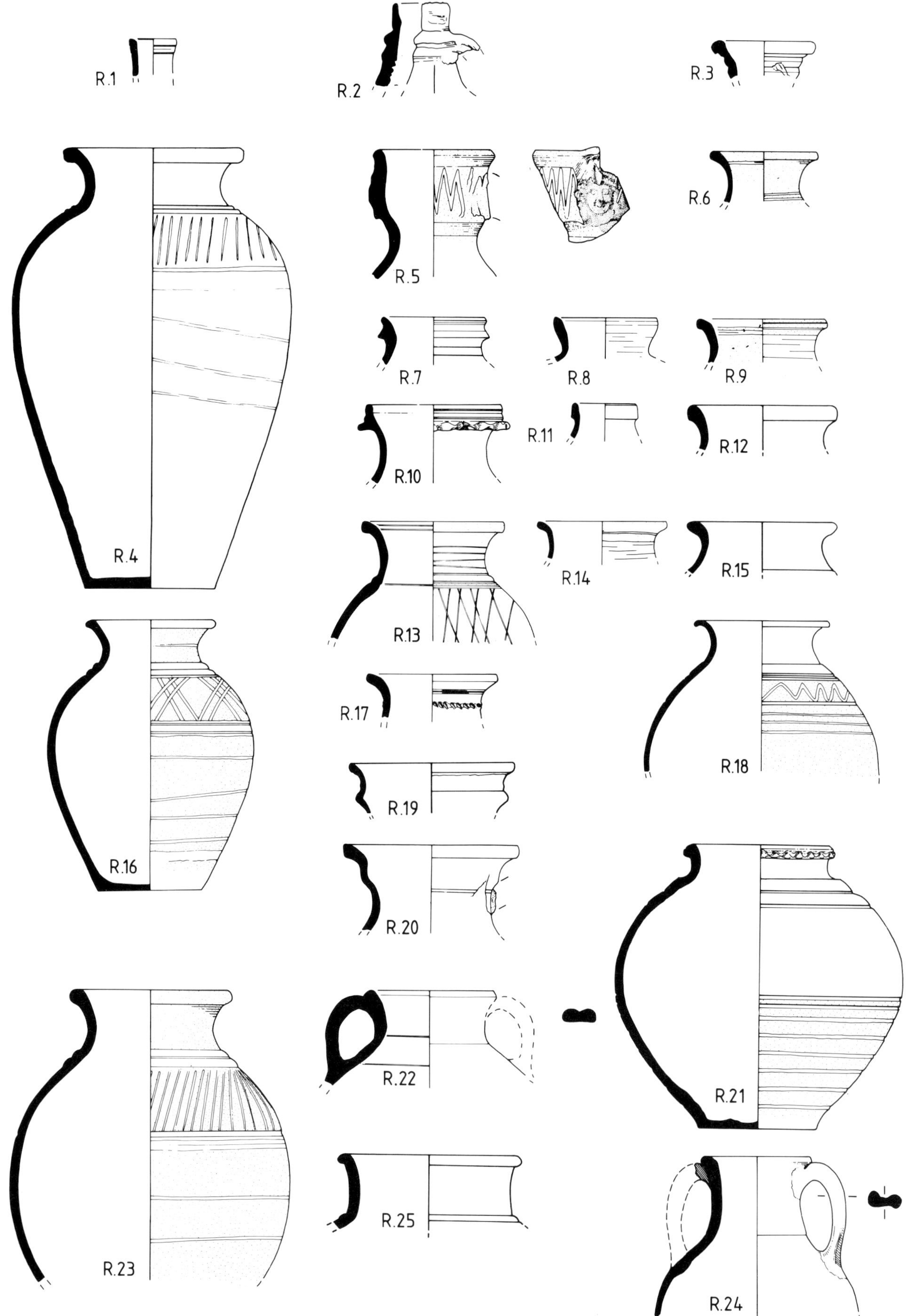

Figure 1 Roman coarse pottery, types R.1–R.25 (1/4 scale)

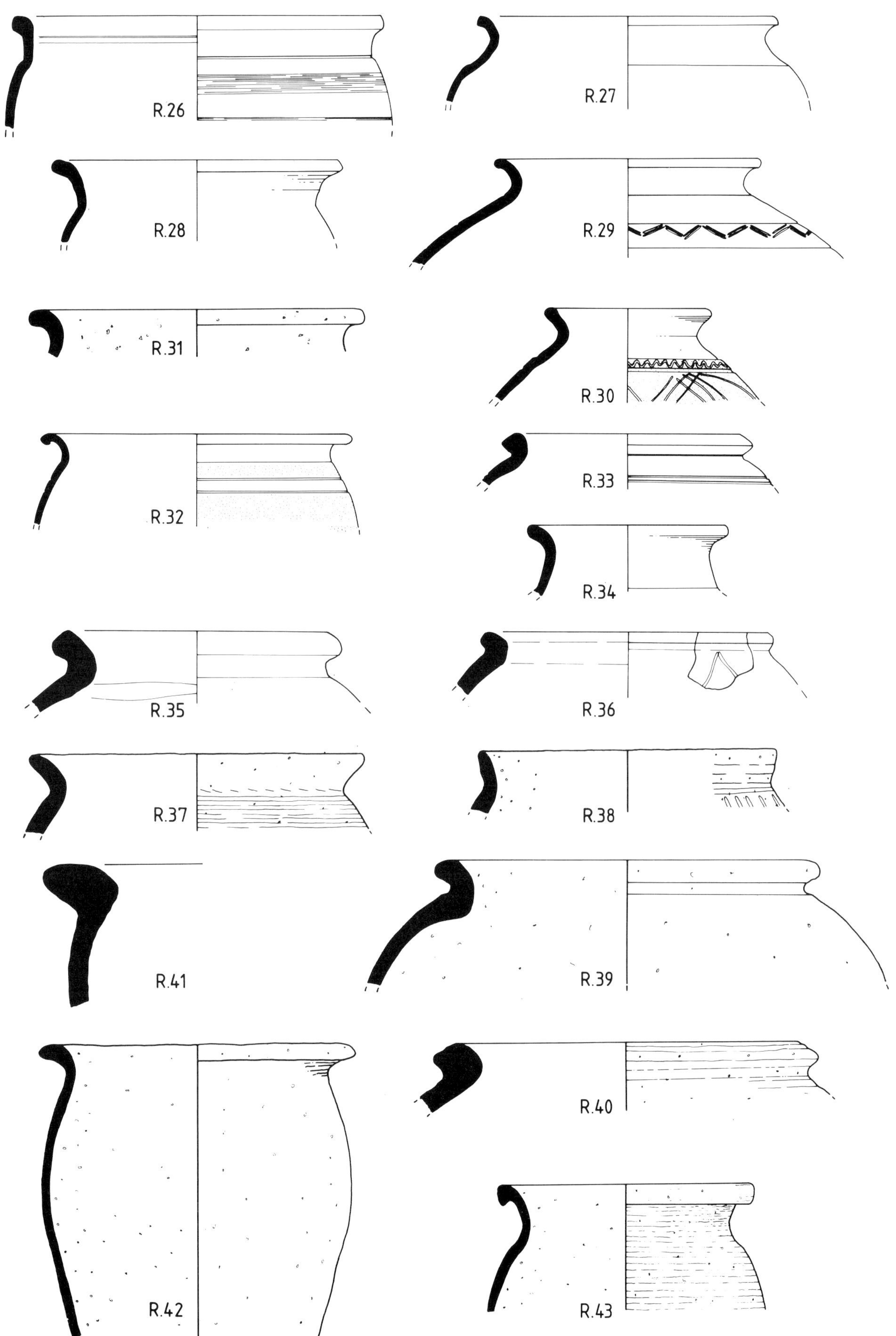

Figure 2 Roman coarse pottery, types R.26–R.43 (1/4 scale)

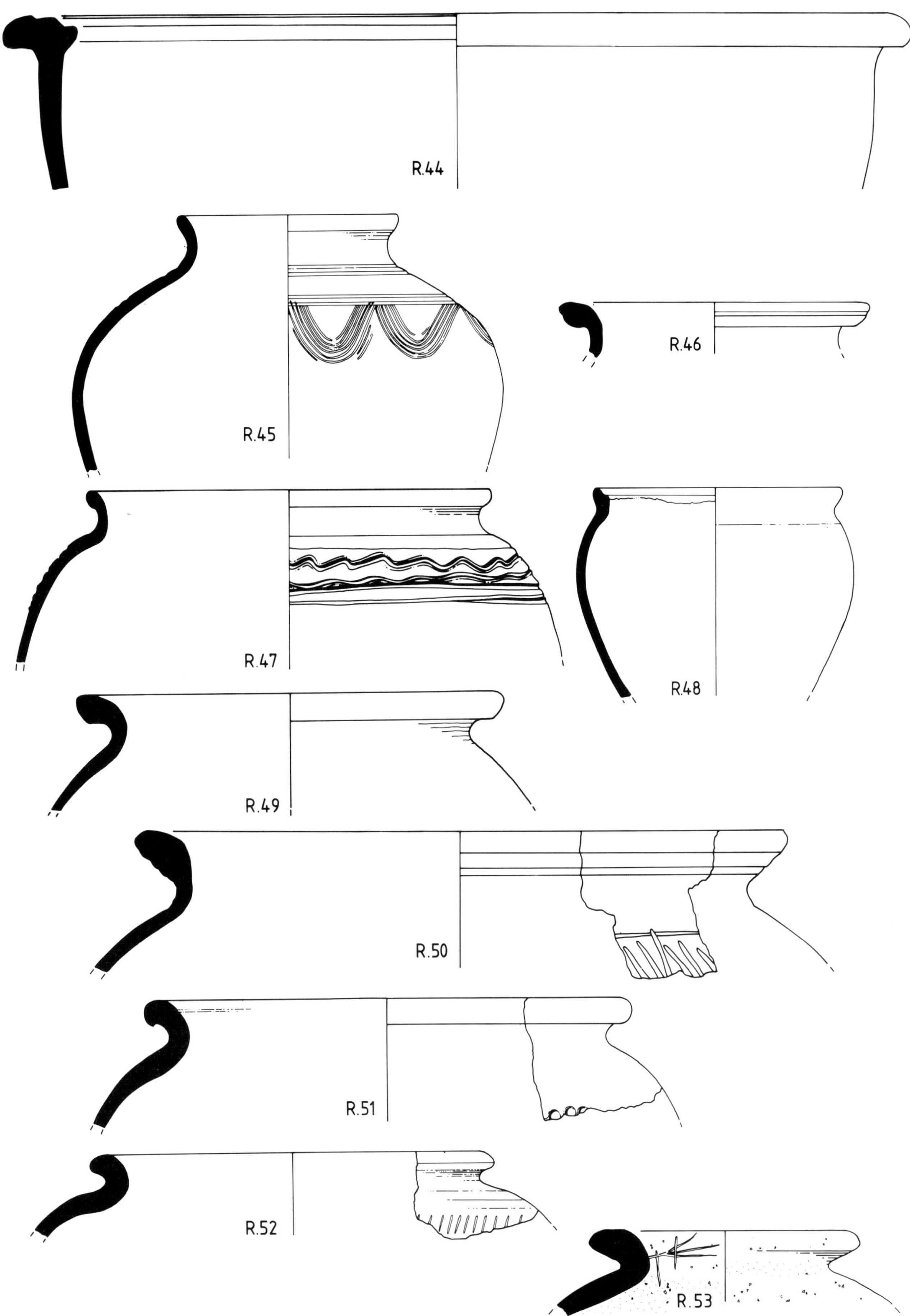

Figure 3 Roman coarse pottery, types R.44–R.53 (1/4 scale)

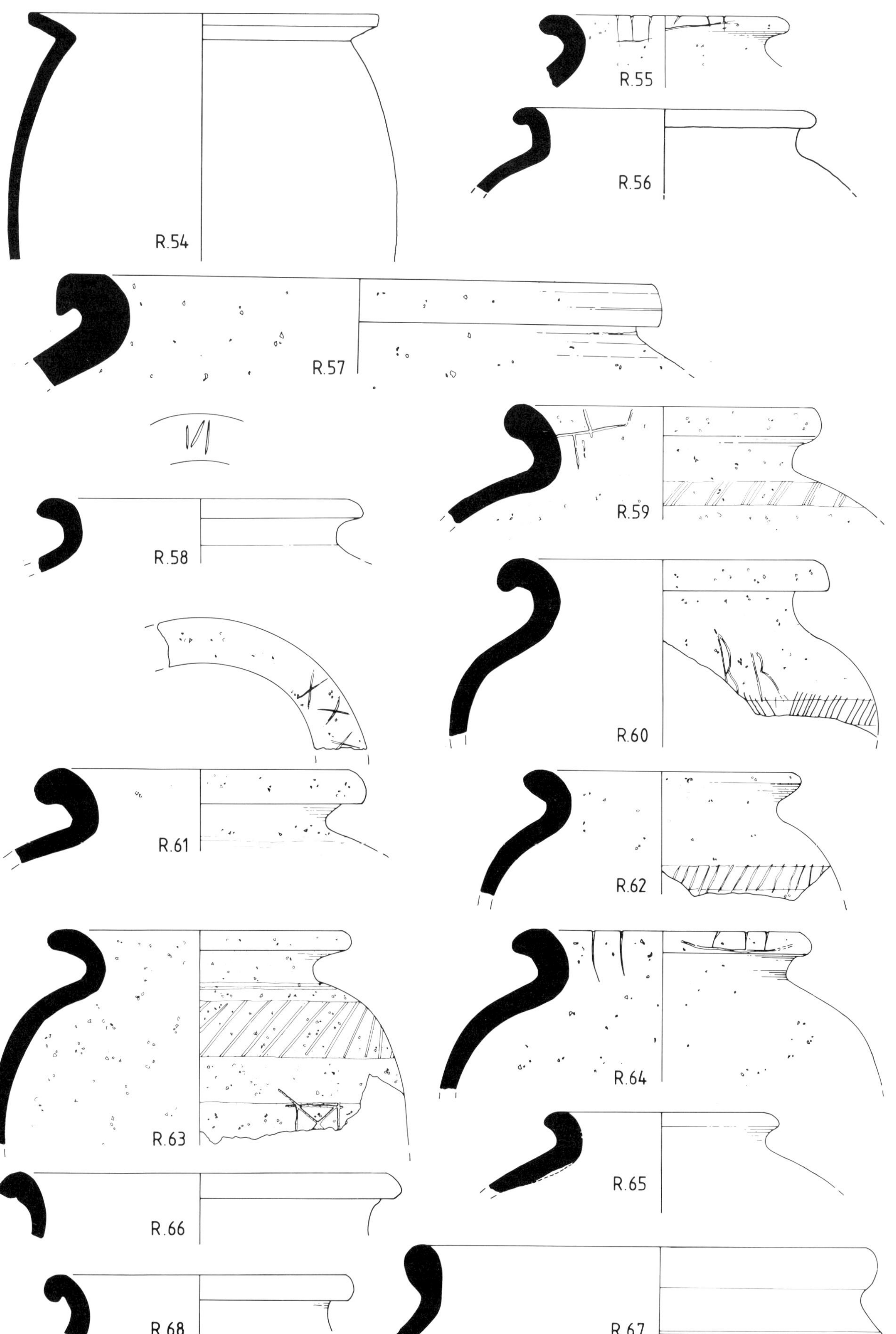

Figure 4 Roman coarse pottery, types R.54–R.68 (1/4 scale)

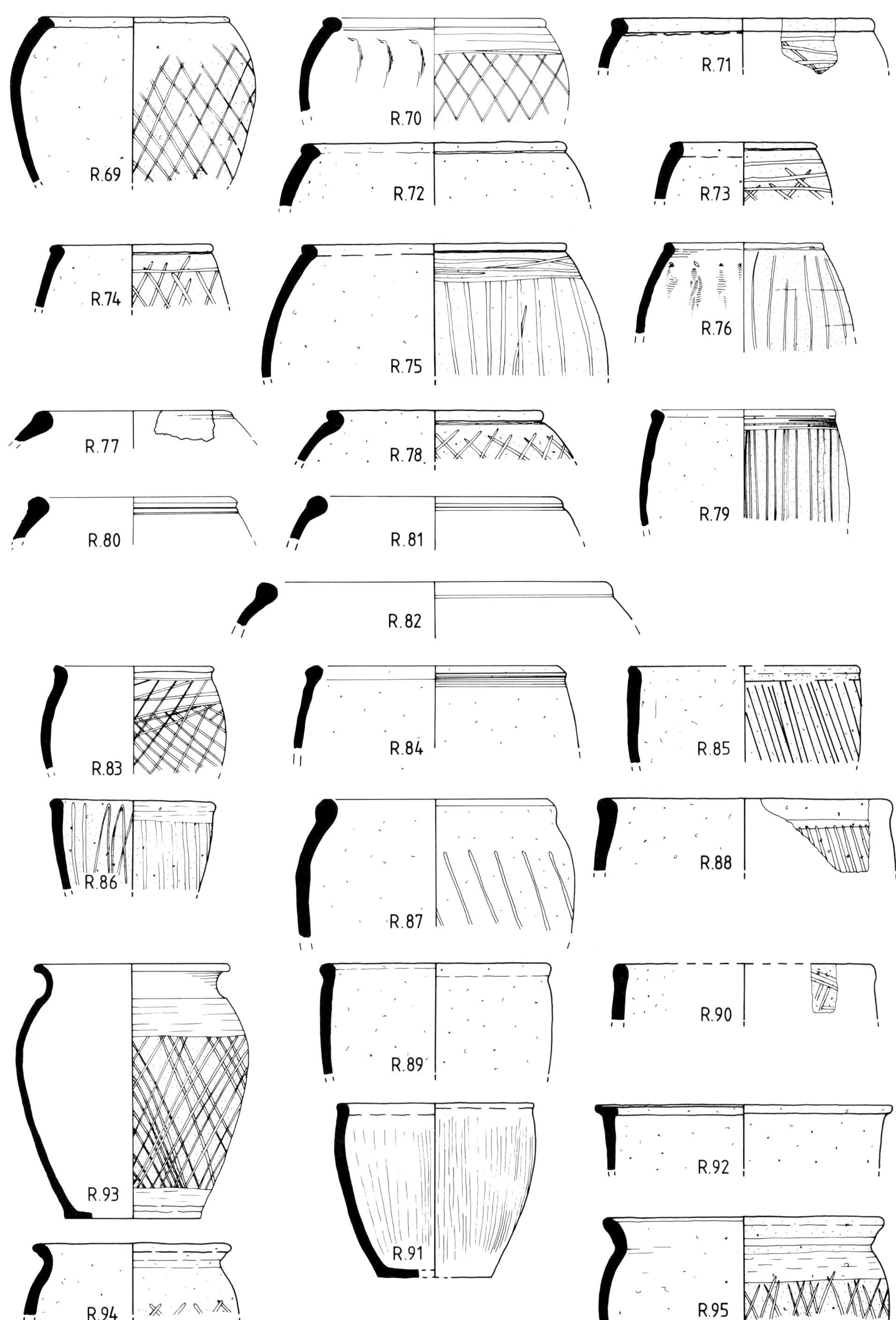

Figure 5 Roman coarse pottery, types R.69–R.95 (1/4 scale)

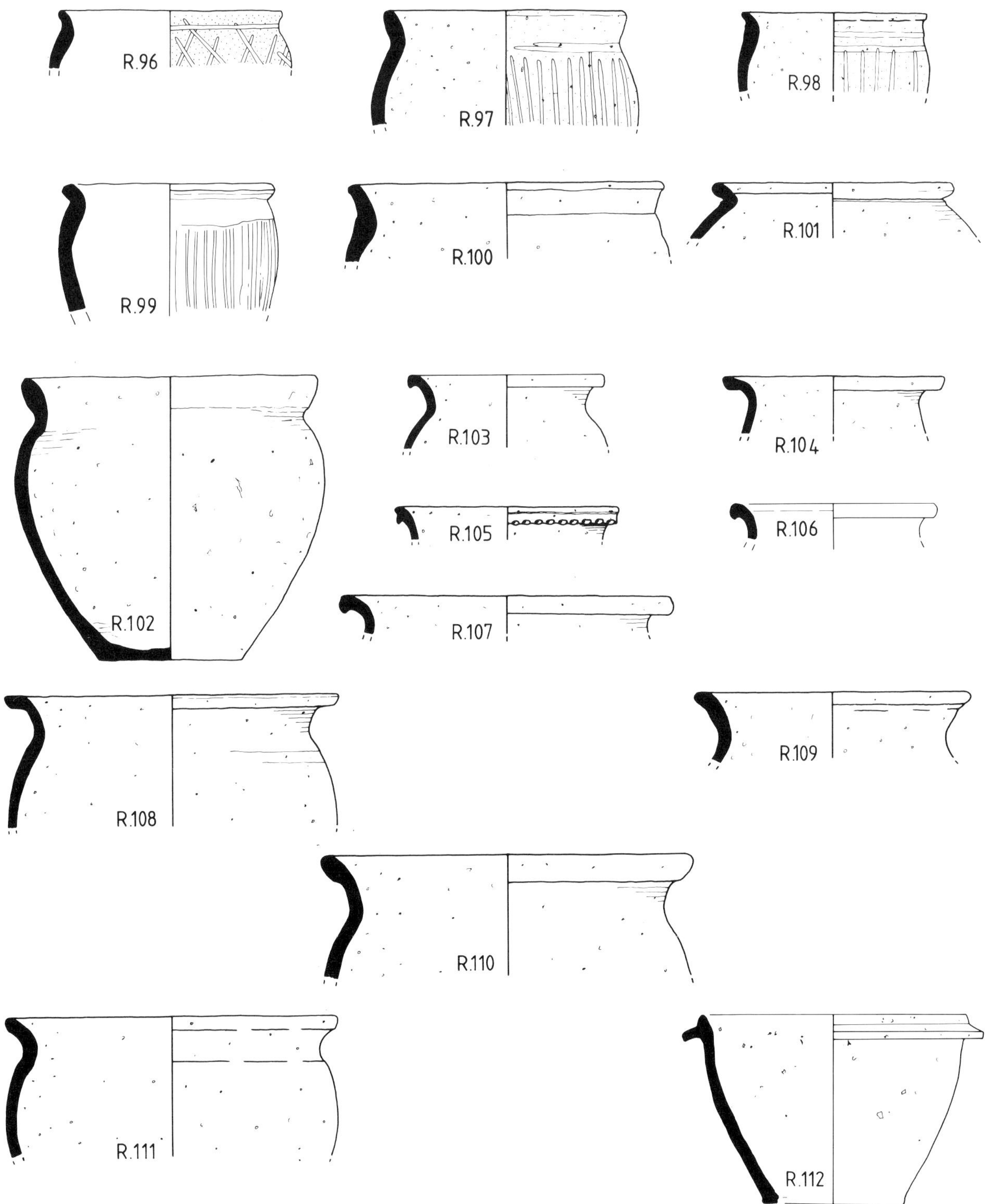

Figure 6 Roman coarse pottery, types R.96–R.112 (1/4 scale)

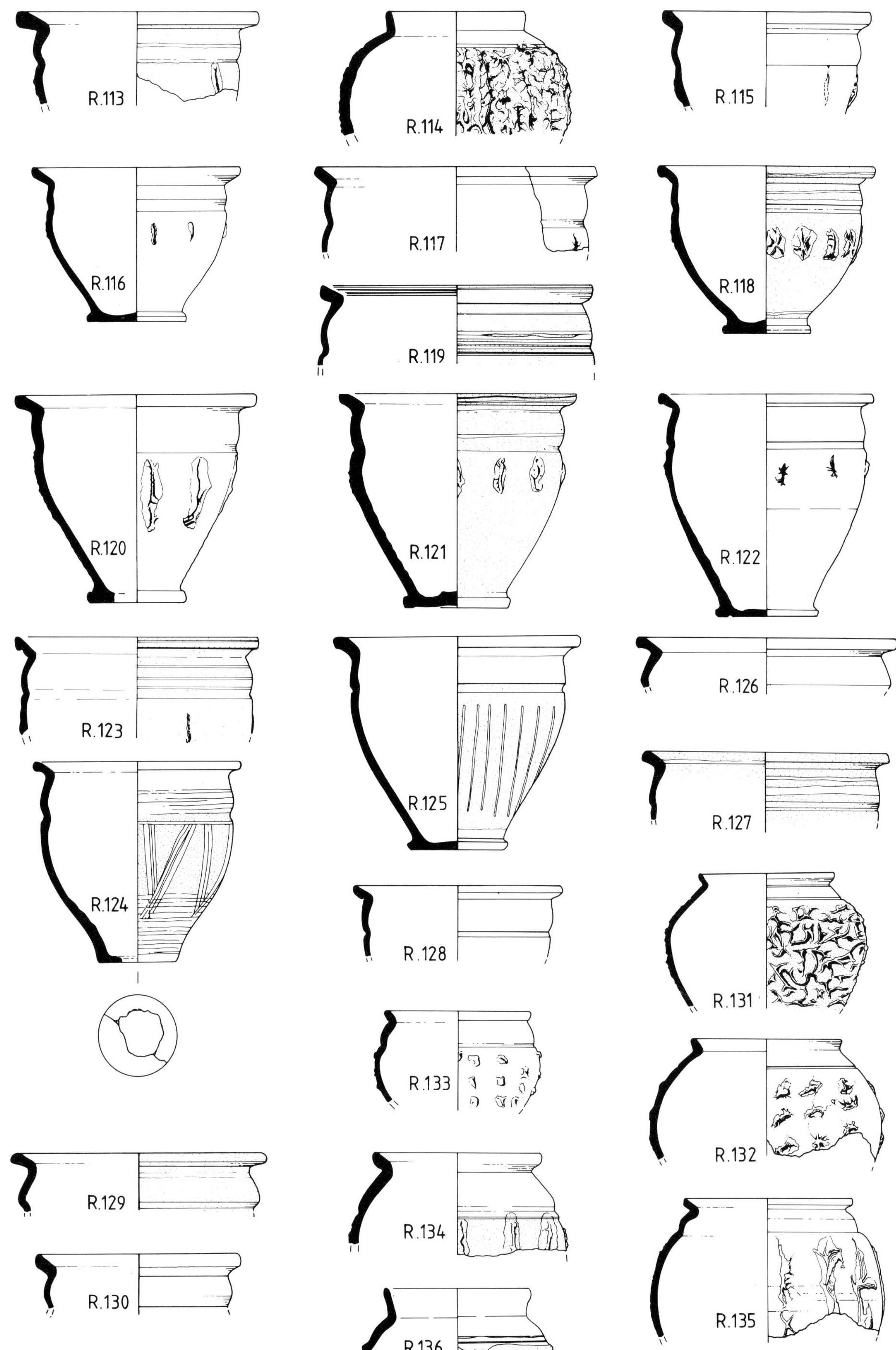

Figure 7 Roman coarse pottery, types R.113–R.136 (1/4 scale)

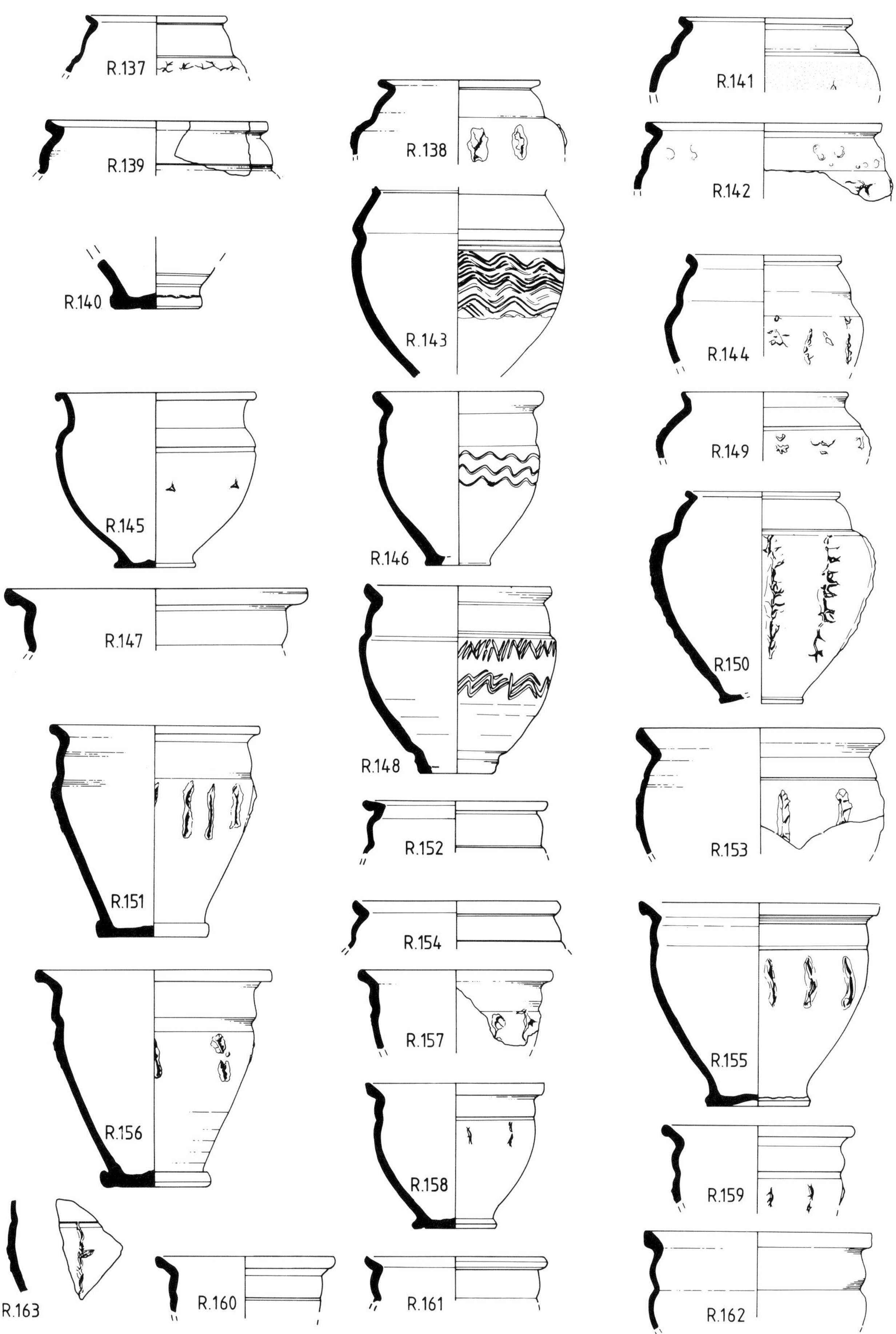

Figure 8 Roman coarse pottery, types R.137–R.163 (1/4 scale)

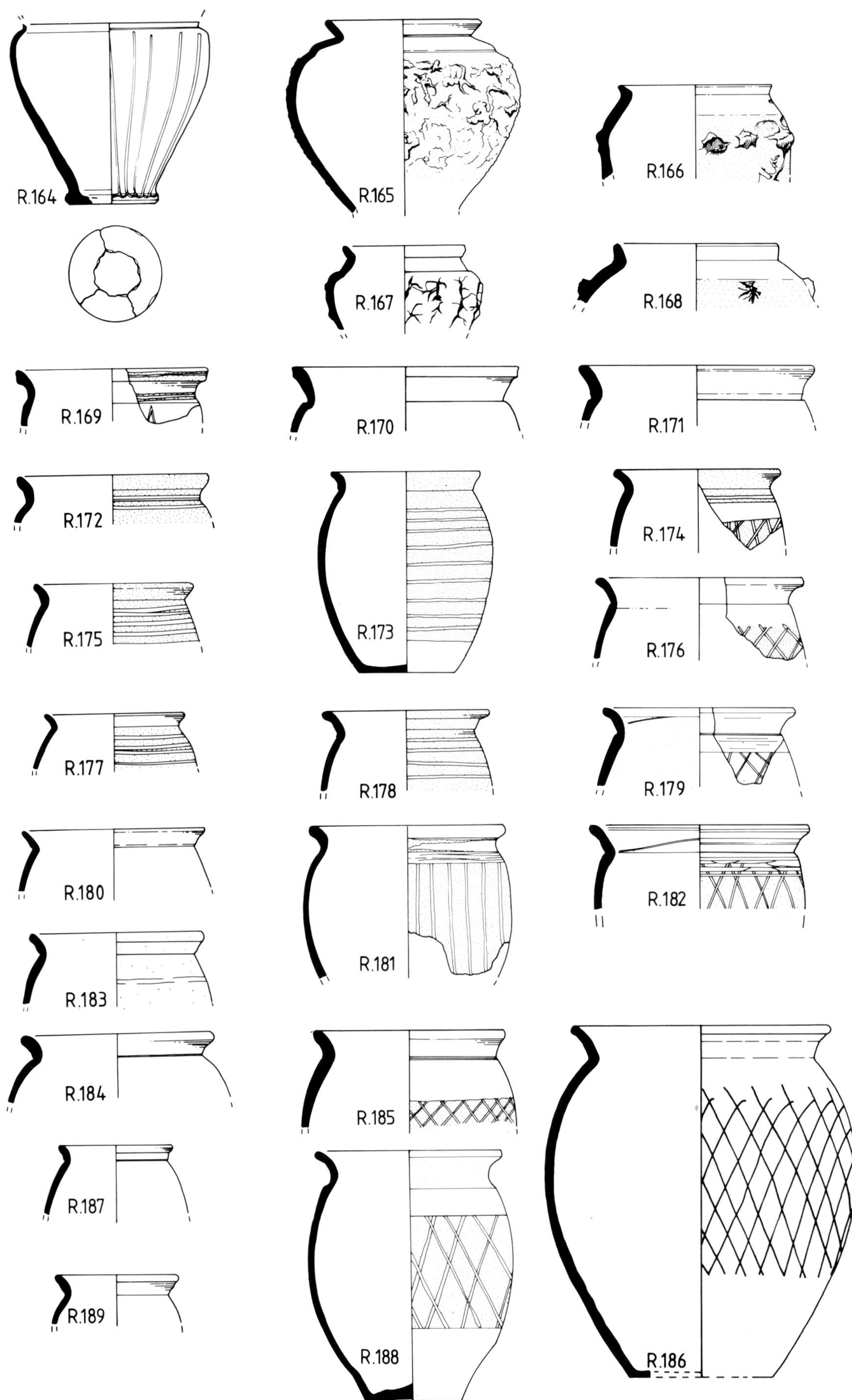

Figure 9 Roman coarse pottery, types R.164–R.189 (1/4 scale)

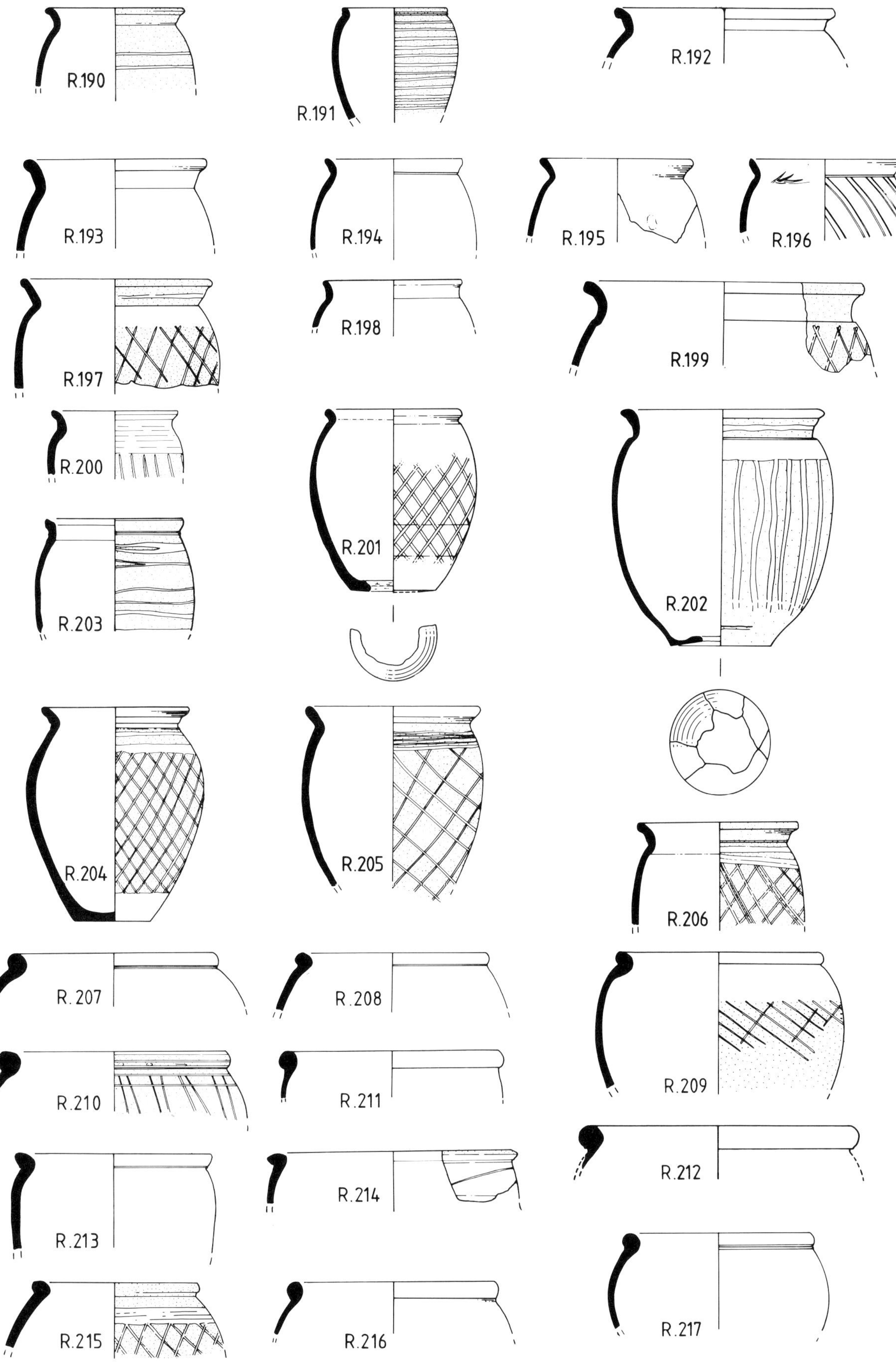

Figure 10 Roman coarse pottery, types R.190–R.217 (1/4 scale)

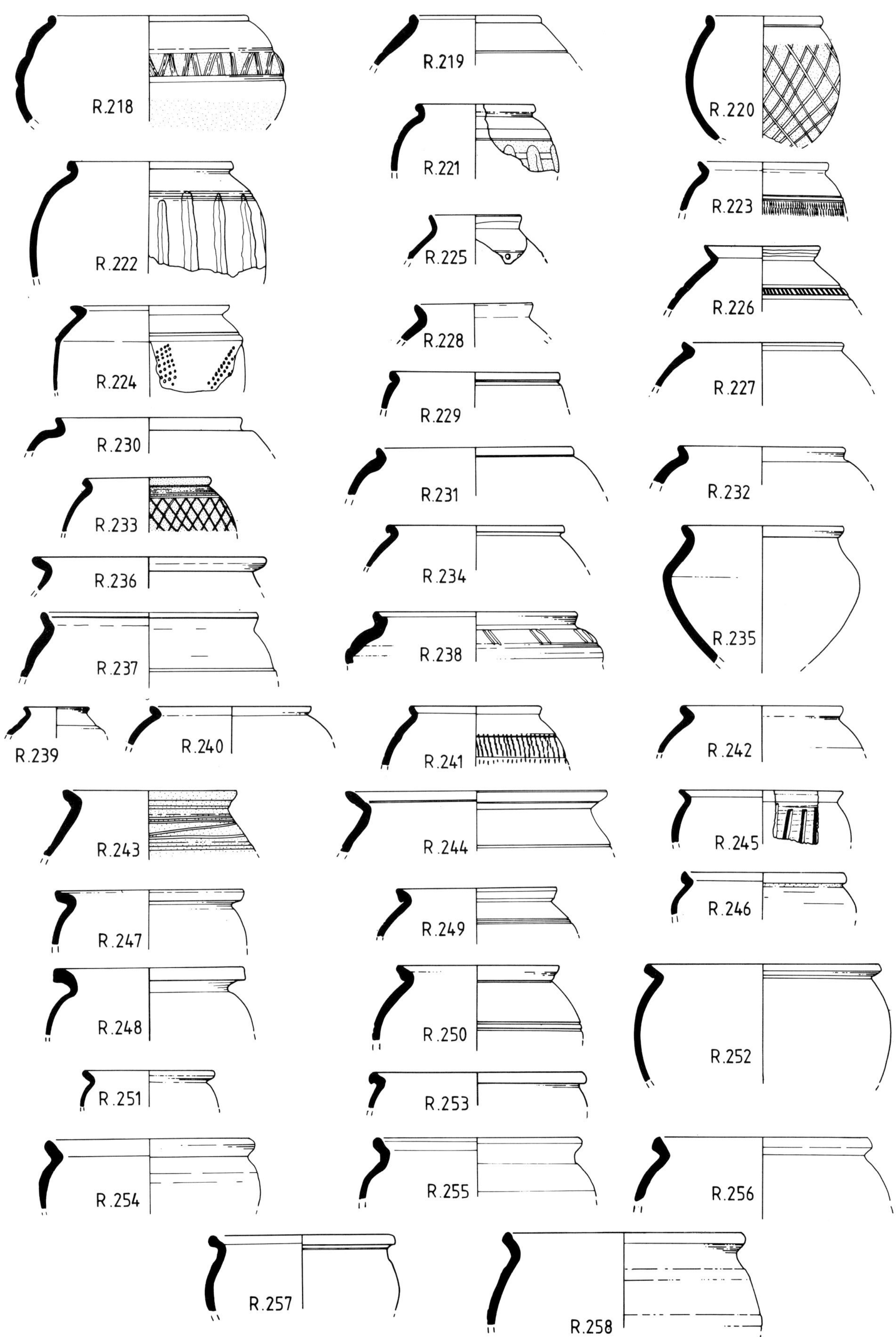

Figure 11 Roman coarse pottery, types R.218–R.258 (1/4 scale)

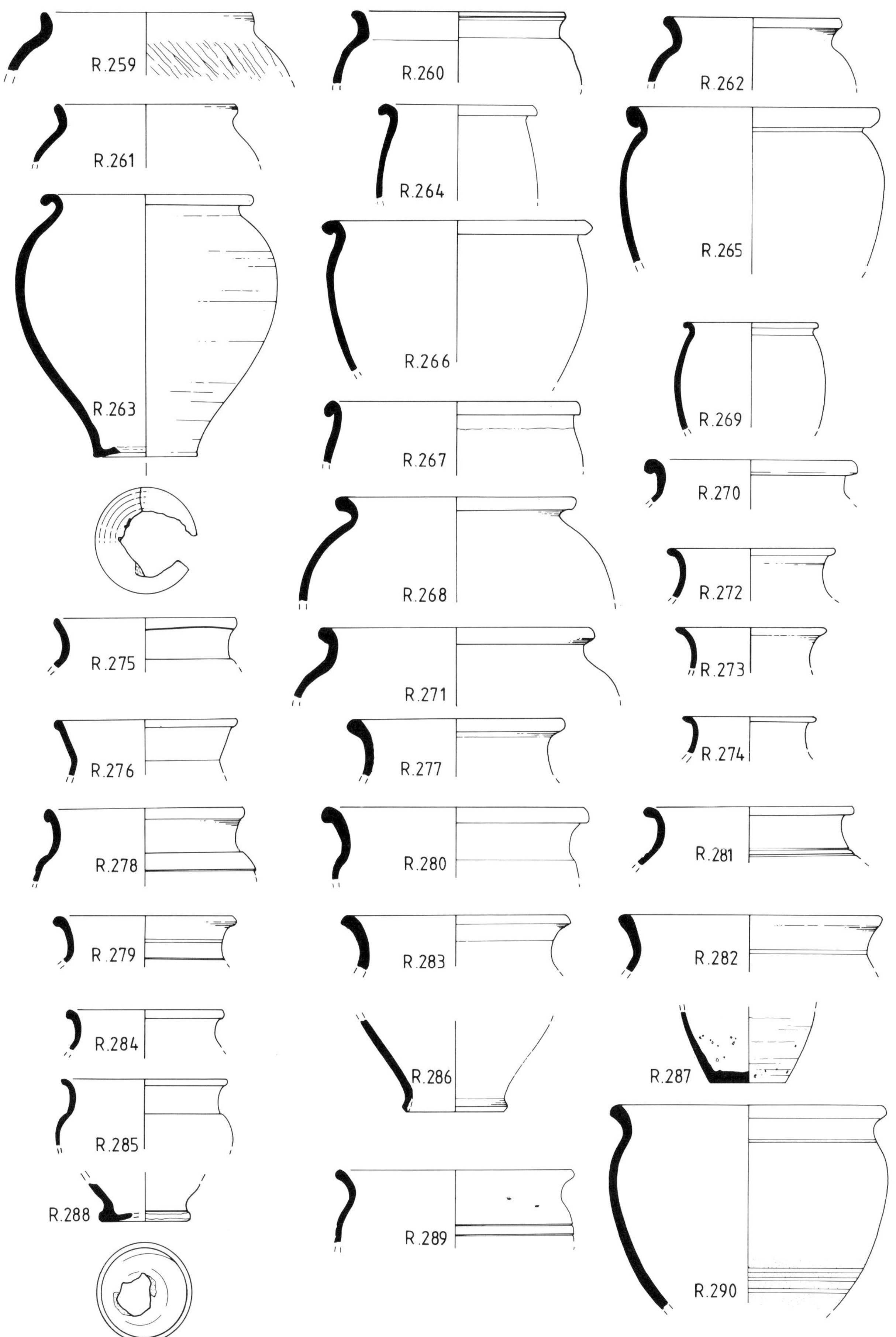

Figure 12 Roman coarse pottery, types R.259–R.290 (¼ scale)

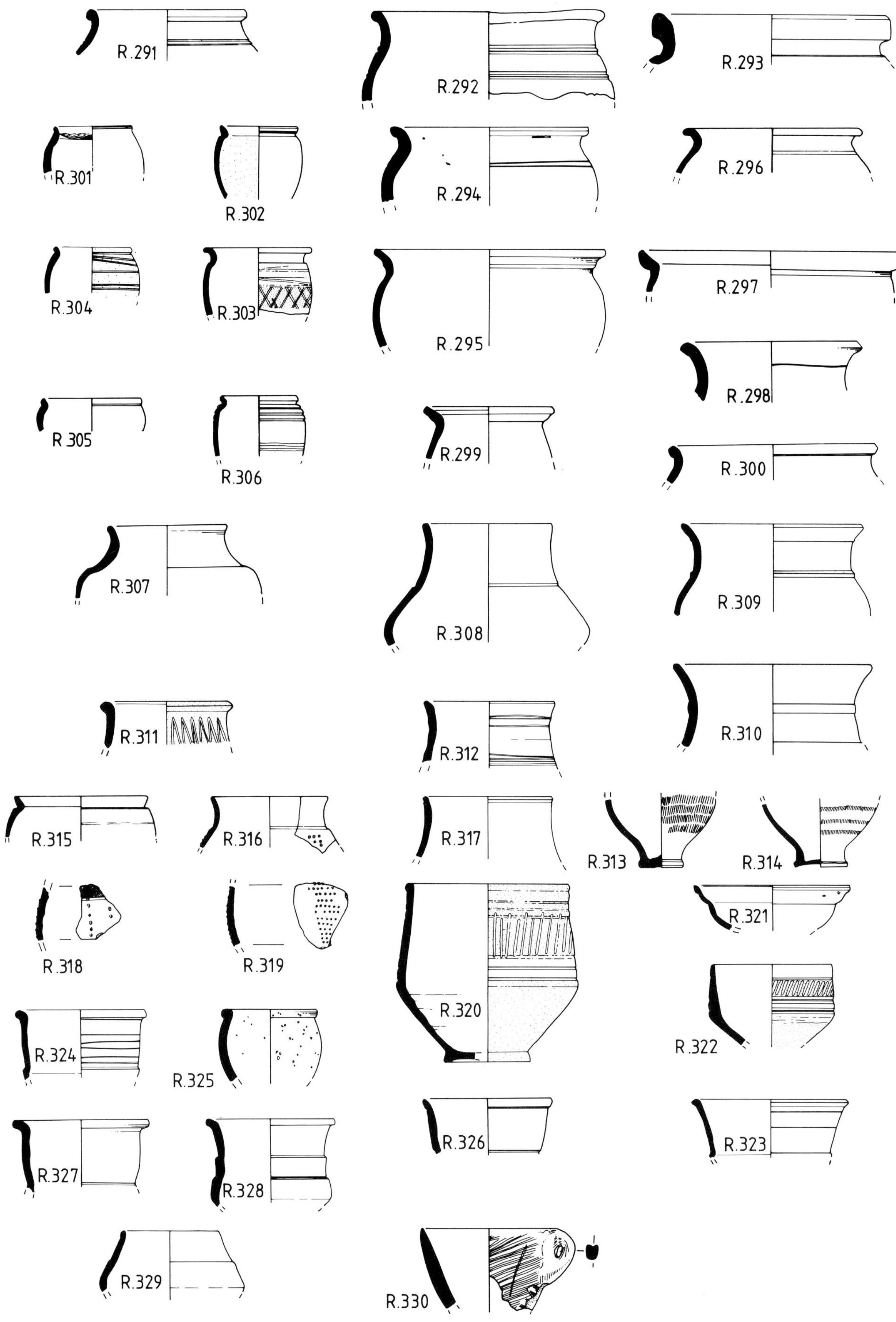

Figure 13 Roman coarse pottery, types R.291–R.330 (¼ scale)

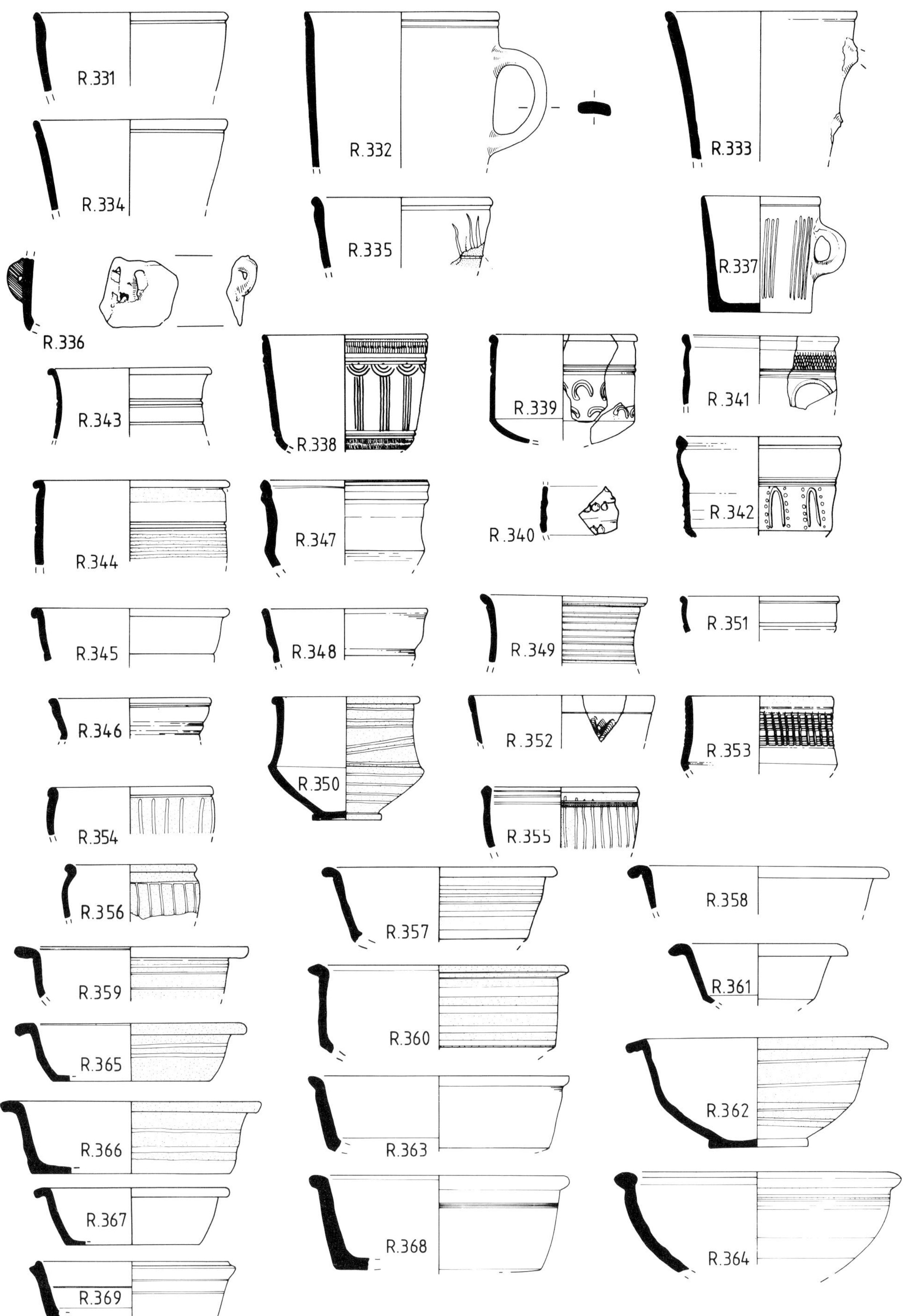

Figure 14 Roman coarse pottery, types R.331–R.369 (1/4 scale)

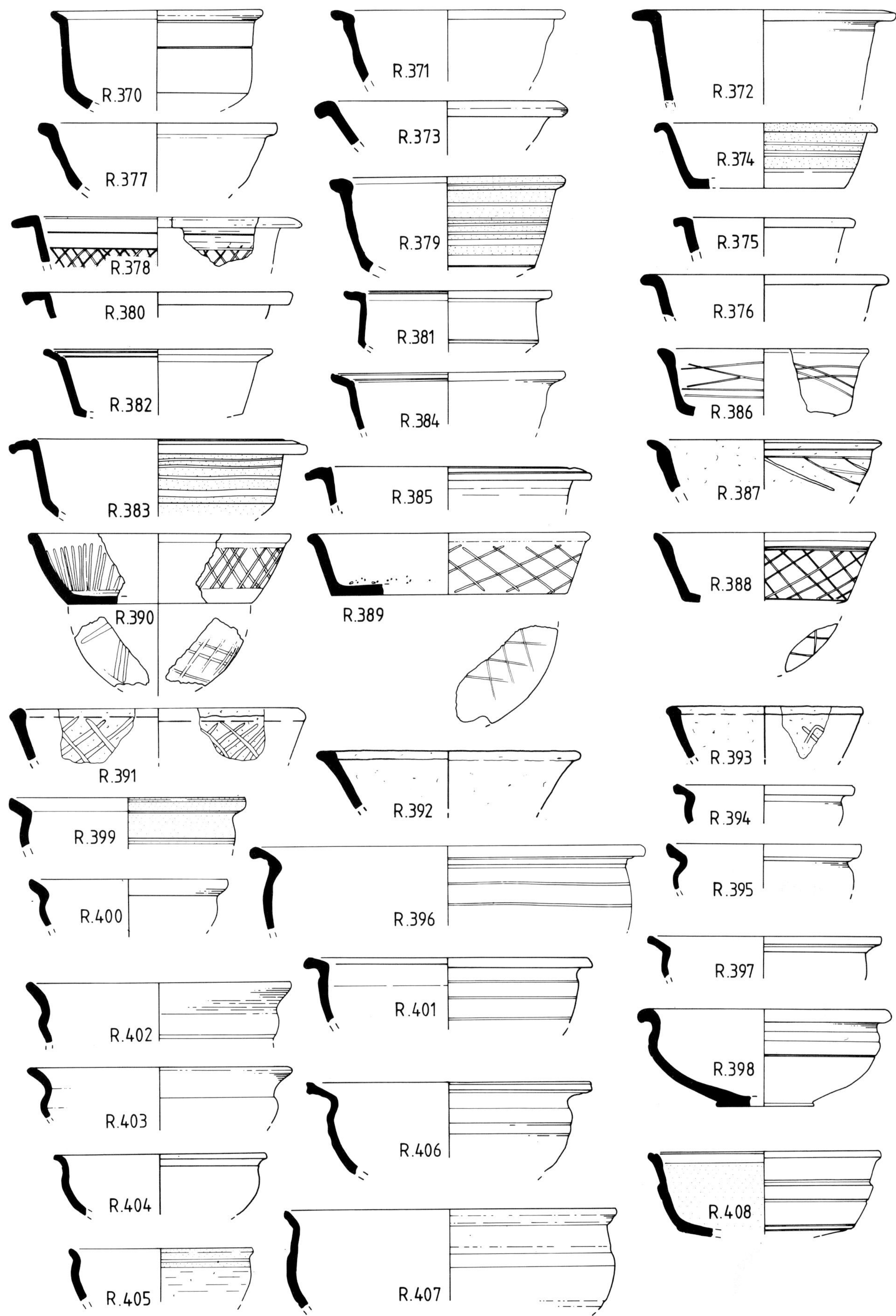

Figure 15 Roman coarse pottery, types R.370–R.408 (1/4 scale)

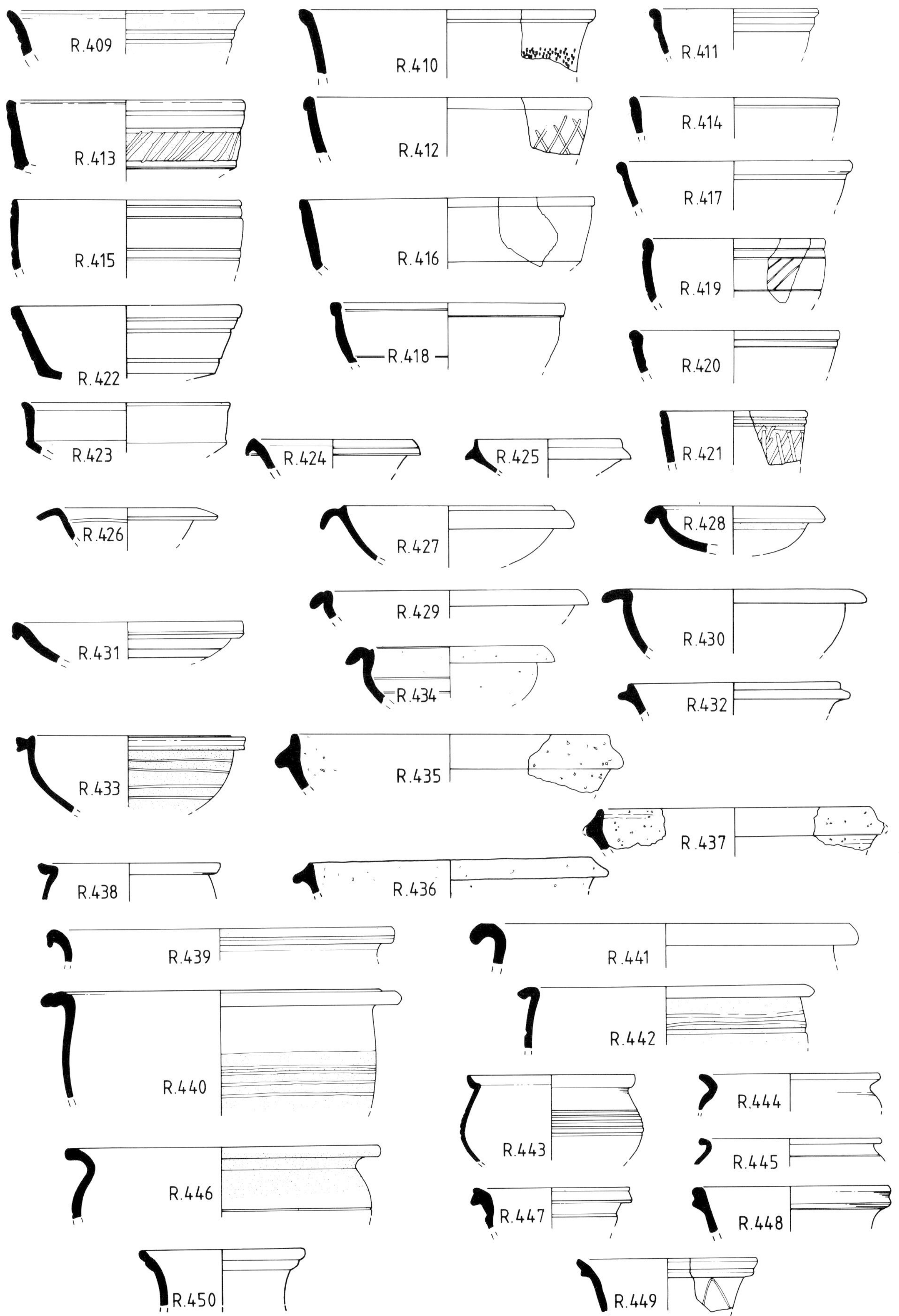

Figure 16 Roman coarse pottery, types R.409–R.450 (1/4 scale)

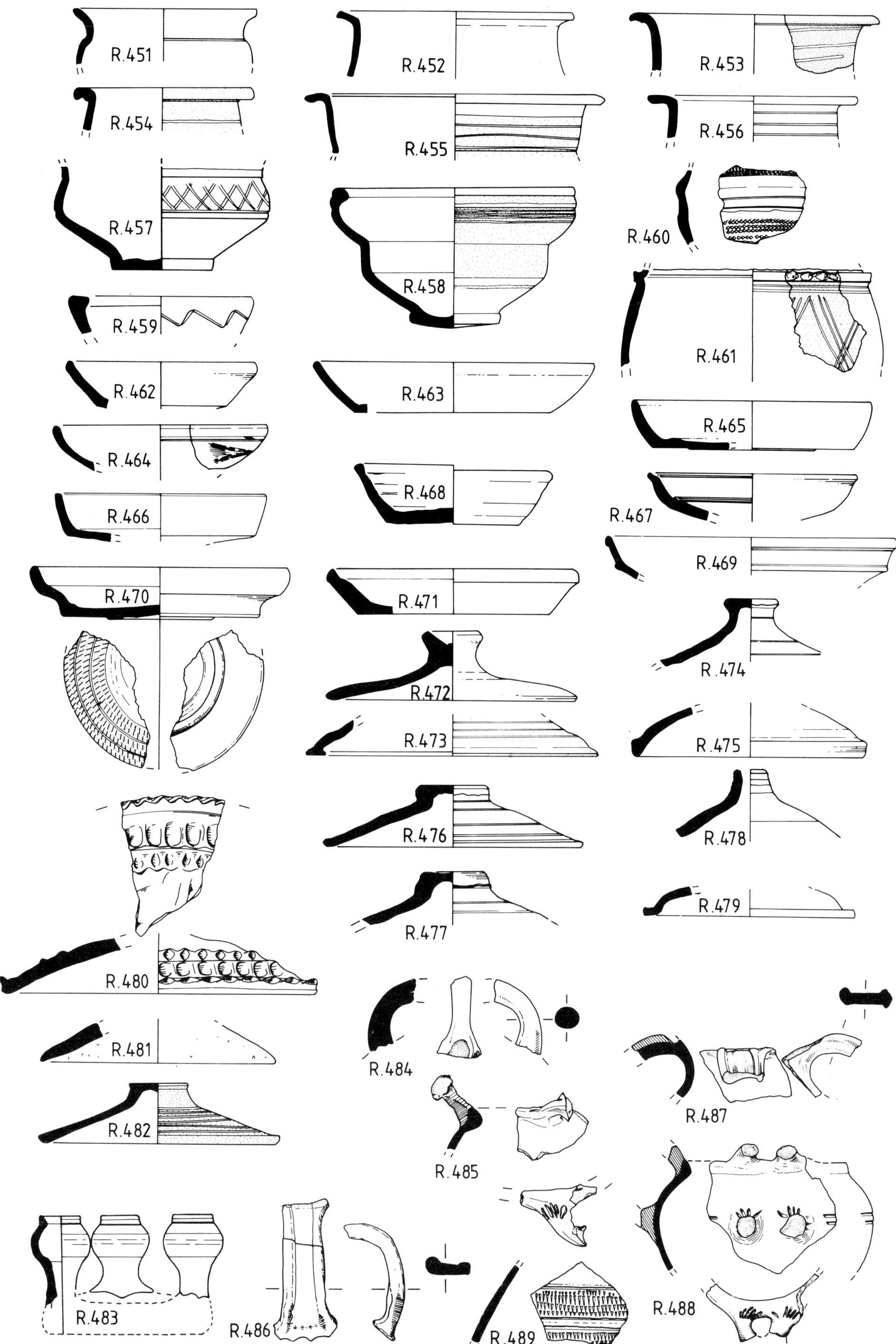

Figure 17 Roman coarse pottery, types R.451–R.489 (1/4 scale)

Black-Burnished wares (figs 18–20)

Black-Burnished ware accounts for *c* 18% of the total number of sherds collected during the excavations at Alcester. It is the hand-made Black-Burnished 1 type and belongs to Alcester fabric CB.

Fabric

CB: Black-Burnished ware is essentially hard, and dark grey to black in colour, although a reddish-grey layer is common immediately beneath the surface. The fabric is close-grained and heavily tempered with medium-grained quartz, and many of the Alcester sherds have chalky calcitic inclusions.

Range of vessel types

The range of types in Black-Burnished fabrics is not very wide, becoming even narrower in the later period. The vessels are all utilitarian in function, the majority being cooking pots, jars, bowls, or dishes.

(i) Cooking pots and jars (B.2–B.29)
(ii) Bowls (B.31–B.57)
(iii) Dishes (B.58–B.75)

There are also examples of jugs and a cup, but these are not forms which are found frequently at Alcester.

Decorative techniques

As the name Black-Burnished ware suggests, the main decorative technique is burnishing. This is found on all vessels, with certain areas denoted for decoration, for example, the rim and shoulder of the jars. Burnished lattices are a common decorative form on the body of the vessel. The latticing may be acute or obtuse but acute latticing is more common.

Typology and origin

The forms are originally derived from the late Iron Age with a continuity of forms between the Durotrigian wares and Black-Burnished ware. For example, the cooking pots with distinctive upright necks and everted rims with a wavy line beneath the neck are directly derived in form from the Durotrigian type.

The heavy mineral analysis carried out by Peacock (1967) produced results with a high tourmaline content that indicate that the Black-Burnished ware from Alcester was manufactured in Dorset, the Black-Burnished 1 factories around Poole Harbour being a possible production site, with the tertiary sands as the source of the tourmaline.

Chronology

Black-Burnished 1 appears in the Hadrianic period at Alcester and is found on the site well into the 4th century.

Illustrated vessels

Jug

B.1 CB 202 Jug with pinched-neck spout. Ext. and handle highly burnished with faintly burnished acute lattice on body ext. (Cf Wallace & Webster 1989, fig 1, no 2). Mid-1st to late 2nd century. (D I 246, phase II, later 2nd to early 3rd century?). WMFC 06.

Cooking pots / jars

These vessels are highly burnished on the exterior with certain areas denoted for decoration. The inner surface and rim are burnished to the junction of the neck while the body interior is always untreated. A broad zone is generally decorated by an acute-angled lattice, a departure from the lattice scheme being very unusual. Wavy lines on the neck of the cooking pot are also common until the end of the 2nd century.

B.2 CB 222 Handleless beaker with well-burnished ext. and patches of oxidation. (Cf Gillam 1976, no 19). Early to mid-2nd century. (D II 29A). WMFC 63.

B.3 CB 110 Cooking pot or beaker with highly burnished ext. (Cf Gillam 1976, no 16). Early to mid-2nd century. (A XVIIA 4). WMFC 26/63.

B.4 CB 204 Cooking pot with upright neck, derived from the Durotrigian jar. Burnished rim and shoulder with acute burnished lattice beneath. (Cf Gillam 1976, nos 3–4). Hadrianic–Antonine. (A XIV 16). WMFC 26.

B.5 CB 44 Cooking pot derived from Durotrigian jar, burnished rim and shoulder with wavy line beneath rim suggesting date in the 2nd century. Below shoulder an acute burnished lattice. (Cf Gillam 1976, no 3). Mid- to late 2nd century. (AA II 87, phase III, 3rd century — residual). WMFC 26.

B.6 CB 87 Cooking pot with burnished rim and shoulder, and with a burnished lattice design on body. 2nd century. (C V 56). WMFC 26.

B.7 CB 223 Cooking pot with acute burnished lattice and burnished rim and shoulder. (Cf Gillam 1976, no 31). Mid-2nd century. (D II 29A). WMFC 26.

B.8 CB 255 Cooking pot with burnished rim and shoulder, a wavy line beneath acute lattice below shoulder, and patches of oxidation. Pre-3rd century because wavy lines suggest an early date. (Cf Gillam 1976, no 1). Early to mid-2nd century. (AA II 73, phase V, later 3rd century on — residual). WMFC 26.

B.9 CB 69 Large jar possibly for storage, with sharply everted rim and tapering slightly angled lip. Rim burnished with upside-down scallop beneath rim ext. and acute lattice on shoulder. Later 2nd century? (C I 61). WMFC 26.

B.10 CB 24 Jar with slightly everted rim and bead-rim. Rim and shoulder burnished. Acute burnished lattice decorates the body. (Cf Gillam 1976, no 2). Mid-2nd century. (A IX 1A). WMFC 26.

B.11 CB 47 Jar with slightly everted burnished rim and shoulder. An acute burnished lattice beneath the shoulder. (Cf Gillam 1976, no 3). Mid- to late 2nd century. (AA I 66, phase VI, late 3rd to early 4th century — residual). WMFC 26.

B.12 CB 206 Jar with everted rim. Highly burnished rim and shoulder. Burnished obtuse lattice decorates the ext. with area of solid burnishing beneath. (Cf Gillam 1976, no 9). Mid- to late 3rd century. (G V 87, phase II?, mid-3rd century?). WMFC 26.

B.13 CB 260 Jar with everted rim and bead lip. Burnished neck, rim, and ext., with oxidized patches on body. (D I 183, phase IV, late 3rd century? — probably residual). WMFC 26.

B.14 CB 232 Small jar/cooking pot with everted curved rim and slightly angled lip. Burnished rim and body. (Cf Gillam 1976, no 7). Early to mid-3rd century. (D II 2, phase IX, late 4th century — residual). WMFC 26.

B.15 CB 85 Cooking pot with everted rim and slight moulding beneath. Burnished rim and ext. (C IIID 1). WMFC 26.

B.16 CB 259 Cooking pot with everted rim and pronounced shoulder; rim and ext. burnished. (Cf Gillam 1976, no 3). Mid- to late 2nd century. (B I 14). WMFC 26.

B.17 CB 194 Jar with sharply everted rim. Beneath rim are burnished hatching marks, and a burnished obtuse lattice. Rim, shoulder, and body below lattice are also burnished. (Cf Gillam

1976, nos 8–9). Mid- to late 3rd century. (D I 36, phase VI, mid- to late 4th century? — residual). WMFC 26.
B.18 CB 211 Cooking pot with sharply everted rim burnished with an incised obtuse lattice on the ext. (Cf Gillam 1976, no 9). Mid- to late 3rd century. (L III 10, phase IV, late Roman/modern — residual). WMFC 26.
B.19 CB 208 Jar with upright rim. Burnished rim and shoulder, with incised zig-zag on neck suggesting a 2nd-century date. (Cf Gillam 1976, no 3). Mid- to late 2nd century. (D I 246, phase II, later 2nd to early 3rd century?). WMFC 26.
B.20 CB 80 Jar with everted rim. Burnished rim and ext. (Cf Gillam 1976, no 10). Late 3rd century. (A XV 11). WMFC 26.
B.21 CB 12 Jar with everted rim and pronounced shoulder. Burnished rim and shoulder. A burnished obtuse lattice on body. (Cf Gillam 1976, no 10). Late 3rd century. (C IIIC 1). WMFC 26.
B.22 CB 235 Small jar with everted rim and burnished ext. On neck are two burnished lines. (E II 9, phase XIII, after AD 353 — residual). WMFC 26.
B.23 CB 10 Jar with everted rim. Burnished rim and shoulder. (C VIA 19, phase IX, mid-4th century on — residual). WMFC 26.
B.24 CB 132 Jar with everted rim. Burnished rim and shoulder. Beneath shoulder is an incised obtuse lattice. (Cf Gillam 1976, no 14). Mid-4th century. (G I 24, phase IX+, late 4th century). WMFC 26.
B.25 CB 253 Jar with everted rim. Rim and shoulder burnished, with obtuse burnished lattice on the body. (Cf Gillam 1976, nos 8–9). Mid- to late 3rd century. (AA II 110, phase VI, early to mid-4th century — residual). WMFC 26.
B.26 CB 225 Jar with everted rim. Well-burnished rim and ext. (Cf Gillam 1976, nos 8–9). Mid- to late 3rd century. (D I 87, phase V, early to mid-4th century? — residual). WMFC 26.
B.27 CB 133 Jar/cooking pot with upright rim. Flange moulded onto neck, with handle moulded onto flange. (Cf Farrar 1977, fig 14.3, no 32.4 from Ower kiln site). 4th century. (G I 24, phase IX+, late 4th century). WMFC 35.
B.28 CB 176 Jar with bead-rim. Rim and shoulder burnished, with acute lattice beneath. (Cf Gillam 1970, no 118). 2nd century. (D II 16). WMFC 38.
B.29 CB 199 Body sherd of jar with counter-sunk handle. Handle moulded on after first indenting the wall. Acute burnished lattice on body. (Cf Farrar 1977, no 41). Probably 1st or 2nd century. (E V 19, phase VI, early 3rd century? — residual).

Cup

B.30 CB 218 Handled beaded rimmed beaker. Highly burnished ext. (L V 1). WMFC 62.

Bowls and dishes

Both bowls and dishes are almost always burnished all over the body, although the bases may be matt with burnished decoration on the exterior.

Upright-moulded or grooved rim dishes

B.31 CB 257 Dish with upright rounded rim with vestigial bead. Int. and ext. burnished, with burnished 'X' decoration on ext. 2nd century. (D I 2, phase VIII, late 4th century — residual). WMFC 82.
B.32 CB 123 Dish with upright rim, handle, and chamfered base. Int. and ext. burnished, with faint open lattice on body. (AA I 30, phase VI, late 3rd to early 4th century). WMFC 82.
B.33 CB 122 Bowl with beaded rim and shallow groove beneath. Int. and ext. burnished, with faint large burnished acute lattice. (Cf Gillam 1976, no 68). Early to mid-2nd century. (D I 19, phase VI, mid- to late 4th century? — residual). WMFC 82.
B.34 CB 191 Bowl with beaded rim and wide shallow groove beneath. Base chamfered with burnished marks radiating towards circumference. (Cf Gillam 1976, no 52). Early to mid-2nd century. (D II 28). WMFC 82.
B.35 CB 230 Bowl with grooved rim. Burnished int. and ext. Arcading-type decoration covers the body ext., while there is a tooled line in the int. Base chamfered. (Cf Gillam 1976, no 52). Mid- to late 2nd century. (D I 6, phase VI, mid- to late 4th century? — residual). WMFC 82.

Pie-dish rim bowls

The rims of these vessels are either flat or gently curved.

B.36 CB 169 Bowl with out-turned rim. Int. and ext. burnished, with acute burnished lattice on the ext. (Cf Gillam 1976, nos 56–9). 2nd century. (D I 109, phase II, later 2nd to early 3rd century?). WMFC 68.
B.37 CB 229 Small flanged bowl, flange broken off, burnished ext. (D I 91, phase VI, mid- to late 4th century?). WMFC 64.
B.38 CB 105 Bowl with out-turned rim and beaded lip. Rim and int. burnished, with a burnished loop decoration on ext. (A XVIIA 2). WMFC 68.
B.39 CB 70 Bowl with a pie-dish rim and chamfered base. The vessel is burnished. (Cf Gillam 1976, no 37). Mid-2nd century. (AA II 109, phase III, 3rd century — residual).
B.40 CB 70 Bowl with pie-dish rim and chamfered base. Int. and ext. burnished. Above the chamfer is large acute burnished lattice. (Cf Gillam 1976, no 40). Mid- to late 2nd century. (D I 2A, phase VIII, late 4th century — residual). WMFC 68.
B.41 CB 60 Bowl with out-turned rim curving over to tapering lip. Int. and ext. burnished, with loop decoration on ext. (Cf Gillam 1976, no 41). Late 2nd century. (C I 53). WMFC 68.
B.42 CB 234 Bowl with pie-dish rim, the lip a thick roll. Int. and rim burnished, with acute angled lattice on ext. (Cf Gillam 1976, no 55). Mid- to late 2nd century. (E IV 22, phase VI, early 3rd century? — residual). WMFC 68.
B.43 CB 237 Bowl with pie-dish rim. Int. and ext. burnished, with acute angled lattice on ext. (Cf Gillam 1976, no 41). Late 2nd century. (D I 23, phase VIII, late 4th century — residual). WMFC 68.

Incipient flanged-rim bowls

This form is only produced in Black-Burnished fabric 1 and appears after AD 200.

B.44 CB 43 Bowl with incipient flanged rim and chamfered base. Large acute lattice on ext. with looped design on base. (Cf Gillam 1976, no 42). Late 2nd to early 3rd century. (C VI 24A). WMFC 68.
B.45 CB 244 Bowl with incipient flange. Well-burnished. (Cf Gillam 1976, no 43). Early to mid-3rd century. (AA I 3). WMFC 68.
B.46 CB 210 Bowl with incipient flange. Rim and int. burnished, with burnished arcading on body ext. Similar looped design on base. (Cf Gillam 1976, no 42). Late 2nd to early 3rd century. WMFC 68.
B.47 CB 254 Bowl with incipient flange. Burnished rim and int. Ext. decorated by an 'X' design. (Cf Gillam 1976, no 42). Late 2nd to early 3rd century. (A V 8, phase VI, late 3rd to early 4th century — residual). WMFC 68.

Flanged bowls

This is a development of the incipient flange and is later in date, first appearing in the late 3rd century.

B.48 CB 95 Bowl with flanged rim. Burnished int. and ext. (Cf Gillam 1976, no 45). Late 3rd century. (C VI 25, phase VIII, early to mid-4th century on). WMFC 68.
B.49 CB 4 Bowl with flanged rim. Burnished int. and ext. (Cf Gillam 1976, no 46). Late 3rd to early 4th century. (A I 4).
B.50 CB 94 Bowl with flange. Int. and ext. burnished with arcading design on body ext. (Cf Gillam 1976, no 46.) Late 3rd to early 4th century. (C II 1). WMFC 68.
B.51 CB 263 Flanged bowl with burnished int. and ext., and the beginnings of lattice decoration on ext. (Cf Gillam 1976, no 46). Late 3rd to early 4th century. (E V 2). WMFC 68.
B.52 CB 245 Bowl with a flanged rim and burnished int. and ext. Intersecting arcs decorate ext. (Cf Gillam 1976, no 42). Late 2nd to early 3rd century. (G I 1). WMFC 68.

B.53 CB 246 Flanged bowl, with an incised groove beneath flange. Int. and ext. are burnished, with looped design on ext. and base. (Cf Gillam 1976, no 42). Late 2nd to early 3rd century. (AA II 51B).
B.54 CB 84 Bowl with flanged rim and well-burnished int. and ext. (Cf Gillam 1976, no 48). Early to mid-4th century. (C IIID 1). WMFC 68.
B.55 CB 205 Bowl with flanged rim and burnished int. A burnished arcading design on ext. (Cf Gillam 1976, no 48). Early to mid-4th century. (A XIV 2).
B.56 CB 20 Bowl with flanged rim. Rim and int. burnished, with ext. decorated by arcade design. (Cf Gillam 1976, no 48). Early to mid-4th century. (A IX 1A). WMFC 68.
B.57 CB 14 Bowl with flanged rim and well-burnished int. and ext. (Cf Gillam 1976, no 48). Early to mid-4th century. (A VI 1). WMFC 68.

Dishes

B.58 CB 220 Dish with pie-dish rim. Int. and ext. burnished with acute lattice on body, and burnished decoration on base ext. (Cf Gillam 1976, no 57). Early to mid-2nd century. (D II 29A). WMFC 80.
B.59 CB 250 Dish with pie-dish rim. Int. burnished and an acute lattice on body ext. (Cf Gillam 1976, no 61). Mid-2nd century. (L XIII 2). WMFC 80.
B.60 CB 221 Dish with a pie-dish rim and lip curving over. Rim and ext. burnished, with acute lattice on ext. Ext. also shows signs of burning. Base has burnished loop or circle design on ext. (Cf Gillam 1976, no 58). Early to mid-2nd century. (D II 29A). WMFC 80.

Shallow lipless dishes

The rims have a flattened or rounded surface and are occasionally everted. The sides of the dish are straight or slightly concave, and are decorated from the groove to the base or chamfer with lattice or arcading. The flattened bases are also frequently decorated. These vessels first appeared on sites around AD 120.

B.61 CB 89 Dish with upright rounded rim and burnished int. and ext. Burnished arcading decorates ext. with looped design on base. Late 2nd century or later. (A XVI 4). WMFC 82.
B.62 CB 224 Dish with upright beaded rim and chamfered base with no decoration. (Cf Gillam 1976, no 72). Early 3rd century. (D II 29A). WMFC 82.
B.63 CB 203 Dish with upright rim and vestigial bead. Int. and ext. burnished with acute lattice on ext. Looped design decorates base. A graffito on base, no 29. (Cf Gillam 1976, no 71). Late 2nd century. (G V 87, phase II?, mid-3rd century?). WMFC 82.
B.64 CB 264 Dish with upright rim and vestigial bead. Int. and ext. burnished, with a burnished lattice on ext. 2nd century. (D II 42). WMFC 82.
B.65 CB 15 Dish with upright rim and tapering lip. Int. and ext. burnished, with acute lattice on ext. (Cf Gillam 1976, no 74). 3rd century. (A VI 4). WMFC 82.
B.66 CB 228 Dish with upright rounded rim and chamfered base. Int. burnished with acute lattice on ext. (Cf Gillam 1976, no 78). Late 2nd to early 3rd century. (D II 7, phase IX, late 4th century — residual). WMFC 82.
B.67 CB 23 Dish with upright rounded rim. Int. and ext. burnished, with burnished loop decoration on base ext. (A IX 8, phase VI, late 3rd to early 4th century). WMFC 82.
B.68 CB 177 Dish with upright rounded rim and burnished int. Ext. has acute lattice, and burnished loop decoration on base. (Cf Gillam 1976, no 69). Mid-2nd century. (D I 135, phase VI, mid- to late 4th century — residual). WMFC 82.
B.69 CB 195 Dish with upright rim and sagging base. Int. burnished, with a burnished arcade on ext. Burnished loop decoration on base ext. (Cf Gillam 1976, no 78). Late 2nd to early 3rd century. (D I 36, phase VI, mid- to late 4th century? — probably residual). WMFC 82.
B.70 CB 219 Dish with upright rim, two handles, and burnished int. Acute burnished lattice on ext., with burnished zig-zag design on the base ext. 2nd century. (D II 29A). WMFC 82.
B.71 CB 239 Dish with vestigial beaded rim. Burnished rim and int. Ext. decorated by a burnished arcade with loop design on base ext. Late 2nd century or later. (F I 99, phase VII, 3rd century?). WMFC 82.
B.72 CB 249 Dish with upright rounded rim and well-burnished int. Burnished diamond design on ext. with looped decoration on base and a line on body int. 2nd century. (D I 90). WMFC 82.
B.73 CB 92 Dish with upright rounded rim and well-burnished int. Looped design on ext. Late 2nd century or later. (C VI 2). WMFC 82.
B.74 CB 2 Dish with upright flattened rim and burnished int. and ext. Burnished arcading on ext. Late 2nd century or later. (A I 2A). WMFC 82.
B.75 CB 165 Dish with upright tapering rim and well-burnished int. and ext. Handle. (Cf Gillam 1976, nos 87–8). 3rd–4th century. (D I 87, phase V, early to mid-4th century?). WMFC 82.

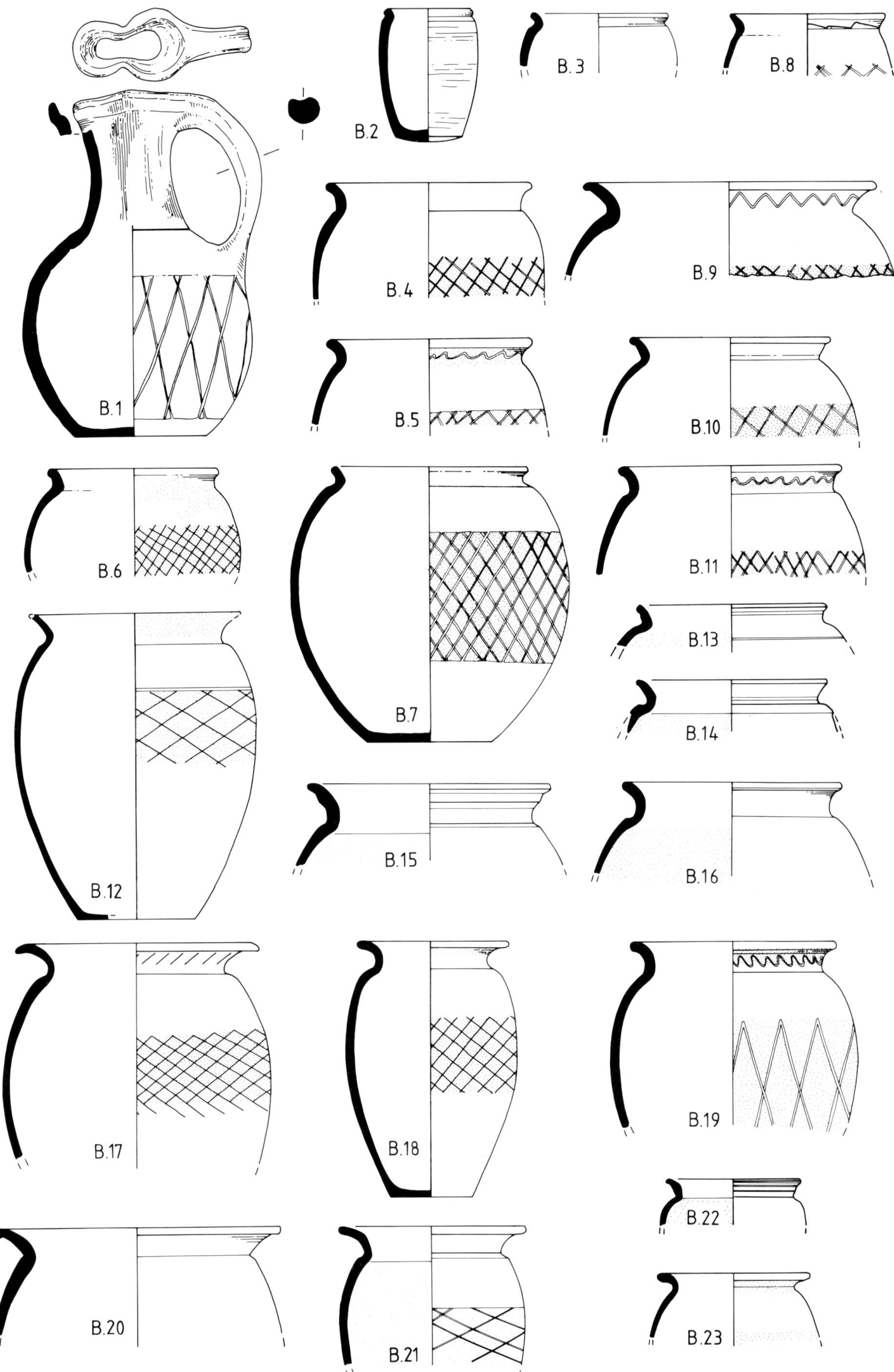

Figure 18 Roman coarse pottery, types B.1–B.23 (1/4 scale)

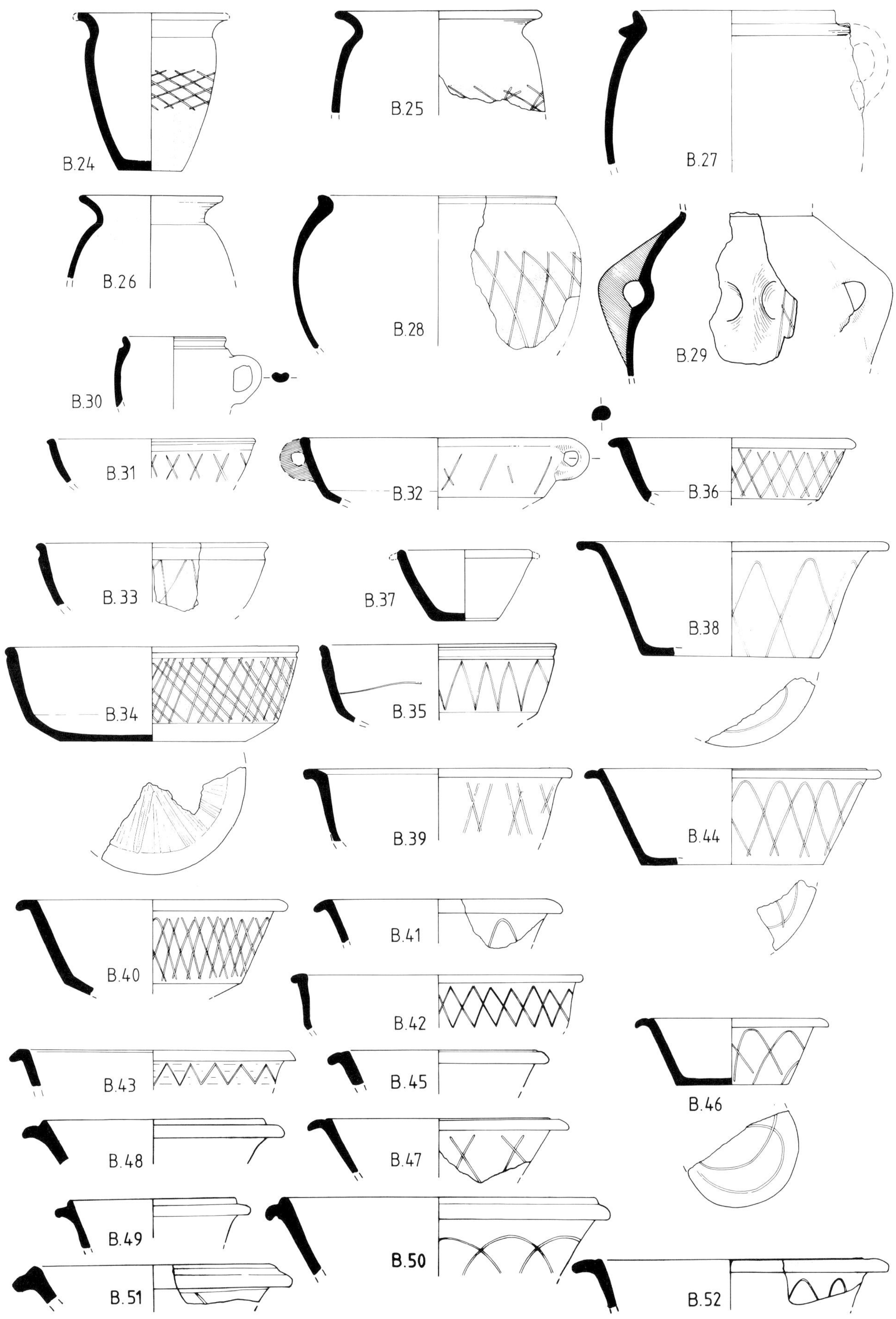

Figure 19 Roman coarse pottery, types B.24–B.52 (1/4 scale)

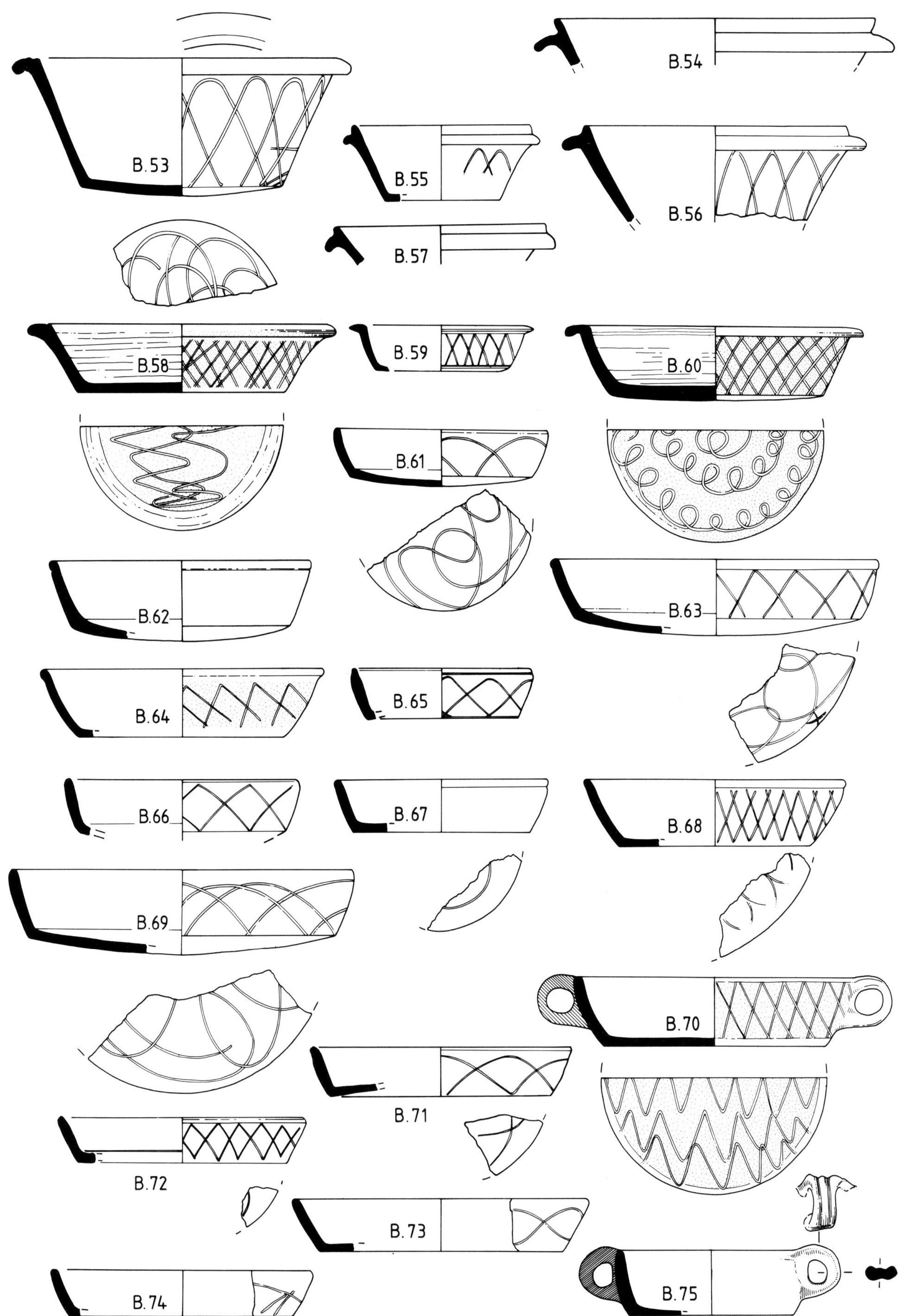

Figure 20 Roman coarse pottery, types B.53–B.75 (1/4 scale)

Oxidized wares (figs 21–38)

Oxidized wares account for approximately 33% of the total sherds retrieved at Alcester. Over 84% of these are in so-called Severn Valley fabrics, which is a general term for a group of fabrics appearing throughout the Severn Valley Basin. All show a similar technique of manufacture and have common stylistic forms and decorative techniques. A number of production centres are known throughout the area but knowledge as to which were supplying Alcester is limited.

Fabrics

Thirty oxidized fabrics can be distinguished in the Alcester pottery (omitting colour-coated vessels). Eighteen of these are minor groups with less than five sherds within each group, another two have less than ten sherds each, leaving only ten major fabric groupings of which eight are known Severn Valley wares (DA, DE, DEA, DI, DIA, DK, DW, and DZ).

BJ: A fairly soft fabric fired to a grey core with reddish-brown surfaces. The fabric is sandy with abundant inclusions of quartz. The form is a wheel-made jar with rouletted decoration. Fabric Group 1.

CH: A hard fabric with sparse inclusions, fired to a grey core with mottled buff and black surfaces. The vessels are highly burnished. All are wheel-made and the vessel types include beakers, jars, bowls, and dishes. Date: 1st–4th century. Fabric Group 2.

CK: A hard fairly fine fabric containing a moderate number of quartz inclusions. The core is a reddish-brown, fired to a mottled black and brown surface. Hand-made. Date: late Roman. Fabric Group 1.

CM: Hard, fine fabric fired to a well-burnished red and black mottled ext. The fabric is sandy with a moderate number of quartz inclusions. All are wheel-made and the vessel types include beakers, bowls, and dishes. Date: 1st–4th century. Fabric Group 1.

DA: Severn Valley ware. A hard fabric fired to a grey core with light buff to red surfaces. The fabric is micaceous, generally vesiculated, with frequent inclusions of charcoal. There are also signs that these vessels were grass-tempered and there are a few inclusions of grog. All the vessels are wheel-made and included storage jars, bowls, tankards, and lids. Probably Warwickshire Museum fabric O21. Date: 1st to early 3rd century. Fabric Group 7.

DE: Severn Valley ware. Hard, fine, smooth fabric fired to a buff/red ext. The vessels are generally homogeneous in colour although some are fired to a grey core. The fabric is distinguishable from fabric DEA on the basis of the quantity and size of the inclusions (see 'Petrology of selected samples' below, p 131). It contains abundant inclusions of sub-angular and rounded limestone, measuring between 0.02 and 0.45mm and with fine inclusions of quartz. The inclusions of limestone suggest a source in a limestone area, for example, Warwickshire. All the vessels are wheel-made with the vessel types including flagons, jars, beakers, bowls, tankards, and dishes. Possibly Warwickshire Museum fabrics O25, O27, and O33. Date: 1st to mid-4th century. Fabric Group 5.

DEA: Severn Valley ware. A hard fabric similar to fabric DE but coarser in texture and distinguishable by its quartz size. All the vessels are wheel-made and include flagons, jars, beakers, tankards, bowls, dishes, and tazzas. Date: 1st to mid-4th century. Fabric Group 1.

DG: A very hard, fine fabric fired to a grey core with red surfaces. The fabric has few or no inclusions. All are wheel-made and the vessel types are represented by beaker body sherds. Fabric Group 2.

DI: Severn Valley ware. A soft reddish-brown fabric with a soapy texture. The fabric is micaceous with few or no inclusions.

DIA: Severn Valley ware. A fairly hard reddish-brown fabric frequently with a red and black mottled exterior. The fabric is sandy with a moderate number of quartz inclusions. All the vessels are wheel-made and include flagons, jars, beakers, tankards, and bowls. Date: 1st–4th century. Fabric Group 1.

DJ: A very hard, sandy fabric with abundant inclusions of quartz. The colour is buff to a light orange with a grey core. All the vessels are wheel-made and include beakers and bowls. Fabric Group 1.

DK: A very hard, fine fabric with few or no visible inclusions. It is fired to a red ext. and frequently covered by a grey slip. The vessels are well burnished and have Severn Valley forms. All are wheel-made and include flagons, jars, tankards, and bowls. Date: 1st–4th century. Fabric Group 2.

DR: A hard, fine, sandy, micaceous fabric. All the vessels are wheel-made and the type sherd is a jar or beaker. Fabric Group 1.

DS: A fairly hard, coarse sandy fabric with abundant inclusions of quartz. The colour range is a dark red to brown and the vessels are self-slipped. All the vessels are wheel-made jars and date to the 4th century. Fabric Group 1.

DU: A hard, red, very sandy fabric with abundant inclusions of quartz. The surfaces are coarse and rough in texture, and frequently very badly pitted. All the vessels are wheel-made jars. Date: 1st–4th century. Fabric Group 1.

DV: A very hard, fine fabric with few or no visible inclusions. The colour is essentially a reddish-orange and the sherds are covered by a pink to cream slip. All the vessels are wheel-made and the forms are bowls. Fabric Group 2.

DW: Fine Severn Valley ware. A hard, very fine fabric. The colour range varies from a light orange to red. The surface has a thin slip or is fired to a brown ext. These are very finely made vessels with few or no visible inclusions and are highly micaceous. Decoration frequently occurs in the form of white paint. Strong parallels can be found in the Oxfordshire kilns; however, the fabric is too coarse for Oxfordshire and a fine Severn Valley ware is more plausible. All the vessels are wheel-made and the forms include jars, beakers, cups, bowls, and dishes. Date: 1st–4th century. Fabric Group 11.

DX: A soft orange fabric covered with a pink slip and with red paint decoration on the exterior. Date: 3rd century. Fabric Group 1.

DZ: A hard, sandy fabric fired to a grey core with a red exterior and generally covered by a thin slip. The fabric is very sandy with frequent inclusions of quartz. The forms are all wheel-made and suggest an origin in the Severn Valley. They include jars, beakers, tankards, and bowls. Date: 1st–4th century. Fabric Group 1.

DZA: Hard, fine, sandy fabric normally fired to an orange colour. All the vessels are wheel-made beakers. Fabric Group 1.

EC: A pink fabric with a white slip and orange paint decoration. The vessel types are all wheel-made and include *mortaria* and bowls. Date: 2nd–4th century. Fabric Group 2.

EG: A hard, fine sandy fabric with a grey core and interior. The exterior is fired orange and covered with a white slip. The form found is a wheel-made body sherd. Date: 2nd century. Fabric Group 1.

EH: A hard, fine fabric with a light grey core and brown interior and exterior. The form is a wheel-made small jar. Date: 3rd century. Fabric Group 2.

EJ: A hard coarse fabric with a grey core, fired to an orange exterior. The vessels are hand-made. Jar. Date: 3rd century. Fabric Group 2.

FA: A hard, fine fabric with fine sand inclusions. The colour is essentially a reddish-orange with a brown slip (self-slipped). Clay particle rough-cast decoration covers the body ext. beneath the shoulder. Close parallels are to be found at Breddon Hill in the Severn Valley. Fabric Group 2.

FB: A soft fabric with a dark core, and red to brown surfaces. The fabric is very sandy with abundant inclusions of quartz. The vessels are wheel-made and thick walled. The types include a coarse cup and jar or flagon. Date: 1st–4th century. Fabric Group 1.

FD: A soft, very micaceous fabric with few visible inclusions. The colour is a reddish-orange and the exterior soot-encrusted. The vessel is a wheel-made jar. Fabric Group 2.

NB: Calcite-gritted storage jar. Fabric Group 4.

PA: Mica-dusted ware. Warwickshire Museum fabric class F20. Date: 2nd to early 3rd century. Fabric Group 2.

Range of vessel types

There are eight main groups, of which a number may be subdivided into minor headings.

Flagons (illustration nos O.1–O.39)

This is a large and important group accounting for the majority of the Alcester flagons. The fabrics are all oxidized and are characterized by a chalky white slip. These vessels are specialist Roman types and may have been produced in specialist workshops, for example, at Gloucester. Their importance lies in their illustration of the pattern of Romanization at Alcester.

Jars (O.47–O.182)

This group has been subdivided into numerous small headings.

(i) Narrow-necked jars (O.47–O.82)
This is a common Severn Valley form with cordons and grooves as typical methods of decoration. These vessels are common throughout the Roman period.

(ii) Storage jars (O.83–O.126)
Almost all of these vessels are in fabric DA and are similar in type to the storage jars manufactured in the reduced fabric GC. Graffiti are not unusual on the rims of these vessels.

(iii) Wide-mouthed jars (O.127–O.157)
This is a typical Severn Valley form derived from Belgic prototypes. It was in use throughout the Roman period and has no chronological significance. Burnishing on the rim and rim int., where it is visible, is a common decorative motif.

(iv) Jars with everted rims (O.157–O.175)

(v) Globular or ovoid jars (O.176–O.194)

(vi) Necked jars (O.195–O.219)
These have prominent shoulders and are developed from the common Belgic jar.

(vii) Rough-cast jars (O.220–O.224)
These occur in the fabric FA and are typified by cornice rims and burnished shoulders above the area of clay particle rough-cast decoration. In origin these vessels seem to be derived from the North Gaulish rough-cast beakers.

Beakers (O.229–O.244)

This is a small category containing only 4% of the oxidized vessels from Alcester.

Cups (O.245–O.260)

These account for 3% of the oxidized assemblage and comprise either carinated or curved-wall vessels.

Tankards (O.261–O.290)

Of the oxidized vessels, 20% fall into this category. They are all in Severn Valley wares and are derived from Durotrigian forms (Webster 1976). Tankards are the most widely distributed of Severn Valley forms with the most common type being the plain straight-sided vessel with a groove immediately beneath the rim, and with a ring groove on the base exterior.

Bowls (O.291–O.425)

Bowls are the largest single oxidized category accounting for 25% of the vessels, with a date range covering the 1st–4th century.

Dishes (O.426–O.435)

Miscellaneous vessels (O.436–O.461)

These include triple vases, spouted jars, tazzas, and a possible skillet.

Decorative techniques

A wide variety of decorative techniques were employed on the oxidized wares but unfortunately very few have any chronological significance. Grooves and cordons are to be found on most categories and throughout the period. They are especially a feature of jars, appearing on the storage, the narrow-necked, and the wide-mouthed vessels. Burnishing is extremely common and is used on all vessel types from the 1st to 4th century. Rims and shoulders are the most frequently burnished areas, with burnished patterns on the shoulder of hatched lines and lattices being a common decorative technique. Incised decoration in the form of combed loop decoration is found on jars and bowls with one example of an incised geometrical pattern on a globular jar (O.176). Rouletting is a common form of decoration on oxidized vessels. It is found on a wide range of vessel types although beakers and bowls are the most common form. The rouletting has no chronological significance. There are very few examples of impressed decoration. A bowl (O.405) with impressed semicircles and a very fine body sherd (O.459) with an impressed bird's foot pattern are the only examples. Pie-crust and flange decoration is unusual and is limited to bowls and tazzas. Paint appears on the fine table ware in particular. The most common colour is white although O.437 was decorated with orange painted circles. Rough-cast decoration occurs exclusively on jars in fabric FA and is made from clay particles. This treatment is not only decorative but is also used to facilitate grip.

Distribution

Severn Valley ware is seen as an industry or as pottery producers working from a variety of centres but banded together by their traditions of vessels type, form, and fabric.

Illustrated vessels

Flagons

Flagons account for approximately 5% of the oxidized assemblage. Of the 39 flagons illustrated from Alcester, 32 have a chalky white slip covering the exterior. The nearest parallels to these flagons are to be found at the College of Arts site, Gloucester, which was producing pottery during the Flavian period (Rawes 1972).

O.1 DA 63 Large flagon with out-turned thickened rim and handle scar. The ext. covered by white slip. (Cf Darling 1977, fig 6.2, no 1, Usk.) AD 55–70. (A IX 1A). WMFC 12.

Grooved-rim flagons

O.2 DE 243 Grooved rim flagon with triple-ribbed handle. Cream slip covers ext. and rim int. (Cf Gillam 1970, type 17). AD 150–250. (D II 29A). WMFC 12.
O.3 DE 247 Flagon with collared rim. Two incised grooves on rim ext. (D II 29A). WMFC 12.
O.4 DE 190 Fine flagon with grooved rim and narrow neck. Handle double-ribbed. Ext. covered with cream/pink slip. (Cf Gillam 1970, type 17). AD 150–250. (H II 68, phase III, Antonine to 3rd century on). WMFC 12.
O.5 DE 251 Small flagon with grooved rim. Cream slip covers ext. and rim int. (Cf Gillam 1970, type 17). AD 150–250. (B I 6). WMFC 12.
O.6 DE 83 Flagon with grooved rim and handle scar; ext. badly pitted. (Cf Gillam 1970, type 17). AD 150–250. (AA II 88, phase III, 3rd century). WMFC 12.
O.7 DE 204 Flagon with grooved rim, double-ribbed handle, and with ring groove on base ext. Ext. covered with cream slip. (Cf Gillam 1970, type 17). AD 150–250. (E II 31, phase VI, early 3rd century?). WMFC 12.
O.8 DE 205 Flagon with thickened grooved rim and double-ribbed handle. At base of neck is an incised line, ext. covered by white slip. (D II 29). WMFC 12.
O.9 DE 319 Flagon with grooved rim and triple-ribbed handle. Ext. covered by cream slip. (Cf Gillam 1970, type 17). AD 150–250. (D II 29A). WMFC 12.
O.10 DEA 98 Very fine flagon with collared rim and two incised grooves on ext. Neck very narrow, with burnished vertical lines; handle has four ribs. (B IA 17). WMFC 18.
O.11 DEA 208 Flagon with out-curved thickened undercut rim, and handle scar. Neck int. covered by a thick black slip. (Cf Darling 1977, fig 6.2, no 1, Usk). AD 55–70. (D II 28). WMFC 12.
O.12 DEA 196 Flagon with collared rim and projecting lower lip, and with handle scar. Ext. and rim int. covered by white slip. Parallel: Gloucester (Rawes 1972, no 129). Flavian. (G I 158, phase V, later 4th century — residual). WMFC 12.

Cupped-mouth flagons

O.13 DEA 407 Flagon with inward-turning rim and shallow groove on neck. Handle scar. Int. covered by cream slip. (H II 2). WMFC 18.
O.14 DEA 212 Flagon with cupped mouth and beaded rim, moulding on neck forms a ridge. Base is flat with ring groove on ext. Int. and ext. white-slipped. (D II 60). WMFC 18.
O.15 DEA 174 Small flagon with cupped mouth and incised groove at base of neck. Handle double-ribbed and ext. covered by white slip which dribbles down into the int. 2nd century. (AA I 46, phase V, later 3rd century on — residual). WMFC 18.
O.16 DEA 358 Flagon with cupped mouth and moulded neck. Handle double-ribbed. At base of neck an incised groove. Ext. covered with pink/white slip. 2nd century. (D II 29A). WMFC 18.
O.17 DEA 320 Flagon with cupped mouth and globular body. Base flat with ring groove on ext., and handle triple-ribbed. Ext. covered by chalky-white slip. 2nd century. (D II 29A). WMFC 18.
O.18 DEA 416 Flagon with grooved rim and moulded neck. Handle double-ribbed. Int. and ext. covered by grey/white slip with spot of green glaze immediately beneath rim on ext. (D II 20). WMFC 18.
O.19 DEA 347 Flagon with thickened rim. White slip. (B I 3, phase II, Antonine to 3rd century). WMFC 18.
O.20 DEA 181 Flagon with upright rim and corrugated neck, with incised line at base. Handle is plaited. Ext. covered with a pink to cream slip. (D I 29). WMFC 18.

Ring-necked flagons

O.21 DE 403 Narrow ring-necked flagon with cupped mouth, globular body and flat, ringed base. Handle double-ribbed and flagon ext. is covered with white slip. (Cf Wilderspool: Webster & Hartley 1973, no 3). Early to mid-2nd century. (D II 29A). WMFC 18.
O.22 DE 232 Large ring-necked flagon with incised line at base of neck, and tooled vertical lines. Handle double-ribbed. Base flat. Similar to forms from Gloucester (College of Art site: Rawes 1972).

Neronian–Flavian. (E III 6, phase XIII, after AD 353 — residual). WMFC 11.
O.23 DE 46 Ring-necked flagon with everted rim and downward-turned lip. A chalky slip covers int. and ext. Flavian–Trajanic. (AA II 91, phase II, late 2nd to early 3rd century — residual). WMFC 11.
O.24 DE 225 Ring-necked flagon with triple-ribbed handle. A cream slip covers rim int. and ext. Flavian–Trajanic. (C I 17). WMFC 11.
O.25 DEA 128 Very sandy ring-necked flagon with cupped mouth, white slip. Fabric: South-Western white slip. Parallel: Cirencester Excavation Committee fabric 88 (J Richardson pers comm). (C VI 37, phase VII, early to mid-4th century — residual). WMFC 11.
O.26 DEA 145 Very sandy ring-necked flagon with thickened rim and white slip on int. and ext. Parallel in form: Gloucester. Fabric: South-Western white slip. Parallel: Cirencester Excavation Committee fabric 88. (C I 90, phase I/II, late 1st to early 3rd century). WMFC 11.
O.27 DEA 262 Ring-necked flagon with thickened rim and white slip on int. and ext. Fabric: South-Western white slip. Parallel: Cirencester Excavation Committee fabric 88. (D I 29). WMFC 11.
O.28 DEA 377 Ring-necked flagon with thickened rim and white slip on int. and ext. Overfired. (Cf Gloucester: Rawes 1972, no 122). Flavian. Fabric: South-Western white slip. Parallel: Cirencester Excavation Committee fabric 88. (A XVI T/S). WMFC 11.
O.29 DEA 185 Ring-necked flagon with thickened rim and double-ribbed handle. Cream slip on ext. and rim int. (H II 48, phase II, Antonine to 3rd century). WMFC 11.
O.30 DEA 211 Regular ring-necked flagon with a pear-shaped body and triple-ribbed handle. Ext. is covered by white slip. Late 1st to early 2nd century. (D I 126A, phase II, later 2nd to early 3rd century? — residual). WMFC 11.
O.31 DEA 203 Ring-necked flagon with a bevelled rim and incised line at base of neck. Handle double-ribbed with thick white slip on the rim int. and body ext. Late 1st to early 2nd century. (E V 6, phase XIII, after AD 353 — residual). WMFC 11.
O.32 DEA 197 Flagon with flat everted rim and handle scar. (D I 107, phase I, 1st century to early Antonine). WMFC 12.

Large flagons

O.33 DEA 389 Large flagon with gently everted rim and burnished neck. (C VI 32). WMFC 17.
O.34 DE 369 Large flagon with upright rim and pointed flange on neck. Int. and ext. have pink/cream slip. Handle scar. (B I 6). WMFC 17.

Miscellaneous flagons

O.35 DI 28 Necked sherd of flagon with traces of cream slip on ext. (B I 3, phase II, Antonine to 3rd century).
O.36 DK 15 Flagon with cupped flanged rim and handle scar. Grey slip on ext. (Cf Gloucester: Rawes 1972, no 129). Flavian. (D I 246, phase II, later 2nd to early 3rd century?). WMFC 12.
O.37 DW 63 Very fine disc-neck flagon with highly burnished ext. (D IV 4). WMFC 14.
O.38 DW 16 Long-necked, very fine bottle with highly burnished ext. (D I 36, phase VI, mid- to late 4th century?).
O.39 DW 47 Bottle or flagon. At base of neck is shallow incised line. Ext. burnished and decorated with white-painted circles and line of white-painted dots decorating shoulder. Foot moulded with a ring-groove on base ext. (D I T/S).

Flask

O.40 DEA 199 Small screw neck flask, *unguentarium*. (D I 176).

Jugs

O.41 DEA 200 Jug with rim pinched in at middle. At base of neck an incised line. Handle triple-ribbed. Raised base. (D I 196). WMFC 06.
O.42 DEA 151 Rim of jug with handle scar. (C VI 69, phase IV, later 3rd century on). WMFC 05.

Spouts

O.43 DA 17 Spout with vertical burnishing on the neck. (H I 9, phase II, Antonine to 3rd century).
O.44 DE 166 Spout. (D II 1).

Lagenae or double-handled jars

O.45 DE 194 Ring-necked jar; probably a double-handled type. (D II 15, phase VIII, late 4th century — residual). WMFC 17.
O.46 DEA 240 Two-handled pitcher. Handles are double-ribbed. Severn Valley ware. (D II 29A). WMFC 17.

Narrow-necked storage jars

This is a common vessel type in Severn Valley ware with cordons and grooves as typical modes of decoration. The cordons occur at the base of the neck on most of the Birch Abbey examples. A band of hatching or of burnished lattices on the shoulder are other typical decorative techniques.

O.47 DA 111 Narrow-necked storage jar with two incised lines below rim and another two at base of neck forming a cordon. Ext. is well burnished. (G IA 7, phase VI?, late 4th century? — residual). WMFC 20.
O.48 DA 52 Narrow-necked storage jar with everted rim. (C VI 32). WMFC 20.
O.49 DA 6 Narrow-necked storage jar with bead-rim and incised line at base of neck. Ext. burnished. (AA I 51). WMFC 20.
O.50 DA 90 Narrow-necked storage jar. Neck has horizontal burnished lines and at base is a cordon. A band of burnished lattice decoration bordered by a pair of incised lines decorates the shoulder. Severn Valley ware. (Cf Webster 1976, no 3). 1st–3rd century. (B I 3, phase II, Antonine to 3rd century). WMFC 20.
O.51 DE 150 Narrow-necked storage jar with incised line beneath rim and a double-ribbed handle. (C VI 69, phase IV, later 3rd century on). WMFC 20.
O.52 DE 244 Narrow-necked storage jar with incised line beneath rim, and a handle. Burnished vertical lines decorate ext. (D II 29). WMFC 20.
O.53 DE 249 Narrow-necked storage jar with double cordon at base of neck. On shoulder a band of burnished hatching. Severn Valley ware. (Cf Webster 1976, no 3). 1st–3rd century. (D I 87A). WMFC 20.
O.54 DE 304 Narrow-necked storage jar with cordon at base of neck. Severn Valley ware. (Cf Webster 1976, no 1). 1st–4th century. (A XVI 1). WMFC 20.
O.55 DE 242 Narrow-necked storage jar with double cordon at base of neck. This vessel contained a cremation. Severn Valley ware. (Cf Webster 1976, no 1). 1st–4th century. (A II 61). WMFC 20.
O.56 DE 245 Narrow-necked storage jar with everted rim and cordon at base of neck. On shoulder a pair of incised lines either side of a band of burnished lattices. Severn Valley ware. (Cf Webster 1976, no 3). 1st–3rd century. (B I 3, phase II, Antonine to 3rd century). WMFC 20.
O.57 DE 110 Narrow-necked jar with everted rim and cordon at base of neck. Neck and shoulder burnished. Severn Valley ware. (Cf Webster 1976, no 1). 1st–4th century. (B IA 8). WMFC 20.
O.58 DE 372 Narrow-necked storage jar with cordon at base of neck. Shoulder decorated by band of burnished hatched lines banded by pair of incised lines. Near base three holes have been drilled. Severn Valley ware. (Cf Webster 1976, no 2). Late 1st to mid-2nd century. (A XVIIB 4). WMFC 20.
O.59 DE 177 Narrow-necked storage jar with flanged rim and two grooves on ext. At base of neck a cordon. Incised groove on shoulder. (Cf Webster 1976, no 12). 2nd–4th century. (AA II 51A). WMFC 20.
O.60 DE 176 Narrow-necked storage jar with flanged rim and pie-crust decoration on flange. (Cf Webster 1976, no 10). 3rd–4th century. (AA II 24). WMFC 20.
O.61 DE 137 Narrow-necked jar with everted rim. (A XVI 6). WMFC 20.

O.62 DE 409 Narrow-necked jar with slightly everted rim and cordon at base of neck. On neck int. is incised graffito, no 35. (G I 59, phase IV, early to mid-4th century). WMFC 22.
O.63 DEA 331 Narrow-necked storage jar with burnished line on neck. (Cf Webster 1976, no 2). Late 1st to mid-2nd century. (D II 29A). WMFC 20.
O.64 DEA 172 Narrow-necked jar with everted rim and cordon at base of neck. Shoulder has pair of incised lines. Severn Valley ware. (Cf Webster 1976, no 4). 2nd–4th century. (H II 1). WMFC 20.
O.65 DEA 387 Narrow-necked storage jar with everted rim and possible cordon at base of neck. Severn Valley ware. (Cf Webster 1976, no 1). 1st–4th century. (G IA 68, phase IV, early to mid-4th century). WMFC 20.
O.66 DEA 218 Narrow-necked jar with two incised grooves on rim. A large cordon at base of neck. (D I 126A, phase II, later 2nd to early 3rd century?). WMFC 20.
O.67 DEA 373 Narrow-necked storage jar with cordon at base of neck. Band of acute latticing bordered by pair of incised lines on shoulder. Severn Valley ware. (Cf Webster 1976, no 1). 1st–4th century. (B I 3, phase II, Antonine to 3rd century). WMFC 20.
O.68 DEA 202 Narrow-necked storage jar with cordon at base of neck. Band of burnished zig-zag. The lead plugs in drilled holes are not rivets, the vessel being complete, perhaps they were for the attachment of a horizontal handle to enable the vessel to be used for drawing water. (D I 126A, phase II, later 2nd to early 3rd century?). WMFC 20.
O.69 DEA 398 Narrow-necked storage jar with cordon at base of neck. Band of burnished latticing bordered by a pair of incised lines on shoulder. Severn Valley ware. (Cf Webster 1976, no 1). 1st–4th century. (B I 3, phase II, Antonine to 3rd century). WMFC 20.
O.70 DEA 391 Narrow-necked storage jar with cordon at base of neck. Shoulder has band of acute burnished latticing bordered by a pair of incised lines. Severn Valley ware. (Cf Webster 1976, no 1). 1st–4th century (B I 3, phase II, Antonine to 3rd century). WMFC 20.
O.71 DEA 8 Narrow-necked jar with cordon at base of neck and incised groove on shoulder. Severn Valley ware. (Cf Webster 1976, no 4). 2nd–4th century. (A V 8, phase VI, late 3rd to early 4th century). WMFC 20.
O.72 DEA 256 Narrow-necked storage jar with simple everted rim and cordon at base of neck. Neck burnished. Burnished line on shoulder. Severn Valley ware. (Cf Webster 1976, no 1). 1st–4th century. (B I 15, phase II, Antonine to 3rd century). WMFC 20.
O.73 DIA 83 Narrow-necked jar with thickened rim and traces of burnishing on ext. (B I 3, phase II, Antonine to 3rd century). WMFC 20.
O.74 DK 8 Narrow-necked storage jar with bead-rim and cordon at base of neck. Three pairs of incised grooves decorate ext. with vertical line decoration between. Severn Valley ware. (Cf Webster 1976, no 3). Mid-1st to 2nd century (G I 110, phase IV, early to mid-4th century — residual). WMFC 20.
O.75 DK 40 Fine closed-mouth jar with bead-rim and double cordon at base of neck. Ext. is well burnished. Severn Valley ware. (Cf Webster 1976, no 2). Late 1st to mid-2nd century. (B IA 5, phase II, Antonine to 3rd century). WMFC 32.
O.76 DU 1 Closed-mouth jar with handle scar and possible cordon at base of neck. (D I 6, phase VI, mid- to late 4th century? — residual). WMFC 20.
O.77 DW 30 Small narrow-necked jar with two shallow incisions at base of neck. On girth is a deep incised groove with burnished horizontal lines on the body. Graffito (no 37) on shoulder reading 'IIPON'. Severn Valley ware. (Cf Webster 1976, no 1). 1st–4th century. (D II 60). WMFC 20.
O.78 DW 67 Fine narrow-necked jar with two cordons at base of neck and highly burnished ext. (C VIA 29, phase VIII, early to mid-4th century on). WMFC 20.
O.79 DZ 39 Narrow-necked jar with cordon at base of neck and burnished horizontal lines on neck and shoulder. (D II 29). WMFC 20.
O.80 DZ 40 Small narrow-necked jar with cordon at base of neck. (A XI 9). WMFC 20.
O.81 DZ 27 Narrow-necked jar with cordon at base of neck, and a grey slip. (Cf Webster 1976, no 2). Late 1st to mid-2nd century. (C IA 11, phase III, 3rd century — probably residual). WMFC 20.

Large storage jars

O.82 CH 62 Narrow-necked storage jar with cordon at base of neck and incised groove on shoulder. Highly burnished. (G IA 68, phase IV, early to mid-4th century). WMFC 21.
O.83 DA 39 Storage jar with everted rim and burnished ext. (D I 173, phase II, later 2nd to early 3rd century?). WMFC 21.
O.84 DA 1 Storage jar with everted rim and high shoulder, calcite-gritted. (C V 79). WMFC 35.
O.85 DA 12 Narrow-necked storage jar with everted rim. (C IXA 18). WMFC 21.
O.86 DA 59 Large narrow-necked storage jar. (D I 246, phase II, later 2nd to early 3rd century?). WMFC 21.
O.87 DA 36 Necked storage jar with everted rim. (D I 173, phase II, later 2nd to early 3rd century?). WMFC 35.
O.88 DA 32 Necked storage jar with high shoulder. (D I 173, phase II, later 2nd to early 3rd century?). WMFC 35.
O.89 DA 9 Large storage jar with everted rim. (AA IIIA 7). WMFC 35.
O.90 DA 47 Necked storage jar with thickened rim and high shoulder. (D I 173, phase II, later 2nd to early 3rd century?). WMFC 35.
O.91 DA 92 Large storage jar with everted rim. Graffito on rim, no 31. (G II 28). WMFC 35.
O.92 DA 93 Wide-mouthed storage jar with cordon at base of neck. On shoulder a band of burnished hatching banded by burnished horizontal bands. Graffito on rim, no 30. (Context unknown). WMFC 21.
O.93 DA 34 Wide-mouthed storage jar with everted rim and high shoulder and burnished ext. (D I 126A, phase II, later 2nd to early 3rd century). WMFC 35.
O.94 DA 76 Wide-mouthed storage jar with everted rim. (D II 29). WMFC 39.
O.95 DA 50 Necked jar with thickened rim and high shoulder. (D I 126A, phase II, later 2nd to early 3rd century). WMFC 35.
O.96 DA 84 Wide-mouthed storage jar with high shoulder and burnished rim and body ext. Severn Valley ware. (Cf Webster 1976, no 24). Late 2nd to late 3rd century. (B I 3, phase II, Antonine to 3rd century). WMFC 39.
O.97 DA 101 Wide-mouthed storage jar with pair of grooves at point of maximum girth. Ext. burnished. Severn Valley ware. (Cf Webster 1976, no 19). 1st–2nd century. (G V 84, U/S). WMFC 31.
O.98 DA 10 Wide-mouthed storage jar with cordon at base of neck and two incised grooves at widest part of girth. Gloucester (cf Webster 1976, no 19). 1st–2nd century. (C V 19). WMFC 35.
O.99 DA 25 Storage jar with thickened everted rim and high shoulder with incised groove. (G IA 68, phase IV, early to mid-4th century). WMFC 39.
O.100 DA 81 Necked storage jar with everted rim, and cordon at base of neck. On shoulder a pair of incised lines. (G IA 63, phase V, later 4th century — residual). WMFC 35.
O.101 DA 3 Storage jar with rolled-over rim and two incised grooves on widest part of girth. Rim and ext. burnished. Gloucester (cf Rawes 1972, no 102). Flavian. (G IA 63, phase V, later 4th century — residual). WMFC 39.
O.102 DA 46 Wide-necked storage jar with burnished rim. (D I 126A, phase II, later 2nd to early 3rd century). WMFC 39.
O.103 DA 79 Wide-necked storage jar with high shoulder and two pairs of incised lines on ext. Ext. and rim burnished. (G IA 68, phase IV, early to mid-4th century — residual). WMFC 39.
O.104 DA 8 Necked storage jar with a downward-turning rim. Severn Valley ware. (Cf Webster 1976, no 7). 2nd–3rd century. (AA II 101, phase I, late 1st to 2nd century). WMFC 35.
O.105 DA 28 Storage jar with thickened rolled-over rim. Severn Valley ware. (Cf Webster 1976, no 8). 3rd century. (B VI 3). WMFC 35.
O.106 DA 112 Storage jar with sharply everted rim and high shoulder. Severn Valley ware. (Cf Webster 1976, no 7). 2nd–3rd century. (AA III 93, phase V, later 3rd century on). WMFC 35.
O.107 DA 22 Closed-mouth storage jar with sharply everted rim and high shoulder. Rim burnished. (G IV 23, phase VI, late 4th century — residual). WMFC 21.
O.108 DA 27 Storage jar, with narrow upright neck. Ext. burnished. (G V 105, U/S). WMFC 22.
O.109 DA 66 Jar with everted rim and burnished ext. (Context unknown). WMFC 22.
O.110 DA 57 Base sherd of storage jar with ring groove on base. (D I 246, phase II, later 2nd to early 3rd century?).

O.111 DA 80 Body sherd with burnished zig-zag between two incised grooves. Typical Severn Valley ware. (A IX 1A).
O.112 DA 83 Body sherd with two drilled holes. (D I 173, phase II, later 2nd to early 3rd century?).
O.113 DA 87 Body sherd with graffito, no 34. (G V 2).
O.114 DA 71 Body sherd with graffito, no 33. (B I 25, phase I, 1st century to Hadrianic).
O.115 DA 68 Body sherd with two incised cuts on the ext. (G IA 63, phase V, later 4th century — residual).
O.116 DA 100 Body sherd with band of vertical burnished lines bordered by pairs of incised grooves. (D I 87, phase V, early to mid-4th century?).
O.117 DA 62 Large body sherd, with incised compass-drawn circle. Graffito, no 39. (A XVIIB 4).
O.118 DA 69 Body sherd reused and made into a disc; burnished vertical lines on ext. (B I 6).
O.119 DE 368 Storage jar with narrow neck and everted rim. Severn Valley ware. (Cf Webster 1976, no 3). Mid-1st to 3rd century. (B IA 25, phase III, Antonine to 3rd century on). WMFC 21.
O.120 DE 371 Necked storage jar. (B I 6). WMFC 21.
O.121 DE 275 Storage jar with cordon at base of neck and burnished rim and ext. Severn Valley ware. (Cf Webster 1976, no 2). Late 1st to mid-2nd century. (B I 6). WMFC 21.
O.122 DE 302 Storage jar with rolled-over rim. (A XVI 1). WMFC 21.
O.123 DE 364 Storage jar with rolled-over beaded rim. (B I 6). WMFC 21.
O.124 DE 285 Large body sherd of storage jar. Ext. burnished. (B IA 8). WMFC 21.
O.125 DEA 220 Necked storage jar with everted grooved rim. Shouldered jar with burnished triple zig-zag lines on shoulder. (D I 87, phase V, early to mid-4th century). WMFC 35.
O.126 DEA 67 Necked jar with groove on rim and high shoulder. (AA II 65B). WMFC 32.

Wide-mouthed jars

These are all represented by Severn Valley ware fabrics. The forms are common Severn Valley family with close parallels in Webster (1976). The decoration is simple with incised grooves frequently found on the shoulder. Burnishing on the rim and neck interior (when visible from above) is a distinguishing feature of the vessel.

Wide-mouthed jars with cordons and grooves on the widest part of the girth

O.127 DEA 217 Wide-mouthed jar with downward-turning rim and two incised grooves. Severn Valley ware. (Cf Webster 1976, no 21). Mid- to late 2nd century. (A X 18). WMFC 37.
O.128 DEA 264 Wide-mouthed jar with cordon at base of neck and a pair of incised grooves on shoulder. Severn Valley ware. (Cf Webster 1976, no 21). Mid- to late 2nd century. (B I 2, phase II, Antonine to 3rd century). WMFC 37.
O.129 DEA 142 Wide-mouthed jar with everted rim and triple zig-zag burnished decoration on shoulder. Severn Valley ware. (Cf Webster 1976, no 20). 1st century. (C IXA 13). WMFC 37.

Wide-mouthed jars with wedge-shaped rims

O.130 DE 330 Wide-mouthed jar. Severn Valley ware. (Cf Webster 1976, no 22). 2nd–3rd century. (D II 29A). WMFC 37.
O.131 DE 376 Wide-mouthed jar with incised groove on body and faint incised loop decoration. Severn Valley ware. (Cf Webster 1976, no 22). 2nd to 3rd century. (B I 14). WMFC 37.

Wide-mouthed jars with simple curved rims

O.132 DE 305 Wide-mouthed jar with downward-curving rim, and high shoulder. Severn Valley ware. (Cf Webster 1976, no 27). Late 3rd to 4th century. (C IIIA 21). WMFC 37.
O.133 DE 305 Wide-mouthed jar with tapering rim. Severn Valley ware. (Cf Webster 1976, no 23). Mid-2nd to late 3rd century. (D I 87, phase V, early to mid-4th century — residual). WMFC 37.
O.134 DE 292 Wide-mouthed jar with everted rim. Severn Valley ware. (Cf Webster 1976, no 22). 2nd–3rd century. (J II 22A). WMFC 37.
O.135 DE 289 Wide-mouthed jar with indentation on neck, before firing. High shoulder with burnished lines on ext. Severn Valley ware. (Cf Webster 1976, no 25). 2nd–3rd century. (J II 22A). WMFC 37.
O.136 DEA 14 Wide-mouthed jar with downward-turning rim and burnished ext. Severn Valley ware. (Cf Webster 1976, no 27). Late 3rd to 4th century. (A VII 19). WMFC 37.
O.137 DEA 45 Wide-mouthed jar with sharply everted rim and burnished ext. Severn Valley ware. (Cf Webster 1976, no 21). Mid- to late 2nd century. (A IX 21). WMFC 37.
O.138 DEA 260 Wide-mouthed jar. (J II 22A). WMFC 35.
O.139 DEA 396 Wide-mouthed jar with everted downward-turning rim. Severn Valley ware. (Cf Webster 1976, no 22). 2nd–3rd century. (J II 22). WMFC 37.
O.140 DEA 303 Wide-mouthed jar with wedge-shaped rim. Severn Valley ware. (Cf Webster 1976, no 22). 2nd–3rd century. (D I 87, phase V, early to mid-4th century? — residual). WMFC 37.
O.141 DEA 268 Wide-mouthed jar with thickened lip. Rim and shoulder burnished up to a pair of incised grooves on shoulder and there is a burnished band above base. (J II 22A). WMFC 37.

Wide-mouthed jars with hooked rims and high shoulders

O.142 DE 96 Wide-mouthed jar with hooked rim and high shoulder. Severn Valley ware. (Cf Webster 1976, no 30). Late 3rd to 4th century (C II 1). WMFC 37.
O.143 DE 113 Wide-mouthed jar with hooked rim and high shoulder. Severn Valley ware. (Cf Webster 1976, no 28). Late 3rd to 4th century (C VI 24, phase VII, early to mid-4th century). WMFC 37.
O.144 DE 301 Wide-mouthed jar with beaded lip and high shoulder. Severn Valley ware. (Cf Webster 1976, no 29). Late 3rd to 4th century. (A XVI 1). WMFC 37.
O.145 DE 311 Wide-mouthed jar with flared, hooked rim. Parallel: Severn Valley ware (Webster 1976, no 27). Late 3rd to 4th century. (A XVI 1). WMFC 37.
O.146 DE 286 Wide-mouthed jar with hooked rim and high shoulder. Rim and ext. burnished. Severn Valley ware. (Cf Webster 1976, no 27). Late 3rd to 4th century. (D I 89). WMFC 37.
O.147 DE 393 Large wide-mouthed jar with hooked rim and high shoulder. Ext. burnished. Severn Valley ware. (Cf Webster 1976, no 27). Late 3rd to 4th century. (D I 6, phase VI, mid- to late 4th century?). WMFC 37.
O.148 DEA 326 Wide-mouthed jar with hooked rim. Severn Valley ware. (Cf Webster 1976, no 27). Late 3rd to 4th century. (D II 29). WMFC 37.
O.149 DEA 224 Wide-mouthed jar with hooked rim, and burnished rim and shoulder. On widest part of girth a pair of incised grooves. Severn Valley ware. (Cf Webster 1976, no 28). Late 3rd to 4th century. (D I 87A). WMFC 37.

Wide-mouthed jars with thick wedge-shaped hooked rims

O.150 DE 154 Wide-mouthed jar with hooked wedge-shaped rim and high shoulder. Rim and ext. burnished. Severn Valley ware. (Cf Webster 1976, no 32). 4th century. (A XVIIA 2). WMFC 37.
O.151 DE 327 Wide-mouthed jar with wedge-shaped rim. Severn Valley ware. (Cf Webster 1976, no 32). 4th century. (M I T/S). WMFC 37.
O.152 DI 8 Wide-mouthed jar with wedge rim. Severn Valley ware. (Cf Webster 1976, no 30). Late 3rd to 4th century. (AA III 11, phase VIII, early to mid-4th century). WMFC 37.
O.153 DIA 45 Wide-mouthed jar with hooked rim. Severn Valley ware. (Cf Webster 1976, no 27). Late 3rd to 4th century. (A XVI 1). WMFC 37.
O.154 DIA 29 Wide-mouthed jar with high shoulder and burnished horizontal lines on the ext. (C VI 32). WMFC 37.

O.155 DK 10 Wide-mouthed jar with hooked rim and well-burnished body ext. Severn Valley ware. (Cf Webster 1976, no 28). Late 3rd to 4th century. (D I 214, phase VIII, late 4th century — residual). WMFC 37.
O.156 DW 26 Very fine, wide-mouthed jar with hooked rim, high shoulder and well-burnished ext. and rim. Severn Valley ware. (Cf Webster 1976, no 31). 4th century. (D IV 6). WMFC 37.
O.157 DZ 44 Large, wide-mouthed jar with thickened rim. Severn Valley ware. (Cf Webster 1976, no 22). 2nd–3rd century. (J II 22A). WMFC 37.

Jars with everted rims

O.158 CH 9 Jar with everted rim and highly burnished ext. (H II 25, phase II, Antonine to 3rd century). WMFC 23.
O.159 CK 2 Jar with everted thickened rim and burnished int. and ext. Vertical burnished lines decorate the ext. A hole has been drilled in the neck and another started. On lower part of pot two more holes have been drilled horizontally, 9mm apart. (D II 22). WMFC 22.
O.160 CM 9 Ovoid jar with everted, well-burnished rim and ext. (D II 29). WMFC 26.
O.161 DE 276 Jar with everted rim and pronounced shoulder. (B I 6). WMFC 26.
O.162 DE 102 Jar with everted rim and pronounced shoulder. Ext. well burnished. (B IA 1). WMFC 26.
O.163 DE 309 Small jar with everted rim and high shoulder. (D I 87, phase V, early to mid-4th century?). WMFC 23.
O.164 DEA 79 Jar with everted rim and high shoulder, burnished ext.; a second. (C IIIB 1). WMFC 26.
O.165 DEA 20 Jar with everted rim and high shoulder. (A IX 1A). WMFC 32.
O.166 DEA 233 Ovoid jar with everted rim. (B I 3, phase II, Antonine to 3rd century). WMFC 22.
O.167 DEA 72 Jar with everted rim. (AA II 78, phase II, late 2nd to early 3rd century). WMFC 22.
O.168 DEA 334 Small jar with everted rim and high shoulder, decorated with burnished horizontal lines on ext. (B I 6). WMFC 22.
O.169 DEA 337 Small jar with everted rim. (J II 22A). WMFC 22.
O.170 DIA 43 Jar with everted rim and burnished design on body ext. in the form of burnished diagonal lines with thick vertical bands of burnishing; very crude. (B I 3, phase II, Antonine to 3rd century). WMFC 26.
O.171 DS 1 Jar with everted rim. (C VI 32B). WMFC 22.
O.172 DW 55 Small jar with closed mouth and burnished ext. (B I 6). WMFC 20.
O.173 DW 49 Jar with everted rim and pronounced shoulder. Ext. burnished. (B I 6). WMFC 26.
O.174 DW 50 Jar with everted rim. Burnished rim and ext. (B IA 1). WMFC 26.
O.175 DZ 37 Jar with everted rim. (B I 3, phase II, Antonine to 3rd century). WMFC 26.

Globular or ovoid jars with small everted rims

O.176 CM 6 Globular closed-mouth jar with burnished ext. There is an inverted 'V' incised decoration immediately below rim and above two incised grooves which form a cordon. Below this a band of incised 'X' decoration. (H I 9, phase II, Antonine to 3rd century — probably residual). WMFC 31.
O.177 DE 44 Small jar with rim prepared to seat a lid and a hole drilled in the body. (A IX 17, phase II, late 2nd to mid-3rd century). WMFC 31.
O.178 DE 209 Jar with small everted rim and pair of incised grooves below rim. On body ext. are two bands of acute lattice decoration bounded by incised grooves. Rim and ext. well burnished. (G IA 84, phase IV, early to mid-4th century — residual). WMFC 31.
O.179 DE 343 Globular closed-mouth jar with burnished ext. (B I 2, phase II, Antonine to 3rd century). WMFC 31?
O.180 DE 261 Jar with small everted rim. Severn Valley ware. (Cf Webster 1976, no 17). (B I 6). WMFC 31.
O.181 DE 180 Small jar with small everted rim and high shoulder. Foot is moulded with ring groove on base ext. (AA III 28). WMFC 34.
O.182 DEA 198 Closed-mouth jar with small everted rim and burnished ext. (D I 173, phase II, later 2nd to early 3rd century?). WMFC 31.
O.183 DEA 163 Globular jar with groove on shoulder and rouletted decoration on body ext. Traces of white slip on int. and ext. (H I 1). WMFC 42.
O.184 DEA 293 Jar with flattened bead-rim. (J II 22A). WMFC 22.
O.185 DEA 167 Globular jar with everted rim and pair of incised grooves at maximum girth. (C VI 125). WMFC 34.
O.186 DEA 167 Globular jar with small everted flanged rim, and pair of incised grooves on int. with a faint zig-zag burnished decoration between them. (E IV 25, phase VI, early 3rd century?). WMFC 58.
O.187 DEA 338 Small jar with a hooked rim. (J II 22A). WMFC 32.
O.188 DEA 124 Jar with everted rim and burnished ext. Ext. decorated by incised vertical grooves at regular intervals. (C IXA 13). WMFC 22.
O.189 DEA 169 Globular jar with everted rim and burnished ext. Graffito beneath rim, no 36. (C VIA 107, phase V, later 3rd century on). WMFC 22.
O.190 DEA 421 Jar with sharply everted rim and constriction on shoulder. Ext. covered with burnished horizontal lines. (C VIA 42C, phase IX+, mid-4th century on). WMFC 24.
O.191 DIA 42 Small jar with everted rim and constriction on shoulder. Possibly rusticated jar form. Ext. badly pitted. (B I 3, phase II, Antonine to 3rd century). WMFC 24.
O.192 DIA 16 Globular jar with small everted rim and burnished acute lattice on ext. (AA II 16, phase V, later 3rd century on — probably residual). WMFC 26.
O.193 DW 27 Globular jar with vestigial beaded rim and highly burnished ext. (D II 39). WMFC 23.
O.194 DW 35 Fine, globular jar with almost vertical rim. Ext. well burnished with pair of incised grooves decorating shoulder and white-painted scallop band. (G V 98, phase II?, mid-3rd century?). WMFC 23.

Necked jars

Necked jars with everted rims and prominent shoulders are developed from the common Belgic jar. These vessels are either completely or partially burnished, frequently with horizontal burnished bands and incised grooves at the maximum girth.

O.195 CH 65 Necked jar with upturned rim and pronounced shoulder. Ext. well burnished with hole drilled through body possibly to hold a rivet. Gloucester (cf Rawes 1972, no 96). Flavian. (D II 22). WMFC 32.
O.196 CH 15 Necked jar with upturned rim and pronounced shoulder. Well-burnished ext. Gloucester (cf Rawes 1972). Flavian. (H II 80, phase II, Antonine to 3rd century). WMFC 32.
O.197 DE 99 Necked jar/bowl with pronounced shoulder. (B IA 5, phase II, Antonine to 3rd century). WMFC 32.
O.198 DE 418 Jar with upright neck and rim curving out. At widest girth are pair of incised grooves. Beneath is area of burnished horizontal bands. Gloucester (cf Rawes 1972, no 100?) Flavian. (D II 22). WMFC 32.
O.199 DE 417 Necked jar with prominent shoulder. Ext. well burnished. (D II 16). WMFC 32.
O.200 DE 146 Necked jar with prominent shoulder and two incised grooves at maximum girth. A hole has been drilled in neck of jar. Well-burnished ext. Severn Valley ware. (Cf Webster 1976, no 20). 1st–2nd century. (B IA 18). WMFC 32.
O.201 DEA 273 Necked jar with rim curving out and prominent shoulder. Burnished ext. (G IA 68, phase IV, early to mid-4th century). WMFC 32.
O.202 DEA 380 Necked jar with groove on rim int. High rounded shoulder. (C V 48). WMFC 32.
O.203 DEA 423 Small jar with upright and everted rim. Shoulder prominent and ext. decorated by regularly spaced horizontal lines. (B I 3, phase II, Antonine to 3rd century). WMFC 32.
O.204 DU 2 Wide-necked jar with curved rim and two incised grooves on girth. Surface badly worn. (D I 173, phase II, later 2nd to early 3rd century?). WMFC 32.

Romano-British coarse pottery

O.205 DZ 29 Small jar with curved neck and prominent shoulder. Incised groove on shoulder. (A IX 24). WMFC 46.
O.206 DZ 24 Jar (a second) with curved everted rim. Burnished vertical lines decorate shoulder. (J II 22A). WMFC 32.
O.207 DZ 21 Jar with upright neck and everted rim. Neck decorated by burnished horizontal lines. Beneath shoulder is burnished acute lattice. (A XVIIA 4). WMFC 32.
O.208 DZ 16 Base sherd jar. (B I 14).

Jars with inward-sloping necks

O.209 BJ 1 Body sherd of jar with two incised grooves on neck. Ext. rouletted. (A IX 28).
O.210 CH 28 Narrow-necked jar with outward-splaying rim. Ext. well burnished. Gloucester (cf Rawes 1972, no 78). Flavian. (D II 38). WMFC 41.
O.211 DA 13 Narrow-necked jar with everted moulded rim and burnished ext. Gloucester (cf Rawes 1972, no 95). Flavian. (B IA 25, phase III, Antonine to 3rd century on — possibly residual). WMFC 41.
O.212 DA 95 Narrow-necked jar with everted rim and straight sides. Gloucester (cf Rawes 1972, no 74). Flavian. (C IXA 13). WMFC 41.
O.213 DE 255 Small narrow-necked jar with prominent shoulder. Burnished rim and neck. (D I 246, phase II, later 2nd to early 3rd century?). WMFC 20.
O.214 DE 313 Small necked jar with grooved rim and prominent shoulder. Shoulder and rim burnished. (D I 87, phase V, early to mid-4th century — probably residual). WMFC 20.
O.215 DEA 421 Jar with everted rim. Gloucester (cf Rawes 1972, no 84). Flavian. (C VIA 42C, phase IX+, mid-4th century — residual). WMFC 32.
O.216 DEA 183 Narrow-necked jar covered with white slip on ext. and decorated by bands of red paint. (G I 4). WMFC 20.
O.217 DK 23 Jar with a thickened rim. (Cf Webster 1976, no 3). 1st–3rd century. (D I 126A, phase II, later 2nd to early 3rd century?). WMFC 32.
O.218 DK 22 Necked jar with incised groove beneath rim ext. (D I 20, phase IV, late 3rd century?). WMFC 32.
O.219 FD 1 Butt beaker with everted rim and two incised grooves at girth defining a band of burnished triple wavy lines. Patches of black soot encrusted on ext. (C II 135). WMFC 49.

Rough-cast jars

The vessels from Birch Abbey are typified by cornice rims and high shoulders. The shoulders are burnished down to an incised groove defining the upper limit of rough-cast decoration. This is formed by clay particles and has a practical as well as decorative function, in that it facilitates grip. Close parallels are to be found at Breddon Hill in the Severn Valley, and the contexts in which the vessels appear here suggest a 2nd-century date.

O.220 FA 10 Jar with cornice rim and incised groove above area of rough-cast decoration. (AA III 28). WMFC 42.
O.221 FA 6 Jar with cornice rim and incised groove above area of rough-cast decoration. (D II 29A). WMFC 42.
O.222 FA 9 Small rough-cast jar/beaker base. (B I 3, phase II, Antonine to 3rd century). WMFC 42.
O.223 FA 13 Jar with cornice rim and incised groove on shoulder above area of rough-cast decoration. (B I 6). WMFC 42.
O.224 FA 1 Base sherd of a rough-cast jar. (A V 12, phase VI, late 3rd to early 4th century? — residual). WMFC 42.

Miscellaneous jars

O.225 DEA 254 Conical rusticated jar with grooved rim above area of regularly spaced linear rustication. AD 70–120. (D I 246, phase II, later 2nd to early 3rd century? — residual). WMFC 24.
O.226 DJ 3 Bag-shaped jar/beaker with sharply everted rim and incised line on shoulder. Ext. lightly burnished. (A I 2). WMFC 42.
O.227 EJ 1 Hand-made jar. Ext. decorated with burnished vertical lines. Copy of a Malvernian cooking pot. Antonine onwards. (D I 25, phase VIII, late 4th century — residual). WMFC 26.
O.228 EH 26 Small jar, very fine. (C V 4). WMFC 22.

Straight-sided beakers

O.229 CM 1 Straight-sided beaker with bead-rim. Ext. has regularly spaced vertical grooves. Well burnished. (G I 85, phase V, later 4th century). WMFC 66.
O.230 CM 3 Straight-sided beaker with three incised grooves below rim. Ext. has burnished vertical lines at regular intervals. (D I 123, phase VI, mid- to late 4th century?). WMFC 66.

Corrugated beakers

O.231 DEA 158 Corrugated beaker. (C VIA 86, phase II, late 2nd century). WMFC 47.
O.232 DEA 296 Base sherd of beaker. (J II 22A).
O.233 DIA 77 Corrugated beaker with burnished ext. (A XIV 29). WMFC 47.
O.234 DIA 85 Corrugated beaker. (A X 2). WMFC 47.
O.235 DEA 253 Bag-shaped beaker. (J II 4A). WMFC 43.
O.236 DI 71 Beaker, possibly carinated. Neck well burnished with pair of incised grooves at waist. Below groove an area of 'X' type decoration at regular intervals. (AA II 102, phase III, 3rd century). WMFC 54.

Necked beakers

O.237 DE 325 Beaker with long curved neck decorated with burnished horizontal lines. (D II 29A). WMFC 41.
O.238 DE 419 Butt beaker with curved neck. On body are three incised horizontal grooves at regular intervals between which a burnished grid. (G IA 89, phase VI, late 4th century — residual). WMFC 49.
O.239 DEA 333 Butt beaker with sloping neck and everted rim. Ext. burnished. A hole has been drilled near rim, possibly for riveting. (D II 29A). WMFC 49.
O.240 DW 33 Curved-neck beaker with incised line on shoulder and well-burnished ext. (D II 60). WMFC 41.
O.241 DZ 45 Beaker with inward-sloping neck and thick everted rim. Neck burnished. Two incised grooves on shoulder. (D II 29). WMFC 49?

Rouletted beakers

O.242 DJ 4 Beaker with sharply everted rim and with rouletted decoration on ext. (D II 29). WMFC 42.
O.243 DZA 42 Rouletted beaker, with sharply everted rim and burnished ext. above rouletting. (D I 138). WMFC 42.
O.244 DZA 41 Beaker with sharply everted rim and buff slip on int. and ext. Well burnished. (C IIIB 1). WMFC 42.

Carinated cups

O.245 DA 96 Carinated cup with bead-rim and cordon at carination. (A IX 4, phase III, later 3rd century — probably residual). WMFC 47.
O.246 DA 114 Carinated cup with line incised above carination. Ext. burnished. (G IA 85, phase I?, late 2nd/3rd century?). WMFC 47.
O.247 DA 113 Carinated cup with fine acute lattice decoration between rim and carination. (H II 64). WMFC 47.
O.248 DE 109 Cup or small bowl. (A XVII 1). WMFC 64.
O.249 DEA 238 Carinated cup with bead-rim and incised line on shoulder above carination. Ext. well burnished and there is a ring groove on base ext. (L XIII 2). WMFC 53.
O.250 DI 24 Carinated cup. (D II 90, phase I, 1st century to early Antonine). WMFC 51.
O.251 DI 22 Carinated cup with cordon at carination. Ext. burnished. (D II 49). WMFC 51.

O.252 DIA 78 Carinated cup with light groove above carination, lightly burnished int. and well-burnished red/black ext. (H I 9, phase II, Antonine to 3rd century). WMFC 51.

Cups with curved body wall

O.253 DA 98 Cup with bead-rim and lightly burnished ext. (D I 238). WMFC 58.
O.254 DE 120 Wide-necked cup/bowl, with high shoulder. (A XVI 6). WMFC 55.
O.255 DEA 336 Base sherd of cup, with dome in base int. Burnished bands decorate the ext. (B I 3, phase II, Antonine to 3rd century).
O.256 DK 38 Cup with everted bead-rim. (A XVI 76). WMFC 58.
O.257 FB 1 Coarse cup with inward-turning rim and burnished ext. (C VIA 2A). WMFC 58.

Miscellaneous cups

O.258 DE 70 Cup with pedestal base. (AA I 66, phase VI, late 3rd to early 4th century).
O.259 DW 64 Campanulate cup. 2nd century. (A IX 11). WMFC 59.
O.260 DW 8 Cup with bead-rim and white paint decoration on the ext. (C VI 8, phase VII, early to mid-4th century). WMFC 42?

Tankards

The most common tankard form at Alcester is the simple straight-sided vessel with an incised groove beneath the rim and a double-ribbed handle. The majority are well burnished. (See microfiche M2:C11 for a discussion of the capacity of the tankards.)

O.261 DA 89 Base sherd of large tankard. Two incised grooves form cordon on body ext; above foot an incised groove. Base raised. (Cf Webster 1976, no 38). Mid- to late 1st century. (D II 29A). WMFC 61.
O.262 DA 42 Tankard with bead-rim. Severn Valley ware (cf Webster 1976, no 39). 2nd century. (C VI 32). WMFC 62.
O.263 DA 51 Tankard with bead-rim and incised groove on body ext. Severn Valley ware (cf Webster 1976, no 39). 2nd century. (B I 6). WMFC 62.
O.264 DE 265 Tankard with incised line beneath rim and pair of incised grooves on body ext. There is a hole which may have been used for the attachment of a handle with an incised groove beneath. Severn Valley ware (cf Webster 1976, no 40). 2nd to early 3rd century. (D I 173, phase II, late 2nd to early 3rd century?). WMFC 62.
O.265 DE 1 Tankard with incised line beneath rim, and ring groove on base. Handle double-ribbed. Severn Valley ware (cf Webster 1976, no 43). Late 2nd to 3rd century. (C III 21). WMFC 62.
O.266 DE 288 Tankard with incised line beneath rim and double-ribbed handle. Base flat and ext. of vessel well burnished. Severn Valley ware (cf Webster 1976, no 43). Late 2nd to 3rd century. (L II 7). WMFC 62.
O.267 DE 362 Fine tankard with two shallow incised lines beneath rim and well-burnished ext. Handle double-ribbed. Severn Valley ware (cf Webster 1976, no 43). Late 2nd to 3rd century. (D II 94). WMFC 62.
O.268 DE 375 Tankard with incised line beneath rim and double-ribbed handle. Severn Valley ware (cf Webster 1976, no 43). Late 2nd to 3rd century. (J II 2). WMFC 62.
O.269 DE 344 Small tankard with bead-rim and well-burnished ext. (B I 3, phase II, Antonine to 3rd century). WMFC 62.
O.270 DE 270 Base sherd of tankard with indentation above base, damaged while clay was still soft. (B IA 8). WMFC 62.
O.271 DE 349 Tankard with incised groove beneath rim and further two incised lines at regular intervals, forming borders of band of acute lattice decoration. Severn Valley ware (cf Webster 1976, no 59). 1st–2nd century. (B I 2, phase II, Antonine to 3rd century). WMFC 54.
O.272 DEA 248 Tankard with incised groove beneath rim and a pair of incised grooves around body ext. Handle double-ribbed. Severn Valley ware (cf Webster 1976, no 38). Mid- to late 1st century. (D I 246, phase II, later 2nd to early 3rd century?). WMFC 61.
O.273 DEA 246 Tankard with beaded rim and double-ribbed handle. Severn Valley ware (cf Webster 1976, no 43). 2nd–3rd century. (D I 246, phase II, later 2nd to early 3rd century?). WMFC 62.
O.274 DEA 143 Tankard with incised groove beneath rim and ring-groove on base ext. Handle is double-ribbed. Severn Valley ware (cf Webster 1976, no 40). 2nd to early 3rd century. (A XVI 14). WMFC 62.
O.275 DEA 258 Tankard? (D I 173, phase II, later 2nd to early 3rd century?). WMFC 61?
O.276 DEA 308 Tankard with incised groove beneath rim and burnished ext. Severn Valley ware (cf Webster 1976, no 43). Late 2nd to 3rd century. (A XVI 1). WMFC 62.
O.277 DEA 354 Tankard with incised groove beneath rim and burnished ext. Severn Valley ware (cf Webster 1976, no 38/39). 2nd century. (B I 3, phase II, Antonine to 3rd century). WMFC 61.
O.278 DEA 402 Tankard with incised groove beneath rim, and double-ribbed handle. On base ext. a ring-groove. Severn Valley ware (cf Webster 1976, no 42/43). 2nd–3rd century. (B I 3, phase II, Antonine to 3rd century). WMFC 62.
O.279 DEA 346 Small tankard with incised line beneath rim. Lightly burnished ext. (B I 3, phase II, Antonine to 3rd century). WMFC 62.
O.280 DEA 406 Tankard with incised line on rim. (Cf Webster 1976, no 43). 2nd–3rd century. (J II 22A). WMFC 62.
O.281 DEA 131 Tankard/mug with incised line on rim. Lightly burnished ext. Severn Valley ware (cf Webster 1976, no 44). 4th century. (C VI 24, phase VII, early to mid-4th century). WMFC 62.
O.282 DIA 21 Tankard with incised groove beneath rim and incised ring-groove on base ext. Ext. well burnished and handle double-ribbed. Severn Valley ware (cf Webster 1976, no 42). 2nd–3rd century. (J II 22A). WMFC 62.
O.283 DIA 32 Tankard with incised groove beneath rim. Burnished ext. (J II 22A). WMFC 62.
O.284 DIA 31 Tankard with incised groove beneath rim. Ext. burnished with acute lattice on body ext. and incised ring groove on base. Handle double-ribbed. Severn Valley ware (cf Webster 1976, no 38). Mid- to late 1st century. (B I 3, phase II, Antonine to 3rd century — residual). WMFC 61.
O.285 DIA 11 Base sherd of mug/tankard with ring groove on base and handle scar. (C IIIA 5).
O.286 DK 12 Fine small tankard/mug with incised groove beneath rim. Surface of vessel is mottled black and red. (Cf Webster 1976, no 43). 2nd–3rd century. (AA II 87, phase III, 3rd century). WMFC 62.
O.287 DW 1 Small fine tankard with incised groove beneath rim. Ext. well burnished. (Cf Webster 1976, no 43). 2nd–3rd century. (AA III 30). WMFC 62.
O.288 DZ 8 Hard, very sandy tankard with incised groove on rim and lightly burnished ext. (C VI 55, phase IV, later 3rd century on). WMFC 61.
O.289 DZ 34 Small mug with incised groove on rim and ring groove on base ext. Handle is double-ribbed and ext. well burnished. (Cf Webster 1976, no 39). 2nd century. (B I 3, phase II, Antonine to 3rd century). WMFC 61.
O.290 DZ 43 Tankard with incised groove beneath rim and on body ext. bordering area of burnished latticing. Severn Valley ware (cf Webster 1976, no 40). 2nd–3rd century. (J II 22A). WMFC 62.

Bowls

This category of the oxidized vessels accounts for 25% of the oxidized assemblage, the majority of which are utilitarian vessels with a few fine wares imitating metal and samian vessels.

Carinated jars / bowls (Iron Age-derived vessels)

O.291 CH 8 Carinated jar/bowl. Rim beaded. Three incised grooves occur at waist. Ext. well burnished. (H II 25, phase II, Antonine to 3rd century). WMFC 53.
O.292 CH 19 Very fine carinated jar/bowl with two grooves beneath rim and cordon on upper part of body. Above the cordon

a band of left-hatching and beneath a band of right-hatching. Traces of another cordon beneath this. (D II 16). WMFC 54.
O.293 CM 5 Bowl probably carinated with rim tapering to a point. Ext. lightly burnished with an acute incised lattice decoration. Below is a band of burnishing. (G IA 71, phase V, later 4th century — residual). WMFC 54.
O.294 DA 77 Carinated bowl/tankard with straight sides and two pairs of incised grooves on body ext. Ext. lightly burnished. (Cf Webster 1976, no 38, mid- to late 1st century). (D I 246, phase II, later 2nd to early 3rd century? — residual). WMFC 61.
O.295 DA 45 Bowl probably carinated. Ext. corrugated by burnishing. (D I 173, phase II, later 2nd to early 3rd century?). WMFC 54?
O.296 DA 97 Jar/bowl carinated with bead-rim and cordon at waist. Ext. burnished. Severn Valley ware (cf Webster 1976, no 59). 1st–2nd century. (A X 26). WMFC 53.
O.297 DE 340 Carinated jar/bowl with bead-rim and double cordon at waist. Severn Valley ware (cf Webster 1976, no 59). 1st–2nd century. (C VI 135). WMFC 53.
O.298 DE 195 Carinated jar/bowl with incised line beneath rim. At waist are a further two incised grooves, and above the carination a cordon. Ext. well burnished. Severn Valley ware (cf Webster 1976, variant of no 59). 1st–2nd century. (D I 148, phase VI, mid- to late 4th century — residual). WMFC 53.
O.299 DE 282 Carinated jar/bowl with bead-rim and three incised grooves at waist. Ext. well-burnished. Severn Valley ware (cf Webster 1976, no 60). Date uncertain, probably 1st–2nd century. (G IA 68, phase IV, early to mid-4th century — residual). WMFC 53.
O.300 DE 234 Very fine carinated bowl, form loosely based on Dr. 30. Rim beaded and a pair of incised lines on the upper body. Beneath carination another incised groove. On base ext. a deep ring groove. (AA III 28). WMFC 53.
O.301 DE 170 Carinated bowl with two incised grooves beneath rim and cordon at carination. Ext. burnished. Cf Gloucester (Rawes 1972, variant of type 26). Flavian. (C VIA 140). WMFC 53.
O.302 DE 431 Carinated bowl with three cordons on body and highly burnished ext. (G IA 63, phase V, later 4th century — residual). WMFC 54?
O.303 DE 420 Bowl, probably carinated with small cordon near rim and large cordon on upper body. Rim burnished, with a burnished zig-zag pattern above and below cordon on upper body. (G I 106A, phase V, later 4th century — residual). WMFC 54.
O.304 DE 425 Body sherd of carinated bowl with two cordons on ext. and burnished hatching lines on ext. (D II 29A). WMFC 54.
O.305 DE 227 Carinated waisted bowl with four cordons on ext. On upper body between the first and second cordon is a decorated band of cross type decoration. (L I 21, phase II, late 2nd century on). WMFC 54?
O.306 DE 117 Bowl, probably carinated. Ext. rouletted. (A XVIII 2). WMFC 54?
O.307 DEA 236 Carinated bowl with everted rim. Upper body has groove. Base raised. Dr. 37 copy. (L XII 7). WMFC 66.
O.308 DEA 229 Carinated bowl with everted rim and incised groove on rim ext. Upper body has incised line. (B I 30). WMFC 52.
O.309 DEA 148 Fine carinated bowl with bead-rim, incised line above carination. Foot moulded. A hole has been punched in the base. (A XVI 12). WMFC 53.
O.310 DEA 351 Carinated bowl with two incised lines on upper body. A combed acute lattice on ext. Severn Valley ware (cf Webster 1976, no 38). Mid- to late 1st century. (B I 3, phase II, Antonine to 3rd century — residual). WMFC 61.
O.311 DEA 201 Simple bowl with possible carination. Under the rim an incised line. Ext. burnished. (G IA 60, phase V, later 4th century — residual). WMFC 51.
O.312 DEA 422 Bowl with small cordon beneath rim, on upper body is area of rouletted decoration. Cf Gloucester (Rawes 1972, no 34). Flavian. (D I 176). WMFC 56.
O.313 DEA 54 Bowl, possibly carinated. The rim curves inward with three incised lines on ext. (Cf Gloucester: Rawes 1972, no 29). Flavian. (C VI 32). WMFC 56.
O.314 DI 12 Carinated bowl with two pairs of incised lines on body ext. Severn Valley ware (cf Webster 1976, no 60). 1st–2nd century. (B IA 1). WMFC 53.
O.315 DI 18 Carinated bowl with bead-rim and double cordon at waist, above the carination is cordon. (C II 125). WMFC 53.
O.316 DIA 76 Bowl, probably carinated. Two incised lines on neck of vessel and body ext. has burnished diagonal lines. (Cf Darling 1977, fig 6.5, no 21, Usk.) AD 55–70. (D I 124, phase VI, mid- to late 4th century — residual). WMFC 56.
O.317 DIA 72 Carinated bowl with bead-rim and two incised grooves at waist. (A VII 9). WMFC 53.
O.318 DJ 5 Carinated bowl with sharply everted rim. Ext. decorated by burnished horizontal lines. 1st century. (G IV 59, phase IV, early to mid-4th century — residual). WMFC 52.
O.319 DK 39 Bowl, probably carinated. (A XIV 33). WMFC 82.
O.320 DZ 9 Small carinated bowl with bead-rim. Ext. decorated by burnished horizontal lines. (C VI 32). WMFC 54.

Bowls reminiscent of Dr. 37 in coarse fabrics

O.321 DA 40 Bowl with bead-rim. (D I 173, phase II, later 2nd to early 3rd century?). WMFC 66.
O.322 DE 328 Bowl with bead-rim and pair of incised grooves on upper body. Ext. well burnished. Severn Valley ware (cf Webster 1976, no 61). Mid-1st to late 2nd century. (D II 29). WMFC 66.
O.323 DEA 112 Bowl with two pairs of incised horizontal lines and covered with white slip on ext. Fabric: South-Western brown slip. Cirencester Excavations Committee Fabric 88 (J Richardson pers comm). (C X 40). WMFC 66.
O.324 DEA 250 Bowl with bead-rim and two incised grooves on body. Foot moulded, with ring-groove on base. Severn Valley ware (cf Webster 1976, no 61). Mid-1st to late 2nd century. (B I 3, phase II, Antonine to 3rd century). WMFC 66.
O.325 DEA 320 Bowl with incised groove beneath rim. (D II 29A). WMFC 66.
O.326 DEA 48 Bead-rim bowl with pair of incised grooves on body ext. Severn Valley ware (cf Webster 1976, no 61). Mid-1st to late 2nd century. (A IX 24). WMFC 66.
O.327 DEA 428 Bead-rim bowl with pair of incised grooves on upper body. Ext. burnished. A ring-groove on base ext. Severn Valley ware (cf Webster 1976, no 61). Mid-1st to late 2nd century. (B I 3, phase II, Antonine to 3rd century). WMFC 66.
O.328 DEA 381 Bead-rim bowl with pair of incised grooves on upper body and ring-groove on body ext. Severn Valley ware (cf Webster 1976, no 61). Mid-1st to late 2nd century. (B I 20). WMFC 66.
O.329 DEA 283 Bead-rim bowl with pair of incised grooves on body ext. Severn Valley ware (cf Webster 1976, no 61). Mid-1st to late 2nd century. (B I 3, phase II, Antonine to 3rd century). WMFC 66.
O.330 DEA 231 Bead-rim bowl with lightly burnished ext. (Cf Webster 1976, no 61). Mid-1st to late 2nd century. (C VI 31, phase III, 3rd century — probably residual). WMFC 66.
O.331 DEA 231 Bowl with pair of incised grooves beneath rim. Ext. has combed wavy lines. (L I 16, phase II, late 2nd century on). WMFC 66.
O.332 DI 54 Bowl with bead-rim and burnished irregular horizontal lines on ext. (D I 177). WMFC 66.
O.333 DIA 59 Small bowl with bead-rim and burnished horizontal lines on ext. (B I 3, phase II, Antonine to 3rd century). WMFC 66.
O.334 DIA 44 Bead-rim bowl with two incised grooves on upper body. Severn Valley ware (cf Webster 1976, no 61). Mid-1st to late 2nd century. (J II 22A). WMFC 66.
O.335 DIA 75 Bead-rim bowl with two incised grooves on upper body. Ext. lightly burnished. Severn Valley ware (cf Webster 1976, no 61). Mid-1st to late 2nd century. (A V 30). WMFC 66.
O.336 DIA 34 Bead-rim bowl with pair of incised grooves on body ext. and ring-groove on base ext. Severn Valley ware (cf Webster 1976, no 61). Mid-1st to late 2nd century. (B I 3, phase II, Antonine to 3rd century). WMFC 66.
O.337 DIA 61 Bead-rim bowl with pair of incised grooves on ext. and ring-groove on base ext. Ext. burnished. Severn Valley ware (cf Webster 1976, no 61). Mid-1st to late 2nd century. (B I 3, phase II, Antonine to 3rd century). WMFC 66.
O.338 DIA 14 Bowl with bead-rim and pair of incised grooves on body ext. Ext. burnished. Cf Gloucester (Rawes 1972, no 27). Flavian. (D I 2, phase VIII, late 4th century — residaul). WMFC 66.
O.339 DIA 19 Bowl with burnished rim. Burnished acute lattice on ext. 2nd century. (D I 46, phase V, early to mid-4th century? — residual). WMFC 82.

Large bowls with thickened rims

O.340 DA 2 Large bowl with bead-rim. (A I 4E). WMFC 66.
O.341 DE 429 Bowl in fine fabric with thick body wall and thickened rim. Ext. lightly burnished and has incised decoration. (Cf Webster 1976, no 52). 2nd–3rd century. (C VI 31, phase III, 3rd century). WMFC 66.
O.342 DEA 367 Large bowl with vestigial beaded rim. Ext. decorated by combed wavy design. (C VI 32). WMFC 69.
O.343 DEA 365 Bowl with bead-rim and incised groove beneath. (B I 6). WMFC 69.
O.344 DIA 40 Large bowl with thickened rim and wide shallow groove beneath. Ext. well burnished. (B I 3, phase II, Antonine to 3rd century). WMFC 69.

Flanged bowls with internal lips

Common decorative techniques employed include burnishing, incised grooves, and wavy lines. Handles in the form of a clay cord beneath the rim are not uncommon. All of these vessels have close parallels in the Severn Valley ware.

O.345 DA 115 Bowl with two incised grooves on top of rim and burnished rim and ext. Severn Valley ware (cf Webster 1976, no 57). 3rd century. (D I 6, phase VI, mid- to late 4th century? — residual). WMFC 67.
O.346 DA 31 Large flanged bowl with very thick rim and burnished ext. (Cf Webster 1976, no 53). Late 3rd to 4th century. (C III 1). WMFC 67.
O.347 DE 186 Flanged bowl with grooved rim and thick clay cord beneath rim to form a handle. Severn Valley ware (cf Webster 1976, no 57). 3rd century. (D I 48, phase VI, mid- to late 4th century? — residual). WMFC 67.
O.348 DE 19 Large flanged bowl with pair of incised grooves on ext. and a burnished wavy line over the first pair. Severn Valley ware (cf Webster 1976, no 50/51). Late 2nd to 3rd century. (A IX 1A). WMFC 67.
O.349 DE 90 Large flanged bowl with pair of incised grooves on ext. Severn Valley ware (cf Webster 1976, no 50/51). 2nd–3rd century. (L III 10, phase IV, late Roman/modern — residual). WMFC 67.
O.350 DE 267 Flanged-rim bowl with internal lip. Pair of incised grooves beneath rim with burnished band beneath. Severn Valley ware (cf Webster 1976, no 48). 2nd–3rd century. (B I 14). WMFC 67.
O.351 DE 105 Flanged-rim bowl with groove beneath rim and burnished towards base. Severn Valley ware (cf Webster 1976, no 50). Late 2nd to late 3rd century. (A XVI 1). WMFC 67.
O.352 DE 39? Triangular flanged-rim bowl with pair of incised grooves on body ext. Severn Valley ware (cf Webster 1976, no 50). Late 2nd to 3rd century. (B I 6). WMFC 67.
O.353 DE 141 Flanged-rim bowl with cordon beneath rim. Three incised grooves on ext. Rim burnished and burnished bands occur on body ext. (Cf Webster 1976, no 47). 2nd–3rd century. (A XVI 1). WMFC 67.
O.354 DIA 86 Bowl with flanged rim and lightly burnished ext. (H II 2). WMFC 67.
O.355 DIA 23 Flanged-rim bowl. (Cf Webster 1976, no 49). 3rd–4th century. (A X 5). WMFC 67.
O.356 DK 13 Flanged-rim bowl. (Cf Webster 1976, no 51). 3rd century. (A XII 2). WMFC 67.

Flanged bowls with grooved or reeded rims

O.357 DE 213 Flanged bowl with grooved rim. Burnished near base. Severn Valley ware (cf Webster 1976, no 57). 3rd century. (L III 10, phase IV, late Roman/modern). WMFC 67.
O.358 DE 165 Bowl with reeded rim. Burnished. Severn Valley ware. (Cf Webster 1976, no 53). Late 3rd to 4th century. (G I 1). WMFC 67.
O.359 DE 101 Bowl with reeded rim. Severn Valley ware (cf Webster 1976, no 56). 3rd century. (B IA 1). WMFC 67.
O.360 DE 214 Bowl with flanged rim and pair of incised grooves on rim. (G V 1). WMFC 67.
O.361 DE 188 Bowl with grooved flanged rim. (E I 16A). WMFC 67.
O.362 DE 207 Bowl with a frilled flange rim. (G IV 23, phase VI, late 4th century). WMFC 67.
O.363 DI 74 Flanged-rim bowl with two incised lines on top of rim. On rim edge is a knife mark. Severn Valley ware (cf Webster 1976, no 56). 3rd century. (B I 14). WMFC 67.

Bowls with beaded or everted rims

O.364 DA 116 Small wide-mouthed bowl with bead-rim and prominent shoulder. (Cf Rawes 1982, no 90). (E V 37, phase V, late 2nd century?). WMFC 65.
O.365 DE 76 Small wide-mouthed bowl with everted rim. Severn Valley ware (cf Webster 1976, no 34). 2nd–4th century. (C II 1). WMFC 65.
O.366 DE 132 Wide-mouthed bowl with everted rim. Severn Valley ware (cf Webster 1976, no 36). 2nd–3rd century. (C VI 24, phase VII, early to mid-4th century — residual). WMFC 65.
O.367 DE 182 Everted bead-rim bowl with prominent shoulder. Burnished above base. Severn Valley ware (cf Webster 1976, no 34). 2nd–4th century. (D I T/S). WMFC 65.
O.368 DE 291 Fine bead-rim bowl. (J II 22A). WMFC 65.
O.369 DE 80 Small bowl with everted rim. Severn Valley ware (cf Webster 1976, no 35). 2nd–4th century. (Context uncertain). WMFC 65.
O.370 DE 257 Fine wide-mouthed bowl. Severn Valley ware (cf Webster 1976, no 35). Probably 2nd–4th century. (D II 29). WMFC 65.
O.371 DE 312 Wide-mouthed bowl with everted rim. Severn Valley ware (cf Webster 1976, no 35). Probably 2nd–4th century. (A XVI 1). WMFC 65.
O.372 DE 332 Fine bowl with beaded rim and three incised grooves beneath. (D II 29). WMFC 65.
O.373 DE 310 Small fine bowl with beaded rim and burnished ext. (A XVI 1). WMFC 65.
O.374 DE 297 Bowl with incised groove beneath rim. Severn Valley ware (cf Webster 1976, no 34). 2nd–4th century. (B I 6). WMFC 65.
O.375 DE 298 Bowl with incised groove on int. and ext. beneath rim. Also an applied cordon on int. Ext. burnished. (D I 246, phase II, later 2nd to early 3rd century?). WMFC 65.
O.376 DEA 324 Small bowl with everted rim and burnished ext. (D II 29). WMFC 65.
O.377 DEA 427 Bowl with everted rim and prominent shoulder. Int. and ext. burnished. (G IV 12, phase V, later 4th century). WMFC 52.
O.378 DEA 342 Fine bowl with everted rim and burnished ext. (J II 22A). WMFC 82.
O.379 DI 70 Bowl with everted rim. Severn Valley ware (cf Webster 1976, no 36). 2nd–3rd century. (C III 4). WMFC 65.

Other flanged bowls

O.380 DE 348 Bowl with flange beneath a vestigial beaded rim. Int. and ext. burnished. Severn Valley ware (cf Webster 1976, no 65). Mid-2nd to early 3rd century. (B I 3, phase II, Antonine to 3rd century). WMFC 67.
O.381 DE 345 Bowl with everted flattened rim; on top of rim an incised line. (B I 3, phase II, Antonine to 3rd century). WMFC 67.
O.382 DEA 299 Flanged bowl with incised groove on rim. (J II 22A). WMFC 67.
O.383 DEA 281 Segmental flanged bowl. (A I 4A?). WMFC 67.
O.384 DEA 116 Flanged bowl with incised groove on rim. (A XVIII 2). WMFC 67.
O.385 DI 56 Flanged bowl with incised groove on rim. Ext. burnished. Form reminiscent of the so-called raetian *mortarium*. Severn Valley ware (cf Webster 1976, no 66). 2nd century. (B I 3, phase II, Antonine to 3rd century). WMFC 67.
O.386 DIA 66 Flanged bowl with moulded foot. Form reminiscent of the raetian *mortarium*. Severn Valley ware (cf Webster 1976, no 66). 2nd century. (C VI 102, phase I, late 1st to 2nd century). WMFC 67.
O.387 DIA 17 Flanged bowl with a bead-rim. (D II 2, phase IX, late 4th century). WMFC 67.

Bowls with everted rims/flanges

O.388 DA 106 Bowl with everted rim and incised groove on rim and ext. Burnished lines on rim int. and ext. (Cf Rawes 1982, no 127). (D I 110). WMFC 67.
O.389 DA 20 Bowl with flanged rim. Int. burnished and burnished horizontal lines cover base and lower body. (Cf Rawes 1982, no 126). (D I 87, phase V, early to mid-4th century? — residual). WMFC 67.

Shallow carinated bowls

O.390 CH 14 Shallow carinated bowl with thickened everted rim. On rim int. are two incised grooves. Groove on shoulder. (D I 87, phase V, early to mid-4th century? — residual). WMFC 52.
O.391 CH 60 Bowl with incised groove on rim and double cordon on shoulder. Ext. well burnished. (B IA 5, phase II, Antonine to 3rd century). WMFC 55.
O.392 DEA 415 Corrugated bowl with incised horizontal groove and burnished ext. (H II 2). WMFC 51.
O.393 DIA 26 Carinated bowl with burnished ext. (C I 25). WMFC 57.
O.394 DW 17 Fine, necked, shallow bowl with carination and burnished ext. (H II 39). WMFC 55.
O.395 DZ 25 Wide-necked bowl with cordon on ext. (AA II 42). WMFC 54.

Bowls with a cornice rim or pie-crust flange beneath rim

O.396 DE 108 Bowl with cornice rim and burnished base, int., and rim. On base ext. are moulded concentric circles. (A XVI 2). WMFC 90.
O.397 DE 226 Bowl with upright rim and pie-crust flange. Int. and ext. covered by white slip. (L I 7). WMFC 90.
O.398 DE 34 Coarse bowl with upright rim and pie-crust flange. (A IX 8, phase VI, late 3rd to early 4th century). WMFC 90.
O.399 DW 56 Bowl with upright rim and finger indentations, a finger-indented flange. White paint decoration occurs beneath flange with descending vertical lines at regular intervals. (L XIII 8, phase II, late 2nd century on). WMFC 90.

Everted rim bowls

O.400 DEA 385 Bowl with short everted rim. Burnished horizontal lines on ext. (AA II 97). WMFC 58.
O.401 DIA 38 Bowl with thick everted rim. Rim burnished and ext. has horizontal burnished lines. (B I 2, phase II, Antonine to 3rd century). WMFC 67.
O.402 DK 35 Jar with everted rim and beaded lip. (AA II 8). WMFC 32.
O.403 DW 34 Fine bowl with everted rim and burnished ext. (A XII 2). WMFC 58.

Miscellaneous bowls

O.404 CH 56 Straight-sided bowl with inward-turning flattened rim and highly burnished ext. (Unstratified). WMFC 65.
O.405 DE 230 Bowl with everted rim and straight sides, with ridge on ext. (possibly carination). Impressed decoration occurs at regular intervals on body ext. in form of semi-circles. (Cf Young 1977, C 84, 350–400). (K I 23). WMFC 66.
O.406 DEA 149 Small bowl with four incised lines on rim. (C IA 2, phase V, later 3rd century on). WMFC 50.
O.407 DEA 125 Bowl, probably carinated, with thickened rim beneath which are two incised grooves. Body ext. has impressed pattern. (C IXA 13). WMFC 66.
O.408 DV 1 Base sherd of bowl with frilled base. Int. and ext. covered by a light pink slip. (C VIA 73, phase VI/VIII, later 3rd century on).
O.409 DZ 20 Bowl with a stepped ext. (L I 16, phase II, late 2nd century on). WMFC 66.

Very fine bowls imitating samian or metalwork forms

All of these vessels are in fabric DW and are frequently decorated with white paint. These vessels have close parallels in Oxfordshire (Young 1977) but are more likely to have been produced closer to Alcester, with a source in the Severn Valley a strong possibility (the fabric being too harsh to be Oxfordshire (Young pers comm)).

O.410 DW 19 Fine carinated bowl with bead-rim and three shallow incised grooves at waist. Base raised. Body ext. has regularly spaced cream/pink paint circles each with a white paint spot at the centre. Ext. burnished. Copy of Dr. 30. (H II 49B, phase II, Antonine to 3rd century). WMFC 51.
O.411 DW 20 Bowl copying Dr. 37. Ext. has two incised grooves and white paint decoration in the form of regularly spaced groups of vertical lines with white paint dots between them. Pedestal base. (Cf Young 1977, O.45). AD 100–200. (H II 49C, phase II, Antonine to 3rd century). WMFC 66.
O.412 DW 15 Bowl copying Dr. 37 with two incised horizontal grooves on ext. Ext. burnished. (Cf Young 1977, no 45). AD 100–200. (H II 33, phase II, Antonine to 3rd century). WMFC 66.
O.413 DW 11 Bead-rim bowl copying Dr. 37, with pair of incised grooves on body ext. Ext. burnished and has concentric circles of dots in white paint with a spot in the centre. (Cf Young 1977, O.45). AD 100–200. (C VI 106, phase I, late 1st to 2nd century). WMFC 66.
O.414 DW 53 Fine bowl with groove beneath rim. (A XVI 6). WMFC 66.
O.415 DW 39 Fine 'pie-dish' bowl with incised groove on rim. Int. and ext. burnished. (Exact angle of rim uncertain.) (B I 3, phase II, Antonine to 3rd century). WMFC 68.
O.416 DW 4 Bowl with two shallow grooves on neck. (C VIA 44). WMFC 66.
O.417 DW 69 Flange of bowl with white paint decoration. (C VI 93, phase II, late 2nd century). WMFC 67.
O.418 DW 70 Segmental bowl with white paint decoration on flange. On girth is shallow double groove. Ext. and int. lightly burnished. (Cf Young 1977, O.39). AD 70–150. (AA II 8A). WMFC 67.
O.419 DW 62 Segmental bowl with white paint decoration on flange. Highly burnished. (Cf Young 1977, O.39). AD 70–150. (H II 6A, phase III, Antonine to 3rd century on). WMFC 67.
O.420 DW 57 Segmental bowl with flange beneath rim. White paint decoration occurs on rim. (Cf Young 1977, O.39). AD 70–150. (C VI 78B, phase II, late 2nd century). WMFC 67.
O.421 DW 72 Segmental bowl with white paint decoration on flange. (A IX 13, phase IV, later 3rd century on — residual). WMFC 67.
O.422 DW 40 Bowl copying Dr. 38. Immediately beneath rim is groove, white paint decoration on flange. Int. and ext. burnished. (Cf Young 1977, O.47). AD 240–400. (B I 3, phase II, Antonine to 3rd century). WMFC 67.
O.423 DW 71 Flanged bowl possibly imitating Dr. 38. Rim beaded, with incised groove beneath. Int. burnished. (E IV 16). WMFC 67.
O.424 DW 65 Bowl reminiscent of Dr. 38. (A XVIII T/S). WMFC 67.
O.425 DW 45 Base sherd of bowl with ring-groove on base ext. (D II 29A).

Dishes

O.426 DA 103 Dish with groove beneath rim and incised ring-groove on base. Int. and ext. burnished. (A IX 8, phase VI, late 3rd to early 4th century). WMFC 82.
O.427 DA 15 Dish with groove beneath rim. Base flat. Int. and ext. of vessel burnished. Severn Valley ware (cf Webster 1976, no 74). Uncertain date. (C VI 81, phase II, late 2nd century). WMFC 82.
O.428 DE 139 Fine dish with pair of incised lines on rim int. (A XVII 2). WMFC 81.

O.429 DEA 162 Carinated dish with incised groove beneath carination. Cf Gloucester (Rawes 1972, no 3). Flavian. (C VI 78, phase II, late 2nd century). WMFC 82.
O.430 DEA 399 Carinated dish with flattened base. (Cf Webster 1976, no 70, 1st to early 2nd century). (AA II 102, phase III, 3rd century — residual). WMFC 81.
O.431 DEA 414 Carinated dish with incised line beneath rim. Ext. burnished. Form derived from Camulodunum 16. Severn Valley ware (cf Webster 1976, no 70). 1st–2nd century. (H I 1). WMFC 82.
O.432 DI 87 Dish with flat base and ring-groove on base ext. Int. and ext. well burnished. (G I 59, phase IV, early to mid-4th century). WMFC 82.
O.433 DIA 80 Dish derived from Belgic or Gallo-Belgic antecedents such as Camulodunum type 24. Burnished int. and ext. Severn Valley ware (cf Webster 1976, variant no 69). 1st to early 2nd century. (D I 176). WMFC 81.
O.434 DW 66 Very fine dish with incised groove beneath carination. Shallow grooves or moulding on body ext. (B I 6). WMFC 81.
O.435 DW 32 Very small fine platter/dish with incised ring-groove on base. Int. and ext. burnished. (G V 2). WMFC 82,

Miscellaneous vessels

O.436 DE 189 Base sherd of triple vase. On upper side of sherd is a hole where rest of vessel was attached. Ext. covered by cream slip. (D I 112, phase IV, late 3rd century?). WMFC 94.
O.437 DX 1 Triple vase. Ext. covered by cream slip, and orange-painted circles on widest part of vessel. (D I 2, phase VIII, late 4th century). WMFC 94.
O.438 FB 2 Miscellaneous vessel, possibly the neck of jar or flagon with well-burnished ext. (B IA 17). WMFC 20.
O.439 DW 37 *Tettina* with well-burnished ext. (G V 100, phase VI, late 4th century). WMFC 99.
O.440 DEA 210 *Tazza* with flange and pie-crust rim covered by cream slip. (G IA 99, phase IA, late 2nd to 3rd century?). WMFC 90.
O.441 DEA 221 *Tazza* with flange and pie-crust rim. (L I 4, phase III, late Roman/post-medieval). WMFC 90.
O.442 DEA 223 *Tazza* with pie-crust rim. The carination is also decorated with pie-crust. Incised groove on rim int. (L I 4, phase III, late Roman/post-medieval). WMFC 90.
O.443 DEA 235 Skillet with cream slip on int. and ext. (Cf Marsh 1978, type 32). 1st–2nd century. (L XII 1). WMFC 99.

Lids

O.444 CH 59 Fine lid with well-burnished int. and ext. (D II 29A). WMFC 86.
O.445 DA 85 Lid with lightly burnished ext. (B I 3, phase II, Antonine to 3rd century). WMFC 86.
O.446 DA 73 Lid? with traces of cream slip. (D II 29A).
O.447 DE 274 Fine lid with rouletted decoration and white slip on ext. (D I 173, phase II, later 2nd to early 3rd century). WMFC 86.
O.448 DIA 39 Lid, burnished with horizontal lines on ext. (B I 3, phase II, Antonine to 3rd century). WMFC 86.
O.449 DW 61 Very fine lid with a very well-burnished ext. (B IA 8).
O.450 EC 1 Lid or dish with orange paint spots on rim. Burnished rim and int. (A IX 21). WMFC 81.

Base sherds

O.451 DE 121 Very fine stepped base. (B IA 14, phase IV, mid- to late 4th century).
O.452 DEA 405 Kick base of dish or bowl. (AA II 106, phase III, 3rd century).

Handles

O.453 DE 266 Four-ribbed handle with a white slip on ext. Probably from a flagon. (D I 173, phase II, later 2nd to early 3rd century).
O.454 DEA 323 Very fine triple-ribbed handle of flagon or jug. (D II 29).

Body sherds

O.455 DA 107 Body sherd of colander with groove on ext. defining area of perforation. (C VIA 140).
O.456 DE 263 Body sherd with large applied loop decoration. (C VIA 5A, phase IX, mid-4th century on).
O.457 DG 3 Body sherd with vertical combed decoration between wide incised horizontal grooves. (A XVI 9).
O.458 DI 73 Body sherd with scallop decoration on ext. and an area of rouletted decoration beneath. (A X 6).
O.459 DIA 2 Body sherd with two holes and a further four marked; a groove surrounds these. Possible colander. (A VI 5).
O.460 DJ 2 Body sherd with rouletted decoration on ext. (A I 2).
O.461 DW 54 Very fine body sherd with an impressed bird's-foot pattern. (G I 148, phase IV, early to mid-4th century).

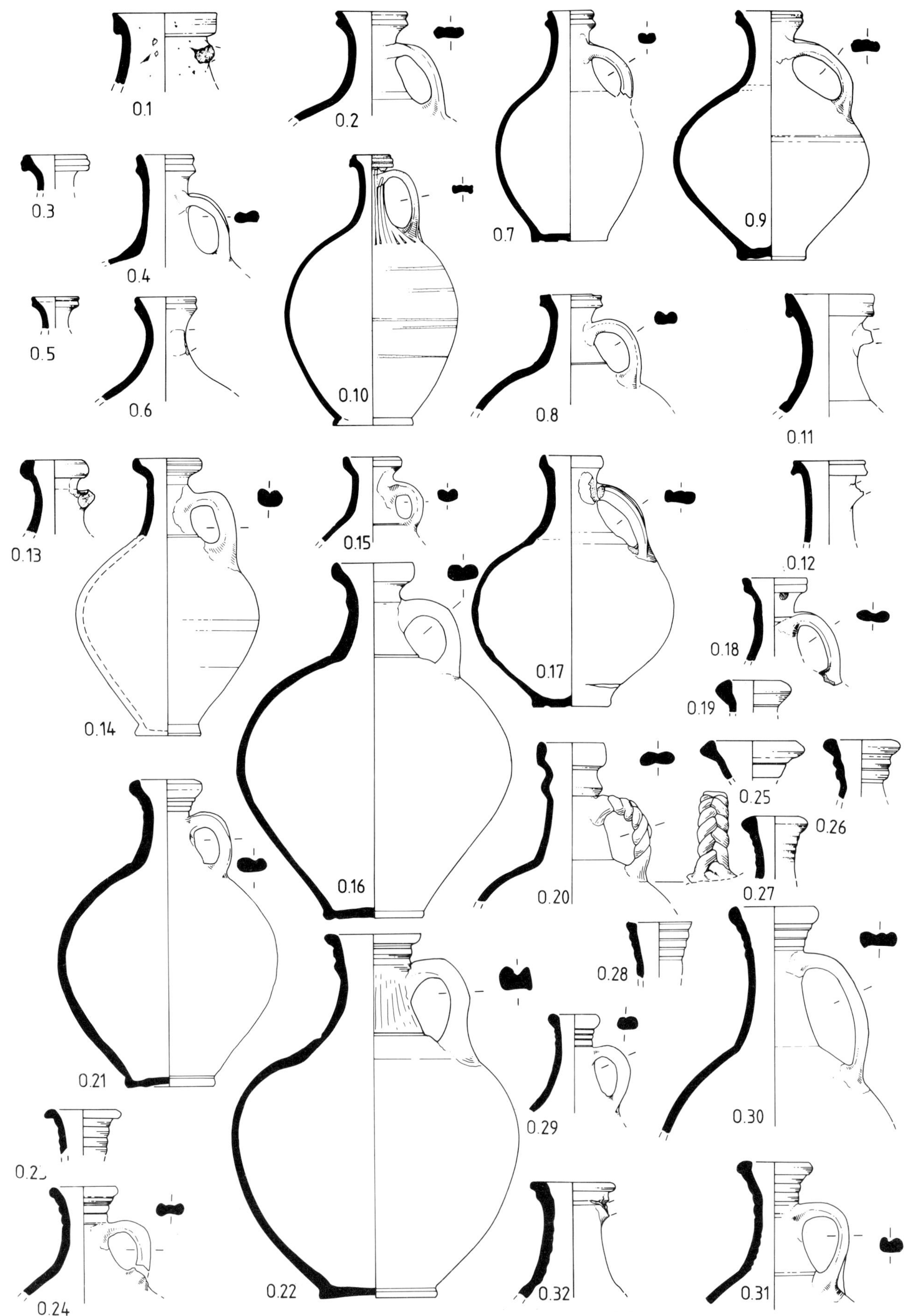

Figure 21 Roman coarse pottery, types O.1–O.32 (1/4 scale)

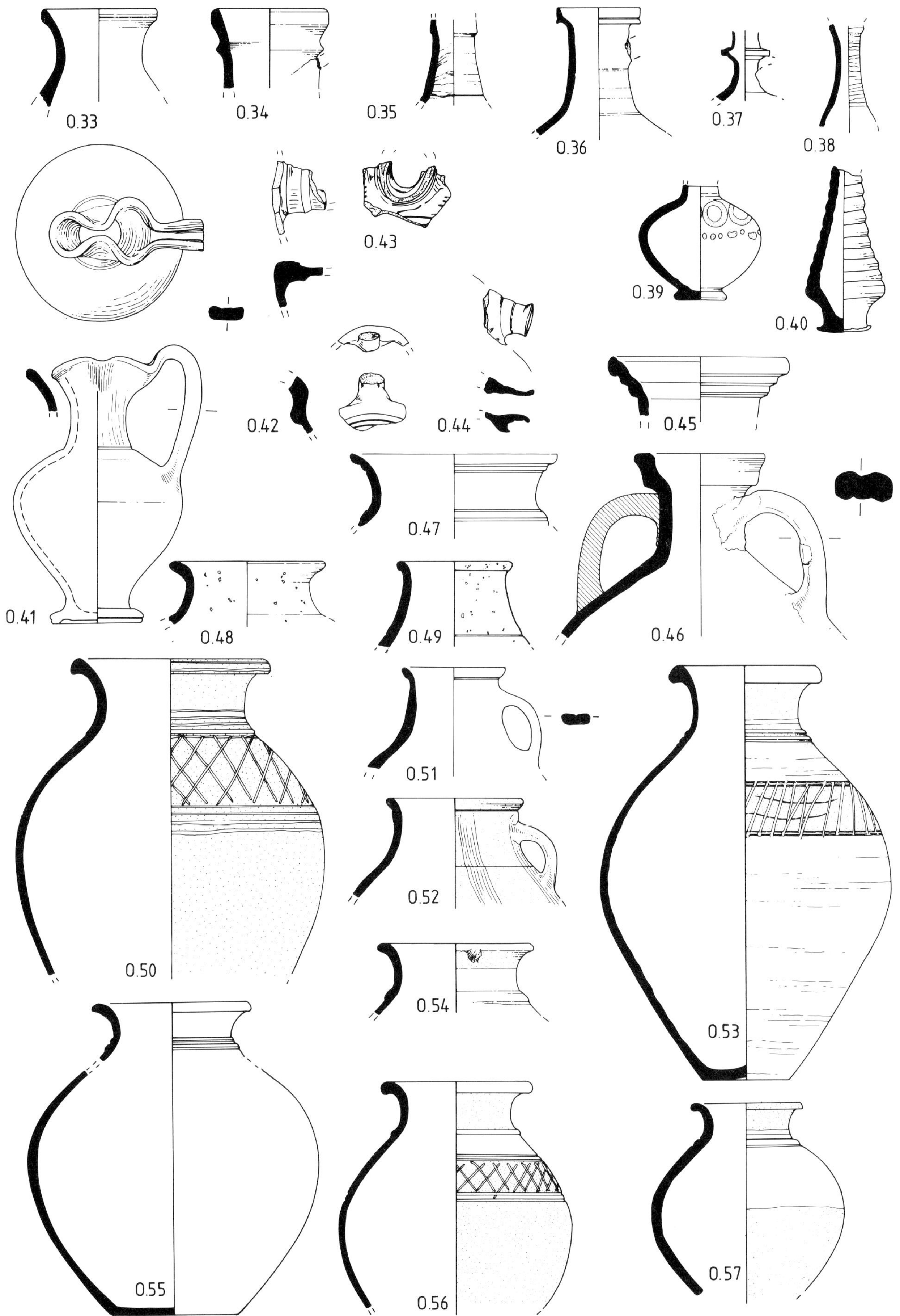

Figure 22 Roman coarse pottery, types O.33–O.57 (1/4 scale)

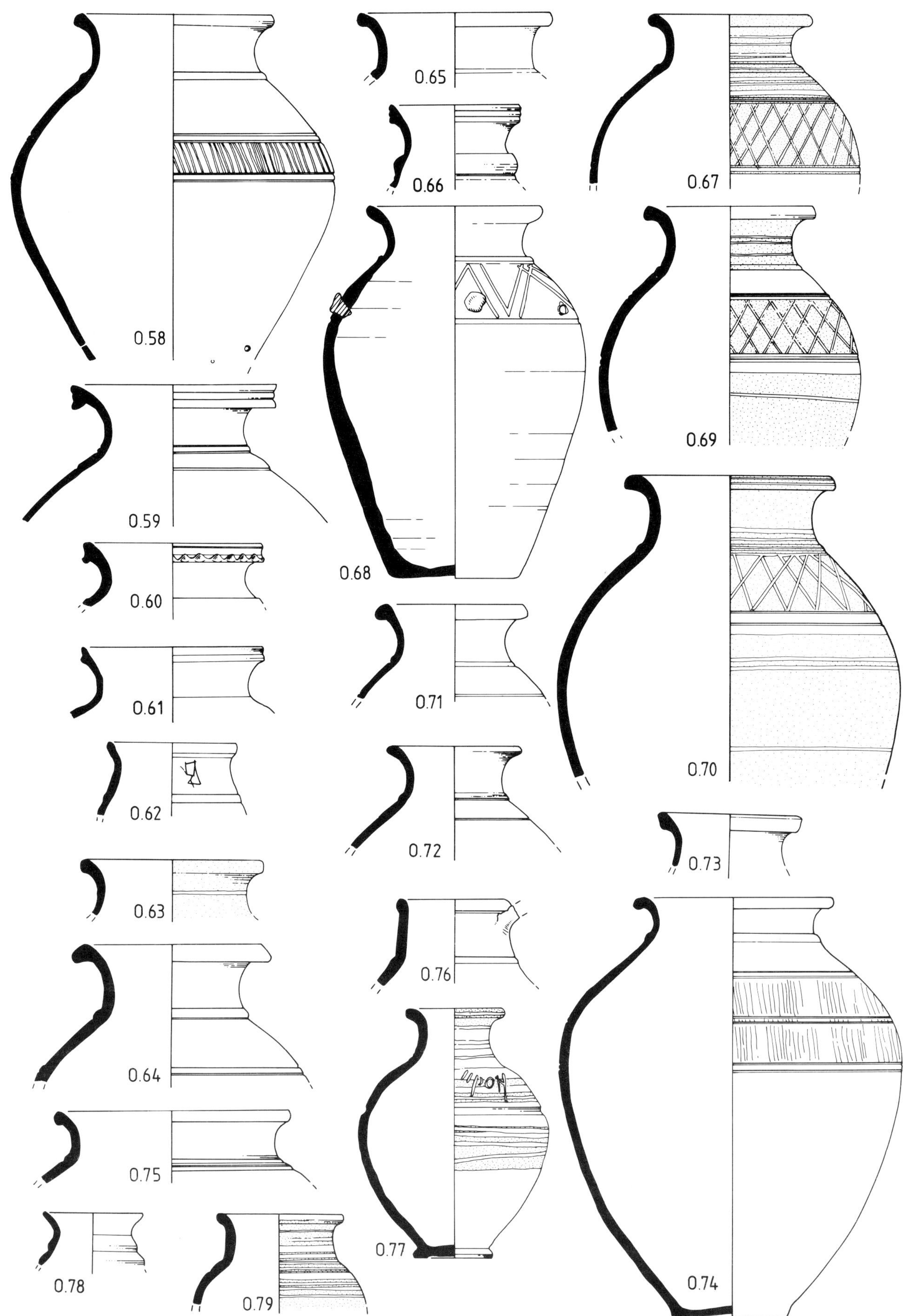

Figure 23 Roman coarse pottery, types O.58–O.79 (1/4 scale)

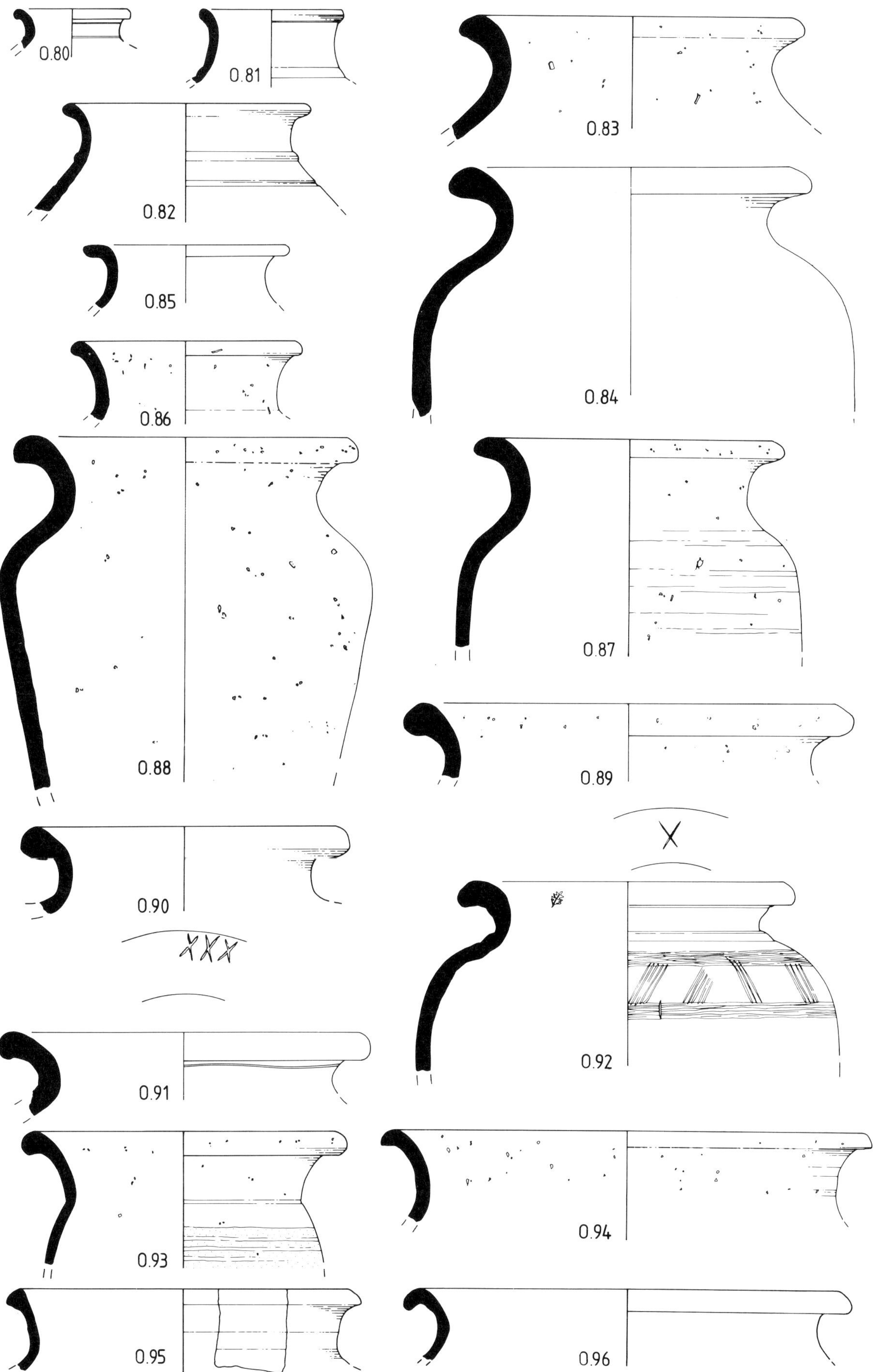

Figure 24 Roman coarse pottery, types O.80–O.96 (1/4 scale)

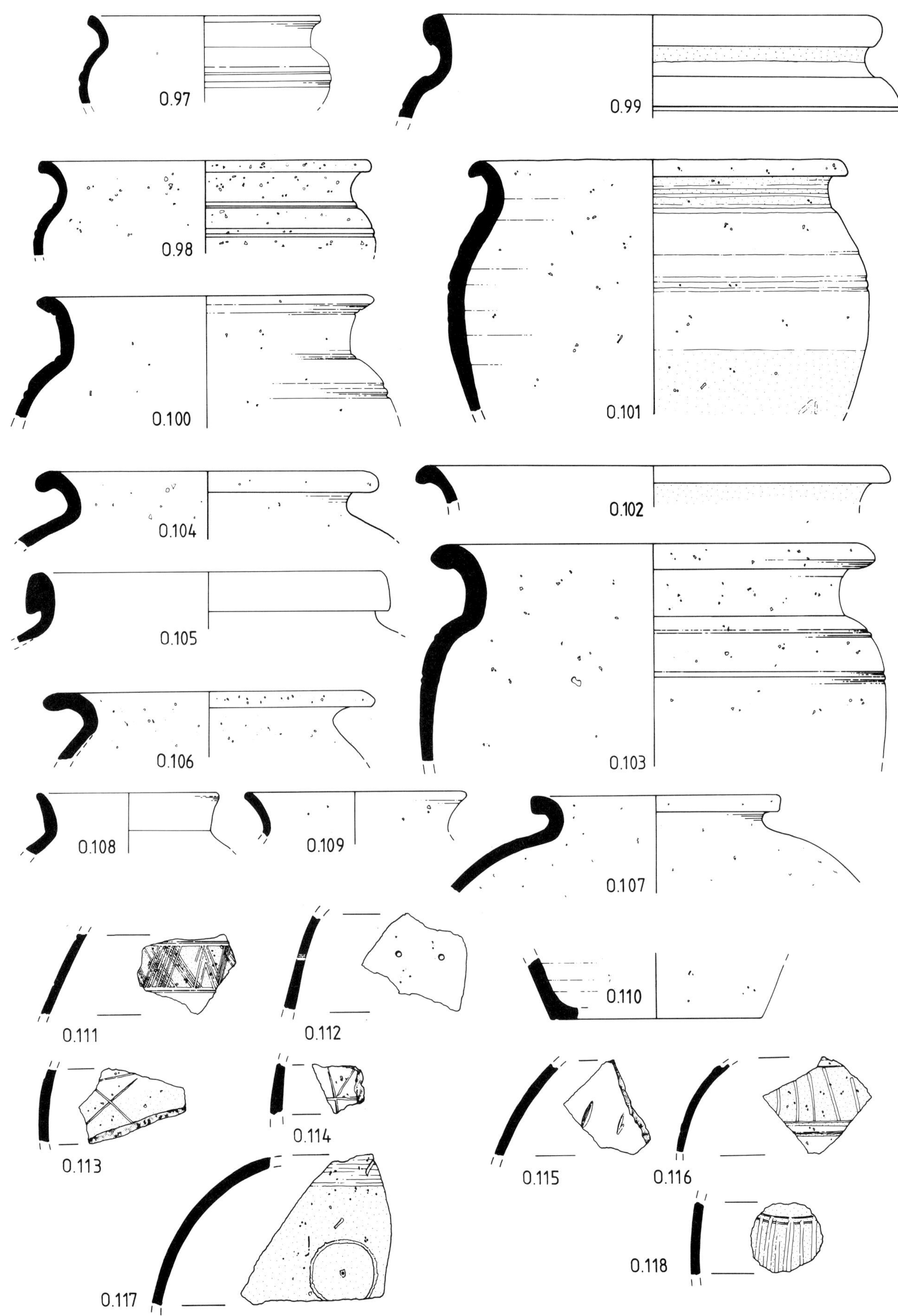

Figure 25 Roman coarse pottery, types O.97–O.118 (1/4 scale)

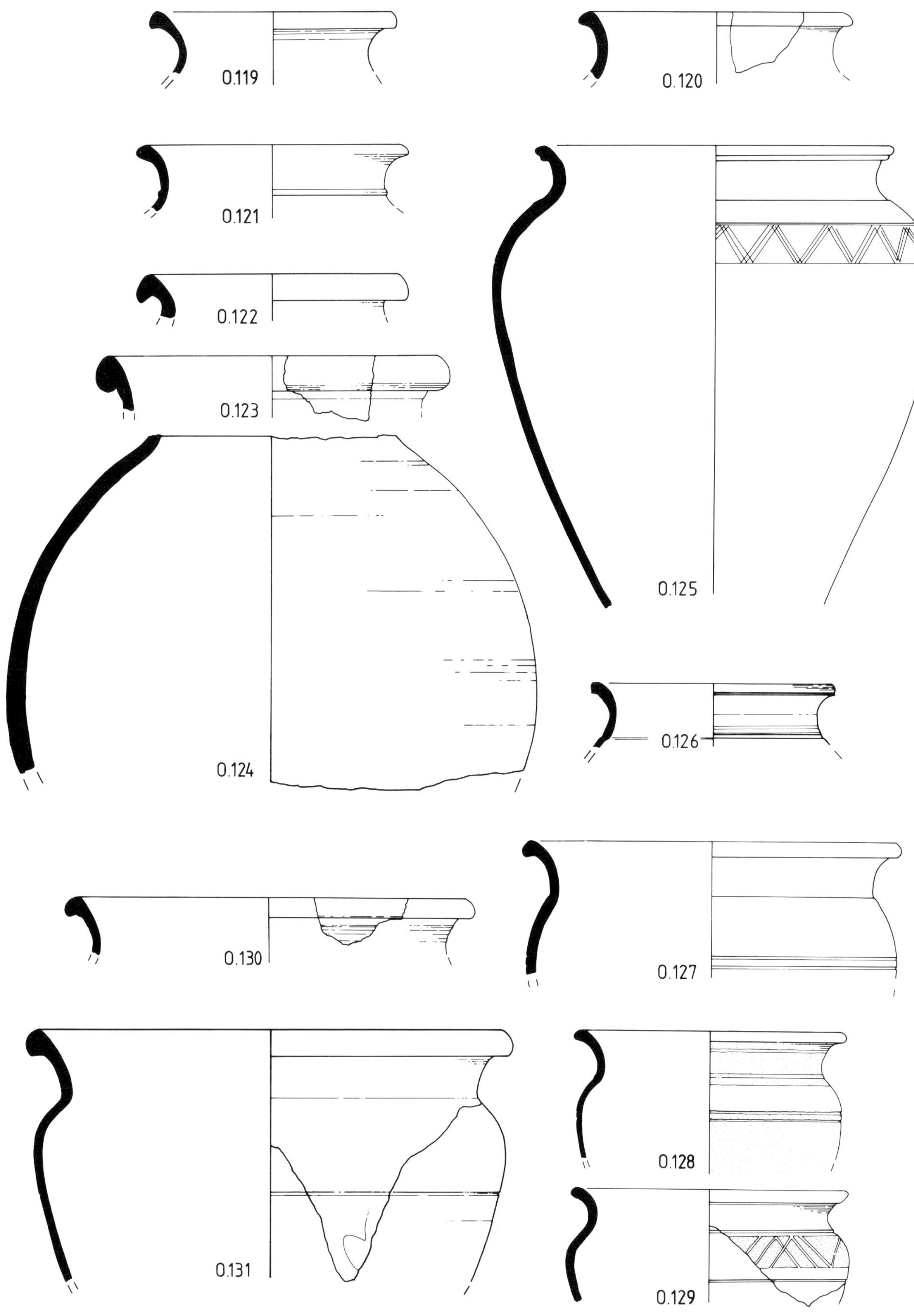

Figure 26 Roman coarse pottery, types O.119–O.131 (1/4 scale)

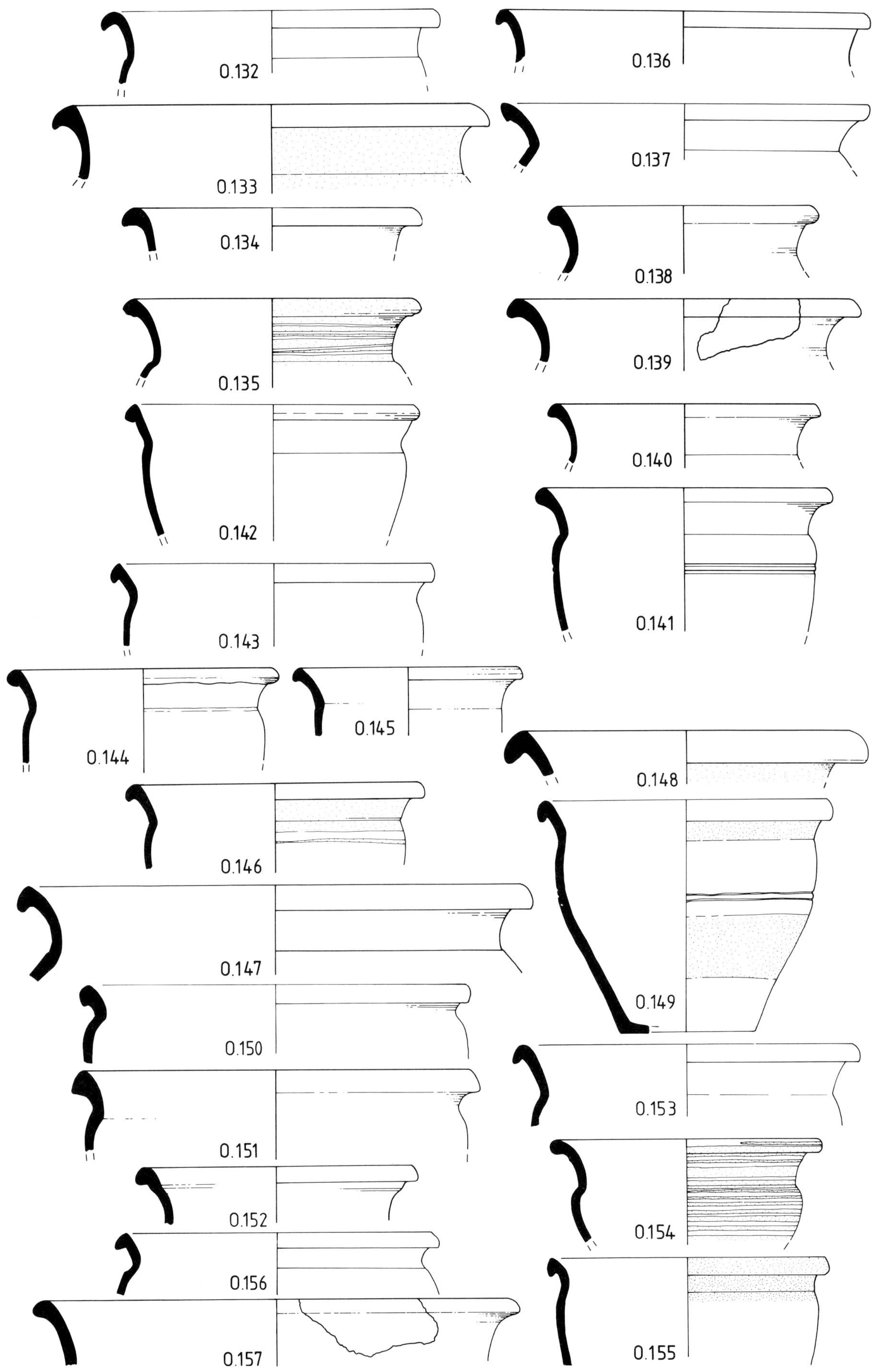

Figure 27 Roman coarse pottery, types O.132–O.157 (1/4 scale)

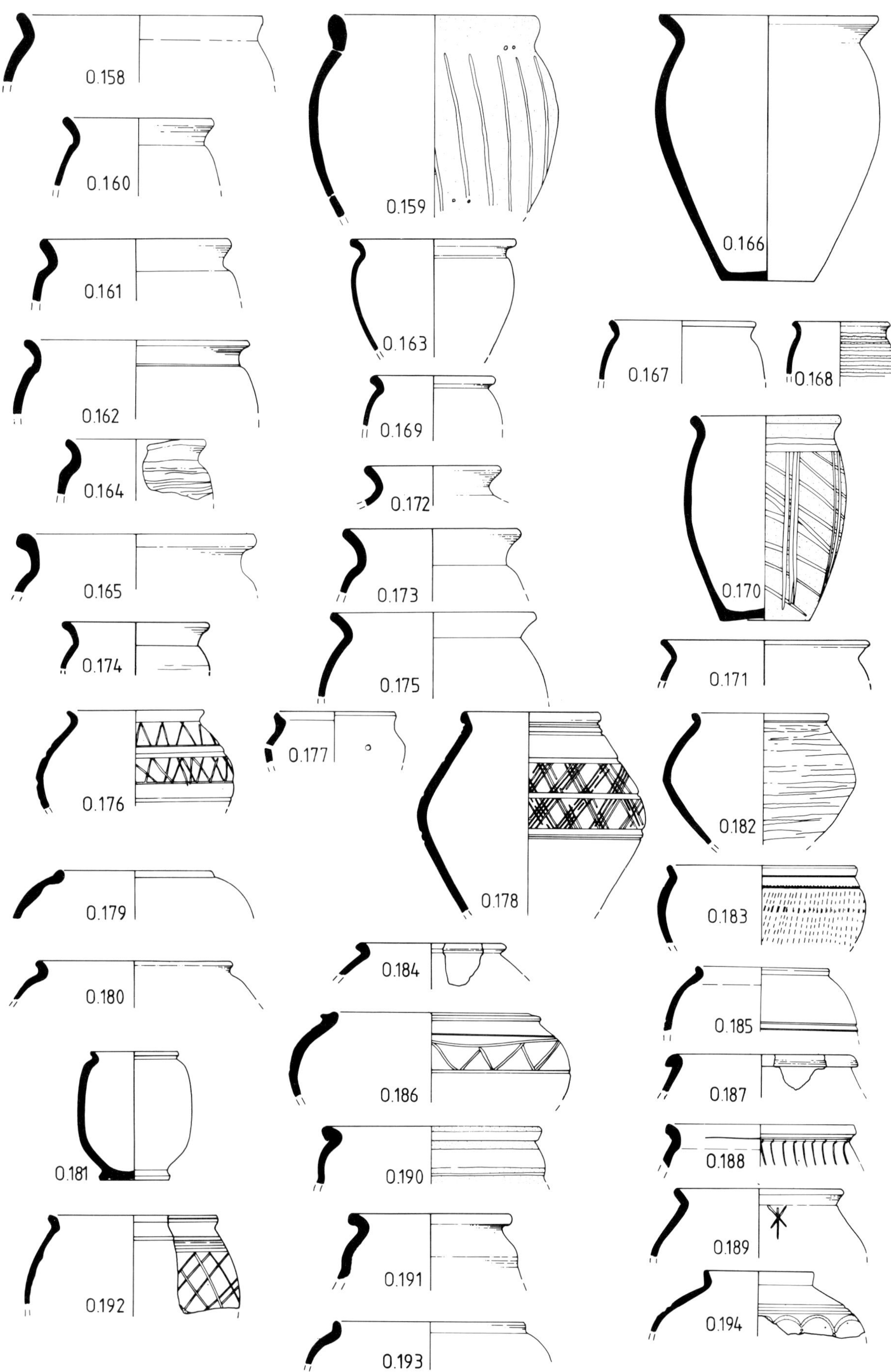

Figure 28 Roman coarse pottery, types O.158–O.194 (¼ scale)

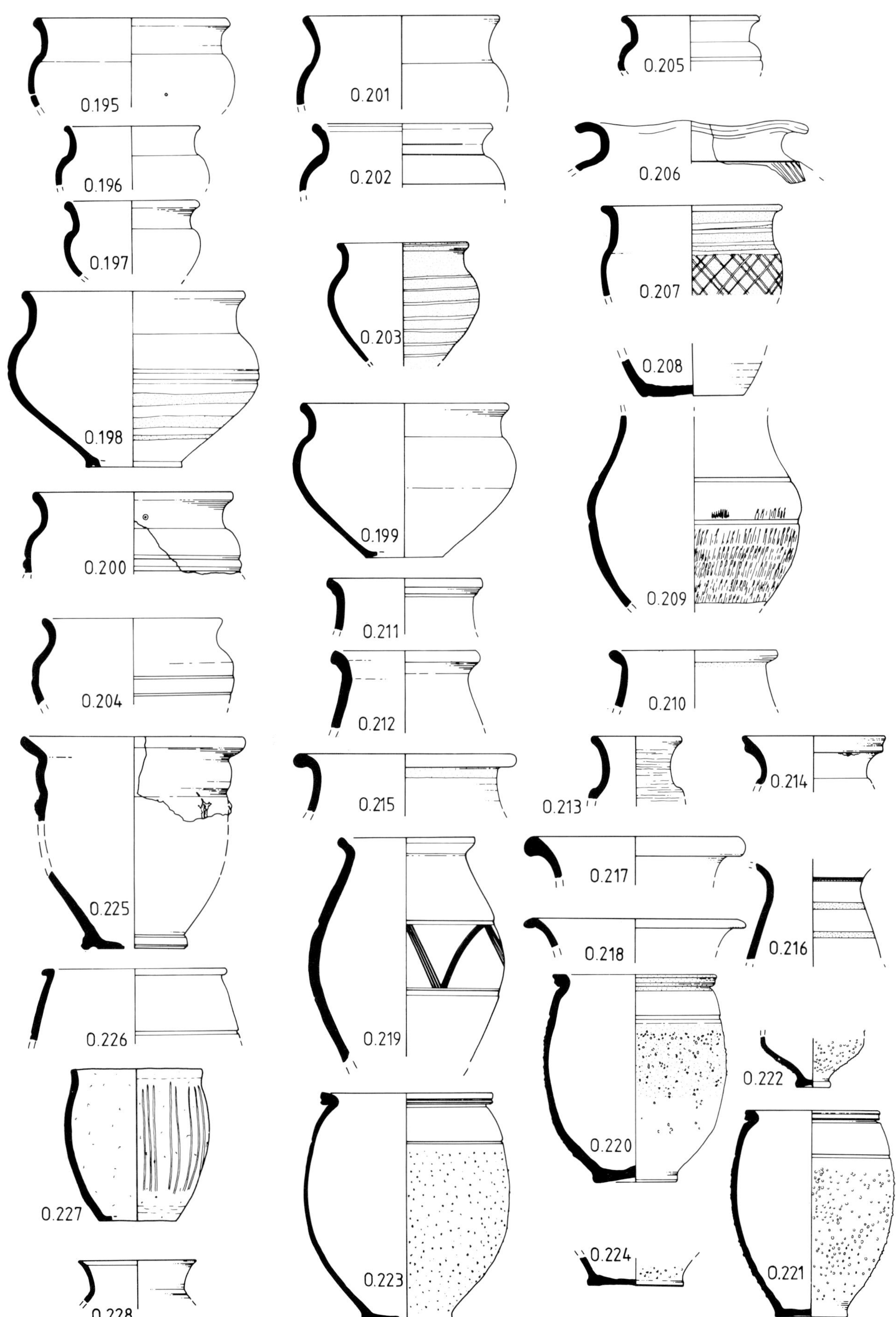

Figure 29 Roman coarse pottery, types O.195–O.228 (1/4 scale)

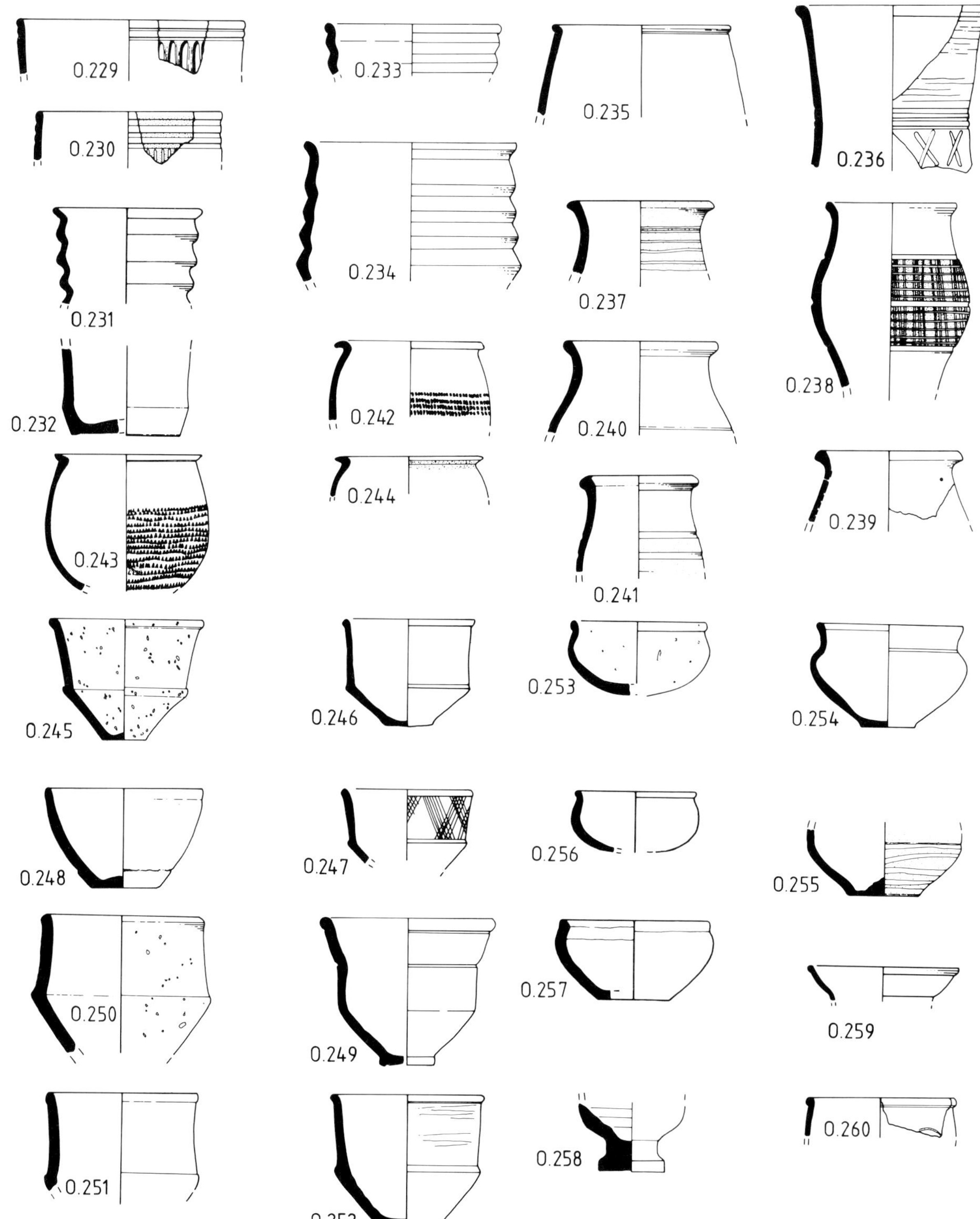

Figure 30 Roman coarse pottery, types O.229–O.260 (1/4 scale)

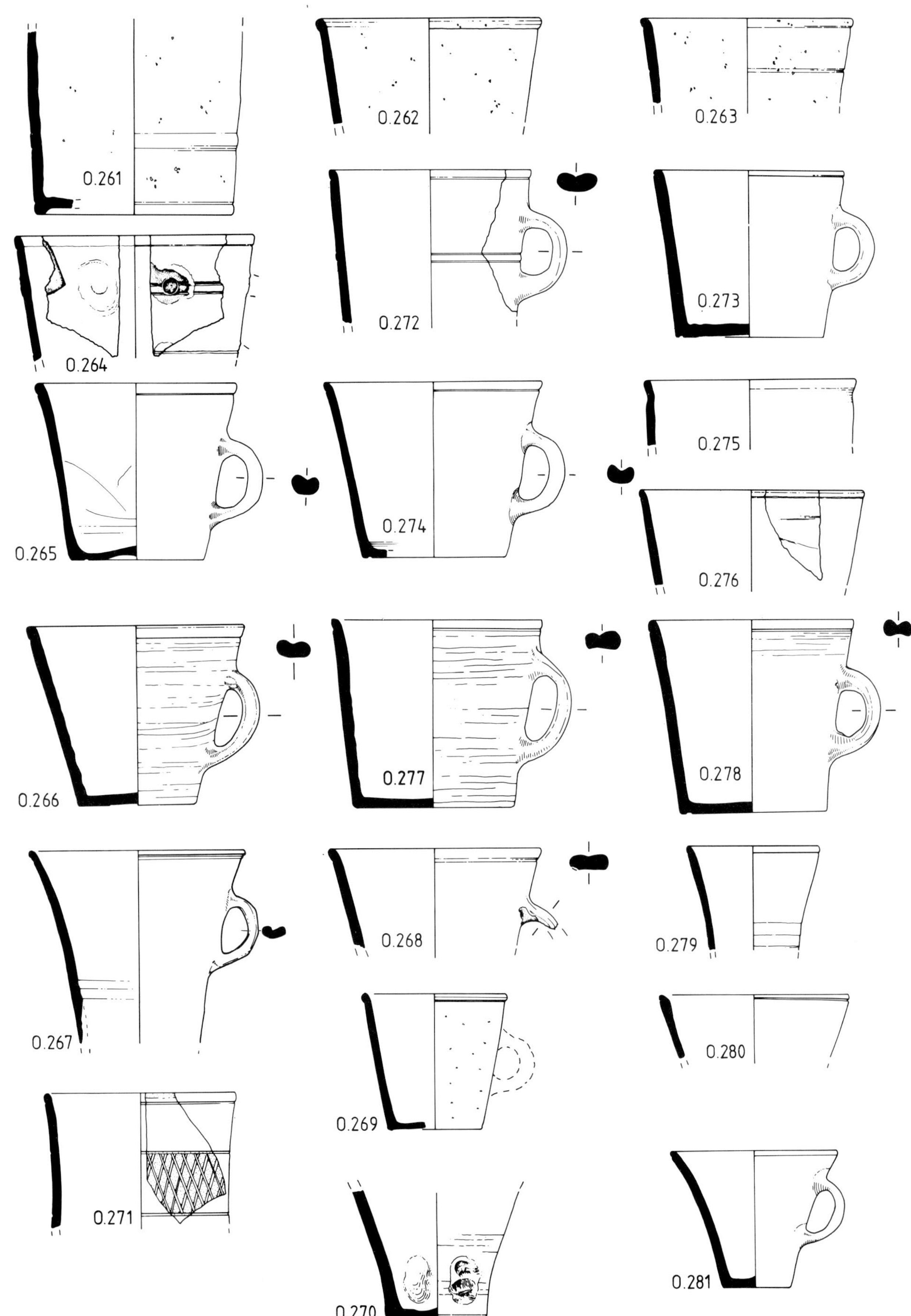

Figure 31 Roman coarse pottery, types O.261–O.281 (1/4 scale)

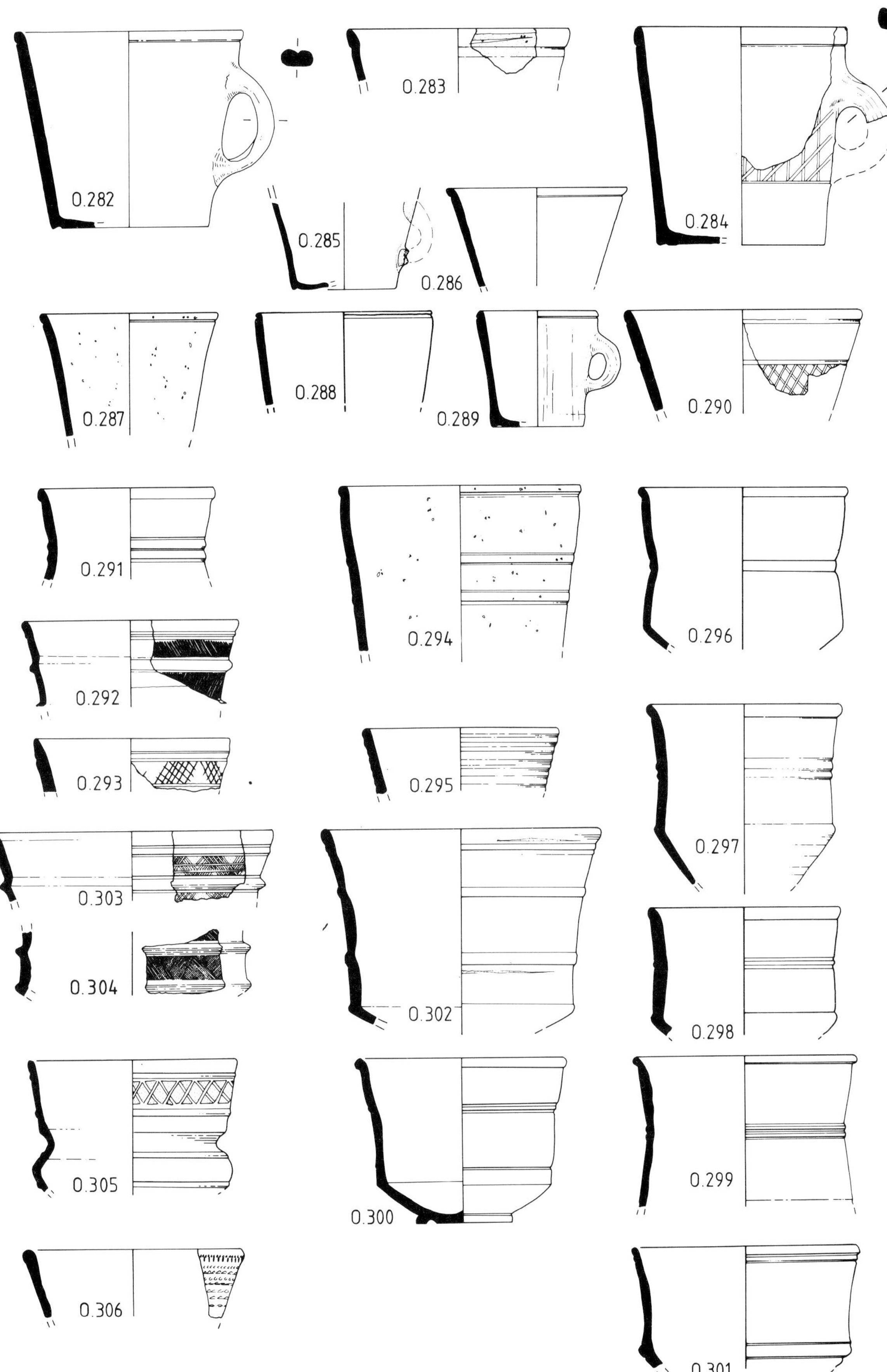

Figure 32 Roman coarse pottery, types O.282–O.306 (1/4 scale)

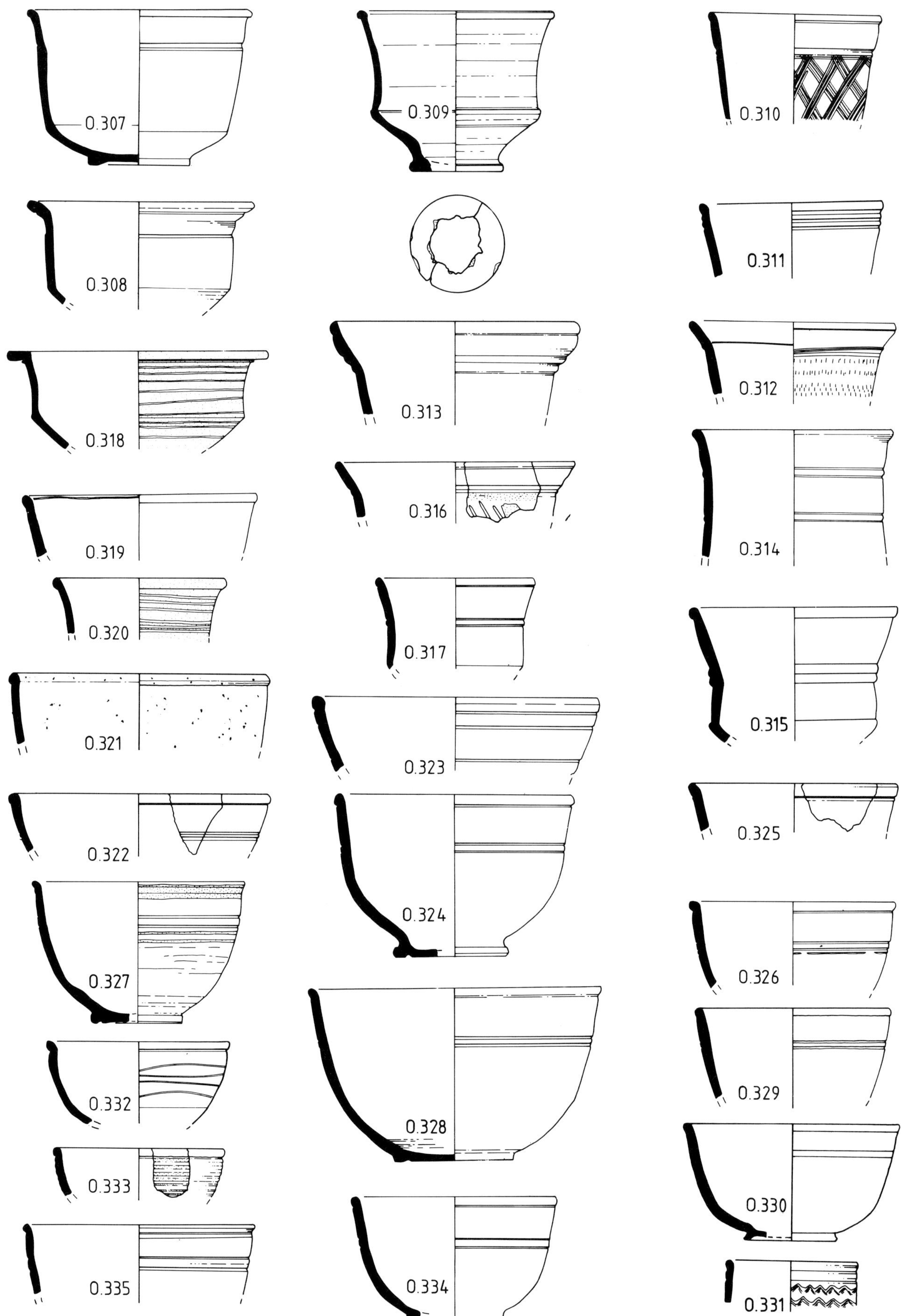

Figure 33 Roman coarse pottery, types O.307–O.335 (¼ scale)

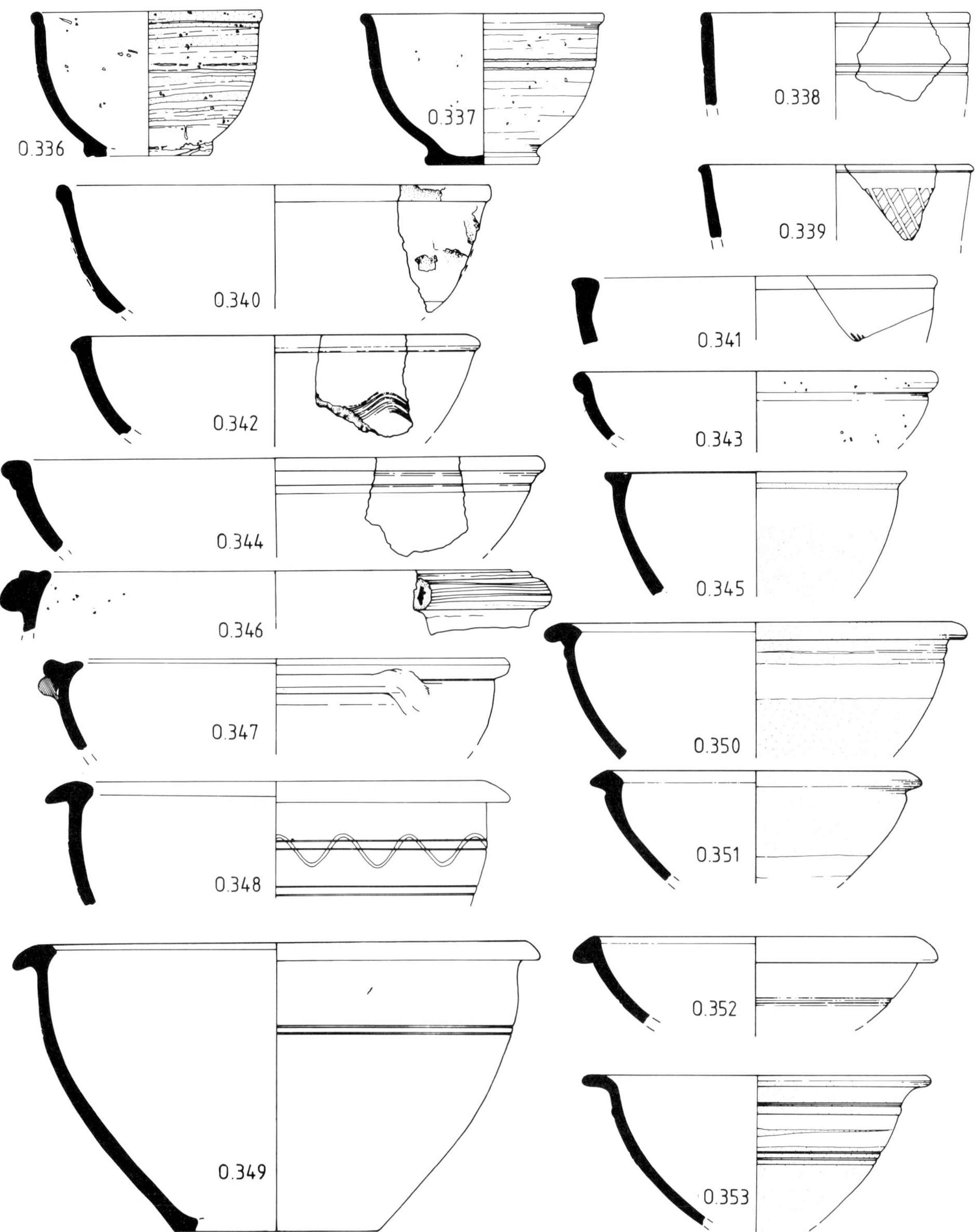

Figure 34 Roman coarse pottery, types O.336–O.353 (1/4 scale)

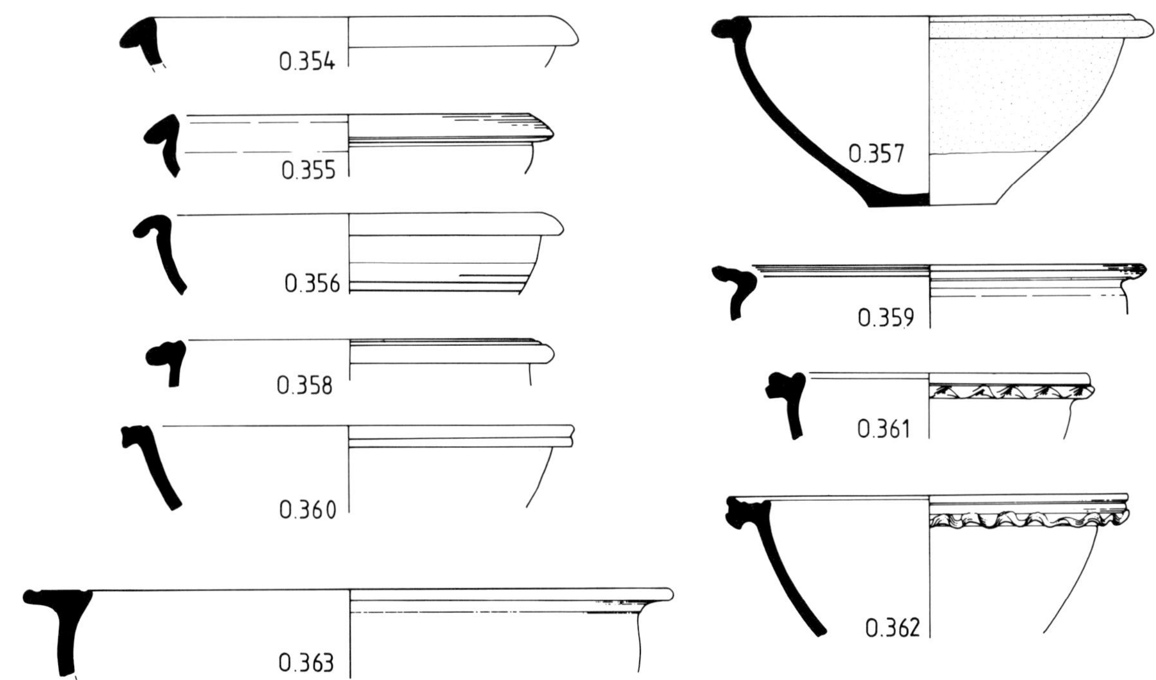

Figure 35 Roman coarse pottery, types O.354–O.363 (1/4 scale)

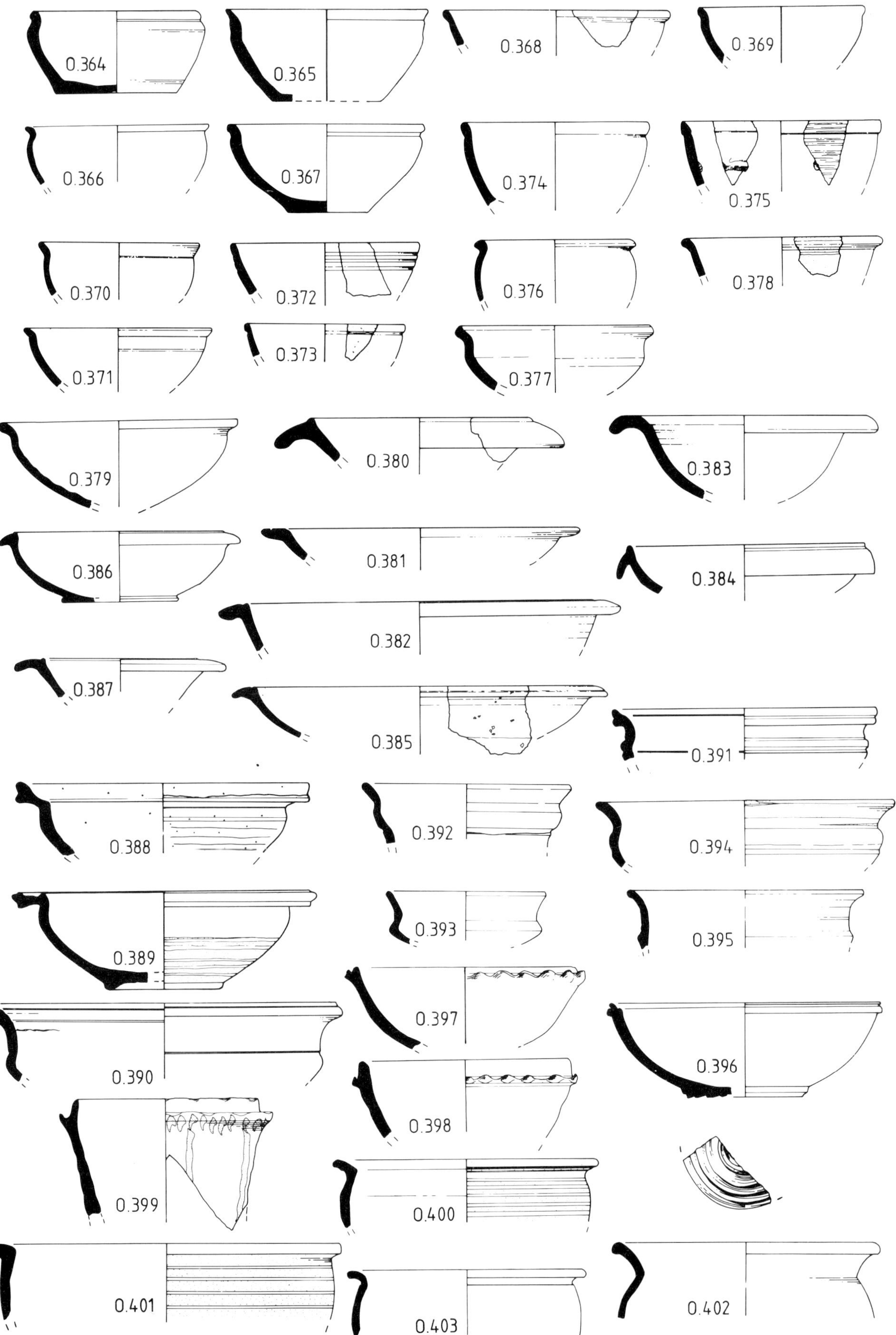

Figure 36 Roman coarse pottery, types O.364–O.403 (1/4 scale)

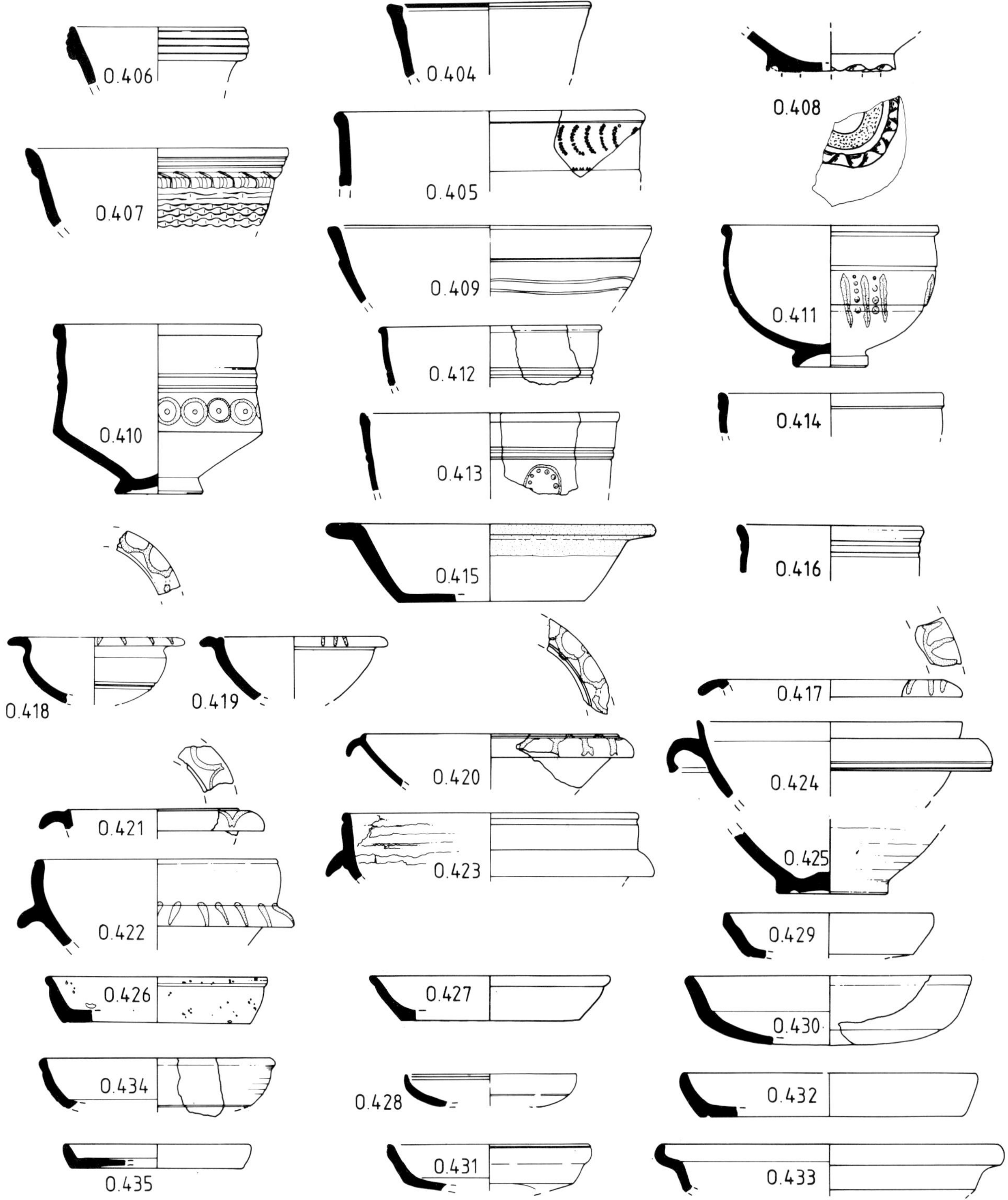

Figure 37 Roman coarse pottery, types O.404–O.435 (1/4 scale)

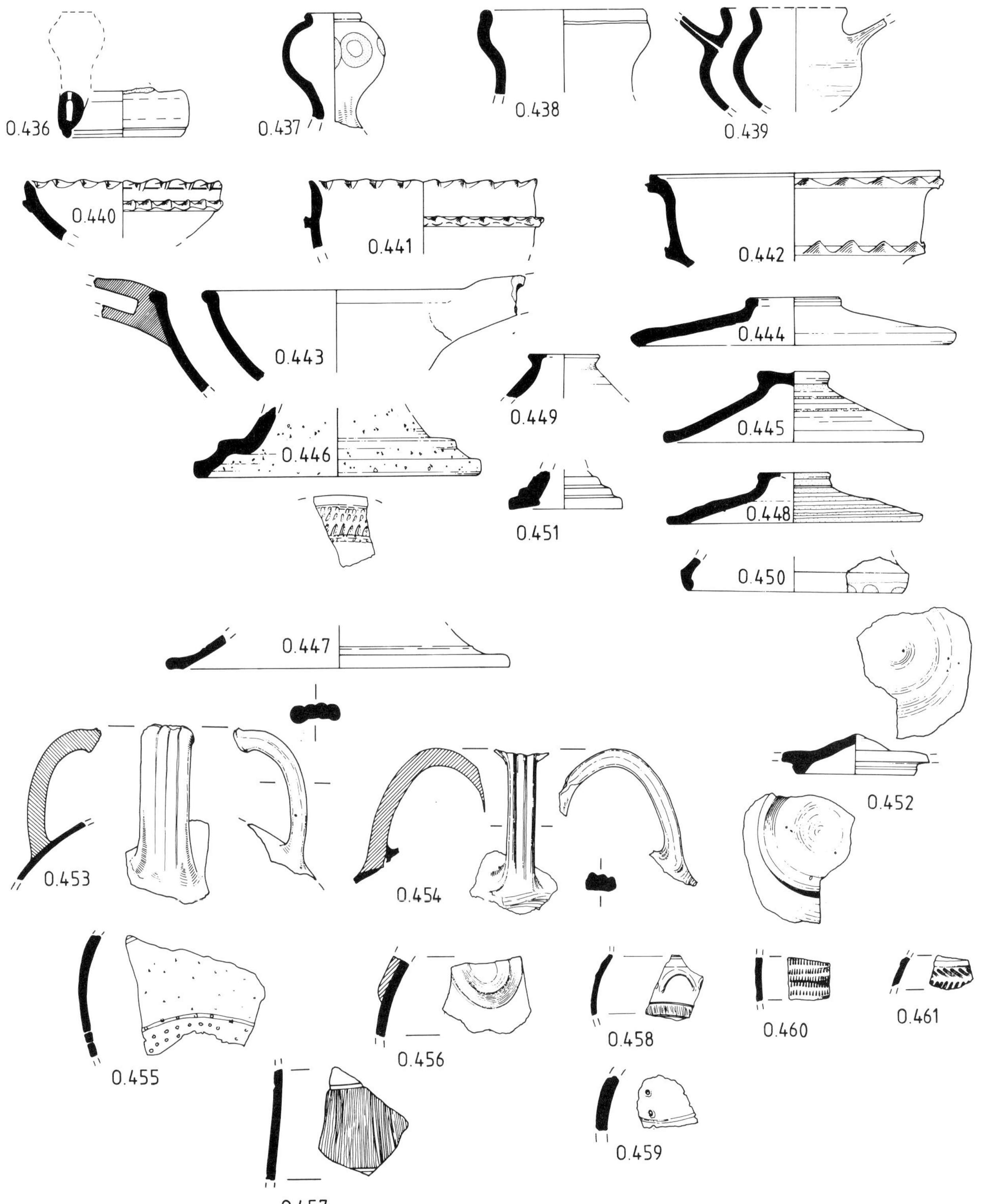

Figure 38 Roman coarse pottery, types O.436–O.461 (1/4 scale)

Oxidized colour-coated wares (figs 39, 40)

The colour-coated wares found at Alcester include most of the fine table wares in the oxidized ceramic assemblage. They include both British and foreign imported vessels (*terra sigillata* excluded). These two groups have distinct chronological divisions, the foreign vessels being the innovators of the colour-coated industry dating to the 1st–2nd century, while the British colour-coated industry did not become independent of the Continent until the late 3rd century.

Fabrics

CI: Fairly hard, micaceous fabric with large inclusions of quartz. The colour range is a red to brown fabric with a black colour-coat and well-burnished exterior. All of the vessels are wheel-made and include jars, beakers, and cups. Date: 2nd–4th century. Fabric Group 9.

DF: Oxfordshire or Oxfordshire-type ware. Hard, fine buff to orange fabric frequently with a grey core and covered by an orange to red colour-coat. The fabric is sandy and frequently micaceous with small black and red inclusions. All are wheel-made and include beakers, bowls, and lids. Date: mid-3rd to 4th century. Fabric Group 18.

DH: South-Western brown slip. A hard, red fabric with a grey core and brown to dark brown colour-coat. The fabric is micaceous with sand tempering and is similar to Cirencester Excavation Committee fabric 105B. All the vessel types are wheel-made and include flagons, beakers, and bowls. Date: 4th century. Fabric Group 20.

DHA: Oxfordshire and Oxfordshire-type wares (similar to fabric DF, but with a brown colour-coat). Hard, fine, micaceous fabric with red and black inclusions. The colour-coat is brown to dark brown in colour. All the vessel types are wheel-made and include flagons, beakers, and bowls. Date: mid-3rd to 4th century. Fabric Group 18.

DO: Gaulish and Rhenish ware. Very hard, fine orange to red fabric, usually very micaceous. The int. and ext. are covered by a very fine glossy black colour-coat, often with a metallic lustre. All the vessel types are wheel-made and include beakers and cups. Date: 2nd–3rd century. Fabric Group 14.

DP: Hard, fine, sandy fabric with a grey interior and orange exterior. The exterior is covered by a dark brown colour-coat. Body sherd. Date: 3rd century. Fabric Group 1.

DQ: Hard, sandy buff fabric, micaceous with sparse inclusions of quartz. The exterior is covered by a dark brown colour, with a red colour-coat on the interior. Wheel-made body sherds. Date: 4th century. Fabric Group 18.

DT: 'North Gaulish' rough-cast beakers (cf Symmonds 1990). Very fine, hard, red fabric occasionally with a grey core. There are no visible inclusions, and the int. and ext. are covered by a dark brown to black colour-coat. All of these vessels are wheel-made. Clay particle rough-cast beakers. Date: AD 80–135. Fabric Group 13.

DTA: Very hard, coarse, sandy fabric, micaceous, with abundant large quartz inclusions. The colour-coat is dark brown in colour. All of the vessels are wheel-made and are thought to have been produced locally. Date: 4th century. Fabric Group 9.

FE: Very hard, fine, micaceous, red fabric with occasional black inclusions. The colour-coat is a reddish-brown often with a metallic lustre. One origin of these rough-cast beakers is Colchester (cf Symmonds 1990). Date: AD 120–80. Fabric Group 16.

EL: Purple and red colour-coated vessels.

Range of vessel types

The range of vessel types is not large. It is dominated by table wares, in particular beakers and bowls, although flagons, jars, and cups do occur.

Flagons (C.1–C.7)

These occur in Oxfordshire and Oxfordshire-type ware, and also in South-Western brown slip.

Jars (C.8–C.11)

The jars produced in colour-coated wares are in the coarser fabrics CT and DTA and are derived from forms which are produced prolifically in the reduced utilitarian wares.

Beakers (C.12–C.41)

These vessels account for over half of the colour-coated assemblage. The most prolific British oxidized colour-coated wares found at Alcester are the Oxfordshire and Oxfordshire-type beaker with its elongated neck. The predominant imported vessels are the 'North Gaulish' rough-cast beaker, and the fine Rhenish and Central Gaulish beakers with their barbotine and rouletted decoration.

Cups (C.42–C.44)

This is a small category, with a coarse example in fabric CI and a couple of fine Central Gaulish examples dating to AD 150–250.

Bowls (C.45–C.67)

Oxfordshire and Oxfordshire-type wares account for almost all the fine bowls in this category. The forms are either derived from samian origins or follow the same tradition. A feature of these bowls is that they are covered with a red to orange colour-coat which is a practice employed by the Oxfordshire potters on open vessel forms. There is one colour-coated bowl in fabric DTA.

Decorative techniques

Colour-coated vessels, and indeed most table wares, were frequently decorated with a wide range of techniques. Grooves are mostly used on the enclosed vessel types, for example beakers, and occur less frequently on the open forms. Indenting is exclusive to beakers, and was first employed by the continental potters, appearing at Alcester on the Rhenish beakers (dated to AD 150–250) with British potters producing forms typologically similar from the late 2nd and early 3rd century. The barbotine tradition persisted throughout the Roman period, but with some variation in style and method. The earliest vessels at Alcester decorated by the barbotine method are Gaulish and Rhenish beakers. The designs are tear-drop leaves and tendrils, with the vessels dating to AD 150–250. The later barbotine decoration on the Oxfordshire vessels is all animal forms. They are to be found on both flagons and hunt cups, and appear on vessels dating from the late 3rd century onwards. Barbotine scales are also found on a South-Western brown slip body sherd, dating to the 4th century. This is a continental technique adopted by the Oxfordshire potters during the late 3rd century (Young 1977); its use by the South-Western brown slip potters provides further evidence for there having been a migration from the Oxfordshire kilns.

Rouletting is a very common technique on colour-coated wares and has little or no chronological significance. However, on the coarser fabrics and South-Western brown slip vessels the quality and definition of the rouletting is poorer and the date late, possibly suggesting that well-defined rouletting may indicate an early date. Impressed decoration occurs only on Oxfordshire and Oxfordshire-type vessels. The vessel forms on which this type of decoration occur are the deeper bowls and beakers; all are dated to the 4th century. Linear comb stamps, circles, and demi-rosettes are all represented. Rough-cast decoration was seen as a cheap and convenient method of decorating fine wares and was employed by the North Gaulish potters and their British counterparts. All employ clay particle rough-casting. Painted vessels are well known throughout the Roman period with a general increase in painted vessels towards the later periods. The paint used on the Alcester colour-coated wares is without exception white.

Illustrated vessels

Flagons

These vessels account for 4% of the colour-coated assemblage. Examples from Alcester are covered with a brown colour-coat which is a feature of Oxfordshire and Oxfordshire-type enclosed vessels.

C.1 DH 31 Flagon with a dark brown colour-coat. Pair of incised lines immediately beneath rim. Flange on neck. South-Western brown slip. Cf Cirencester Excavation Committee fabric 105 (Richardson pers comm). Mid- to late 4th century. (A IX 21). WMFC 14.

C.2 DH 13 Cupped-mouth flagon with incised groove beneath rim and covered with dark brown colour-coat. South-Western brown slip. Cf Cirencester Excavation Committee fabric 105 (Richardson pers comm). Mid- to late 4th century. (G IV 1A). WMFC 18.

C.3 DHA 18 Flagon with tall neck and flange mid-way. Immediately beneath rim a groove. Handle scar. (Young 1977, C8, AD 240–400+). (G III 2, phase X, late 4th century). WMFC 14.

C.4 DHA 24 Body sherd of flagon with burnished ext. Between two grooves is a barbotine hunting scene and beneath lower groove is a band of rouletting. Oxfordshire (Young 1977, C.8). AD 240–400. (C IIIA 21). WMFC 14.

C.5 DHA 41 Body sherd of flagon or beaker, with barbotine decoration on ext. Oxfordshire. AD 240–400. (C IIIA 32).

C.6 DHA 44 Body sherd of flagon or beaker with barbotine animal on ext. and a line of rouletting beneath. Oxfordshire. AD 240–400. (G IV 1).

C.7 DHA 43 Body sherd of flagon or beaker with barbotine decoration on ext. Oxfordshire. AD 240–400. (C III U/S).

Jars

Few examples at Alcester occur in colour-coated wares. The main types are in coarser fabrics.

C.8 CI 7 Narrow-necked jar with blue-black colour-coat and well-burnished ext. (H II 63, phase II, Antonine to 3rd century). WMFC 20.

C.9 CI 6 Small fine jar with black colour-coat. Well-burnished ext. (AA I 51). WMFC 23.

C.10 DF 24 Narrow-necked jar with out-turned rim and an orange/red colour-coat. Oxfordshire (Young 1977, C.16). AD 270–400. (G I 24, phase IX+, late 4th century). WMFC 20.

C.11 DF 51 Wide-necked jar/bowl with everted rim and red/brown colour-coat. (Young 1977, C75). AD 325–400+. (K II 2). WMFC 66.

Beakers

This is the largest group in the colour-coat category, with over 54% of the vessels accounted for by beakers.

Rough-cast beakers

These are foreign imports from Northern Gaul with the exception of two copies produced in the Severn Valley and a further two vessels from Colchester.

North Gaulish fabric

C.12 DT 24 Rough-cast beaker with grooved cornice rim and small rough-cast particles. The colour-coat is a blue-black with diagonal wipe marks on rim int. 'North Gaulish fabric 1' (Anderson 1980, fig 11, no 1). AD 80–135. (D II 60). WMFC 40.

C.13 DT 23 Base of rough-cast beaker with a dark brown colour-coat. 'North Gaulish fabric 1' (Anderson 1980, fig 11). AD 80–135. (B I 3, phase II, Antonine to 3rd century).

C.14 DT 2 Rough-cast beaker with cornice rim, and thin groove on shoulder defining upper extent of rough-cast decoration. The colour-coat is dark brown with wipe marks on rim int. 'North Gaulish fabric 1' (Anderson 1980, fig 11). AD 80–135. (A XVIIA 4). WMFC 40.

C.15 DT 8 Rough-cast beaker with grooved cornice rim. Covered by dark brown colour-coat. 'North Gaulish fabric 1' (Anderson 1980, fig 11, no 6). AD 80–135. (B IA 7). WMFC 40.

C.16 DT 6 Rough-cast beaker with grooved cornice rim. Covered by dark brown colour-coat. 'North Gaulish fabric 1' (Anderson 1980, fig 11, no 6). AD 80–135. (D II 90, phase I, 1st century to early Antonine). WMFC 40.

C.17 DT 22 Small rough-cast beaker with cornice rim and dark brown colour-coat. Incised line defines upper limit of rough-cast decoration. 'North Gaulish fabric 1' (Anderson 1980, fig 11, no 2). AD 80–135. (D II 28). WMFC 40.

C.18 DT 26 Small beaker with grooved cornice rim covered by dark brown colour-coat. Incised line defines upper limit of rough-cast decoration. Stylistically this form has parallels with Lezoux (Anderson pers comm). Trajanic. (E II 46, phase V, late 2nd century?). WMFC 40.

C.19 DT 1 Large rough-cast beaker with deep groove immediately beneath rim; a dark brown colour-coat. (D I 126A, phase II, later 2nd to early 3rd century). WMFC 40.

C.20 DT 20 Rough-cast beaker covered by dark brown colour-coat. Origin local (Anderson pers comm). (AA II 87, phase III, 3rd century). WMFC 40.

Romano-British coarse pottery

C.21 DT 5 Rough-cast beaker with deep groove immediately beneath rim, very micaceous and covered with a dark brown colour-coat. Copying 'North Gaulish fabric 2'. Locally made? perhaps at Gloucester (Anderson pers comm). (C VI 131, phase III?, 3rd century?). WMFC 40.
C.22 FE 1 Very fine, rough-cast beaker with everted rim and self colour-coated. 'Colchester' (Anderson 1980, fig 13). AD 120–150. (B I 3, phase II, Antonine to 3rd century). WMFC 43.
C.23 FE 2 Fine base of rough-cast beaker with iridescent colour-coat. Cf 'Colchester' (Anderson 1980, fig 13, no 1). AD 120–150. (B I 3, phase II, Antonine to 3rd century).

Gaulish and Rhenish wares

C.24 DO 9 Beaker with incised line on body ext., and two pairs of bands of rouletting with single band between. Rhenish ware (Greene 1978, fig 2.3, no 4). AD 150–250. (D I 36, phase VI, mid- to late 4th century? — residual). WMFC 48.
C.25 DO 3 Very fine small beaker. Rhenish. AD 150–250. (B IA 1). WMFC 46.
C.26 DO 7 Very fine indented globular beaker with two bands of rouletting on shoulder. Central Gaulish (Greene 1978, fig 2.3, no 6). AD 150–250. (G V 100, phase VI, late 4th century — residual). WMFC 46.
C.27 DO 4 Two body sherds from hunt cup, with barbotine decoration. Rhenish. AD 150–250. (C IIIA 3).
C.28 DO 8 Very fine body sherd from beaker with barbotine decoration. A rouletted band on ext. above incised line. Central Gaulish (Greene 1978, fig 2.3, no 9). AD 150–250. (A XVI 7).

Other beakers

C.29 CI 3 Beaker with everted rim and a brown-black colour-coat. Ext. is rouletted. (G IA 60, phase V, later 4th century). WMFC 42.

Oxfordshire and Oxfordshire-type beakers

C.30 DF 22 Beaker with sloping neck and everted rim. A standard late Roman form. Oxfordshire (Young 1977, C.23). AD 270–400. (AA I 17, phase VI, late 3rd to early 4th century). WMFC 44.
C.31 DF 41 Beaker with sloping neck and everted rim. Oxfordshire (Young 1977, C.23). AD 270–400. (D I 2, phase VIII, late 4th century). WMFC 44.
C.32 DF 12 Beaker base with well burnished ext. and red colour-coat. (C IIIC 1).
C.33 DF 55 Cut-off base of beaker, reused as small cup with traces of red paint on the interior. (AA II 25).

South-Western brown slip-type beakers

C.34 DH 40 Beaker with straight sides and burnished ext. Dark brown colour-coat. South-Western brown slip. Cf Cirencester Excavation Committee fabric 105 (Richardson pers comm). Mid- to late 4th century. (A IX 21). WMFC 46.
C.35 DH 51 Fine, globular, indented beaker with vertical comb-stamping on ext. with a reddish-brown colour-coat. Similar to Cirencester Excavation Committee fabric 105B but with added temper (Richardson pers comm). (A IX 1C). WMFC 46.
C.36 DH 47 Body sherd of beaker with indented comb-and-rosette stamp decoration, covered by brown colour-coat. South-Western brown slip. Cf Cirencester Excavation Committee 105B (Richardson pers comm). Mid- to late 4th century. (G IA 17, phase VI?, late 4th century?).
C.37 DH 5 Body sherd of a pentice-moulded beaker with brown colour-coat. Ext. beneath shoulder rouletted. Similar to Cirencester Excavation Committee fabric 105B with added sand temper. (A IX 1C).

Indented or folded beakers

C.38 DHA 49 Fine indented beaker with two shallow incised lines and a single pair of rouletted lines. Ext. well burnished with a reddish-brown colour-coat (found at foot of coffin HB 65). Oxfordshire (Young 1977, C.29 variant). AD 270–400. (G V 6, phase VI, late 4th century). WMFC 46.
C.39 DHA 16 Very fine beaker with downward-turning rim and globular indented body. Oxfordshire (Young 1977, C.31 variant). AD 300–400. (G I 24, phase IX+, late 4th century). WMFC 46.
C.40 DHA 17 Base sherd of beaker with brownish-red colour-coat. Oxfordshire. AD 240–400. (D II 1).
C.41 DTA 11 Base sherd of beaker with brown colour-coat. (A IX 1A).

Cups

C.42 CI 1 Carinated cup with black colour-coat. Well-burnished ext. (G IA 60, phase V, later 4th century — probably residual). WMFC 51.
C.43 DO 14 Fine, small cup, well burnished. Central Gaulish (Greene 1978, fig 2.3, no 7). AD 150–250. (A IX 6). WMFC 40.
C.44 DO 6 Pedestal base sherd of cup. Central Gaulish (Greene 1978, fig 2.3, no 7). AD 150–250. (G I 47).

Bowls

This is the second largest category in the colour-coated wares, and is almost entirely composed of forms in fabric DF. It is significant that all the open Oxfordshire ware vessels are covered with an orange/red colour-coat, whereas all the enclosed vessels, for example beakers and flagons, have brown colour-coats. This practice is so consistent that it must have been deliberate.

Oxfordshire and Oxfordshire-type bowls

All of these vessels are covered by a red/orange colour-coat unless otherwise stated.

C.45 DF 45 Wall-sided, bead-rim, carinated bowl. Beneath rim is band of rouletting, and above and below the carination two more bands. Oxfordshire (Young 1977, C.81). AD 300–400. (B I 6). WMFC 66.
C.46 DF 38 Bowl with double-beaded rim. Probably a full-bellied form from Oxfordshire (Young 1977, C.71). AD 300–400. (AA II 1). WMFC 66.
C.47 DF 46 Base sherd of bowl with circular lines of rouletting on int. of base. Oxfordshire (Young 1977, C.44/45). AD 270–400. (A XVI 1).
C.48 DF 10 Wall-sided, bead-rim carinated bowl with rouletted decoration immediately beneath rim, and midway down body between two parallel lines. Area of rouletting beneath carination. Oxfordshire (Young 1977, C.81). AD 300–400. (AA III 9). WMFC 66.
C.49 DF 31 Full-bellied bowl with a double-beaded rim and lightly burnished body. Oxfordshire (Young 1977, C.71). AD 300–400. (G II 3, phase V, later 4th century). WMFC 66.
C.50 DF 14 Necked bowl with out-turned beaded rim and full curved body. Pronounced shoulder at base of neck. Neck decorated by rouletted band. On body ext. is white painted pattern in form of large spots bordered by S-shaped design. Beneath paint is a band of rouletting. Oxfordshire (Young 1977, C.77). AD 340–400. (B IA 15, phase IV, mid- to late 4th century). WMFC 66.
C.51 DF 29 Necked bowl with out-turned rim and full curved body. Neck rouletted. Rows of deep-impressed rosettes decorate ext. Oxfordshire (Young 1977, variant C.78). AD 340–400. (F IV 14, phase XIII, after AD 353). WMFC 66.
C.52 DF 48 Bowl with everted rim. Oxfordshire (Young 1977, variant C.48). AD 270–400. (B I 6). WMFC 67.
C.53 DF 27 Shallow bowl with wide rolled-over rim. Form copying Dr. 31. Rim decorated with white paint. Oxfordshire (Young 1977, C.48). AD 270–400. (G IA 1A). WMFC 67.
C.54 DF 36 Shallow bowl with large fat beaded rim, copying Dr. 31 with well-burnished int. and ext., and chamfered base. Oxfordshire (Young 1977, variant C.45). AD 270–400. (AA II 45, phase VI, early to mid-4th century). WMFC 69.
C.55 DF 47 Shallow bowl copying Dr. 31 with bead-rim. Oxfordshire (Young 1977, C.45). AD 270–400. (B I 6). WMFC 69.

C.56 DF 13 Shallow bowl with large bead-rim, copying Dr. 31. Int. highly burnished. Oxfordshire (Young 1977, C.45). AD 270–400. (A XV 15). WMFC 69.
C.57 DF 35 Shallow bowl copying Dr. 31 with bead-rim and well-burnished int. and ext. Oxfordshire (Young 1977, C.45). AD 270–400. (D I 2A, phase VIII, late 4th century). WMFC 69.
C.58 DF 43 Shallow bowl copying Dr. 31 with bead-rim and well-burnished int. and ext. Oxfordshire (Young 1977, C.45). AD 270–400. (D I 120, phase VI, mid- to late 4th century). WMFC 69.
C.59 DF 18 Shallow bowl copying Dr. 31 with slightly hooked rim. Oxfordshire (Young 1977, variant C.44). AD 270–350. (C IIIA 12). WMFC 69.
C.60 DF 37 Shallow bowl copying Dr. 31 with bead-rim and shallow incised line on ext. Int. and ext. well burnished. Oxfordshire (Young 1977, variant C.45). AD 270–400. (B III 4). WMFC 69.
C.61 DF 52 Flanged bowl copying Dr. 38. Beneath flange an incised line. Oxfordshire (Young 1977, C.51). AD 240–400. (K II 2). WMFC 67.
C.62 DF 20 Flanged bowl with missing flange (form copying Dr. 38). Oxfordshire or Oxfordshire imitation (Young 1977, C.51). AD 240–400. (AA I 3). WMFC 67.
C.63 DF 16 Flanged bowl with stubby flange. Oxfordshire (Young 1977, C.53). No dating evidence. (C VI 24, phase VII, early to mid-4th century). WMFC 67.
C.64 DF 30 Shallow bowl with out-turned rim. Probably derived from Dr. 36 and Curle 15. Oxfordshire (Young 1977, C.49). AD 240–400+. (D III T/S). WMFC 81.
C.65 DH 19 Flanged bowl copying Dr. 38. Int. and ext. well burnished. Similar to Cirencester Excavation Committee fabric 105B, but with exceptionally good brown colour-coat. (A IX 24). WMFC 67.
C.66 DH 50 Body sherd of flanged bowl with brown colour-coat. Oxfordshire (Young 1977, C.51). AD 240–400. (E VII 1). WMFC 67.
C.67 DTA 21 Bowl with flanged pie-crust rim. A dark brown colour-coat. Local brown-slipped ware. (E IV 7, phase XIII, after AD 353). WMFC 90.

Body sherds

C.68 DF 34 Body sherd with two bands of rouletting and with rosette stamp beneath. Red colour-coat. Oxfordshire. Probably AD 340–400. (AA III 37).
C.69 DF 49 Body sherd with two bands of rouletting and white paint decoration on ext. Red/orange colour-coat. Oxfordshire-type ware. Late 3rd to 4th century. (C VIA 10, phase IX, mid-4th century on).
C.70 DH 46 Body sherd with barbotine decoration and a brown colour-coat. (C IIA 16).
C.71 DH 33 Body sherd with rouletted band and rusticated scallop decoration. A dark brown colour-coat. South-Western brown slip. Cf Cirencester Excavation Committee fabric 105 (Richardson pers comm). Mid- to late 4th century. (F IV 2, phase XIII, after AD 353).
C.72 DHA 6 Body sherd with rouletted decoration. (A IX 7).
C.73 DF 1 Body sherd with an area of rouletted decoration. Dark brown colour-coat. (A I 4, phase VI, early to mid-4th century).
C.74 DQ 1 Body sherd with knife marks on ext. Dark brown colour-coat on ext. and red colour-coat on int. (A I 2A).
C.75 DTA 19 Body sherd with area of coarse rouletting on ext. Probably local. (AA II 97).
C.76 DTA 12 Body sherd. Well burnished with raised white paint decoration on ext. and dark brown colour-coat. (C VI 12A, phase VI, early to mid-4th century).
C.77 DTA 9 Body sherd with white paint decoration and rouletted line. Dark brown colour-coat. Coarse, probably local. (C VI 12A, early to mid-4th century).

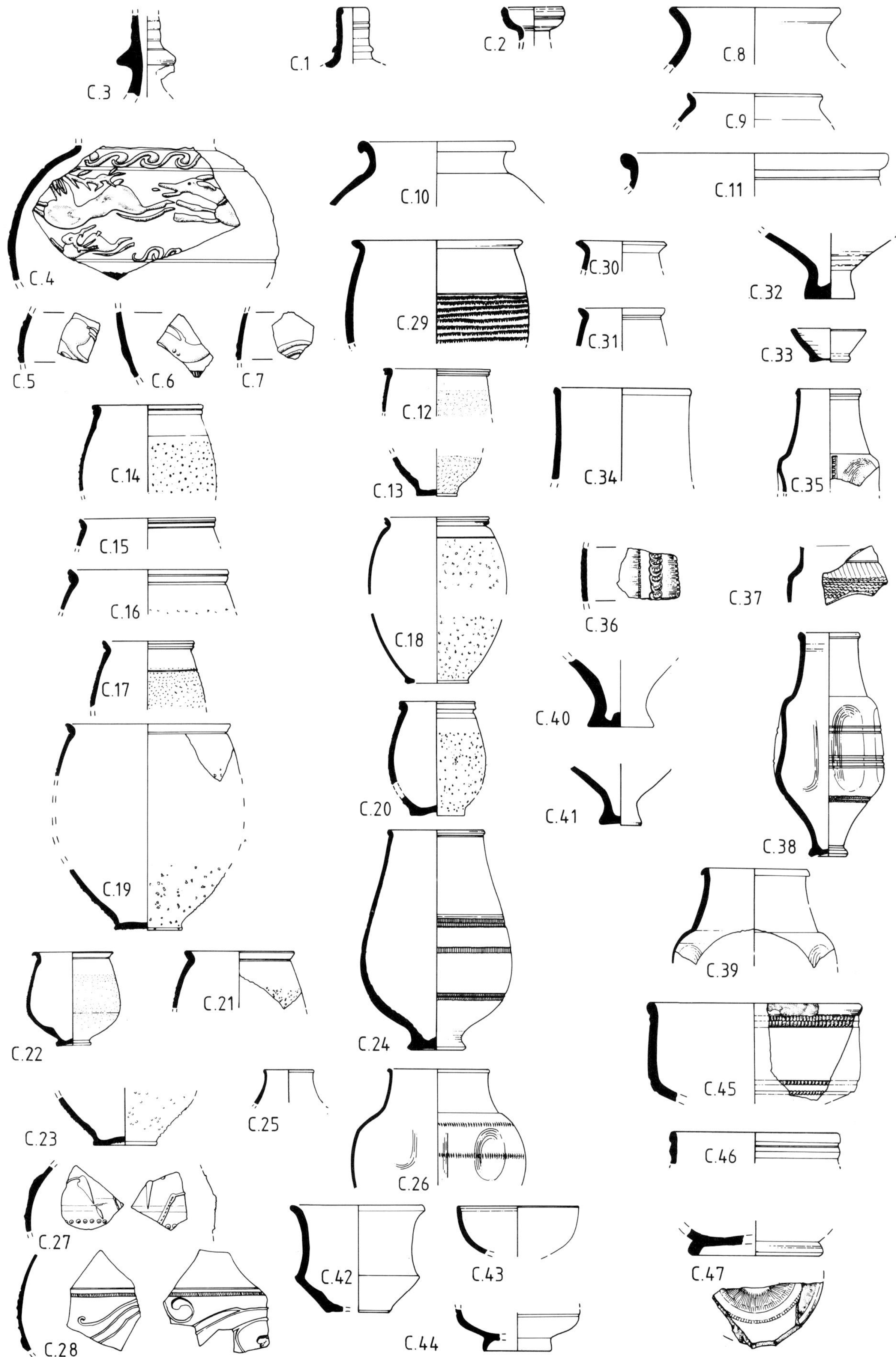

Figure 39 Roman coarse pottery, types C.1–C.47 (1/4 scale)

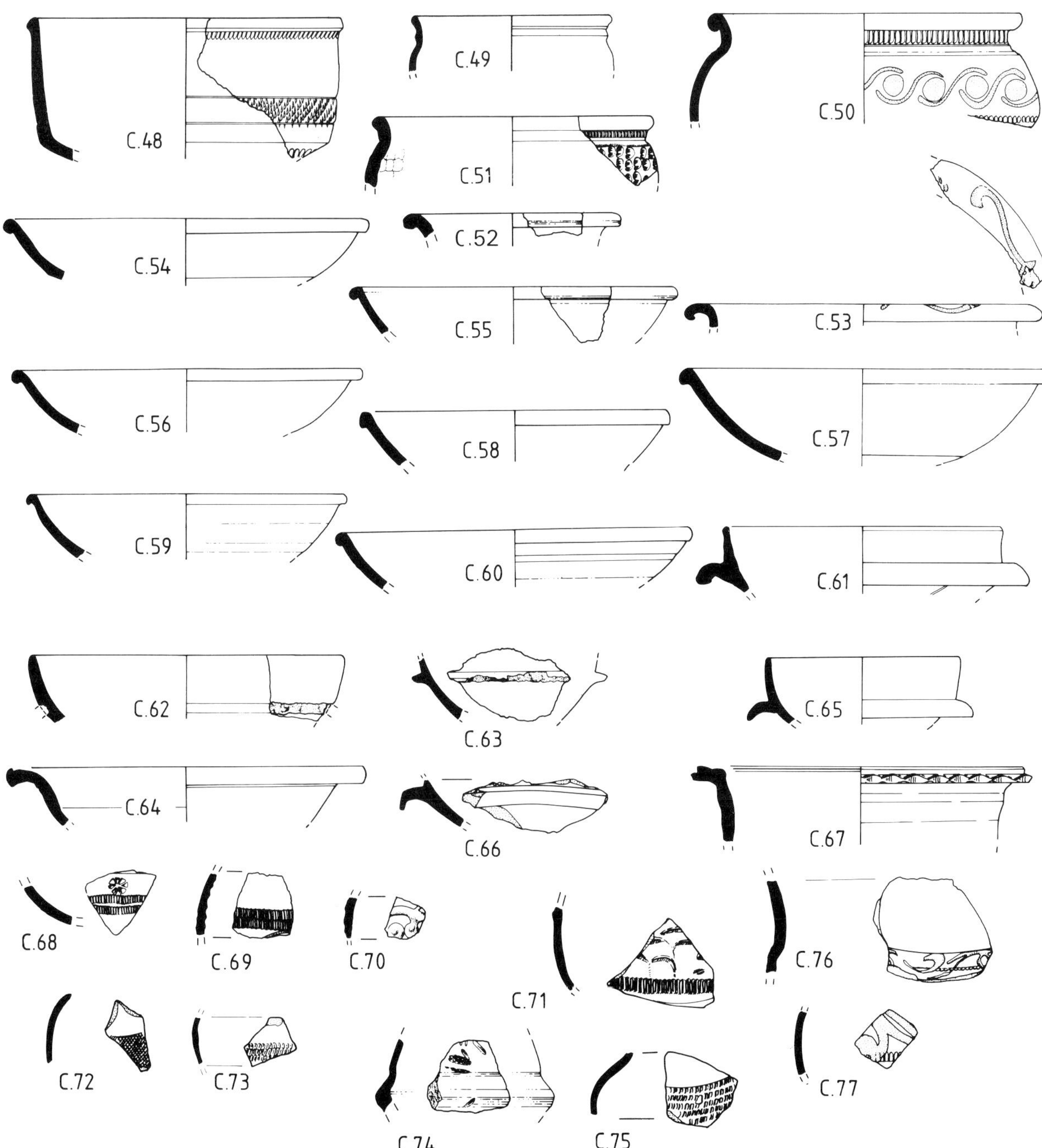

Figure 40 Roman coarse pottery, types C.48–C.77 (1/4 scale)

White wares (figs 41, 42)

This is the smallest of the three major fabrics groupings. White wares represent 2% of the total sherd count for the coarse ware pottery (excluding *mortaria*) and are mainly table wares and other specialist types, for example, flagons and bowls. The range of products is limited, and each form is only represented by one or two vessels. Both the Mancetter and Oxfordshire kilns manufactured white ware vessels during the Roman period and their fabrics and vessel types can be identified at Alcester.

Fabrics

Two major fabric groupings and two small ones are distinguishable in the white ware assemblage. The main fabrics are divided by a difference in the coarseness of the fabric.

AB: A hard, coarse, sandy fabric with a pink core and covered with a thick white slip, tempered with large quartz inclusions. All the vessels are wheel-made and include flagons and tazzas. Fabric Group 1a.

BL: A hard, very fine, white fabric with no inclusions and a grey flecked ext. The vessel is a beaker and wheel-made. 2nd century. Fabric Group 19.

EB: Hard, fine, white to off-white fabric, occasionally with a pink core. The fabric is tempered with fine sand and frequently with small red and black inclusions. All the vessels are wheel-made, fine, and well finished, with red paint a common form of decoration. The vessel forms include flagons, beakers, cups, bowls, and a candlestick. 1st–4th century. Fabric Group 19.

ED: Hard, very sandy vessels (much coarser than the previous group), white to cream in colour, tempered with abundant inclusions of medium-sized quartz grains, and red and black grits. The surface is frequently rough and plastery in appearance. All the vessels are wheel-made and include flagons, beakers, and bowls. 1st–4th century. Fabric Group 1a.

Range of vessel types

Six groups of vessels are distinguishable among the white wares at Birch Abbey.

Flagons and bottles (illustration nos W.1–W.13)

These account for approximately 34% of the white ware vessels, the most dominant form being the ring-necked flagon (W.1–W.7). Bottles, however, are not common and only one example occurs in this ware (W.10).

Jugs (W.14–W.16)

Pottery jugs are uncommon in Roman Britain; there are only three examples amongst the white wares.

Beakers (W.17–W.25)

Beakers are not common in white wares.

Cups (W.26–W.28)

There are three examples; all are very fine, well-finished vessels.

Bowls (W.29–W.45)

This is the largest of the white ware groupings, comprising 47% of the white wares. Many of the forms are samian-derived and a number are from either Oxfordshire or Mancetter.

Miscellaneous vessels (W.46–W.47)

Decorative techniques

A variety of methods was employed. Grooves and cordons occur on all categories of vessels throughout the Roman period. Stabbing occurs directly beneath the rim on illustration no W.21.

Rouletting is found only on beakers and flagons. Incised decoration occurs in a variety of styles: incised acute lattices (W.48), zig-zag or incised wavy lines (W.31), or incised vertical knife slashes (W.28). The use of red or orange paints is a well-known decorative technique in the Roman period, and becomes more common in fine white wares towards the late Roman period. Burnishing occurs on a number of vessels but is not as common as it is on oxidized and reduced vessels.

Tazza frilling is exemplified by illustration no W.46.

Illustrated vessels

Ring-necked flagons

W.1 AB 9 Ring-necked flagon with everted rim and thick white slip. (G V 49). WMFC 11.

W.2 EB 6 Screw-necked flagon with simple bead-rim and handle scar. This is a common flagon type of the 2nd century. (AA II 87, phase III, 3rd century — probably residual). WMFC 11.

W.3 EB 12 Ring-necked flagon, a 'second' with a lop-sided neck. Fabric similar to Mancetter wares (Booth pers comm). Late 1st to early 2nd century. (C I 90, phase I/II, late 1st to early 3rd century). WMFC 11.

W.4 EB 25 Ring-necked flagon with simple bead-rim and double-ribbed handle. Ext. and visible rim int. covered with orange slip. Fabric: possibly Mancetter. Late 1st to early 2nd century. (D I 126A, phase II, later 2nd to early 3rd century?). WMFC 11.

W.5 ED 18 Ring-necked flagon with rim inturned at tip; double-ribbed handle. Late 1st to early 2nd century. (D I 246, phase II, later 2nd to early 3rd century? — probably residual). WMFC 11.

W.6 ED 15 Narrow ring-necked flagon with beaded rim. Late 1st to early 2nd century. (D I 126A, phase II, later 2nd to early 3rd century? — probably residual). WMFC 11.

W.7 ED 21 Ring-necked flagon with beaded rim. Late 1st to early 2nd century. (G I 93). WMFC 11.

Other flagons

W.8 EB 32 Flagon with cupped mouth and two deep incised lines on the rim; handle scar. 2nd century. (L III 10, phase IV, late Roman/modern — residual). WMFC 18.
W.9 EB 22 Flagon with flange on neck; handle scar. Fabric similar to Mancetter wares. (D I T/S). WMFC 14.
W.10 EB 20 Flagon or bottle with tapering rim; no evidence for handle. Orange slip on ext. (G IA 26, phase V, later 4th century). WMFC 13.
W.11 EB 33 Very fine base sherd of flagon with ring-groove on base. (D II 29A).
W.12 ED 29 Large flagon with thickened rim and pair of incised lines on neck. Single handle. Fabric similar to Mancetter wares (Booth pers comm). Perhaps later 2nd century. (E V 31, phase XIII, after AD 353 — residual). WMFC 10.
W.13 ED 35 Flagon with thickened rim and handle scar. (D II 14). WMFC 10.

Jugs

W.14 EB 65 Jug with bead-rim and grooved handle. (H II 74A, phase II, Antonine to 3rd century). WMFC 17.
W.15 EB 21 Cupped mouth jug. Fabric similar to Mancetter wares (Booth pers comm). Later 2nd to 3rd century. (G I 93). WMFC 17.
W.16 ED 30 Trefoil-lipped jug with moulded rim and cordon on neck and shoulder. Triple-ribbed handle. Fabric similar to Mancetter wares (Booth pers comm). (A XVIIB 2). WMFC 06.

Beakers

W.17 BL 1 Poppy-headed beaker with three incised grooves on neck. 2nd century. (AA II 7). WMFC 54.
W.18 EB 46 Globular beaker with everted rim and two shallow grooves on shoulder. (D II 2, phase IX, late 4th century — residual). WMFC 23.
W.19 EB 14 Narrow-necked beaker/jar. (E II 1). WMFC 20.
W.20 EB 3 Beaker with everted rim and upward-sloping neck. Ext. fired to yellow/cream colour. (A IX 4, phase III, later 3rd century — probably residual). WMFC 20.
W.21 EB 30 Narrow-necked beaker/jar with grooved rim and regularly spaced stab marks decorating rim ext. (G I 24, phase IX+, late 4th century). WMFC 20.
W.22 EB 61 Base of beaker with trace of paint on body ext. Well-finished ext. (D I 36, phase VI, mid- to late 4th century?).
W.23 EB 43 Body sherd of beaker with rouletted decoration on ext. (D I 173, phase II, later 2nd to early 3rd century?).
W.24 ED 17 Beaker with rolled-over everted rim. Faint burnished regularly spaced quadruple of vertical lines on body ext., intersected by light incised horizontal lines. (C I 33A). WMFC 32.
W.25 ED 28 Large butt-beaker with well-burnished rim int. and ext. 1st century. (H I 27, phase I, 1st century to Hadrianic). WMFC 49.

Cups

W.26 EB 16 Fine carinated cup with cordon beneath rim and pair of incised grooves beneath cordon. Ext. well burnished. (AA I 35, phase VI, late 3rd to early 4th century — residual). WMFC 51.
W.27 EB 59 Very fine cup with three grooves immediately beneath rim. Ext. decorated by regularly spaced orange paint. (D II 2, phase IX, late 4th century — residual). WMFC 40.

Bowls

W.28 EB 29 Carinated bowl with bead-rim and moulded body wall. Incised slash decoration above carination in form of quadruple of vertical lines at regular intervals. Ext. well burnished. (G IV 33, phase VI, late 4th century — residual). WMFC 54.
W.29 EB 48 Bowl probably carinated, with cordon on neck and burnished ext. (AA III 79, phase II, late 2nd to mid-3rd century). WMFC 54.
W.30 EB 18 Fine bowl with corrugated body wall. Two incised horizontal lines on ext. form cordon on middle corrugation. Ext. well burnished. (G I 35, phase IX, late 4th century — residual). WMFC 55.
W.31 EB 24 Hemispherical bowl, with two incised horizontal lines beneath rim forming upper limit of two bands of incised wavy decoration. Another incised groove divides the two bands. (G I 106A, phase V, later 4th century). WMFC 66.
W.32 EB 31 Wall-sided bowl with incised groove beneath beaded rim and with regularly spaced vertical lines cut by two horizontal lines. Dr. 37 copy. (B III 61). WMFC 66.
W.33 EB 41 Very fine, wall-sided bead-rim bowl with pair of incised horizontal lines on body, carinated with foot-ring base. Dr. 37 copy. (A V 16, phase VI, late 3rd to early 4th century). WMFC 66.
W.34 EB 26 Very fine, wall-sided bowl, based on Dr. 29 and 30. Rim beaded with cordon beneath. Below cordon is an orange paint design in form of semi-circles bordered on upper edge by orange paint spots. Cf Oxfordshire (Young 1977, W.53:1). Late 1st to early 2nd century. (E IV 28, phase VI, early 3rd century? — residual). WMFC 51.
W.35 EB 13 Bowl with everted rim and full curved body. On body ext. are three incised horizontal grooves. Ext. well burnished. (C VIA 98, phase V, later 3rd century on). WMFC 58.
W.36 EB 1 Shallow bowl with vestigial flanged rim and handle scar. Cream/yellow int. and ext. Cf Oxfordshire (Young 1977, P.14). AD 300–400. (B III 16). WMFC 67.
W.37 EB 17 Bowl with flanged rim and red paint decoration on rim. Fabric and form similar to vessels from Mancetter (Booth pers comm). (D I 25, phase VIII, late 4th century — residual). WMFC 67.
W.38 EB 19 Bowl with moulded rim and incised groove on flat top of rim, which has red paint decoration. Oxfordshire (Young 1977, P.24). AD 240–400. (D I 65, phase IV, late 3rd century?). WMFC 56.
W.39 EB 62 Bowl with thickened moulded rim and two incised grooves. Traces of orange paint. Oxfordshire (Young 1977, P.24). AD 240–400. (E IV 15, phase XIII, after AD 353). WMFC 56.
W.40 EB 28 Wall-sided bowl with carination. Rim moulded and a moulded cordon above the carination. Red paint bands on int. Oxfordshire (Young 1977, P.24). AD 240–400+. (G II 12, phase V, later 4th century). WMFC 56.
W.41 EB 63 Bowl with moulded rim and dark orange paint. Oxfordshire (Young 1977, P.24). AD 240–400+. (A XI 2). WMFC 56.
W.42 EB 33 Body sherd of small carinated bowl with incised groove beneath rim and above carination. Ext. burnished. (AA II 85, phase III, 3rd century).
W.43 ED 27 Bowl with bead-rim and pair of horizontal incised grooves. Rim and ext. burnished. (E IV 20). WMFC 66.
W.44 ED 32 Shallow bowl with upturned flanged rim and pink-orange slip on int. and ext. Oxfordshire (Young 1977, P.15). AD 300–400+. (B IA 7). WMFC 69.
W.45 ED 24 Bowl with out-turned rim and straight sides. Decorated with red paint; horizontal stripes on body ext. and rim. (A XI 3). WMFC 68.

Miscellaneous

W.46 AB 10 Coarse ?*tazza* with pie-crust rim. (L III 14, phase II, 3rd century). WMFC 90.
W.47 EB 60 Candlestick with cordon on neck and another cordon on base ext. Red paint on ext. and a hole in base. (Unstratified). WMFC 91.

Body sherds

W.48 EB 54 Very fine body sherd with incised 'X' decoration and traces of brown paint on ext. White fabric with grey core. (AA II 41, phase III, 3rd century).
W.49 EB 54 Body sherd with orange painted dots in diamond zig-zag. Probably from a ring and dot or poppyhead beaker. Neronian to 2nd century. (AA II 85, phase III, 3rd century — residual).
W.50 EB 4 Body sherd with orange paint decoration in form of vertical painted line bordered on each side by a line of dots. (A IX 12, phase V, later 3rd century on).

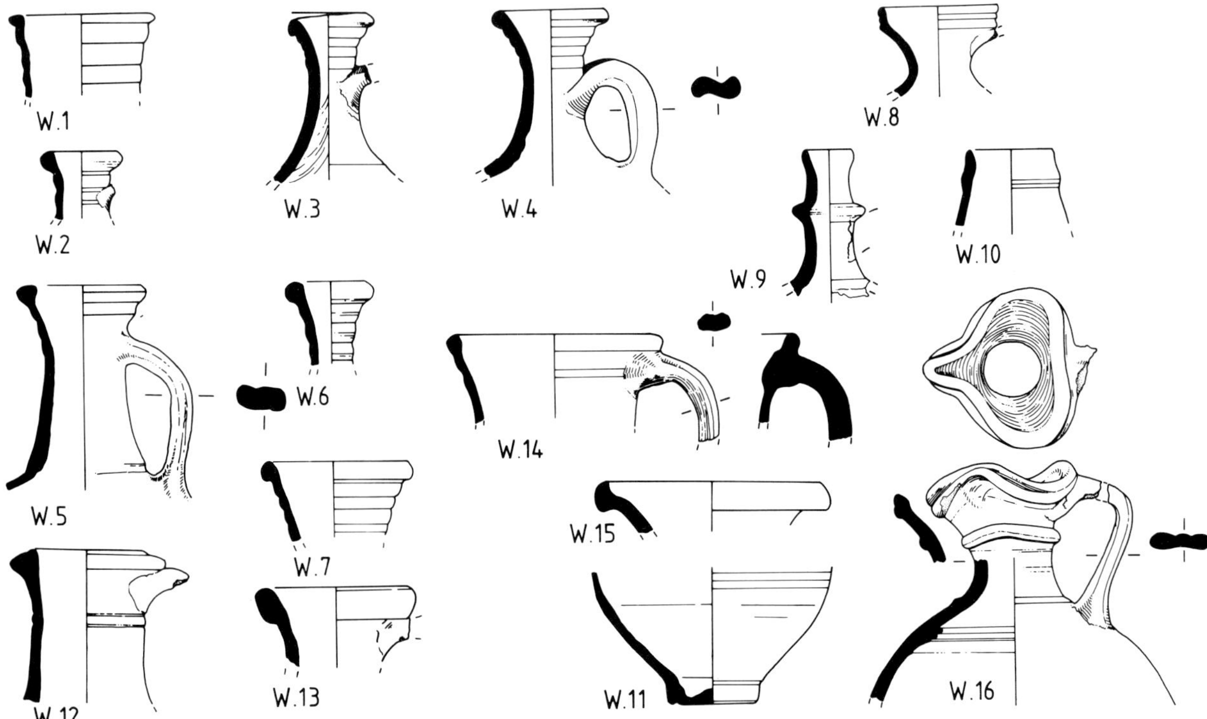

Figure 41 Roman coarse pottery, types W.1–W.16 (1/4 scale)

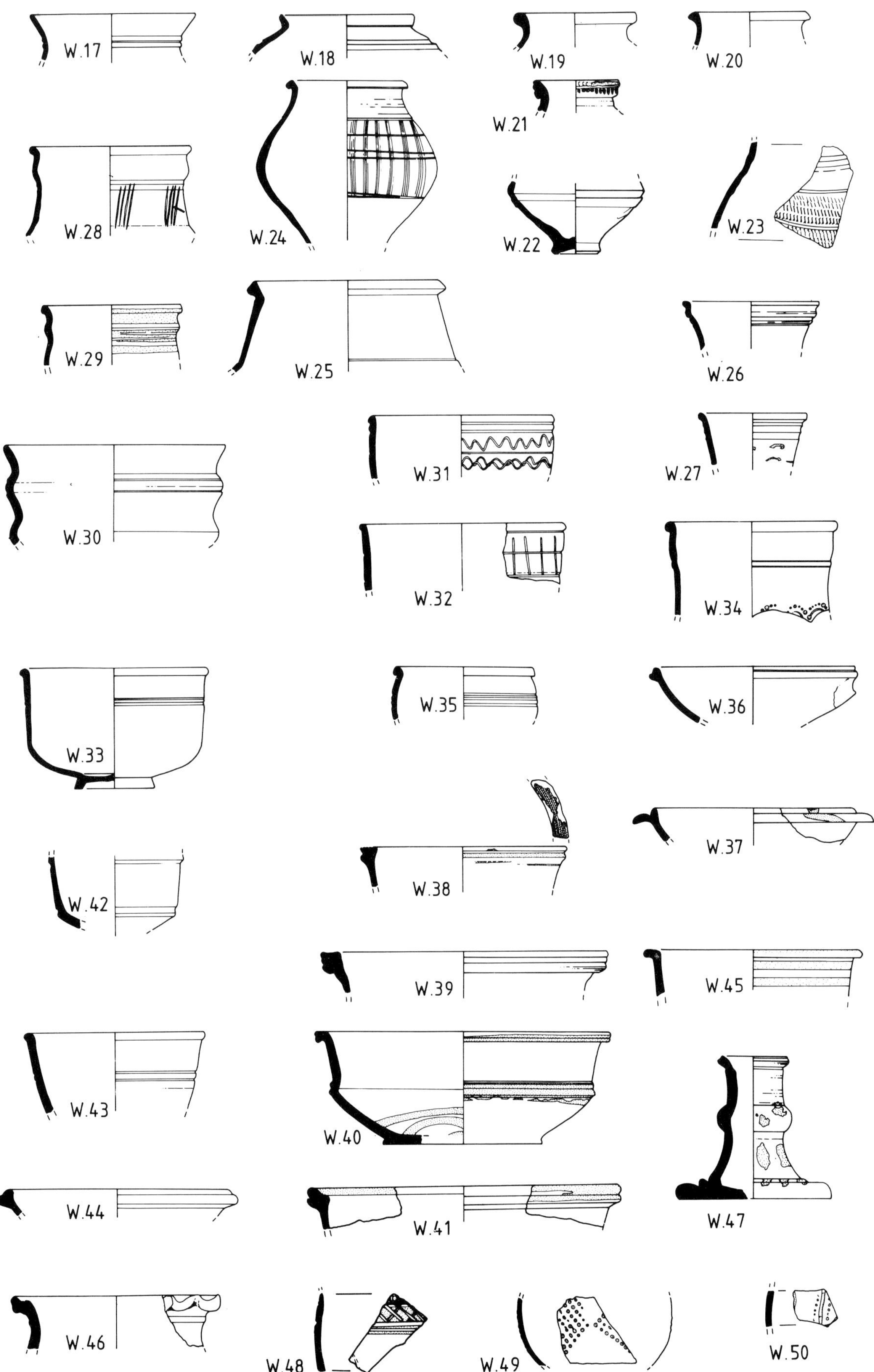

Figure 42 Roman coarse pottery, types W.17–W.50 (1/4 scale)

White colour-coated wares (fig 43)

Vessels in this group, with only one exception, were produced in the Nene Valley, and are dated to the late 2nd to 4th centuries. The isolated exception is a body sherd manufactured in the Lower Rhineland and dated to the late 2nd to 3rd century.

Fabric

The majority of the vessels (illustration nos CW.1–CW.19) are in fabric DM (Fabric Group 19) — 'Nene Valley ware'. This is a hard, fine, sandy white/cream fabric, with a few black inclusions and occasionally with red sand. The surfaces are covered with red/brown or dark brown/black colour-coat and all the vessels are wheel-made. The body sherd from the Lower Rhineland (no CW.20) is in fabric DN (Fabric Group 20): this is a very fine wheel-made white fabric with no visible inclusions and covered with a blue-black colour-coat.

Range of vessel types

Four groups of products can be identified and date to the 3rd and 4th centuries.

Jars (CW.1–CW.2)

Beakers (CW.3–CW.11)

This is the largest group and includes two sub-groups. The earliest group includes the fat squat beakers, and hunt cups, decorated with barbotine-type decoration. The later vessels are elongated beakers with long necks and are closer to the Rhenish forms.

Flanged bowls (CW.12–CW.13)

Castor boxes and lid (CW.14–CW.17)

The earlier examples are small with angular profiles and well-defined rouletting. The later vessels are larger with less well-defined rouletting.

Decorative techniques

Rouletting is one of the most characteristic traits of Nene Valley ware and occurs in both the 3rd- and 4th-century examples. The standard of rouletting provides a chronological indicator, with the earlier examples more defined and of a higher standard, whereas the later ones are much less clearly defined. Barbotine was applied under the colour-coat and includes tendril-motif dots and animal subjects. White-painted decoration is used in the later periods, applied over the dark colour-coat.

Illustrated vessels

Jars

CW.1 DM 25 Wide-mouthed jar with prominent shoulder and curved body. Dark red/brown colour-coat. Nene Valley (Howe *et al* 1980, no 75). 4th century. (F IV 14, phase XIII, after AD 353). WMFC 32.
CW.2 DM 15 Base of jar, dark brown colour-coat. (B IA 15, phase IV, mid- to late 4th century).

Beakers

CW.3 DM 35 Hunt cup with simple curved rim. Tall globular profile with barbotine animal decoration under dark brown colour-coat. Nene Valley ware (Howe *et al* 1980, no 26). Later 2nd to 3rd centuries. (D II 24). WMFC 43.
CW.4 DM 46 Pentice-moulded beaker with everted rim and reddish-brown colour-coat. Nene Valley ware (Howe *et al* 1980, no 56/57). 4th century. (AA III 9). WMFC 44.
CW.5 DM 29 Beaker with neck, well-burnished int. and ext. and covered with dark brown/black colour-coat. Nene Valley ware (Howe *et al* 1980, no 49/52). Later 3rd to 4th centuries. (C VIA 52, phase IX, mid-4th century on). WMFC 44.
CW.6 DM 19 Pentice-moulded beaker, rouletted on most of body (containing skeleton of a bird). Nene Valley ware (Howe *et al* 1980, no 56). 4th century. (AA II 45, phase VI, early to mid-4th century). WMFC 44.
CW.7 DM 5 Small beaker with very dark brown colour-coat. (A IX 8, phase VI, late 3rd to early 4th century). WMFC 44.
CW.8 DM 22 Pentice-moulded beaker with everted rim. Covered by very dark brown colour-coat. Nene Valley ware (Howe *et al* 1980, no 55/56). 4th century. (AA II 50, phase VI, early to mid-4th century). WMFC 44.
CW.9 DM 47 Small beaker base with reddish-brown colour-coat. Nene Valley ware (Howe *et al* 1980, no 44). Late 2nd to early 3rd century. (G IV 5, phase X, late 4th century — residual).
CW.10 DM 35 Beaker base with very dark brown colour-coat. (B IA 8).
CW.11 DM 33 Beaker base with dark brown colour-coat. (A V 6).
CW.12 DM 23 Flanged bowl with dark reddish-brown colour-coat. Nene Valley ware (Howe *et al* 1980, no 79). 4th century. (F I 8, phase XIII, after AD 353). WMFC 68.
CW.13 DM 31 Flanged bowl with reddish-brown colour-coat. Nene Valley ware (Howe *et al* 1980, no 79). 4th century. (F IV 14, phase XIII, after AD 353). WMFC 68.

Castor boxes and lid

CW.14 DM 41 Fine castor box with orange colour-coat. Nene Valley ware (Howe *et al* 1980, no 89). Late 2nd to 4th century. (G I 12, phase VIII, late 4th century). WMFC 95.
CW.15 DM 32 Castor box with red/orange colour-coat. Nene Valley ware (Howe *et al* 1980, no 89). Late 2nd to 4th century. (AA I 3). WMFC 95.
CW.16 DM 28 Castor box with red/brown colour-coat. Nene Valley ware (Howe *et al* 1980, no 89). Late 2nd to 4th century. (C IIIA 14). WMFC 95.
CW.17 DM 48 Lid of castor box with a rouletted ext. and blue-black iridescent colour-coat. Nene Valley ware (Howe *et al* 1980, no 89). Late 2nd to 4th century. (A XVIIIB 2). WMFC 98.

Body sherds

CW.18 DM 6 Two body sherds probably of flagon with handle scar and two incised lines on neck, with rouletting beneath. Cream/white paint decoration applied over colour-coat. Nene Valley ware (cf Howe *et al* 1980, no 68). 4th century. (A IX 21).
CW.19 DM 36 Body sherd probably of jar with cordon. Rouletting and white paint decorate the ext. Nene Valley ware. Later 3rd to 4th century. (M I 1).
CW.20 DN 5 Body sherd of beaker with barbotine decoration under the blue-black colour-coat, Lower Rhineland. Late 2nd to early 3rd century. (AA I 17, phase VI, late 3rd to early 4th century — residual).

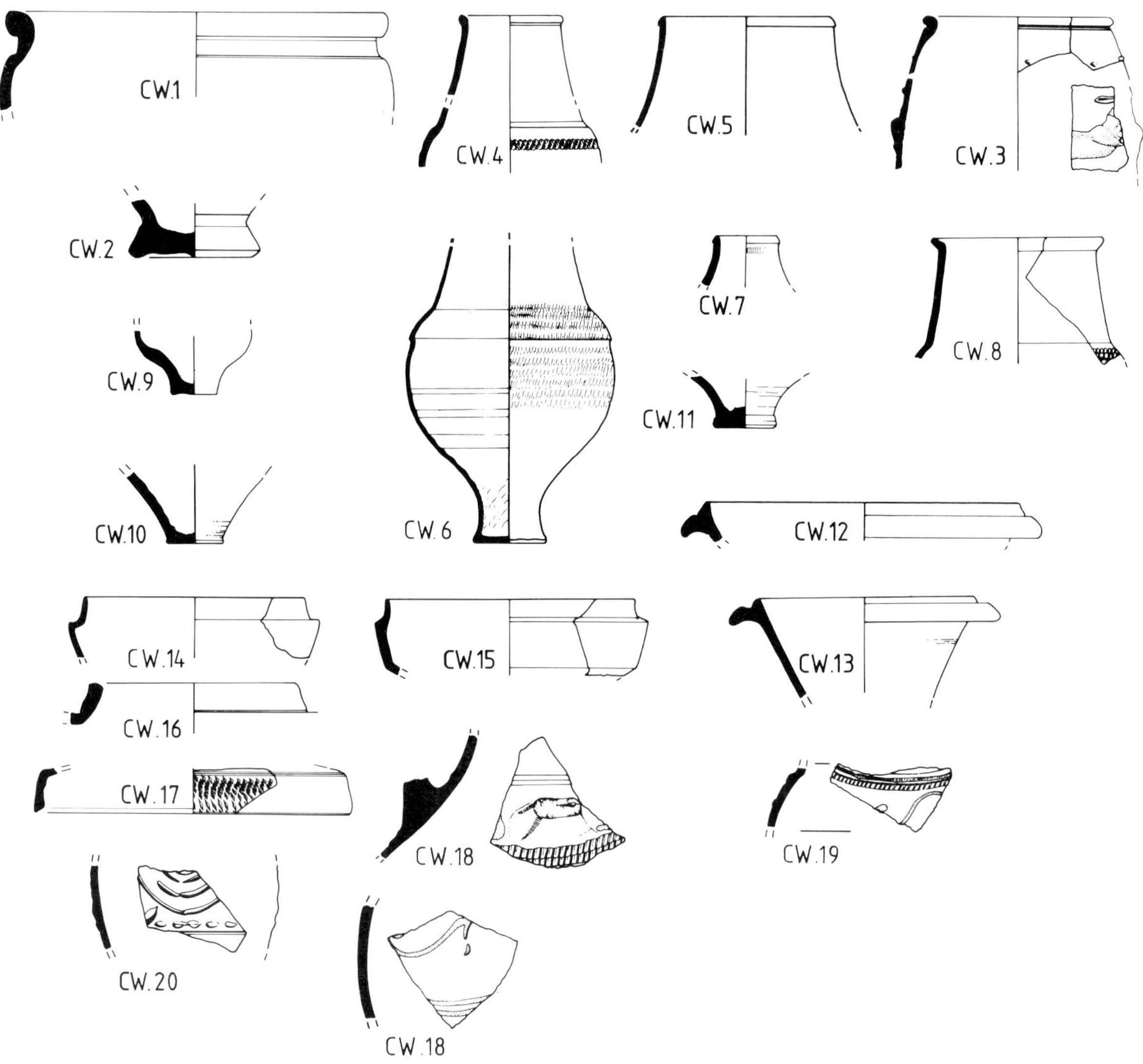

Figure 43 Roman coarse pottery, types CW.1–CW.20 (1/4 scale)

List of illustration numbers and the fabric groups to which the illustrated pots belong.

R.1, 2; R.2, 1; R.3, 1; R.4, 2; R.5, 2; R.6, 2; R.7, 2; R.8, 2; R.9, 2; R.10, 2; R.11, 1; R.12, 1; R.13, 1; R.14, 1; R.15, 1; R.16, 1; R.17, 1; R.18, 1; R.19, 1; R.20, 1; R.21, 1; R.22, 1; R.23, 2; R.24, 2; R.25, 7; R.26, 2; R.27, 1; R.28, 1; R.29, 1; R.30, 1; R.31, 1; R.32, 2; R.33, 2; R.34, 2; R.35, 2; R.36, 3; R.37, 3; R.38, 4; R.39, 4; R.40, 4; R.41, 3; R.42, 6; R.43, 6; R.44, 8; R.45, 8; R.46, 8; R.47, 8; R.48, 8; R.49, 8; R.50, 8; R.51, 7; R.52, 7; R.53, 7; R.54, 7; R.55, 7; R.56, 7; R.57, 7; R.58, 7; R.59, 7; R.60, 7; R.61, 7; R.62, 7; R.63, 7; R.64, 7; R.65, 7; R.66, 7; R.67, 7; R.68, 7; R.69, 3; R.70, 3; R.71, 3; R.72, 3; R.73, 3; R.74, 3; R.75, 3; R.76, 3; R.77, 3; R.78, 3; R.79, 3; R.80, 3; R.81, 3; R.82, 3; R.83, 3; R.84, 3; R.85, 3; R.86, 3; R.87, 3; R.88, 3; R.89, 3; R.90, 3; R.91, 3; R.92, 3; R.93, 3; R.94, 3; R.95, 3; R.96, 4; R.97, 4; R.98, 4; R.99, 4; R.100, 4; R.101, 4; R.102, 4; R.103, 6; R.104, 6; R.105, 6; R.106, 6; R.107, 6; R.108, 6; R.109, 6; R.110, 6; R.111, 6; R.112, 6; R.113, 2; R.114, 2; R.115, 1; R.116, 1; R.117, 1; R.118, 1; R.119, 1; R.120, 1; R.121, 1; R.122, 1; R.123, 1; R.124, 1; R.125, 1; R.126, 1; R.127, 1; R.128, 1; R.129, 1; R.130, 1; R.131, 1; R.132, 1; R.133, 1; R.134, 1; R.135, 1; R.136, 1; R.137, 1; R.138, 1; R.139, 1; R.140, 1; R.141, 1; R.142, 1; R.143, 1; R.144, 1; R.145, 1; R.146, 1; R.147, 1; R.148, 1; R.149, 1; R.150, 1; R.151, 2; R.152, 2; R.153, 2; R.154, 2; R.155, 2; R.156, 2; R.157, 2; R.158, 2; R.159, 2; R.160, 2; R.161, 2; R.162, 2; R.163, 2; R.164, 1; R.165, 2; R.166, 2; R.167, 2; R.168, 2; R.169, 2; R.170, 2; R.171, 2; R.172, 2; R.173, 1; R.174, 1; R.175, 1; R.176, 1; R.177, 1; R.178, 1; R.179, 1; R.180, 1; R.181, 1; R.182, 1; R.183, 1; R.184, 1; R.185, 1; R.186, 1; R.187, 1; R.188, 1; R.189, 1; R.190, 1; R.191, 1; R.192, 1; R.193, 1; R.194, 1; R.195, 1; R.196, 1; R.197, 1; R.198, 1; R.199, 1; R.200, 1; R.201, 1; R.202, 1; R.203, 1; R.204, 1; R.205, 1; R.206, 1; R.207, 1; R.208, 1; R.209, 1; R.210, 1; R.211, 1; R.212, 1; R.213, 1; R.214, 1; R.215, 1; R.216, 1; R.217, 1; R.218, 1; R.219, 1; R.220, 1; R.221, 2; R.222, 2; R.223, 2; R.224, 10; R.225, 10; R.226, 10; R.227, 10; R.228, 2; R.229, 2; R.230, 1; R.231, 1; R.232, 1; R.233, 1; R.234, 1; R.235, 1; R.236, 1; R.237, 1; R.238, 1; R.239, 1; R.240, 1; R.241, 2; R.242, 2; R.243, 2; R.244, 2; R.245, 1; R.246, 1; R.247, 1; R.248, 1; R.249, 1; R.250, 1; R.251, 1; R.252, 1; R.253, 2; R.254, 1; R.255, 1; R.256, 1; R.257, 1; R.258, 1; R.259, 1; R.260, 1; R.261, 1; R.262, 1; R.263, 1; R.264, 1; R.265, 1; R.266, 1; R.267, 1; R.268, 1; R.269, 2; R.270, 2; R.271, 1; R.272, 2; R.273, 2; R.274, 2; R.275, 2; R.276, 2; R.277, 2; R.278, 10; R.279, 2; R.280, 1; R.281, 1; R.282, 1; R.283, 2; R.284, 2; R.285, 2; R.286, 2; R.287, 2; R.288, 2; R.289, 2; R.290, 2; R.291, 10; R.292, 1; R.293, 1; R.294, 1; R.295, 1; R.296, 1; R.297, 2; R.298, 2; R.299, 1; R.300, 1; R.301, 2; R.302, 10; R.303, 2; R.304, 1; R.305, 2; R.306, 10; R.307, 1; R.308, 1; R.309, 1; R.310, 1; R.311, 2; R.312, 2; R.313, 2; R.314, 2; R.315, 10; R.316, 10; R.317, 10; R.318, 10; R.319, 10; R.320, 1; R.321, 10; R.322, 1; R.323, 1; R.324, 1; R.325, 1; R.326, 1; R.327, 2; R.328, 2; R.329, 1; R.330, 1; R.331, 2; R.332, 1; R.333, 1; R.334, 1; R.335, 1; R.336, 1; R.337, 2; R.338, 10; R.339, 10; R.340, 10; R.341, 10; R.342, 10; R.343, 1; R.344, 1; R.345, 1; R.346, 1; R.347, 1; R.348, 2; R.349, 2; R.350, 1; R.351, 10; R.352, 1; R.353, 1; R.354, 2; R.355, 2; R.356, 1; R.357, 2; R.358, 1; R.359, 1; R.360, 1; R.361, 1; R.362, 1; R.363, 1; R.364, 1; R.365, 1; R.366, 1; R.367, 1; R.368, 1; R.369, 1; R.370, 1; R.371, 1; R.372, 1; R.373, 1; R.374, 1; R.375, 1; R.376, 2; R.377, 1; R.378, 1; R.379, 1; R.380, 6; R.381, 2; R.382,

1; R.383, 1; R.384, 1; R.385, 1; R.386, 3; R.387, 3; R.388, 3; R.389, 3; R.390, 3; R.391, 3; R.392, 3; R.393, 3; R.394, 2; R.395, 1; R.396, 1; R.397, 1; R.398, 1; R.399, 2; R.400, 2; R.401, 2; R.402, 2; R.403, 2; R.404, 2; R.405, 2; R.406, 1; R.407, 1; R.408, 1; R.409, 1; R.410, 1; R.411, 1; R.412, 1; R.413, 1; R.414, 1; R.415, 1; R.416, 1; R.417, 1; R.418, 1; R.419, 2; R.420, 2; R.421, 2; R.422, 1; R.423, 1; R.424, 2; R.425, 2; R.426, 10; R.427, 10; R.428, 1; R.429, 1; R.430, 1; R.431, 1; R.432, 1; R.433, 1; R.434, 1; R.435, 6; R.436, 6; R.437, 6; R.438, 2; R.439, 2; R.440, 1; R.441, 1; R.442, 1; R.443, 1; R.444, 2; R.445, 1; R.446, 1; R.447, 2; R.448, 2; R.449, 1; R.450, 7; R.451, 2; R.452, 1; R.453, 1; R.454, 1; R.455, 2; R.456, 2; R.457, 2; R.458, 1; R.459, 1; R.460, 1; R.461, 1; R.462, 2; R.463, 10; R.464, 10; R.465, 1; R.466, 1; R.467, 1; R.468, 1; R.469, 1; R.470, 1; R.471, 1; R.472, 1; R.473, 1; R.474, 1; R.475, 1; R.476, 1; R.477, 1; R.478, 1; R.479, 1; R.480, 3; R.481, 3; R.482, 1; R.483, 8; R.484, 1; R.485, 1; R.486, 1; R.487, 1; R.488, 1; R.489, 2;

B.1, 12; B.2, 12; B.3, 12; B.4, 12; B.5, 12; B.6, 12; B.7, 12; B.8, 12; B.9, 12; B.10, 12; B.11, 12; B.12, 12; B.13, 12; B.14, 12; B.15, 12; B.16, 12; B.17, 12; B.18, 12; B.19, 12; B.20, 12; B.21, 12; B.22, 12; B.23, 12; B.24, 12; B.25, 12; B.26, 12; B.27, 12; B.28, 12; B.29, 12; B.30, 12; B.31, 12; B.32, 12; B.33, 12; B.34, 12; B.35, 12; B.36, 12; B.37, 12; B.38, 12; B.39, 12; B.40, 12; B.41, 12; B.42, 12; B.43, 12; B.44, 12; B.45, 12; B.46, 12; B.47, 12; B.48, 12; B.49, 12; B.50, 12; B.51, 12; B.52, 12; B.53, 12; B.54, 12; B.55, 12; B.56, 12; B.57, 12; B.58, 12; B.59, 12; B.60, 12; B.61, 12; B.62, 12; B.63, 12; B.64, 12; B.65, 12; B.66, 12; B.67, 12; B.68, 12; B.69, 12; B.70, 12; B.71, 12; B.72, 12; B.73, 12; B.74, 12; B.75, 12;

O.1, 7; O.2, 5; O.3, 5; O.4, 5; O.5, 5; O.6, 5; O.7, 5; O.8, 5; O.9, 5; O.10, 1; O.11, 1; O.12, 1; O.13, 1; O.14, 1; O.15, 1; O.16, 1; O.17, 1; O.18, 1; O.19, 1; O.20, 1; O.21, 5; O.22, 5; O.23, 5; O.24, 5; O.25, 1; O.26, 1; O.27, 1; O.28, 1; O.29, 1; O.30, 1; O.31, 1; O.32, 1; O.33, 1; O.34, 5; O.35, 2; O.36, 2; O.37, 11; O.38, 11; O.39, 11; O.40, 1; O.41, 1; O.42, 1; O.43, 7; O.44, 5; O.45, 5; O.46, 1; O.47, 7; O.48, 7; O.49, 7; O.50, 7; O.51, 5; O.52, 5; O.53, 5; O.54, 5; O.55, 5; O.56, 5; O.57, 5; O.58, 5; O.59, 5; O.60, 5; O.61, 5; O.62, 5; O.63, 1; O.64, 1; O.65, 1; O.66, 1; O.67, 1; O.68, 1; O.69, 1; O.70, 1; O.71, 1; O.72, 1; O.73, 1; O.74, 2; O.75, 2; O.76, 1; O.77, 11; O.78, 11; O.79, 1; O.80, 1; O.81, 1; O.82, 2; O.83, 7; O.84, 7; O.85, 7; O.86, 7; O.87, 7; O.88, 7; O.89, 7; O.90, 7; O.91, 7; O.92, 7; O.93, 7; O.94, 7; O.95, 7; O.96, 7; O.97, 7; O.98, 7; O.99, 7; O.100, 7; O.101, 7; O.102, 7; O.103, 7; O.104, 7; O.105, 7; O.106, 7; O.107, 7; O.108, 7; O.109, 7; O.110, 7; O.111, 7; O.112, 7; O.113, 7; O.114, 7; O.115, 7; O.116, 7; O.117, 7; O.118, 7; O.119, 5; O.120, 5; O.121, 5; O.122, 5; O.123, 5; O.124, 5; O.125, 1; O.126, 1; O.127, 1; O.128, 1; O.129, 1; O.130, 5; O.131, 5; O.132, 5; O.133, 5; O.134, 5; O.135, 5; O.136, 1; O.137, 1; O.138, 1; O.139, 1; O.140, 1; O.141, 1; O.142, 5; O.143, 5; O.144, 5; O.145, 5; O.146, 5; O.147, 5; O.148, 1; O.149, 1; O.150, 5; O.151, 5; O.152, 2; O.153, 1; O.154, 1; O.155, 2; O.156, 11; O.157, 1; O.158, 2; O.159, 1; O.160, 1; O.161, 5; O.162, 5; O.163, 5; O.164, 1; O.165, 1; O.166, 1; O.167, 1; O.168, 1; O.169, 1; O.170, 1; O.171, 1; O.172, 11; O.173, 11; O.174, 11; O.175, 1; O.176, 1; O.177, 5; O.178, 5; O.179, 5; O.180, 5; O.181, 5; O.182, 1; O.183, 1; O.184, 1; O.185, 1; O.186, 1; O.187, 1; O.188, 1; O.189, 1; O.190, 1; O.191, 1; O.192, 1; O.193, 11; O.194, 11; O.195, 2; O.196, 2; O.197, 5; O.198, 5; O.199, 5; O.200, 5; O.201, 1; O.202, 1; O.203, 1; O.204, 1; O.205, 1; O.206, 1; O.207, 1; O.208, 1; O.209, 1; O.210, 2; O.211, 7; O.212, 7; O.213, 5; O.214, 5; O.215, 1; O.216, 1; O.217, 2; O.218, 2; O.219, 2; O.220, 2; O.221, 2; O.222, 2; O.223, 2; O.224, 2; O.225, 1; O.226, 1; O.227, 2; O.228, 2; O.229, 1; O.230, 1; O.231, 1; O.232, 1; O.233, 1; O.234, 1; O.235, 1; O.236, 2; O.237, 5; O.238, 5; O.239, 1; O.240, 11; O.241, 1; O.242, 1; O.243, 1; O.244, 1; O.245, 7; O.246, 7; O.247, 7; O.248, 5; O.249, 1; O.250, 2; O.251, 2; O.252, 1; O.253, 7; O.254, 5; O.255, 1; O.256, 2; O.257, 1; O.258, 5; O.259, 11; O.260, 11; O.261, 7; O.262, 7; O.263, 7; O.264, 5; O.265, 5; O.266, 5; O.267, 5; O.268, 5; O.269, 5; O.270, 5; O.271, 5; O.272, 1; O.273, 1; O.274, 1; O.275, 1; O.276, 1; O.277, 1; O.278, 1; O.279, 1; O.280, 1; O.281, 1; O.282, 1; O.283, 1; O.284, 1; O.285, 1; O.286, 2; O.287, 11; O.288, 1; O.289, 1; O.290, 1; O.291, 2; O.292, 2; O.293, 1; O.294, 7; O.295, 7; O.296, 7; O.297, 5; O.298, 5; O.299, 5; O.300, 5; O.301, 5; O.302, 5; O.303, 5; O.304, 5; O.305, 5; O.306, 5; O.307, 1; O.308, 1; O.309, 1; O.310, 1; O.311, 1; O.312, 1; O.313, 1; O.314, 2; O.315, 2; O.316, 1; O.317, 1; O.318, 1; O.319, 2; O.320, 1; O.321, 7; O.322, 5; O.323, 1; O.324, 1; O.325, 1; O.326, 1; O.327, 1; O.328, 1; O.329, 1; O.330, 1; O.331, 1; O.332, 2; O.333, 1; O.334, 1; O.335, 1; O.336, 1; O.337, 1; O.338, 1; O.339, 1; O.340, 7; O.341, 5; O.342, 1; O.343, 1; O.344, 1; O.345, 7; O.346, 7; O.347, 5; O.348, 5; O.349, 5; O.350, 5; O.351, 5; O.352, 5; O.353, 5; O.354, 1; O.355, 1; O.356, 2; O.357, 5; O.358, 5; O.359, 5; O.360, 5; O.361, 5; O.362, 5; O.363, 2; O.364, 7; O.365, 5; O.366, 5; O.367, 5; O.368, 5; O.369, 5; O.370, 5; O.371, 5; O.372, 5; O.373, 5; O.374, 5; O.375, 5; O.376, 1; O.377, 1; O.378, 1; O.379, 2; O.380, 5; O.381, 5; O.382, 1; O.383, 1; O.384, 1; O.385, 2; O.386, 1; O.387, 1; O.388, 7; O.389, 7; O.390, 2; O.391, 2; O.392, 1; O.393, 1; O.394, 11; O.395, 1; O.396, 5; O.397, 5; O.398, 5; O.399, 11; O.400, 1; O.401, 1; O.402, 2; O.403, 11; O.404, 2; O.405, 5; O.406, 1; O.407, 1; O.408, 2; O.409, 1; O.410, 11; O.411, 11; O.412, 11; O.413, 11; O.414, 11; O.415, 11; O.416, 11; O.417, 11; O.418, 11; O.419, 11; O.420, 11; O.421, 11; O.422, 11; O.423, 11; O.424, 11; O.425, 11; O.426, 7; O.427, 7; O.428, 5; O.429, 1; O.430, 1; O.431, 1; O.432, 2; O.433, 1; O.434, 11; O.435, 11; O.436, 5; O.437, 1; O.438, 1; O.439, 11; O.440, 1; O.441, 1; O.442, 1; O.443, 1; O.444, 2; O.445, 7; O.446, 7; O.447, 5; O.448, 1; O.449, 11; O.450, 2; O.451, 5; O.452, 1; O.453, 5; O.454, 1; O.455, 7; O.456, 5; O.457, 2; O.458, 2; O.459, 1; O.460, 1; O.461, 11;

C.1, 20; C.2, 20; C.3, 18; C.4, 18; C.5, 18; C.6, 18; C.7, 18; C.8, 9; C.9, 9; C.10, 18; C.11, 18; C.12, 13; C.13, 13; C.14, 13; C.15, 13; C.16, 13; C.17, 13; C.18, 13; C.19, 13; C.20, 13; C.21, 13; C.22, 16; C.23, 16; C.24, 14; C.25, 14; C.26, 14; C.27, 14; C.28, 14; C.29, 9; C.30, 18; C.31, 18; C.32, 18; C.33, 18; C.34, 20; C.35, 20; C.36, 20; C.37, 20; C.38, 18; C.39, 18; C.40, 18; C.41, 9; C.42, 9; C.43, 14; C.44, 14; C.45, 18; C.46, 18; C.47, 18; C.48, 18; C.49, 18; C.50, 18; C.51, 18; C.52, 18; C.53, 18; C.54, 18; C.55, 18; C.56, 18; C.57, 18; C.58, 18; C.59, 18; C.60, 18; C.61, 18; C.62, 18; C.63, 18; C.64, 18; C.65, 20; C.66, 20; C.67, 9; C.68, 18; C.69, 18; C.70, 20; C.71, 20; C.72, 18; C.73, 18; C.74, 18?; C.75, 9; C.76, 9; C.77, 9;

W.1, 1a; W.2, 19; W.3, 19; W.4, 19; W.5, 1a; W.6, 1a; W.7, 1a; W.8, 19; W.9, 19; W.10, 19; W.11, 19; W.12, 1a; W.13, 1a; W.14, 19; W.15, 19; W.16, 1a; W.17, 19; W.18, 19; W.19, 19; W.20, 19; W.21, 19; W.22, 19; W.23, 19; W.24, 1a; W.25, 1a; W.26, 19; W.27, 19; W.28, 19; W.29, 19; W.30, 19; W.31, 19; W.32, 19; W.33, 19; W.34, 19; W.35, 19; W.36, 19; W.37, 19; W.38, 19; W.39, 19; W.40, 19; W.41, 19; W.42, 19; W.43, 1a; W.44, 1a; W.45, 1a; W.46, 1a; W.47, 19; W.48, 19; W.49, 19; W.50, 19;

CW.1, 17; CW.2, 17; CW.3, 17; CW.4, 17; CW.5, 17; CW.6, 17; CW.7, 17; CW.8, 17; CW.9, 17; CW.10, 17; CW.11, 17; CW.12, 17; CW.13, 17; CW.14, 17; CW.15, 17; CW.16, 17; CW.17, 17; CW.18, 17; CW.19, 17; CW.20, 15;

Samian ware

B R Hartley, Hedley Pengelly, and Brenda Dickinson

The areas involved in these excavations produced large quantities of samian, most of which comes from either La Graufesenque or Lezoux. Some East Gaulish ware is present, but in a lower proportion than for Britain in general, though the result is not abnormal for Midland sites. There are two vessels from Banassac and one example of 2nd-century Montans ware. There is also a stamped dish in 1st-century Lezoux ware.

The histogram, fig 44, based on the average annual loss of stamped plain ware and moulded bowls with identifiable decoration, shows that small amounts of samian were in use at Alcester in the pre-Flavian period, and suggests that the initial occupation of the areas dug in 1964–6 took place in the early 60s of the 1st century. By *c* AD 75–80, samian was prolific on the site, but its use seems to have declined gradually from *c* AD 80 to a trough in the period *c* AD 90–125. The maximum use of samian here was in the period *c* AD 150–65, after which it gradually declined again, so that by *c* AD 180 the quantities being discarded were not much greater than in the early years of the occupation of the site.

The drop in supply in the Trajanic period presents no particular problems. Many British sites with continuous occupation in the 1st and 2nd centuries show a reduction in the level of samian in the early 2nd century which cannot be explained by historical evidence, and must surely be related to a temporary scarcity of samian. The main exporter at this time was Les Martres-de-Veyre, whose output seems to have been relatively modest, compared with those of La Graufesenque and Lezoux.

No such argument can be used to explain the decline in the use of samian at Alcester in the later Antonine period. Lezoux was still producing on a

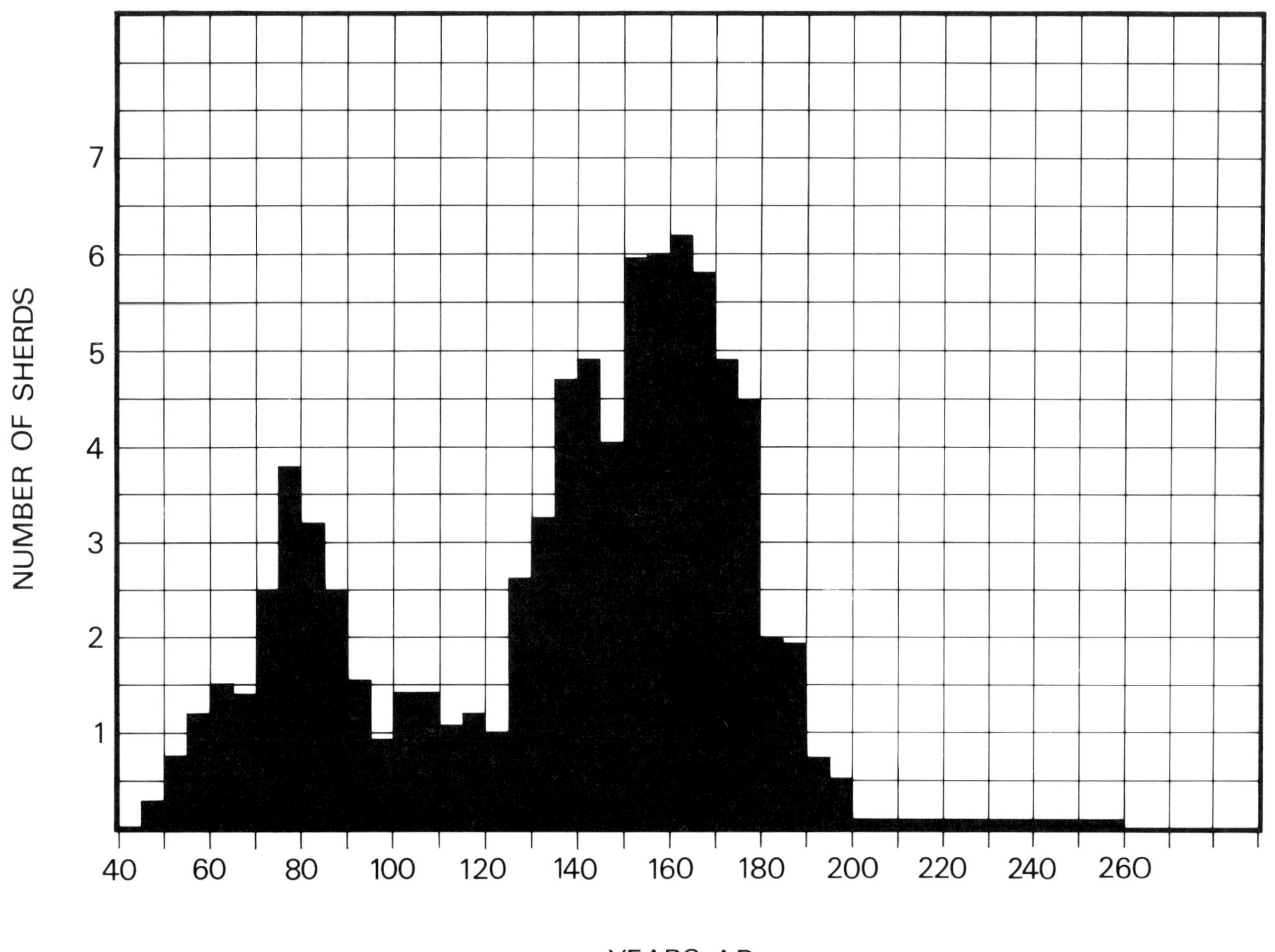

Figure 44 Histogram representing average annual losses of decorated samian and stamped plain ware

massive scale and was exporting large quantities of samian to Britain, as evidenced by the finds from northern forts reoccupied *c* AD 160. The supply of samian to Alcester begins to drop again by *c* AD 165, according to the histogram. However, other evidence suggests that a peak may have been reached in the 150s. The stumbling-block is the uncertain closing dates for potters such as Cerialis ii and Paullus iv, collectively known as the Cerialis ii-Cinnamus ii group. In the absence of such evidence, a range *c* AD 135–70 has been allowed, although it is more likely that most of the group had ceased production by *c* AD 160. The argument for this is based on the comparative proportions of these potters' decorated bowls from Scotland and the Hadrian's Wall system (Hartley 1972b, 33). Furthermore, the number of decorated bowls from Alcester assignable to other potters who were not at work after *c* AD 160 is 67, against 45 by potters who were not producing before this date. The proportion of bowls by Cinnamus ii to those of Paternus v is also striking, 50 to 8. In view of this, one wonders whether the large group of samian from the pit D II 29A (discussed on pp 106–7), dated by us *c* AD 150–60, is due to something more than an accidental breakage in one pottery store.

The evidence of the samian, therefore, suggests that after *c* AD 170, occupation continued on a much reduced scale in these particular areas of the town. It is equally clear, however, that it did not cease entirely, since some of the East Gaulish decorated ware cannot have arrived at Alcester before *c* AD 175. It is by no means certain that samian was in use here in the 3rd century. Rheinzabern ware is notoriously difficult to date closely, but the potters represented by decorated bowls all began work in the 2nd century, though some of them may have continued into the 3rd century. No samian is likely to have reached the excavated areas after *c* AD 220 at the latest.

Decorated ware (figs 45–53)

This comprises the latest samian vessels in the contexts concerned and/or any pieces of intrinsic interest, illustrated where appropriate in figs 45–53. The phase and phase date, where known, are entered in parentheses after the context number. (Additional datable samian from phased contexts is listed in table M8.)

Site A

1 (A V 4, phase VIII, early to mid-4th century) See A V 7.
2 (A V 7, with A V 4, 10) Five fragments, two joining, of form 37, Central Gaulish. The bowl seems to have been removed from the mould while the clay was still plastic, and the decoration is badly distorted. It varies enormously in thickness and the rim is not horizontal. The surviving traces of ovolo (Rogers B231) suggest some connection with Cinnamus ii, but the workmanship is so poor that the bowl is more likely to be by one of his less-experienced workmen. *c* AD 150–80.
3 (A VII 9) Form 37, Central Gaulish. The ovolo (Rogers B12) and bird (O.2298) are on a signed bowl of Criciro v from Cardurnock (S & S 1958, pl 117, 2). *c* AD 135–170.
4 (A IX 1A) See A IX 21.
5 (A IX 1C) Form 37, East Gaulish. The arcades (Ricken & Fischer 1963, KB112) and small rosette between them (041) were both used at Rheinzabern by Cerialis v (Ricken 1948, Taf 42–69). *c* AD 160–90.
6 (A IX 10) See A V 7.
7 (A IX 11) Form 37, with Cinnamus ii's ovolo 2 (Rogers B231). *c* AD 150–80.
8 (A IX 13, phase IV, later 3rd century on) See D I 109.
9 (A IX 21, with A IX 1A) Form 30, Central Gaulish. A bowl with panels:
1) A figure to right.
2) A seated Cupid (D.260) and D-monogram.
3) Dolphins on a basket (Rogers Q59).
4) An athlete (D.394), cornucopia (Rogers U246) and rosette (S & S 1958, fig 44, 5).
All the details were used at Lezoux by Do(v)eccus i. *c* AD 165–200, cf A XVI 7.
10 (A IX 25, phase VI, late 3rd to early 4th century) Form 37, East Gaulish. The figure-type is probably a Minerva (Ricken & Fischer 1963, M29A?), used at Rheinzabern in the late 2nd century.
11 (A IX 29, phase VI, late 3rd to early 4th century) Form 37, Central Gaulish, in the style of Tetturo of Lezoux. For the ovolo see S & S 1958, pl 131, 1 which also has an impression of the vine-scroll of which part occurs on this piece. *c* AD 135–65.
12 (A XI 14) Form 37, in the style of Tetturo of Lezoux. The wavy-line borders and rosette at the panel junctions are characteristic of his style, as is the leafy festoon which occurs on a bowl from Corbridge. The hare to left is perhaps O.2132. *c* AD 135–65.
13 (A XII 17?, in a bag marked A XII 17 on one side and AA II 69 on the other) Form 37, with an ovolo used at Lezoux by potters such as Sacer i and Criciro v (Rogers B12). *c* AD 130–60.
14 (A XVI 2) Form 37, in the style of Butrio or Ianuaris ii of Lezoux, with a seated figure (D.555). *c* AD 125–45.
15 (A XVI 6) Form 37, Central Gaulish. The scroll includes a seated figure (D.55) and a rosette (Rogers C227?) in the lower concavity and a tier of cups (Rogers Q77, upside-down) in the upper concavity. All the details were used at Lezoux by both Butrio and Ianuaris ii. Cf S & S 1958, pl 119, 5, 11, 57, 655; 59, 666, 672. *c* AD 125–45.
16 (A XVI 7) Form 30, stamped DOIICCI by Do(v)eccus i of Lezoux (see stamp no 25). The decoration includes ovolo Rogers B161 and a kneeling figure (D.394). Perhaps from the same bowl as A IX 21. *c* AD 165–200.
17 (A XVI 14) Form 37, Central Gaulish, with Cinnamus ii's ovolo 2 (Rogers B231). *c* AD 150–80.
18 (A XVI 26?, sherd marked A XVI 76, though in a bag apparently marked A XVI 26) Form 37, with T-tongued ovolo used at Lezoux by the Quintilianus i and Paternus v groups (Rogers B206). The fabric suggests Paternus, or an associate. *c* AD 150–90.
19 (A XVIIB 2) Form 37, Central Gaulish. The ovolo (Rogers B32) and boar (D.826) occur on a bowl in the style of Stanfield & Simpson's X-6 (S & S 1958, pl 75). *c* AD 125–50.
20 (A XVIIB 3) Form 37, Central Gaulish. The main zone of decoration consists of repeated small vine-scrolls (Rogers M8). The basal wreath of chevrons suggests the work of X-6 (S & S 1958, pl 75, 15), and he is known to have used the scroll. *c* AD 125–50.
21 (A XVIIB 4) i) Form 37, Central Gaulish. The ovolo (Rogers B231) and spirals occur on bowls almost certainly by Cinnamus ii, but not in one of his standard styles. The chevron and ovolo are on a bowl from Little Chester (Hartley 1961b, 97, no 20). The trifid motif (close to Rogers G8, but not exactly the same) appears on bowls more closely related to the Paternus v group. This will be one of the earlier styles used by Cinnamus. *c* AD 140–60.
22 (A XVIIB 4) ii) Form 37, Central Gaulish, with ovolo 1 of Cinnamus (Rogers B223). *c* AD 150–80.
23 (A XVIIB 4) iii) Form 37, Central Gaulish, with unusual, inverted festoons (Rogers F11) at the bottom of the decoration. One probably contains a bird to the right. Hadrianic or early Antonine.
24 (A XVIIB 11) See A XVIIB 12.
25 (A XVIIB 12, with A XVIIB 11) Three fragments of form 37, Central Gaulish. The decoration includes a gladiator (a smaller version of O.1002), pygmy (D.437a), lioness, etc to left (a large version of D.805) and cushion motifs. The ovolo is perhaps Rogers B230. The gladiator is on bowls from London (S & S 1958, pl 154, 19) and Chester, both of which suggest some connection with Pugnus ii or one of his associates. Hadrianic–Antonine.
26 (AA I 11, phase IX, mid-4th century) Form 37, Central Gaulish. The ovolo is perhaps Rogers B70. Almost certainly Antonine.
27 (AA I 17, phase VI, late 3rd to early 4th century) i) (with AA I 18, 30, 66; AA II 2, 8). Ten fragments, some joining, one burnt and

with a rivet-hole, from a bowl of form 37 assignable to Birrantus of Lezoux. The ovolo (Rogers B108) is his commonest one, and the rows of fine beads and the frequent use of astragali as space-fillers are characteristic of his bowls. The surviving pieces allow an almost complete reconstruction of the design.

1) A divided panel with a festoon (Rogers F42) containing a lion (D.765 bis) above and a hare to right (O.2057) below, over two large rings.

2) Horseman (D.157) over repeated impressions of a serpent on a rock (a variant of D.960 bis).

3) Mercury (D.289A). All these types except for the horseman have been recorded previously on bowls from Birrantus's stamped moulds, or in his style. His work occurs at Lezoux in association with the wares of Austrus, Butrio and other primarily Hadrianic potters. A date *c* AD 125–45 would fit this evidence. His work is not very common in Britain.

27A (AA I 17, phase VI, late 3rd to early 4th century) ii) Form 37, Central Gaulish, with Cinnamus ii's ovolo 2 (Rogers B231) and a horseman (D.157). Possibly from the same bowl as AA I 27, which has the same figure-type. *c* AD 150–80.

28 (AA I 18, phase VII, late 3rd to early 4th century) See AA I 17, i. NB This sherd is marked AA I 18, but comes from a bag marked AA I 17.

29 (AA I 29, phase IX, mid-4th century) i) Form 37, stamped [CI]NNAM[I] retrograde (Cinnamus ii, Die 5b; stamp no 18). A narrow panel contains the stamp, flanked by partly impressed leaves (Rogers H101). The adjacent panel has a double medallion with a sea-cow (D.29). *c* AD 150–80. Cf AA II 25.

29A (AA I 29, phase IX, mid-4th century) ii) Form 37, with an ovolo (Rogers B12) used at Lezoux by Sacer i, Criciro v and rarely, Cinnamus ii. The panels include:

1) A single festoon with an acanthus (one of the series Rogers K10–12).

2) Chevron medallion (Rogers E21), containing a partly impressed animal to right, with its hind-quarters masked by the same acanthus as in panel 1. The animal may be the bear D.808. This bowl is most likely to be by Cinnamus, though he only used the medallion and ovolo occasionally. Partly impressed animals appear on three bowls in his style from Lauriacum (Karnitsch 1955, Taf 5, 1; 6, 1–2). *c* AD 150–80.

30 (AA I 30, phase VI, late 3rd to early 4th century) i) Two joining fragments of form 37, Central Gaulish. The single-bordered ovolo (Rogers B12) was used by several Lezoux potters and appears occasionally, as here, on bowls of Cinnamus ii. The panels include:

1) A single festoon, containing an acanthus (Rogers K12), over an unidentified, perhaps trifid, motif, impressed sideways.

2) A chevron medallion (Rogers E21), containing a hare (O.1588), partly impressed and with its hind-quarters masked by an acanthus (as in 1). The use of partly impressed animals is common on Cinnamus bowls. He used the ovolo and festoon less often; they occur on a bowl from Corbridge with his large label stamp, CINNAMI retrograde. *c* AD 150–65.

30A (AA I 30, phase VI, late 3rd to early 4th century) ii) See AA I 17.

31 (AA I 42, phase V, later 3rd century on) Form 37, Central Gaulish, with the same decorative elements as F I 50b.

32 (AA I 62, phase II, late 2nd to mid-3rd century) Form 29, South Gaulish. Part of the lower zone, with a conventional tree in a medallion. This style is common at La Graufesenque in the pre-Flavian period, and the fabric of this piece would fit such a date.

33 (AA I 66, phase VI, late 3rd to early 4th century) See AA I 17.

34 (AA I 74) Form 37, East Gaulish. The ovolo (Ricken & Fischer 1963, E26), small bird (T250), bear (T54A) and festoon (KB136) were all used at Rheinzabern by several potters. The closest parallel, in general style, is with the work of Ricken's B- F- Attoni (1948, Taf 35ff).

35 (AA II 2) See AA I 17.

36 (AA II 8) i) Form 37, in the fabric of Les Martres-de-Veyre. Traces of a sharp, zig-zag line suggest the work of Igocatus (X-4). *c* AD 100–30.

36A (AA II 8) ii) See AA I 17.

37 (AA II 8A) Form 30, Central Gaulish. The ovolo (Rogers B52) occurs on bowls by Criciro v and Divixtus i. The surviving decoration consists of a narrow panel between two wider ones, both containing medallions. This narrow panel has a mask (D.696), impressed sideways over a trophy-like motif (Rogers Q10). The top of the motif is impressed behind a caryatid on stamped Divixtus bowls from Carlisle and Leicester (S & S 1958, pl 116, 8) and the mask on its side is on a stamped bowl from London (14). This bowl is more likely to be by Divixtus than Criciro, in view of the rosette junction-mask. *c* AD 150–80. Probably from the same bowl as AA III 41.

38 (AA II 13, phase III, 3rd century) Fragments of a burnt Central Gaulish bowl of form 37, with a freestyle scene including a lion (O. 1450) and lioness (D.793?). Antonine. Cf 13A.

39 (AA II 13A) Form 37, possibly an unburnt part of the same bowl as 13. The ovolo has been almost completely obliterated by careless workmanship and the figure-types are badly blurred. They include a lion (O.1450), sea-horse (D.35?), bear (D.808?), and warrior (D.125). There is also an acanthus. In view of the state of the ovolo, it is impossible to say who is responsible for this bowl, but it is likely to be later than *c* AD 160.

40 (AA II 16, phase V, later 3rd century on) i) Form 37, Central Gaulish, with bead-rows above and below the ovolo. This is probably one of the ovolos of Attianus ii of Lezoux. *c* AD 125–45.

41 (AA II 16, phase V, later 3rd century on) ii) A small fragment of form 37, Central Gaulish. The ring-terminals at the bottom of the bead-rows suggest the work of Criciro v of Lezoux. Cf S & S 1958, pl 117, 4, which has the same mask and caryatid (D.656). *c* AD 135–65.

42 (AA II 25) Form 37, Central Gaulish. One panel contains a festoon with a sea-cow (D.29). The rosette used as a space-filler in the corner of the adjacent panel is unusual for Cinnamus ii, but he used the sea-cow and the ovolo (Rogers B223). Almost certainly from the stamped Cinnamus bowl in AA I 29. *c* AD 150–80.

43 (AA II 28, phase V, later 3rd century on) i) Form 29, a weathered fragment from one of the comparatively rare Central Gaulish bowls of this form. The upper zone has panels divided by a wavy line, but only a cockerel (D.1025) survives. The lower zone is very blurred, but seems to have small, double medallions containing plain rings, with a bird used as a space-filler between them. Hadrianic.

44 (AA II 28, phase V, later 3rd century on) ii) (with AA II 87). Fragments from the bottom of a panelled bowl of form 37, in the style of one of the Cerialis ii-Cinnamus ii group at Lezoux. The decoration includes:

1) A vine-scroll (Rogers M31) and lozenge (Rogers U36).

2) A leopard (D.797). *c* AD 135–70.

45 (AA II 28, phase V, later 3rd century on) iii) Form 37, Central Gaulish. Three joining fragments, giving a substantial part of the base and lower decoration of a small bowl in the style of Cinnamus ii. Three panels, repeated four times, have:

1) A mask (D.675).

2) A small medallion.

3) A standing figure.

The foot-ring is unworn. *c* AD 150–80.

46 (AA II 28, phase V, later 3rd century on) iv) Form 37, Central Gaulish. Three fragments from a small bowl with Cinnamus ii's ovolo 2 (Rogers B231). The panels include:

1) A candelabrum (Rogers Q43).

2) A festoon over a large lozenge (S & S 1958, pl 161, 50). *c* AD 150–80.

47 (AA II 29, phase V, later 3rd century on) Form 37, Central Gaulish, with Cinnamus ii's ovolo 2 (Rogers B231). The panels include:

1) A double medallion.

2) A Cupid with torches (D.265). *c* AD 150–80.

48 (AA II 50, phase VI, early to mid-4th century) Form 37, Central Gaulish. The panels include:

1) A gadroon over a leaf (Rogers H136?).

2A) A double medallion, containing a Pan mask (D.675), impressed sideways;

2B) two astragali, side-by-side.

3A) A festoon or medallion;

3B) a cup (Rogers T13?), impressed sideways. All the details, apart from the gadroon, are known for Banuus. *c* AD 160–90.

49 (AA II 60, phase III, 3rd century) Four joining fragments of form 30, South Gaulish. The ovolo closely resembles one used at La Graufesenque by Iustus i, and may indeed belong to him. It occurs on form 30 from Augsburg, together with the goose to right (Hermet 1934, pl 28, 68), similar arcades, and a row of (different) leaf-tips below the figure (Roger 1913, Taf I, 1). The Augsburg bowl is from the same mould as one from a group of samian from the York fortress belonging to the early 70s. The leaves in the sides of the saltire and below the Cupid (Hermet 1934, pl 18, 37) are on

bowls from Valkenburg ZH and de Meern, respectively, both with Iustus's mould-stamp. *c* AD 70–90.
50 (AA II 69, phase VI, early to mid-4th century) See A XII 17.
51 (AA II 78, phase II, late 2nd to early 3rd century) Form 37, Central Gaulish. The panelled decoration includes a medallion with a hare (D.2057a). The rosette on the bead-row suggests a member of the Sacer i group at Lezoux. Hadrianic.
52 (AA II 87, phase III, 3rd century) See AA II 28.
53 (AA II 97) Form 37, South Gaulish, with panelled decoration. For the ovolo and the trifid motif (here in a saltire), see Mercator i (Knorr 1919, Taf 57, 19, 10 respectively). *c* AD 85–110.
54 (AA II 106, phase III, 3rd century) Form 29, South Gaulish. The upper zone contains a four-petalled rosette and a row of pomegranates. The latter were used at La Graufesenque by the Bassus ii-Coelus partnership (Knorr 1919, Taf 13L) and the rosette is on a bowl from Aislingen stamped by Bassus (Knorr 1952, Taf 8A). *c* AD 55–65.
55 (AA III 1) Form 37, Central Gaulish, with panels:
1) A hare (D.950a) in a chevron festoon (Rogers F41), with a ring below.
2) A dog to left.
Cinnamus ii used the hare and festoon on a stamped bowl from Housesteads and the beads would fit his style. *c* AD 150–80.
56 (AA III 27, phase III, later 3rd century) Two fragments of form 37, probably from the same bowl, South Gaulish. The trident-tongued ovolo was used at La Graufesenque by several potters. The decoration includes a chevron festoon containing a goose to right and plain medallion containing a large rosette and surrounded by pointed leaf-tips. The rosette is probably one used by the Bassus i-Coelus firm (Knorr 1919, Taf 13, 6). *c* AD 75–95.
57 (AA III 41) See AA II 8A. This sherd has the ovolo only.
58 (AA III 49, phase IV, later 3rd century on) i) Form 37, with an ovolo used at Les Martres-de-Veyre by a potter who supplied moulds to Donnaucus (S & S 1958, fig 11). *c* AD 100–25.
59 (AA III 49, phase IV, later 3rd century on) ii) Form 37, from Les Martres-de-Veyre. The lozenge (Rogers U4) and a row of beads below the decoration occur on a bowl from London, from a mould by a potter who supplied Donnaucus (S & S 1958, pl 44, 508). *c* AD 100–25.
60 (AA III 57, phase III, later 3rd century) Form 37, in the fabric of Les Martres-de-Veyre. The small beads, ovolo and dancer (O.361) suggest that this bowl is from a mould made by a potter who supplied moulds to Donnaucus (cf S & S 1958, pl 47, 559, etc). *c* AD 100–25.
61 (AA III 61, phase II, late 2nd to mid-3rd century) Form 37, South Gaulish. The ovolo is an unusual one, with badly formed egg and a tongue too large in proportion. It, and the straight line below it, suggest that this is very late South Gaulish ware, comparable to some of the products of the Natalis group at Banassac. For the dog (D.926), cf a Banassac bowl from the Bregenz Cellar (Jacobs 1913, no 34). Trajanic or early Hadrianic?
62 (AA III 77, phase III, later 3rd century) Form 37, Central Gaulish. The ovolo, similar to Cinnamus ii's ovolo 5, coarse zig-zag border, single medallion, putto (D.240), beaded ring (Rogers C120), and small bird (smaller than D.1042) were all used at Lezoux by Tetturo. *c* AD 135–65.

Site B

63 (B I 1) Form 64, see B I 3.
64 (B I 1A) Form 37, in the fabric of Les Martres-de-Veyre. A bowl in the so-called Medetus-Ranto style, with large arrowheads in the lower part of the lower concavities of a scroll with winding tendrils in the upper concavities. Cf S & S 1958, pl 28, 334. *c* AD 110–25.
65 (B I 3, phase II, Antonine to 3rd century) See the pit groups.
66 (B I 6) i) Form 37, Central Gaulish. Scroll decoration, with a large leaf (Rogers H13) and a 'bud' (Rogers J178, partly impressed), both used at Lezoux by the Cerialis ii-Cinnamus ii group. *c* AD 135–70.
67 (B I 6) ii) Form 37, Central Gaulish, with ovolo (Rogers B208). Freestyle decoration, with a lion (O.1403A) and stag (O.1822K). The ovolo was used at Lezoux by both Docilis i and Casurius ii. The heavy bead-row suggests Casurius, but he is not known to have used the figure-types, while Docilis is. It seems likely that the two potters were connected for a time, and transference of poinçons would not be impossible. Casurius used a larger version of the lion. *c* AD 155–85.
68 (B I 6) iii) (with a sherd in B I 14). Two sherds from a jar, Central Gaulish, with appliqué Silenus mask, as on a vessel from a late 2nd-century layer at *Verulamium* (Hartley 1984, 199, 1), and Bacchus with a kneeling figure (not in Déchelette). Light grainy body fabric, with the masks in mixed clay, but showing normal samian colour in streaks. The interior is brown and the exterior blue-grey. Second half of the 2nd century.
69 (B I 8) Form 37, in the style of Butrio of Lezoux. The ovolo (not in S & S 1958 or Rogers) is one of the commoner ones. He is also known to have used the leaf-spray (Rogers J160), depending from the upper border (S & S 1958, pl 60, 678) and the Bacchus (D.449a). *c* AD 120–45.
70 (B I 14) i) Form 37, in the style of Cettus of Les Martres-de-Veyre. The decoration includes the ovolo (Rogers B97?, but with the tongue at the other side of the egg) and a panel with a single festoon depending from his S-shaped motif. The festoon contains a lion (O.1403A?). *c* AD 135–60.
71 (B I 14) ii) Form 37, with Cinnamus ii's ovolo 2 (Rogers B231) and a large scroll. *c* AD 150–80.
72 (B I 14) iii) See B I 6, iii.
73 (B I 15, phase II, Antonine to 3rd century) i) Form 37, Central Gaulish. The unusual, shallow festoon, topped by bulbous astragali, and the lozenge (Rogers U31 or 33) are all on a bowl from *Verulamium* with an ovolo used by Rogers's P-15. One of this potter's bowls is in Antonine I at Newstead and the decoration of others suggests a range *c* AD 130–50.
74 (B I 15, phase II, Antonine to 3rd century) ii) Form 37, Central Gaulish, with ovolo (Rogers B208) and untidy beads, as used at Lezoux by Docilis i. The decoration is probably zonal, with panels in an upper zone including:
1) A small, double medallion.
2) A festoon (Rogers F71), containing the same medallion. All the details are common in his work. Cf S & S 1958, pl 91–2. *c* AD 135–65.
75 (B I 15, phase II, Antonine to 3rd century) iii) Form 37, Central Gaulish, with Cinnamus ii's ovolo 5 (Rogers B182). The decoration consists of a large scroll; one lower concavity includes a double medallion with an erotic group (Oswald 1937, pl XC, B). *c* AD 150–80.
76 (B I 16, phase II, Antonine to 3rd century) Two fragments of form 37, in the style of Cinnamus ii, with his ovolo 1 (Rogers B223) and panels including:
1) A double medallion containing a stag (D.852).
2) A candelabrum (Rogers (Q43). *c* AD 150–80.
77 (B I 20) i) Form 37, Central Gaulish, with panels including:
1) A tree motif (Rogers Q6).
2A) A chevron festoon (Rogers F41);
2B) A bird (O.2250A) over an acanthus (Rogers K20?).
3) A double medallion, with a partial impression of the leaf (Rogers H101). Astragali are placed diagonally across the panel corners. All the details are attested for Cinnamus ii, though he only used the tree motif rarely. *c* AD 150–80.
78 (B I 20) ii) Form 37, Central Gaulish, probably with freestyle decoration, including an Apollo (D.73). The ovolo is perhaps one used at Lezoux by Belsa (S & S 1958, pl 130, 4). Antonine, probably after AD 160.
79 (B I 22) Form 37, Central Gaulish. The lower zone of decoration, or the lower half of the panel, contains a large double medallion with a vine-scroll (Rogers M2). Probably by Cinnamus ii, cf S & S 1958, pl 160, 41. *c* AD 150–80.
80 (B IA 1) i) Form 37, Central Gaulish. Both surviving panels contain large, double medallions, one with a Cupid with torches (D.265) and an eleven-petalled rosette (Rogers C227). The vertical border of squarish beads is topped by a trilobed motif (Rogers G159). Astragali are placed diagonally across the panel corners. A bowl in the style of Laxtucissa (cf S & S 1958, pl 97, 7; 100, 4). *c* AD 145–75.
81 (B IA 1) ii) Form 37, Central Gaulish, with Cinnamus ii's ovolo 4 (Rogers B145). The surviving panel contains a double medallion with a Venus (D.184). Cinnamus's striated spindle is across one corner of the panel. *c* AD 150–80.
82 (B IA 1) iii) Form 37, Central Gaulish. The ovolo (Rogers B258), festoon (Rogers F2), bird (O.2250A) and panel border of rhomboidal beads were all used at Lezoux by Mercator iv. Cf S & S 1958, pl 145, 9 for the ovolo and bird. The festoon is on a stamped bowl from Lezoux. *c* AD 160–90.
82A (B IA 1) iv) A sherd with the same basal wreath as B 1A 9, no 72, and perhaps from the same vessel.

83 (B IA 7) Form 37, Central Gaulish. A freestyle bowl, with a pygmy used at Lezoux by members of the Cerialis ii-Cinnamus ii group of potters. The unusual foliage occurs on one of their bowls from Little Chester (Hartley 1961b, 96, no 21). *c* AD 135–70.
84 (B IA 9) Fragments from a bowl of form 37, Central Gaulish. The panels, some divided horizontally, include a Vulcan (O.68) and birds to left and right (D.1010–11). The basal wreath of chevrons (Rogers K35), birds and general arrangement recall the work of Butrio (S & S 1958, pl 59, 664, 672). The Vulcan is not recorded for him, but is known for Libertus. *c* AD 120–45. Cf B 1A 1, iv.
85 (B IA 17) Form 37, in the fabric of Les Martres-de-Veyre. A scroll encloses large spirals, in the manner of Silvius ii/Silvio (S & S 1958, pl 33, 400). Trajanic or early Hadrianic.

Site C

86 (C II 119) Central Gaulish. The bold basal ridge between two slighter ridges and vertical and horizontal series of rings are common features of the style of X-6. The decoration is divided into panels by striated columns, which he is not known to have used, however. *c* AD 125–50.
87 (C III 1) i) Form 37, Central Gaulish, from a cracked mould. The ovolo (Rogers B19) was used by a Lezoux Paternus (iv), who signed moulds in the nominative. Cf a bowl from the Barnsley Park villa (Hartley 1983, 171, fig 57, no 9), which also has the kneeling stag (O.1704A). The figure in the adjacent panel is a Venus (one of the variants of D.179). The rosette junction mask has seven beads. *c* AD 140–70.
88 (C II 119) ii) Form 37, by the same potter as the last. The panels contain a Venus (D.175), as on the Barnsley Park bowl above, and a warrior (not in D. or O.). *c* AD 130–60.
89 (C IIIA 14, medieval corn dryer walls) Form 37, Central Gaulish, with freestyle decoration. The ring-tongued ovolo (Rogers B105), dog (D.919), *bestiarius* (D.631), and bear (as on S & S 1958, pl 106, 22) all occur on stamped bowls of Paternus v. *c* AD 160–95.
90 (C III 15) Form 37, Central Gaulish. The ovolo (a version of Rogers B223), with a straight line below, and the six-petalled rosette are on a stamped bowl of Pugnus ii from Gloucester (S & S 1958, pl 155, 20). The surviving panel includes a chevron festoon (Rogers F19?) with a hare (O.2120A). *c* AD 150–75.
91 (C V 56) i) Form 37, Central Gaulish, drilled for a rivet. Probably from a freestyle bowl by a member of the Sacer i group at Lezoux, which used closely packed conventional vegetation (here partly impressed acanthi) in this manner. Cf a stamped bowl of Attianus ii from London (S & S 1958, pl 85, 9), which has a stag (D.867), whose forelegs probably appear on this piece. *c* AD 125–45.
92 (C V 56) ii) Form 37, Central Gaulish, with ovolo (Rogers B35). A bowl in the style of Stanfield & Simpson's X-6, with rings below the ovolo in one panel (cf S & S 1958, pl 74, 11). The adjacent panel has a saltire with a top section identical to that on one of his bowls from Corbridge (S & S 1958, 8). *c* AD 125–50.
93 (C V 56) iii) Form 37, Central Gaulish, with a basal wreath of trifid motifs and a zone containing a crane (D 1001). Hadrianic or early Antonine.
94 (C V 62) Form 37, in the style of Drusus i (X-3) of Les Martres-de-Veyre. A band of conjoined dolphins replaces the ovolo. The main zone of decoration includes a pair of gladiators (one D.611, the other not in D. or O.), a Cupid (?), seven-beaded rosette (Rogers C280), and the festoon Rogers F21. See S & S 1958, pl 11, 141 for a close parallel to this arrangement, but on a bowl with an ovolo. *c* AD 100–25.
95 (C VI 3, phase VIIIA, early to mid-4th century on) Form 37, Central Gaulish. The decoration probably consists of a single-bordered scroll, with a draped man (a smaller version of D.372) and serpentine motif (Rogers U261?). Both details were used at Lezoux by Do(v)eccus i, though he rarely used scrolls. *c* AD 165–200.
96 (C VI 22, phase VIII, early to mid-4th century on) Form 37, Central Gaulish. Scroll decoration, with leaves (Rogers H13 and J90(?)). The larger leaf is attested for Cinnamus ii (S & S 1958, pl 161, 53) and the smaller one is on a mould in his style from Lezoux. *c* AD 150–80.
97 (C VI 32A) i) Form 37, with the small vine-scroll used at Lezoux by Drusus ii and some of his contemporaries (Rogers M10). *c* AD 125–45.
98 (C VI 32A) ii) Form 37, with an ovolo used at Lezoux by Pugnus ii, X-6, etc (Rogers B233?). *c* AD 125–50.
99 (C VI 51, phase IV, later 3rd century on) See C VI 66.
100 (C VI 60, phase IV, later 3rd century on) Form 37, with rivet-holes, South Gaulish. The main zone includes a saltire and a panel with tassel in at least one corner. Both the ovolo (Knorr 1919, Taf 57, 19) and the trifid motif of which the basal wreath is composed (Knorr 1919, 12) were used at La Graufesenque by Mercator i. *c* AD 85–110.
101 (C VI 66, phase IV, later 3rd century on, with C VI 51) Fragments of form 37, Central Gaulish, with scroll decoration. The ovolo is one chiefly associated with the Cerialis ii-Cinnamus ii group at Lezoux (Rogers B144), and the leaf (Rogers H37) is on a bowl from Castleford by one of these potters. *c* AD 135–70.
102 (C VI 99, phase IV, later 3rd century on) Form 37, with rivet-hole, South Gaulish. The trident-tongued ovolo is blurred. The zone of triple festoons containing stirrup leaves, with wavy lines or tassels between, is reminiscent of some of the 1st-century form 37s in Scotland. *c* AD 75–90.
103 (C VI 102, phase I, late 1st to 2nd century) Form 37, South Gaulish. The decoration includes a winding scroll, with leaves in the lower concavities (Hermet 1934, pl 10, 13 and a smaller, unidentified, one) and birds (blurred) in the upper concavities. The basal zone contains a roundel (Hermet 1934, pl 15, 76?). The fabric and the sharpness of the detail suggest a date *c* AD 70–85.
104 (C VIA 42C) Form 29, South Gaulish. The upper zone includes panels with a stag (Hermet 1934, pl 27, 15 or 16) and diagonal wavy lines. The workmanship and quality of the moulding suggest that this is one of the latest South Gaulish examples of the form. *c* AD 75–85.
105 (C VIA 59, phase VII, early to mid-4th century) Form 30, with an ovolo used at Lezoux by Pugnus ii, X-6, etc (Rogers B233). *c* AD 125–50.
106 (C VIA 87, phase V, later 3rd century on) Form 37, Central Gaulish. The ovolo (Rogers B12) was used at Lezoux by Hadrianic and Antonine potters. This piece is probably Antonine.
107 (C VIA 96, phase VI, early to mid-4th century) Form 37, in the fabric of Les Martres-de-Veyre. The panels include:

1) A festoon or medallion.
2) A tendril ending in a leaf (Rogers J89). The twist motif (Rogers U103) is impressed over the panel border and in panel 2. For bowls with these details, in the so-called Medetus-Ranto style, see S & S 1958, pl 32, 374, 378, etc. *c* AD 110–25.

108 (C VIA 108, phase IV, later 3rd century on, with C VIA 116) Form 37, South Gaulish, in the style of one of the potters whose work is common in the Pompeii Hoard of AD 79. See Atkinson 1914, nos 48, 50, 51 for the ovolo, with a chevron wreath below. *c* AD 75–85.
109 (C VIA 116, phase V, later 3rd century on) See C VIA 108.
110 (C VIA 137) Form 37, South Gaulish. The surviving panels contain:

1) A Victory (Hermet 1934, pl 20, 104) and corner tassels.
2) A saltire. All the details were used at La Graufesenque by Mercator i, and his stamp may be impressed below the Victory, though no letters are clearly visible. *c* AD 85–110.

111 (C IXA 13) Form 37, Central Gaulish. A small bowl, with freestyle decoration, including a boar (D.834), Amazon (D.155), pygmy (D.442 reduced), a partly impressed trifid motif (of the type Rogers G62–76) and, perhaps, a bear impressed vertically. There are remains of a cursive signature below the decoration (unidentified). The boar, Amazon, pygmy, and trifid motif were all used by Acaunissa, who may have made this bowl. *c* AD 125–45.

Site D

112 (D I 2A, phase VIII, late 4th century, with D I 25, D I 114, D I 173, and, probably D I U/S and D I 176) Form 37, Central Gaulish. A standard freestyle bowl by a member of the Cerialis ii-Cinnamus ii group, with ovolo (Rogers B144), dog (D.934), bear (D.820), panther (D.799), stag (D.874), athlete (D.403), and leaf-tips. The cursive signature below the decoration is largely obliterated. *c* AD 135–70.
113 (D I 6, phase VI, mid- to late 4th century?) i) Form 37, burnt, with ovolo 2 of Cinnamus ii of Lezoux (Rogers B231). *c* AD 150–80.
114 (D I 6, phase VI, mid- to late 4th century?) ii) Form 37, Central Gaulish. A freestyle bowl is the style of Casurius ii, with a cow (D.900), hare (D.949) and bear (D.808?). *c* AD 160–90.
115 (D I 14, phase V, early to mid-4th century?) Form 30, Central Gaulish, with a blurred, ring-tongued ovolo (Rogers B107). The

panelled decoration includes a double medallion and a seven-petalled rosette, probably by Q I Balbinus. *c* AD 150–80. Cf S & S 1958, pl 124, 1.
116 (D I 25, phase VIII, late 4th century) i) See D I 2A.
117 (D I 25, phase VIII, late 4th century) ii) Form 37, Central Gaulish, in the style of Laxtucissa, with a panel border of squarish beads (Rogers A40), topped by a trifid motif (Rogers G97). The panel contains a tripod (Rogers Q16). The upper border consists of fine beads. *c* AD 145–75.
118 (D I 36, phase VI, mid- to late 4th century?) A pedestal beaker, with barbotine decoration, probably close in form to Ludowici VMc (cf O & P 1920, pl LXXX, 7). The form of the barbotine leaves is closely matched at Rheinzabern (O & P 1920, 5), though the glaze is unusually good for Rheinzabern ware. Late 2nd or early 3rd century.
119 (D I 40, phase V, early to mid-4th century?) Form 37, Central Gaulish. The decoration includes a large shield used at Lezoux by Servus iv, Cinnamus ii and Do(v)eccus i (Rogers U210). This piece is probably by Do(v)eccus, in view of the large beads in the border. *c* AD 165–200.
120 (D I 70, phase IV, late 3rd century?) Form 30, South Gaulish. The ovolo was used at La Graufesenque by C Valerius Albanus and M Crestio. The decoration includes a saltire with a trifid motif at the top, flanked by arrowheaded buds. The adjacent panel includes a corner-tassel. The trifid motif is on a stamped bowl of C Valerius Albanus from Wroxeter (Atkinson 1942, pl 68, 51A). *c* AD 75–100.
121 (D I 75, phase IV, late 3rd century?) Form 37, in the so-called Medetus-Ranto style, with the ovolo usually associated with this style (S & S 1958, fig 9, 1). The decoration includes a leaf (Rogers H96) and double medallion or scroll containing a panther (D.799). Bowls in this style occur in the fabrics of both Les Martres-de-Veyre and Lezoux. It is possible that mould-makers at Les Martres sold these moulds to Lezoux, but Medetus, at least, is known to have stamped plain ware at Lezoux. This particular bowl is in Lezoux fabric. Cf S & S 1958, pl 32, 377 and 386 for parallels for the decoration. This type of bowl does not occur in Scotland, except for Birrens. *c* AD 120–40.
122 (D I 87, phase V, early to mid-4th century?) i) Form 37, with an ovolo used at Lezoux by Advocisus and his associates (Rogers B102). *c* AD 160–90.
123 (D I 87, phase V, early to mid-4th century?) ii) Form 37, Central Gaulish, with the smaller of Do(v)eccus i's common ovolos (S & S 1958, fig 44, 2) and a border of large beads below. *c* AD 165–200.
124 (D I 89) Form 29, South Gaulish. A small fragment of the upper zone, probably with a scroll including a trilobed motif. *c* AD 55–75.
125 (D I 91, phase VI, mid- to late 4th century?) Form 37, in the style of Casurius ii of Lezoux. The surviving panels include:

1) A long, winding tendril impressed vertically.
2) A large, double festoon or medallion containing a cow (D.900), over winding tendrils with leaves (Rogers H42, J56?). Cf S & S 1958, pl 132, 11; 133, 20). *c* AD 160–90.

126 (D I 98, phase V, early to mid-4th century?) Form 37, stamped [S]ERVM retrograde; Servus iv of Lezoux, Die 1b (see stamp 66). The ovolo is Rogers B27 and the panels are divided by his coarse, zig-zag borders. The large double festoon contains the leaf Rogers H78. *c* AD 160–90.
127 (D I 109, phase II, later 2nd to early 3rd century?) i) (with A IX 13, D I 116 and G I Topsoil). Form 29, South Gaulish, stamped]NDVILMA (see stamp 45). The scroll in the upper zone has striated spindles, spirals with thirteen-petalled rosettes, roundels, and bifid bindings. Similar scrolls, but with smaller motifs, are on a stamped Manduilus bowl from Nanstallon (Hartley 1972a, 101, no 1), and on one from Mainz stamped by Namus (Knorr 1952, Taf 46A). The composite motifs in the lower zone are unusual. The bowl is probably from a partly cracked mould. The foot-ring is well worn. *c* AD 55–75.
128 (D I 109, phase II, later 2nd to early 3rd century?) ii) Form 37, South Gaulish. The motifs in the two different straight wreaths were used at La Graufesenque by Germanus i (Knorr 1919, Taf 35, 59, and 85). The wreaths occur together on a bowl in his style from La Graufesenque (Hermet 1934, pl 99, B1). This piece is not necessarily by Germanus himself but, if not, is certainly by one of his associates. *c* AD 70–85.
129 (D I 110) i) (With another sherd in D I 87). Form 29, South Gaulish. The scroll in the upper zone has birds (O.2230 and 2258) in the upper and low concavities, respectively. The bird in the lower concavity stands amid pointed leaf-tips. There is a straight wreath of leaves below the central moulding. This and the sharp carination suggest a date *c* AD 60–80.
130 (D I 110) ii) Form 29, South Gaulish. A small fragment from the upper zone, which consists of a scroll. *c* AD 65–85.
131 (D I 110) iii) Form 37, South Gaulish. The trident-tongued ovolo was used at La Graufesenque by Severus iii and Pontus. The decoration includes a zone of triple festoons containing spurred leaves. *c* AD 70–90.
132 (D I 110) iv) Form 29 rim, South Gaulish. Neronian–Flavian or early Flavian.
133 (D I 114, phase VI, mid- to late 4th century?) See D I 2A.
134 (D I 115, phase VI, mid- to late 4th century?) Form 37, South Gaulish. The rosette-tongued ovolo is on a signed bowl of Calvus, from La Graufesenque, and on one in his style from Doncaster. The chevron wreath below the ovolo recalls bowls in the Pompeii Hoard (Atkinson 1914, *passim*). *c* AD 70–90.
135 (D I 116, phase III, later 2nd to early 3rd century on) i) Form 29, South Gaulish. The scroll in the upper zone includes a hare (similar is Hermet 1934, pl 26, 72) in one of the lower concavities. *c* AD 55–70.
135A (D I 116, phase III, later 2nd to early 3rd century on) ii) See D I 109.
136 (D I 126A, phase II, later 2nd to early 3rd century?) See G I 88.
137 (D I 134) Form 64, Central Gaulish. The decoration includes a standing figure (a smaller version of O.637), between tiers of cups (Rogers Q84). Hadrianic.
138 (D I 145, phase I, 1st century to early Antonine) Form 37, Central Gaulish. The festoon (Rogers F32) is on a stamped mould of Priscinus from Lezoux (Roanne Museum) and the plant (Rogers J41) is on a bowl in his style from Corbridge. *c* AD 145–75.
139 (D I 155) i) Form 37, with panels bordered by bead-rows ending below in small, hollow rosettes. By Criciro v or Divixtus i. *c* AD 135–75.
140 (D I 155) ii) Form 37, Central Gaulish. The combination of T-tongued ovolo (Rogers B206) and wavy-line border suggests a member of the Quintilianus i group, probably Quintilianus himself. The twenty-six fragments, some joining, give a series of three panels:

1) A warrior (D.114).
2) A double medallion with a cockerel (D 1023, reduced).
3) A Jupiter (D.4).

The trifid motif is on a stamped bowl of Quintilianus from Chesters (S & S 1958, pl 68, 2). The bifid motif is not known. *c* AD 125–50.
141 (D I 155) iii) Form 37, Central Gaulish, with a border of rhomboidal beads topped by a trifid motif (Rogers G159). Almost certainly by Laxtucissa. *c* AD 145–75.
142 (D I 170, phase II, later 2nd to early 3rd century?) See G I 88.
143 (D I 173, phase II, later 2nd to early 3rd century?) i) Form 30, South Gaulish. The ovolo, with sloping sides and tongue with large rosette, is one of a series used at La Graufesenque in the Claudio-Neronian period, based on Arretine prototypes. Knorr 1919, Taf 95D and 97C have similar ovolos. Claudio-Neronian.
143A (D I 173, phase II, later 2nd to early 3rd century?) ii) See D I 2A.
144 (D I 176) i) Form 37, almost certainly from the same bowl as D I 2A (no 112), with the same dog, ovolo, and leaf-tips. *c* AD 140–70.
145 (D I 176) ii) Form 37, Central Gaulish. The surviving panel contains a corner-tassel ending in a leaf (Rogers G208) and the arm of an unidentified figure. The border consists of large, rhomboidal beads. By a member of the Paternus v group. *c* AD 150–90.
146 (D I 176) iii) Form 37, Central Gaulish. The ovolo (a version of Rogers B223) and panther were used at Lezoux by Casurius ii. This figure-type (D.804=O.1569) appears, with the tail broken off, on bowls in his style from Corbridge and Cirencester (S & S 1958, pl 136, 51; 137, 60). The Alcester piece comes from a mould in which the tail has been restored, freehand. *c* AD 160–90. Cf G IA 2.
147 (D I 208, phase VIII, late 4th century) Form 37, in the style of Cinnamus ii of Lezoux, with a large double medallion containing a horse and rider (D.156) over a naked man (D.403). *c* AD 150–80.
148 (D I 230) Form 37, with the same ovolo as D I 110, iii, and with a similar zone of decoration. *c* AD 70–90.

149 (D I 239, phase I, 1st century to early Antonine) Form 37, South Gaulish. The decoration includes a double medallion containing a griffin (Hermet 1934, pl 25, 2). *c* AD 70–90.
150 (D I 246, phase II, later 2nd to early 3rd century?) i) Form 30, South Gaulish. The ovolo is perhaps one used at La Graufesenque by Memor, Mommo, and a potter whose name begins in Trim . . . *c* AD 70–90.
151 (D I 246, phase II, later 2nd to early 3rd century?) ii) Form 37, Central Gaulish. An almost complete bowl of sixteen panels, thus:

1) a candelabrum (Rogers Q40).
2) A vine-scroll (Rogers M2), with a bird to right, looking back.
3) Osiris (D.413).
4) Pan (a much reduced version of D.415).

The order of panels is 12131214, repeated. The rosette-tongued ovolo is Rogers B24. All the details apart from the Osiris appear on bowls in the style of the Large S Potter. The foot-ring is only slightly worn and there is kiln-grit inside the bowl from the foot-ring of the vessel stacked above it (off-centre) in the kiln. The small diameter of this ring of grit suggests plain ware. *c* AD 125–40.
152 (D II 1) i) Form 37, Central Gaulish. The decoration involves a (chevron?) festoon or medallion over a shallow zone divided vertically by astragali and containing beaded rings (Rogers C290) with blurred beaded rosettes between. The astragali are joined to the basal ridge by the same rosette. Probably by a member of the Quintilianus group. *c* AD 125–50.
153 (D II 1) ii) A small bowl of form 37, Central Gaulish, with ovolo 2 of Cinnamus ii (Rogers B231). The scroll contains two leaves in the upper concavity (a variant of Rogers H99, which also occurs in the lower concavity, and one not illustrated by him but similar to H140). The way in which the tendrils spring from the scroll is diagnostic of Cinnamus, though the smaller leaf is not known from him. *c* AD 150–80.
154 (D II 2, phase IX, late 4th century) See stamp 15.
155 (D II 3) Form 37, Central Gaulish. The single-bordered ovolo (Rogers B28), in conjunction with a guide-line, suggests a member of the Quintilianus i group. Quintilianus himself is known to have used the boar (D.829), stag (D.879), and festoon (Rogers F42) and the motif in the corner of one panel (Rogers G259) is on bowls in his style. The use by this group of potters of beaded borders with this ovolo is unusual and the border between the festoons is not known. *c* AD 125–50.
156 (D II 14) Form 37, in the style of Cettus of Les Martres-de-Veyre. The decoration includes two of his S-shaped motifs, with a large *pelta* and a tree (Rogers N6) between. The ovolo is probably Rogers B266, not previously recorded for him. *c* AD 135–60.
157 (D II 16) Two joining fragments from a freestyle bowl with the end of Cinnamus ii's commonest label stamp, CINNAMI, retrograde (Die 5b; see stamp 19). The decoration includes a stag. *c* AD 150–80.
158 (D II 20) Form 37, Central Gaulish. The ovolo (Rogers B208), uneven beds and chevron (in a festoon or narrow panel) were all used at Lezoux by Docilis i. *c* AD 135–65.
159 (D II 24A) Form 37, Central Gaulish. One of the surviving panels is divided horizontally. The adjacent panel contains a double medallion with a naked man (D.402). One of the lower corners of this panel has a leaf (Rogers G204). All the details are on a stamped bowl of Do(v)eccus i from Lezoux (S & S 1958, pl 149, 27). *c* AD 165–200.
160 (D II 28) i) Form 37, Central Gaulish. A large bowl, complete, with a very slightly worn foot-ring. The ovolo (Rogers B144) was commonly used at Lezoux by members of the Cerialis ii-Cinnamus ii group, one of the features of whose style is the lavish use of buds in the background of the decoration, as here. The upper concavities of the scroll contain a large leaf (Rogers H24), goat (D.889), and kneeling horse (not in D. or O.). The lower concavities have Cupid (D.254), large goat (D.893), leaping animal (dog?, not in D. or O.), Pan (D.419), pugilist (D.383), woman in tunic (O.363 variant), Hercules (D.467), Victory (D.484), Venus (D.177), dancer (D.216), and Bacchus (D.361). The buds are partial impressions of Rogers J178. It seems that most of these figures were used only on large scroll bowls, which are comparatively rare at Lezoux, and most of them are not associated with this group of potters. However, the buds are on many signed bowls of Cerialis ii and these, and the ovolo, make attribution to him almost certain. An unstamped bowl from Wels (Karnitsch 1959, Taf 70, 2) is perhaps from the same mould. *c* AD 135–70.
161 (D I 28) ii) Form 37, with a fragment of Cinnamus ii's ovolo 1 (Rogers B223). *c* AD 150–80.
162 (D II 29) i) Form 37, Central Gaulish, with beaded rings (Rogers C290) in the bottom part of a panel. The adjacent panel has the motif Rogers G259, impressed sideways. An eight-beaded rosette (Rogers C281) acts as a junction-mask. Almost certainly by a member of the Quintilianus i group. *c* AD 125–50.
163 (D II 29) ii) (with D II 70) Form 37, Central Gaulish. The rosette-tongued ovolo (Rogers B24) was used at Lezoux in the Hadrianic and Antonine periods. This particular piece is Antonine.
164 (D II 29) iii) Form 37, in the style of Cettus of Les Martres-de-Veyre. The panels include:

1) A hare to left (D.950A), in a single medallion.
2A) Bear (D.820);
2B) A small, double medallion.
3) Hare to right (O.2061), in a single medallion. The ovolo is Rogers B97. Cf S & S 1958, pls 141–4. *c* AD 135–60. (With D II 39 & 60).

165 (D ii 29) iv) Form 30, with one of the ring-tongued ovolos used at Lezoux by Paternus v and some of his associates. *c* AD 150–90.
166 (D II 29) v) A fragment from a Central Gaulish jar, with appliqué decoration. The figure-type, a seated figure, bearded, is not one illustrated by Déchelette. However the fabric suggests origin at Lezoux, where such jars were made in the second half of the 2nd century.
167 (D II 29A) See pit groups.
168 (D II 39) i) See D II 29, iii.
169 (D II 39) ii) Two joining fragments from a freestyle bowl of form 37, Central Gaulish. The ovolo (Rogers B143), lion (D.766), dog (D.934), and corn-stock (Rogers N15) were all commonly used by Cinnamus ii. The large boar to right (not in D. or O.) is rare for him, but occurs on a stamped bowl from Caerleon. *c* AD 150–80.
170 (D II 39) iii) Six fragments from a freestyle bowl in the style of the Cerialis ii-Cinnamus ii group at Lezoux. The decoration includes this group's common ovolo (Rogers B144), a lion (D.766), stag, and partly impressed leaf-tips. *c* AD 135–70. (With D II 60).
171 (D II 60) i) See D II 29, iii.
172 (D II 60) ii) See D II 39, iii.
173 (D II 60) iii) Two fragments from a panelled bowl of form 37, with Cinnamus ii's ovolo 2 (Rogers B231) and medallions. *c* AD 150–80.
174 (D II 60) iv) Form 37, Central Gaulish. A badly made bowl in the style of Cinnamus ii, with the same ovolo as the last. The surviving panels contain:

1) A chevron medallion (Rogers E2) containing a sea-creature (D 38).
2) A Vulcan (D.39, without tongs). *c* AD 150–80.

175 (D II 70, phase VIII, late 4th century) See D II 29, ii.
176 (D II 76) i) Form 37, Central Gaulish. A poorly moulded bowl in the style of Arcanus of Lezoux, with ovolo (S & S 1958, fig 20), zig-zag borders, beaded rosette and a panel containing a man with draperies (D.330). *c* AD 125–45.
177 (D II 76) ii) Form 37, in the style of the Cerialis ii-Cinnamus ii group at Lezoux, with the group's common ovolo (Rogers B144). The freestyle scene includes a stag (D 867), a lion (D 766), and partly impressed leaf-tips. Cf D II 39, iii. *c* AD 135–70.
178–9 (D II 76) iii) Bowls of form 37, Central Gaulish, with Cinnamus ii's ovolos 2 (Rogers B231) and 3 (Rogers B143). *c* AD 150–80.
180 (D II 76) iv) Form 37, Central Gaulish, with a ring-tongued ovolo (Rogers B105) used at Lezoux by Paternus v and some of his associates. *c* AD 150–90.
181–2 (D II 76) v) Forms 37 and 30, Central Gaulish. Antonine and late Antonine, respectively.
183 (D II 76) vi) Fourteen fragments from a Central Gaulish freestyle bowl. The decoration includes the ovolo (Rogers B208), a horseman (D.157), bear (D.807), panther (D.789), and leafy spray (Rogers H118). Perhaps by Illixo, who used the astragalus border (Rogers A10), horseman, and spray, though he is not known to have used the ovolo. *c* AD 150–80.
184 (D II 77, phase III, later 2nd to early 3rd century on) Form 29, South Gaulish. The scroll in the lower zone is exactly paralleled on a bowl from La Graufesenque (Millau Museum) with a stamp of the Bassus ii/Coelus association. The trilobed motifs and small leafs in the lower concavities (Knorr 1919, Taf 13, 4 and 9, respectively) are common on bowls with the joint stamp of these two potters, but the tulip-shaped leaves in the upper concavities are not. *c* AD 60–80.

185 (D III 2) i) Two fragments from a Central Gaulish bowl of form 37, with Cinnamus ii's ovolo 3 (Rogers B143) and a winding scroll. *c* AD 150–80.
186 (D III 2) ii) Form 37, Central Gaulish, with scroll decoration. Probably by Paternus v, who used the ring-tongued ovolo (Rogers B105) and dog (O.1926A). *c* AD 160–95.
187 (D IV 10) Two joining fragments from a jar (probably Déchelette 72 variant). Central Gaulish. Barbotine decoration is combined with the leaf D. (appliqué) type 157. Cf Brodribb, Hands & Walker 1971, 63, 79. Second half of the 2nd century.

Site E

188 (E II 2) See E VI 2.
189 (E V 22, phase V, late 2nd century?) i) Approximately one-third of a badly moulded bowl of form 37, South Gaulish. The decoration consists of a zone of chevron festoons, separated by poppy-head tassels and containing stirrup-leaves, between an upper wreath of trifid motifs and a basal wreath of chevrons. The rosette-tongued ovolo was used at La Graufesenque by Frontinus, whose bowls from stamped moulds also have the pendant and basal wreath (Knorr 1952, Taf 25C) and trifid motif (Knorr 1952, D). The festoon and stirrup-leaves are on a bowl in his style from Doncaster. Most of the elements of the decoration appear on bowls from Camelon and the rest occur at Inchtuthil. *c* AD 70–95.
190 (E V 22, phase V, late 2nd century?) ii) Form 37, South Gaulish. The upper zone has coarse, chevron festoons, separated by tassels. One festoon contains a bird (O.2290). The lower zone includes a dog (O.1925), leaping over conventional grass-tufts, partly impressed. The festoons suggest that this is the work of Biragillus i, and all the details, apart from the dog, are on a stamped bowl from Rottweil (O & P 1920, pl XIX, 5). *c* AD 90–110.
191 (E VI 2, with E II 2) Form 37, Central Gaulish. A freestyle scene includes a hare to left (O.2120A) and bear to right (D.807). Mid- to late Antonine.

Site F

192 (F I 50B, phase III/IV, Neronian–Antonine) Form 37, Central Gaulish. The ovolo (Rogers B52) appears on bowls in the style of Secundus v of Lezoux, and the straight line below it makes the attribution almost certain. The decoration includes a crouching panther (D.792) which is on a bowl from Corbridge with the ovolo which occurs on Secundus's stamped bowls (S & S 1958, pl 155, 28, there assignable to Pugnus). *c* AD 150–80. Cf AA I 42.
193 (F I 161, phase XIII, after AD 353) Form 37, Central Gaulish. The surviving panels contain:

1) A fleur-de-lys (Rogers G56), in the upper part of the panel.
2) A double medallion, with thick borders. For both details, see stamped bowls of Paternus v from Wels (Karnitsch 1959, Taf 44, 1–2). *c* AD 160–95.

194 (F I 187B) Form 37, Central Gaulish, almost certainly with scroll decoration. The ovolo (Rogers B234) and leaf (Rogers H75) were used at Lezoux by Iustus ii and Paternus v, but the horizontal border of rhomboidal beads makes this bowl more likely to be by Iustus. The decoration also includes a blurred ring, which is on a stamped bowl from Malton (S & S 1958, pl 110, 6). *c* AD 160–90.
195 (F I 187D, phase XIII, after AD 353) Three joining fragments of form 37, with panels:

1) A leopard to right (D.787).
2) A lion to left (O.1426), over a goat (O.2127) and a small leaf.
3) A narrow panel with a *bucranium* (Rogers G372). This motif is also impressed over the border dividing panels 2 and 3.
4) (Lower half) leopard, as in 1. All the details, except for the lion and the leaf, occur on bowls stamped by, or in the style of, Secundus v, and the absence of junction-masks makes the attribution likely. *c* AD 150–80.

196 (F III 15, phase XIII, after AD 353) Form 37, South Gaulish. A panelled zone includes an unusually wide saltire, with narrow leaves at the sides and at the bottom a four-bladed plant flanked by striated spindles. The adjacent panel has a corner-tassel. The zone below includes a festoon with a stirrup-leaf. The spacing of the saltire is unusual, suggesting that the decoration was perhaps laid out by an inexperienced potter. *c* AD 85–110.
197 (F V 8) Form 37, Central Gaulish. A fragment from a freestyle scene, including a bear (D.810), dog (O.2007A, used twice), and horse and rider (D.157). All the details are on a stamped bowl of Paternus v from Wingham, Kent (S & S 1958, pl 106, 22). *c* AD 160–95.
198 (F V 12, phase XIII, after AD 353) Form 37, with ovolo Rogers B27, used at Lezoux by Servus iv (S & S's Servus 2). *c* AD 160–90.
199 (F V 14B) Form 37, Central Gaulish. The leaf in the scroll (Rogers H13) and the buds in the background (partial impressions of Rogers J178) occur on bowls by the Cerialis ii-Cinnamus ii group at Lezoux. *c* AD 135–70.

Site G

200 (G I 2A) See G I 4A.
201 (G I 4A, phase X, late 4th century, with G I 2A) Two joining fragments of form 37, Central Gaulish. All the details on this scroll bowl are on a bowl from York, which may well be from the same mould (S & S 1958, pl 50, 598). Although these bowls have an ovolo so far only attested at Lezoux for Libertus ii and Butrio (Rogers B213), the figure-type suggests that they are by Attianus ii, or an associate. The details are: panthers to left and right (O.1566, D.799), birds (O.2298, 2278, 2252), and leaves (Rogers J4 and one not illustrated by him). The ovolo and panthers are also on an unpublished bowl from Newstead, the decoration of which does not suggest Libertus or Butrio. *c* AD 125–45.
202 (G I 7, phase IX, late 4th century) Form 37, Central Gaulish, with an ovolo used by Iullinus ii (Rogers B184). The surviving panels contain:

1) A double medallion with a leaf (Rogers H14?). Iullinus's tiny ring appears in one corner of the panel.
2) A candelabrum (Rogers Q43). *c* AD 160–90.

203 (G I 9) Form 37, South Gaulish, slightly burnt. Probably Banassac ware, with a straight-tongued ovolo (cf Walke & Walke 1968, Taf 33, 17 from Gauting) and leaf-tips (*ibid*, 1968, Taf 42, 7) in both surviving panels. Probably Hadrianic.
204 (G I 17, phase VI, late 4th century) Form 37, Central Gaulish, in the style of Iullinus ii. The upper part of a panel contains a double medallion or festoon, containing an astragalus and a *cantharus* (?). The lower part contains a pair (?) of *canthari* (Rogers T16). *c* AD 160–90.
205 (G I 24, phase IX+, late 4th century) Form 37, East Gaulish, with ovolo (Ricken & Fischer 1963, E25) and a stag (T98 or 98a). Rheinzabern ware, probably by Comitialis. Late 2nd or 3rd century.
206 (G I 24A) Form 37, in the style of Servus iv (S & S's Servus 2) of Lezoux. A panel contains a Diana with hind (O 107), between tripods (Rogers Q16?), probably supporting an arcade, as on a stamped bowl from Castor (S & S 1958, pl 181, 1). *c* AD 160–90.
207 (G I 36) Form 37, Central Gaulish. One panel includes a double medallion and an eight-petalled rosette with a hollow centre. The beads and medallion suggest Paternus v or one of his associates. *c* AD 150–90.
208 (G I 59, phase IV, early to mid-4th century, with G I 89, G IA 66) Form 29, South Gaulish. Three fragments from the lower zone, with a basal wreath of four-bladed motifs, probably with straight gadroons above. Neronian.
209 (G I 60D, with G I 137) Form 29, South Gaulish with a lower zone of straight gadroons. The scroll in the upper zone has corded medallions containing large rosettes and spirals with tendrils ending in fan-shaped plants. The medallion and rosette are similar to, but smaller than, ones on bowls stamped by Labio (Knorr 1919, Textbild 43; 1952, Taf 52, 6, 9). The rosette was probably also used on plain forms. The plant occurs on bowls stamped by Felix i, Pass(i)enus, and Rufinus iii; also (with the rosette) on a bowl from Period 2 construction at Fishbourne (Dannell 1971, no 23). *c* AD 65–80.
210 (G I 66, phase VIII, late 4th century) Form 37, Central Gaulish. The ovolo (Rogers B233) was used by Pugnus ii and associated potters. It occurs with the goose (D.1013), and leaf impressed over the festoon, on a bowl from Leicester by a member of this group. *c* AD 130–50.
211 (G I 88, with D I 126A, D I 70 and D I 246A) Form 37, South Gaulish. The upper concavity of a scroll contains a tapering leaf. The lower concavity has a Cupid (close to O.435), over pointed leaf-tips. A tendril is attached to the scroll by a rosette, to the left of the Cupid. The basal wreath consists of chevrons. The blurred ovolo is perhaps one used by M Crestio, but this leaf is slightly different from his usual one. *c* AD 75–100.
212 (G I 89, phase IV, early to mid-4th century) See G I 59.

213 (G I 115, phase V, later 4th century) i) Form 29, South Gaulish. A fragment from the lower zone, with large and small webbed leaves. Not strictly assignable, but cf Knorr 1919, Taf 31E, stamped by Daribitus. *c* AD 45–65.
214 (G I 115, phase V, later 4th century) ii) (With eleven fragments in G I 151, most joining). Form 30, South Gaulish. Signed bowls of Masc(u)lus i from Southwark (Bird & Marsh 1978, I, 77, 2) and the Tongres area (Knorr 1952, Taf 36B) have the same arcade with spirals, but with different ovolos. The leaf in the lower corner of this panel and the spindle in the saltire were also used by him (de Groot 1960, Abb 5, 15, and Knorr 1952, Taf 36A, respectively). The ovolo and plant in the top of the saltire are on an unsigned bowl from York in a group of samian of the 70s. The ovolo is probably the one used by Martialis i on a bowl from Usk (Boon 1962, 2) and occurs also on a signed bowl of Masclinus from Canterbury. *c* AD 50–70.
215 (G I 115, phase V, later 4th century) iii) Two joining fragments of form 37, South Gaulish. The decoration includes a saltire panel with a trifid motif in the lower part, as on a signed bowl of Memor in the Pompeii Hoard (Atkinson 1914, no 73). The S-shaped gadroons in the basal wreath do not seem to be his normal ones, however. The tendrils in the side sections of the saltire end in bottle-shaped buds. *c* AD 70–90.
216 (G I 137, phase IV, early to mid-4th century) See G I 60D.
217 (G I 151, almost certainly from the same bowl as G I 115, ii, no 186). Form 30, South Gaulish, with panels including:
1) A saltire, with striated spindle in the upper section.
2) A corner tassel. *c* AD 50–70.
218 (G I 161) Form 29, South Gaulish. A fragment of rim and upper zone, with the upper concavity of a scroll containing a rosette, a spiral, ending in the same rosette, and a tendril with trifid motif. Neronian.
219 (G I 168, phase IV, early to mid-4th century) Form 29, South Gaulish. The lower zone has short, straight gadroons over a zone of fine chevron festoons, one containing a stirrup-leaf. The arrangement of this zone is paralleled in the late Neronian and early Flavian periods on bowls from London (stamped by Meddillus; Knorr 1952, Taf 40B) and Rottweil (unstamped; Knorr 1912, Taf V 3). *c* AD 65–80.
220 (G IA 2, with G IA 7, phase IX, late 4th century) Form 37, Central Gaulish. A freestyle scene includes a dog (D.934), a panther (D.804=0.1569, with a broken tail restored freehand) and leaf (Rogers H167). All the details were used at Lezoux by Casurius ii. Cf D I 176, v. *c* AD 160–90.
221 (G IA 7, phase VI, late 4th century?) See G IA 2.
222 (G IA 17B) Form 29, slightly burnt, South Gaulish. A fragment of the lower zone, with a saltire between panels with striated medallions. The trilobed motif in the top of the saltire and the rosettes in the corners of the other panels suggest a Neronian date. The bud-clusters in the saltire are on a bowl from Vechten (?) with a stamp of Bassus ii-Coelus. *c* AD 55–70.
223 (G IA 25, phase VI, late 4th century) Form 37, Central Gaulish, with ovolo Rogers B102. The sherd shows two double festoons, side-by-side, with a trifid tassel (Rogers G73) between them. One festoon contains a mask (not in D. or O.). All the details, apart from the mask, are known for Advocisus, though this arrangement is not paralleled on his stamped bowls. *c* AD 160–90.
224 (G IA 53, phase VIII+, late 4th century) Form 37, burnt, in the fabric of Les Martres-de-Veyre. The upper part of a panel contains arrowheads, probably flanked by diagonal wavy lines (as in S & S 1958, pl 47, 549). The lower part of the panel has a boar (D 826). The bowl has wavy-line borders and seven-beaded rosette junction-masks (Rogers C280). Not assignable to a particular potter, but certainly belonging to the period *c* AD 100–25.
225 (G IA 66) See G I 59.
226 (G IA 68, phase IV, early to mid-4th century, with G IV 20) Two fragments of form 29, South Gaulish. The upper zone has a winding scroll, with spirals and an uncommon five-petalled plant, or a trifid motif in a bifid cup. The four-beaded binding, used at La Graufesenque in the Claudian and Neronian periods, occurs on bowls from Camulodunum (Hawkes & Hull 1947, pl XXV, 2, 9). *c* AD 50–65.
227 (G IA 78) Form 37, South Gaulish. A fragment from a bowl with the panel border over-running into the zone occupied by the ovolo. The trident-tongued ovolo was used by Mommo and occurs also on a bowl from the Pompeii Hoard (Atkinson 1914, no 76) *c* AD 70–90.
228 (G II 2) i) Form 37, with an ovolo used at Lezoux by Cinnamus ii, Carantinus and Illixo (Rogers B145). *c* AD 150–80.
229 (G II 2) ii) Form 37, Central Gaulish. The lower concavity of a scroll has a double medallion with widely spaced borders, perhaps containing a leaf. The medallion suggests Paternus v, and he is known to have used the ovolo (Rogers B163). *c* AD 160–95.
230 (G II 14, phase I?, late 2nd/3rd century?) Eleven fragments from form 37, Central Gaulish. The (repeated) panels include:
1A) A crane to right (not in D or O);
1B) A pygmy (D 405).
2) A man with staff (perhaps O.583 variant).
3) A panther to left (O 1566).
4) = 2.
The ovolo (similar to Rogers B203, but smaller) was used by a Central Gaulish potter whose most characteristic motif is a small, beaded medallion. Bowls in his style are published from Ashfurlong, near Olney, Bucks (Simpson 1965, 7) and Watercrook (Potter 1979, 280, 48). It occurs also on bowls in his style from Abingdon (with the pygmy), Rochester, and Towcester. This potter cannot yet be closely dated, but his figure-types and motifs suggest a range *c* AD 135–70.
231 (G IV 1A) i) Form 29, South Gaulish. A fragment from the upper zone, with a winding scroll with large and small spirals and tendrils ending in a four-petalled plant (Knorr 1919, Taf 9, 48). The scroll has bead-and-chevron bindings. All the elements occur on bowls stamped by Aquitanus, and most of them are on a stamped example from Lake Farm, Wimborne. *c* AD 45–60.
232 (G IV 1A) ii) (with G IV 12) Form 37, Central Gaulish. The decoration includes a beaded circle (Rogers C290) and distinctive, heavy festoon (Rogers F33). Both are on a bowl by a member of the Quintilianus i group at Lezoux. *c* AD 135–50.
233 (G IV 1A) iii) Form 37, East Gaulish, in the style of either Atto or Belsus of Rheinzabern. The decoration includes the ovolo Ricken & Fischer 1963, E25 and an arcade supported on columns (Ricken & Fischer 1963, 0214) and containing a satyr (Ricken & Fischer 1963, M166). Late 2nd or early 3rd century.
234 (G IV 20, phase VI, late 4th century) See G IA 68.
235 (G IV 23, phase VI, late 4th century) Form 37, Central Gaulish. The decoration includes a panel with a tripod (Rogers Q16). The adjacent panel is divided horizontally. The vertical border of rhomboidal beads suggests a member of the Paternus v group. *c* AD 150–90.
236 (G IV 39, phase IV, early to mid-4th century) Form 37, South Gaulish. The ovolo was used at La Graufesenque by Memor, Mommo and a potter whose name begins in Trim . . . . The decoration consists of a panelled zone between an upper chevron wreath and a basal wreath of S-shaped gadroons. The surviving panels have a saltire and two dogs (smaller than O.1921), impressed one over the other. The gadroons are on a stamped form 29 of Iucundus iii from Strasbourg, and the fan-shaped plant in the saltire (Knorr 1919, Taf 43, 8) and, probably, the dog (Knorr 1919, 24?) are associated with his stamps. The scheme of decoration is reminiscent of bowls in the Pompeii Hoard (Atkinson 1914, pls VII–XVI). *c* AD 70–90.
237 (G IV 89) Form 37, Central Gaulish. The trilobed motif topping a panel border (Rogers G113) was used at Lezoux by Attianus ii and Martialis ii. This bowl is probably by Attianus, since Martialis is not known to have used a wavy line below the ovolo. The chevron festoon (Rogers F41?) is probably the same as one on stamped bowls of Attianus (S & S 1958, pl 87, 26, from Leicester, London, and Wroxeter), which also appear to have the same ovolo (Rogers B61). *c* AD 125–45.
238 (G V 29, 50, 51, NB the sherd in bag G V 29 is marked 28) Three fragments of form 37, Central Gaulish. The scheme of decoration is far from clear, but it is divided into panels by borders of untidy beads with astragali at the bottom. The figure-types include a naked man (O.637), and a seated satyr (D.362 variant). The motifs include a column (Rogers P10?) used both vertically and horizontally, cushion (Rogers U2), and acanthus (Rogers K16?). Some of these details were used by X-5, others by Docilis i, and some are common to them both. The beaded borders tip the balance in favour of Docilis though the arrangement of festoon and medallion is not otherwise known for him. *c* AD 135–50.
239 (G V 58) Form 37, Central Gaulish, with freestyle decoration including a dog (D.934) and, probably, a lion (D.766), and panther (D.787?). A spiky leaf (Rogers H101) was used at Lezoux by Cinnamus ii, as were the animals, but it is equally possible that this bowl is by Secundus v, since all the details occur on bowls in

his style. Cf Karnitsch 1959, Taf 68, 8, from Wels, which is not in Cinnamus's usual style, but might be by Secundus. *c* AD 150–80.

Site H

240 (H I 1) See H I 5.
241 (H I 5, phase II, Antonine to 3rd century) i) (with H I 1, 19). Three fragments of form 37, with an ovolo used at La Graufesenque by Memor, Mommo, and a potter whose name begins in Trim . . . (Knorr 1952, Taf 53A, under Sasmonos, ie Memoris). *c* AD 70–90.
242 (H I 5, phase II, Antonine to 3rd century) ii) Two fragments of form 37, South Gaulish. The ovolo with large rosette tongue was used at La Graufesenque by Calvus i. The decoration includes a scroll, a chevron wreath, and a zone of straight gadroons. *c* AD 70–90.
243 (H I 14) Five fragments, two joining, of form 29, South Gaulish. Two wide panels in the upper zone are separated by multiple wavy-line borders. One contains rows of pointed leaf-tips. The other has a saltire, with diagonals ending in poppy-heads, and spirals between them. For the use of spirals, cf Knorr 1919, Taf 13M, which has a stamp of the Bassus ii-Coelus firm and a bowl from Aislingen (Knorr 1912a, Taf X, 15), which may be from the same workshop. The multiple borders are on a Bassus-Coelus bowl from Risstissen. *c* AD 60–80.
244 (H I 19, phase II, Antonine to 3rd century) See H I 5, i.
245 (H II 5, phase III, Antonine to 3rd century on) Form 37, with ovolo Rogers B144 and a pygmy (O.696A), both used at Lezoux by the Cerialis ii-Cinnamus ii group. *c* AD 135–70.
246 (H II 6A, phase III, Antonine to 3rd century on) Form 37, Central Gaulish. The single-bordered ovolo with beaded tongue (Rogers B12) was used at Lezoux by Sacer ii, Criciro v, Cinnamus ii, and some of their associates. A panel includes a single festoon containing a dolphin. The ovolo and festoon are on a stamped bowl of Cinnamus ii from Corbridge, and the beads are consistent with his style. *c* AD 150–80.
247 (H II 74, phase II, Antonine to 3rd century) Form 37, Central Gaulish, with a single-bordered scroll. The ovolo (Rogers B144), birds (D 1019, 1038), and bud (Rogers J178, partially impressed) were all used at Lezoux by members of the Cerialis ii-Cinnamus ii group. The details, and particularly the ovolo, are unusually sharp, and the bowl is probably from a fairly new mould. *c* AD 135–70.
248 (H II 74A, phase II, Antonine to 3rd century) Two fragments of form 37, Central Gaulish, with scroll decoration. The ovolo (Rogers B143), large leaf (Rogers H31), and rosette (Rogers C98) were all used at Lezoux by Cinnamus ii. *c* AD 150–80.
249 (H III 1) Form 37, Central Gaulish, stamped CI[NNAMIOF] (see stamp 17). The decoration includes his ovolo 3 (Rogers B143) and a panel containing a festoon. *c* AD 150–80.

Site L

250 (L I 7) i) (with L VI 1) Form 37, in the style of Drusus i (X-3) of Les Martres-de-Veyre. The decoration includes his single-bordered ovolo (Rogers B28) and panels:
1) A saltire, with acanthi (Rogers K25) in all four sections.
2A) A pygmy (O.692A variant) and seven-beaded rosette (Rogers C280), in a double festoon;
2B) acanthi (Rogers K25), impressed horizontally, stem-to-stem. The basal wreath consists of beaded rings (Rogers C294).
Cf S & S 1958, pl 13, 160, 153 for the details. *c* AD 100–25.
251 (L I 7) ii) Form 37, Central Gaulish, with panelled decoration. The ovolo (Rogers B82, with the tongue incompletely impressed) and vertical borders of rhomboidal beads topped by masks are on a stamped bowl of Butrio (S & S 1958, pl 58, 659). The Pudicitia (D.40) is on a bowl in his style from Chester (S & S 1958, pl 59, 669). *c* AD 125–40.
252 (L VI 9) Form 29, South Gaulish. The lower zone consists of straight gadroons. The upper zone has festoons containing fan-shaped plants and separated by pendant leaves. The plant and leaf are on forms 29 and 37 respectively, from Wels (Karnitsch 1959, Taf 3, 8; 8, 7). *c* AD 60–80.
253 (L VIII 3, phase IV, mid-4th century) Form 37, Central Gaulish, with one of Iullinus ii's ovolos (Rogers B156) and a border of rhomboidal beads. The decoration includes a leaf (not in Rogers, and not known for Iullinus). The scheme of decoration is not clear. *c* AD 160–90.
254 (L IX 1) Form 37, Central Gaulish, in the style of Geminus iii (Stanfield's G Iulius Vibius). The decoration includes his commonest ovolo (Rogers B76) and a zone of small, double medallions containing birds and pairs of dolphins (O.2298 and 2407A), alternately. The medallions have trilobed motifs below (Rogers G112) and between them (Rogers G173) and are flanked in the upper part of the zone by the smaller of these motifs. All the details, apart from the ovolo and larger trilobed motif, are on a signed bowl from Catterick. The bird and dolphin are also on one of his bowls, from Berghausen (S & S 1958, pl 66, 20). This piece is slightly burnt and has traces of a lead rivet. The wall is shallow and thick and the bowl seems, from the grooving below the decoration, to have been removed from the mould with a wire, which also obliterated some of the design. The foot-ring is worn. Geminus iii may have started work at Les Martres-de-Veyre, but this bowl is in Lezoux fabric. *c* AD 125–40.
255 (L XII 6) Form 37, Central Gaulish, with scroll decoration. The naked man (D.403) and pygmy (O.656A) were both used at Lezoux by members of the Cerialis ii-Cinnamus ii group. *c* AD 135–70.
256 (L XII 10) i) Form 37, Central Gaulish, with freestyle decoration.
Probably by Paternus v, who used the dog (O.1926A) and horse and rider (D.157). Cf S & S 1958, pl 106, 22. *c* AD 160–95.
257 (L XII 10) ii) Form 37, Central Gaulish. A fragment from a thick-walled bowl with a hare (close to D.950A), repeated on either side of a bifurcated tendril. The style is not diagnostic, but the bowl is certainly mid- or late Antonine.

Site M

258 (M III 3, phase IV, Roman/post-Roman) i) Form 37, Central Gaulish, with ovolo 3 of Cinnamus ii (Rogers B143). *c* AD 150–80.
259 (M III 3, phase IV, Roman/post-Roman) ii) Form 30, Central Gaulish, in the style of Do(v)eccus i. The decoration includes an arcade with a Cupid (D.251). The arcade is joined to a column by an eight-petalled rosette (Rogers C167). The adjacent panel has a festoon (Rogers F61) in the upper part. The ovolo is Rogers B161. *c* AD 165–200.

Potters' stamps

The entries run number, potter (i, ii, etc, where homonyms are involved), die, form, reading, pottery kilns of origin, and are arranged in alphabetical order by potter's name. These stamps are not illustrated as they will appear in the corpus presently being prepared.

Superscript a, b, and c indicate:

[a] A stamp attested at the pottery kilns in question.
[b] Not attested at the pottery kilns in question, but the potter is known to have worked there.
[c] Assigned to the pottery kilns on the evidence of form, fabric, etc.

The stamps from pit groups are listed separately, below.

S1 (C III 15) Advocisus 2a 79 (?) ADVO[CISI·O] Lezoux.[a]
A stamp from a die used on forms 31R, 79, 80, and Ludowici Tx. It is recorded from Bainbridge, Catterick (2) and Malton. *c* AD 160–90.
S2 (C III 1) Aisius 3a 27 A ISI·I'IIC retrograde Lezoux.[c]
Aisius's range of forms includes 18/31–31, 31, 31R, 80 and 81, but the only other recorded example of this particular stamp is also on form 27. *c* AD 140–60.
S3 (G IA 17A) Albucius ii 3c 79 (?) [ALBVC]I OF Lezoux.[b]
This stamp occurs on forms 31R and 80, but also on form 27, showing that it was in use before *c* AD 160. *c* AD 150–80.
S4 (D IV 16) Andegenus 3a 33 (?) A NDEGENI[·F] Lezoux.[b]
Andegenus's stamps occur in the Antonine fire deposits at

Verulamium, in a group of burnt samian of *c* AD 170 from Tác (Hungary), and at Alcester, in the D II 29A pit. His range of forms includes 18/31, 18/31R, 27, and 79. There is no internal dating evidence of this particular stamp. *c* AD 150–80.

S5 (D I 71, phase V, early to mid-4th century?) Anius (?) 6b 27g [A]NI La Graufesenque.[c]
A stamp noted elsewhere on forms 24 and Ritt.9. Neronian.

S6–7 (AA I 43; C III I) Annius ii 6a 27; 33 ANN[I·M]; AN[NI·M] retrograde Lezoux.[a]
Annius ii almost certainly started work at Les Martres-de-Veyre, though it is not likely that Die 6a was used there. His earliest and latest stamps occur in the Second Fire groups from London and *Verulamium*, respectively. This particular stamp has been noted from Corbridge and Falkirk, and on forms 18/31, 18/31R, and 31. *c* AD 130–50.

S8 (G I 119, phase IV, early to mid-4th century) Ardacus 12a 15/17 AR[DACI] La Graufesenque.[b]
Ardacus's output is entirely pre-Flavian. His wares turn up at Velsen (before *c* AD 47) and in a large pit group of samian of *c* AD 50–60 at La Graufesenque. This particular stamp occurs on forms 24, 29, and Ritterling 9. *c* AD 40–65.

S9 (C I 14) Asiaticus 6a 33 [ASIATC]IM (sic) Lezoux.[b]
Asiaticus's output includes several examples of forms 79 and 79R, though this particular (misspelled) die seems to have been used only on forms 31 and 33. *c* AD 160–90.

S10 (D IV 2) Attianus iii (probably) 4c (probably) 31R [ATTIA]ИVS Rheinzabern.[a]
This potter is best dated by his forms, which include 32, 36, and 36R. Whether by him or not, the dish is East Gaulish and late 2nd or early 3rd century.

S11 (AA I 1) Attillus v 2a 33 AT·T[ILLIM] Lezoux.[b]
This stamp occurs at Corbridge and at northern forts reoccupied in the 160s. His range of forms includes 32, 31R, and 80 and his decorated ware is early Antonine. *c* AD 150–80.

S12 (G I 34) Avitus iii 10a 33 [AVIF Lezoux.[b]
An uncommon stamp of a potter whose plain wares turn up in Antonine Scotland. His decorated bowls are Hadrianic. *c* AD 125–50.

S13 (AA III 17) Balbinus 2a 18/31 IIИI[BINI·M] Les Martres-de-Veyre.[a]
This stamp is noted in the London Second Fire deposits and on form 15/17, showing that the die was in use in the Trajanic period. The clearest examples give BALBINI·M, but cleaning of the die blurred the letters, so that the stamp usually appears as at Alcester, and is often taken to belong to a non-existent Ainibinus or Enibinus. *c* AD 100–25.

S14 (G V 1) Belinicus i 11a 31 BE[LINICIM] retrograde Lezoux.[a]
Some of this potter's stamps occur both at Les Martres-de-Veyre and Lezoux but this, one of his latest, comes from a die used only at Lezoux. There are examples from Hadrian's Wall, Antonine Scotland and the Wroxeter forum destruction, and it occurs on forms 15/31 and 80. *c* AD 140–65.

S15 (D II 2, phase IX, late 4th century) Cabucatus 4a 29 CABV [CAF] La Graufesenque.[b]
A stamp of the potter whose name is often taken as Canrucatus (Hermet 1934, pls 103–5), or Canrugatus. Some of his work is Flavian, but this stamp, from one of his less common dies, occurs on form 24 and at Aislingen (before *c* AD 75). *c* AD 60–75.

S16 (D I 83) Caratus ii 2b 33 CARA]TI·M Les Martres-de-Veyre,[a] Lezoux.[b]
Although this stamp is attested at Les Martres, the fabrics of most of the examples noted belong to the Lezoux range. The site records include Corbridge and, almost certainly, Newstead, and the forms include 18/31 and 27. *c* AD 130–60.

S17 (H III 1) Cinnamus ii 1a 37 CI[NNAMIOF] Lezoux,[a] Lubié,[a] Vichy (Terre-Franche).[a]
A stamp noted on decorated bowls from Wroxeter (with a stamp of Mercator iv applied, after moulding, below the decoration) and Halton Chesters. *c* AD 150–80.

S18–19 (AA I 29, phase IX, mid-4th century; D II 16) Cinnamus ii 5b 37 (2)]NNAM[; CINNAMI retrograde Lezoux,[a] Lubié,[a] Vichy (Terre-Franche).[a]
Decorated bowls with this stamp are common on both Hadrian's Wall and the Antonine Wall, but are slightly more numerous in Scotland. *c* AD 150–80.

S20 (A XVII B2) Clemens iii 2a 38 CLE[MENTI] Lezoux.[a]
A stamp noted from Hadrian's Wall and Piercebridge, and on forms 31R and Ludowici Tg. Clemens was associated with Priscus iii in the production of decorated ware, and their stamps appear together on a mould from Lezoux. *c* AD 160–90.

S21 (H II 1) Cornutus iii 1a 27 CORNVTVS Lezoux.[c]
The only other example noted of this stamp is on form 18/31 from York. The fabric of this and the glaze of the Alcester piece suggest origin at Les Martres-de-Veyre. Trajanic or Hadrianic.

S22 (C VI 2A) Crestus 2a′ 27g OFCRES<T> La Graufesenque.[b]
Crestus's earliest work includes early Flavian form 29s, but stamps from the full version of this particular die occur at Domitianic foundations, such as Cannstatt, Wilderspool, and the main site at Corbridge. The range for the die is *c* AD 80–100, but later versions from which fewer stamps are recorded cannot be precisely dated within the range.

S23 (A XI 15) Cucalus 1a 33 CVC[AKIMI] Lezoux.[b]
Cucalus's stamps turn up in Antonine Scotland and at Corbridge. His range of forms includes 18/31R, 27, 79, and 80. There is no dating evidence for this particular stamp. *c* AD 140–70.

S24 (C VI 40) Dagomarus 4c 18/31 DAGO[MARVS·F] Les Martres-de-Veyre, Lezoux.[bc]
Some of Dagomarus's dies were used at both Les Martres and Lezoux, but the fabrics associated with this stamp suggest that it came from a die used only at Les Martres. There are examples from Catterick, Hadrian's Wall (Chesters Museum), and *Verulamium* (Period IIB; *c* AD 110–40), and on forms 18/31 and 27. One of his other stamps occurs in the London Second Fire deposits. *c* AD 110–25.

S25 (A XVI 7) Do(v)eccus i 5a 30 DOIICCI Lezoux.[a]
There are several decorated bowls with this stamp from Hadrian's Wall and Hinterland forts, including Brougham, where the samian from the cemetery is mostly late Antonine. *c* AD 165–200.

S26 (H II 91, phase III, Antonine to 3rd century on) Do(v)eccus i 11a 38 (burnt) DO[VIICC]VS Lezoux.[b]
This occurs on form 15/31 at Rough Castle and is one of the latest stamps recorded from a Scottish fort with a normal Antonine occupation. It appears also on Hadrian's Wall (Chesters Museum) and was used on dishes, form 31R. *c* AD 160–90.

S27 (L IX 1) Do(v)eccus i 11b 79 [DOVII]CCVS Lezoux.[b]
A stamp recorded from Catterick and on form 31R. *c* AD 165–200.

S28–29 (D I 48; D I 109, phase VI, mid- to late 4th century, and phase II, later 2nd to early 3rd century? respectively) Dontio 6a 27g; 27]NTIOI[; DONTIOIIICI La Graufesenque.[b]
Dontio's output is mainly Flavian, though this stamp occurs at the pre-Flavian cemeteries at Nijmegen and one of his less common dies was used on form 24. *c* AD 65–90.

S30 (G I 60E) Felix i 4b′ 18 [OF·FE]ΓIC<I> La Graufesenque.[a]
Felix's stamps occur in the Boudiccan burning at Colchester and on forms 24 and Ritterling 9, but some of his wares reached Flavian foundations. There is no dating evidence for either Die 4b or its broken version. *c* AD 60–75.

S31 (E II 71, phase III, Neronian–Trajanic) Firmo ii 4a 27 OF.FIRMo La Graufesenque.[b]
Firmo ii's wares occur in a Tiberian pit at La Graufesenque and his forms include 16 and Ritterling 5. There is no dating evidence for this particular stamp, and an example from Chester may be a survival. Die 4a is perhaps to be dated *c* AD 45–60, since it has not been noted on any of the earliest samian forms.

S32 (E II 71, phase III, Neronian–Trajanic) Frontinus 33b 27 FR[ON]La Graufesenque.[b]
This stamp is from one of Frontinus's less common dies, for which no dating evidence has been noted. His wares reached sites such as Cannstatt, Camelon, and the Saalburg, but his frequent use of form 29 suggests that he began work in the early Flavian period. *c* AD 70–95.

S33 (H II 1) Gallus ii 4a 15/17 or 18 GALLIO+ La Graufesenque.[a]
Gallus ii's stamps occur in Claudio-Neronian groups of samian from La Graufesenque and Narbonne (La Nautique). This particular one appears at the Kingsholm site at Gloucester, from which most of the material is pre-Flavian. *c* AD 50–65.

S34 (D I T/S) Geminus vi 6a 31 GEM[INIF] Lezoux.[a]
Much of this Geminus's output consists of samian mortaria of form 45. No stamps from this die have been recorded on such vessels, but its use on forms 31R and 79 attests a mid- to late Antonine date. *c* AD 160–200.

S35 (D II 60) Habilis (?) 4a 18/31 ABILI·M Lezoux.[a]
It is not certain whether this stamp belongs to Habilis or to an Abilus, for whom no other dies are known. The open B, which occurs on some of Habilis's stamps, may tip the balance in his favour. His forms include 27, 79, 80, and Ludowici Tg and his

stamps occur at Chester-le-Street and at forts on Hadrian's Wall reoccupied *c* AD 160. The uneven foot-ring of this dish and the finger-nail marks on the surface suggest that it is by an apprentice, and so the shallowness of the wall may not be an indication of date. *c* AD 150–80.

S36 (D I 25, phase VIII, late 4th century) Ianuarius ii 5a 33 (heavily burnt) IANVARI Lezoux.[b]
This stamp has been recorded so far only on cups of form 33, one of which is more likely to be Hadrianic than later. His range also includes forms 18/31, 18/31R, 27, 38 (?), and 42. One of his stamps comes from Ebchester. *c* AD 120–50.

S37 (L V 9) Iullinus i (probably) 7a (probably) 15/17 [IVL]LI[N] La Graufesenque.[a]
The site record for this stump includes Domitianic foundations, such as Butzbach (2) and the main site at Corbridge (2). There is also an example from the Inchtuthil Gutter. The form of the dish suggests a date *c* AD 70–85.

S38 (D I T/S) Lentiscus 2a 18/31R LENTISCVS Les Martres-de-Veyre.[a]
A stamp recorded from the London Second Fire groups and on forms 18/31, 18/31R, 27 and the earlier type of form 33. *c* AD 100–25.

S39 (L XVI 8) Libertus i 4a 27g IBERTVS La Graufesenque.[b]
This stamp is perhaps from a broken die. There are several examples from Flavian foundations, but also two from Hofheim (before *c* AD 75). Stamps from one of his other dies occur at Camulodunum (2) and on forms 24, 29 (with pre-Flavian decoration), and Ritterling forms 8 and 9. *c* AD 65–85.

S40 (C II 111) Luppa 2a 33 [LV]PPA Lezoux.[b]
Luppa's wares, including ones with this particular stamp, reached the Rhineland and Scotland, suggesting activity in the Hadrianic–Antonine period. Stamps from Die 2a occur on forms 18/31, 27, and 81. *c* AD 130–55.

S41 (G I 44) Macrinus iii 5b 31 M[ACRINI] Lezoux.[a]
Apart from one example on form 27, all the stamps recorded from this die are on either form 31 or 33. It is attested at Chesters, South Shields and Newstead and, twice, from the Wroxeter Gutter. *c* AD 150–80.

S42 (G IV 22, phase VI, late 4th century) Mainacnus 2a 31 MAI[NCNI] (sic) Lezoux.[b]
The site record for this stamp includes Rudchester and South Shields. There are six examples from Pudding Pan Rock. *c* AD 160–200.

S43 (D II 28) Malliacus 3f 18/31 MALLIACI Lezoux.[b]
Malliacus's stamped vessels reached Corbridge (2), Scotland, and northern forts evacuated when Hadrian's Wall was built. Stamps from one of his dies occur in a group of burnt samian of *c* AD 140–50 at Castleford. His forms include 18/31R, 27, and 31. *c* AD 140–60, in view of the form.

S44 (C VIII, with big pot) Malluro i 7a 31 [MALL] V RVF Lezoux.[a]
The stamp is recorded on a wide range of forms, including 18/31, 27, 31, 42, 79, and 80, but there is no site dating for it. Stamps from his other dies occur on Hadrian's Wall, in the Rhineland and at Bar Hill. *c* AD 140–70.

S45 (D I 109, phase II, later 2nd to early 3rd century?) Manduilus 6a 29 [MAN]DVILMA La Graufesenque.[a]
Decorated bowls with this stamp occur at Nanstallon (on form 29 with the same upper zone as a bowl stamped by Senicio), Chester, York, and in the Pompeii Hoard. *c* AD 60–80.

S46 (AA II 2) Mapillus 2a 33 MA PIKKI ·M[v] Lezoux,[b] Vichy (Terre-Franche).[b]
An unusually large example of the form, in coarse orangey fabric with dull, red-brown glaze. The stamp has not been noted before and no other examples of stamps in . . . MV (ie m(an)u) are known. Mapillus's stamps occur on forms 27 and 79/80 and at Corbridge. His decorated style is connected with one of those used by Pugnus ii. *c* AD 130–60.

S47 (D I 246, phase II, later 2nd to early 3rd century?) Marcellinus i 1c′ 18/31 MARCIIKK IN<I> Les Martres-de-Veyre.[a]
The original version of this die was used at Les Martres on forms which are normally Trajanic or Hadrianic. Several burnt examples from London are likely to have been involved in the Second Fire. However, both the original and the secondary versions occur on forms 79 and 79/80 (one each), which presupposes pre-Antonine versions of the form at Les Martres. Probably c AD 115–35.

S48 (L IX 1) Martinus iii 1a 31R MAR[TIN]IM Lezoux.[b]
A stamp recorded from Malton and twice, on form 79, from Pudding Pan Rock. *c* AD 160–200.

S49 (H II 75, phase II, Antonine to 3rd century) Masc(u)lus i 19a 15/17 or 18 MASCV]LVS La Graufesenque.[a]
Though Masc(u)lus i's output is mostly pre-Flavian, this particular stamp has been noted from Caerleon, Chester (2), and the Nijmegen fortress, and so the die will probably have been in use after AD 70. *c* AD 55–75.

S50 (G IV 46, phase I?, late 2nd/3rd century?) Murranus 10d′ 27g FM[VRR/] La Graufesenque.[b]
This die, in both its original and recut state, was used on form Ritterling 8. Other stamps of Murranus occur in the Boudiccan burning at Colchester, in Period I at *Verulamium*, and in a Claudio-Neronian group of samian at La Graufesenque. *c* AD 50–65.

S51 (D I 87B) Muxtullus 1a 31R MVXTVLLIM Lezoux.[b]
One of Muxtullus's later stamps, noted from Hadrian's Wall, Chester-le-Street, and the Wroxeter Gutter. It was, however, used on form 18/31R. *c* AD 155–75, on the form.

S52 (D I 109, phase II, later 2nd to early 3rd century?) Nequres 1a, a′ or a″ 27g NEQ[VRES] etc La Graufesenque.[a]
Four distinct stages can be seen in the life of this die. The latest gives -EQVRE, but the others all have NE. All the possible versions for this stamp appear both at pre-Flavian and Flavian foundations, but are slightly more common at the latter. *c* AD 60–80.

S53 (AA III 39) Pass(i)enus 9a′ 15/17 or 18 (FP)ASSE.
One of the potter's latest stamps, not uncommon at Flavian foundations, including Camelon. An earlier version of the die from which it comes was used in the pre-Flavian period, but perhaps also in the 70s. The modified die, 9a′, had swallow-tails cut into the ends of the frame, presumably to disguise a small chip. 9a gave OFPASSE, but stamps from 9a′, including this piece, often look almost like FPARE. *c* AD 70–85.

S54 (D II 36, phase I, 1st century to early Antonine) Pass(i)enus 16a′ 15/17 or 18 (burnt) <O>PASSEN La Graufesenque.[a]
The die from which this stamp comes was used, in both the original and recut versions, on form 29s with decoration typical of the period. *c* AD 50–65.

S55 (G IA 49, phase IX, late 4th century) Pass(i)enus 60a 15/17 or 18 PASSIEN La Graufesenque.[b]
A few of Pass(i)enus's stamps, though not apparently this one, were in use in the early Flavian period. It has been noted from Aislingen (2) and the Kingsholm site at Gloucester. *c* AD 50–65.

S56 (E II 78, phase III, Neronian–Trajanic) Patricius i 17e′ 27g [<P>A]TRI<C> La Graufesenque.[b]
There is no site dating for the stamps from the full die, but examples from the broken die occur at Caerleon, Chester, York, and the main site at Corbridge. *c* AD 75–95.

S57 (L III 10, phase IV, late Roman/modern) Paullus v 8c′ 79 (?) PAAAKJI Lezoux.[a]
There are five stamps from the original die (8c) from Pudding Pan Rock, all on form 79. Die 8c′ is presumably later than 8c, since some recutting of the letters seems to have been involved. *c* AD 175–200.

S58 (H II 61) Primus iii (probably) 12r (probably) 15/17 or 18 [OFPRIA]MI La Graufesenque.[a]
Although stamps from Die 12r seem to read OFPRIAMI
there is no doubt from the lettering that they belong to the later La Graufesenque Primus. The die is used mainly on rouletted dishes and on bowls of form 29, the decoration of which suggests a range *c* AD 50–70.

S59 (AA I 32, phase VI, late 3rd to early 4th century) Reditus 3a 33 REDITI·M Lezoux.[c]
Reditus's stamps occur in the Saalburg Erdkastell (before AD 139) and in a group of burnt samian of *c* AD 170 at Tác (Hungary). This particular one occurs in the Rhineland, suggesting that it was in use in the first half of the 2nd century, and examples from Camelon and Corbridge show that it was current after AD 140. The forms include 18/31 and 27 (?). *c* AD 135–60.

S60 (AA I 19, phase VII, late 3rd to early 4th century) Regalis i 3a′ 18/31R [RI]IGALI<S·M> Lezoux.[b] Stamps from this broken die appear on forms 27 and 80, on Hadrian's Wall (Chesters Museum) and at Corbridge and Newstead. Regalis also made forms 79 and Ludowici Tg. *c* AD 150–80.

S61 (D I 2, phase VIII, late 4th century) Rentus 1a 27 RENTI.OF Lezoux.[a]
A stamp used on forms 18/31 and 31. Other stamps occur on decorated ware, including form 29, which was occasionally made at Lezoux in the Trajanic and Hadrianic periods. *c* AD 120–40.

S62 (A XIV 30, T) Rufinus iii 4c′ 27 (complete)]FRVFIA La Graufesenque.[a]
Stamps from both the full die (giving OFRVFIN) and the broken version occur at Flavian foundations. Rufinus ii started work in the 60s, but most of his output is Flavian. *c* AD 75–90.
S63 (A XVI 26) Samogenus 1a 33 SAMOGE[NI] Lezoux.[c]
There is no site dating for this stamp, but its use on forms 27 and 80 suggests a date *c* AD 140–70.
S64 (E II 37, phase IV, Hadrianic–Antonine) Sarrutus 1a 15/17 or 18 OF.SARRVT La Graufesenque.[a]
A stamp noted from Domitianic foundations, such as Butzbach and the main site at Corbridge, but also at Risstissen (before *c* AD 75) and on form 29. *c* AD 70–90.
S65 (D I 46, phase V, early to mid-4th century?) Secundus ii 25a 15/17 or 18 SECVN[DVSF] La Graufesenque.[a]
This stamp occurs at the Nijmegen fortress (2) and Camelon. The latter perhaps suggests that this die was not in use in the pre-Flavian period, though he may have started work as early as *c* AD 60. *c* AD 70–90.
S66 (AA II 87, phase III, 3rd century) Sedatus iv 2a 33 SEDA[TI·M] Lezoux.[a]
This stamp was also used on forms 18/31, 27, and 31. One of his other stamps comes from Corbridge and his signature appears on the base of a jar mould also signed by Paullus iv, who was associated with Cinnamus ii in the early part of his career. *c* AD 125–50.
S67 (D I 98, phase V, early to mid-4th century?) Servus iv 1b 37 [S]ERVM retrograde Lezoux,[a] Vichy (Terre-Franche).[a]
The style of decoration used by Servus iv suggests a date of *c* AD 160–90.
S68 (A XI 1) Severianus i 2a 33 [SEVER]IANIMA Lezoux.[a]
A stamp noted on forms 79 (including one from Pudding Pan Rock), 80, and 31R. *c* AD 160–200.
S68A (D I 87D, phase V, early to mid-4th century?) Severus vi 3d 33 SIIVIIRIM Lezoux.[b]
There is no internal dating evidence for this stamp, but Severus vi used other dies on forms which were not normally made before *c* AD 160, such as 31R, 79, and 80, and his stamps turn up at forts in northern Britain reoccupied about that time. The evidence of his decorated ware, too, is consistent with a date *c* AD 160–90. The cup has graffiti inscribed under the lower wall and inside the foot-ring, after firing. The absence of internal glaze on the outer edge of the base suggests that liquid had been stirred in the cup.
S69 (C VI 11, phase VI, early to mid-4th century) Severianus i 3a 31 SEVE[RIANI· W] Lezoux.[a]
For Severianus i's date, see no 111. This particular stamp occurs at Stanwix. *c* AD 160–200.
S70 (D I 2, phase VIII, late 4th century) Suadullius 3a 37 rim SVADV·LLIVS Ittenweiler,[b] Rheinzabern.[b]
This stamp occurs on the rim of a bowl from Carlisle from a mould made by Reginus vi and there is an example of plain ware from Great Chesters. Suadullius's range includes form 40, which was probably not made at Rheinzabern before the late Antonine period, but he is not likely to have worked in the 3rd century, since he started his career at Ittenweiler. This piece is almost certainly from Rheinzabern. *c* AD 160–90.
S71 (E I 19, phase III, Neronian–Trajanic) Sulpicius 8c 18 SVLPICI La Graufesenque.[b]
This die was also used to stamp decorated moulds and the stamp appears on form 37 at Wilderspool. Some of his stamps occur at other sites founded under Domitian, such as Cannstatt, the Saalburg, and the main site at Corbridge. *c* AD 80–110.
S72 (M III 17, phase I, late 2nd to early 3rd century) Tempera 1a 31 TEM[PERA] Lezoux.[c]
The fabric and glaze suggest an Antonine date.
S73 (H I 1) Verecundus ii 8a 27 [VE]RECV La Graufesenque,[a] Banassac.[b]
This stamp is from a die which was apparently used only on form 27. Other examples have been noted from Binchester, Caerlon, and Watercrook. Verecundus ii seems to have begun work in the 50s, since one of his stamps appears in a group of samian of that date from La Graufesenque, but Die 8a is almost certainly Flavian. *c* AD 70–85.
S74 (D I 87D, phase V, early to mid-4th century) Victor iv 1a 31 VIC[TORIM] Lezoux.[a]
A stamp noted in a grave at Sompting, Sussex, on the late Antonine form 79R, together with stamps of Rheinzabern and other Lezoux potters and a scarcely worn coin of Geta as Caesar (Dannell & Hartley 1974, 312). *c* AD 170–200.
S75 (A XIV 24) Virtus i 8b 15/17 or 18 VIRTVTI[S] La Graufesenque.[b]
This is from a die which seems to have been used only in the Flavian period. Stamps from it occur on dishes only, including one from Camelon. Virtus i was at work by AD 60 at the latest, however, as one of his stamps occurs in the Boudiccan burning at Colchester. *c* AD 70–90.
S76 (B I 2, phase II, Antonine to 3rd century) Vitalis iii 2a 18/31 [V]ITALIS ·M· S·F Les Martres-de-Veyre.[a]
This stamp occurs at Malton and Corbridge and in groups from the London Second Fire. It was used occasionally on form 15/17, which at Les Martres was not normally made after the Trajanic period. *c* AD 100–25.

Illiterate

S77 (D I 176)]IIIИ on form 27, South Gaulish. Flavian or Flavian–Trajanic.
S78 (A XVI 8) AVI·IV on form 31, Central Gaulish. Antonine.

Rosette, etc

S79 (AA I 12, phase VI, late 3rd to early 4th century) A six-petalled rosette on form Curle 15 or 23, Central Gaulish. Antonine.
S80 (G V 100, phase VI, late 4th century) A fragmentary rosette on form 46, Central Gaulish. Antonine.
S81 (G IV 38, phase I?, late 2nd/early 3rd century?) A rosette with eight (?) radiating spokes on form 32 etc, East Gaulish. Late 2nd or 3rd century.
S82 (A XVI 7) A herringbone stamp on form 31, Central Gaulish. Antonine.
S83 (H II 1) A fragmentary herringbone stamp on form 33, Central Gaulish. Antonine.
S84 (G I 56, phase V, later 4th century) A fish on form 32 etc, East Gaulish. Late 2nd or early 3rd century.

Unidentified

S85 (G I 90) An illegible stamp on form 27, South Gaulish. Neronian.
S86 (F V 14A) O[or]O on form 27, South Gaulish. Pre-Flavian.
S87 (G I 89, phase IV, early to mid-4th century) OF[on form 18, South Gaulish. Neronian or early Flavian.
S88 (G I 106A, phase V, later 4th century)]PANI on form 15/17 or 18, slightly burnt. The coarse, micaceous fabric and orange-brown glaze suggest origin at Lezoux in the 1st century. The stamp probably belongs to Campanus i, two of whose stamps have already been noted from Alcester. In view of the comparative scarcity of 1st-century Lezoux ware in Britain, it is likely that the three vessels arrived at the site in the same consignment. Neronian or early Flavian.
S89 (H II 74, phase II, Antonine to 3rd century) O[or]O on a dish, South Gaulish. Flavian.
S90 (C VI 66, phase IV, later 3rd century on)]SF on form 18, South Gaulish. Probably Flavian.
S91 (E IV 46, phase VI, early 3rd century?) O[or]O on form 27, South Gaulish. Flavian or Flavian–Trajanic.
S92 (L VI 9) O[or]O on a dish, South Gaulish. Flavian or Flavian–Trajanic.
S93 (D II 27)]VI[on form 15/17 or 18, South Gaulish. Flavian or Flavian–Trajanic.
S94 (AA I 41, phase VIII, early to mid-4th century) A[on form 33a (?), South Gaulish. 1st-century.
S95 (B IA 9)]INVS·FE on form 18/31 or 31, Central Gaulish. Hadrianic or early Antonine.
S96 (B I 4, phase II, Antonine to 3rd century)]F on form 44/81, Central Gaulish. Hadrianic or early Antonine.
S97 (D I 87, phase V, early to mid-4th century?)]M on form 31, Central Gaulish. Antonine.
S98 (A XVI 1) T[on form 33, Central Gaulish. Antonine.
S99 (D I 102, phase VI, mid- to late 4th century?)]M on form 31, burnt, Central Gaulish. Antonine.
S100 (A V 3, phase VI, late 3rd to early 4th century) S[or]S on form 31, Central Gaulish. Antonine.

S101 (A IX 1C) O[or]O on form 31, Central Gaulish. Antonine.

S102 (G I 34) [illegible] on form 33, Central Gaulish. Perhaps an illiterate stamp. Antonine.
S103 (L IX 1)]N or]M on form 80, Central Gaulish. Mid- to late Antonine.
S104 (AA II 8A) Λ . . . . . M on form 33 or, less probably, 27, Central Gaulish (?). Second century (?).
S105 (A IX U/S) ƳTTX/FEC retrograde on form 33, Central Gaulish (?). Antonine.
S106 (B I 14) An illegible stamp on form 31, East Gaulish. Antonine or later.
S107 (C V1)]ĸMMI on form 31, East Gaulish. Late 2nd or early 3rd century.

Pit B I 3

A pit group of Hadrianic or early Antonine samian, including four more-or-less complete pots which, apart from one (the dish of Calava), had certainly been used before breakage. A date *c* AD 145–55 seems likely for the filling of the pit. (B I 3, phase II, Antonine to 3rd century).

Decorated ware (fig 49)

This consists of single sherds only, apart from 260.

260 (With another sherd in B I 1). A thick-walled cup of form 64, Central Gaulish. The surviving panels contain:
1) An athlete (D.388).
2) A caryatid (O.1195A).
3) A satyr (D.364).
4) = 2)
5) A satyr (D.355).
The figure-types were used variously by Butrio, Libertus ii and Austrus. In view of the masks at the top of the borders, the piece is more likely to be by Libertus or Butrio than Austrus. *c* AD 120–45.
261 Form 37, Central Gaulish, with wavy-line borders and a scarf-dancer (O.360 variant), in a panel. The borders suggest a member of the Quintilianus i group at Lezoux. *c* AD 125–50.
262 Form 37, crudely finished inside, and with an internal groove at the level of the ovolo. The ovolo is replaced by spirals, and is separated by a thick, wavy line from a series of elliptical festoons containing similar spirals. These festoons are on a bowl from Périgueux stamped, after moulding, by Malcio. One of his others, from Montans, has the spirals. An unstamped and unassigned bowl from Strageath has similar, but larger, festoons and similar spirals. Typologically, Malcio seems rather earlier than most of the 2nd-century Montans potters and his work may be Trajanic, though this piece looks later. Hadrianic–Antonine?
263 Form 37, Central Gaulish. The single-bordered ovolo was used at Lezoux by several potters, including Sacer ii and occasionally, Cinnamus ii. Hadrianic or early Antonine.
264 Form 37, Central Gaulish. The ovolo (Rogers B231) is chiefly associated with Cinnamus ii, but was almost certainly also used by members of the Sacer ii group. The decoration consists of a scroll, including a leaf and a bird to left, looking back. Neither is precisely identifiable. Hadrianic or early Antonine.
265 Form 37, Central Gaulish, with freestyle decoration. Hadrianic or early Antonine.
266 Form 37, Central Gaulish, with the ovolo chiefly associated with the Cerialis ii-Cinnamus ii group at Lezoux (Rogers B144). The beads in the tongue show clearly, but the border below the ovolo is unusually blurred. The scroll includes a large leaf (Rogers H99). The bud in the background is a partial impression of a leafy spray (Rogers J178). *c* AD 135–70.
267 Form 37, Central Gaulish, with ovolo as last. The scroll includes a bird (D.1038). *c* AD 135–70.
268 Form 37, Central Gaulish, by a member of the Cerialis ii-Cinnamus ii group. The freestyle scene includes a bear (D.820), leopard (D.798), and animal to left. All the figure-types are on a signed bowl of Paullus iv from Leicester (S & S 1958 pl 165, 4). The foot-ring is unworn. *c* AD 135–70.
269 Form 37, Central Gaulish. The wavy line below the ovolo and the sphinx (D.497), probably in a festoon, suggest the work or Paullus iv. *c* AD 140–70.
270 There are also several fragments from a two-handled jar of Déchelette form 74, Central Gaulish, in orange fabric with iridescent, brownish slip, inside and out. The decoration consists of appliqué masks of slaves and pine cones, alternating. There is no exact published parallel for the slave, but the cone is on a similar jar from York (Simpson 1957, pl XIV, 29). This type of jar occurs at *Verulamium* in Period IID occupation (Hartley 1972c, 254). Mid-2nd century.

Potters' stamps

S108 Banvillus 2a 18/31 BANVILLIM.
Stamps from this die are known from Les Martres-de-Veyre, but a few of his vessels, including this one, are almost certainly in Lezoux fabric. The stamp was also used on forms 18/31R and 27, and occurs at Balmuildy, Camelon, and Corbridge. Almost complete, with slightly worn foot-ring. *c* AD 135–55.
S109 Calava 2b 18/31 CAĸAVA·F Lezoux.[a]
Stamps from this die occur in the Rhineland, at Corbridge and Chesters (where it presumably belongs to Period I) and, probably, at Camelon. There are eleven examples from a pottery shop of *c* AD 140–50 at Castleford. Almost complete; the foot-ring is slightly worn, but there is still kiln-grit inside the base. *c* AD 125–50.
S110 Caratedo 1a 31 [C]ARATEDO·FE Lezoux.[c]
These are three examples of this stamp from the Castleford pottery shop (see above). It was used on forms 18/31 and 18/31R. Kick only. *c* AD 125–50.
S111 Criciro v 2a 31 CRICIRO·[OF] Lezoux.[a]
A stamp used on forms 18/31, 27, 31, and 81. It occurs on Hadrian's Wall (Chesters Museum) and at Corbridge. Kick only, worn on top. *c* AD 135–60.
S112 Doccalus 5c 81 DOCCALI (on the collar and inside the base). Doccalus is known to have worked at Lezoux and may also have worked earlier at Les Martres-de-Veyre. The bowl is from Lezoux. The stamp occurs on forms 18/31, 18/31R, and 27 and there are eleven examples from the Castleford pottery shop (see no 2). One of his other stamps occurs in the D II 29A pit. Approximately three-fifths complete, with worn foot-ring. *c* AD 130–50.
S113 Silvius ii 1j (probably) 18/31R [SILV]I·OF Lezoux.[b]
Silvius ii's output includes the plain forms 18/31, 18/31R, 27, 33a, and 42. His decorated ware is Hadrianic. Kick only, from an unusually thin base. *c* AD 125–50.
S114 Vespo 2b 27 VESPOF Lezoux.[b]
A stamp used mainly on form 27, but with a few examples of forms 33 and 42. His other stamps occur on forms 18/31, 18/31R, 81, and 79(?), in Antonine Scotland, at Corbridge and in the Castleford pottery shop (eight examples). Almost complete but riveted and with worn foot-ring. *c* AD 135–65. The plain ware also includes fragments of forms 18/31(2), one with a worn foot-ring, and 18/31R (riveted).

Pit D II 29A

The 69 vessels in this pit include stamps or signatures of 30 Lezoux potters. There are 33 stamps on plain ware, from 25 different dies, and 12 stamps on decorated bowls, from 6 different dies. There are also three cursive signatures on decorated ware.

Most of the plain ware consists of substantial fragments. Many of the vessels are almost complete and most of the others are more than half-complete. Of the six vessels which are less than half-complete, only the form 31R of Advocisus does not seem to accord with the rest of the group, and one wonders whether it is intrusive.

Apart from one very fragmentary pot (Musicus ii), the foot-stands are either unworn or have wear which could have been caused by moving the pots on shelves. Such a substantial contemporary group is most likely to have come from a shop selling pottery.

There are no examples of form 18/31, but there are two (Banoluccus and Muxtullus) which are intermediate between forms 18/31 and 31, and nine dishes are certainly of form 31. In the rouletted series there are ten dishes of form 18/31R, as opposed to one (Maturus ii) classed as an early example of form 31R and another classed as a standard form 31R (Advocisus). Cups are comparatively rare, with four examples each of forms 27 and 33, and a single example of form 35. The larger form 35/36 and the full form 36 are both represented by single examples, as are bowl forms 38 and 44. Curle form 23 has three examples, two stamped with the same rosette.

Many of the potters involved made mid- to late Antonine forms, such as 31R, 79, 80, and the Ludowici forms Tg and Tx, but it is interesting to note that the particular stamps present in these groups are from dies used on earlier 2nd-century forms, such as 18/31, 18/31R, and 27. Only three examples are found on forms 79 and 80. One is the stamp of Advocisus. The others are stamps of Duppius and Laxtucissa, but these two were also used on form 27.

Three of the stamps (Cracissa, Muxtullus, and Pugnus ii) occur in a group of burnt samian of *c* AD 140–50 from Castleford, one (Secundus v) in Antonine I in Scotland, and two (Andegenus and Duppius) in the Period IID fire at *Verulamium* (before *c* AD 160). Four of the plain ware stamps (Banoluccus, Cracuna, Muxtullus, and Tauricus i), the decorated stamp of Cinnamus ii and the signatures of Cassius i and Criciro v occur in Antonine Scotland. The stamps of Cinnamus ii, Cobnertus iii, Laxtucissa, and Sennius turn up on Hadrian's Wall or at the Hinterland forts founded, or reoccupied, *c* AD 160. The stamps of Cobnertus iii, Titus iii, and Uxopillus are represented in a group of burnt samian of *c* AD 170 from Tác (Hungary). It is noticeable that none of the stamps is paralleled at Pudding Pan Rock, or in the Wroxeter Gutter.

The bulk of the decorated ware belongs to the main period of Cinnamus ii (ie after *c* AD 150). The typologically earlier bowls, of Sacer i, Cassius i, Tittius, and Pugnus ii, are all from moulds which were worn, or probably worn. The remaining bowls are probably all contemporary with the Cinnamus ones and it is noticeable that Paternus v and his associates are only represented by Laxtucissa and Maccius ii, who were both early members of the group.

The single sherds or less complete vessels range from the Flavian to the early Antonine period and include fragments from three more bowls in the style of Cinnamus.

On balance, therefore, it is clear that the group as a whole was deposited *c* AD 150–60.

The decorated ware (figs 49–53)

All the bowls are of form 37 and come from Lezoux, unless otherwise stated.

271 Sacer ii: stamp SACERFEC retrograde, Die 12a (S39).
Almost complete, with unworn foot-ring, but from a very worn mould. Rim diameter 219mm.
Ovolo Rogers B16(?). The upper zone has festoons containing birds (O.2317, 2324) and separated by trifid tassels (Rogers G76). The freestyle lower zone has alternating stags (D.874) and bear (D.818 bis) between trees (Rogers N16). Partly impressed leaf-tips (Rogers K10 and 22?) are used as space-fillers. All the main figure-types and motifs are already attested on stamped and signed bowls of Sacer i. The letters of the stamp are scarcely visible, but the length of the label is the same as that of the Sacer stamp on a bowl from London (S & S 1958, pl 83 10). This stamp is much less common than his large label one. Sacer often preferred the zonal style to the more unusual vertical division of the decoration into panels (S & S 1958, pl 82, 2–3, etc). *c* AD 125–45.

272 Maccius: stamp MACCIVSF retrograde, Die 5d (S32).
Almost complete, in six pieces, with unworn foot-ring. Rim diameter 158mm.
Ovolo Rogers B114. Freestyle decoration, with lion (O.1459?), horse (D.905), tree (Rogers N9), pillar (Rogers P59), and leafy sprays (Rogers J169, 170). Very few decorated bowls by Maccius are known. Stylistically, he is closest to Butrio, though not all his details come from Butrio's repertoire. There are also connections with some of the earlier members of the Paternus v group. *c* AD 130–60.

273 Tittius-Cassius i: stamp TITTIVS retrograde (Die 4c) in the decoration (S9) and cursive signature Cassi— retrograde, below the decoration.
Almost complete, in one piece, with scarcely worn foot-ring. The quality of the moulding is very poor, and the mould may have been rather worn. Rim diameter 224mm.
Ovolo Rogers B32. Scroll decoration with warrior (O.1061), erotic group (Oswald, pl XC, L), panther (O.1566), bear (O.1630 variant), hare (D.950A?), leaves (Rogers G143?, H73, and H131), and bifid bud used here as a scroll binding (Rogers G297). The grapes are not illustrated by Rogers. The motifs used by these potters show clear connections with X-6, though the arrangement of the scroll is somewhat idiosyncratic. Another Tittius bowl, from Wels (Karnitsch 1959, Taf 40, 7) has the same type of scroll, with a joining band of rings, the bifid bindings, and the erotic group. Another, from London, with the same combination of stamp and signature (S & S 1958, pl 146, 2), has the leaf Rogers H131. *c* AD 130–60.

274 Pugnus ii: stamp PVGNI.MA retrograde, Die 1b (S37).
Almost complete, in ten pieces, with unworn foot-ring. The bowl is probably from a worn mould. Rim diameter 195mm.
Ovolo Rogers B41, sheared off unevenly, in careless finishing of the rim. Semi-freestyle decoration. Festoons, suspended from astragali and containing panthers (D.799), are flanked by candelabra (a small version of Rogers Q42), with (alternating) panthers (D.971) and partly impressed dogs (D.934) chasing stags (D.885?). This bowl is in one of the several styles used by Pugnus ii, and is probably the work of his middle period of production. Cf S & S 1958, pl 153. *c* AD 140–50.

275 Style of Tetturo.
Complete, in three pieces, with unworn foot-ring. The clay which joined the foot-ring to the bowl has not been completely smoothed off. Rim diameter 181mm.
Two panels, repeated four times, with slight variations in the position of the space-fillers. The figure-types are a Hercules with snakes (D.464) and a stag to left (D.874). The space-fillers are astragali (Rogers R17?) and beaded rings (Rogers C125?). A signed bowl of Tetturo from Corbridge has rings, the astragalus, and the zig-zag borders (S & S 1958, pl 131, 3). The ovolo is on a bowl in his style from Camelon. Tetturo was somewhat ecletic in his choice of decorative details, and there are no strong links with any other Central Gaulish potter, or group of potters. His plain ware includes forms 18/31, 27, and 80, with emphasis on the two earlier forms. *c* AD 135–65.

276 Laxtucissa: stamp LAXTVCISF retrograde, Die 5a (S29–30).
Complete, or almost complete. State of wear and rim diameter are not noted. Ovolo, with tip of tongue bent to right, Rogers B245. Scroll decoration with leaves (Rogers H29 & J146), goose (D.1041), rosette (Rogers C194?), and two different astragali. All the details are known for Laxtucissa, but the goose is not one of his commoner figure-types. *c* AD 145–75.

277 Laxtucissa: stamp as last.
Complete, in five pieces, with unworn foot-ring. Rim diameter 188mm. Ovolo Rogers B114. The decoration is divided into panels by a combination of wavy lines and borders of rhomboidal beads. It comprises a seated figure (D.566), Cupid with torches (D.265), dolphins (D.1050, 1051), a festoon (Rogers F15), an obelisk (Rogers P68), and a rosette (Rogers C194?). Most of the details are already known for Laxtucissa; some were used by other members of the Paternus v group. There are also links with Quintilianus i and his associates, some of whom, like Laxtucissa, were later associated with Paternus. *c* AD 145–75.

278 Criciro v: signature Criciro, retrograde, below the decoration (S18). Almost complete, with very slightly worn foot-ring. Rim diameter 257mm.
Ovolo B204. The main zone of decoration is divided into sixteen panels, thus: abcdefcda (without caryatid) bcdefcd. The details are: Apollo (a larger version of D.55), Diana with hind (D.64), Cupid (a larger version of D.255), caryatid (D.656), erotic group (a smaller version of Oswald, pl XC, B), two pairs of birds (O.2250A, 2295A and O.2252(?), 2298), hares (D.950A (?), O.2061, 2129A), panther (D.799), trifid motif (Rogers G67), tulip leaf (Rogers G138), rosette (Rogers C125), and pediment (Rogers U269) containing a head. The arrangement of the decoration is more elaborate than Criciro's usual style (cf S & S 1958, pls 117–18). Several of the details, including the ovolo, were also used by Attianus ii. *c* AD 135–65.

279 Criciro v: signature CI, retrograde, below the decoration, and mostly obliterated by the addition of the foot-ring (S19). Complete, with badly finished rim. The foot-ring is slightly worn, but there is still kiln-grit inside the base. Rim diameter 156mm.
Ovolo S & S 1958, fig 22.1. The decoration is divided into sixteen panels, thus: abcb, four times. The figure types comprise a Hercules with snakes (D.464), a caryatid (a smaller version of D.656), and an erotic group (Oswald, pl XC, B). The rosette is probably Rogers C125. The ovolo is more commonly associated with Sacer i, who also used the same beads, but the rosettes are diagnostic of Criciro, and all the figure-types have been previously noted for him. *c* AD 135–65.

280 Style of Cinnamus ii.
Approximately three-quarters complete, with unworn foot-ring and a little kiln-grit inside the base. Rim diameter 175mm.
Ovolo 2 (Rogers B231). The decoration consists of three panels, repeated four times. The figure-types comprise a Vulcan (D.39, without tongs) and a sea creature (a larger version of D.38). The motifs are a medallion (Rogers E27), 'cushion' and chevron festoon (neither illustrated by Rogers). Apart from the festoon, all the details are attested for Cinnamus's developed style. An unstamped bowl from the same mould occurs at Mumrills. (Hartley 1961a, 110, 1). *c* AD 150–80.

281 Style of Cinnamus ii, with the same ovolo as the last.
Approximately two-thirds complete, in thirteen fragments, with unworn foot-ring. Rim diameter 202mm.
The decoration comprises a horse and rider (D.156, but with cloak and spear), stags (D.852, O.1822I), a horse (D.908), a dog (D.934), and a cornstook (Rogers N15). A typical Cinnamus freestyle bowl, similar to one from Wels (Karnitsch 1959, Taf 77, 2). *c* AD 150–80. All the details are known for him, though the stag O.1822I was only used occasionally.

282 Cinnamus ii: stamp CINNAMI, retrograde, Die 5b (S10–15).
Approximately two-thirds complete, in four pieces, with unworn foot-ring. Rim diameter 234mm.
Ovolo 3 (Rogers B143). The decoration consists of four panels, repeated three times. The figure-types comprise a philosopher (D.523), a man with a staff (larger version of D.331), a hare (D.950A), and a dolphin (D.1050). The motifs include a vine-scroll (Rogers M2), lozenge (Rogers U33), and medallion (Rogers E16). The bowl is from a mould inscribed X after firing, below the decoration. The front end of the stamp label is visible. *c* AD 150–80.

283 Cinnamus ii: stamp and ovolo as last.
Approximately three-quarters complete, in 25 pieces, with unworn foot-ring. Rim diameter 234mm.
The decoration is divided into sixteen panels, thus: abcdaebcdbfdaecd. The figure-types comprise Vulcan (D.39), Venus (D.176), a warrior (D.614 variant), masks (D.675, 705), sphinxes (O.858, D.496), a goat (D.889), and dolphins on a basket (D.1069A). The motifs are a double festoon, a large, double medallion, a tree (Rogers N2), a plant (Rogers H109), and a chevron (Rogers G284). The stamp is surrounded by partly impressed leaves (Rogers H101). The decoration is unusually fussy for Cinnamus, and the rows of rings without a border below are not paralleled elsewhere. Some of the details, particularly the warrior and sphinx, occur on bowls by potters with whom he worked in the earlier part of his career, such as Paullus iv. This bowl is in transitional style between Cinnamus's earlier work and bowls such as D15, below, but is closer to his developed style. Three rivet-holes have been cut, but not used; one of them looks incomplete. *c* AD 145–65.

284 Style of Cinnamus ii, with ovolo as D12.
Almost complete, in nineteen fragments, with unworn foot-ring. Rim diameter 232mm.
The decoration consists of three panels, repeated four times. The figure-types are an Apollo (D.52, with both feet complete), a philosopher (D.523), a leopardess (D.793, partially impressed), and a bird (D.1038). The motifs include a rosette (Rogers C98) and a chevron festoon (Rogers F41). The rear quarters of the leopardess are masked by leaves, here acanthus tips (Rogers K12), in typical Cinnamus fashion (cf S & S 1958, pl 162, 60 and D.15 and 21, below). All the details are previously recorded for him, though this particular bowl is perhaps by an apprentice. The ovolo is badly moulded and the ridge below the decoration has been almost entirely smoothed away and a groove inserted, cutting through the bottom of the decoration. *c* AD 150–80.

285 Cinnamus ii: stamp and ovolo as D12.
Almost complete, in five pieces, with slightly worn foot-ring. Rim diameter 220mm.
The decoration consists of three panels, repeated four times. The figure-types comprise a Victory (D.474), an athlete (D.394), a stag (D.852, partially impressed), a bear (D.820), and a hare on a log (not in D. or O., but known for Cinnamus). The motifs include a chevron festoon (Rogers F41) and a large lozenge (Rogers U1). The hind-quarters of the stag are masked by acanthus tips, as in D14 (Rogers K12). *c* AD 150–80.

286–7 Style of Cinnamus ii, with ovolos as D12 (2).
The details and general layout are exactly the same, but slightly different spacing shows that two moulds were involved, and the bowls are in very different fabrics. Both were almost complete, in nine and five fragments, respectively, with unworn foot-rings. Rim diameters 215mm, 222mm.
The details include a bird (O.2239B) and three types of leaf (Rogers H13, 101; J153). The two larger leaves are on a stamped Cinnamus bowl from London (S & S 1958, pl 162, 61). The use of leaves in both concavities of a scroll is unusual for him, though not unprecedented (S & S 1958, pl 162, 62). *c* AD 150–80.

288 Style of Cinnamus ii, with ovolo as D12.
Almost complete, in sixteen pieces, with unworn foot-ring. Rim diameter 211mm.
The scroll is similar to the last, with the same leaves and bird in the upper concavities. The lower concavities contain chevron medallions (Rogers E16) with hares (D.950A), over dogs (D.934). All the details are known for Cinnamus. *c* AD 150–80.

289 Cinnamus ii: stamp and ovolo as D12.
Almost complete, in 29 pieces, with unworn foot-ring. Rim diameter 227mm.
The scroll is similar to the last, and the bird, dog, and larger leaf are the same. The decoration also includes a heart-shaped leaf (Rogers J15), a Pan-mask (D.675), and dolphins on a basket (D 1069A). Cinnamus frequently used this type of scroll (cf S & S 1958, pl 162). *c* AD 150–80.

290 Cinnamus ii: stamp as D12.
Almost complete, in two pieces, with foot-ring definitely worn. Rim diameter 224mm.
Ovolo 1 (Rogers B223). The decoration consists of three panels, repeated four times. The figure-types are a Perseus (D.146), a warrior (D.117), a hare (D.950), and dolphins (D.1050, 1057). The leaf-tips are not closely identifiable. This is not quite a standard range of figure-types for Cinnamus, though he is known to have used them all. The hare and smaller dolphin are more usually associated with his contemporary, Secundus v. *c* AD 150–80.

291 Cinnamus ii: stamp as D12.
Almost complete, in eight pieces. Foot-ring very slightly worn. Rim diameter 244mm.
Ovolo as D20. The decoration consists of three panels, repeated four times, except that the sea-creatures (D.36 and 38, with pectoral fin) alternate. The other figure-types are a horse and rider (D.156), athlete (D.403), Minerva (O.126B), and lioness (D.793, partially impressed). The motifs include a lozenge (not in Rogers,

but known for Cinnamus). For the acanthus tips (Rogers K12), see D.14–15. *c* AD 150–80.

More fragmentary bowls and single sherds

291 Form 29, South Gaulish. Flavian.
292 Form 37. Style of Arcanus. Ovolo Rogers B45. Panelled decoration with candelabrum (Rogers Q40), vine-scroll (Rogers M2), man with draperies (D.330), seven-beaded rosette (Rogers C280), and beaded spindle. An exact parallel occurs at Carlisle (May & Hope 1917, pl iv, 47). *c* AD 125–45.
293 Form 37. Three fragments of a bowl in the style of Cettus of Les Martres-de-Veyre. Ovolo Rogers B97. Semi-freestyle decoration, with a hare (O.2061) in a single-bordered medallion and a man (cf S & S 1958, pl 142, 17–18), between rings. Cf Terrisse 1968, pl XX, 519 for the medallion and figures. *c* AD 135–60.
294 Form 37. A fragment from a panelled bowl. The ring-tongued ovolo and vertical astragaloid border suggest Albucius ii, who used the stag (D.860). The figure in the adjacent panel is probably a Cupid with torches (D.265), which is one of his commonest figure-types. He is not known to have used double festoons, but an arcade of the same size occurs on several of his stamped bowls. *c* AD 150–80.
295 Form 37. A small fragment of ovolo, probably Rogers B28, used at Lezoux by several members of the Quintilianus i group. *c* AD 125–50.
296–7 Form 37. Style of Cinnamus ii: two bowls, one with ovolo Rogers B231, the 297 other with ovolo B223. *c* AD 150–80.
298 Form 37. Style of Cinnamus ii. Panelled decoration with a hare to left (D.950), sea-creature (D.38 variant) over acanthus tips, in a double medallion, and a trifid plant (Rogers H109). *c* AD 150–80.
299 Form 37. A fragment from a panelled bowl, with unidentified figure-type. Antonine.

Potters' stamps

S115 Advocisus 1b 31R (approximately one-quarter complete, with unworn foot-ring) ADVOCISI·OF Lezoux.[b]
A stamp noted from Ilkley and on forms 79 and 80. Advocisus's wares reached Pennine forts reoccupied *c* AD 160 and his range of forms includes 31R, Ludowici Tg and Tx, and decorated bowls of mid- to late Antonine date. *c* AD 160–90.
S116 Andegenus 1a 31 (approximately half-complete, with slightly worn foot-ring) ANDEGENIM Lezoux.[c]
This stamp appears on forms 18/31, 18/31R, and 27 and in the Antonine fire deposits at *Verulamium*. His later wares include form 79 and a vessel in a group of burnt samian of *c* AD 170 from Tác (Hungary). His range is *c* AD 140–75, with 140–60 for Die 1a.
S117 Aprilis ii 3a 18/31R (almost complete, with unworn foot-ring). A[R[ILIS·F] Lezoux.[b]
A stamp recorded on forms 18/31, 27 and, probably, 80. Stamps from his other dies occur at Corbridge, Piercebridge, and South Shields. *c* AD 145–75.
S118–19 Banoluccus 1e 18/31–31 (almost complete); 31 (half the base only); both with unworn foot-rings BΛNOLVCCI;]NOLVCCI Lezoux.[b]
Banoluccus's stamps occur at Corbridge and Binchester and his forms include 18/31R and 80. This particular one turns up at Balmuildy and Newstead. *c* AD 140–70.
S120–21 Burdo 2b 27 (2; half-complete and two-fifths complete, both with unworn foot-rings). BVRDONIS·OF Lezoux.[a]
Burdo's range of forms includes 15/31R, 42, 79, and 80 and his stamps turn up in a group of burnt samian at Castleford dated *c* AD 140–50. A date *c* AD 140–60 is likely for these cups, in view of the forms.
S122 Burdo 6b 31 (base only, with unworn foot-ring) BVRDO·F Lezoux.[a]
This stamp occurs also on form 27, and the date-range is likely to be the same as for nos 6–7, though Burdo was almost certainly still at work in the 160s.
S123 Cassius i cursive; Tittius 4c 37 (almost complete, with scarcely worn foot-ring) Cassi . . . retrograde; TITTIVS retrograde Lezoux.[b]
The signature below the decoration belongs to a potter whose name was presumably Cassius. He normally signed moulds and stamped plain ware Cassia.of, for Cassia(na) of(ficina). His decorated ware occurs at Balmuildy and Brough-under-Stainmore and his plain ware is in a group of burnt samian of *c* AD 140–50 at Castleford. The stamp of Tittius, here in the decoration, was also used on plain ware, including form 18/31. Stamps from his other dies appear at Newstead, on Hadrian's Wall (Chesters Museum), and in the same group at Castleford as one of Cassius's stamps. His forms include 18/31R and 27. See also the decorated ware, D3. *c* AD 130–60.
S124–9 Cinnamus ii 5b 37 (6; three almost complete, two two-thirds, one three-quarters complete; five with unworn foot-rings, S15 with scarcely-worn foot-ring) CINNAMI retrograde Lezoux.[a]
Decorated bowls with this stamp are common on Hadrian's Wall and in Antonine Scotland, but are slightly more numerous in Scotland. For decoration, see D12, 13, 15, 19–21. *c* AD 150–80.
S130 Cobnertus iii 1a 18/31R (almost complete, with moderately worn foot-ring) COBNERTI·M Lezoux.[a]
A stamp noted on form 18/31R, at Ilkley and Corbridge and in a group of burnt samian of *c* AD 170 from Tác (Hungary). His output also includes forms 31R, 79, and 80. His range is *c* AD 155–85, but the form of the Alcester piece suggests a date *c* AD 155–65.
S131 Cracuna i 2a 31 (complete, with unworn foot-ring). CRACVNA·F Lezoux.[a]
There are several examples of this stamp from both Hadrian's Wall and Scotland. It occurs also in a group of burnt samian of the 140s from Castleford, and on forms 18/31 and 27. *c* AD 130–60.
S132–3 Criciro v cursive 37 (almost complete) Criciru retrograde: Lezoux.[a] C[retrograde; the rest of the signature is obliterated by the foot-ring.
Signed bowls of Criciro v occur several times in Antonine Scotland. One is in a group of burnt samian of *c* AD 140–50 from Castleford, and there are examples from Catterick and in the Aquincum Hoard. *c* AD 135–65. For decoration, see D8–9.
S134 Doccalus 6a 18/31R (almost complete, with unworn foot-ring with kiln-grit inside the base) DOCCALVSF Lezoux,[b] Les Martres-de-Veyre.[b]
A dish in Lezoux fabric. The stamp was used on form 27 and early varieties of form 33. Many of his stamps (from two different dies) are in a group of burnt samian of *c* 140–50 at Castleford, and there is one in the B I 3 pit at Alcester. Doccalus's decorated ware is similar to that of Docilis i. *c* AD 130–50.
S135–6 Duppius 1b 27 (2; one complete, the other almost complete, both with unworn foot-rings) DVPPIVSF Lezoux.[b]
This stamp was used on forms 79 (once) and 80, but is more common on form 27. It occurs in Period IID at *Verulamium* (after AD 150). His other stamps appear at Chester, Mumrills, and *Brigetio*. His range is therefore *c* AD 150–80, with 150–60 for the Alcester pieces.
S137–9 Genialis iv 6c 18/31R (2); 31 (one almost complete, one two-thirds, one half-complete, all with unworn foot-rings) GENIALISF Lezoux.[a]
There is no site dating for this stamp. Ones from other dies are on forms 79, 79R and at Carrawburgh and Chester-le-Street (on form 18/31R) and the Corbridge Pottery Shop. If this stamp belongs to the same man, it must be from an early die, but one surely later than *c* AD 150. The dishes of form 18/31R are unlikely to be later than AD 165, however.
S140–1 Gongius 2b 31 (2; one approximately half-complete, the other approximately two-thirds complete, both with unworn foot-rings) GONGI·M;]GI·M Lezoux.[c]
An uncommon stamp, always on form 31, but with no site dating. It seems to be from a die made, by *surmoulage*, from a vessel stamped with his common die. This was used on forms 18/31, 18/31R, and 27, and stamps from it occur at Old Kilpatrick and Camelon (2, one in Antonine I or primary Antonine II context). *c* AD 140–70.
S142 Lallus i 2a 33 (complete; state of wear not noted) LALLI·MA Lezoux.[b]
A stamp used on forms 18/31R, 27, and 38 or 44 (with clubbed foot-ring). There are examples from Newstead and Hadrian's Wall (Chesters Museum). One of Lallus's other stamps occurs on form 79. *c* AD 150–80.
S143–4 Laxtucissa 5a 37 (2, complete) LAXTVCISF retrograde Lezoux,[a] Lubié.[b]
This die was also used on plain ware, including forms 27, 31R, 79, and 80, with form 27 almost as common as form 79. The site record includes Ilkley and Halton Chesters. For the description, see D6–7. *c* AD 145–75.

S145 Maccius ii 5a 33 (almost complete, with slightly worn foot-ring) MACCIVS·I Lezoux.[a]
A stamp used on forms 18/31R and 27. Maccius ii is dated by his forms and by his decorated ware (cf D2), which is linked stylistically with Butrio and the earlier products of the Paternus v group. *c* AD 130–60.
S146 Maccius ii 5b 37 (almost complete, with unworn foot-ring) MACCIVSF retrograde Lezoux.[b]
This stamp occurs also on plain ware, including form 31. For the decoration, see D2 and for Maccius's date, see S30.
S147 Marcius (?) i 1a 33 (almost complete with slightly worn foot-ring) ·MARCII·MA· Lezoux.[c]
The lettering of this stamp does not suggest that it belongs to the Lezoux Marcus and the reading seems to rule out Marcellus iii, though the lettering is not dissimilar to his. It occurs on forms 18/31, 31, and 33, and is presumably Antonine.
S148 Maturus ii 1c 31R (an early variety, one-third complete, with unworn foot-ring and kiln-grit inside the base) [M]A TVRI·M Lezoux.[a]
Two other stamps from this die occur on form 27. Maturus's range (with other dies) includes forms 31R, 79, and 80. One of his stamps comes from Turret 52a of Hadrian's Wall. *c* AD 150–80.
S149 Musicus ii 2b 33 (approximately one-sixth complete, with worn foot-ring) MVSICI·M Lezoux.[b]
There is no site dating for this stamp, though there is a burnt example from Gauting, which could be either Hadrianic or Antonine. It occurs on forms 18/31, 18/31R, and 31 and Musicus's other stamps are on forms 18/31R, 27, and 38. *c* AD 140–70.
S150 Muxtullus 1b 18/31–31 (complete, state of wear not noted) MVXTVLLIM Lezoux.[a]
A stamp from one of Muxtullus's earlier dies, recorded from Camelon (2), the Castleford pottery shop destroyed by fire in the 140s (13), and Mumrills. The forms include 18/31, 18/31R, and 27. His later stamps occur in the Wroxeter Gutter and at Chester-le-Street. *c* AD 140–60.
S151 Pugnus ii 1b 37 (almost complete, with unworn foot-ring) PVGNI·MA retrograde Lezoux.[b]
A stamp used on both decorated and plain forms (27, 33 and 81?). There are two examples on plain ware from a group of burnt samian of *c* AD 140–50 at Castleford, and a decorated bowl from Munningen carries both this stamp and one of Tittius (Simon 1976, no 49). *c* AD 130–50 on the evidence of the stamp, 140–50 on the style of the decoration. See also D4.
S152 Ruttus 1a 18/31R (almost complete, with unworn foot-ring and kiln-grit inside the base) RVTTIOFFIC Lezoux.[a]
Ruttus's output consists almost entirely of forms 18/31R and 33, though one form 18/31 has been noted. Apart from the Lezoux examples, all the stamps recorded are from Britain. One, from the complete die, occurs at Corbridge and stamps from a broken version of the die (giving TTIOFFIC) come from Benwell and Newstead. *c* AD 140–65.
S153 Sacer i 12a 37 (almost complete, with unworn foot-ring) SACERFEC retrograde Lezoux.[b]
The letters are scarcely visible, but the label matches that of the only other recorded example of this stamp (on form 37 from London) and the decoration (see D1) is consistent with Sacer's. His plain forms include 18/31 and 27. *c* AD 125–45.
S154 Secundus v 4a 18/31R (approximately two-fifths complete, with unworn foot-ring) SECVNDVS·F Lezoux.[a]
A stamp from a die used on both plain and decorated ware, the latter connected stylistically with Cinnamus ii. The plain forms include 18/31, 18/31R, and 33 and the stamp occurs at Birrens (in Antonine I) and Camelon. *c* AD 150–70.
S155 Sennius 2a 31 (approximately two-thirds complete, with unworn foot-ring and kiln-grit inside the base) SENNIVSF Lezoux.[c]
A stamp noted from Chester-le-Street. It appears on forms 27, 31, and 38, and on the rim of a decorated bowl, with an ovolo of Cinnamus ii (S & S 1958, pl 166, 4, there completed as [A]NNIVSF). *c* AD 150–80.
S156 Tauricus i 8a 31 (two-thirds complete, with unworn foot-ring) TAVRICVSF Lezoux.[b]
A stamp used on forms 18/31 and 27, and noted from Mumrills. Stamps from his other dies occur at Bewcastle, on Hadrian's Wall (Chesters Museum), in the Wroxeter Gutter (7), and on forms 18/31R, 27, 79, and 80. *c* AD 150–80.
S157 Tittius 4c 37 (almost complete) See S9 and D3.
S158 Titus iii 8b 18/31R (almost complete with unworn foot-ring) TITIM Lezoux.[b]
A stamp noted from Mumrills and in a group of burnt samian of *c* AD 170 from Tác (Hungary). The rouletted dishes on which it appears are all form 18/31R, though Titus used other dies on form 31R. *c* AD 145–75.
S159–60 Uxopillus 4a 18/31R (2; both almost complete, and with unworn foot-rings and kiln-grit inside their bases) VXOPILLI·M Lezoux.[a]
This stamp is in a group of burnt samian of *c* AD 170 from Tác (Hungary), but occurs on form 27 also, which suggests that the die was in use by AD 160, at the latest. His later stamps occur at Catterick, Ilkley, and in the Wroxeter Gutter, and on forms 31R and 80. *c* AD 150–80.
S161–2 An eight-petalled rosette on form Curle 23 (2; both complete, one with unworn, the other with slightly worn foot-ring). This stamp occurs on form 46 at Lezoux. Antonine.
Also in this group are the following forms, either unstamped, or without surviving stamps: 35 (almost complete), 35/36 (almost complete), 36 (complete), 38 (approximately half-complete), 44 (approximately two-thirds complete) and Curle 23 (approximately one-third complete). The form 44 has a slightly worn foot-ring. The foot-ring on the form Curle 23 has not survived, but there is kiln-grit on the inside of the base. All the others have unworn foot-rings.

Figure 45 Samian nos 6–69

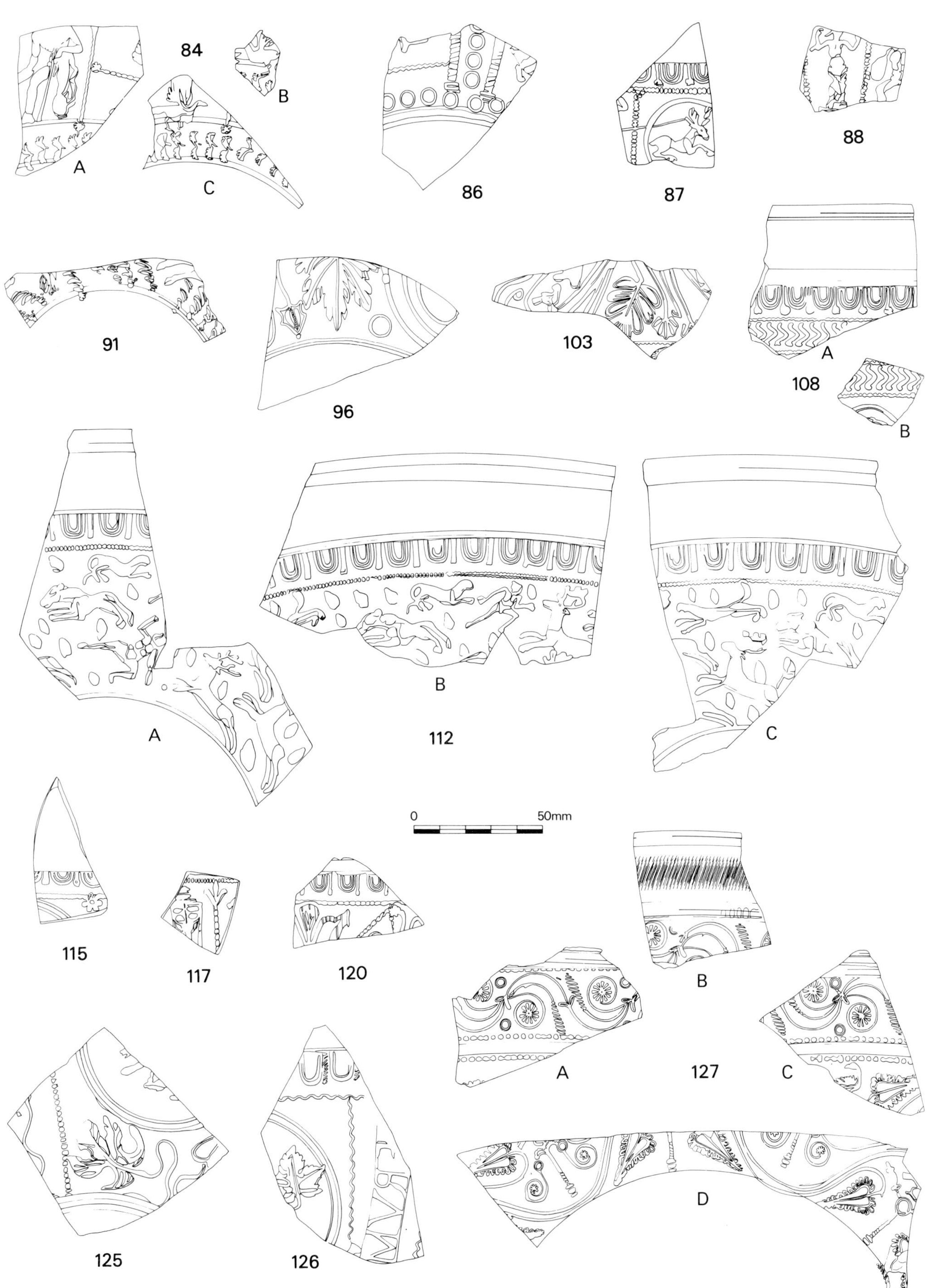

Figure 46 Samian nos 84–127

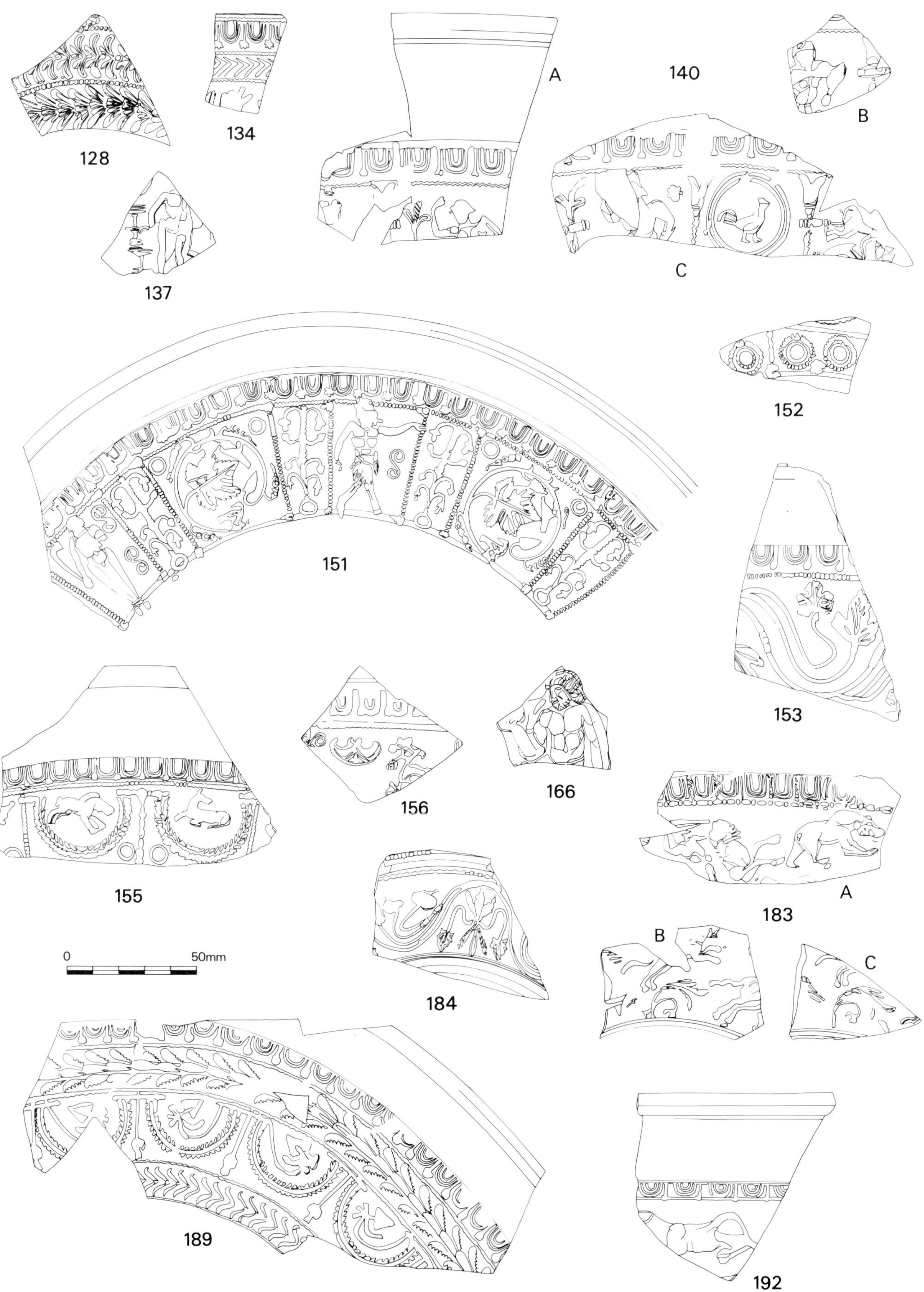

Figure 47 Samian nos 128–92

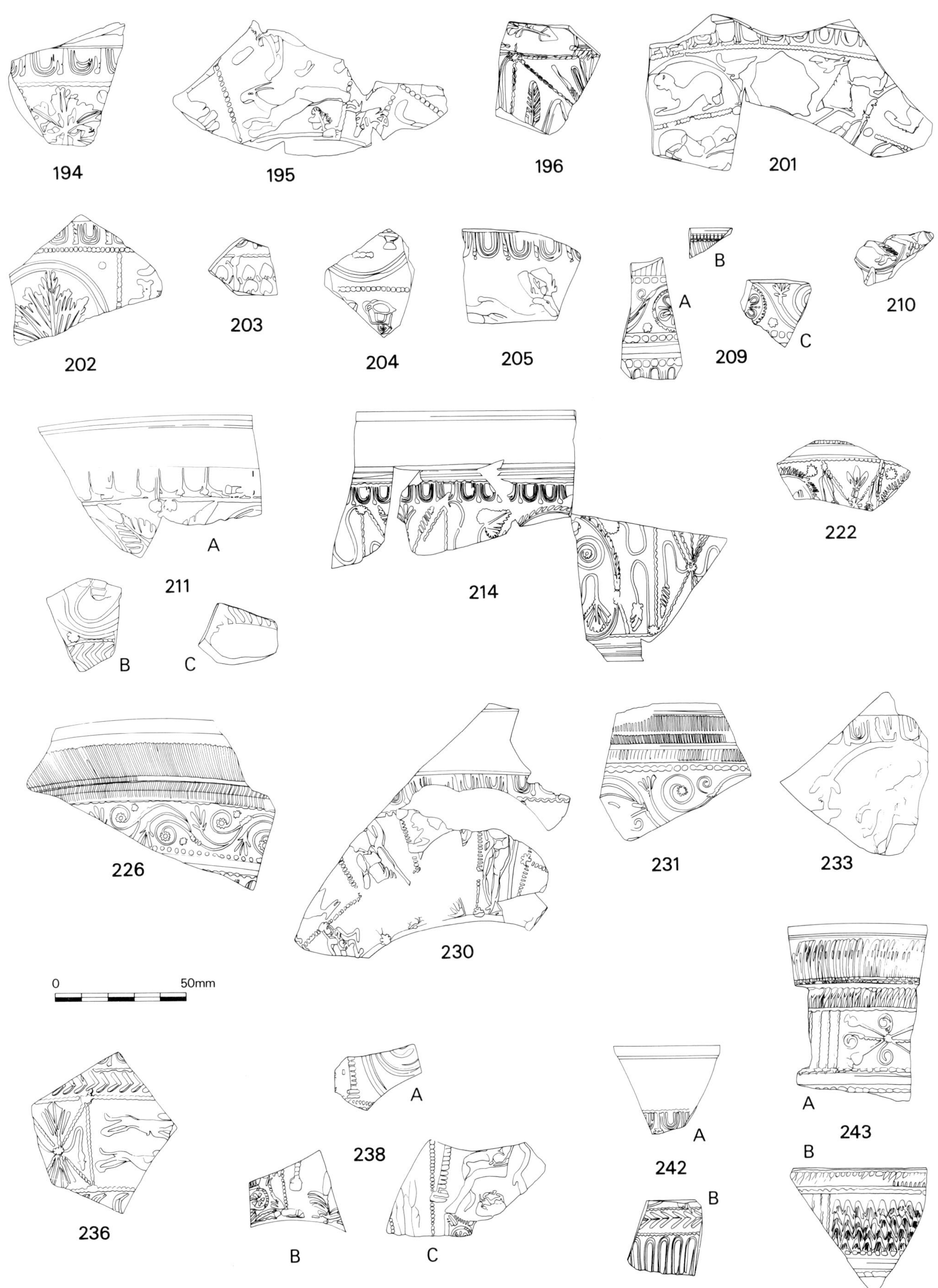

Figure 48 Samian nos 194–243

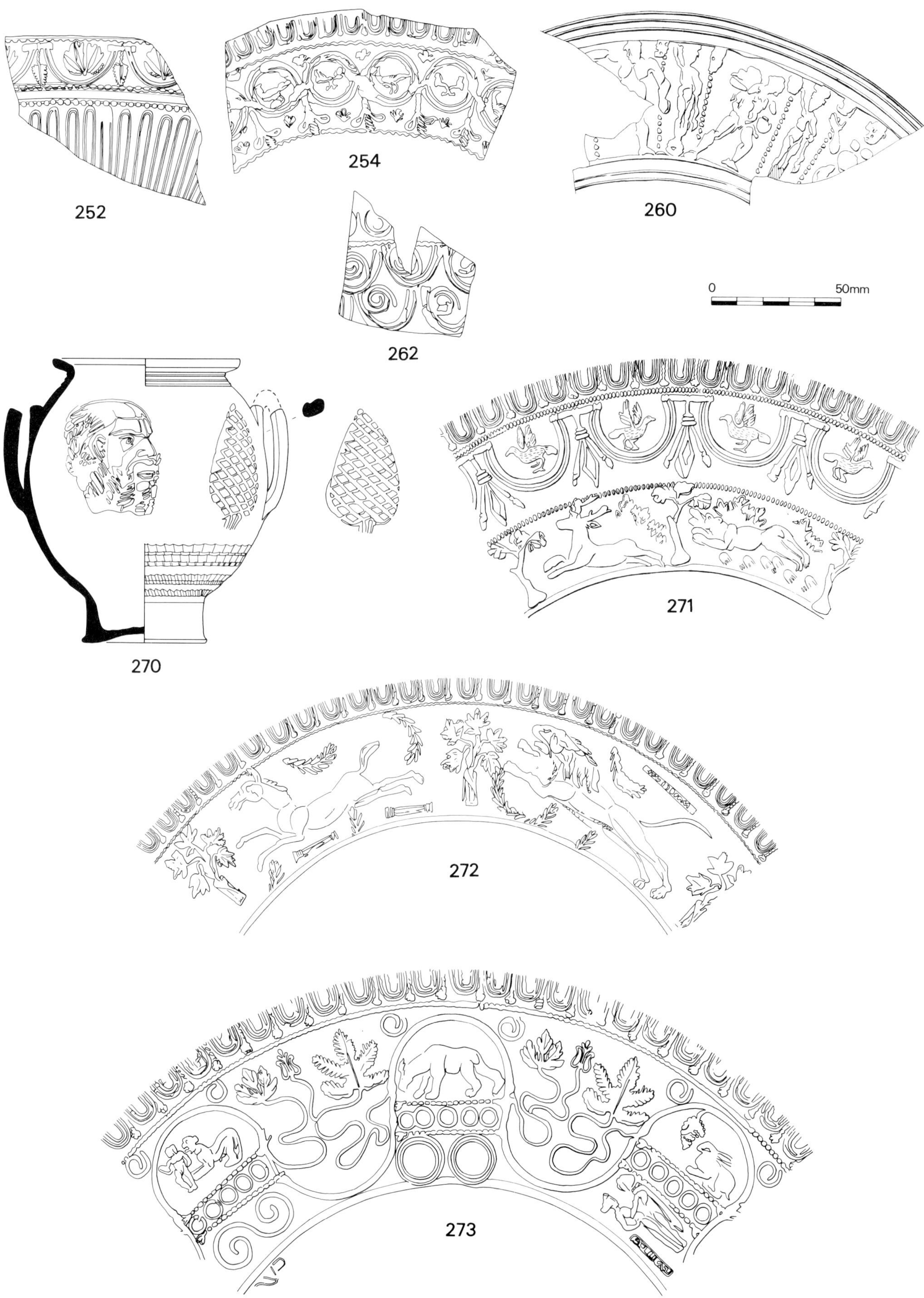

Figure 49 Samian nos 252–73

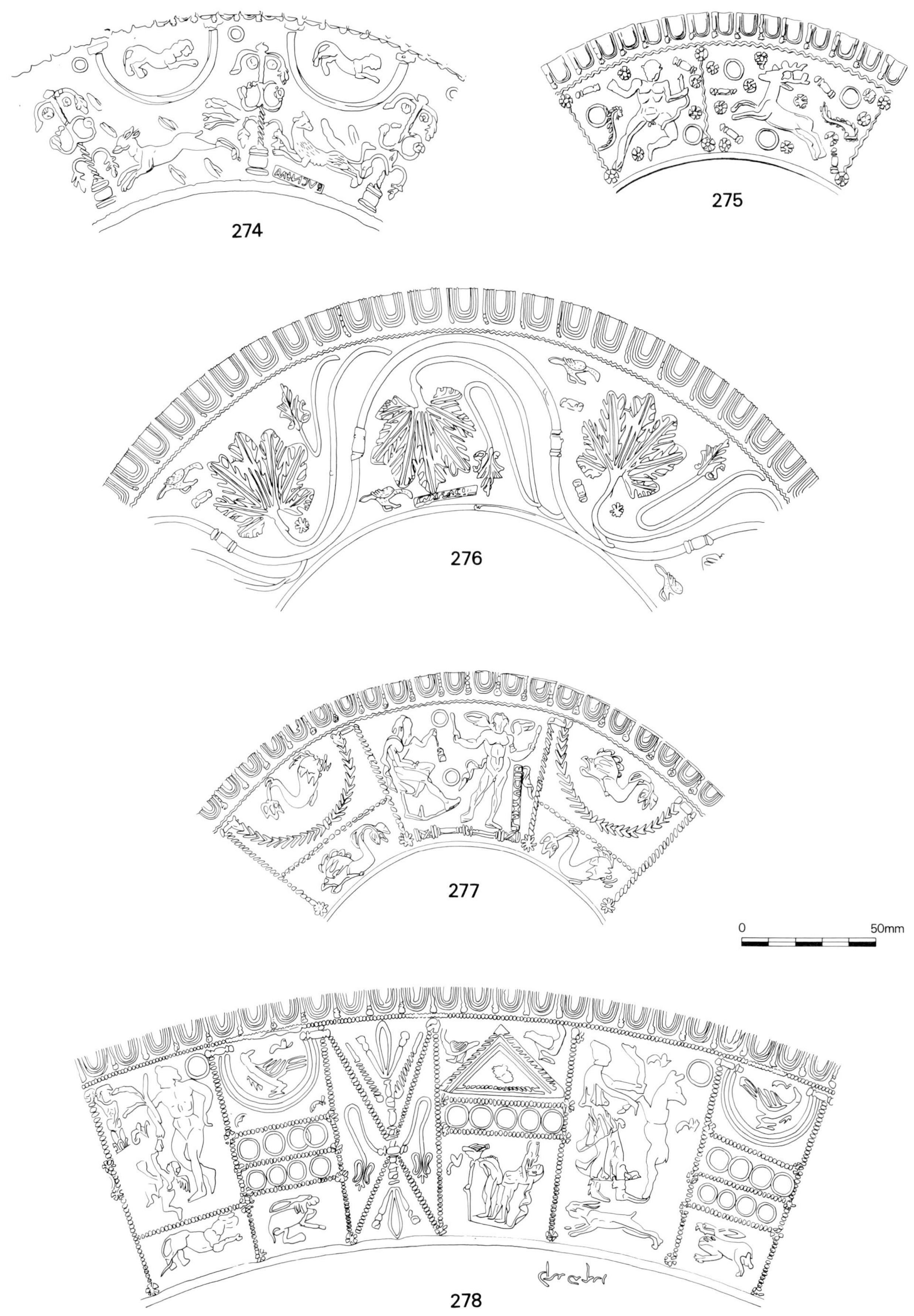

Figure 50 Samian nos 274–8

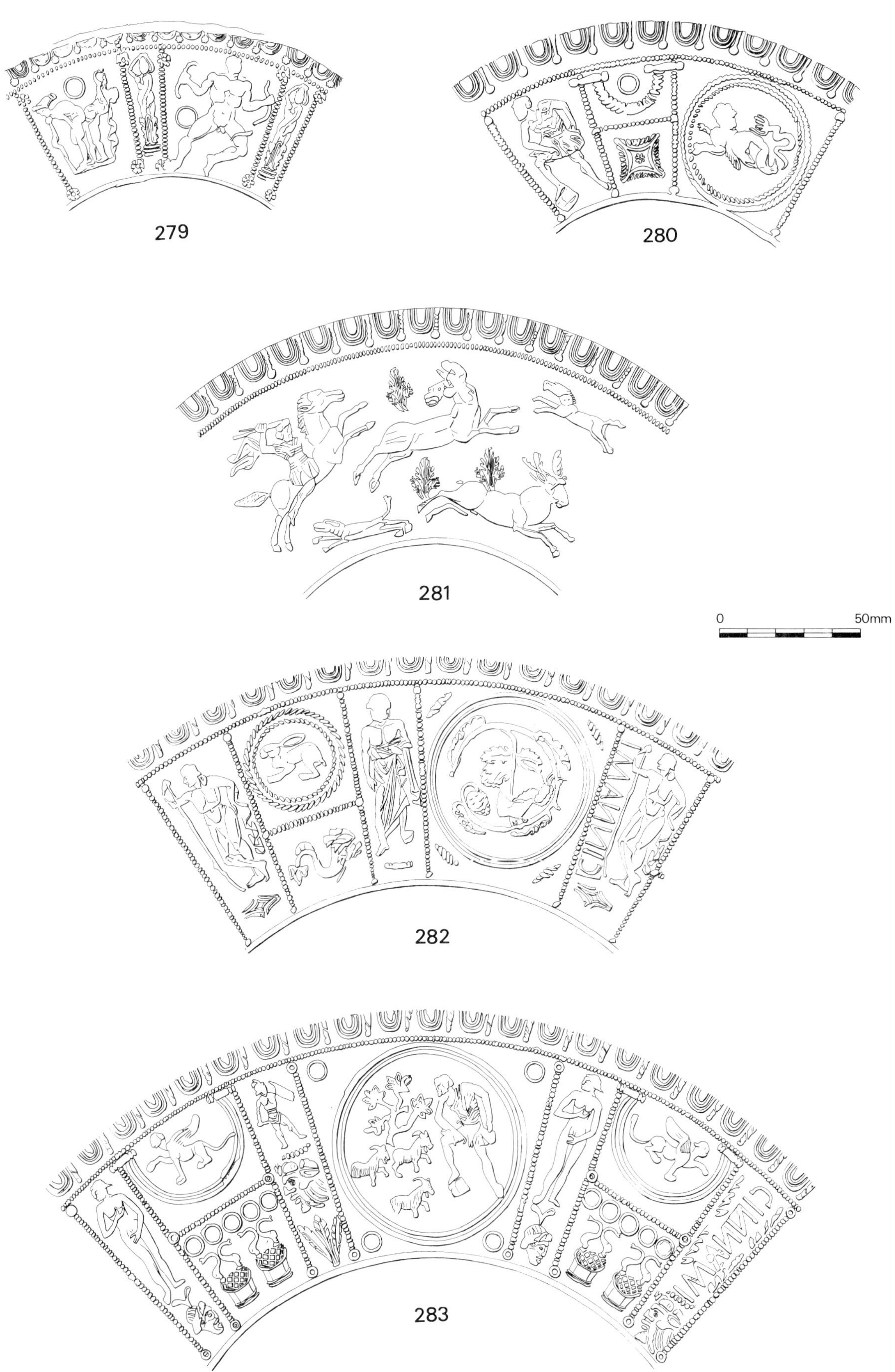

Figure 51 Samian nos 279–83

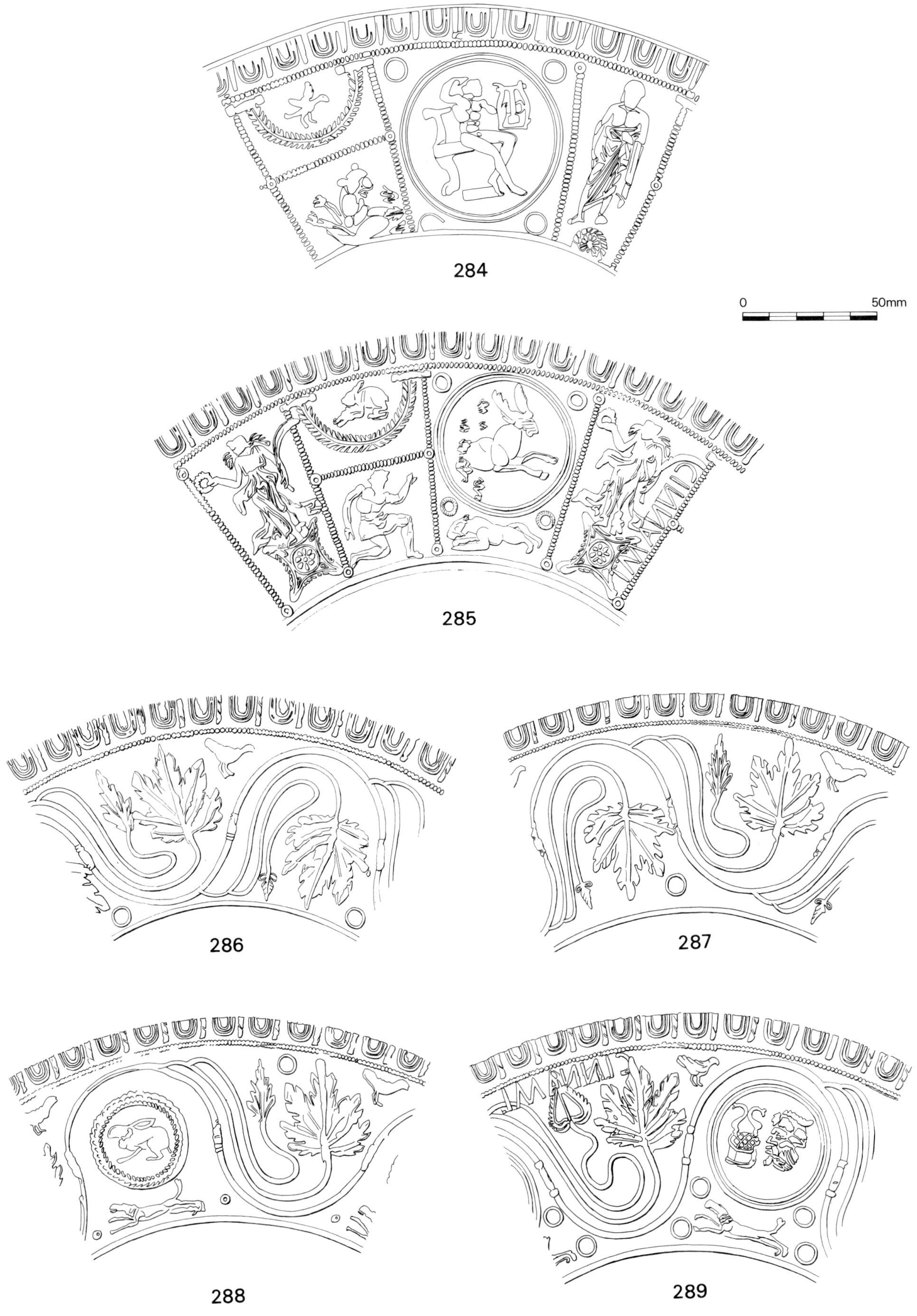

Figure 52 Samian nos 284–9

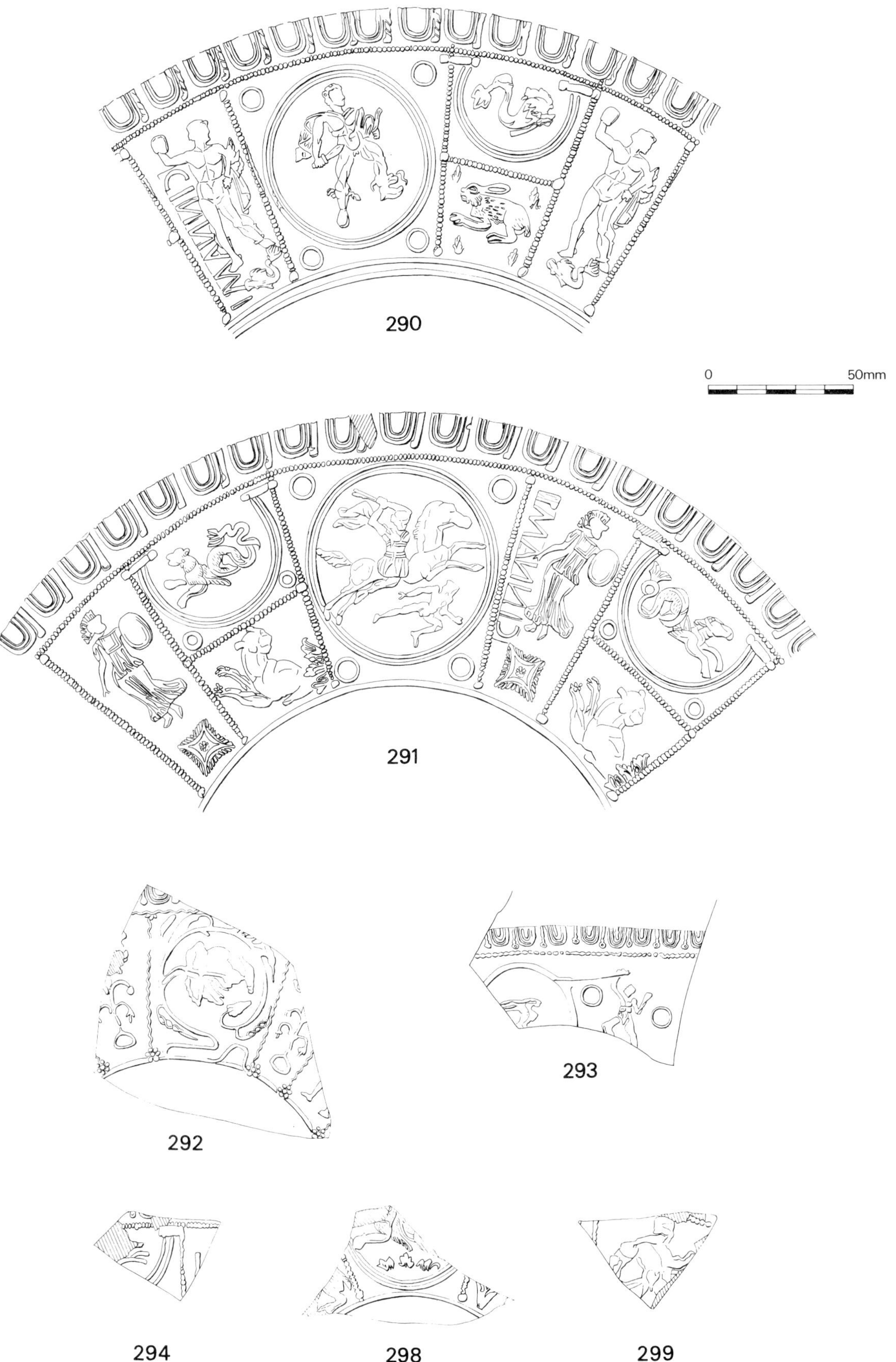

Figure 53 Samian nos 290–9

Roman *amphorae* *D F Williams*

Apart from no 15, these are not illustrated.

Pélichet 47/Gauloise 4

1 Rim sherd of the flat-bottomed wine *amphora*, form Pélichet 47/Gauloise 4. This form was predominantly made in southern France, more particularly around the mouth of the Rhône in Languedoc, where a number of kilns have been discovered in recent years (Laubenheimer 1985). This *amphora* type started arriving in Britain sometime after the early 60s AD (Peacock 1978). During the 2nd century AD it was the most common wine *amphora* in Britain, and importation continued during the 3rd and possibly into the early 4th century AD (Peacock & Williams 1986, Class 27). (AA6, D I 1A, unphased).

Dressel 20

Dressel 20 is the most common *amphora* type found in Roman Britain, while recent research has shown that it was already present in some numbers during the late Iron Age (Williams & Peacock 1983). This form of *amphora* was made in the southern Spanish province of Baetica, along the banks of the river Guadalquivir and its tributaries between Seville and Cordoba, and carried the locally produced olive-oil (Ponsich 1974; 1979). The Dressel 20 type of *amphora* has a wide date-range. The Augustan prototype (Oberaden 83) has a fairly upright rim, a short spike, and less of a squat bulbous body than the later types. It developed into the well-known globular form which, with some typological variation, was in use until the second half of the 3rd century AD (Zevi 1966).

Eight rims are present at Alcester, all of which can be paralleled with examples from Augst illustrated by Martin-Kilcher (1983) in her scheme for the chronological development of the Dressel 20 rim.

2 Rim. Dated at Augst mid-2nd century AD to the beginning of the 3rd century (Martin-Kilcher 1983, no 36). (AA1, A V 6, unphased).
3 Rim (AA2, A IX 8, phase VI, late 3rd to early 4th century).
4 Basal wort (AA4, AA IIIA 7, unphased).
5 Rim. Dated at Augst late 1st century AD to mid-2nd century (Martin-Kilcher 1983, no 26). (AA5, C IXA 13, unphased).
6 Four body sherds showing part of the neck which has been deliberately smoothed over. (AA7, D I 173, phase II, later 2nd to early 3rd century?).
7 Bodysherd (AA8, B I 3, phase II, Antonine to 3rd century).
8 Rim. Dated at Augst about mid-2nd century AD (Martin-Kilcher 1983, no 27). (AA9, D I 165A, unphased).
9 Rim. Dated at Augst mid-1st century AD to mid-2nd century (Martin-Kilcher 1983, nos 15 or 17). (AA21, G IV 66, unphased).
10 Bodysherd (AA23, B I 3, phase II, Antonine to 3rd century).
11 Rim. Dated at Augst about mid-2nd century AD (Martin-Kilcher 1983, no 29).(AA24, D I 244, phase VI, mid- to late 4th century?).
12 Rim. Dated at Augst *c* AD 40–75 (Martin-Kilcher 1983, nos 8–11).

Also handles with stamp. The stamp HLO appears *in ansa*. The nearest parallel quoted by Callender is HLQ from London and Richborough, both unpublished (Callender 1965, no 711). (AA25, G I 168, phase IV, early to mid-4th century).
13 Stamped handle. This stamp is quite faint and difficult to make out. It is possible that it may be QVINT (or I), *in ansa*. This stamp appears in Callender on Dressel 20 vessels, one from Colchester is dated to Period VI (AD 61–5), while an example from Richborough was dated to the 1st century AD (Callender 1965, no 1514). (P82, G IA 70, phase IV, early to mid-4th century).
14 Rim. Dated at Augst *c* AD 110–85 (Martin-Kilcher 1983, nos 32–4). (P68, D II 29, unphased).
15 Large part of the body with *tituli picti*, and handles — see separate report below (P68, D II 29A, unphased). See fig 54.
16 Unmarked handle bagged with the *tituli picti* sherds but representing a different vessel. The first letter of an incomplete stamp M . . . appears *in ansa*.

The majority of the above rims date to about the mid-2nd century AD, which appears to be the apogee of Spanish olive-oil exportation to Roman Britain (Williams & Peacock 1983, fig 2).

Dressel 20 *titulus pictus*

Pedro Funari and D F Williams

Introduction

This globular *amphora* had, on the outer surface, a *titulus pictus* in black paint and a graffito which had been scratched into the clay before the vessel was fired in the kiln (fig 54, D II 29A, unphased, *c* AD 150–60 from the associated samian). The inscription and graffito were first published in 1966 (Wright 1966; see note 1). Since this date our knowledge of the typology of the Dressel 20 form and the range of inscriptions associated with it have increased considerably (Martin-Kilcher 1983; Rodriguez-Almeida 1986; Funari in press).

It is therefore the purpose of this brief note to re-examine both the inscription and graffito and the actual *amphora* itself, in the light of our present understanding of these matters.

Amphora type
D F Williams

The Dressel 20 (Peacock & Williams 1986, Class 25) is a form that is commonly found on a wide variety of sites in Britain from the pre-Roman Iron Age until the second half of the 3rd century AD (Williams & Peacock 1983).

The Dressel 20 form shows some typological variation over the 300+ years of its production, mainly in the shape of the rim and to a lesser extent in the shape of the handles and the 'globular' shape of the body (Martin-Kilcher 1983; Funari in press). Unfor-

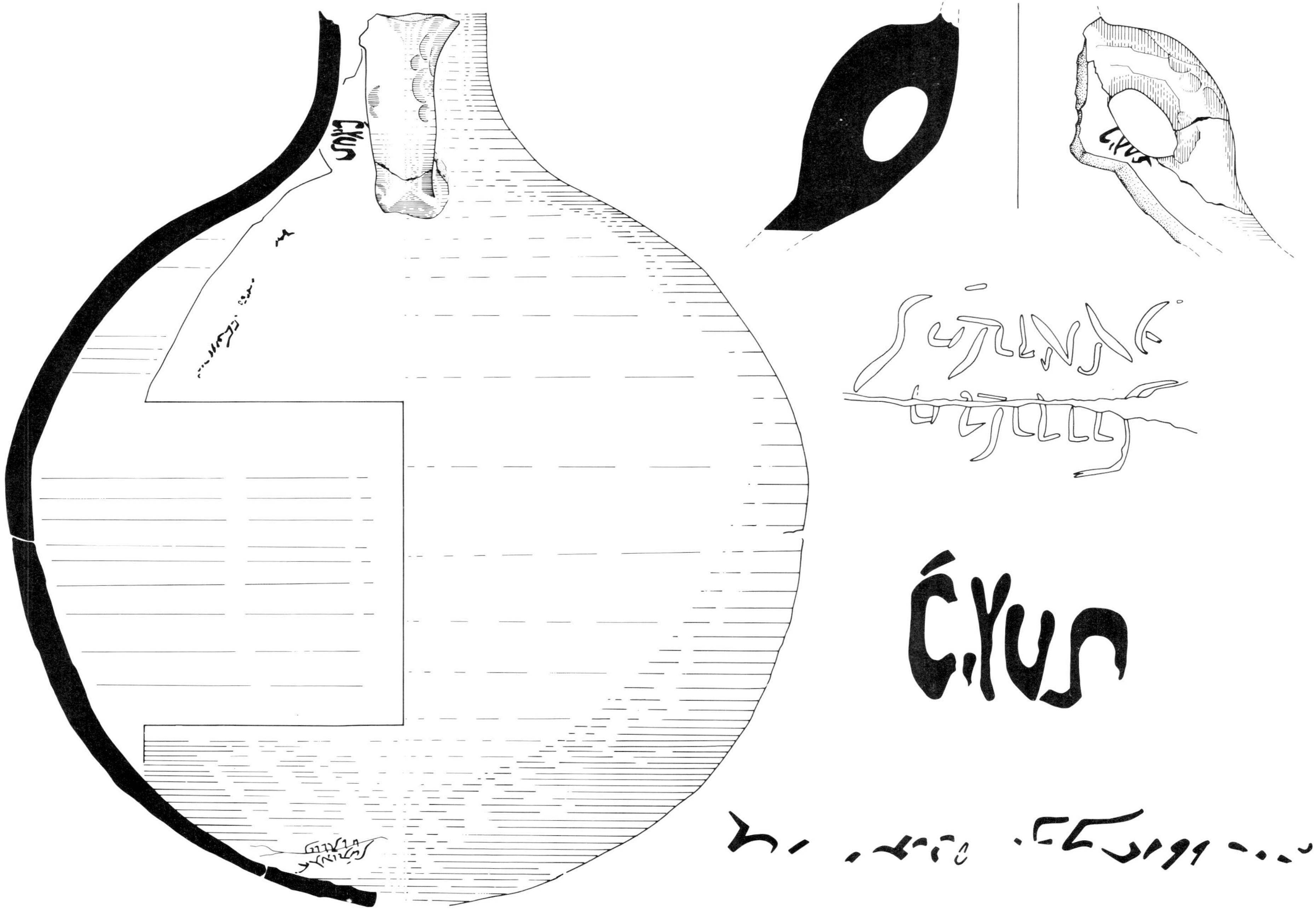

Figure 54 Amphora from pit group D II 29A (1/4 scale) with inscriptions and depinto (full size)

tunately, the Alcester vessel is lacking its rim, but taking into account the short handles, circular in section, and the well-rounded body, a date about the middle to the end of the 2nd century AD might be suggested. The fabric of the body and handles is hard, rough and sandy, with dark, buff-coloured surfaces (Munsell 7.5YR 7/4) and a light brownish-buff core. Thin sectioning and study under the petrological microscope shows a fairly fine-textured matrix containing a scatter of large subangular grains of quartz, quartzite, and potash felspar, with lesser amounts of chert, sandstone, quartz-mica-schist, and flecks of mica, all set in an anisotropic matrix of fired clay.

The fabric associated with Dressel 20 *amphorae* is a fairly standard one although, given the large number of known production sites scattered over a relatively wide area, some nuances of fabric are to be expected and these can sometimes be recognized in the hand-specimen. This has been confirmed by a small method-testing programme of petrological analysis based on stamped Dressel 20 material, much of which can be fairly confidently allocated to suspected kiln sites strung out along the banks of the river Guadalquivir (Pieksma 1982).

A comparison of the fabric of the Alcester vessel with this material shows a close similarity with a group of sherds centred on the region around the villa site at Berro II (Cortijo de), which is situated on the north bank of the river Guadalquivir, about halfway between Seville and Cordoba (Ponsich 1979, 91; Pieksma 1982). However, at this stage it is probably best to regard this result as no more than a possible indication of origin. It should be emphasized that the original number of stamped sample sherds analysed by Pieksma was relatively small, and more work will have to be done before undesignated Dressel 20 sherds can be more confidently allocated to specific kiln sites.

Inscriptions and graffito (figs 54, 55) *Pedro Funari*

Dressel 20 *amphorae* normally display a standard scheme of *tituli picti* which refer:

(i) to the weight of the vessel in Roman pounds,
(ii) to the weight of the olive-oil they invariably carried, also in Roman pounds,
(iii) to a tradesman (in capital letters), and
(iv) to a control or customs point (in cursive script) which mentions a consular date, plus sometimes other information (Rodriguez-Almeida 1986, 207–60).

Graffito

A Graffito was cut into clay before the vessel was fired, and was thus accomplished in Baetica. The inscription covers two lines of clearly cut letters and reads SVRINAE/VIRILIS (see note 2). This possibly refers to a Surina Virilis. The genitive may not indicate the owner or producer of the vessel (*officinator*), as is the normal interpretation (Dressel 1978, 212; Rodriguez-Almeida 1986, 254). In this case it could simply indicate the owner of the inscription itself, thus giving a reading of the 'graffito of Surina Virilis' (*titulus Surinae Virilis*) (see note 3).

Titulus pictus

There are two inscriptions, published originally as CAVS and SCO. FLOS. SCROM(BRI) (Wright 1966). The first, written in capital letters, probably reads CXVS. The second letter should not be an A, for then it would be difficult to explain the right apex. It seems more reasonable to suppose that it is an X (cf *CIL* XV 4340; Rodriguez-Almeida 1979, 921–2, no 31A). It could thus refer to a number CXVS(emis) or CXVI or to a number CXV followed by S(). Such a number, which may possibly have been written in Britain (Hamp 1975), could refer to a batch of *amphorae*, or to a sequential number relating to this particular vessel. It might, for example, refer to the weight of a possible product put inside the vessel once the original contents were removed.

The cursive inscription that runs down vertically from the lower junction of one handle was originally read as SCO. FLOS. SCOM(BRI) and translated as 'prime extract of mackerel' (Wright 1966). However, this appears to be untenable on both palaeographical and semantic grounds. Indeed, the proposed shape of the letters is completely unparalleled, as fig 55 shows. The only clearly recognizable letter is C, while the identification of the others is somewhat speculative. Last, but not least, although the published photograph is not particularly clear, it does seem that the last visible letter at the right end is probably an S or a T, adding to the difficulty of palaeographically interpreting this inscription.

On semantic grounds the published reading is even less convincing for the following reasons:

(i) The normal order of these inscriptions seems to be *flos scombri*, not the other way round (cf *CIL* IV 2574 to 2578), although we do find some *garum scombri flos* (*CIL* XV 4687, 4692, 4697), but always preceded by *garum* ('fish sauce').
(ii) The ordinary abbreviation used is *f* for *flos* (*CIL* XV 4722; *CIL* IV 2574 *inter alia*; cf Zevi 1966).
(iii) The repetition of *sco* is unparalleled.
(iv) The use of stops, as after *sco* and *flos*, is most unusual in these inscriptions.
(v) Similar inscriptions are normally written with capital letters, not with cursives as we have here (*CIL* XV 4687–731, *CIL* IV 2562–738).
(vi) As *scomber* is a mackerel, a fish, there would be no reason to refer to 'the best kind' (= *flos*) of mackerel, for it was not the fish that was very good, but the fish sauce or *garum*. The absence of the word *garum*, always quoted both in inscriptions and in the literary sources, makes no real sense in this context (see note 4).
(vii) The use of a Dressel 20 *amphora* to hold fish sauce would be surprising, taking into account that *garum* was usually exported inside *amphorae* of different forms from Dressel 20, and it would not be usual to transfer it from its original vessel to one already used for a different purpose.

Unfortunately, it is impossible to propose an alternative reading given the fragmentary nature of the inscription.

Notes

1 The original report on the *titulus pictus* and graffito was published by Wright in *J Roman Stud* 56 (1966, 224). It is quoted in full here to allow a better understanding of the remarks made in this note.

Globular *amphora* restored from several fragments found in 1965 at Alcester. (a) A black 'dipinto' in cursive letters ¾in high runs vertically downwards to the left of one handle and reads: CAVS. (b) A second black 'dipinto' in cursive letters ¼in high runs down vertically from the lower junction of one handle and reads: SCO. FLOS SCOM(BRI). (c) With the vessel inverted a graffito has been cut before firing near the knob of the base reading: SVRINAE/VIRILIS
Note 59 (a) No interpretation has been found for CAVS, recorded at Pompeii, *CIL* IV 5989. In (b) FLOS SCOMBRI 'prime extract of mackerel', is well attested, eg *CIL* IV 2576, 5679, 9397–9; XV 4687. The terminal mark which resembles a large T on the photograph seemed on inspection to be due to chance. (c) For the 'nomen' SURINUS see *CIL* V 483, 544. The second name seems to be VIRILIS although the writer of it cut III instead of ILI. It is not clear whether the genitive case marks this vessel as the product or the property 'of Surina Virilis'.

2 All the letters are very clear (contra Wright 1966, quoted above at note 1), as *CIL* XV 3616 shows beyond dispute.

3 This is an unverifiable supposition, but it is based on the existence of graffiti written on walls at Pompeii which contain names in the genitive, and which it would be difficult to interpret as meaning 'wall of *someone*'. The suggestion here is that the genitive could not only refer to artefacts, *'amphora* of . . . ' 'wall of . . . ', but also to the inscription itself, eg 'this inscription is of . . . ' (*CIL* IV 8813, 8893, 8957).

4 Cf Pliny *Naturalis Historia*, 31, 94: *'garum nunc e scombro pisce laudatatissimus in Carthaginis spartariae ceteriis; sociorum id appellatur'*. Martial, 13, 102: *'Experantis adhuc scombri de sanguine accipe fastosum, munera cara, garum'*.

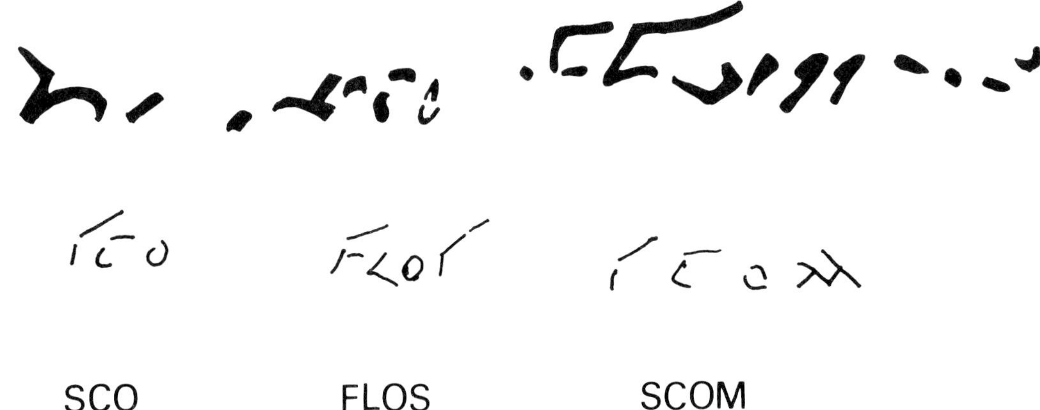

Figure 55 Disputed interpretation of depinto on Dressel 20 amphora from pit group D II 29A

Vessels with incised graffiti

Jeremy Evans, Frances Lee, and Gerda Lindquist

The Alcester graffiti assemblage exhibits a number of strikingly unusual features. There are 43 graffiti on 38 coarse ware vessels and 8 on 7 samian vessels. This is a striking reversal of the usual pattern for small towns where 57% of graffiti are on fine wares (Evans 1987, table E), almost always on samian.

Catalogue of graffiti (figs 56–8)

In this section the first number is the illustration number, followed by the type fabric series number.

Reduced wares

1 GC 34 Grey storage jar with everted rim; rim and shoulder are burnished. Graffito in form of a square with a vertical line through the centre on rim. (G I 168, phase IV, early to mid-4th century).
2 GC 36 Storage jar with graffiti along rim interior. There is a graffito of a horizontal line terminating in a bisected angle. This seems to have been cut later by two vertical lines. (G IA 85A).
3 GC 22 Storage jar with well-burnished rim and body. On shoulder a zone of right-hatched burnished lines. Graffito of three perpendicular lines, two downwards and one upwards from a horizontal line. (G IA 70, phase IV, early to mid-4th century).
4 GC 42 Storage jar with burnished rim. Graffito of two parallel vertical lines incised on rim interior joining a line at right angles. (G I ?42).
5 GC 29 Storage jar with burnished rim and shoulder. Below shoulder a band of right-hatched lines. Graffito of a single line on rim incised after firing. (D II 83, phase IX, late 4th century).
6 GC 21 Storage jar with burnished rim and body exterior. Graffito of three crosses, possibly more, incised on rim, perhaps denoting the number 30. Two of the three crosses were incised heavily, the third lightly incised at a different time. (G IA 63, phase V, later 4th century).
7 GC 20 Storage jar with burnished rim and shoulder. Graffito in form of line along edge of rim with two large perpendicular lines running from it towards the pot interior and a third similar but shorter line. (G IA 68, phase IV, early to mid-4th century).
8 GC 45 Storage jar with burnished rim and shoulder. Graffito of a vertical line on the rim. (G IV 26, phase VI, late 4th century).
9 GC 44 Storage jar with burnished rim. Graffito in form of three lines incised on rim before firing. Two are parallel and another is diagonal, probably indicating the number 6. (D I 28).
10 GC Grey storage jar with burnished rim and shoulder. On rim, an incised graffito of three vertical lines cut through by a horizontal line with 'VI' incised above this, perhaps indicating the number '6' with the number '3' cancelled out. On the shoulder another graffito 'MAR'. Beneath this a band of right-hatched burnished decoration and another band of burnishing. Context not recorded.
11 GC 31 Storage jar with well-burnished rim and shoulder. On shoulder a decorated band with sloping burnished lines. A complete graffito on the shoulder of reads 'RR'. (G IA 63, phase V, later 4th century).
12 GC 5 Storage jar with burnished exterior and graffito of a square with a vertical line through the centre. (D II 22).
13 GC 1 Storage jar with burnished shoulder followed by band of right-hatched burnished lines beneath. Body burnished. Graffito of a square with an 'X' within it, on body exterior. (G IA 63, phase V, later 4th century).
14 GC Body sherd of storage jar with burnished exterior. Graffito of a square with a cross inside it. (D I 25, phase VIII, late 4th century).
15 GC 24 Body sherd of storage jar with burnished left-hatched lines in a band bordered by another band of solid burnishing. Graffito of a square with a cross inside. A drilled circular rivet-hole to side of the graffito. (G V 1).
16 GC 35 Body sherd of storage jar. Exterior burnished with graffito of a square with a cross within it. (G I 90).
17 GC 28 and GC 37 Two body sherds of grey storage vessel with burnished exterior. Graffito of rhomboid divided by a sloping line probably with its mirror-image adjacent to it. (G IA 68, phase IV, early to mid-4th century).
18 GC 26 Body sherd of storage vessel. Graffito in form of line bisecting a 90 degree angle, incised after firing. (G IA 68, phase IV, early to mid-4th century).
19 GC 27 Body sherd of grey storage jar. Graffito in form of a vertical line bisecting a right angle, incised after firing. (H II 10, phase II, Antonine to 3rd century).
20 GC 30 Body sherd of grey storage jar with burnished exterior. Graffito of a square with ?triangle inside. (G IA 63, phase V, later 4th century).
21 GC 32 Body sherd of grey storage jar with burnished exterior. Graffito of a cross on body exterior. (G IA 63, phase V, later 4th century).
22 GC 38 Body sherd of grey storage jar. Graffito of a large 'V' with a smaller 'V' inside, incised on neck. Context not recorded.
23 GC Body sherd of grey storage jar. Graffito of a horizontal line with vertical lines intersecting it, and bisected angle terminals. (G IA 63, phase V, later 4th century).
24 GC 23 Body sherd of grey storage jar. Shoulder burnished with a zone of three left-hatched burnished lines, alternating with three right-hatched burnished lines, and a burnished band beneath. Graffito in form of an incised 'X' on body exterior. (G IA 63, phase V, later 4th century).
25 GC 33 Body sherd of storage jar with burnished shoulder and a zone of burnished right-hatched lines, a burnished band beneath. Graffito of cross, scratched repeatedly rather than made by two single strokes, after firing. (G II 21, phase VI, late 4th century).
26 GC Body sherd of storage jar with burnished band and an inscribed triangle. (G IA 63, phase V, later 4th century).
27 GC Body sherd of storage jar with a graffito of a diamond enclosing a vertical line of four drilled holes bisecting it vertically, with drilled holes at the angles of the horizontal. (G IA 63, phase V, later 4th century).
28 GC 25 Body sherd of storage jar with sloping burnished lines and a burnished band beneath, graffito of a pair of incised vertical lines. (G IA 72A)

Black-Burnished ware

29 CB 203 Dish with upright rim, burnished int. and ext. Burnished acute lattice on ext. and loop decoration on base ext. A graffito 'X' has been scratched on to dish base, after firing. Context not recorded.

Oxidized wares

30 DA 93 Wide-mouthed storage jar with cordon at base of neck and a burnished band of hatching on shoulder, bounded by horizontal burnished bands. Graffito of an 'X' on rim and an incised leaf motif, on interior of rim. Context not recorded.
31 DA 92 Large storage jar with graffito of three crosses on top of rim. (G II 28)
32 DA 1 Large storage jar with band of diagonal burnished lines on shoulder. Graffito of two incised lines on rim. There are a couple of other slash marks on rim, probably accidental. Context not recorded.

33 DA 71 Body sherd of storage jar with incised graffito of an 'X' probably surrounded by a square. (B I 25, phase I, 1st century to Hadrianic).
34 DA 87 Body sherd of storage jar with graffito of a cross. (G V 2).
35 DE 409 Narrow-necked jar with slightly everted rim and cordon at base of neck. Graffito in a letter 'g'-shape inscribed after firing. (G I 59, phase IV, early to mid-4th century).
36 DEA 169 Globular jar with everted rim and burnished exterior. Incised graffito in form of cross bisected by vertical line through centre. (C VIA 107, phase V, later 3rd century on).
37 DW 30 Small narrow-necked jar with deep incised groove on girth. On shoulder incised graffito reading 'IIpon', Epon(ae). Presumably used to contain an offering to the goddess. The inscription added after firing. Previously published in *J Roman Stud* 56 (Wright 1966, 224). (D II 60).
38 GCA storage jar rim, rim and shoulder burnished with zone of burnished sloping lines on shoulder. Cut into the top of the rim are two parallel incised vertical lines. (C VI 135).
39 DA 62 Body sherd from storage jar with a wheel-burnished zone towards shoulder above an undecorated zone which has an inscribed circle with a central compass hole made *post cocturam*. Diameter of circle 49mm. (A XVIIB 4).
40 P34 Two joining bodysherds from a Dr. 31R (CGS) with a complete graffito SCAMNVS scratched on the base. (D I T/S, unphased).
41 P14 Stamped base of a Dr. 33 (SG), with Die 9a′ of Pass(i)enus, *c* AD 75–80. See stamped samian no S53. A small base sherd, stamped and slightly burnt. A large graffito 'X' has been inscribed on the underside of the base, probably an illiterate mark of ownership or apotropaic rather than a numeral (cf Evans 1987, 200–1). After this was done a hole was drilled through the centre of the base from the underside. This may be a rivet-hole, but it is not certain. (AA III 39).
42 Body sherd of Dr. 31R? East Gaul. Four parallel sloping lines scratched into exterior 'IIII' perhaps an illiterate mark of ownership. However, the marks could, possibly, be the result of accidental abrasion. (G IA 1A).
43 Burnt body sherd, form indeterminable, CGS. The outer surface is abraded possibly to efface the graffito which is a single letter 'M'. Presumably the owner's initial. (G IA 13, phase VII+, late 4th century).
44 Base of a Dr. 27, see stamp no 31, SG, AD 45–60. Graffito in centre of footring base, a single letter 'T'. Presumably the owner's initial. (E II 71, phase III, Neronian–Trajanic).
45 Half of a Dr. 27, SG, only a fragment of the stamp border survives. A deeply incised graffito in the centre of the foot-ring base would seem to have been the single letter 'N' although there is probably space for a second letter. Probably the owner's initial. (A BDS).
46 Part of Dr. 18/31R or 31R (CGS). The bottom of the foot-ring has two parallel incised lines 5mm apart, either the number 'II' or an illiterate mark of ownership. (B I 23).
47 Around a quarter of a Dr. 38 (CGS). In the centre of the foot-ring base are the ends of three strokes of a graffito suggesting at least two letters if it were literate. The first two vertical strokes are 2mm apart and the third is 11mm distant. (G I 4A, phase X, late 4th century).
48 Base of a Dr. 33 (CGS) worn around the edge of the interior, as if by stirring. Stamped SIIVIIRIM, die 3d of Severus iv, *c* AD 160–90, reported in *J Roman Stud* 56 (Wright 1966, 223). This bears two graffiti:
(i) in the centre of the foot-ring base, and
(ii) on the chamfer between the base and the wall of the vessel.
(i) A series of intersecting triangles read as M AXIM[I].
(ii) M AXIM[I], the name Maximus in the genitive. (D I 87D, phase V, early to mid-4th century?).

Discussion

The graffiti on coarse ware are not randomly distributed throughout the range of fabrics, but are limited to two main groups: the reduced, hand-made fabric GC, which accounts for 78% of the vessels, and the oxidized fabrics, particularly fabric DA. All the graffiti are cut after firing. This concentration on fabric GC might suggest that the bulk of the graffiti can be explained as potters' tally marks, especially since most of the marks on fabric GC are either numbers or symbols, although such marks might more usually be expected to be incised before firing, especially if the aim was to separate the products of different potters. However, this interpretation is unlikely for two reasons. First, although similar marks are found on some of the Severn Valley ware vessels, this does not seem to be a general phenomenon on Severn Valley ware material elsewhere. Second, the distribution of graffiti on the site suggests a different interpretation (see below).

Turning to the types of graffiti, nine (on eight vessels) are of names or initials, probably those of their owners, although no 37 — Epon[a] — could well be a dedicatory inscription to the goddess (Wright 1966, 224). This suggestion is strengthened by its being on a complete vessel deposited in a pit (D II 60) since votive deposits commonly occur in such contexts and complete vessels are rather rare outside funerary or votive contexts. Fifteen graffiti on twelve vessels could be interpreted as being numerical (see table 2 and figs 56–8).

However, numbers often appear, in fact, to be illiterate marks of ownership, generally being represented by 'X' and this seems likely for no 29, on a dish base, no 44 on a samian foot-ring and perhaps for nos 21 and 24 on storage jar walls, together with the four sloping parallel lines on no 40, a samian bowl.

The remainder, nevertheless, are on the rims of storage jars and might well be intended to indicate the quantity of the contents, or the empty weight of the vessel. The numerals on the storage jar rims would have been visible when the vessels were packed close together, for example when transporting them or while they were in storage.

The bulk of the graffiti, some 25 examples, are symbols. The commonest would seem to be a cross within a square, of which there are five or six examples (nos 13, 14, 15, 16, 34, and perhaps 33). The other recurring motifs are the right-angle bisected by a long horizontal line (nos 2, 19, and the related no 23) and the square with a vertical line dividing it in half (nos 1 and 12). These are all on the exteriors and rims of storage jars and must represent either a mark of ownership or a symbol of the contents.

The fairly high proportion of numbers and the frequent occurrence of symbols, whilst forming an unusual assemblage, are not untypical once the type of vessel receiving the bulk of the graffiti, storage jars, is taken into consideration. In a general survey (Evans 1987) 21% of graffiti on storage jars were numbers and 58% were marks other than personal names, numerals, or literate indications of the contents. The really unusual feature of this assemblage is the high proportion of graffiti on storage jars.

Fig 59 shows the distribution of graffiti across the excavations, subdivided by the type of graffiti and fabric (fine or coarse). This proves most interesting, with a major concentration of material in trench G IA, and a scatter through the rest of site G quite probably derived from this. A concentration of graffiti like this would seem to be a very unusual feature.

Table 2 Numerical interpretation of some graffiti

Illus no	Type series	Graffito	Numerical interpretation
5	GC 29	single incised line 'I'	1
6	GC 21	three crosses 'IXXX' the final one cut later	30
9	GC 44	three incised lines in arrangement 'VI' or 'N' retrograde	6
10	GC	three incised lines 'III' cut by horizontal line and with a 'VI' beside them	figure 3 crossed, 6 beside
21	GC 32	a cross 'X'	10
24	CG 23	a cross 'X'	10
28	GC 25	two vertical lines 'II'	
29	GC 203	'X' on a Black-Burnished 1 dish base	10
30	DA 93	single cross	10
31	DA 92	three incised crosses 'XXX'	30
32	DA 1	two incised lines 'II'	2
38	GC	two incised vertical lines 'II'	2
40	Dr. 31R? (EG)	four sloping incised 'IIII'	4
44	Dr. 18/31R or 31R (CGS)	two incised lines 'II'	2

Examination of the phasing of those graffiti from this area which are provenanced and phased shows six from phase IV, nine from phase V, two from phase VI, one from phase VII+, one from phase X and eight unphased. Especially given that there is no structure on the site in phase V, it seems highly probable that many of the graffiti derive from the phase IV hall-like structure, GC or the earlier structure GA. The latter may be more likely as most of the intrinsically datable pieces appear to be of 1st- to 2nd-century date. The concentration here is principally of numbers and symbols on storage jars; names and graffiti on samian are more evenly distributed across the site. If the graffiti from site G are disregarded then the collection from the rest of the site looks more typical, although it still shows a higher proportion of coarse ware than might be expected. The concentration in trench G IA clearly suggests that the graffiti were made here on vessels and were not some form of potters' marks. The number of personal graffiti do seem to imply, at least, some communal function to the structure, in which possessions might be confused, rather than the dwelling of a single nuclear family.

The total number of graffiti from the site, 51, seems high even allowing for the extensive nature of the excavations (*c* 6000–7000 pottery rims, perhaps 60,000–70,000 sherds) compared with 70 graffiti from extensive work spread over 30 years at Catterick, North Yorkshire.

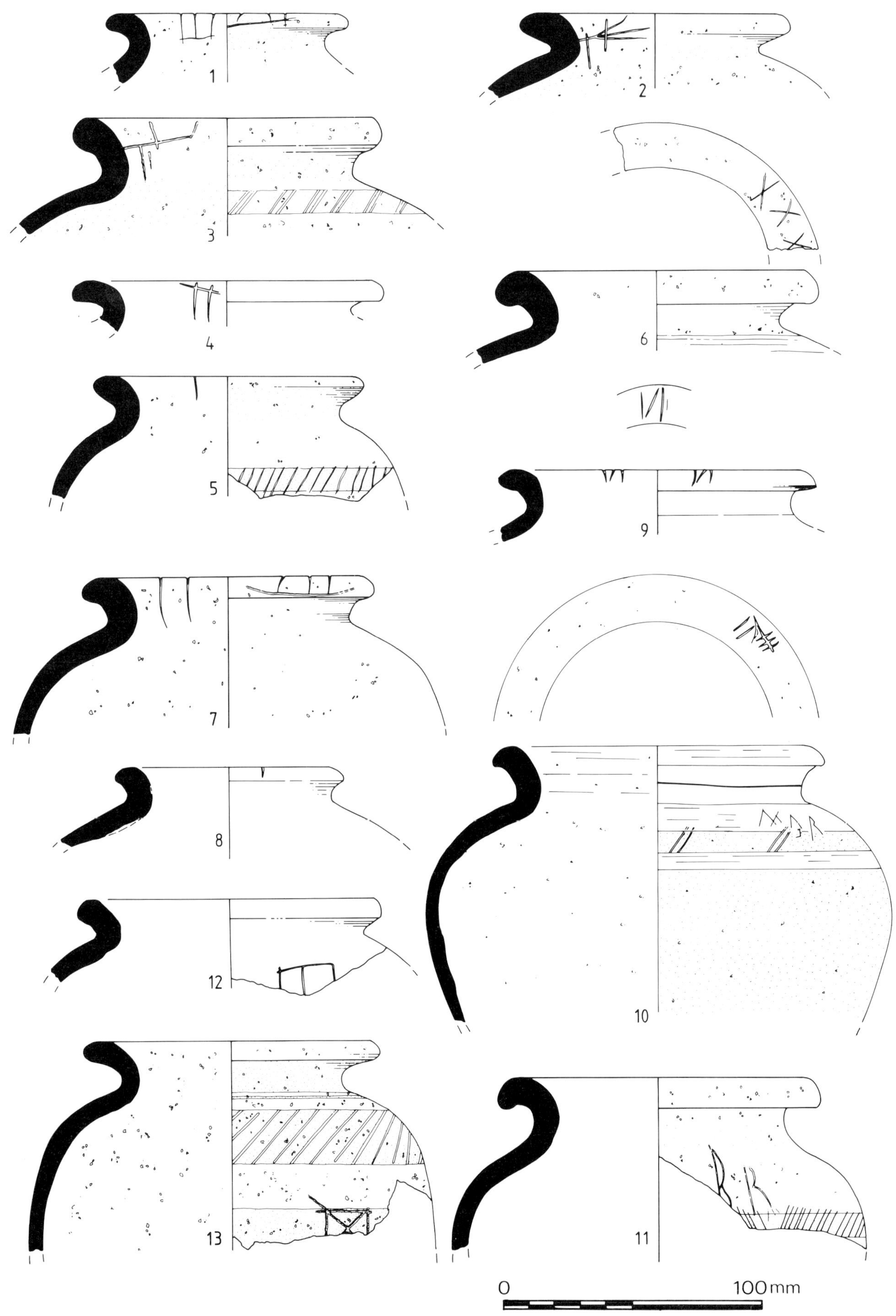

Figure 56 Graffiti, nos 1–13 (1/4 scale)

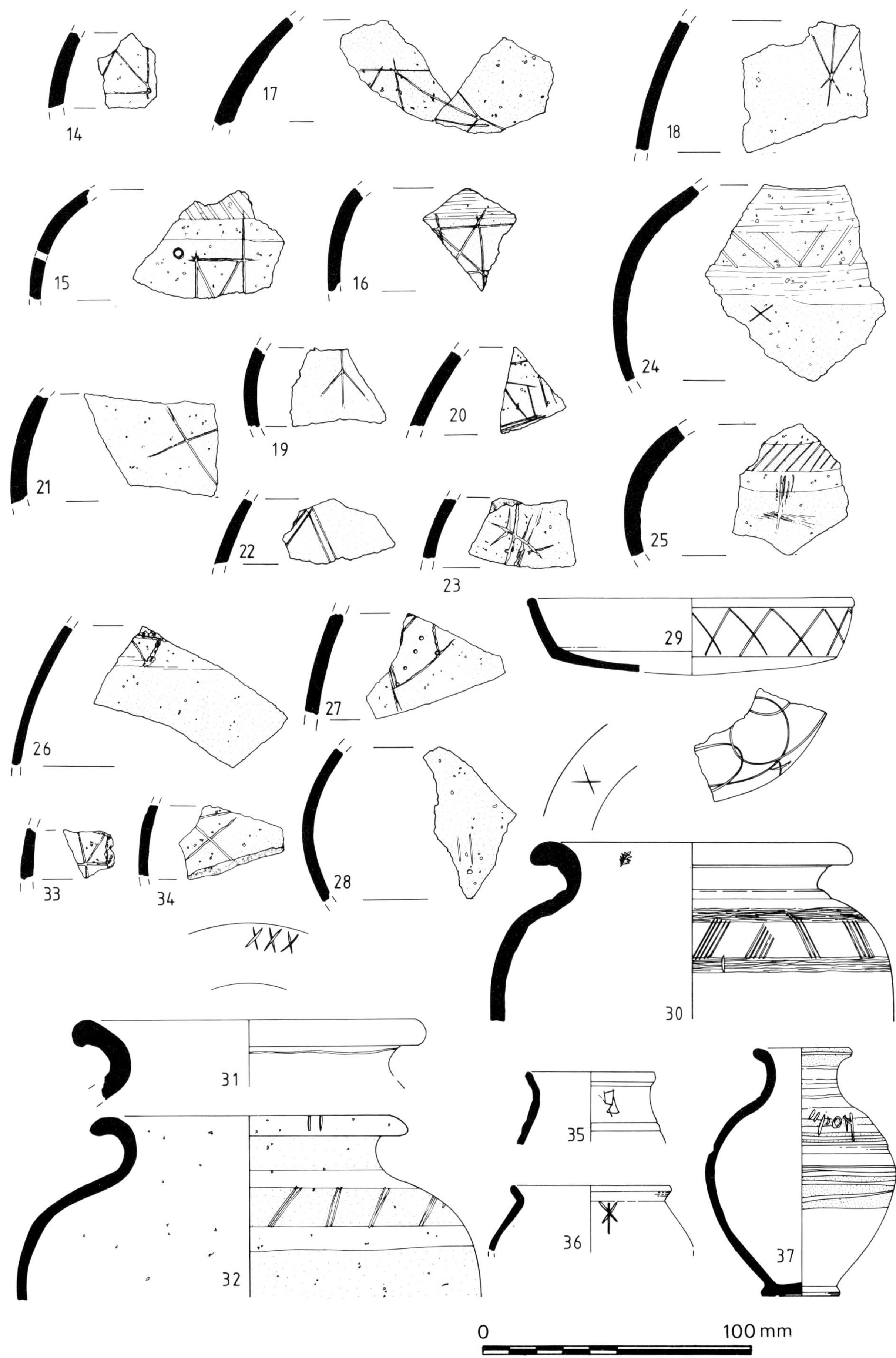

Figure 57 Graffiti, nos 14–37 (1/4 scale)

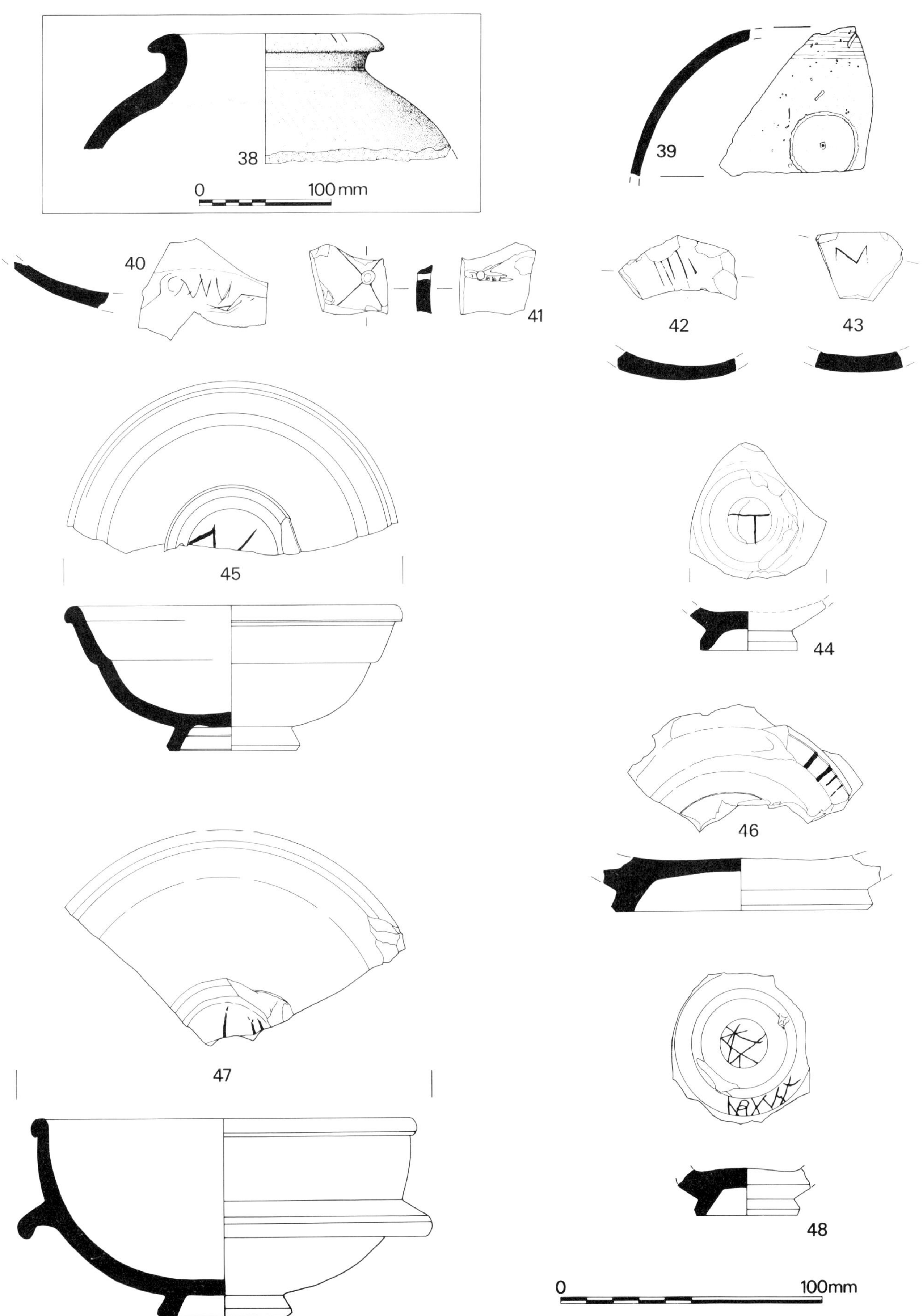

Figure 58 Graffiti, nos 38–48

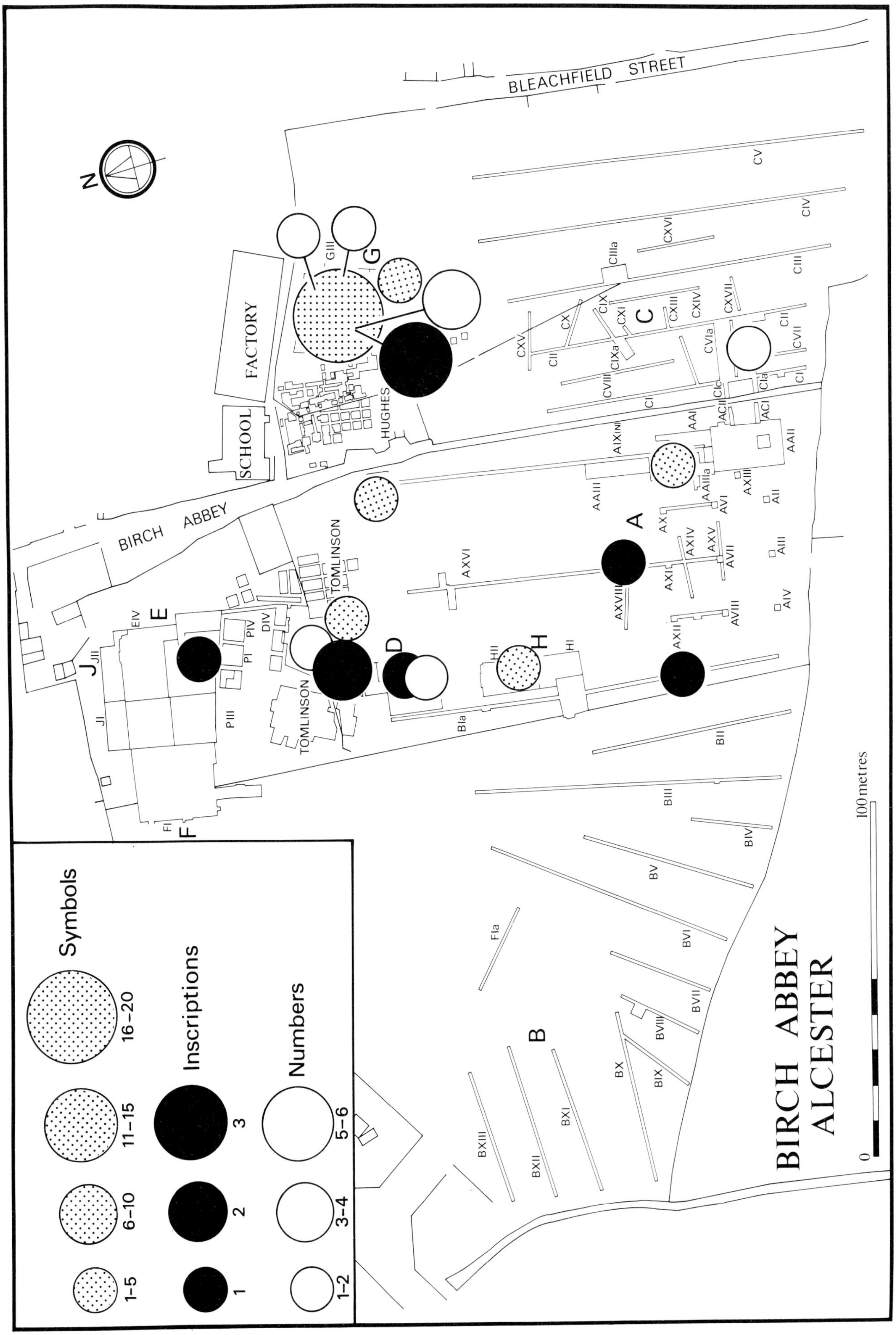

Figure 59 Distribution of pottery with graffiti

Roman pottery: notes

Stamped grey ware base

Val Rigby

There was a central stamp on the upper side of the base of a bowl or platter with a moulded scarcely functional foot-ring, in a light grey sandy ware, with a burnished finish (fig 60; P 55, D I 173, phase II, later 2nd to early 3rd century?). The reading is uncertain, but it is likely to be 'SCVTILLIVO' or 'SCVTILLI A[V]O[TIS]', in either case giving a previously unknown potter's name.

Name stamps on coarse ware products are rare in Britain, while illiterate 'marks' are comparatively common and widely found. The main period for the use of stamps was AD 80–180, although their use continued sporadically throughout the Roman period. The Alcester piece is unique but may well be the product of a workshop which also supplied the settlement at Tiddington (Fieldhouse *et al* 1931, 64).

The narrow rectangular die face most closely resembles those of some samian dies of South Gaulish origin in the Flavian–Trajanic period and also some of Central Gaulish origin in the 2nd century. The comparatively long and complex inscription suggests either that it was imported, or that a considerable period of Romanization occurred before its manufacture. A tentative date for its manufacture is AD 100–40.

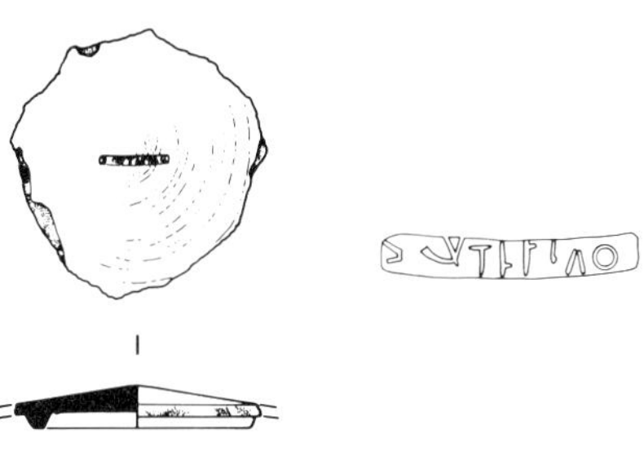

Figure 60 Stamped grey ware base (1/4 scale); stamp full size

Petrography of selected samples of Severn Valley ware

[M2:C8] Dr Roberta Tomber examined five sherds of Severn Valley ware from the excavations as part of a more general survey of the fabric (Tomber 1980). In summary, the five sherds could be divided into two major fabric groups: a coarse-textured ware distinguished on the basis of quartz size, and a finer-textured ware with limestone inclusions. (Perhaps equivalent to Warwickshire Museum fabrics O24 and O27 respectively.)

Mortaria *Paul Booth,*

incorporating notes on the stamps by K F Hartley

Introduction

[M2:C4] All the extant *mortaria* from the 1964–6 excavations were examined. The resulting data were intended to supplement the dating evidence for the site (see table M8) and answer questions relating to the development of pottery trading patterns. The *mortaria* have not been considered in the context of the pottery assemblage as a whole since there are no reliable quantified data for the other coarse pottery. There were 565 *mortarium* sherds, weighing 42.597kg and totalling 23.01 EVEs (estimated vessel equivalents), with an estimated 188 different vessels represented by rims. The use of several different quantification techniques is justified in demonstrating the apparent integrity of the group (see below) and in allowing comparison with a number of other assemblages for which varying methods have been used.

All the *mortarium* sherds found on the site were retained, in contrast to the policy on coarse wares. This can be confirmed by comparison with other sites in the vicinity. For example, the average sherd weight of 75g compares closely with an average of 71g for 282 *mortarium* sherds from the 'unweeded' assemblage from the 1980–1 excavations at Tiddington, Warwicks (Booth forthcoming (a)), and the high representation of rim sherds (just under one in three) is also paralleled at Tiddington, where the figure was nearer one in two (*ibid*). A further check on the integrity of the 1964–6 figures is in the comparison of figures for EVEs (based on a count of rim percentages) and sherd count. In the 1964–6 excavations the average rim percentage per sherd was 4.0% (dividing the total EVEs by the total sherds). At 1–5 Bleachfield Street, Alcester (Booth forthcoming (c)), excavated in 1976–7 and where all sherds were retained, the closely comparable figure was 3.7%.

Some less common fabrics were represented largely by rim sherds, for example three of the four Nene Valley sherds were rims. This feature has been noted also at Tiddington and Wasperton (Booth forthcoming (b)), but is not explained (at least at Alcester) by the difficulty of distinguishing between body sherds of Nene Valley origin and those from Mancetter/Hartshill, since this problem was very carefully considered during the processing of the material.

Fabrics

Seventeen different *mortarium* fabrics were identified (excluding *mortaria* in samian ware). The fabric classification followed is that of the Warwickshire

Table 3 Quantification of *mortarium* fabrics

Fabric	Total Sherds	%	Weight (g)	%	Vessel Count	%	Eves	%
M12	27	4.8	2896	6.8	14	7.9	1.43	6.2
M21	20	3.5	2204	5.2	11	5.8	1.39	6.0
M22	205	36.3	14363	33.7	64	33.9	8.01	34.8
M23	144	25.5	9010	21.1	56	29.6	5.77	25.2
M25	4	0.7	283	0.7	3	1.6	0.27	1.2
M26	57	10.1	3807	8.9	9	4.8	1.56	6.8
M34	5	0.9	691	1.6	1	0.5	0.30	1.3
M41	7	1.2	424	1.0	3	1.6	0.29	1.3
M43	10	1.6	263	0.6	6	3.2	0.37	1.6
M44	24	4.2	1935	4.5	6	3.2	0.84	3.7
M45	7	1.2	549	1.3	4	2.1	0.21	0.9
M46	1	0.2	153	0.4	1	0.5	0.01	–
M49	7	1.2	2042	4.8	1	0.5	1.00	4.3
M51	19	3.4	2691	6.3	4	2.1	0.84	3.7
M52	2	0.4	551	1.3	2	1.1	0.44	1.9
M53	1	0.2	342	0.8	1	0.5	0.15	0.7
M71	25	4.4	393	0.9	2	1.1	0.13	0.6
TOTALS	565		42597		188		23.01	

Museum Roman pottery recording system, used on all sites excavated by the Museum since 1980. This facilitates comparison with other recorded assemblages. The overall quantities of each fabric, with the various quantification methods compared, can be seen in table 3, while their descriptions and possible sources are presented below.

The fabrics fall into six main subgroups of the *mortarium* class, based on broad characteristics of colour and surface treatment. M12 is the only representative of a group of buff wares, most of which were probably imported. It has minor variations which may represent the products of several different industries of differing dates. It includes vessels usually assigned a South-East England/North Gaul origin (Hartley 1977, 11–13).

The M20 group comprises white and cream fabrics, including all the major central England industries (*Verulamium* Region — M21, Mancetter/Hartshill — M22, Oxfordshire — M23, Nene Valley — M25) along with a further group of vessels (M26) from one or possibly more Midland sources. On the basis of the distribution of potters' stamps in this fabric, Wroxeter is almost certainly a principal (perhaps the sole) source for M26. This fabric is not easily distinguished from some products of the Mancetter/Hartshill industry, and some of its rim forms are also very similar to Mancetter/Hartshill types. All examples are likely to be of 2nd-century date.

M34 was the sole example of a group of oxidized fabrics which do not seem to have had a white slip. The parallels both of form and fabric (see discussion of no 45 below) suggest that it originated at Gloucester. The M40 group was more diverse, consisting of a range of oxidized fabrics with white or cream slip. The best known of these is the Oxfordshire white slipped fabric (Young 1977, fabric WC), of late 3rd- to 4th-century date. On the basis of the rim forms the other fabrics in this group are likely to be of 1st- to 2nd-century date, and most were probably reaching Alcester in the period *c* AD 100–60. Fabric M46 may have had a Gloucestershire origin. There was considerable similarity between some of the fabrics in this group, however. M41, M44, and M49 were clearly in the same broad tradition in terms of fabric and trituration grits. Only M44 was relatively common, amounting to 4.2% of all *mortarium* sherds. The source of this and other fabrics in this group is uncertain, though some may have been relatively local to Alcester.

Oxidized fabrics in the M50 group were characterized by the occurrence of a red-brown slip on the flange of the vessel. This technique is characteristic of 'raetian type' *mortaria*, but not all the vessels in this group necessarily had the distinctive rim characteristic of the raetian type. A Wroxeter origin is likely for the principal fabric in this group, M51; the source of the other two is unknown.

The remaining fabric, M71, was the Oxfordshire oxidized colour-coated ware (Young 1977, fabric C). Sherds in this fabric and in the white slipped Oxfordshire fabric M43 were generally quite small, and much below the overall average *mortarium* sherd weight. This seems to reflect both the relatively small size of vessels in these fabrics, and perhaps particularly the fact that they are much thinner-walled than other fabrics.

Fabric descriptions

Only those fabrics for which no clear published definition can be found are described here. Reference is made to existing corpora for the description of well-known fabrics.

M12: ?North-East Gaul/South-East England. cf Hartley 1985, 330 (fabric 103). There attributed to the Pas de Calais. For wider discussion see Hartley 1977.

M21: *Verulamium* Region. cf Saunders and Havercroft 1977, 119.

M22: Mancetter/Hartshill. cf Hartley 1967, 29.

M23: Oxfordshire White Ware. cf Young 1977, 56, fabric M.

M25: Lower Nene Valley. cf Hartley 1989, 132, fabric 4f.

M26: ?West Midlands/Wroxeter. Hard, fairly coarse brown-buff to cream or off-white fabric, often with a pink core and sometimes with a pale orange-brown slip. Moderate subangular quartz inclusions and occasional subrounded red-brown and black inclusions. Subangular quartz and much less common subrounded red-brown and black (sandstone and iron ore?) trituration grits.

M34: ?Gloucester. Fine, buff to light buff-brown fabric. Very slightly micaceous, with sparse to moderate subrounded quartz sand grains and sparse rounded black ?iron and red-brown ?sandstone inclusions. Subangular quartz trituration grits, plus sparse black ?slag and opaque, fine-grained grey grits.

M41: Source uncertain. Fairly fine orange-brown fabric with pinkish-cream to white slip. Sparse subrounded quartz sand and occasional rounded red-brown ?iron inclusions. Subangular quartz and small red-brown trituration grits.

M43: Oxfordshire White Colour-Coated Ware. cf Young 1977, 117, fabric WC.

M44: Source uncertain. Hard, fairly fine red-brown fabric with a cream slip. Occasional rounded quartz and rounded brown-black ?iron ore inclusions. Sparse irregular voids may indicate some organic tempering. Large subangular white and grey quartz and red-brown ?sandstone trituration grits.

M45: Source uncertain. Hard, very fine orange brown fabric with cream-white slip. Micaceous, with occasional subrounded quartz sand grains. Subangular quartz and large sandstone trituration grits.

M46: Source uncertain, perhaps Gloucestershire. Hard, red-brown fabric with grey core and white slip. Moderate to common quartz sand and very occasional rounded black ?iron inclusions. Occasional voids on surface indicating organic inclusions. White and grey quartz trituration grits, scarce in the only example of this fabric. The fabric is comparable to the description of Cirencester fabric 88 (Keeley 1986, 159–60).

M49: Source uncertain. Hard, fine buff-red fabric with off-white slip. Slightly micaceous, with very sparse red-brown inclusions and occasional small voids. Subangular white quartz and brown sandstone trituration grits, the latter more common.

M51: ?West Midlands/Wroxeter. Hard, fairly fine red-brown fabric with red-brown slip over flange and upper part of vessel interior. Sparse small quartz inclusions and occasional very small specks of black ?iron ore. Subrounded quartz and angular brown ?sandstone trituration grits.

M52: Source uncertain. Fairly fine, red-brown fabric usually with grey core, probably with a micaceous dark red-brown slip. Sparse subrounded quartz sand, sparse burnt organic and occasional black ?iron inclusions. Occasional angular to subrounded quartz trituration grits.

M53: Source uncertain. Fine, hard orange-red fabric with a dark red-brown ?slip. Occasional subrounded quartz sand inclusions. Subrounded quartz grits densely packed on the rim and upper part of the vessel interior.

M71: Oxfordshire Red Colour-Coated Ware. cf Young 1977, 123, fabric C.

Forms and chronology

Detailed typological discussion is confined to the catalogue of illustrated vessels, but for the purposes of assessing broad chronological trends in *mortarium* supply the vessels were recorded under six main typological headings. These were A, hook flanged (broadly mid-1st to 2nd century); B, 'dropped' flange with very tall bead (mainly late 2nd to 3rd century); C, dropped straight flange (eg Oxfordshire type M22, mid-3rd to 4th century); D, collared (mainly late 2nd to mid-3rd century); E, hammer-headed (broadly 3rd–4th century); F, wall-sided (mainly mid-3rd to 4th century).

More precise details of form were recorded in the case of fabrics for which there is a standard typology (eg Oxfordshire, Young 1977). The breakdown of type by fabric can be seen in table 4 and a listing of Oxfordshire types represented is given in table 5.

The most common overall form was the hook-rimmed type A. Even allowing for the fact that some vessels of this type were of 1st-century date, 2nd-century *mortaria* can be seen to have been more common than those of other centuries. An estimate of the number of vessels per century is provided in table 6. The figures are based on known chronologies where possible, but for broad groups such as A and E an arbitrary proportional division has been made, based on the approximate overall date-range of the type. For example, as type A is assigned to the period *c* AD 60–180, two-thirds of the vessels of this type are allotted to the 2nd century and one-third to the 1st (occupation has been assumed to have started *c* AD 60). The method of calculation is very crude, but the figures give an order-of-magnitude impression of the chronological breakdown of the *mortaria*.

It is likely that the 1st century is over-represented at the expense of the 2nd as a result of the proportional division, and the 4th century may be slightly under-represented, if more of the Mancetter/Hartshill hammer-headed vessels were of this date. Nevertheless the figures suggest steady use of *mortaria* in the 1st and 2nd centuries, with some fall-off in the

Table 4 Mortarium types by fabric (quantification by vessel count)

Fabric	Type A	Type B	Type C	Type D	Type E	Type F	Total
M12	14						14
M21	11						11
M22	38				26		64
M23	9	31	12	4			56
M25		1			2		3
M26	9						9
M34	1						1
M41	3						3
M43	6						6
M44	6						6
M45	4						4
M46	1						1
M49	1						1
M51	4						4
M52	1				1		2
M53	1						1
M71		1				1	2
TOTAL	103	39	12	4	29	1	188

For a definition of types see text.

3rd and particularly in the 4th. This may reflect some reduction in the scale of activity in the 4th century, or alternatively a change in culinary/dietary practice.

Table 4 shows that a much wider range of fabrics was in use for vessels of type A (and by definition in the 1st and 2nd centuries) than for other types. Only three fabrics (Nene Valley ware and the two oxidized Oxfordshire wares) were not used for this type, and eleven fabrics were used exclusively for it, demonstrating the radical changes in *mortarium* supply after the end of the 2nd century (see below).

Stamps (fig 61)

S1 (Illustrated vessel no 11, fig 62.) Fabric M21. ALBINUS, incomplete, stamped diagonally across the flange. This stamp always appears in conjunction with a counterstamp apparently reading VIANVACA FE. Cf Hartley 1972, 371 and 373, nos 3 and 4. For the dating, however, see Hartley 1984, 282, where a range of AD 60–90 is suggested. (C IXA 17, unphased)
S2 Fabric M21. ALBINUS, incomplete, from one of his dies usually counterstamped F.LVGVDV. Date AD 60–90 as above. (L XII 7, unphased)
S3 Fabric M22. BRUSCIUS, retrograde, incomplete. Kilns of Bruscius are known at both Mancetter and Hartshill, where he worked in conjunction with Iunius. *c* AD 140–80. (D I 25, phase VIII, late 4th century)
S4 Fabric M26. DECANIUS, incomplete. The distribution of his stamps points very firmly to production in the area of Wroxeter, where at least 28 examples have been recorded. Date *c* AD 110–60. (H II 1, unphased)
S5 (Illustrated vessel no 42.) Fabric M26. DOCILIS.F. Docilis I was probably also producing *mortaria* in the Wroxeter area, where the stamp occurs quite commonly (eg Bushe-Fox 1914, 57 and 60, no 47). The rim forms of vessels associated with this stamp suggest a date in the period *c* AD 100–40. (D II 2, phase IX, late 4th century and D II 3, unphased)
S6 (Illustrated vessel no 41.) Fabric M26. DOCI, incomplete. Probably for Docilis II. A Wroxeter source is again likely, and the date is probably within the range *c* AD 110–60. (AA III 102, unphased)
S7 Fabric M21. DOINUSF, incomplete. An early die in use in the period *c* AD 70–100 (cf Hartley 1984, 284). (H II 39, unphased)
S8 Fabric M21. DOINUS, incomplete. From one of his later dies dated *c* AD 85–110 (Hartley 1984, 284). (1966 U/S)
S9 (Illustrated vessel no 19.) Fabric M22. IUNIUS, retrograde, incomplete. This is one of the more prolific Mancetter/Hartshill potters, with kilns at both centres. *c* AD 150–90. (D II 14, unphased)
S10 (Illustrated vessel no 18.) Fabric M22. IUNIUS LOCCIUS and LOCCIUS PRO, incomplete. This vessel is of particular interest in having stamps of two potters. That of Loccius Pro is fragmentary but the letters and border make the identification certain. The similarity of their names makes some connection between these and a third potter, Loccius Vibius, very likely, a supposition which is reinforced by this vessel, though the exact nature of the connection is uncertain. All three potters worked in the Mancetter/Hartshill industry. Stamps of Loccius Pro are considerably more common than those of Iunius Loccius. A date in the range *c* AD 140–85 is likely. (G V 5, phase VI, late 4th century)
S11 Fabric M41. MOF.F, retrograde, incomplete. See S12 below. (E V 22, phase V, late 2nd century?)
S12 (Illustrated vessel no 46.) Fabric M41. MOF.F, retrograde, incomplete. The reading of these stamps is not altogether certain; MOF.E is possible, but less likely than MOF.F, the last letter presumably representing FECIT. Both stamps are positioned diagonally across the rim, a characteristic most notably associated with Flavian *mortaria* from the *Verulamium* region (cf eg S1 above). No other examples of this stamp are known. The fabric suggests origin in the west Midlands and the rim form of no 46 a date *c* AD 120–60. (E II 34, phase V, late 2nd century?)
S13 (Illustrated vessel no 17.) Fabric M22. SARRIUS, fragmentary. See S14 below. (AA II 2, unphased)
S14 (Not drawn, for rim see illustrated vessel no 21.) Fabric M22. SARRIUS, incomplete and very poorly impressed. This and S13 are probably both from a die which reads SARIUS with the final S reversed. Kilns of Sarrius have been found at Mancetter and

Table 5 Oxfordshire *mortarium* types (types after Young 1977; quantification by vessel count)

Type	M2	M3	M11	M12	M17	M18	M19	M20	M21	M22	M23	Uncertain	Total
Probable	2	4	5	1	6	5	3	3	3	11		3	46
Possible	1	1		1	2	3			1		1		10
Total	3	5	5	2	8	8	3	3	4	11	1	3	56

Type	WC4	WC5	WC7	C97	C100
Probable	1	1	2	1	1
Possible			2		

Table 6 Breakdown of mortaria by century (based on vessel count)

Century:		1st	2nd	3rd	4th	Total
Type:	A	34	69			103
	B		1	32	6	39
	C			4	8	12
	D		1	3		4
	E		2	14	13	29
	F				1	1
Total		34	73	53	28	188

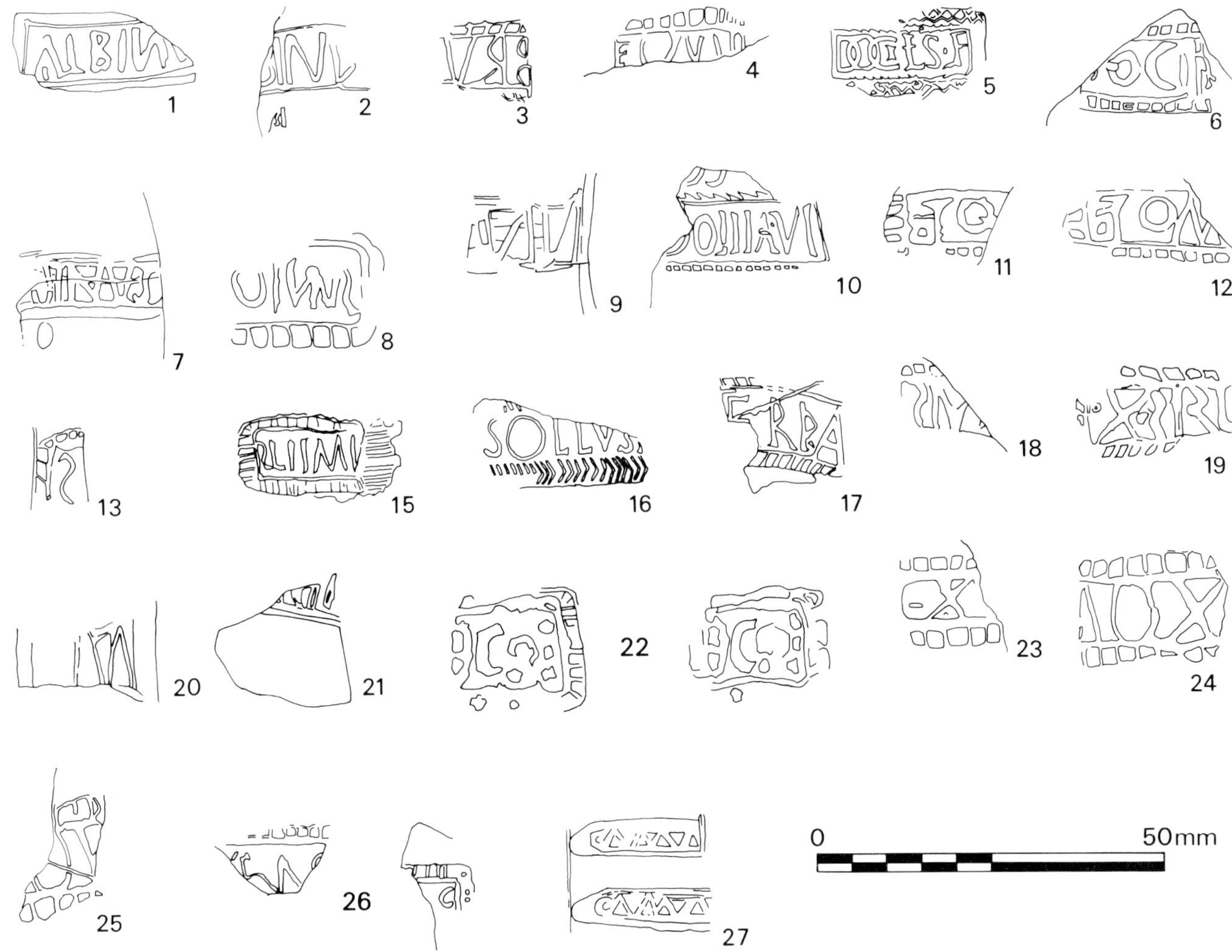

Figure 61 Mortaria stamps

Hartshill, the source of these two pieces, as well as at Rossington Bridge, where a rather different fabric was used, *c* AD 140–70. (D I 87D, phase V, early to mid-4th century?)

S15 (Illustrated vessel no 20.) Fabric M22. SIMILIS, retrograde, incomplete. Another potter with a known kiln at Mancetter. *c* AD 140–70. (E IV 1, U/S)

S16 (Illustrated vessel no 13.) Fabric M21. SOLLUS, incomplete. Probably *c* AD 60–100 (Hartley 1984, 287). (G I 2A)

S17 Fabric M41. A. TERE RIPANUS, incomplete. This die may have read A. TE RIPANUS, being abbreviated to fit the name into a single line. The distribution of this stamp includes Exeter, Caerleon, Gloucester, and Wroxeter as well as Castleford and London. A west Midlands or south-west England origin is likely on fabric grounds. Date *c* AD 60–85. (C V 48, unphased)

S18 Fabric M41. Unknown, incomplete. The stamp is placed diagonally across the flange of the vessel (cf S11 and S12 above, in the same fabric). Another stamp from this die is known from Penydarren Park. A date in the first half of the 2nd century is likely. (C IX 11, unphased)

S19 (Illustrated vessel no 15.) Fabric M22. Illiterate. A trademark perhaps imitating a stamp of Sarrius, for whom it is sometimes misread. The fabric and the limited distribution indicate production at Mancetter (other stamps have been found at Wroxeter and Templeborough). An Antonine date seems certain. (B I 14, unphased)

S20 (Illustrated vessel no 22.) Fabric M22. Uncertain, incomplete. The stamp is poorly impressed and cannot be identified with certainty. The vessel is from the Mancetter/Hartshill industry and probably of Antonine date. (J II 1, unphased)

S21 Fabric M22. VBHC, fragmentary. From the same die as an old find from Alcester. This may be the full reading for the stamp, but its significance is unclear. The potter may have been illiterate. The fabric indicates an origin in the Mancetter/Hartshill industry, and the vessel form and type of lettering can be compared to the work of another illiterate potter who had a kiln at Hartshill. He was probably working in the period *c* AD 135–80. (AA II 16A, phase V, later 3rd century on)

S22 (Illustrated vessel no 58.) Fabric M49. Illiterate. Two stamps, one on each side of the spout. A possible reading is BCO. No other examples are known. The fabric suggests a west Midlands origin, and the vessel form a date in the first half of the 2nd century. (D II 29A, unphased)

S23 Fabric M26. Illiterate, incomplete. See S24 below. (B IA 9, unphased)

S24 (Illustrated vessel no 43.) Fabric M26. Illiterate. These stamps appear to be from two different dies used by an illiterate potter or potters. The similarities between these dies and a further seven presumably used by the same group suggest that if more than one man was involved they were members of the same workshop. Two of these other stamps are also represented at Alcester among material from excavations by H V Hughes. The stamps are almost never intact; only three of the nine dies can be more or less completed. They do not appear to represent names, but usually give some combination of the letters X, H, V, A, O, and C. Some 50 stamps are known from this group of dies, about half from Wroxeter and most of the rest from the west Midlands and Wales, although two examples occur on the Antonine Wall. The distribution suggests manufacture at Wroxeter. The presence of two stamps on the Antonine Wall suggests that the potters were active in the early Antonine period. Their overall period of activity must fall in the period *c* AD 100–60. (D III 2, unphased)

S25 (Illustrated vessel no 16.) Fabric M22. Uncertain. Fragmentary. The two surviving parts of the stamp do not join and it is not possible to read the stamp with any certainty. A Mancetter/

Hartshill origin is certain. The rim form suggests a date *c* AD 110–40. (D I 2, phase VIII, late 4th century and D IIA 1, unphased)
S26 (Illustrated vessel no 35.) Fabric M23. Illiterate. Two stamps occur side by side, with a third on another sherd probably from the same vessel. A trademark used at Littlemore in the Oxfordshire industry (cf Young 1977, 59, no 18). The early rim form of this vessel suggests a date in the range *c* AD 110–40. (D I 34, phase VI, mid- to late 4th century?, D I 36, phase VI, mid- to late 4th century?, D I 126A, phase II, later 2nd to early 3rd century?, and D I 246, phase II, later 2nd to early 3rd century?)
S27 (Not illustrated.) Fabric M22. Unknown, fragmentary. A tiny fragment too small to identify. Mancetter/Hartshill in origin and the rim form probably datable *c* AD 120–60. (A XVIII U/S)

Catalogue of illustrated vessels (figs 62–5)

The illustrated vessels are grouped by fabric in simple numerical order, rather than presented as an overall type series.

1 Fabric M12. Type A. (G IV 39, phase IV, early to mid-4th century)
2 Fabric M12. Type A. (H II 88?, phase II, Antonine to 3rd century?)
3 Fabric M12. Type A. Nos 1–3 are characteristic of the Flavian potters of Hartley group II (Hartley 1977, 9 and 16). (G IA 6, phase IX, late 4th century)
4 Fabric M12. Type A. (A XVIII U/S)
5 Fabric M12. Type A. (AA III 98, phase I, late 1st to early 2nd century)
6 Fabric M12. Type A. (E VI 8, unphased)
7 Fabric M12. Type A. (F I 33, unphased)
8 Fabric M12. Type A. Nos 4–8 are comparable to Bushe-Fox types 26–30 (Bushe-Fox 1913, 77) though the tip of the flange of all the present examples is more sharply hooked back. In this respect they are closer to a vessel from Dover for which a Gaulish origin and a date range of *c* AD 90–150 are suggested (Hartley 1981a, 204–5, no 368). These vessels are not necessarily from the same source as nos 1–3, though the fabric appears to be very similar. (E V 22, phase V, late 2nd century?)
9 Fabric M12. Type A? This *mortarium*, which on fabric grounds is likely to be an import is, like nos 4–8 above, comparable to vessels from Dover, particularly Hartley 1981a, 204–5, no 375. The parallel is not exact but the differences, particularly in the relative lack of definition of an internal bead or lip on the Alcester example, are not great. The Dover vessel, and the related examples nos 376 and 377, are suggested as possible Gaulish imports and dated *c* AD 100–60 (*ibid*). (D II 20, unphased)
10 Fabric M21. Type A. (C I 25, unphased)
11 Fabric M21. Type A. With a diagonal stamp of ALBINUS (S1), within the period AD 60–90 (Hartley 1984, 282). (C IXA 17, unphased)
12 Fabric M21. Type A. (D II 60, unphased)
13 Fabric M21. Type A. Stamp of SOLLUS (S16), probably within the range AD 60–100 (Hartley 1984, 287). (G I 2A)
14 Fabric M21. Type A. The *Verulamium* region vessels span the period from mid-1st to mid-2nd century, though the majority are likely to have arrived at Alcester in the first part of this period. The two stamped pieces are of 1st-century date. No 12 is paralleled by a vessel now assigned a range AD 80–120 (Frere 1972, 316–17, no 751; 1984, 273) and no 14 by a vessel dated AD 120–60 (Frere 1972, 339–40, no 1026). No 10, however, is not closely paralleled amongst the *mortaria* from *Verulamium*, though there is no doubt as to its source as the fabric is characteristic of the area. This vessel and nos 12 and 14 were all very worn and had no surviving trituration grits. (D II 2, phase IX, late 4th century)
15 Fabric M22. Type A. Stamp of an illiterate Antonine potter (S19). (B I 14, unphased)
16 Fabric M22. Type A. Unidentifiable stamp (S25), but on the basis of the rim form assigned to the period AD 110–40. (D II 2, phase IX, late 4th century and D IIA 1, unphased)
17 Fabric M22. Type A.2 Fragmentary stamp of SARRIUS (S13), dated *c* AD 140–70. (AA II 2, unphased, AA II 8, unphased, and AA II 78, phase II, late 2nd to early 3rd century)
18 Fabric M22. Type A. Stamp of IUNIUS LOCCIUS and LOCCIUS PRO (S10), dated *c* AD 140–85. (G V 5, phase VI, late 4th century)
19 Fabric M22. Type A. Stamp of IUNIUS (S9), dated *c* AD 150–90. (D II 14, unphased)
20 Fabric M22. Type A. Stamp of SIMILIS (S15), dated *c* AD 140–70. (E IV 1, U/S)
21 Fabric M22. Type A. Fragmentary stamp of SARRIUS (S14), dated *c* AD 140–70. (D I 87D, phase V, early to mid-4th century?)
22 Fabric M22. Type A. Stamp (S20). (J II 1, 7, 150 and 152, unphased)
23 Fabric M22. Type A. The majority of the hook-rimmed *mortaria* from Mancetter/Hartshill date to the Antonine period. Only no 16, with the steeply humped flange, is typologically earlier. (D II 29A, unphased)
24 Fabric M22. Type A? Vessel with very straight down-sloping flange, almost a transitional form between hook-rimmed and hammer-headed types. A late 2nd- to early 3rd-century date is likely. (L XII 1, unphased)
25 Fabric M22. Type E. A small *mortarium* with a very short, hooked hammer-head. Broad, irregular bands of red-brown paint on the rim. (AA I 11, phase IX, mid-4th century)
26 Fabric M22. Type E. (L VI 9, unphased)
27 Fabric M22. Type E. (B IA 1, unphased)
28 Fabric M22. Type E. (D I 124, phase VI, mid- to late 4th century?)
29 Fabric M22. Type E. (AA II 51, phase VI, early to mid-4th century)
30 Fabric M22. Type E. (AA II 51A)
31 Fabric M22. Type E, with elaborate linear decoration in red paint. Provenance uncertain.
32 Fabric M22. Type E, with a three-pronged motif in red paint. This was probably repeated at intervals around the rim. (G IV 1, unphased)
33 Fabric M22. Type E. (C IIID 1, unphased?)
34 Fabric M22. Type E, with irregular broad oblique bands of red paint, the most common form of painted decoration on these vessels. Nos 25–34 demonstrate some of the diversity of rim forms to be found in the hammer-headed type. Reeded examples are considerably more common than plain ones (eg nos 33 and 34) in this group. It is unclear, however, if this is of any chronological significance. The overall date-range for these vessels is *c* AD 240–370. (G II 2, U/S)
35 Fabric M23. Type A. Young Type M2 (Young 1977, 68–9) with particularly sharply hooked flange and pronounced internal step. Stamped with a double trademark stamp (S26), probably on each side of the spout (the double stamp and a fragment of a separate stamp survive). This stamp was used at Littlemore in the Oxfordshire industry, and Hartley suggests that the rim form, which is early, should date *c* AD 110–40. (D I 34, phase VI, mid- to late 4th century?; D I 36, phase VI, mid- to late 4th century?; D I 126A, phase II, later 2nd to early 3rd century?; and D I 246, phase II, later 2nd to early 3rd century?)
36 Fabric M23. Type A. Young type M3 (Young 1977, 68–9), but not exactly paralleled in Young's corpus. Dated *c* AD 140–200. (D II 2, phase IX, late 4th century)
37 Fabric M23. Type B. Young type M11 (Young 1977, 70 and 73), but again not exactly paralleled. The simple spout is formed by breaking the top bead of the rim. *c* AD 180–240. (G V 5, phase VI, late 4th century)
38 Fabric M23. Type C. Young type M22 (Young 1977, 76–7), but not precisely paralleled. This type, in particular, is subject to great variation in rim form. (F I 5, phase XIII, after AD 353)
39 Fabric M25. Type B. (F I U/S)
40 Fabric M25. Type E. Markedly concave rim with two small central ridges defined by deep grooves. Both these vessels are presumably of 4th-century date. It is unfortunate that the phasing of the context of no 40 is uncertain. (D IV 13, unphased)
41 Fabric M26. Type A. Stamp of DOCILIS (S6), dated *c* AD 110–60. (AA III 15, phase VII, late 3rd to early 4th century and AA III 102, unphased)
42 Fabric M26. Type A. Stamp DOCILIS F (S5), dated *c* AD 100–40. (D II 2, phase IX, late 4th century)
43 Fabric M26. Type A. Illegible stamp (S24), dated within the period *c* AD 100–60. (D III 2, unphased)
44 Fabric M26. Type A. The rim form of this *mortarium* is consistent with the evidence of the stamped vessels nos 41–3 in suggesting a date in the first half of the 2nd century. (B I 3, phase II, Antonine to 3rd century)

45 Fabric M34. Type A. Hartley considers that this vessel is pre-Flavian, but the earliest context in which it occurs is dated to the late 1st century. There are some similarities between the rim form of this vessel and one from Cirencester, of Gloucester origin and also dated pre-Flavian (Rigby 1982, 162 and 164, no 10). Gloucester products from Kingsholm (Hurst 1985, 73 and 81, nos 99–102) also closely parallel this vessel and a Gloucester origin seem almost certain. (AA III 75, phase II, late 2nd to mid-3rd century, AA III 83, phase II, late 2nd to mid-3rd century, AA III 94, unphased, and AA III 95, phase I, late 1st to early 2nd century)
46 Fabric M41. Type A. Stamp of MOF.F (S12). The rim form of this vessel is likely to date within the period *c* AD 120–60. (E II 34, phase V, late 2nd century?)
47 Fabric M43. Type B. A vessel with characteristics of both Young forms WC5 and WC6 (Young 1977, 121–2), with consequent problems for dating since the two types are dated AD 240–300 and 350–400 respectively. The small size of the vessel suggests, however, that Young's type M23, usually very large, is unlikely to have been the prototype. The present piece should probably therefore be assigned to WC5 and a 3rd-century date. (C III 1A, unphased)
48 Fabric M44. Type A. (D I 49, phase VI, mid- to late 4th century?)
49 Fabric M44. Type A. (D I 126A, phase II, later 2nd to early 3rd century?)
50 Fabric M44. Type A. (D III 2, unphased)
51 Fabric M44. Type A. (D I 1A, unphased)
52 Fabric M44. Type A. The rim forms in this fabric demonstrate considerable diversity, but all are likely to fall within the first half of the 2nd century AD. A notable feature of nos 51 and 52 is the lack of a distinct inner lip or step at the junction of the flange and body wall. Nos 49 and 50 also have a slightly unusual feature in common, in this case a groove on the outer face of the flange. No 49, in particular, is in this respect slightly reminiscent of some examples of the Oxfordshire form M2 (Young 1977, 68–9). (D I 246, phase II, later 2nd to early 3rd century?)
53 Fabric M45. Type A. (H II 3, phase III, Antonine to 3rd century on)
54 Fabric M45. Type A. (J II 13, unphased)
55 Fabric M45. Type A. (G I 193, phase II?, mid-3rd century?)
56 Fabric M45. Type A. The range of rim types in fabric M45 is similar to that in fabric M44. Nos 53 and 54, with only a slight internal step, are comparable to nos 51 and 52 and the occurrence of an external groove on the flange of no 56 is paralleled in nos 49 and 50. A date-range for these vessels primarily in the first half of the 2nd century seems likely. (H II 2, unphased)
57 Fabric M46. Type A. The date-range for Cirencester fabric 88, with which M46 is probably equivalent, is 2nd–3rd century and possibly also 4th century (Keeley 1986, 160). This vessel must be of 2nd-century date. (D I 173, phase II, later 2nd to early 3rd century?)
58 Fabric M49. Type A. Illiterate stamp (S22) on each side of the spout. A complete vessel, likely to date to the first half of the 2nd century on the basis of the rim form. (D II 29A, unphased)
59 Fabric M51. Type A. (D I 21, phase IX, late 4th century)
60 Fabric M51. Type A. This vessel comes the closest of any of the M50 group to the so-called 'raetian type' (cf Hartley & Webster 1973, 89–103). This type is known from 64 Bleachfield Street, Alcester (eg Booth 1983, 29–30, no 20), a vessel for which a Wroxeter origin was postulated. Nos 59 and 60 here appear to be in the same fabric and a Wroxeter origin is suggested for them too. A date in the period *c* AD 120–60 seems likely for both, though it is perhaps possible that production of raetian *mortaria* continued at Wroxeter after AD 160, as seems to have been the case at Wilderspool (Hartley 1981b, 473). (D II 29A, unphased)
61 Fabric M52? Type A. This vessel has no trace of the red-brown slip characteristic of this group of fabrics, indeed one or two tiny patches may suggest the presence of a white slip. In all other respects, however, the fabric is consistent with the normal description of M52. The identification remains uncertain, however, and it is possible that this vessel is from a different source from the other sherds attributed to M52. It is certainly rather earlier in date than no 62, and a 1st-century date may be possible on the basis of the form. (D I 173, phase II, later 2nd to early 3rd century?)
62 Fabric M52. Type E. Probably an early form of hammer-headed rim, dating to the late 2nd to early 3rd century. (B I 12, unphased)
63 Fabric M53. Type A. Rectangular impression for a possible potter's stamp along the flange of the vessel, but completely illegible. The red slip covers the upper surface of the flange, except where worn away, and the upper interior of the vessel. Date uncertain, but perhaps about the middle of the 2nd century. (G V 98, phase II?, mid-3rd century?)

Areas

The distribution of *mortaria* by excavated site was studied; tables showing quantities of *mortaria* by fabric and excavated site can be found in the microfiche (tables M2–5). Site D produced the greatest quantity of *mortaria* (ranging from 43.6% of the material by weight to 29.8% by vessel count) and thus had the widest range of fabrics. Fabrics M46, M49, and M51 occurred there exclusively, and all but one sherd of M44 was also confined to that area. Fabric M34 was confined to site AA, and the single sherd of M53 came from site G. Otherwise there was little clear patterning in the data. Most of the major fabrics were widely distributed. The relative proportions of the two most common fabrics (Mancetter/Hartshill (M22) and Oxfordshire (M23) white wares) varied from site to site, but it was in site D that the preponderance of M22 in relation to M23 was most noticeable.

Distinctively late fabrics such as the Oxfordshire products M43 and M71 were widely distributed; neither was particularly concentrated in any one site. The absence of both fabrics from site E, and a strong representation of Mancetter/Hartshill and North-East Gaul/South-East England products, might argue a general lack of late Roman occupation on this site, although the group in question was relatively small. Site B also produced predominantly early *mortaria*, with only a single sherd of the Oxfordshire colour-coated fabric, a good representation of M22 and a particularly high proportion of the 2nd-century fabric M26 (22 out of 48 sherds from the site).

Discussion: the supply of *mortaria* to Alcester

The 1st and 2nd centuries AD saw *mortaria* reaching Alcester from a wide variety of sources, including both major and minor industries. The principal suppliers in the later 1st and early 2nd centuries included ?North-East Gaul and the *Verulamium* region. Mancetter/Hartshill probably became more important towards the middle of the 2nd century; there is a relative lack of very early types from this industry. Oxfordshire products were also reaching Alcester by this time, but type M2 (Young 1977, 68) is not very closely dated, so it is not possible to say exactly when they first appeared. Young's type M1 is absent in this assemblage, though present at nearby Tiddington.

The later 1st and 2nd centuries are also characterized by the occurrence of vessels in a variety of oxidized fabrics, most with white/cream or red/brown slip. The sources of many of these fabrics are unknown, but some may be Wroxeter products. The evidence of potters stamps and typological considerations suggests that most of the oxidized fabrics and the white ware M26, also probably of Wroxeter origin, were much more common in the period up to *c* AD 160 than later. These fabrics may have held, along with the *Verulamium* industry and continuing imports (represented by the vessels of Bushe-Fox type 26–30, nos 4–8 here), a dominant position in the supply of *mortaria* to the town in the first half of the 2nd century. None of these fabrics definitely occurred after the late 2nd century, and it seems clear that they were supplanted at Alcester in the Antonine period by the increasingly important Mancetter/Hartshill and Oxfordshire industries. The one possible exception is the occurrence of a hammer-headed type (no 62) in fabric M52, but this is likely to be early in the sequence for vessels of this type, and a late 2nd-century date is possible.

The cessation of recognizable imported *mortaria* and the demise of the *Verulamium* region industry and the various 2nd-century oxidized fabrics left the supply of *mortaria* exclusively in the hands of three industries from the end of the 2nd century at the latest. Of these, one, the Nene Valley industry, was only lightly represented, at a level comparable to that of other recently examined Warwickshire assemblages such as Tiddington and Wasperton. Nene Valley *mortaria* may have been traded with colour-coated wares. They were much less common than these in terms of vessel numbers in 3rd- and 4th-century contexts at Alcester (this is certainly true of 1–5 Bleachfield Street, where no Nene Valley *mortaria* were identified). Their occurrence on Warwickshire sites seems to have been consistently in 4th-century deposits.

The main late Roman *mortarium* suppliers were therefore the Mancetter/Hartshill and Oxfordshire industries. These lie respectively about 50 and 70km (in a direct line) from Alcester and the distribution of the products of both to Alcester must have been mainly if not entirely by road. In overall terms Mancetter/Hartshill was better represented than Oxfordshire in the 1964–6 collection by all methods of quantification, though the combined Oxfordshire products (fabrics M23, M43, and M71) equalled the Mancetter/Hartshill total in terms of numbers of vessels. However, the period in which Mancetter/Hartshill really seems to have dominated the *mortarium* supply is the mid- to late 2nd century. It is therefore somewhat surprising that collared forms from Mancetter/Hartshill, generally datable to the late 2nd and early 3rd centuries, are completely absent from the assemblage. The few vessels recorded as being of this broad type (type D above) were Oxfordshire products, of Young type M11 (Young 1977, 70 and 73).

For the 3rd and 4th centuries the total numbers of hammer-headed *mortaria*, a Mancetter/Hartshill type *par excellence*, were outweighed by Oxfordshire products of comparable date, particularly in the 3rd century (see table 6). A similar pattern can be seen at 1–5 Bleachfield Street, where the late 3rd- to early 4th-century phase in particular was dominated by Oxfordshire vessels. Here, as in the 1964–6 assemblage, M17 and M18 were the principal types.

The closing date of the Mancetter/Hartshill industry is still uncertain, but if it was out of production before the end of the 4th century AD, as seems likely, it must be assumed that the final phases of *mortarium* supply to Alcester were completely dominated by the Oxfordshire industry. It is probably at this time that the colour-coated fabric (M71) became really important. This can be demonstrated at 1–5 Bleachfield Street, where 54% of later 4th-century *mortarium* sherds were of this fabric (non-Oxfordshire products amounted to only 12% of *mortarium* sherds in this phase). Elsewhere in the town there is evidence that the white colour-coated fabric M43 was of greatly increased importance at the very end of the Roman period (eg at the Gateway supermarket site, R Ferguson pers comm). This is not necessarily the case from the evidence of the 1964–6 excavations, however, since two of the six vessels recorded in this fabric were 3rd-century types (one each of Young types WC4 and WC5). The significance of this is unclear. The representation of M43 in the 1964–6 assemblage is quite high in comparison to that of M71 (in complete contrast to 1–5 Bleachfield Street where there were respectively 6 and 114 sherds of M43 and M71). It may be that localized, very late Roman occupation produced the majority of the sherds of M43, the relatively poor representation of M71 perhaps suggesting a somewhat reduced general level of activity in the second half of the 4th century (not necessarily borne out by the structural sequence). It seems less likely that the pattern of *mortarium* supply to the Gateway supermarket and 1–5 Bleachfield Street sites (at the latter, M43, though scarce, occurred only in the very latest Roman deposits) would have been completely different from that to the 1964–6 sites.

The occurrence of apparently 3rd-century types in M43 in the 1964–6 assemblage is of some interest since it is apparently atypical. Young's typological framework for this fabric is, however, possibly open to question as the published examples do not always correlate well with their suggested models (Young 1977, 120–2). The significance of the occurrence of types WC4 and WC5 at Alcester therefore remains uncertain.

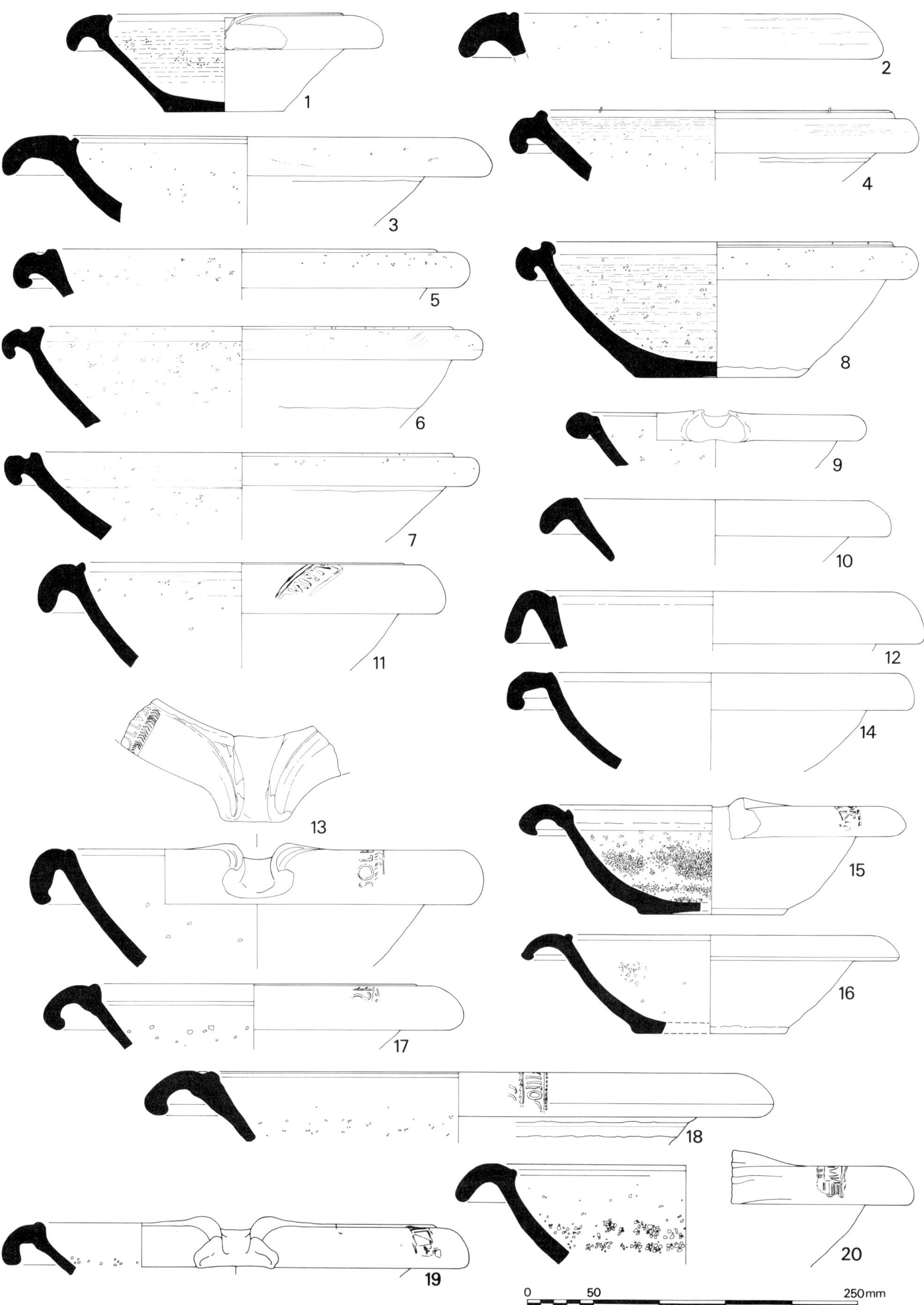

Figure 62 Mortaria, nos 1–20

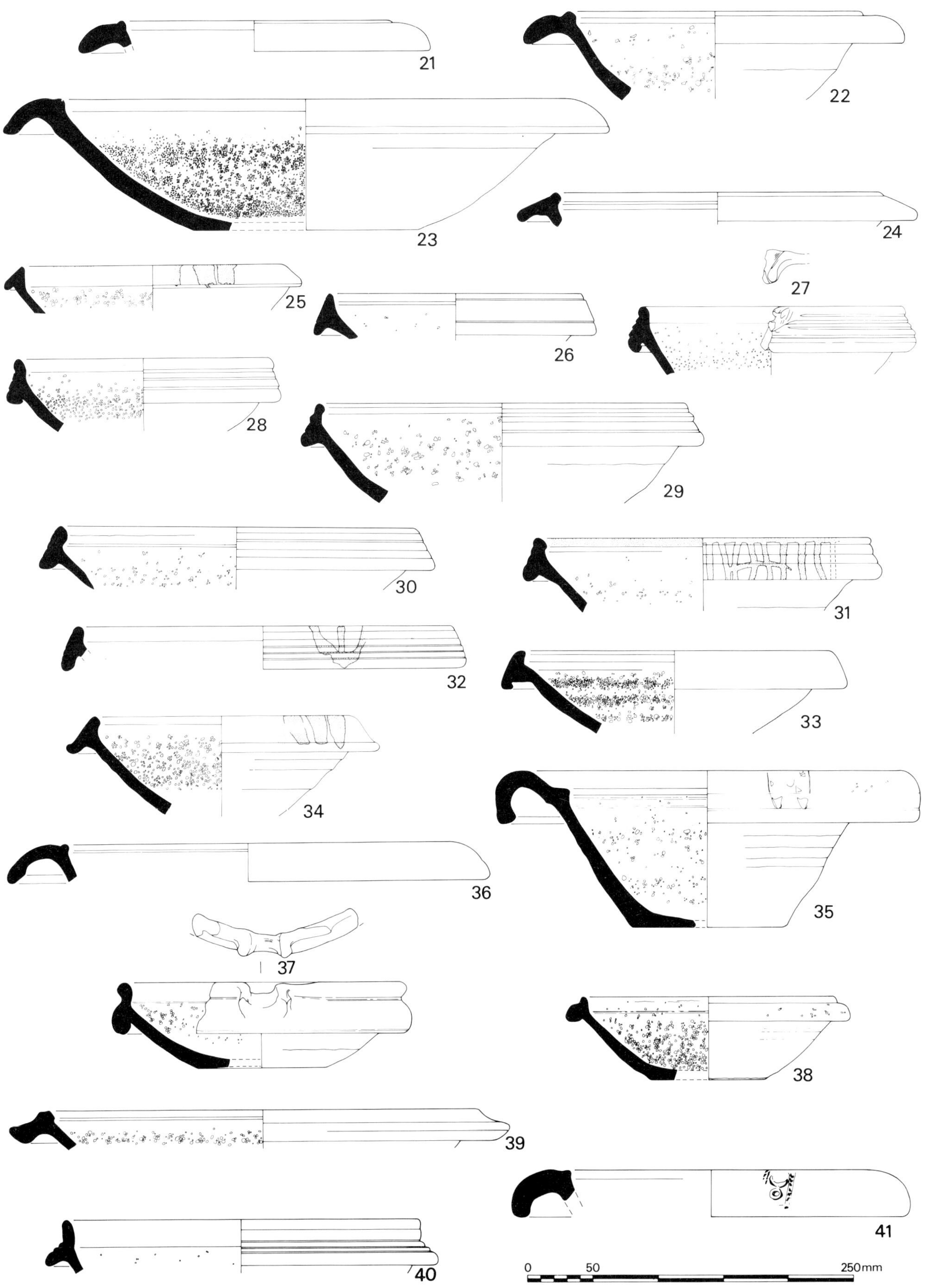

Figure 63 Mortaria, nos 21–41

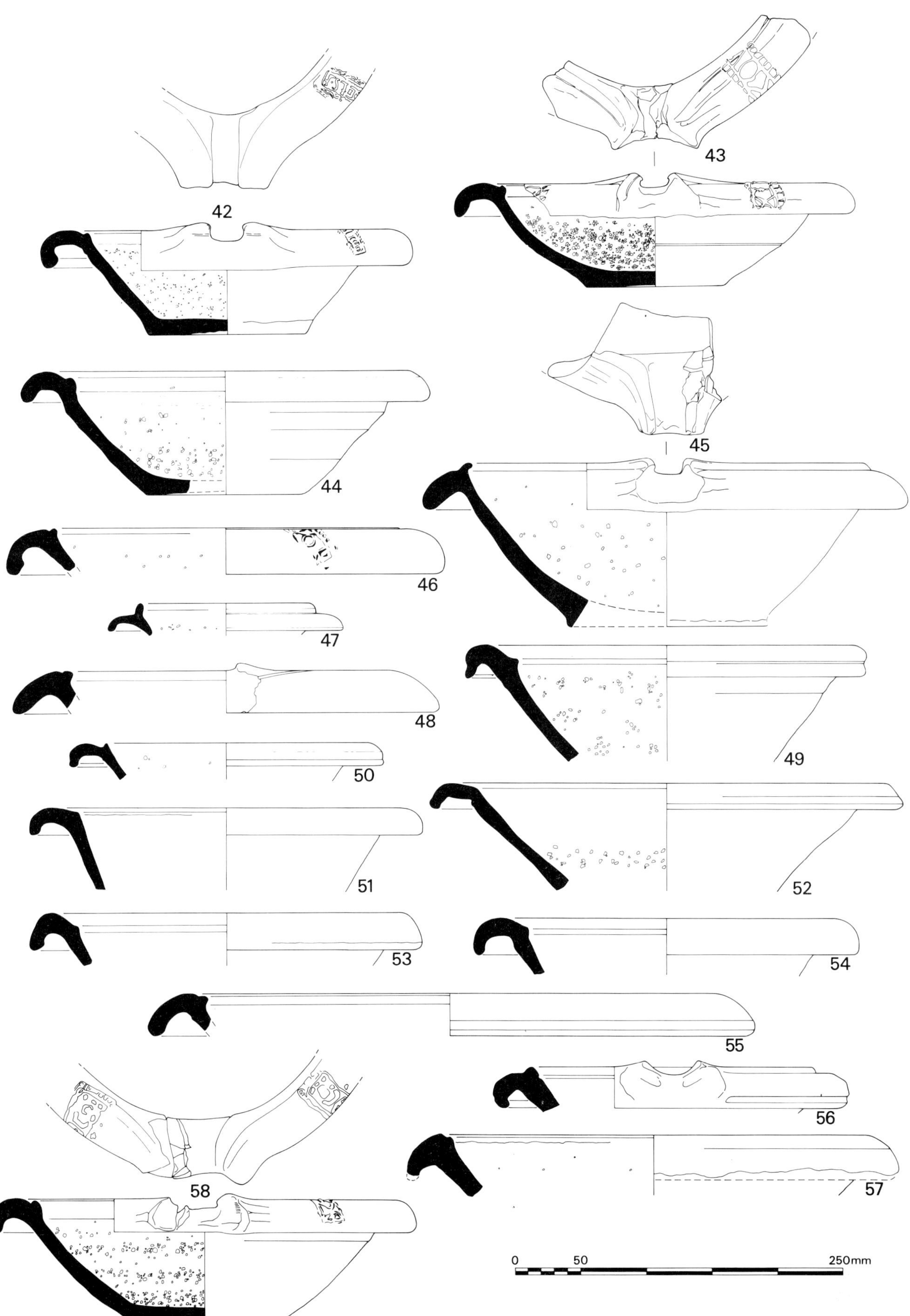

Figure 64 Mortaria, nos 42–58

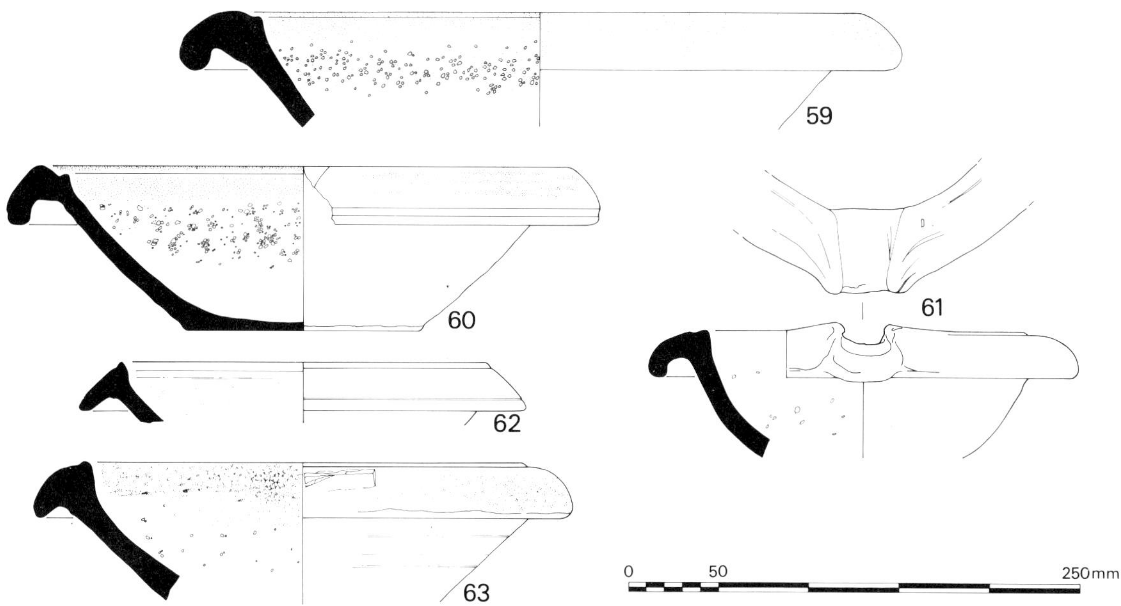

Figure 65 Mortaria, nos 59–63

Discussion of the pottery in the context of Roman Alcester *Jeremy Evans*

There is no direct evidence of Iron Age occupation in the Birch Abbey area from the structural sequence and this is reflected in the lack of Iron Age material amongst the ceramics. There are, however, a few brooches of Iron Age date and there is some very slight evidence of Iron Age occupation within the area of the later walled town at Tibbet's Close (Ferguson 1985) and Gas House Lane (Evans in prep), but the lack of any substantial quantity of Iron Age ceramics from the town demonstrates the absence of any Iron Age nucleated settlement in the environs.

The site samian list suggests that the town was founded in the AD 60s and the South Gaulish list rises to a peak in the AD 80s as is usual (Marsh 1981). There is little evidence in the samian list for an early fort on the site, although there are twelve items of military equipment from Birch Abbey. However, these, many of which are legionary-associated pieces (see Copper alloy cat nos 130–9, pp 181–2 and Iron cat nos 1–3, p 195), may well be casual losses rather than material associated with a military phase at the town. Both the strong concentration of *militaria* and the samian list suggest that an early military phase in the town is present to the north of Birch Abbey at the Baromix site in Bleachfield Street (sites ALC 69, ALC 72/2, and AL 28 (see Part 1, p 165)).

Samian

The Birch Abbey samian list is of interest in that it falls much more into the northern English pattern than into the usual southern town list, with a much stronger Central Gaulish than South Gaulish peak (cf York: Marsh 1981, fig 11.8, or Catterick: Dickinson forthcoming). This would seem to suggest that much of the development of the site took place in the Hadrianic–Antonine period rather than in the 1st century. Hartley *et al* point out that there is a notable decline in the later Antonine samian supply to the site and 'after *c* AD 170 occupation continued on a much reduced scale in these particular areas of the town' (see p 94).

Black-Burnished 1

The collection of Black-Burnished 1 from the Birch Abbey excavations seems fairly typical for a site with continuous occupation from the 2nd century which is located beyond the core area of the fabric. There are, however, a few pieces of intrinsic interest; the flagon (B.1) is not a common type and is not listed in Gillam (1976), but it has been studied recently (Wallace & Webster 1989) and is widely if thinly distributed, apart from a surprising concentration at Catterick (Central Excavation Unit site 46: Bell & Evans forthcoming). The countersunk handled jar (B.29) is a rare type, Gillam (1976, type 15) cites four others outside the Black-Burnished 1 core area, two from western Scotland, one from the west of Hadrian's Wall, and one from Derbyshire. B.27 is also of a rare type, not illustrated in Gillam (1976), but probably related to Ower types 32–4 (Farrar 1977). It is from a late 4th-century context and the Ower report principally cites 4th-century parallels, noting that it is a type usually restricted to the Dorset core area. B.27 has close parallels with a vessel in an imitation Black-Burnished 1 produced in the Catterick area, probably in the early to mid-4th century (Bell & Evans forthcoming). None of these types has been found elsewhere in the town (with the exception of a single flagon rim fragment from Gas House Lane (Evans forthcoming). Although it is not possible to gain any very reliable statistics about the proportions or frequency of types because of the method of on-site recording (see above, 'Roman coarse pottery', p 3), it is of note that much of the illustrated material is Hadrianic–Antonine and the percentages of the recorded occurrence of the types by context (fig 66) also reflects this. Fig 66 shows that the numbers of recorded types rise to a peak in the later 2nd century then decline very strongly in the early to mid-3rd century before rising to their greatest peak in the late 3rd century and declining in the 4th century.

Overall the number of 3rd-century types does seem to show a decline on the number of 2nd-century ones, and there are again fewer 4th-century ones (see above, pp 43–8). However, this does not mean that proportionately in the assemblage Black-Burnished 1 was in decline, and the picture from elsewhere in the town (Ferguson forthcoming (b), fig 42; Evans forthcoming) shows clearly that this was not the case, with Black-Burnished 1 probably becoming most important in supply in the 3rd and early 4th centuries. The numbers shown in fig 66 seem rather to coincide with Going's (1992) economic cycles.

Reduced wares

There is a considerable range of reduced types illustrated in the corpus which may be roughly divided into three categories — grey wares, Malvernian ware, and shell-tempered ware — of which the great majority is of grey wares and the smallest group is the shell-tempered ware. The reduced ware group is recorded as comprising *c* 50% of all recorded pottery from the site, which is interesting given that none of the material illustrated in the corpus, excepting the shell-tempered ware, need be later

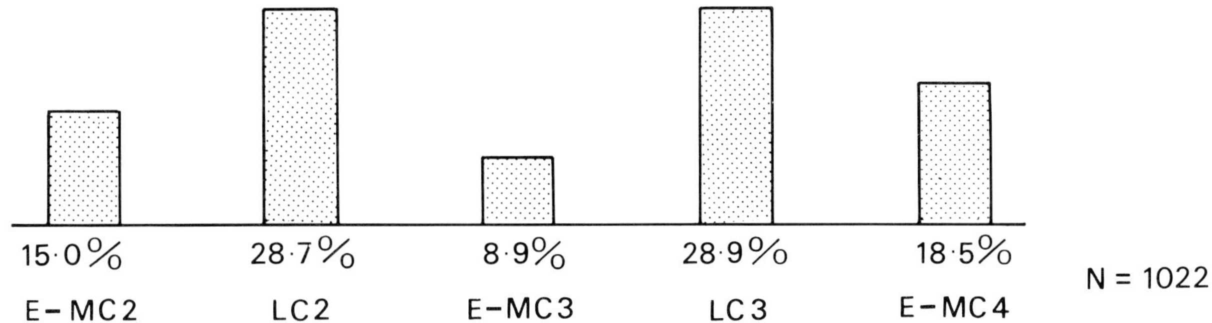

Figure 66 Percentage of recorded occurrence of Black-Burnished ware 1 by date

than the end of the 2nd century. The evidence from elsewhere in the town, especially from the Gas House Lane site (Evans in prep), suggests that grey wares virtually ceased to be used after the end of the 2nd century. As some of the oxidized wares must be 1st or 2nd century, much of the Black-Burnished 1 is 2nd century and, of course, nearly all the samian is 1st or 2nd century, especially the latter, once more the figures tend to suggest that much of the ceramic from the site is 1st or 2nd century, and probably much of this is 2nd century.

Amongst the grey wares is a large collection of late 1st- to early 2nd-century rusticated jars, the vast majority of which are in a distinctive wide-mouthed conical form with an indented shoulder (eg nos R.115–R.130). This form is typical in much of Warwickshire and was produced at a number of kiln sites, including Tiddington and Lapworth. There are no examples yet from pre-Flavian contexts in Alcester, but it occurs from the Flavian period until the earlier 2nd century in considerable numbers.

The distribution of forms in this tradition is geographically very limited (fig 67(a)). No vessels are illustrated by Thompson (1958) in his general survey of rusticated wares, although there is one vessel (*ibid*, Plate VII, f) from Chester which seems to be related to it. Large numbers of vessels in this type also come from Tiddington (Booth forthcoming (a)) where the type seems to have been made in kiln 2. Another kiln site at Lapworth (material in Warwickshire Museum, personal inspection) also seems to produce the type. The geographical range of the type extends well into north Warwickshire where it is found at Coleshill (Booth forthcoming (b)) and at *Tripontium* (Cameron & Lucas 1967, no 225; Cameron & Lucas 1973, nos 380, 401, 422). There are also a number of examples from the Lunt (Hobley 1966, fig 13, nos 25, 27, and 28 — TR20 ditch end, early Flavian). It is of note that here the type does not occur in pre-Flavian deposits.

Surprisingly the type has not been published from Mancetter (Hemsley 1959; Mahany 1970; Scott 1984), despite its occurrence on so many neighbouring sites. The form, however, was produced there (Booth pers comm) although it is not clear that rusticated decoration was used with it. Further north the type seems to be generally absent from Leicester (Kenyon 1948), there being a single example from the town (Pollard pers comm), and it is absent from Wall (Gould 1967). It also fails to travel much west of Alcester with only a few examples of rusticated jars being in this form from Worcester (Jane Evans & Victoria Buteux pers comm) and it is absent from Droitwich (Derek Hurst pers comm). To the south-east down Watling Street the type is absent from Milton Keynes (Marney 1989) and *Verulamium* (Frere 1972). To the south the type does not seem to occur at Cirencester (Rigby 1982) but does occur, at least occasionally, at Gloucester (Hassall & Rhodes 1974, fig 17, no 37).

It is notable that rustic ware consumption in the north of England is predominantly military, presumably, like the use of reeded-rimmed bowls, conditioned by the demand for ceramic types derived from a tradition with which the army was familiar. This may also have been the case in this region for the pre-Flavian rustic wares, but vessels in this tradition seem to be predominantly found on civilian sites, with the Lunt and Gloucester being the only military sites in the distribution shown here (fig 67(a)). It may be that after the establishment of the rustic tradition as a military type it acquired a certain desirability as a 'Romanized' type in the wider civilian market in this region.

In addition there is quite a large collection of Hadrianic–Antonine grey ware Black-Burnished copies, which are also likely to be local products, Tiddington kiln 2 producing similar vessels. Storage jars in fabric GC (Warwickshire Museum fabric R31) are also likely to be fairly local products. The same forms and fabric are found at Tiddington (Booth forthcoming (a)) but are less common in the north of the county at Coleshill (Booth pers comm).

Oxidized wares

Oxidized wares are recorded as producing 33% of the types recorded at Birch Abbey, of which a majority are undoubtedly in Severn Valley wares. Severn Valley wares are generally much commoner at Alcester in the 3rd and 4th centuries (cf Ferguson forthcoming (b); Evans forthcoming) than in the 1st to 2nd centuries. It is of note, therefore, that a reasonable number of 1st-century and a fairly high proportion of 2nd-century examples are illustrated

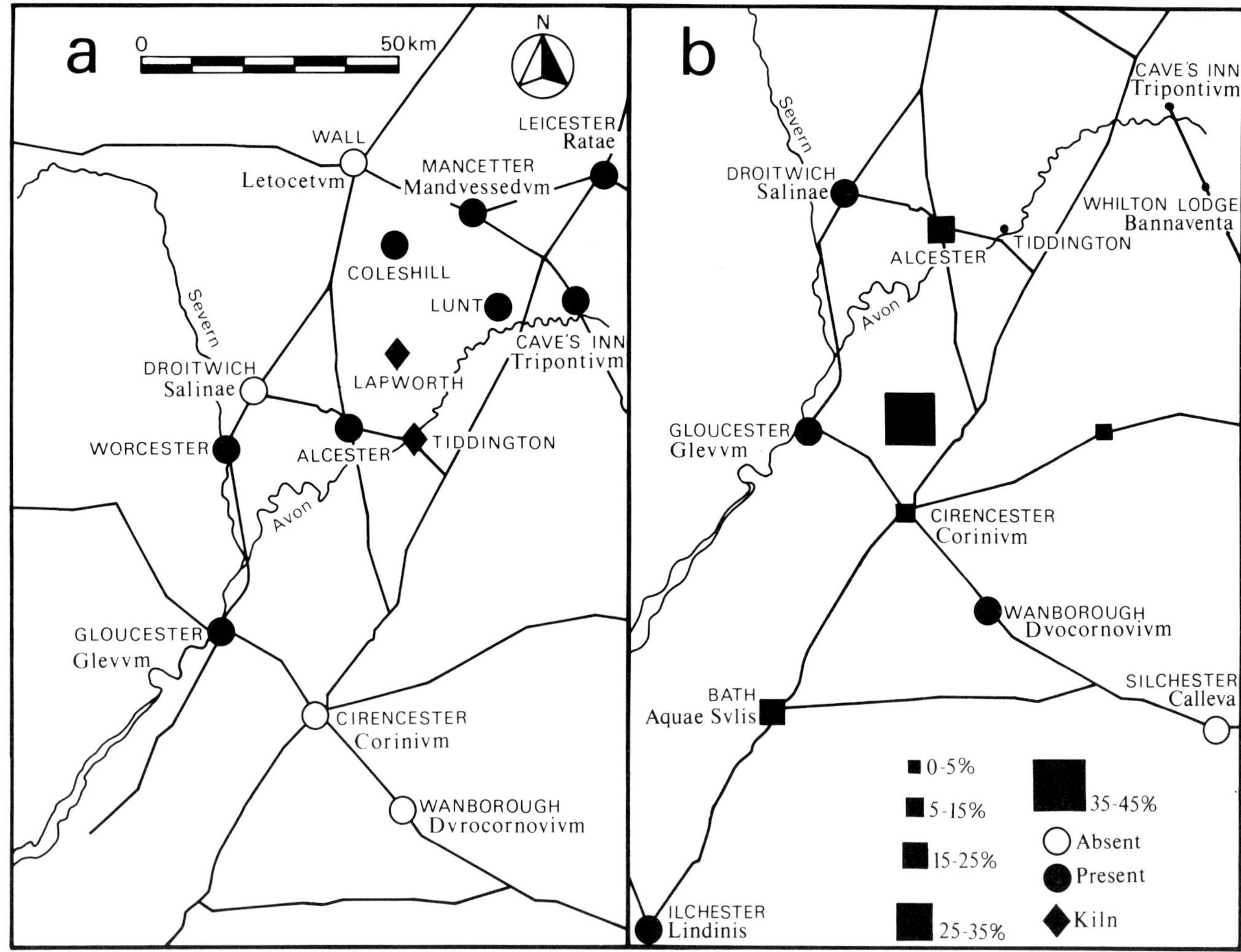

Figure 67 a) Point distribution map of rustic ware jars with indented shoulders, and known kiln sites
b) Quantified distribution map of South-Western brown slipped ware

amongst the material, once more emphasizing the apparent peak of 2nd-century pottery use on the site.

Shell-tempered ware

The collection of shell-tempered ware (fabric GA) from the site is quite extensive. This type of fabric occurs at Alcester from the 3rd century, but these early occurrences are in hand-made fabrics (Evans in prep); the later type, wheel-made, does not appear before the mid-4th century. The earliest occurrence of the early everted-rimmed jar type (R.42, R.109, and R.111) occurs in the Antonine to 3rd-century layer H II 74 and other examples are found in 3rd- and early 4th-century contexts (AA II 13, G IV 61, and D I 30), with residual examples in late 4th-century contexts. The undercut beaded rimmed, wheel-made, late type, which is dated after *c* AD 340 in East Anglia (Plouviez 1976; types R.43, R.103, R.104, R.106, and R.107) occurs in two contexts phased to the mid- to late 4th century (D I 6 and D I 34) and in a large number phased to the late 4th century, with one example in a context phased to the early to mid-4th century (G V 10). The bowl types (R.435–R.437) which are unusual outside the east Midlands are exclusively from late 4th-century contexts, as might be expected.

The occurrence of the late Roman southern shell-tempered ware types on the Birch Abbey site is concentrated in sites F and G, suggesting that these may have been *foci* of activity on the site in the later 4th century. Further hints at the spatial distribution of late activity on the site may be derived from the distribution of Oxfordshire types dated after *c* AD 270, 4th-century Nene Valley types, and Black-Burnished 1 developed flanged bowls, although the last had probably gone out of use on the site before the end of the 4th century. The later Oxfordshire types are concentrated on sites AA and G, whilst the only sites with more than a single late Nene Valley type are AA, F, and G. Black-Burnished 1 flanged bowls are concentrated on sites G, A, and AA (in order of descending magnitude). Allowing for the fact that little pottery comes from site F it would seem to represent a late focus, as would site G, with further concentrations in sites AA and A, perhaps declining earlier.

The source of the late Roman southern shell-tempered ware is almost certainly Harrold, Bedford-

Table 7 Cirencester III, Period III fine ware fabric proportions (RE)

	Area CQ %	Area CX/CY %	Area DE/DF %
South-Western brown slipped ware	15.5	7.2	10.8
Oxfordshire ware	76.5	82.8	81.4
Nene Valley ware	8.0	9.9	7.9
New Forest ware	0	*	*

* — present

shire (Sanders 1973; Swan 1984, microfiche 1.208) and it is found in quantity as far as Wroxeter in the late 4th century and occurs at Dinorben and *Segontium* in north Wales (Webster 1993). The quantity at sites such as Wroxeter, compared with a much lower level of *c* 5% at Bath (Green & Young 1985), and its deeper penetration of north rather than south Wales tends to suggest that the main route for this material into the region was overland along Watling Street.

South-Western brown slipped ware

This fabric group has been discussed by Young (1980) who suggested that it might be a Gloucestershire product. Young identified it at Wycombe and pointed to its occurrence at Gloucester and Cirencester and suggested a late 3rd- to 4th-century date for it. As with the Wycombe material the Alcester collection shows strong affinities with the Oxfordshire industry, the exception being the use of barbotine scale decoration on some beakers (cf Young 1980, fig 11, no 13, and Birch Abbey C.71, fig 40).

Young noted that 'as yet the dating of the industry is uncertain. Its appearance in the Andoversford ditch suggests a late 4th-century date. This must be treated with a little caution since the ditch clearly contained residual material. The Oxford originals copied by this industry were all current in the 4th century but some were current in the late 3rd century also. At present therefore it can only be suggested that this industry is late Roman' (1980, 44). Further evidence has now come to light at Bath (Green & Young 1985), where fabrics 6.5 and 6.6 which are identified with Cirencester fabric 105 first appear in Period 5, dated to around the middle of the 4th century. At Cirencester 'the examples published in CEII came from upper levels of the cemetery site, thought to date from the mid-4th century, though largely unstratified. At the Beeches these vessels were confined to levels dated to post AD 350 (Period II/III)' (Keeley 1986, 161). Similarly most of the Birch Abbey examples from phased contexts come from mid- and late 4th-century contexts, and this picture seems to be generally true of the town. (There is one exception from Birch Abbey, an example of type C37 from AA II 78, phased to the late 2nd to early 3rd century; this seems very likely to have been misidentified or intrusive.)

The figures published by Young (1980, table 1) from Wycombe show that this fabric comprised 44% of the colour-coated fine wares (excluding *mortaria*) compared with 50% from Oxford and 6% from the Nene Valley (fig 67(b)). These compare with *c* 67% Oxford, 9% New Forest, 0% Nene Valley, and 24% South-Western brown slipped ware from Bath Period 5C; and *c* 70% Oxford, 9% New Forest, 5% Nene Valley, and 16% South-Western brown slipped ware from Period 5D (Bath figures calculated from Green & Young 1985, fig 84). Absolute figures cannot be calculated with reliability for Birch Abbey, but the ratios of Oxfordshire to South-Western brown slipped ware are clearly much closer to those from Bath than to the Wycombe figures. However the figures from Cirencester, where 'they represented 8% of the total non-residual fine wares from occupation and rubble levels, which is a measure of their limited success' (Keeley 1986, 171), suggest that the fabric was not produced in the environs of that town. The South-Western brown slipped ware totals at Cirencester listed in the tables are a little higher than Keeley's comments (1986, 171) suggest for Period III deposits when presented as a proportion of the major fine ware industry products on a comparable basis to the Bath and Wycombe figures (table 7).

However the proportion is still rather low given the fairly central location of the site in the fabric's distribution and this presumably reflects the town's importance as a marketing centre for Oxfordshire wares, especially as a provincial capital, as well as major efforts paid to the Cirencester market by the Oxfordshire distributors. The fabric has also been identified at Droitwich and Beckford (Worcestershire), Wanborough (Wiltshire), and Shakenoak (Oxfordshire) (Keeley 1986, 161). At the last site 89% of the colour-coated wares were Oxfordshire, 10% Nene Valley, and only 1.5% from all other sources (Brodribb *et al* 1973, 88). A few examples of the fabric have been identified as far afield as Exeter (Holbrook & Bidwell 1991, fig 23, nos 24–7), all being beakers, and all from late 4th-century contexts. As at Shakenoak they seem to represent *c* 0.9% or less of the late Roman fine wares compared with 41.6% each for Oxford and the New Forest, 10% for the Nene Valley, and 5.7% for *céramique à l'éponge* (data derived from Holbrook & Bidwell 1991, table 10). Other possible examples have been published from Ilchester (Leach 1982, fig 67, nos 16 and 31) and Catsgore (Leech 1982, fig 100, no 74). The data available must suggest that the production centre was located somewhere very close to the Wycombe site given that it has the highest recorded proportion of the fabric amongst colour-coated wares and that the flanged bowl forms were present there but not noted at Bath, Alcester,

Table 8 Functional analysis of South-Western brown slipped ware from Alcester and Wycombe

	Alcester %	Wycombe %
Flagons	12	} 56
Beakers	76	
Table ware bowls	12	6
Other bowls	–	39
	n = 17	n = 114

or Cirencester. This is further strengthened by Wycombe lying very nearly in the centre of the geographical distribution of the fabric.

The Alcester functional breakdown of the vessels in this fabric (table 8) shows that as at Wycombe the bulk of the vessels are in forms which Oxford did not specialize in, especially beakers. It is of note that only 6% of all colour-coated non-*mortaria* 4th-century fine wares at Wycombe were from the Nene Valley, and that at that site South-Western brown slipped ware produced many of the 'other bowls', that is dog dishes and flanged bowls usually provided by the Nene Valley. Whilst an exact figure for Nene Valley wares as a proportion of the late fine wares cannot be calculated for Birch Abbey with certainty, the figure was clearly much higher than at Wycombe, and the 'other bowl' category is not found in the fabric, suggesting that it could not successfully compete with Nene Valley supplies at Alcester. The location of a fine ware industry in Gloucestershire, right on the edge of the New Forest distribution and at a considerable distance from the Nene Valley, no doubt gave it a reasonable competitive advantage provided that it stuck to its niche marketing of desired fine ware forms not produced in quantity by the Oxfordshire industry. Its location was approximately on the boundary of competition in beaker production between the New Forest and Nene Valley industries although there must be some doubt if it had not specialized in a generally declining market, that is that the demand for beakers was falling (cf Evans 1990). However, even if the latter point proves generally true, it may not be so for the Severn Valley region where the collapse of the Severn Valley industries in the last quarter of the 4th century may have increased demand for a substitute to the tankard.

The industry itself has parallels with that at the Obelisk kilns, Harston, Cambridgeshire (Pullinger & Young 1981) which produced Oxfordshire copies in the later 4th century, presumably marketing into East Anglia, where the Oxford industry achieved a market in the later 4th century.

Oxfordshire industry

Whilst exact figures cannot be calculated, the Oxfordshire industry would seem to have been the predominant fine ware supplier at Alcester throughout its fine ware production period. Around 45 Oxfordshire forms are recorded giving 15 of Young's (1977) types. It is interesting that at Bath 18 of Young's types are recorded (Green & Young 1985) from an assemblage of just over 6,000 sherds and, although this is mainly a 4th-century group whilst the Alcester assemblage spans the Roman period, the latter must have been at least 10 times larger. Similarly at Wycombe 114 Oxfordshire vessels are recorded, more than twice the Alcester tally, but the number of types (Young 1980) represented is only 22. It is of note that these three sites, all of which seem to span the same period, have only four of the Oxfordshire types in common, C.23, C.48, C.51, and C.75. This phenomenon is not likely to be merely a product of the assemblage size as even amongst closely contemporary groups of samian ware only a few types were common to many groups (Millett 1983, section C1.4.2 and Appendix C20); instead the frequency of the common types increases.

Nene Valley wares

The collection of Nene Valley ware from the Birch Abbey site is not extensive, with the Oxfordshire industry providing the bulk of the later Roman fine wares from the site. There is some interest in the collection, however. It has been noted above that the bulk of the ceramics from the site tend to be of 2nd-century date, although the samian list does suggest a decline after *c* AD 170. Given that so many of the ceramics are of 2nd-century date and the lack of any major fine ware competitor in the period *c* AD 170–240, it might be expected that later 2nd- to early 3rd-century material would be well represented amongst the collection. However, in fact, the reverse proves strongly to be the case with only three 2nd- to mid-3rd-century types but eighteen later 3rd- to 4th-century forms present. Competition with Nene Valley wares in this crucial early period of the industry mainly came from continental sources, with a few local imitations of them and it is thus surprising if this resulted in the exclusion of Nene Valley wares from the market, especially when Nene Valley products were the predominant, non-samian fine ware in northern England in this period. It seems more likely that the Nene Valley industry simply did not attempt marketing in this region at this time; it was, after all, more successful in the 4th century when fairly direct competition was present from the Oxfordshire and the South-Western brown slipped ware industries.

This trend in Nene Valley material is not a product of the Birch Abbey recording method but seems generally borne out throughout the town.

Cultural links

Alcester is generally reckoned to be within the tribal territory of the Dobunni, although it is on the north-eastern fringe of the coinage zone centred on that group (Millett 1990, fig 3 after Haselgrove 1987) and is very close to the boundary with the Catuvellauni (Cunliffe 1974, fig 7:11) or the Corieltauvi (Millett 1990, fig 16).

In the Iron Age within this region much of the area north of the Bristol Avon was supplied by ceramics from the Malvern area (Peacock 1968b), but to the south in north Somerset the dominant tradition was of locally produced Glastonbury wares (Peacock 1969; Cunliffe 1974). A parallel to this has been found in the coinage distributions: 'In the last two decades before the invasion the territory appears to have been split between two ruling households. Comux, followed by Boduoc, controlled the Gloucestershire–Oxfordshire, Worcestershire area while Corio remained dominant in northern Somerset' (Cunliffe 1974, 100). This statement does indeed reflect the distribution map from which it is drawn (Hawkes 1961, fig 20), but this also shows a predominance of Corio's coinage in Warwickshire and Worcestershire. The north Somerset area of Corio's distribution is attributed to the *civitas* of the Belgae by Millett (1990) following Rivet (1958) despite the coinage zone (Millett 1990, fig 3; cf Sellwood 1984, fig 13.11).

Within the Dobunnic *civitas* defined by the Iron Age coin distribution there are remarkable contrasts of material culture in the Roman period. Villas are almost entirely confined to the east of the Severn on the Cotswolds and Mendips (Branigan & Fowler 1976, fig 23). Mosaics show a similar distribution, not merely owing to a lack of villas, as urban mosaics are similarly lacking (Millett 1990, fig 76).

This major division in material culture is reflected in the ceramics of the region with grey wares being predominant in Somerset (Green & Young 1985; Evans forthcoming (Chew Down report)), and even at Cirencester (Rigby 1982; Keeley 1986), although some (oxidized) Severn Valley wares occur there. Oxidized wares, namely Severn Valley wares, in contrast form the dominant tradition throughout the lower Severn basin. Alcester falls strongly within this tradition, in interesting contrast to Tiddington only 12km to the east. Here 'Severn Valley wares only amounted to 6.9% of [the total] pottery from the 1981 excavations, but only 3.4% from the 1982 site (where occupation is principally 1st to 2nd century)' (Booth 1988, 35). A similar picture is obtained from the rural site of Wasperton, about 17km east of Alcester, where Severn Valley wares also only comprised *c* 6% of the total assemblage (Booth forthcoming (c)). The Severn Valley tradition is represented to some extent in central and northern Warwickshire with tankards being produced at Mancetter and the Birmingham, Perry Bar kiln site (Hughes 1961). However, Booth (1988, 32) points out that the Severn Valley tradition is only represented second-hand by the Perry Bar kiln site, which is best seen as an offshoot of the Mancetter/Hartshill industry.

It is of note that the sharp fall-off in Severn Valley wares to the east of Alcester coincides remarkably with the putative boundary between the Dobunni and the Corieltauvi (cf Millett 1990, fig 61).

Pottery supplies at Alcester also show little impact of supplies from the east Midlands before the very end of the 4th century, when local industries seem to have collapsed. Nene Valley products are very poorly represented considering that the kilns were only 1.6 times the distance of the Oxfordshire kiln site and were producing fine wares earlier. The Oxfordshire kiln site was, of course, located on the postulated boundary of the Dobunnic *civitas* (Millett 1990, fig 68).

Pottery and ceramic small finds

Rowan Ferguson with Don Bailey and Jeremy Evans

Microfiche [M2:C13]

Pottery objects (fig 68)

1 Tubular hand-made object in Roman grey ware. 119mm long × 25mm diam. Oval section. Possibly a handle (P 36, C I 24A, unphased).

2 Zoomorphic object. Severn Valley ware.

Dog/pig. Stumps of legs remain on one side with scars only on the other. It is possible that this was originally part of a pot. There are examples of Severn Valley ware hemispherical bowls with laterally placed tubular handles (Webster (1976) notes them from Gloucester and Malvern kiln II). The curvature of the animal's body would make it suitable for this purpose although no parallels with zoomorphic handles have been found. However the scars are very worn suggesting reuse as a toy, figurine, or amulet (P 23, C II 111, unphased).

Both of these objects were found within a 15m radius in Area C.

3 Ceramic lamp in parchment ware with orange-brown slip (P 66, E II 46, phase V, late 2nd century?). Mr D Bailey kindly writes: Top of a *Firmalampe* of Loeschcke (1919) type IXa, with shallow nozzle-groove interrupted by an air-hole. Loeschcke's shoulder-form IXa, with two unpierced lugs. On the discus, a dramatic mask of a youth, with high *onkos* (compare that on Webster 1969, pl IVd). Buff white clay, with orange-brown slip. Made in Gaul (probably North-Western Gaul) in late Flavian or Trajanic times.

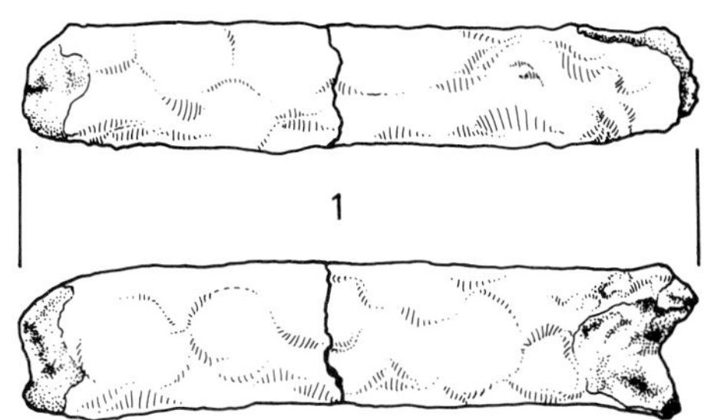

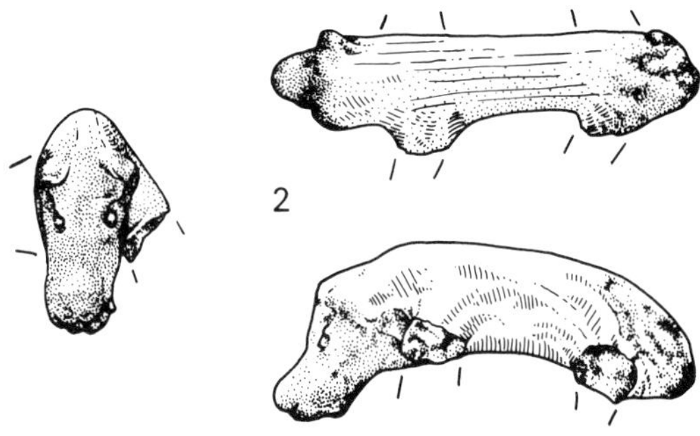

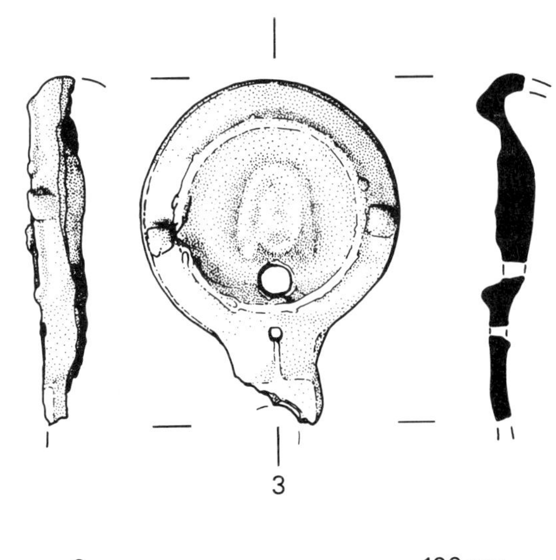

Figure 68 Pottery objects

Repaired sherds

Some 44 samian sherds were found with rivet-holes or surviving rivets, probably from around 36 vessels; and four coarse ware sherds from four vessels had also been repaired. Nine sherds from six samian vessels still had attached lead rivets, as did the Dressel 20 amphora body sherd and the body sherd of a hand-made storage jar in Malvernian metamorphic fabric. The three other coarse ware sherds with rivet-holes were also from storage jars, one a hand-made Severn Valley ware vessel (fabric DA) and the other two on hand-made jar body sherds (in fabric GC).

The rivet-holes on the coarse ware sherds were all of the drilled circular type as is usual for circular rod-like rivets attached by lead strips on both surfaces. Those on samian vessels were both of this type (20 sherds) and of the less visually obtrusive X type (21 sherds). Presumably the latter type were generally restricted to samian vessels as they looked better but were probably much weaker. There is no evidence for any riveting in iron, unlike the 19th- and 20th-century practice. The massive preponderance of riveting on samian is usual.

The riveting of three storage jars is of slight note, in that they are a less common type of vessel to be riveted. In comparison with the size of the assem-

Table 9 Size and fabric groupings of pottery discs and counters

	mm							
Fabric	**10–19**	**20–9**	**30–9**	**40–9**	**50–9**	**60–9**	**70–9**	**Total**
Samian	2	2	4	1				9
Black-Burnished type 1	1			1				2
Severn Valley		1	2	1	2	1		7
Grey wares		1			2			3
Malvernian							1	1
Total	3	4	6	3	4	1	1	22

blage the rate of riveting is not high, and some riveted sherds may well have been discarded.

The distribution of riveted sherds by site area shows little sign of spatial patterning. A full list of the contexts and types of riveted sherds is in microfiche [M2:D2].

Reused sherds

Discs and counters (see table 9)

There were 22 of these in all. A 'counter' is considered less than 50mm in diameter. Using this criterion there were 16 'counters' and 6 'discs'. A range of fabrics was utilized: samian, Severn Valley ware, Black-Burnished ware, grey wares, and the Malvernian fabric. Samian and Black-Burnished ware were only used for counters. All of the sherds had been quite roughly shaped except for the Black-Burnished ware counter P 11 which had been very neatly sanded down. Where a decorated vessel had been reused (as in four cases) there had been little attempt to centre the decoration on the finished counter. The most effective was the samian counter P 6, AA III 1, which had a ?peacock on it. The Severn Valley ware disc, P 69, D II 15, was made from a small pedestal base. This may well have been used as a palette as the interior of the base was slightly dished.

There was also a fragment from the base of an 18R, 18/31R or 31R (CG), from which the foot-ring had been cut, presumably to act as a stopper or pot lid, the omphalos base being especially suitable for this. (Context A II 78).

Pierced sherds

Most of the sherds in this category are discussed below under 'Evidence for textile manufacture'. There remains one pierced sherd which had been worked into a square and would therefore have been unsuitable as a spindle whorl. This is P 54, D I 176, a grey ware fragment about 35mm across from a carinated vessel with very neatly finished edges.

Evidence for textile manufacture

Fragments from nine baked clay loomweights have been identified. The fabric is of clay with some coarse sand and gravel and a certain amount of vegetable tempering. This type of triangluar weight was commonly found in Roman Britain (Liversidge 1968). A list of the contexts of the loomweights and their phasing is in microfiche [M2:D8]. The most complete example, BC 148, from G IV 10A, phase VI, is illustrated in fig 69, no 1.

The spindle whorls had all been neatly trimmed and smoothed into circular or sub-circular shapes. Five examples were found, of which two were in grey wares; one Black-Burnished ware and one Severn Valley ware whorl were reused bases and there was also a decorated turned limestone whorl. One example, P 49, F I 5, showed signs of use as the central hole was worn. A catalogue of spindle whorls is in microfiche [M2:D8].

The small numbers found and the way in which these finds were scattered over the whole southern part of the town would suggest a low level of spinning on a domestic scale.

Ceramic disc

A fragment from the circumference of a flat ceramic disc, hand-made, with a well-shaped and finished edge in a pale orange-brown fabric with some shell inclusions *c* 2–10mm (fig 69, no 2, BC 158, G I 23, unphased). The function of these plates is unclear. Other examples are known from Warwickshire at Tiddington and Wasperton (Booth pers comm) and from Farmoor, Oxon (Sanders 1979, fig 28, nos 124–7).

Burnt clay block

A fragmentary block of burnt clay (fig 69, no 3, BC140, D I 222, unphased). It is in a burnt clay with large, white, rounded, quartzite inclusions up to 10mm. It is not a loomweight. It has a flat base, upon which it rests well and a curved front and concave back face which is more irregularly surfaced with finger-tip marks. The right side curves outwards by at least 20mm. Surviving height: 135mm, surviving width: 115mm; thickness: 75mm.

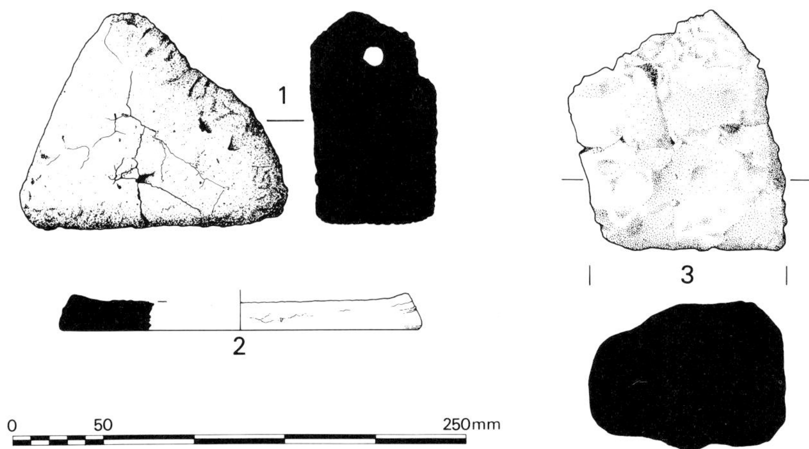

Figure 69 Loomweight, clay block, and disc

Iron Age sherds from site M

Jeremy Evans

See figure 70.

1 Jar rim with simple insloping profile and grooved top of rim in hand-made, Malvernian metamorphic-tempered fabric, with a row of horseshoe stamps just below the top of the rim. Beckford form 2, Beckford ceramic phases B and C, mid-Iron Age. (M III 27, phase I, late 2nd to early 3rd century)

2 Fragmentary rim sherd with splayed, flattened rim (caused by pressing down top of rim whilst leather-hard) in a reduced fabric with abundant organic tempering voids and some moderate sand temper. (M III 30, phase I, late 2nd to early 3rd century)

3 A body sherd and a jar rim sherd with simple insloping profile and grooved rim top. In Malvernian metamorphic-tempered ware with two lines of impressed dots immediately below the top of the rim. Beckford form 2, Beckford ceramic phases B and C, mid-Iron Age. (M III 28, phase I, late 2nd to early 3rd century)

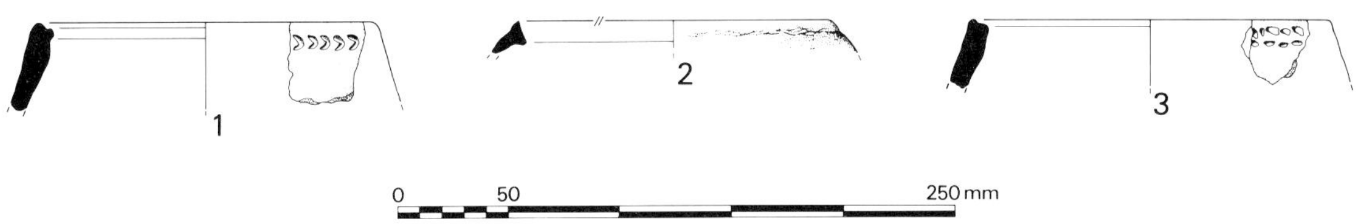

Figure 70 Iron Age pottery from site M

Medieval pottery *Stephanie Ratkai*

The medieval pottery from the Birch Abbey site consisted of 183 sherds. The pottery kept during the excavations was only a sample of what was found and there is only a little information regarding the contexts from which the medieval pottery came. The one exception to this is the corn drier/malting kiln in site C IIIA. In view of the nature of the assemblage it was decided to treat the pottery, with the exception of that from site C IIIA, as an unstratified assemblage. The use of statistics was precluded by the original method of pottery collection and the small number of sherds. The assemblage was therefore simply examined for hitherto unrecorded non-local pottery fabrics or unusual forms in the local Alcester fabric (Cracknell & Jones 1985). Any attempt at a chronological sequence is suspect but it was thought reasonable to try to date the malting kiln and the earliest and latest pottery from the site in general. It is unfortunate that the medieval pottery from excavations so far in Alcester has been mainly unstratified. It has therefore not yet proved possible to establish a firm ceramic chronology for Alcester or to establish the pattern of trade in non-local vessels.

Illustrated vessels (fig 71)

1 Straight-sided Malvernian cooking pot with infolded rim. Hand-made, wheel-finished. External sooting on base, internal calcareous deposit. (C IIIA 27).
2 Straight-sided cooking pot, local Alcester fabric. Hand-made, wheel-finished. External sooting on walls and base. Central external area of base unsooted. (C IIIA 27).
3 Unsooted cooking pot/jar. Hand-made, wheel-finished Alcester fabric. (C IIIA 1A).
4 Sooted cooking pot. External sooting, internal lime deposit. Hand-made, wheel-finished, Alcester fabric. (C IIIA 7 and 1A).
5 Unsooted cooking pot/jar. Hand-made, wheel-finished, with grooved rim. Alcester fabric. (C IIIA 11, 12, and 13)
6 Jug with external spots of tan glaze. Hand-made, wheel-finished Alcester fabric. (C IIIA 11, 12, 13, and 24).
7 Unsooted cooking pot/jar. Internal lime deposit. Cracking along internal and external face of rim from ?overfiring. Hand-made, wheel-finished Alcester fabric. (C IIIA 24).
8 Cooking pot with sooting along the external edge of the rim. Hand-made, wheel-finished Alcester fabric. (C IIIA 24).
9 Jug/pitcher with slightly sagging base, patches of internal blackening, pronounced internal finger-marks, and external olive glaze splashes. Alcester fabric. (C IIIA 9 and 24).
10 Jug, carinated profile. Hand-made, wheel-finished Alcester fabric. (C IIIA 7).
11 Unsooted cooking pot/jar with incised wavy line on body and on rim. Hand-made Alcester fabric. (C IIIA 1C).
12 Jug/pitcher with pronounced irregular horizontal grooving around neck. External patchy opaque olive glaze. Hand-made, wheel-finished Alcester fabric. (C IIIA 1).
13 Jug/pitcher with pronounced irregular grooving around neck. Applied decoration of thumbed strips and an axe. External patchy opaque glaze. Hand-made, wheel-finished Alcester fabric. (C IIIA 1)
14 Small hand-made cooking pot, local Alcester fabric. External and internal sooting. (D II 23).

Discussion

Site C IIIA

Earliest activity

Beneath the end of the drying kiln flue was a pit (C IIIA 27) which may have formed the stoke pit of an earlier kiln. The pit was remarkable for the presence of two upturned cooking pots (fig 71, nos 1 and 2). The complete vessel was made in the local Alcester fabric (no 2); the other, which lacked a section of the base, was made in a Malvernian fabric (no 1). No satisfactory explanation has been found for their presence. It seems likely that both pots were complete when placed in the pit and that the one lost its base when the drying kiln was rebuilt. These pots must have served a function within the pit. There were four other sherds from the pit. Of the two in the local Alcester fabric (Cracknell & Jones 1985) one came from a straight-sided cooking pot with an angled thickened rim springing from the shoulder. There were also two other sherds: a Malvernian base sherd with an internal white deposit and another sherd in a presumed local fabric (fabric 31).

The dating for the pit (C IIIA 27) is dependent on the Malvernian pottery. Straight-sided Malvernian cooking pots were made from the 12th century to the 14th century (Vince 1977). The greatest extent for their distribution was during the 13th century. The Alcester example (fig 71, 1) appears to be a 13th-century type, that is, there are traces of wheel-finishing on the upper half of the vessel. On the evidence of this cooking pot, the pit would seem to be 13th century. The presence of Malvernian wares in small but regular quantities (up to 5%) is seen in every medieval pottery assemblage from Alcester. The pottery is nearly always unglazed. Vince (1977) thinks that the presence of Malvernian cooking pots is, in many cases, the result of lack of competition. This is clearly not the case in Alcester, with its own pottery production. The lack of glazed Malvernian vessels together with the presence of glazed Worcester vessels suggests that the mechanism for distribution of Malvernian wares in Alcester is indirect, possibly via Worcester (23km (14.5 miles) from Alcester) or Droitwich (26km (16 miles) from Alcester) where, in the 13th century, 50% of cooking pots were from the Malverns. As has been suggested elsewhere (Ratkai forthcoming (a)), the saltway from Droitwich to Alcester may have acted as trading conduit.

Malting kiln/corn dryer (C IIIA 31, 1A, 11, 12, 13, 8, 21, 24)

There were two sherds in fabric 1 from context C IIIA 31, a primary deposit in the rebuild of the oven; one

Table 10 Medieval pottery

	No sh	Rims	Base	Handle	Local fabric	Non-local fabric
Site						
A	7	3	1	1	3	4
B	3	1	2	–	1	2
C	138	17	10	1	101	37
D	5	2	–	1	–	–
E	2	2	–	–	2	1
G	6	4	1	–	4	2
K	21	3	9	2	16	5
J	1	1	–	–	–	–

is a ridged neck sherd from a jug similar to nos 12 and 13. The other sherd is from a jug or pitcher decorated with irregular bands of wide-spaced rectangular rouletting of poor quality and with a patchy olive glaze. The sherd probably comes from a vessel like that illustrated in Cracknell & Jones (1985, no 22). The form and decoration is common in Warwickshire, being found in both Warwick (Ratkai 1987) and Coventry (I Soden and R Wallwork pers comm) where they are dated to the 12th century and early 13th century.

The relining of the kiln contained fabric 1 (nos 3 and 4) and a Malvernian sherd with spots of tan glaze. Pottery from the rebuilt flues and hard standing behind the stoke area of the rebuilt kiln (11, 12, and 13) had been recorded as one, that is, the finds from the contexts were not labelled separately. There were six sherds in fabric 1 including two rims (nos 5 and 6) and a ridged neck sherd with a patchy olive glaze. One other sherd had a patchy olive glaze and there was also one Malvernian sherd.

The flue deposit C IIIA 8 and the soil deposits C IIIA 21 and 24 below C IIIA 13 produced a greater variety of fabrics. The dominant fabrics were fabric 1 and fabric 31, both local to Alcester. There was a Malvernian sherd and two glazed Worcester ware sherds, one with incised horizontal lines. Also present were two 'white slip decorated' sherds and two sherds in an oolitic tempered fabric not hitherto found in Alcester. Both were glazed and one was decorated with horizontal combing. They are presumably from the same vessel. The 'white slip decorated' ware occurs in the 13th century and 14th century. The remaining pottery associated with the malting kiln/corn dryer suggests a 13th-century date.

Contexts later than the kiln (C IIIA 1, 1C, 7, 9, 10, 14, 25)

Only 26 sherds were recovered from these contexts, mainly in fabric 1. There were four glazed sherds and three unglazed Malvernian sherds. There was surprisingly no Boarstall-Brill pottery or any other fine glazed ware.

The pottery from site C IIIA, with the exception of the oolitic fabric (see above), was made in fabrics already recorded in Alcester. The general character of the pottery suggests that the kiln was in use during the 13th century.

Pottery from other areas

Most of the sherds from these areas were made up of fabric 1 (see table 10). There is some evidence that the vessels were finished on a slow wheel, this being most apparent around the necks and rims of the vessels. The typical form is a rounded cooking pot with a sagging base and an everted, angled, thickened rim, often internally thickened. There was also one thickened rim. In addition there were some undiagnostic glazed body sherds and the lower part of a straight-sided cooking pot, a less common form in fabric 1, but recorded by Cracknell & Jones (1985). There was a marked ridge at the base angle suggesting that the base was attached to the completed body of the pot.

Non-local pottery came from a variety of sources. The best-represented non-local fabric was Boarstall-Brill ware, mainly jugs but one rim sherd may have been from a cup. Worcester, Malvernian, white slip decorated and Chilvers Coton products were represented as was a fine red ware with a mottled glaze similar to Canon Park ware (see Redknap 1985, 65–77). The range of non-local fabrics is the same as that from other excavations in Alcester.

Fuller details of Alcester fabrics may be found in the medieval pottery reports for the Gateway supermarket site (Ratkai forthcoming (c)) and the Explosion site (Ratkai forthcoming (d)). The date-ranges of the pottery from the 1964–6 Birch Abbey excavations seem to be concentrated in the 13th century, with the possibility that some of the undiagnostic body sherds in local Alcester fabrics or in Malvernian ware may be earlier. Some of the glazed sherds such as white slip decorated, Chilvers Coton, and Boarstall-Brill, may belong to the 14th century or in the case of Chilvers Coton 15th century. The presence of a possible cup rim in Boarstall-Brill ware would also suggest a later medieval date.

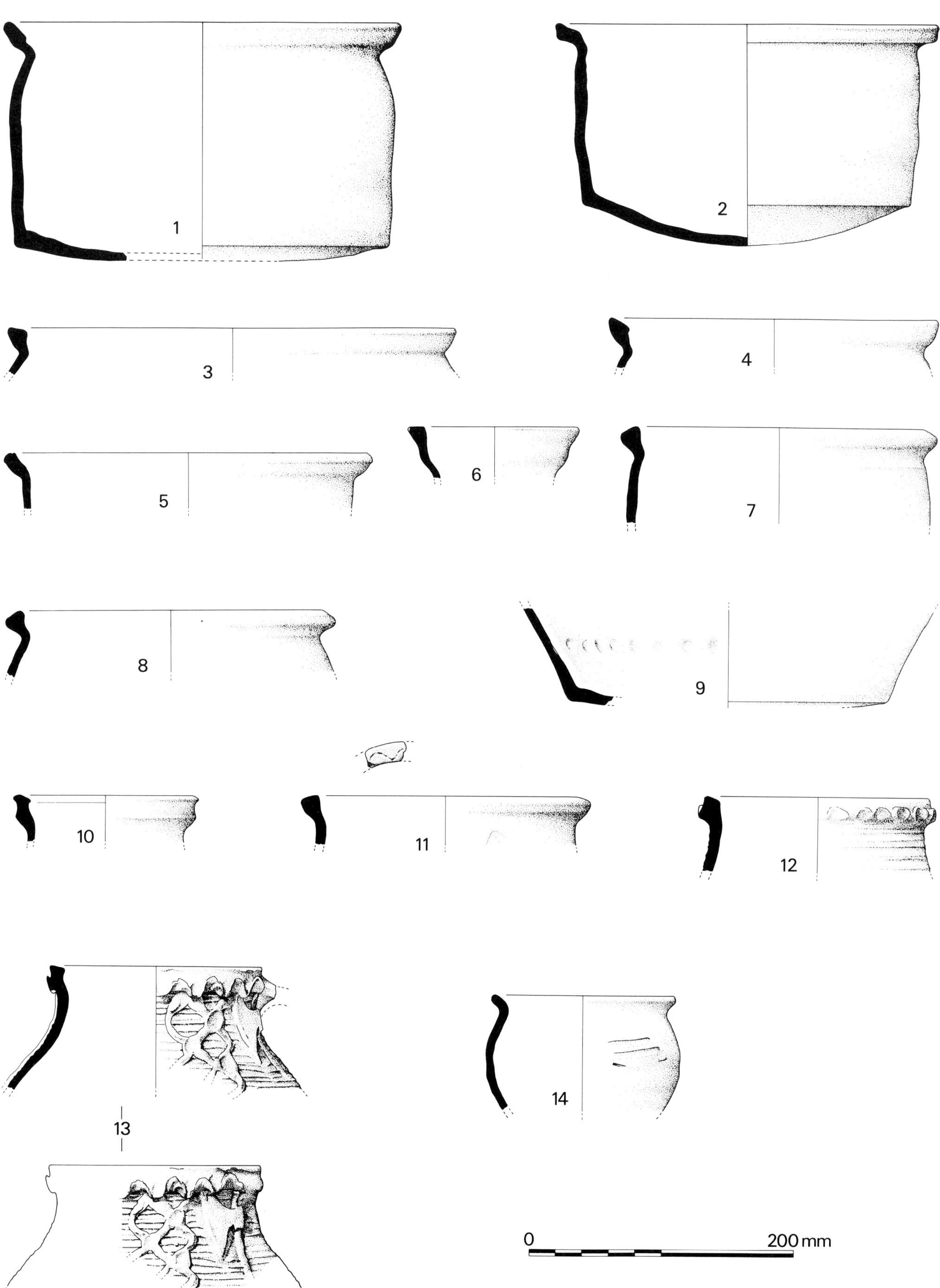

Figure 71 Medieval pottery

Metal artefacts

Coins

Richard Brickstock and P J Casey

[M2:F5] The Celtic and Roman coins discussed in this report are those from the 1964–6 excavations of Mahany together with other coins with an Alcester provenance assembled for study by Mr W Seaby. The latter comprise coins from a number of private collections, from early excavations, and material in regional and national museums. The accumulated total of coins from the town available for study amounts to 1,525.

Since very few of the coins are in a stratified sequence discussion will be based on the graphs in figs 72–4, both in relation to material recovered by Mahany and to the pattern of deposits exhibited by the composite spectrum of Alcester coins. These graphs are based on the standard format established by Casey (1986). The periods into which the coins are divided is as follows:

1. Claudian 43–54
2. Neronian 54–68
3. Flavian I 69–81
4. Flavian II 81–96
5. Trajanic 96–117
6. Hadrianic 117–38
7. Antonine I 138–61
8. Antonine II 161–80
9. Antonine III 180–92
10. Severan I 193–217

11–17. Severan II 218–59 (Elagabalus, Severus Alexander, Maximinus, Gordian III, Philip, Trajan Decius, Valerian)

18. Gallic Empire 260–73
19. Aurelianic 273–86
20. Carausian 286–96
21. Diocletianic 296–317
22. Constantinian I 318–30
23. Constantinian II 330–48
24. Constantinian III 348–64
25. Valentinianic 364–78
26. Theodosian I 378–88
27. Theodosian II 388–402

A single coin from the site is of numismatic importance (catalogue no 168) and this will be discussed in its own right below. The complete coin list with indexes can be found in microfiche (tables M9–12).

One factor which limits the reliability of the coin series is the nature of their discovery. Mahany reports that during the first few months of the excavation few coins were handed in. She then instituted a system whereby the finders received a payment for each coin. In the following weeks the number of coins 'found' increased dramatically. The context of these coins is in some doubt.

The coin pattern suggests that the inception of the Birch Abbey site should be in the middle Neronian period. The bulk of the coins bearing the name or image of Claudius are copies (92%). Of these the majority are degraded copies, light of weight and poor of execution, characteristic products of the period between AD 54 and 64. This decade saw a sharp decline in Claudian coin consignment to Britain (issues with the title P(ater) P(atriae) are distinctly scarce; the title does not appear on copies) and the total cessation of the production of *aes* coinage for the first ten years of the reign of Nero. Copies of the latest circulating coins, Claudian *asses*, filled the gap left by the absence of official supplies (Boon & Hassall 1982). The attenuated grade of the bulk of the copies in the present collection points to a period towards the end of this decade for the production of the deposited material. The presence of late Dobunnic coins, in a normal distribution of types, need not contradict this statement or be construed as evidence for the presence of a pre-conquest site: native silver enjoyed a circulation on military sites, such as Kingsholm (Gloucester) into the Neronian period (Haselgrove forthcoming) and is present with Claudian issues in the Nunney Hoard (*Num Chron* 1861, 1–17). The graph shows the normal heavy input of coinage in the Flavian period (Periods 3–4) which is associated with renewed military activity in the province.

Thereafter, the graph follows the well-established pattern for the bulk of developing towns in Roman Britain with substantial deposits of Trajanic, Hadrianic, and early Antonine *sestertii*, *dupondii* and *asses* (Periods 5–7). These remained in the circulation pool into the middle of the 3rd century, as their well-worn condition attests. There is the normal fall-off in the late Antonine period (Periods 8–9), reflecting the change-over from a currency system in which base metal coins dominated in day-to-day transactions to one where increasingly debased silver coins made up the bulk of new material put into circulation. The concomitant effect of this change was that with fewer, higher-value units of currency in circulation, fewer were available to be deposited.

The scarcity of coins of Period 10 is, perhaps, a little unusual. *Denarii* of Septimius Severus and his family are not uncommon, often being represented by plated counterfeits. On the other hand the subsequent Severan periods (Periods 11–12) are normally represented, possibly indicating some enhanced site activity, or the dispersal of a hoard. The large representation of Elagabalus (Period 11) is of no significance, being the product of the inherent statistical over-representation of a small number of coins

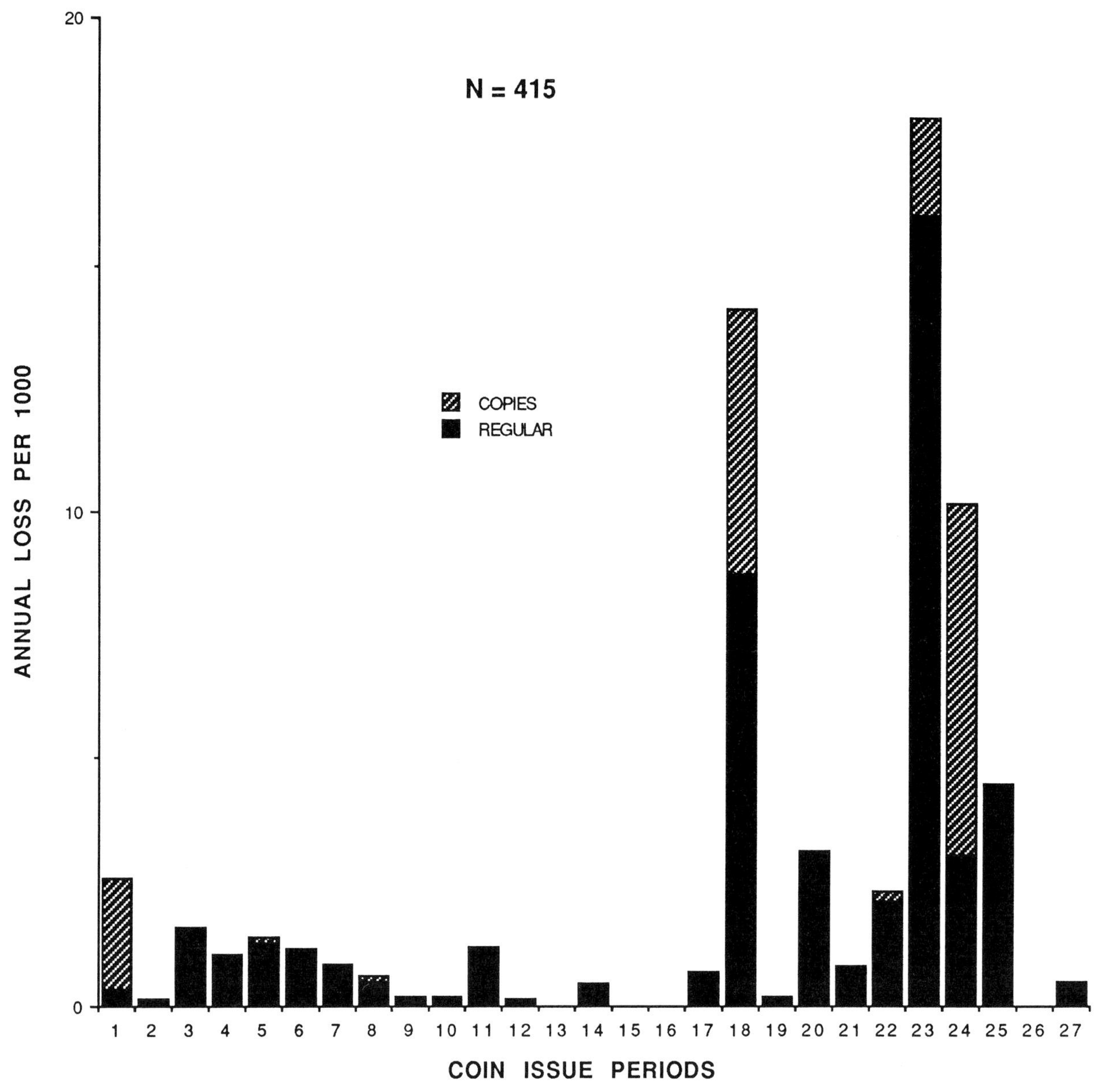

Figure 72 Coins from the 1964–6 excavations (for coin issue periods see text)

in a very short time period. These coins should be regarded as part of the overall coin provision of Periods 11–13. There is a general dearth of coinage of the first half of the 3rd century as a whole, a characteristic of all sites in Britain, which does not seem to have shared in the distribution of the otherwise abundant *aes* coinage of such rulers as Gordian III, Philip, and Trajan Decius. The reason for this monetary neglect of the province is as yet not understood.

The latter half of the 3rd century and the 4th up to and including Period 24 show strict conformity to provincial norms. Period 18 (The Gallic Empire) demonstrates the usual peak of discarded base '*antoniniani*' and copies thereof. These copies circulated in Period 19, the era of the Aurelianic reform, and ceased to form a component of the circulating currency with the introduction of a large-volume coinage by Carausius (Period 20). The introduction and decline of the Diocletianic reformed coinage can be traced in Periods 21–2 and the hyperinflation of the later years of Constantine (Period 23) is, as usual, strongly marked with an abundance of site finds representative of an immense currency pool.

These observations indicate that the coinage of Alcester lies well within the usual limitations imposed on losses by problems of supply. They also show that it is difficult, if not impossible, to establish variation of economic or occupation behaviour against this strong 'background noise' of overall normality. Periods 24–5 offer a contrast to this situation.

The coin reform of AD 348 (Period 24), which introduced a short-lived high-value billon coinage (which after AD 354 was maintained without a silver content), and the introduction of a silver-free petty currency in the Valentinianic period (Period 25),

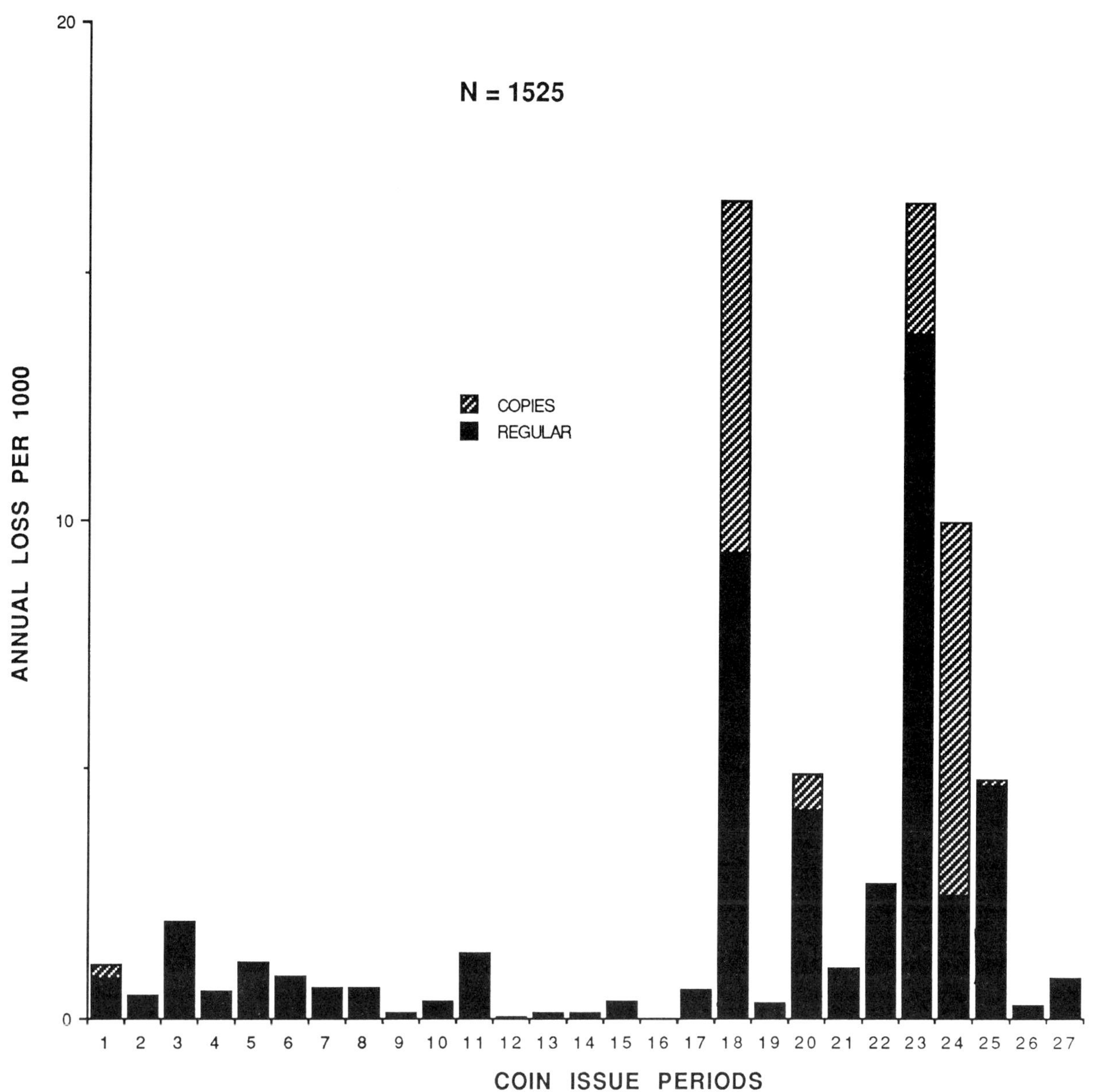

Figure 73 Coins from Alcester excavations to 1985 (for coin issue periods see text)

normally results in a dearth of coinage in the former period and a peak of deposits in the latter. Frequently, Valentinianic values approximate to those of Periods 18 and 23. Alcester shows a reverse trend in these periods. As normal the bulk of the Period 24 coin comprises copies of the official issues. This reflects a situation brought about by the demonetization of earlier issues by an imperial rescript of Constantius II, issued in AD 354, coupled with a failure to provide sufficient coin in the north-western provinces to make good the resulting currency deficit.

The reverse pattern observed at Alcester has been observed in other urban sites, notably by Ravetz (1964) in her pioneer study of 4th-century coinage patterns in Britain. Ravetz's conclusion was that sites which were long established, and had a large currency pool of Constantinian coinage, did not need a large injection of coins in the 360s. This argument does not take into account either the legal background to the currency history of the period or the hoard evidence; nor is it consonant with subsequent archaeological investigations of Roman urban sites. It is clear from the numbers of discarded coins both of the Constantinian period (especially Period 23) and of Magnentius, which are normally found in unworn condition, that the rescript of 354 was effectively and rigorously applied. Further, the overstriking of Constantinian official issues of higher intrinsic value to produce copies of the 'acceptable' coinage of post-354 shows that the earlier coinage was effectively demonetized. We have already seen that post-354 coinage of Constantius II was not well supplied in the West — an unsuccessful tactic to thwart any ambition to revolt by the Caesar Julian — but what was supplied is not hoarded with pre-348 issues. More to the point coins of Period 24 do not appear to be hoarded with those of Period 25, and thus appear to have no value in the Valentinianic

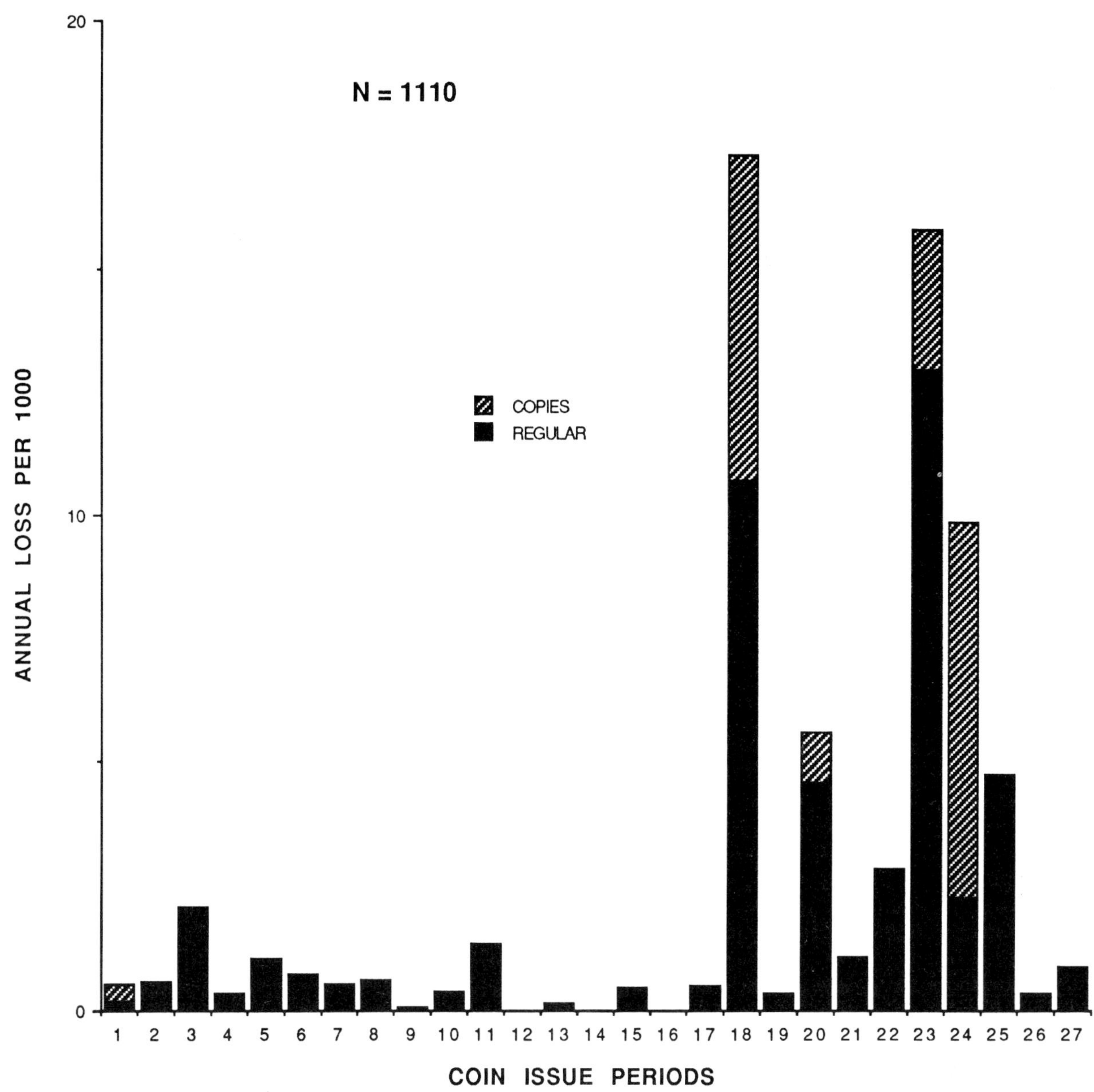

Figure 74 Coins from Alcester excavations to 1985 but excluding those from the 1964–6 excavations

period (Brickstock 1987). In these circumstances it is difficult to maintain that the pre-existing coinage supplied the deficit of the later period.

An alternative view to that of Ravetz is that the dearth of Valentinianic issues is a yardstick of the decline of urban population, or its relocation to new areas. To give but two examples of sites with a low Valentinianic deposit rate: at *Verulamium*, which shows a relative weakness, there is evidence for the abandonment of city centre properties at this period (Frere 1983b), whilst Catterick shows centrally located dwellings probably being converted to store buildings (Wacher 1971). While these conclusions are at present tentative, they have the merit of accommodating the contemporary legal position and its archaeologically observable results.

A modest up-swing of deposits representing the coinage of the years 388–402 (Period 27) is normal for all areas outside Wales and the west Midlands. There the latest coins are issues of 388–93, probably reflecting a military situation brought about by the withdrawal of forces from north Wales, and probably some sites in the west Pennine area, by Arbogastes in 392 (Casey 1989).

It is clear from a comparison of the histogram of coins from the excavations of 1964–6 (fig 72) with the composite graph of the town (fig 73) that there is little or no variation between the numismatic history of the town as a whole and the area investigated by Mahany. This conclusion is reinforced when the Mahany coins are deducted from the town total and the result expressed as a separate histogram (fig 74). The only significant variation is in the larger proportion of Claudian copies recorded by the present excavations. Differences in the proportions of copies represented elsewhere are a product of variations in cataloguing practices over the long period through which the Alcester coin lists have been assembled.

A report on the X-ray fluorescence analysis of the Dobunnic coins can be found in the microfiche [M3:D5].

Caravsivs et fratres svi

Description (see plate 1):

Obv. CARAVSIVS ET FRATRES SVI
Conjoined busts, radiate, cuirassed, l. of Maximian, nearest, Diocletian, centre, and Carausius, farthest.

Rev. PAX AVGGG
Pax std. l. holding in right hand branch, in left vertical sceptre.
Mintmark $\frac{S|P}{C}$. Wt 4.2 gr. Die axis ↑↓
(cat no 168, CO 19, AA I 2)

Plate 1 Caravsivs et fratres svi coin

As far as can be ascertained from the illustrations in the current corpus, the new coin has no die links with any recorded specimen.

Coins issued by the rebel Carausius in the names of his rivals, Diocletian and Maximian, with the portrait of one or other of the legitimate emperors are not uncommon, but those which display the conjoined busts of the three emperors are very rare. Eighteen specimens of this class are known, including that from Alcester, and one of us (PJC) has seen another coin in trade which has not been the subject of academic review (Shiel 1978; Carson 1987). These coins offer a unique iconographic and political insight into the last years of the reign of Carausius.

Sixteen of the recorded specimens, including the Alcester coin, are products of 'C' mint and bear the mint mark $\frac{S|P}{C}$, or its variant SPC. We may confidently assign this mint to Camulodunum both on the grounds of the distribution of 'C' products in the Essex region and on their absence from the region of *Clausentum*, to which some have assigned this atelier (Casey 1977). One specimen (Shiel 1978, no 17) was produced by the London mint, bearing the mintmark MLXXI. This contrasts with the issues of gold in the names of Diocletian and Maximian which are exclusively products of the London mint. All of the triple portrait coins are billon 'Aureliani', probably intended as 5-*denarius* pieces.

On all but two of the hitherto recorded specimens (Shiel 1978, nos 15 and 17) the emperors face to the left in a rank order which ignores strict protocols of seniority. Diocletian is placed centrally in the triumvirate with Maximian on his inferior, left side and Carausius on his right. On the two variants with the emperors facing right the same order of precedence is preserved, with Carausius now nearest the spectator. The obverse inscription normally reads CARAVSIVS ET FRATRES SVI ('Carausius and his brothers'), a variant type (two specimens) has the name of Diocletian. The majority of the coins under review bear the reverse type PAX AVGGG. No coins acknowledging Carausius were issued by the legitimate emperors.

The order of issues of Carausius's coins is well established through the medium of sequential mint marks and hoard evidence (Carson 1971). The mark $\frac{S|P}{C}$, and the variant SPC, is the last used in the reign of Carausius by the 'C' mint and the first used by the mint on the coinage of Allectus. The relative date of the issue is thus firmly fixed. Coins from the London mint alluding to the collegiality of Carausius with Diocletian and Maximian (by use of the formula AVGGG on the reverse), but without the triple portraits, bear the mint mark $\frac{S|P}{MLXXI}$. Similar issues of Colchester are marked, as are the triple portrait coins $\frac{S|P}{C}$. The single triple-headed London issue is signed MLXXI but, as has been observed, 'such is the nature of its reverse type that there is no room left for any letters in the field' (Shiel 1978, 9).

On the basis of the mint mark sequence, the triple portrait coins and the cognate AVGGG issues appear to have been issued in AD 292/3. The $\frac{S|P}{MLXXI}$ mint mark was superseded at London by a very short-lived mark, $\frac{S|P}{ML}$, which is evidently the last of the reign since it is also the first mark of Allectus. No collegiate issues are known for this mark. On the combined evidence of the London and 'C' mint marks the collegiate issues can be placed at the end of the reign, but not at the very end. It is possible that they were issued in anticipation of, or as an overture to secure, some sort of recognition by Diocletian and Maximian in the period immediately before the creation of the Caesar Constantius in early 293. The creation of the Caesar cannot have taken place without preliminary speculation and investigation of his loyalty and suitability for the task of extirpating the usurper. Since at this time Carausius was well established on the Continent, and cannot but have maintained an intelligence service, we may see the issue of these coins in a context of diplomacy provoked by the imminent creation of a ruler devoted to his destruction. Their issue ceased when the elevation of Constantius extinguished the hopes of a peaceful solution to the crisis.

The use of the Colchester mint to strike the bulk of this coinage is in line with the function of that mint in producing the overwhelming proportion of what may be termed 'ceremonial' coins of the reign — those in which the emperor is depicted conjoined with deities, such as Sol, or depicted in heroic posture with shield and spear. These are all rare coins, suggesting that they formed a component of the coinage designed for presentation. It seems probable that the Provincial Council of Britain still met regularly at Camulodunum, or its functions were restored by Carausius, and that the 'ceremonial' coins of the 'C' mint were struck for participants in its deliberations. In such circumstances overtly propagandizing issues, such as the *Carausius et fratres sui* coins, would have had a direct political value to the regime.

Copper alloy and iron brooches

D F Mackreth

All are made of copper alloy, unless otherwise stated.

Except for one feature, this collection is typical of a site lying in the west Midlands and the report below deals with the distribution and dating of individual types. The unusual element which deserves some discussion is the presence of iron brooches belonging to a very restricted range and including a *Kragenfibel*. Apart from that, the discussions of the individual brooches do not lead to a clear view of when the purely Roman site was founded (see 'Discussion' at end).

Catalogue (figs 75–81)

Colchester

1 Iron. The X-ray confirms that there are six coils. The hook is moderately long and the bow is plain. The catch-plate is lost. (FE 276, G I 89, phase IV, early to mid-4th century)

The Colchester type was made from the very end of the 1st century BC until about AD 40. During this time, the profile became bowed and the elaboration of the catch-plate was reduced to a fairly simple fretting (at best). There were other changes, but they are of little moment here. The profile of brooch 1 is not very bowed and, assuming that the catch-plate was below the surviving end, the brooch is fairly long in proportion to the width of the head. Iron was commonly used before the Conquest for brooches and many Colchesters in iron are known. The typological form of the brooch suggests that it should date to the first three decades of the 1st century; it may have survived in use until *c* AD 45/55 by which time a host of the derivative forms was in production.

Colchester derivatives

2 The spring was once held to the body of the brooch by a rearward-facing hook at the end of a ridge on the head of the bow. Each wing is curved to seat the spring and has a pair of grooves at its end. Apart from the ridge, the bow is plain. The lower bow and the catch-plate are missing. (CA 431, G IA 89, phase VI, late 4th century)

3 Very badly corroded. The better-preserved wing had two sunken mouldings — one beaded — separated by a wide flute, with another next to the bow. The strongly swollen front of the bow has a step along each margin and a median ridge with a sunken bead-row down the middle. The lower bow is missing. (CA 347, G I 91, unphased)

Brooch 3 is placed here for two reasons. First, the style of decoration is most common on Rearhooks. Second, the remains will not allow the spring-fixing arrangement to belong either to the Polden Hill method (see below 4) or to the other main system which has a plate pierced by two holes behind the head of the bow. Better-preserved examples of the Rearhook show that the hook only kept the chord from moving, the spring being secured by solder behind the left-hand wing. The homeland of the Rearhook is Norfolk and the adjacent parts of Suffolk and the Fens. The fringe of the main distribution runs into Essex and the western Fen margins. Recent discussion (Mackreth forthcoming (d)) has shown that there is a very precise terminal date, AD 60/65. This coupled with the distribution of the type indicates that it was specifically Icenian and came to an end with the suppression of Boudicca's rebellion. These two brooches, 2 and 3, could have been acquired then and, therefore, stand a chance of having survived beyond the end of the type in general.

4 The spring is held in an open-backed case by an axis bar fixed in the pierced ends of the case. The case was made of folded sheet metal separately from the bow. It has swivelled on the rivet joining the two. There is no decoration. (CA 207, D I 29A, phase IV, late 3rd century?)

Brooches 5–23 and possibly 24 have or had their springs held in the Polden Hill manner: an axis bar through the coils was fixed in pierced plates at the ends of the wings, the chord being held either by a hook or by a pierced plate.

5 The spring has at least seventeen coils. Each wing has three sunken bead-rows. There is another on the head of the otherwise plain bow which tapers to a very thin section at the break. Only the top of the catch-plate is present. (CA 166, C II 134, unphased)

6 A repeat of 5, but with only two sunken mouldings on each wing and with no good trace of bead-rows. The catch-plate has part of a large triangular piercing. (CA 129, AA II 109, phase III, 3rd century)

The relationship between 4 and these two (5 and 6) is not immediately obvious and examples of each basic variety are not common enough to reveal the full connection between them. However, both 5 and 6 have broad hooks to hold the chord, a feature to be found on multiple-part brooches, some of which have mouldings down the head of the bow (eg Webster 1963, 133, fig 33, 1; Rowley's House Museum, Shrewsbury, Y17). The available dating for multiple-part brooches is weak: Broxtowe, before AD 75 (Campion 1938, 11, pl II, 1); Watercrook, *c* 90–?110 (Potter 1979, 206, fig 84, 3). The other feature of the basic type to which both 5 and 6 belong is the very thin sectioning used, with a suggestion that the plates at the ends of the wings were cold-forged into position. Again, dating is weak: Derby, 1st–2nd century (Mackreth 1985, 281–3, fig 123, 2).

Multiple-part brooches have no marked distribution, but lie generally in the western parts of England south of Wroxeter. Brooches with thin sections, on the other hand, are at home in the southern Severn Valley and its eastern catchment area. The exact dating of the Alcester examples is obscure, but is strongly indicated by two factors. First, catch-plates with large piercings are not 2nd century and are a mark of brooches earlier than *c* AD 75. Second, there is a definite development towards the family to which brooches 11–17 belong. Therefore the terminal date of the present type is conditioned by the beginning of that: before *c* AD 70–80. One stage in this development is shown by a brooch from the Lunt, Baginton, Warwicks, which has the overall design of brooches 5 and 6 coupled with a beaded half-round plate on each side of the head. This brooch is dated before *c* 75 (Hobley 1973, 66, fig 19, 7). A similar brooch to the one from the Lunt comes from Bagendon and is dated *c* AD 50–60 (Clifford 1961, 173, fig 36, 5). This should point to the period AD 50–70 for Alcester brooches 4–6.

7 The spring is as that in 5. Each wing has a moulding at the end. There is a plain moulding next to the bow which is itself plain apart from a ridge on the head. The catch-plate has a small triangular hole. (CA 425, D I 173, phase II, later 2nd to early 3rd century?)
8 The same as the last; the mouldings on either side of the head project much further forward. The lower bow is missing, but the top of a piercing is present. (CA 494, E I T/S, unphased)
9 The same as the last two, with a pair of mouldings at the end of each wing. In this example the moulding on each side of the head is now a plate masking the junction with the wing. (CA 484, L I 9, unphased)
10 The basic form is identical to that of the last three brooches. There is a single moulding at the end of each wing and a prominent half-round plate on each side of the head. The lower bow is straight-sided with a flat front. The catch-plate has a triangular hole and the return has a sunken moulding at the top and the bottom with a pair in the middle. (CA 501, F I 124A, phase VI, early 3rd century?)

On typological grounds, these four brooches (7–10) would be placed between the previous three (4–6) and the next group (11–16) and would be dated AD 50/60–75/85. But this does not allow for developments in parallel. However, these four all have pierced catch-plates and the decorated catch-plate return of 10 is not a 2nd-century characteristic. The available dating is, as before, poor: Wroxeter, second half of the 2nd century (Bushe-Fox 1916, 23, pl XV, 6).

11 The spring is held as before. Each wing has a pair of mouldings at its end. The plate on each side of the head is beaded. The plain bow has an incised line on each side of the hook. The foot-knob has a cross-moulding above. The catch-plate has a line of rocker-arm ornament on each side next to the bow. (CA 423, F I 39, unphased)
12 As the last but plain; the moulding at the end of each wing is more marked than usual. The end of the bow is missing. (CA 167, C VI 36, phase V, later 3rd century on)
13 The spring is held as before. Each wing has a pair of mouldings at its end. The plain bow ends in the usual foot-knob. The catch-plate return has a groove across it. (CA 124, A XV 18, unphased)
14 The spring is held as before. The outer of the two mouldings at the end of each wing is beaded, so is the plate on either side of the head. The upper bow has a moulded ornament made up of a pair of ridges with a line of punched dots between. The ridges end with a small excrescence on each side. The foot-knob has three cross-mouldings, the central one being beaded. The catch-plate has, on the back, a line of rocker-arm ornament next to the bow and at the start of the return. This has a series of grooves arranged as a chevron. (CA 28, B I 1, unphased)
15 The spring is held as before. Each wing has a pair of mouldings at the end. The bow has a groove, with punched dots along it, down the centre. On each side is another groove from which rises a line of Vitruvian scrolls. These have traces of inlay, probably niello. The foot-knob has two mouldings across its top. (CA 185, E III 1, unphased)
16 The spring is held as before. The wings are plain. The bow has down most of its length a central sunken ridge with cross-cuts in it and divided lenticular bosses arranged to form three four-petalled flowers, with a half one at the bottom, lying across the bow. The foot-knob has a prominent central moulding. (CA 29, B I 1, unphased)

Brooches 11–16 all belong to a single family whose main area of distribution is the Severn Valley and its eastern catchment, although examples are to be found over the whole of Roman Britain. The type, once established, could be plain or highly ornamented, and the designs here are known ones. The earliest stages in the development of the type bridge the gap between brooches 7–10 and the full form shown best by 11 and lack the foot-knob: see an example from the Lunt, Baginton, Warwicks, before AD 75 (Hobley 1966, 107, fig 19, 3). The presence of the Polden Hill spring system is not an essential characteristic for defining members of the family as there is a group centred in the southern Pennines which has all the necessary qualifications save for having a hinged pin. At first sight, brooch 16 looks as though it ought to be excluded, but it belongs to the one design (eg Rowley's House Museum, Shrewsbury, X9; Hume 1863, 72, pl IV, 4; Hattatt 1985, 84, fig 36, 379) which leads to a different shape. The dating has recently been reviewed (Mackreth forthcoming (d)) and its *floruit* is firmly fixed as *c* AD 75–150, with a few surviving possibly as late as AD 175.

17 The spring is held as before except for the chord which passes through a pierced crest on the head of the bow. The pin is bent into a loop with its end tucked under the chord. Mounted on the loop is an object consisting of two large bosses linked by a bar with two beaded mouldings. There is to one side of this a smaller bar forming a loop through which passes the pin. The wings are plain. The broad bow has a flat front tapering to a small projecting foot. The crest at the top rises from one end of a small flat-topped ridge. The other end finishes in a diamond boss. Down each side of the bow is a groove and the central part of the margin so formed is serrated. (CA 437, J I 11, phase VIII, 3rd century?)
A member of a not large and mainly unpublished family whose homeland is essentially Gloucestershire down to Wiltshire, but which spreads into Somerset; examples are also thinly distributed across the whole of southern England. Variations in design are few and the common form has an enamelled rectangle containing two reserved lozenges just under the ridge. Apart from that, there are cross-cuts or cut chevrons on the same position. The ridge may be absent, but the lower boss is usually present as here, or as a stud. In two examples recorded by the writer this is replaced by a face in relief (Hull 1967, 62, fig 24, 245; Somerdale Villa, Keynsham, to be published). Dating is sparse: Caerleon, with abundant Flavian pottery, (Wheeler & Wheeler 1928, 162, fig 13, 7); Dorchester-on-Thames, pre-Antonine? (Frere 1962, 137, fig 27, 6); Shakenoak Farm, probably late 3rd century (Brodribb *et al* 1978, 100–1, fig 41, 245). The best indications are that the type runs from the late 1st century into the 2nd; any later than AD 200 should be residual.
18 The spring is mounted like that on 17. Each wing has a sunken moulding at the end. There is a half-round plate masking the junction of the wing with the bow. The bow itself is long and tapers to a pointed foot. The crest runs into a wide V-shaped hollow down the bow which has a bordering groove on each side. The catch-plate has a large triangular hole. (CA 159, C VI 26, phase IV, later 3rd century on)
19 A repeat of the last, but with plain wings and no grooves down each side of the bow. (CA 411, E IV 68, phase V, late 2nd century?)
20 The lower bow of a brooch almost certainly of the same type as the previous two. Here the groove down the bow runs to the foot which has a narrow squared end. (CA 345, D I 134, unphased)

The distribution of this style (18–20) appears to be Gloucestershire and the Avon Valley, but there are outliers. The V-shaped hollow down the bow is distinctive enough, coupled with the spring mounting, for variations in ornament, especially on the wings, to count for little. Dating evidence is very limited: the Lunt, Baginton, Warwicks, before AD 75 (Hobley 1966, 111, fig 19, 10); Nettleton, with 1st- to 2nd-century pottery (Wedlake 1982, 123, fig 52, 35). The large opening in the catch-plate certainly suits the dating of the one from the Lunt and the type is probably 1st century with, perhaps, a few lasting into the 2nd.

21 The head only of a brooch whose spring is mounted like those of the last group. The outer half of each wing has a pair of mouldings separated by a flute. The crest runs down onto the upper bow which has a step down each side. (CA 460, E II 37, phase IV, Hadrianic–Antonine)

Little can be said about this fragment. The phase on this site to which it belongs almost certainly marks the time it passed out of use.

22 The spring is mounted as before. Each wing has a sunken moulding at the end. The bow is well rounded in front and the crest continues as a ridge, cross-cut on the upper part, to a pointed end. The lower bow is missing. (CA 389, D I 176, unphased)

23 The spring is mounted as before. The wings are plain and have a flat front face. The bow also has a flat front face with a groove down each side. The catch-plate has a small triangular piercing. (CA 476, D II 84, phase VIII, late 4th century)

24 Very badly corroded, the details are unclear. The chord of the spring passes through a lug behind the head of the bow and was probably mounted in the Polden Hill manner (see above 5), although the very long surviving wing has no sign of the plate at its end. The stub of the other wing has traces of mouldings. The junction of the bow with the wings is masked by added mouldings running back under the head to meet in a point. There are traces of a ridge down the bow which is otherwise plain. The lower bow is missing. (CA 412, G IA 70, phase IV, early to mid-4th century)

None of 22–4 belongs to a recognized group. Only 23, with its piercing in the catch-plate, is likely to be 1st century and the way in which the mouldings meet under the head on 24 also points to the 1st century. Otherwise, only the most general dating can be given: from the later 1st century to *c* AD 150/75, by which time standard bow brooches such as these had ceased to be made.

25 The whole is badly corroded. The pin is hinged and the short wings have a circular section. The bow is straight in profile with a slight taper to the squared-off foot when viewed from the front. Slight traces on the front of the bow suggest reeding, as in the Langton Down type. (CA 366, G I 163, phase IV, early to mid-4th century)

Langton Down imitations are rare outside a group made out of forged folded sheet metal, 1st century in date, and at home in the south-west. Even without reeding on the bow, the form of this brooch is hard to match and, if it was a conscious copying, the date should be 1st century.

Fragments

26 The lower bow only of a brooch with a plain bow having a triangular opening in the catch-plate. The large hole in the catch-plate suggests that this brooch is 1st century in date. (CA 375, D I 107, phase I, 1st century to early Antonine)

27 A completely rotten brooch whose catch-plate is the only feature which can be distinguished. It has a triangular opening with the upper edge being concave. The large hole in the catch-plate suggests that this brooch is 1st century in date. (CA 382, D I 175, phase I, 1st century to early Antonine)

28 Only the plain lower bow survives and it ends in a two-part foot-knob. The form of the foot-knob may suggest that the type had been a Trumpet. The other possibility is the Hod Hill, but the shape of the top of the catch-plate is against this. (CA 475, J II 19, unphased)

29 The lower bow with a damaged catch-plate, the front is flat and plain. The foot ends in a cross-moulding with a small boss under. (CA 61, AA III 4, phase VI, late 3rd to early 4th century)

30 The head is missing. The bow is a flat plate, almost straight-sided, with a pointed foot. On each side is a groove; there is another pair in the middle with a flute between. (CA 348, E V 2, unphased)

Although it has the appearance of a poorly made Langton Down, the form of the catch-plate does not suit that type. The comments made about 25 apply here.

31 The lower bow only of an unidentified type, it is flat with bowed sides and squared-off foot. (CA 406, D I 176, unphased)

32 The head only of a corroded brooch whose spring was mounted in the Polden Hill manner (see above 5). There are no distinctive features visible. Before *c* AD 150/75. Not illustrated. (CA 251, D II 3, unphased)

33 The lower bow of a Colchester Derivative with a pierced catch-plate. There are no distinguishing marks. Before *c* AD 125? (CA 344, G I 91, unphased)

Headstuds

34 The spring is of the Colchester type. From the back of the head of the bow issue two wires: the long lower one is coiled to form the usual bilateral spring, the short upper one is bent forward to form a hook for the chord. There is an axis bar through the coils. The hook has a slightly expanded pointed end. The bow is a plain flat plate, expanded at the top to form wings whose fronts curve out from the bow. It has a slight taper to the foot. On this is a separately made double-moulded foot-knob. The distorted catch-plate seems to have had its return on the left instead of to the right as is usual. (CA 191, D II 1, unphased)

Only not a 'true' Headstud in that it has no stud, the form is obviously closely related: the shape of the head and the general appearance of the foot-knob are not to be expected on any other type.

The initial development of the Headstud is imperfectly understood. Most examples have hinged pins. Of sprung-pin ones, the spring is usually made separately to be mounted on a single loop behind the head. The spring is kept in place by a wire loop, bound by a collar, whose ends are seated in the ends of a rolled sheet tube through the coils. The Colchester system on what may be termed proto-Headstuds is rare and the writer knows of none with a cast-on stud. Three show the relationship with the Headstud proper more clearly than the present piece: at Catterick, a brooch with a separately made foot-knob as here has stepped wings as on 36 (Mackreth forthcoming (e)); at Corbridge, Red House Fort, the separately made foot is also seen, but the two brooches have a ridge down the centre of the bow. These specimens are dated AD 75–90/95 (Hanson *et al* 1979, 61–2, fig 21, 1, 2). There are too few specimens for it to be certain where the development towards the full Headstud began: the three from the north of England and the one from Alcester *may* indicate that the north is the preferred area, but a brooch from Silchester could indicate otherwise. It has the Colchester spring system, the full loop and collar, a separately made foot-knob, a ridge down the bow and a stud riveted through the bow next to the end of the hook (Reading Museum, 03190).

Typologically, the Colchester spring system should come first, followed by the spring mounted on a single loop and finally by the hinged pin. To some extent, this sequence can be demonstrated by the style of enamelling on the bow. So far, no brooch of this series with the Colchester spring system has enamelling and only one noted by the writer has a stud (see above). On other sprung-pin Headstuds, the enamelling can be of three general styles, ignoring aberrant forms which occur throughout the Headstud varieties. The first is the least common and consists of a single cell running the full length of the bow: Wall, Staffs, *c* AD 60–80/3 (Gould 1964, 43, fig 18, 3). The enamel in the strip tends to be in alternating blocks of colour. The second design has a series of rectangular cells: Baldock, with aberrant ornament in the middle of the bow, *c* AD 55–90 (Stead & Rigby 1986, 67, fig 29, 10); Corbridge, Red House bath house, two examples with an aberrant design partly enamelled in this style, AD 75–90/95 (Daniels 1959, 156). The third scheme is the lozenge-and-triangle pattern commonly found on hinged-pin Headstuds. The dating available for sprung-pin Headstuds is: the Lunt, Baginton, Warwicks, without a stud, before AD 75 (Hobley 1973, 66, fig 19, 9); Colchester, AD 80/85 to *c* 100 (Crummy 1983, 13, fig 9, 65). This analysis confirms a 1st-century date for the whole development. It appears to show that examples like the three whose springs are mounted on loops and the two with Colchester systems at Red House, Corbridge were passing out of use during the period AD 75–90/95. It also indicates that those using the Colchester system should belong to the earlier end of this range. It should only be a matter of time before these and others like the Alcester specimen can be shown to date before AD 75, like the unstudded lozenge-and-triangle design from the Lunt.

35 The pin is hinged, its axis bar being housed in a half-round projection behind the wings. On the head are the stubs of a cast-on loop. The fronts of the wings have steps running back from the bow. The stud appears to be plain, and the bow below has a groove down each side with the lozenge-and-triangle pattern between. The foot-knob is of the common form: two mouldings beneath three lesser ones at the bottom of the bow. (CA 194, E III 1, unphased)

Although the casting is larger and appears more robust than most of this variety, there is no reason to suppose that this has any chronological significance. The distribution of this type is wide, covering all or most of Roman Britain. The dating is: Nettleton, with a coin of Nero (Wedlake 1982, 128, fig 53, 59); Harlow, AD 80–100 (France & Gobel 1985, 79, fig 41, 72); Newstead, two examples, AD 80 to *c* 200 (Curle 1911, 323, pl LXXXVI, 19, 20); Cologne, with coin of Trajan and samian of the second half of the 1st century (Exner 1939, 73, *Taf* 6, 1.I.1); Doncaster, *c* AD 80–110 (Buckland & Magilton 1986, 84–5, fig 19, 2); Camelon, *c* AD 80–90 or AD 143 to *c* 160/165 (Christison 1901, 405–6, pl A, 5; Hartley 1972b, 8); Wall, before AD 200 (Gould 1964, 43, fig 18, 2); Harlow, *c* 200+? (France & Gobel 1985, 79, fig 41, 71). The best date-range is from the late 1st century to the middle of the 2nd century. The coin of Nero from Nettleton almost certainly does not date that brooch, and the brooch from Harlow may well have been residual. The two from Newstead would fit well with the suggested *floruit*.

36 The axis bar of the hinged pin is housed like that in the last. The ends of the wire loop were fastened into the ends of the hole for the axis bar. The waist of the loop was bound by a collar across whose front is the lozenge-and-triangle design, which is repeated on the wings and the bow, the lozenges containing blue enamel. Each wing has a curved front and a groove at the end. On the head of the bow is a crest, with a groove along its top, above the stud which has a deep conical hollow with a hole for a rivet to hold the filling in place. The foot-knob is a broad moulding beneath two smaller mouldings and is hollow underneath for another setting. (CA 326, E IV 25, phase VI, early 3rd century?)

Another distinctive variety of Headstud, its distribution is mainly in southern England with examples in the north and in Scotland. The dating is: Harlow, before AD 80 (France & Gobel 1985, 79, fig 41, 73); Chichester, after the early 2nd century (Mackreth 1978, 279–80, fig 10.26, no 11); Derby, second half of the 2nd century (Brassington 1980, 18, fig 8a); Cold Knap, Barry, after AD 150? (Evans *et al* 1985, 109, fig 15, 1). All examples later than AD 200 have been omitted as they would have been residual in their contexts. Although the writer has recorded as many of this variety as the last, the relatively looser character of the dating evidence may suggest that this type is more 2nd century than the last. Production and use would still have ended *c* AD 150/175.

Late La Tène

37 Very corroded. The four-coil spring has the usual internal chord. The bow has a thin rectangular section and tapers to a pointed foot. (CA 408, G IA 68, phase IV, early to mid-4th century)
38 The spring is missing. The bow has the same section as the last but is more elongated and tapers to a pointed foot. Across the middle of the bow is a pair of grooves and, above these, the edges of the bow have a series of diagonal cuts. (CA 34, B III U/S, unphased)

Both brooches 37 and 38 descend from the Nauheim, but only 38 bears any trace of the ornament found on the upper bow of the parent type. The development from the middle of the 1st century BC to the middle of the 1st century AD is obscure. Most, including those which descend from the *Drahtfibel*, date to after the Conquest running on to very near the end of the 1st century. Of the present examples, 38 is likely to date before AD 75.

39 Iron. The spring has the usual four coils. The bow is thin and has a rectangular section with rounded corners. The profile is almost straight with a marked bend down at the top towards the start of the spring. (FE 262, D II 22, unphased)
40 Iron. Like the last, but the section of the bow is more square. (FE 297, G I 59, phase IV, early to mid-4th century)
41 Iron. A repeat of the last, only with the catch-plate and lower bow missing. Not illustrated. (FE 373, D II 90, phase I, 1st century to early Antonine)
42 Iron. A repeat of 39, but the profile of the bow is much slacker. Not illustrated. (FE 400, M III 14, phase II, late 2nd to early 3rd century on)
43 Iron. Only the spring and pin are present with the very top of the bow, which had a rectangular section. Not illustrated. (FE 75, B I 3, phase II, Antonine to 3rd century)
44 Iron. Part of the pin and one coil from a brooch which was almost certainly of the same type as the preceding examples. The pin is broken and is unlikely to have been less than 70mm long. The single surviving coil gives no hint of whether the chord was internal or external. Not illustrated. (FE 301, G I 148, phase IV, early to mid-4th century)

The five brooches 39–43, with their thin rod-like bows, derive from the *Drahtfibel*. Brooch 44 may have been of the same type, but could have been a Nauheim Derivative. There is little to date any particular specimen of either derivation to one part of the overall *floruit* rather than another. In general, both types run from the latter part of the 1st century BC to near the end of the 1st century AD. However, the use of iron for these brooches suggests that they had all been made before the Roman Conquest when iron was much more commonly used than it was after.

45 Iron. The spring has six coils and an internal cord. The section of the bow is almost square. The profile has a marked kink, possibly due to distortion. The catch-plate, in contrast with the preceding iron specimens, is tall. (FE 303, G IV 12, phase V, later 4th century)

Multi-coil sprung-pin brooches of this kind are uncommon and it is far from certain that all should belong to the same time span. One from Fishbourne was dated AD 43 to *c* 75 (Cunliffe 1971, 100, fig 37, 15); another from Werrington, Cambs, was dated *c* AD 50/60–100 (Mackreth 1988, 91, fig 20, 2). These merely indicate the general period during which post-Conquest brooches of the Nauheim and *Drahtfibel* types were in use. However, the use of iron may point to pre-Conquest manufacture.

Aesica

46 The spring is held in the Polden Hill manner (see above 5), the chord passing through a pierced crest. The details of the brooch are masked by corrosion. Each wing is short and appears to have a moulding at the end. The crest is continued as a ridge down the centre of the strongly arched upper bow which ends in the centre of a disc at the top of the fantailed lower bow. The top of the disc joins the top of the upper bow. There is a projecting moulding along the bottom. (CA 152, C VI 37, phase VII, early to mid-4th century)
47 The spring is held by the same method as that in 46. Each wing has a groove at the end. The crest lies at the top of a beaded ridge running between a hollow down each side of the upper bow. The upper bow itself splays out to a knob on each side before returning in a concave curve to the top of the lower bow. This has a series of cross-mouldings above a fantail foot which has a moulding across the bottom edge and a pair of dot-and-circle motifs in the middle. (CA 53, AA III 1, unphased)

Discussion of the origins and distribution of the Aesica type (46–7) has shown conclusively that it is derived from the Rosette, possibly more from the *Kragenfibel* version than the standard one (see brooch 64), and that this development took place in southern England (Mackreth 1982). Of these two examples, 46 is typologically the earlier as its construction shows that it is closer to the parent. Dating is still very rare and there is not enough to give good sense of direction in the developments which can be seen. The type must have evolved when the full-blown Rosette was both popular and frequently seen and that could hardly be later than ten to five years before the Conquest. The earliest dated Aesica, however, still remains the one from Waddon Hill, Stoke Abbott: *c* AD 50–60 (Webster 1981, 60, fig 25, 2). It has the Polden Hill spring system and the same form of casting as 46, although the form of the upper bows differ and the Waddon Hill example is relatively highly decorated. Because these closely copy the full Rosette, and have a more complicated casting to achieve this, such brooches should not have remained long in manufacture after the demise of the parent type and survivors-in-use may all have been discarded by AD 65/70. A good sign that a great many, if not most, Aesicas belong to the period before AD 60/65 is the large number using the Rearhook method of holding the chord of the spring (see 2) which has a terminal date of AD 60/65 (Mackreth forthcoming (d)). Brooch 47 on the other hand is not only later, but also belongs to what is perhaps the most widespread and common of the main varieties. Dating is still exiguous: Camelon, *c* AD 80–90 or AD 143–160/165 (Christison 1901, 403, fig 42; Hartley, 1972b, 8). That some Aesicas run well into the 2nd century is shown by an example from Osmanthorpe, Notts, which is tricked out with enamel and applied silvery trim (Mackreth 1993, 184–5, fig 10,3) and a recent survey of the dating of the Osmanthorpe brooch strongly suggested that it is hardly earlier than *c* AD 125 (Mackreth forthcoming (d)). The use of prominent dot-and-circle on 47 can be paralleled on another group of brooches (eg Wheeler & Wheeler 1936, 206, fig 43, 19) which runs from the late 1st century well into the 2nd, perhaps as far as AD 150/175. This *might* be an indicator in general terms of the proper *floruit* of 47.

Trumpets

Brooches 48–9, 51–2, and 54 have their springs mounted like that on brooch 36. Brooch 49 has the whole system surviving. On brooches 53, 56–8, and probably 54, where there is a cast-on loop or tab and no need for a wire loop, reliance seems to have been placed on a plain axis bar with the chord tucked firmly into a notch in the bottom of the loop behind the head of the bow. Brooches 50 and 59 have their springs seated between pierced plates in what is a version of the Polden Hill method (see above 5).

48 The trumpet head is decorated with relief ornament. Round the base are three bosses each rising from a hollow. Two more occur on either side of the head and are linked by relief versions of the comma motif so common in late Iron Age art. The bosses at the bottom are linked by ridges above them. The ridges sweep up to form a pair running up the centre. The knob consists of three groups of triple mouldings, the central one being very prominent. The lower bow has a median ridge with another down each side. In each panel so formed is another ridge forming a wavy line. The foot-knob is separated from a cross-moulding at the base of the bow by a flute and again has three mouldings with the middle one being large. (CA 283, E II 9, phase XIII, after AD 353)

Brooches with either relief or inlaid ornament belong to the upper Severn Valley, although outliers occur. There seems to be no distinctive chronological span within the overall *floruit* (see after 59).

49 The collar has a triple moulding across its front. The trumpet head is plain with a groove around the top. The knop is of the common petalled form with a triple moulding above and below. The lower bow has a median arris and a groove down each side. The foot-knob has three cross-mouldings. (CA 357, E IV 37, phase VI, early 3rd century?)

This is the only example in this collection of the standard plain trumpet whose distribution is mainly up the eastern side of England from East Anglia to the north and into Scotland.

50 On the head is a cast-on loop on a pedestal. The trumpet head has a groove around it and a median arris. The knop is a simplified version of that on the last with only a single moulding above and below. The lower bow and the foot-knob repeat those of the last. Both the knop and the foot-knob are not carried right round the bow. (CA 428, E V 1, unphased)

Only two precise parallels have come to the notice of the writer: Harlow, Essex (France & Gobel 1985, 79, fig 41, 74); Ware, Herts (excavations by C Partridge).

51 The trumpet head is narrow and runs into the middle of a dished head-plate with diagonal cross-cuts on the border moulding. The knop is like that of the last with two mouldings top and bottom. The lower bow is narrow, plain, and runs down to a foot-knob consisting of a boss beneath two mouldings. (CA 427, E II 32, phase IV, Hadrianic–Antonine)

52 The same as the last, but with three triangular cells for enamel on each side and with a knop made up of three mouldings with a pair of mouldings above and below. The catch-plate return has a sunken moulding at the top and a pair in the middle. (CA 360, E IV 23, phase III, Neronian–Trajanic)

Only one close parallel to 51 is known to the writer: Wycomb, Glos (Rawes 1980, 48, no 3). However, the head, lower bow, and foot-knob of 52 are so similar that it almost certainly came from the same manufactory as 51. The presence of cells for enamel is no hindrance and there is evidence elsewhere in other groups of brooches that a repertoire of ornament was used to produce variations on a basic theme. The decorated catch-plate of 52 is an early feature and should serve to place this brooch in the first half of the overall *floruit* (see after 59).

53 There is a large disc cast on the head. The trumpet is small and plain. The knop consists of three cross-mouldings, the middle one being large, separated from the rest of the brooch, top and bottom, by a flute and then a pair of 'petals'. The lower bow is plain, tapering to a small foot-knob with a moulding above. (CA 438, D IV 2, unphased)
54 The same as the last, but without the disc and with a ridge down the trumpet and an arris on the lower bow. (CA 123, C I U/S, unphased)

The group to which brooches 53 and 54 belong lies basically in the south-western parts of England, including the lower Severn Valley.

55 The head is lost and the rest is corroded. The brooch appears to have been broadly similar to the last two. (CA 145, C II U/S, unphased)
56 Very corroded. The spring-fixing arrangement is like that of the previous brooches. There are the stubs of a cast-on loop on the plain head. The knop here is made up of three cross-mouldings of almost equal size. The lower bow is plain and ends in a triple-moulded foot-knob. (CA 445, E II 27, phase V, late 2nd century?)
57 The trumpet head has been reduced to a moulding round the straight-sided upper bow which ends in a head-plate describing a curve with a lozenge-shaped tab on the top. The knop is like that of the last brooch. The lower bow is plain, narrow, and ends in a simple projecting foot-knob. (CA 426, E IV 38, phase IV, Hadrianic–Antonine)
58 The upper bow has no mouldings around its top and the head-plate has been reduced, but there is now a very large pierced round-headed plate on top only visually separated from the lower part by a cut-out on each side. The knop repeats those of the previous two brooches. The lower bow is broad with a central arris and a small projecting moulding at the bottom. (CA 112, AA II 66, phase III, 3rd century)

The fairly even-sized mouldings on the knops of 56–8 are distinctive, but not very many brooches with this type of spring arrangement have them. However, a group having the same spring system as 59 is marked by this type of knop, although there are usually four mouldings (eg Hattatt 1985, 111, fig 45, 439). The distribution of this group lies in the southern Pennines and spreads out more to the west and north-east than in any other direction. If the few specimens of the same basic style as brooches 56–8 are looked at, they seem to belong to the periphery of this distribution.

59 On the head is a broken cast-on loop on a cross-moulded pedestal. The trumpet has a groove round the upper edge and a marked arris down each side. The knop is unusual in having a central groove with a pair of divided lenticular bosses above and below. The lower bow has a groove down the middle and ends in a prominent foot-knob with a chevron groove around the side. (CA 503, M III 13, phase III, mid-4th century)

The last brooch does not belong to any sub-variety of Trumpet so far isolated by the writer. The Trumpet brooch is sometimes thought to be of northern origin. The comments on the distributions of the Alcester Trumpets should show that this does not hold and, while no satisfactory origin for the type has yet been brought forward, the earliest dated pieces belong to southern England in a broad sense. The dating of the type has recently been discussed (Mackreth forthcoming (c)) and the list runs from before *c* AD 75 to 150/175. Brooches 56–7 may be added to the list.

Unclassified

60 The spring was held like that in 52. The head-plate has a squared top and a rounded bottom to suit the chord of the spring. On top is a cast-on loop on a pedestal. The upper bow is straight-sided, has a flat top, with two longitudinal cells for enamel, and is rounded underneath. There is a knop made up of three cross-mouldings. The lower bow has a central arris and a groove down each side. The foot-knob has a projection on each side. The catch-plate return has a vertical ridge at its start, a groove at the top and in the middle, and a diagonal one in the panels so formed. (CA 209, D I 1A, unphased)
61 The spring was mounted on a single loop. The head-plate is like that of 58. The upper bow, damaged by corrosion, is almost straight-sided, has a nearly rectangular section, is flat at the top, and has a median arris at the bottom. At the junction of the upper and lower bow is a line of three bosses. The lower bow has a central ridge, a groove down each side, and its sides sweep up behind the lower part of the upper bow. The foot-knob consists of two mouldings. (CA 147, C VI 37, phase VII, early to mid-4th century)
62 The spring is mounted like that on 59. The head-plate is like the previous two, but with slightly rounded top corners. It has a cast-on loop and pedestal. The upper bow is damaged by corrosion and all the lower bow is missing. Down the centre are the remains of a ridge, with cross-cuts, relieved on each side by a step. On each side are two, possibly three, divided ridges. (CA 67, B I 20, unphased)

The complete form of 62 is shown by a brooch from Cirencester (excavations by J S Wacher) which reveals that the lowest decorative element at the end of the surviving bow on the Alcester example is another pair of divided ridges but dipping in the centre. The lower bow has a marked recurve and the foot-knob probably had two projections. These two features are represented on brooches 60 and 61 here. The origins of the basic design are obscure and there are examples using several spring systems. The commonest, however, is that on 60 and 62. The dating evidence for the developed version is: Silchester, AD 100–20 (Cotton 1947, 145, fig 8, 3); Derby, AD 115–40 (Mackreth 1985, 293–4, fig 128, 33); Biglands, Cumbria, AD 125–180/200 (Potter 1977, 171, fig 11, 16). Considering the size of the group, the dating is limited, but the range indicated is the 2nd century to about AD 150/175, roughly the same as the Trumpet with which it usually bears a close affinity.

Late La Tène

63 Corrosion hides any traces of decoration on the spring case. The rest of the brooch is set off from the spring-case by a short and plain bridge. The main part was a single plate shaped as a disc with a fantail foot. Only the disc survives, it has three peripheral grooves and a rivet through the middle. Trapped under the rivet are the remains of a repoussé plate which once covered the disc. Not illustrated. (CA 144, C IXA 4, unphased)

The reduction of the full Rosette to a simple plate occurs at the end of the sequence and the final forms have a hinged pin. The British dating for the present type is: Verulamium, King Harry Lane cemetery, phase 2, two examples, AD 30–55 (Stead & Rigby 1989, 290, fig 99, 67.2, 3); Bagendon, two examples, AD 20/25–43/45 and AD 43/45–47/52 (Clifford 1961, 175, fig 32, 2, 3); Colchester, AD 44–60 (Niblett 1985, 116, fig 74, 22), AD 49–61 (Hawkes & Hull 1947, 316, pl XCIV, 81); Baldock, AD 50–70 (Stead & Rigby 1986, 113, fig 46, 100); Colchester, AD 54–60 (Niblett 1985, 116, fig 74, 24), AD 60–80? (Crummy 1983, 8, fig 3, 17). The range is reasonably restricted: maximum, AD 30–80?, but most had passed out of use by *c* AD 55/60.
64 Iron. The spring is mounted in the Colchester manner (see brooch 1), the hook being lost. The wings are short and plain. The

upper bow is thin with a broad top and splays outwards towards the base where it returns in a shallow curve to form a thin stem which passes through a separately made disc. The lower bow is a much narrower version of the upper. The only decoration which can be seen is a groove around the sides and bottom of the upper bow and one, possibly two, grooves across the foot of the lower bow. However, there may have been a pair of grooves down the centre of the upper bow. (FE 314, D I 109, phase II, later 2nd to early 3rd century?)

An example of the *Kragenfibel*, a rare type in Britain, only four having been recorded by the writer: Colchester (Hawkes & Hull 1947, 313, pl XCIII, 67); Odell, Beds (excavations by B Dix); Holbrooks, Old Harlow (Harlow Museum, C259); Abbotstone, Hants (information from N A Griffiths). Only one came from a dated context: Odell, late 1st to early 2nd century AD. The *Kragenfibel* is Feugère's Type 10 and the present example is a cross between his Type 10a1 and 10a2 (Feugère 1985, 243–4). Feuègre points out (1985, 246) that the dating is partially fixed by the probable appearance of the type on the coins of Criciru (Allen 1972). The alternative candidate for the type on the coins is the one of the earliest kinds of Rosette. However, the very high arched bow of the Criciru brooch is better suited to *Kragenfibel* of Feugère's Type 10a1. The earliest manifestation of the type seems to be the first quarter of the 1st century BC. Although examples have been recovered from contexts dated to the early 1st century AD (Feuègre 1985, 246), the actual form of the Alcester brooch with its disc is more typical of the middle of the 1st century BC. The writer would not care to place this example later than that century for, had it been in full production along with the typical Augustan–Tiberian Rosettes, some at least would surely have been found in this country associated with them, yet it appears to be singularly absent from assemblages producing those.

Aucissa–Hod Hills

65 The head-plate has a central flute, a bead-row next to the pin and, faintly, the name AVCIS|SA in relief, the A lacking the cross-bar. The upper bow is of the normal form: a sunken bead-row down the middle of a swollen front and a ridge on each border. The lower bow is flat with a minimal moulding at the top. The usual two-part foot-knob is sweated or brazed on. (CA 433, J I 11, phase VIII, 3rd century?)

66 A very large version of the last. Uninscribed, the head-plate has the bead-row next to the bow. Three small cross-mouldings divide the two parts of the bow; the lower part has chamfers meeting in an arris. The foot-knob is like that of 65. (CA 122, AA I 71, unphased)

No named Aucissa or any which can be attributed to the manufactory has been found in an undoubtedly pre-Conquest context. The distinction between the kind of Aucissa exemplified by 65 and 66 and others lies in the simplicity of the head-plate which has, at best, a small cut-out at the end of the flute, but never 'eyes' or elaborate cut-outs. As the descendant of the Aucissa and its parallel forms, the Hod Hill, arrives in great quantity at the Conquest, the end of the manufacture and use of the Aucissa must fall very early in the Roman period. The best evidence would suit *c* AD 50–60 for the end of the period of use.

67 In five pieces and heavily corroded, the design can be reconstructed to give, on the upper bow, a panel with four vertical ridges divided by flutes, with a pair of cross-mouldings above and below. The lower bow is flat and tapers to the usual two-part foot-knob. (CA 415, D I 210, unphased)

68 The upper bow has three cross-mouldings above and below a pair of prominent ones. The lower bow is short, flat, and tapers to a two-part foot-knob. There are traces of tinning or silvering. (CA 369, D I 107, phase I, 1st century to early Antonine)

69 The upper bow is straight-sided with a rounded front which has a groove down it. There is a pair of bold cross-mouldings at the bottom. The lower bow is damaged and the foot-knob is missing. The upper edges sweep out to each side and there signs of a taper to the foot. There are lines of punched dots on the front and traces of tinning or silvering. (CA 453, F I 89, unphased)

Only one Hod Hill has been published from an unequivocal pre-Conquest context: Baldock, AD 1–25 (Stead & Rigby 1986, 120, fig 47, 112). However, as it would predate its own parent, there must be something wrong with this attribution. The distribution of Hod Hills in Britain shows clearly that they were in common use until the decade AD 60–70, but had largely passed out of use by the latter date as it is rare in the lands taken into the province by Petillius Cerialis. Only one strain of the type survived beyond this and, on the Continent, developed into new types with enamelled ornament. None of the present examples is a member of this group and all should have been consigned to the ground by AD 75.

Unclassified

70 The spring is mounted between two pierced lugs. There had been a cast-on loop on the head. The upper bow is a trumpet and is plain apart from a groove across it near the top. At the bottom of the trumpet is a boldly projecting semi-circular plate. The lower bow is flat with a rounded bottom ending in a nib. On the front face are faint traces of applied ornament, mainly of two circles one above the other. (CA 160, A XVI T/S, unphased)

The nearest relative to this brooch appears to be a group based on Almgren's 101 occurring both on the German *limes* and along the Elbe. Its origins have been placed between AD 80 and 120 (Fischer 1966). The type is often tricked out with applied silver trim, a striking resemblance to the treatment of the British type. The British dating is weak: Camerton, 2nd century, probably Antonine (Wedlake 1958, 223, fig 52, 16); Leicester, before *c* AD 220 (Kenyon 1948, 251, fig 80, 15). However, this meagre information can probably be assisted by the general conclusion arrived at elsewhere (Mackreth forthcoming (d)) that the use of applied trim in Britain is basically after AD 125.

71 The head and spring are missing. The latter would have been like that of a Colchester (see 34) with very short and plain wings. The upper bow is straight-sided with a swollen front. At the point of inflection in the profile there is a small cross-moulding. The lower bow is like the upper, only flatter. There is no trace of decoration. (CA 346, E I 93, unphased)

A variety of the *Augenfibel*, the British dating is: Richborough, AD 50–120 (Bushe-Fox 1932, 77, pl IX, 7); Baldock, AD 90–120 (Stead & Rigby 1986, 112, fig 42, 49). This is not a good guide in itself to the correct *floruit* as the main type should be expected in this country in the earlier years of the Roman occupation, but it is noticeable that none of the present variety is evidenced from forts of exclusively early date. It is tempting to see it as the final version of the type and belonging mainly to the last few decades of the 1st century.

Plate

72 The circular plate has four projections, the one above the head of the pin having a cast-on loop. Most of the face of the brooch is taken up by a shallow dome rising from a groove. In the centre is a dimple and around that are two zones of triangular cells for enamel now alternately blue and green. (CA 424, F IV 55, unphased)

One of the commonest of British plate brooches, the design varies only in the number, rows, and style of triangular cells and the presence or absence of a border, scalloped or with projections. The dating is: Wroxeter, *c* AD 100 (Bushe-Fox 1913, 26, fig 10, 9); Harlow, AD 120–200 (France & Gobel 1985, 80, fig 41, 82); Ravenglass, AD 130–200 (Potter 1979, 67, fig 26, 2); Canterbury, mid-2nd century (Williams 1947, 84, fig 9, 1); Alchester, 3rd century and later (Hawkes 1927, 181, fig 11, 3). The date-range, therefore, is certainly 2nd century and a few may have survived in use into the 3rd. Examples from later contexts are probably residual.

73 The bilateral spring is mounted on a single pierced lug. The front of the circular plate is gilded. In the centre is a raised setting for a paste gem in the form of a ring doughnut. Between this and the bordering ridge is a series of S-shaped stamps. (CA 321, G II 2, unphased)

The dating evidence for this British type has recently been reviewed: first half of the 3rd century (Mackreth forthcoming (d)).

74 The brooch is very corroded. The pin appears to have been sprung. The shape of the plate is either that of a lozenge or of a vesica; its edges are scalloped. In the centre is a raised vesica-shaped area with a cell for enamel in the top. All that can be seen in the cell are traces of three glass dots. (CA 213, H II 1, unphased)

75 The pin is hinged. The plate is lozenge-shaped with a boss on each corner and nine cells filled with enamel, now discoloured, of two tones arranged checky fashion. (CA 227, D I 18A, phase VI, mid- to late 4th century?)

76 The pin is hinged. The plate is lozenge-shaped and its surface entirely given over to enamel, now completely corroded, but betraying signs that it might have been in blocks recalling the use of millefiore. (CA 536, M III 32, phase I, late 2nd to early 3rd century)

None of 74–6 belongs to a well-defined group. The use of enamel to cover large areas such as on 75 and 76, and the presence of raised platforms and scalloped edges like those on 74, are marks of 2nd-century brooches.

77 The sprung pin is mounted between two pierced lugs. The shape of the plate is that of a shoe-sole with a loop attached to the heel. The surface was enamelled in two colours, now decayed. Two curved reserved bars form first, a closed cell at the toe end and, secondly, an open one near the heel. (CA 104, AA III U/S, unphased)

The shoe-sole is the commonest shape of everyday object used for a brooch. Others include flagons, purses, lamps, axes, daggers, and shields. There is no reason to suppose that the various enamelled examples have different date-ranges from each other and the evidence is: *Verulamium*, shield, AD 80–150 (Wheeler & Wheeler 1936, 209, fig 45, 34); Quinton, plain, AD 100–70 (Friendship-Taylor 1979, 138, fig 63, 478); Shakenoak Farm, Wilcote, Oxon, 2nd century (Brodribb *et al* 1973, 108, fig 53, 179); Augst, Hadrianic to early 3rd century (Riha 1979, 203, *Taf* 68, 1749–56, *passim*); *Verulamium*, AD 135–45 (Frere 1984, 29, fig 9, 50); Cramond, purse, *c* AD 140–200+ (Rae and Rae 1974, 193, fig 14, 2); Caerleon, AD 160–230 (Brewer 1986, 172, fig 55, 14); Camerton, axe, AD 180–350 (Wedlake 1958, 232, fig 54, 55); Dover, flagon, *c* AD 190–210, later? (Philp 1981, 150, fig 32, 71). All those without the mention of a shape are shoe-soles. The date-range is obviously the 2nd century with the possibility that a few continued into the earliest 3rd.

Penannulars

78 The ring has a circular section. Each terminal is turned back along the ring and the surviving one has four cross-mouldings across the top. After the loss of one terminal, the rest was bent to form a ring. Not illustrated. (CA 422, G IA 68, phase IV, early to mid-4th century)

The actual number of mouldings, or cross-cuts, in this type of design must, on occasion, have been dictated by both the length of the terminal and the eye of the manufacturer. Therefore, no distinction is made between those with three or more mouldings or cross-cuts. Even so the dating is sparse: Longthorpe, Cambs, Claudian–Neronian (Dannell & Wild 1987, 87, fig 21, 12). If those with two depressions are looked at, the picture is a little better: Bagendon, AD 43/45–47/52 (Clifford 1961, 184, fig 36, 9); Longthorpe, *c* AD 45–60/65 (Frere & St Joseph 1974, 46, fig 24, 15); Waddon Hill, Stoke Abbott, Dorset, two examples *c* AD 50–60 (Webster 1960, 97, fig 7, 21; Webster 1981, 62, fig 59, 13); *Verulamium*, AD 80–150 (Wheeler & Wheeler 1936, 210, fig 45, 39); Shakenoak Farm, Wilcote, Oxon, later 3rd century (Brodribb *et al* 1971, 110, fig 47, 71). The impression is that this group matches the one with three or more depressions: there *may* be no significant difference in date.

79 In very poor condition, the ring has a circular section. The terminals are turned back along the ring. The better-preserved terminal has a hollow in the top. Not illustrated. (CA 72, B I 16, phase II, Antonine to 3rd century)

80 Iron. Heavily corroded; the details show best on the X-ray. The ring appears to have a circular section. Each terminal is turned back along the top of the ring and probably has a dip in the centre of the top surface. The pin is nearly straight and has a plain wrap-round. (FE 255, G I 90, unphased)

There is no sure guide as to what the proper design of the terminals of 79 and 80 had been. It is likely that both brooches date to the first two centuries AD, except that the use of iron for 80 suggests the mid-1st century at the latest. The lack of a bow in the pin of 80 shows that it does not belong to the 1st century BC.

81 Now twisted, this may not be a brooch but some form of handle. However, the terminals are not really coiled enough to loop round anything. The ring has a vertical oval section. Each terminal is turned back along the ring, is plain, and narrows almost to a point at the end. Not illustrated. (CA 32, A XI 2A, unphased).

82 A brooch too corroded for comment except for the terminals which are turned back along the ring. Not illustrated. (CA 55, B III 4, unphased)

83 Iron. Most of a ring with no trace of terminals. Not certainly a Penannular. Not illustrated. (FE 24, A IX 6, unphased)

Fragments (Not illustrated)

84 The pin and fragmentary spring from a Colchester Derivative brooch with an axis bar through the coils. Before *c* AD 150/175. (CA 318, G I 90, unphased).

85 A pin from a penannular brooch. (CA 52, AA III 1, unphased)

86 A pin from a brooch. (CA 169, C VIA 84, phase III, 3rd century)

87 A brooch pin. (CA 274, E III 34A, phase VIII)

88 A spring and pin. (CA 164, C IIIA 6, unphased)

89 A spring and pin. (CA 363, E IV 22, phase VI, early 3rd century?)

90 A pin and part spring. (CA 373, J II 1, unphased)

91 A part spring and broken pin. (CA 138, B IA 17, unphased)

92 A coil and part of a chord from a brooch spring. (CA 447, G IV 41, phase I?, late 2nd/3rd century?)

93 A hinged brooch pin. (CA 410, G IV 12, phase V, later 4th century)

94 Two shapeless lumps. (CA 351, E IV 35, phase V?, late 2nd century?)

95 A fragment of a bow with only part of the catch-plate and without the head. The bow has a prominent central ridge with a beaded top. (CA 212, D I 23, phase VIII, late 4th century)

Discussion

The iron brooches consist of a single example of the Colchester type (the only one from the excavations), 1, seven late La Tène brooches with internal chords, 39–45 (the last having six coils instead of the usual four), and a *Kragenfibel*, 64.

The use of iron for making brooches in quantity lies before the Conquest and iron brooches dating only after then are hard to find. The Colchester, or any *one* of the other brooches, except for the *Kragenfibel*, could have arrived with the earliest occupants of the purely Roman site, but the number involved does not suit the period after the Conquest. On these grounds, therefore, the presence of eight bow brooches in iron points to a pre-Roman site in the very near neighbourhood of the excavation.

Relatively extensive excavation of lowland Iron Age sites in south-east England has not been matched by the number of excavations in the west of England and this has tended to mask what kind of brooch spectrum should be expected there in the last hundred years before the arrival of the Roman army. Two sites, however, offer some aid: Beckford, Worcs (Wilson 1973; 1974; Goodburn 1978; 1979) and Wasperton, Warwicks (Rankov 1982; Frere 1983a). Beckford produced two or three Colchesters (including a possible one in iron), three late La Tène brooches like those here (of which two were in iron), one Langton Down and eight or ten iron brooches of the early and middle Iron Age, mainly the latter (Mackreth forthcoming (a)). Wasperton had three Colchesters, an iron Colchester Derivative and the lower bow of an unidentified type in iron, an iron *Drahtfibel* and a Langton Down. On these sites there can be little doubt that the bulk of these brooches should be associated with the Iron Age occupation there. The eight iron bow brooches from Alcester should indicate the same and the chance that the *Kragenfibel* could have survived in use to have been brought to the site after *c* AD 45 is very remote. It is a moot point whether the Rosette, 63, should be placed in this group or not.

When it comes to assessing the date of the initial purely Roman occupation, and ignoring the group just discussed, the number of useful brooches is pitifully small, but there are just enough to lessen almost to nil the possibility that all had survived in use beyond their natural term. There are five: 2, and almost certainly 3, belong to the Rearhook type, 63 is a Rosette (but see above) and 65 and 66 are Aucissas, the first being inscribed. Brooches 2 and 3 have a clear terminal date of AD 60/65, unless they were spoils derived from the suppression of Boudicca's rebellion, in which case they might have continued to AD 70/75. The Rosette, however, should have been discarded before AD 60. The same terminal date should apply to the Aucissas, but could be earlier as the best group for 'late' dating is that from Wroxeter which places them in full use in the period AD 55/60. However, the brooch assemblage from the fortress is completely unlike contemporary and earlier military sites elsewhere in Roman Britain (Mackreth forthcoming (b)).

There is perhaps little direct evidence for a fort as such at Alcester, and there are not enough relevant brooches to discuss what would form a typical military assemblage in any case (Mackreth forthcoming (b) and (c)). Discussion, therefore, is confined to these five: there are also three Hod Hills (67–9) which might have been brought into the argument, but their terminal date could have been as late as AD 70/75 and so they need not have arrived as early as the others. The possibility that the Rearhooks may have been collected after the collapse of Boudicca's revolt can perhaps be discounted: there are no other brooches belonging to the same date-range from the eastern parts of Britain. The geographical bias of the other Colchester Derivatives which may go back to AD 60 (4–6), as well as those which follow directly, is towards the south-west. Therefore, the probability is that the Rearhooks arrived on the site within their normal *floruit*. This being so, these few early brooches point to a foundation date for the site of *c* 50–60 or 55–65 depending on whether the latest date is taken, or an optimum range is preferred. However, the possibility of an earlier site being close by may remove the Rearhooks from the argument as this type had a tendency to spread sporadically to the west across the Midlands and at a site like Bagendon (Clifford 1961, 172, fig 31, 1, 2, 4) they probably arrived very early and independently of any Roman activity.

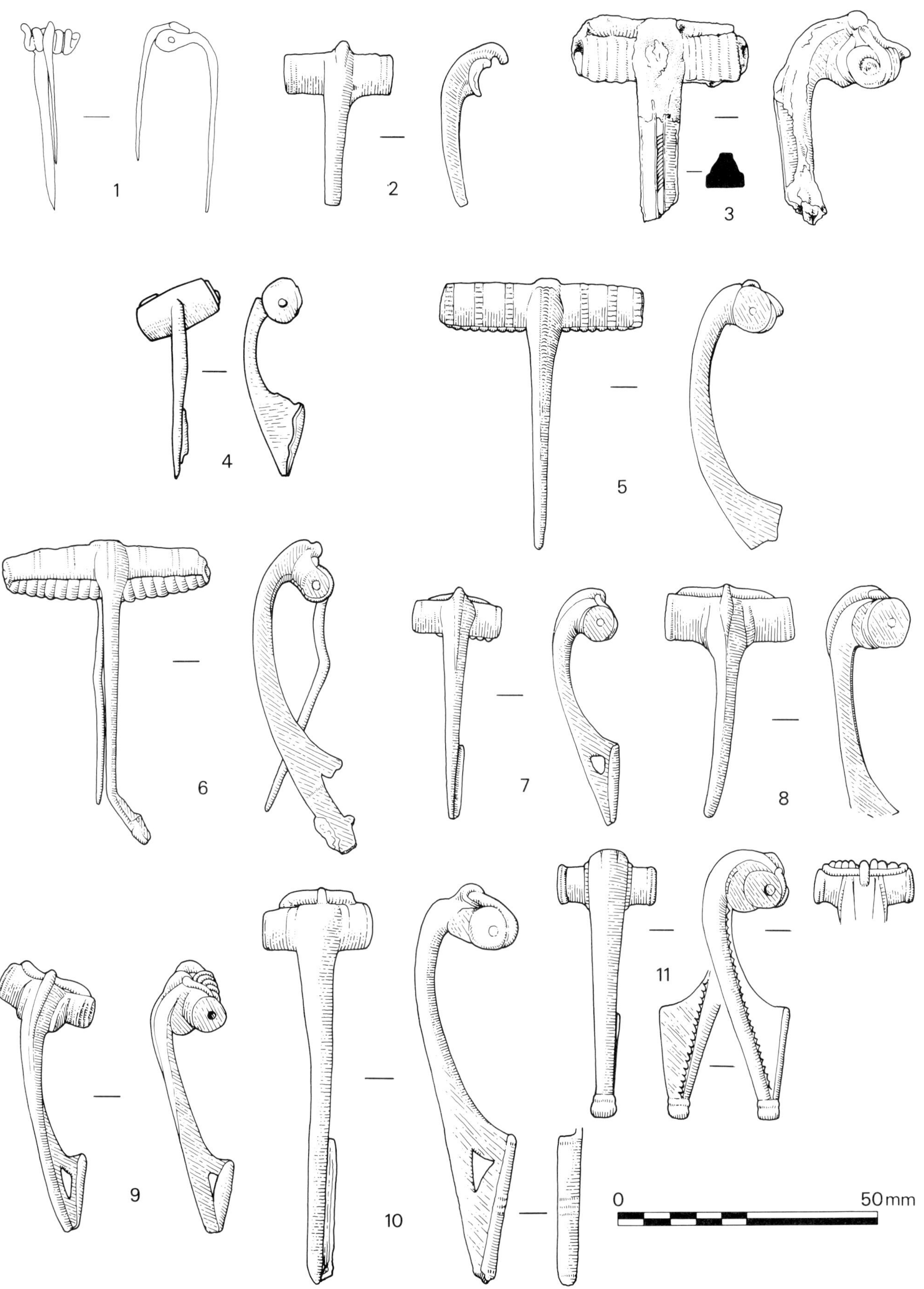

Figure 75 Copper alloy and iron brooches, nos 1–11

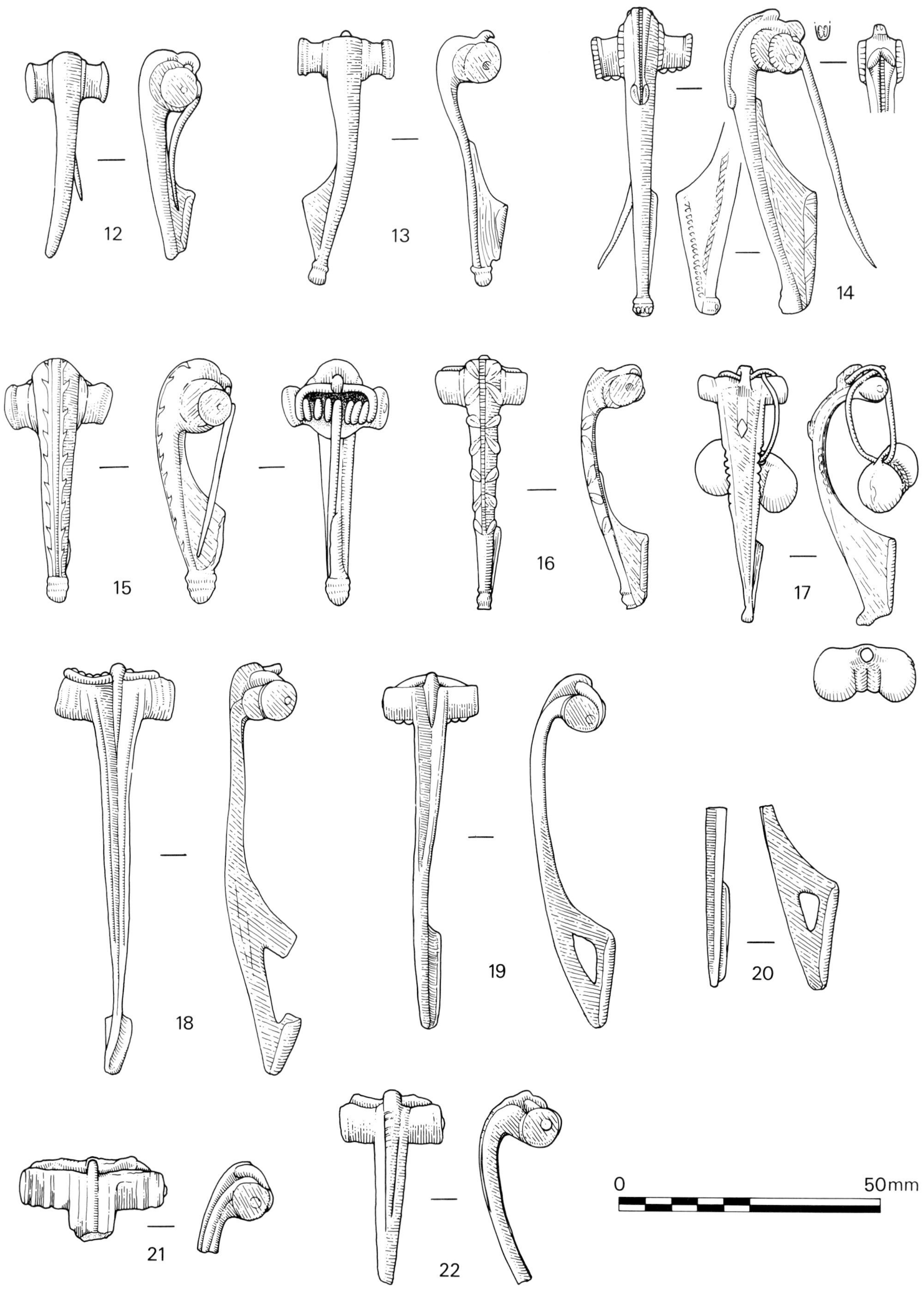

Figure 76 Copper alloy and iron brooches, nos 12–22

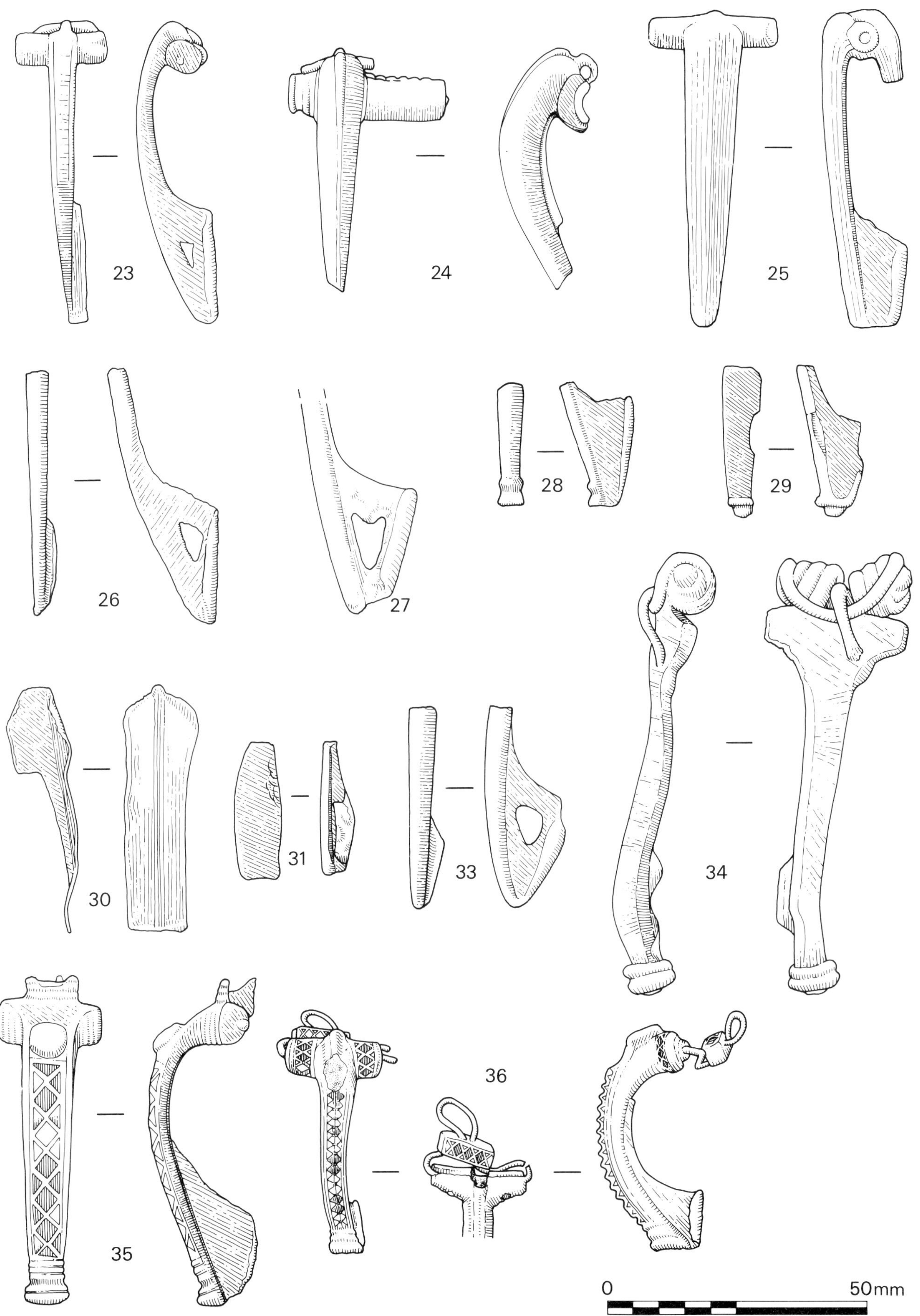

Figure 77 Copper alloy and iron brooches, nos 23–36

Figure 78 Copper alloy and iron brooches, nos 37–51

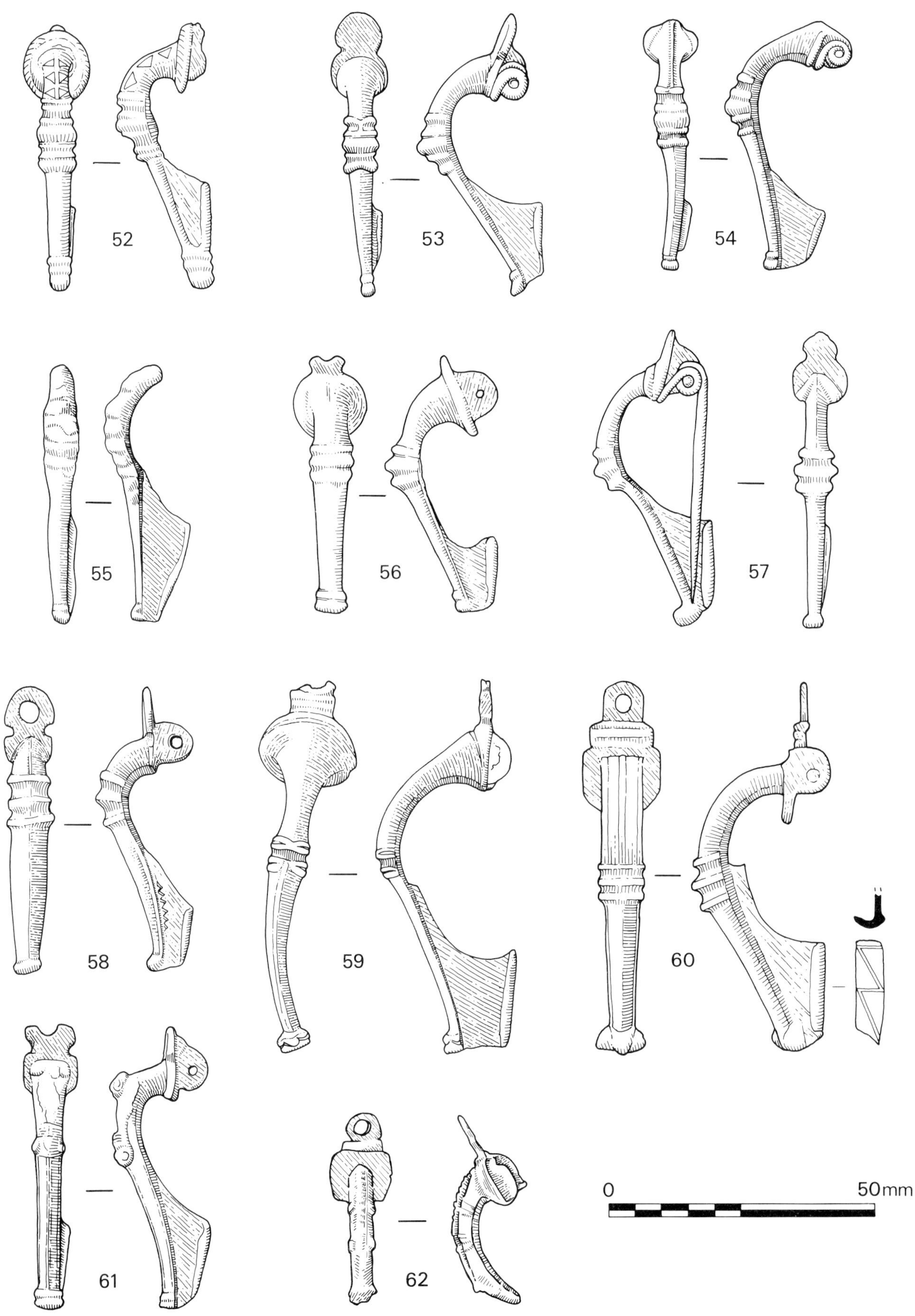

Figure 79 Copper alloy and iron brooches, nos 52–62

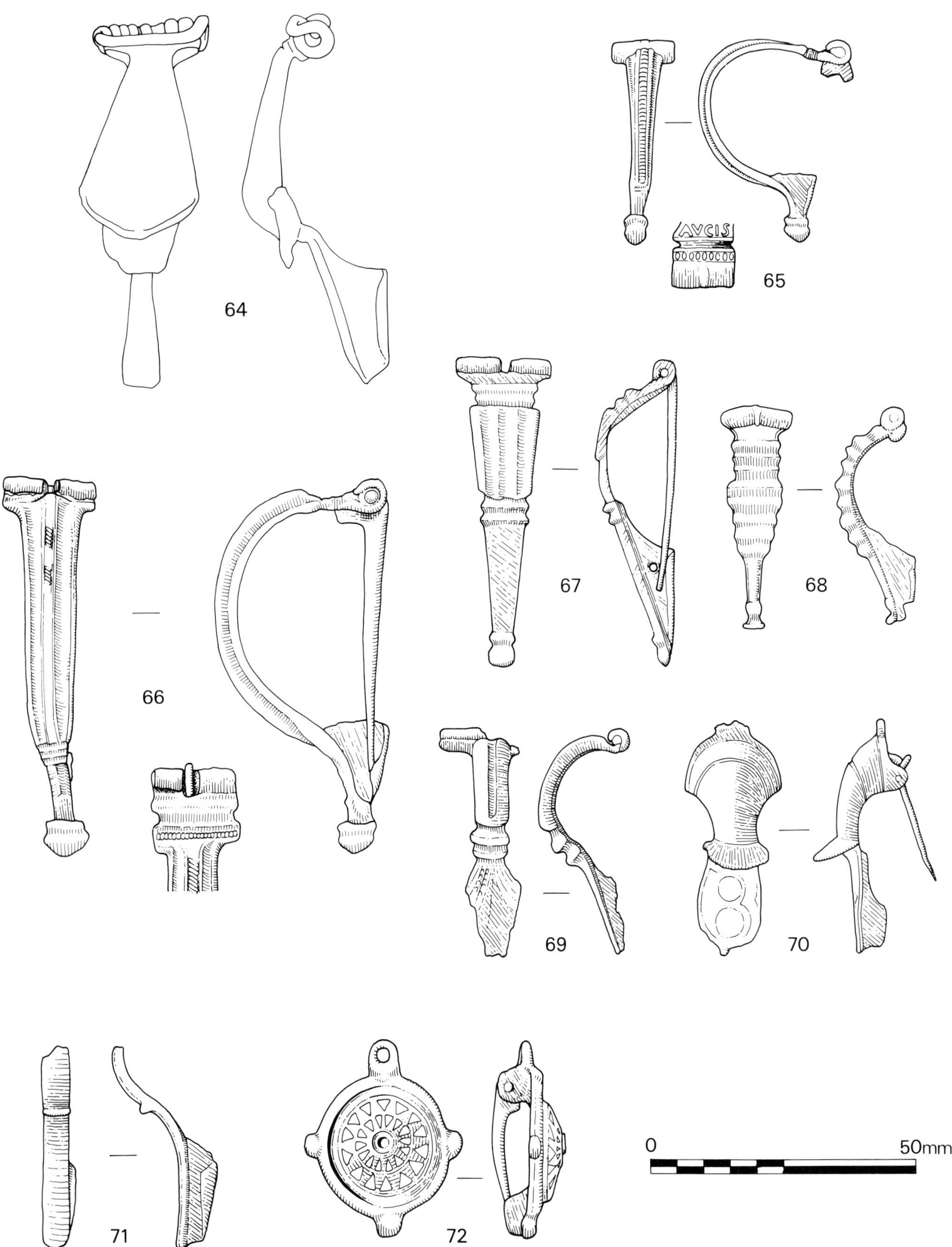

Figure 80 Copper alloy and iron brooches, nos 64–72

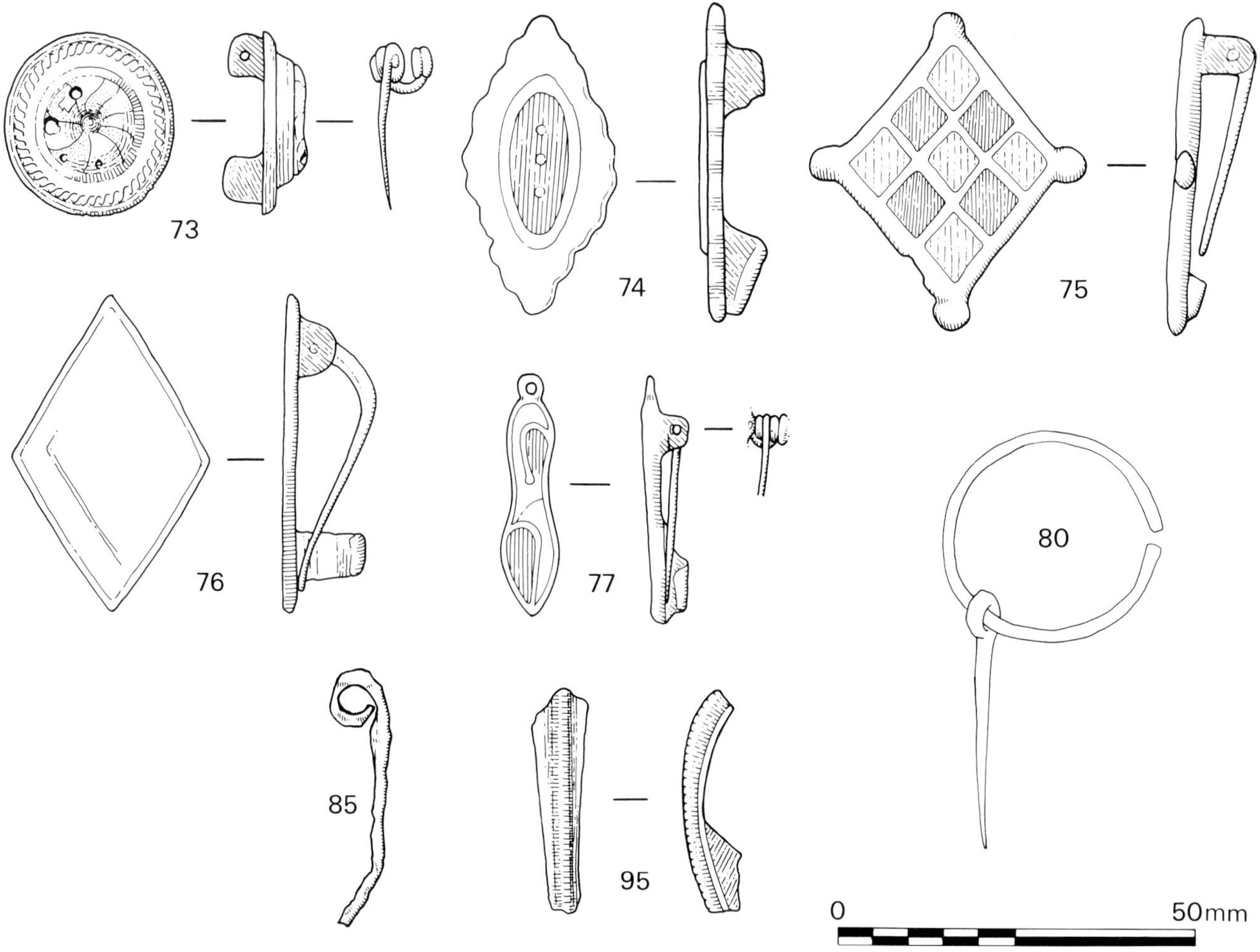

Figure 81 Copper alloy and iron brooches, nos 73–95

Copper alloy objects excluding brooches

G Lloyd-Morgan

[M3:D12] All Roman and possibly Roman items have been included. The list below comprises illustrated objects only (figs 82–92); the full list of objects can be found in the microfiche. Details of post-Roman items are available in the archive.

Dress fasteners

1 Dress fastener with plain disc-shaped head, and solid triangular shaped loop, complete. Diam head 14.9mm × 15.8mm, overall length *c* 23.5mm. (CA 328, F I 1, unphased)

This piece belongs to Wild's class Vc, with a suggested 2nd-century date (Wild 1970b, 140, fig 1). However, recent excavations at the Fortress Baths, Caerleon, produced a piece from a context dated to before AD 100/110 (Zienkiewicz 1986, 173, no 12, fig 56). Another piece now in the Yorkshire Museum was formerly thought to have been associated with the hoard of cavalry fittings found at Fremington Hagg (Webster 1971, cf 118, no 77, fig 15).

Rings

3 Finger-ring with raised cylindrical mount on oval bezel set with a blue glass gem *en cabuchon*. The hoop is incomplete and a little distorted, the one surviving shoulder being decorated with five transverse hatchings. Internal diam front to back *c* 12mm, bezel *c* 7.3mm × 9mm, ht bezel 7mm. (CA 506, M III 13, phase III, mid-4th century)

This type of ring is not uncommon, and a parallel example also set with a blue glass gem is briefly discussed in Allason-Jones & Miket (1984, 125, no 3.194, also listed as no 10.22 on p 347). Another example from Woodeaton, Oxon has a green glass inset (Kirk 1949, 22, no 4, fig 5, no 10), as does another ring from Cirencester (McWhirr *et al* 1982, microfiche BO8, B10, fig 54, no 35).

4 Finger-ring with raised subhexagonal mount on an oval bezel, set with a blue glass gem, the hoop is in five separate fragments but no decoration can be identified. Bezel 7mm × 7mm, ht bezel 6.3mm. (CA 419, G IV 23, phase VI, late 4th century)

Like the other finger-ring, no 3 (CA 506) above, which it closely resembles, it belongs to Henig's Group VIII series which can be dated to around the 3rd century (Henig 1974, part 1, 49, fig 2).

5 Ring with octagonal outer face and circular inner one, otherwise undecorated. Outer diam 22.6–23mm, inner diam *c* 18mm, depth 2.6mm. (CA 450, G IV 41, phase I?, late 2nd/3rd century?)

The ring belongs to Henig's Type IX polygonal rings, dating to the 3rd century. They are found in precious metals as well as copper alloy. Two examples were reported from Neatham, Hants. One nonagonal example came from a late 3rd-century context, and an octagonal silver ring was unstratified (Millett & Graham 1986, 103, fig 71, no 17; and 111, fig 75, no 150 respectively). A copper alloy ring from South Shields is slightly smaller than this one (Allason-Jones & Miket 1984, 122, fig on p 121, no 3.166). Also another piece from *Verulamium* which is described as coming from a context dated AD 365–80, though it is noted that a 3rd-century date is probable (Frere 1984, 31, no 62, fig 10).

6 Curved and moulded fragment, possibly part of the shoulder of a finger ring. Length *c* 11mm, ht 6.4mm. (CA 417, G IV 23, phase VI, late 4th century)

Bracelets

15 Bracelet made of two wires twisted together. Incomplete with about one-third of the hoop surviving, and has an oval cross-section. Length *c* 78mm, cross-section 3.4mm × 2.6mm. (CA 223, H II 1, unphased)

One example from Colchester came from a context dated AD 320–450 (Crummy 1983, 38, no 1611, fig 41); other more closely dated examples come from the Lankhills cemetery, all from graves of around AD 350–70 (Clarke 1979, Type 1a, cf 302, Grave 139, fig 76, no 108, 111; Grave 117, fig 75, no 143; Grave 168, fig 78, no 279). Compare also the piece from Tiddington M45.

19 Incomplete bracelet made of five wires twisted together giving a roughly circular cross-section; one damaged terminal survives. Length 82mm, cross-section *c* 4–4.8mm. (CA 316, G II 2, unphased)

Compare the unstratified example from Whitton, Glamorgan (Jarrett & Wrathmell 1981, 185, no 73, fig 73).

20 Wire with subrectangular cross-section and wound about with *c* four turns of wire at one end. Possibly part of a bracelet with terminal? Length *c* 80mm. (CA 353, F IV 2, phase XIII, after AD 353)

Compare two pieces from South Shields (Allason-Jones & Miket 1984, 132, no 3.249, 3.250, figs on p 133); and another from Colchester (Crummy 1983, 38, no 1601, fig 41, from a grave deposit dated *c* 3rd–4th century AD).

21 Incomplete bracelet with loop terminal and the end turned back on itself and wound round the hoop. Undecorated, and with an oval cross-section. Length 114mm, cross-section 2.8mm × 2.1mm. (CA 317, F I +, unphased)

Compare the complete example from Gestingthorpe (Draper 1985, 29, no 31, fig 10) and a fragment from Bleachfield Street, Alcester which may be related (ALC 1976–7, no 443).

22 Fragment of penannular bracelet with a lightly moulded terminal, oval in cross-section and slightly wider than the hoop. Length 38mm, cross-section hoop *c* 4.8mm × 1.8mm. (CA 31, A X 22, unphased)

Compare the closely related example from Puckeridge-Braughing, Herts (Potter & Trow 1988, 63, fig 26, no 78); and another from Baldock, Herts, found in a late 3rd- or 4th-century context (Stead & Rigby 1986, 125, 128, fig 53, no 188).

25 Fragment of bracelet with slightly expanded terminal, with geometric and linear incised patterns and circles applied, probably in imitation of the snake's head type decoration? The hoop has a rectangular cross-section. Present length *c* 70mm, cross-section hoop 6.2mm × 2mm, max width terminal 9.7mm. (CA 43, B X U/S, unphased)

Compare the complete example from Brockworth, Glos, with a simpler form of decoration on the terminals (Rawes 1981, 66, fig 8, no 8); also the slighter, unpublished pieces from Thistleton, Rutland (THZ 3482 BZ 101 474); and Malton, Yorks 1968–9 (unnumbered).

26 Fragment of bracelet with one terminal in the form of a stylized snake head. Length *c* 55mm, width hoop 6.5mm. (CA 343, D II 21, unphased)

One example of a snake's head bracelet from Canterbury was dated to AD 270–90 (Frere, Stow & Bennett 1982, 124, fig 61, no 31); another from an inhumation grave at Colchester was dated 3rd–4th century (Crummy 1983, 44, fig 45, no 1711).

27 Incomplete strip metal bracelet with rectangular cross-section. The wider outer face is decorated with an incised line as border at each edge, with panels of incised upright hatching lines alternating with others making a rough zig-zag pattern. Part of the eyelet for the fastening survives; the other, hooked terminal is lost. Length 135mm, cross-section 4mm × 1mm. (CA 371, F IV 14, phase XIII, after AD 353)

An exact parallel comes from Dinorben, Denbighshire (Gardner & Savory 1964, 138, fig 18, no 2). Other similar pieces have been reported from *Vindolanda* in a context dated *c* AD 400 or later (Bidwell 1985, 122, fig 41, no 41); Baldock, Herts (Stead & Rigby 1986, 125, fig 52, no 173 where a 4th-century date is suggested); and Lankhills cemetery, Winchester (Clarke 1979, Type D1c, 305, Grave 139, fig 76, no 107, dated AD 350–70).

28 Incomplete strip metal bracelet with rectangular cross-section as above, with one end tapering towards the broken ?hook terminal. The outer face is decorated with an irregular incised wave pattern. Length *c* 68mm, max cross-section 3.8mm × 0.9mm. (CA 495, F V 3, unphased)

29 Strip of slightly varying width in two adjoining pieces with some surviving traces of linear incised decoration. Probably part of a bracelet as CA 371 and 495 above. Length *c* 36mm, max cross-section 6.4mm × 0.9mm. (CA 396, D I 109, phase II, later 2nd to early 3rd century?)

30 Fragment of bracelet with notched 'chip-carved' decoration on the wider outer face, now rolled into a ring with ends overlapping. Length 64mm, max cross-section 3.2mm × 1.6mm. (CA 327, G IV 1, unphased)

Compare the identical decoration on a piece from the Roman theatre at *Verulamium*, said to be from a late 4th-century context (Kenyon 1934, 259, fig 12, no 1); and the one from the Roman cemetery at Lankhills (Clarke 1979, Type D1g, Grave 268, 305, fig 83, no 265, dated AD 350–70, cf also table 2, pp 58–9).

31 Complete bracelet of strip metal tapering towards the terminals, with 'chip-carved' decoration, now come apart at the rivet, which is still *in situ* at one end. The pattern is symmetrical about the centre of the piece. The first section from the terminal is decorated with a central incised line with hatching on either side at the edge; the second section has two small panels with a dot-and-double-circle inside each, and separated from each other, and the sections either side by a transverse incised line; the third and central section consists of three panels with facetted corners to give a raised diamond-shaped effect, each panel being marked off from the other by incised transverse lines. Length *c* 196mm, max cross-section 5mm × 1.2mm. (CA 237, G IA 1A, unphased)

The first two sections are exactly paralleled by examples from Great Dunmow, Essex (Wickenden 1988, 39, 41, fig 31, no 11); and the Fens (Potter 1981, 98, fig 8, no 9 where the bracelet is dated 3rd–4th century). An unpublished fragment from Thistleton, Rutland (THZ 2224 BZ 66 286) has the same diamond-shaped patterns.

32 Hooked terminal of a strip of metal bracelet with moulded and 'chip-carved' decoration, consisting of a diamond-shaped panel similar to the ones found on the bracelet noted above (31), and a long panel with longitudinal moulding with hatching along the outer edges. The remains of transverse moulding can be seen at the break. Length *c* 45mm, max cross-section 5.4mm × 1.5mm. (CA 342, F I 2, unphased)

Similar to the first section of a bracelet also with hooked terminal from Tiddington, Warwicks (TD 81 654).

33 Fragment with rectangular cross-section. The outer narrow edge appears to have traces of light hatching alternating on either side to produce a zig-zag effect. Length *c* 69mm, cross-section 1.2mm × 4.5mm, diam *c* 80mm. (CA 141, C VI 4, phase IX, mid-4th century on)

Compare with examples from Gestingthorpe (Draper 1985, 29, fig 10, no 37); Winterton Villa, Lincs, dated 3rd or 4th century (Stead 1976, 202, fig 103, no 44); and Lankhills cemetery from contexts dated respectively AD 350–70, and 310–350/370 (Clarke 1979, Grave 117, 306, fig 47, no 141, and fig 75; Grave 155, 306, no 196, fig 78). Compare also the example from Alcester, Bleachfield Street, 1976–7, 276.

34 Fragment of a bracelet similar to CA 141 above, but nicked at intervals on the outer narrow edge. Length 17mm, cross-section 1.3mm × 3.3mm. (CA 180, E II 1, unphased)

Two pieces from Shakenoak were dated to the later 3rd century (Brodribb, Hands & Walker 1971, 110, fig 48, no 73, 77); a complete piece from Butt Road, Colchester was found in a grave deposit dated *c* AD 320–450 (Crummy 1983, 38, no 1654, fig 43).

Necklaces and other ornaments

35 Fragments of a necklace, consisting of the fastening section of which one piece is a crook-shaped hook of sheet metal, and the other has the ring-shaped terminal to take it; two almost complete links and four more fragmentary pieces survive, each link being made of wire with a disc-shaped bead of blue or amber-coloured glass threaded on to the middle. Each end of the wire is turned back into a loop and wound round itself for several turns. Length of hook-shaped section of fastener 25.6mm, length of ring-shaped section of fastener 20.2mm, diam of blue beads 4.1mm, length of link with blue bead 12.2mm, diam of amber-coloured bead 4.2mm, length of link with amber-coloured bead 11.4mm. (CA 153, C VIA 12, phase IX, mid-4th century on)

Guido notes that these biconical beads of blue- and amber-coloured glass are datable to the 4th–5th centuries AD (Guido 1978, 97, 98, fig 37, no 12, 13). The hook of this necklace can be paralleled by one from Nettleton found in 'a 4th-century level' — though *pace* Wedlake it is not an earring (Wedlake 1982, 204, fig 85, no 1) — and by another on a necklace from a grave dated AD 350–70 in the Lankhills cemetery, Winchester (Clarke 1979, Grave 336, fig 90, no 363, pl. Ia top, discussed 297, 299, also table 2, p 71).

36 A fragmentary necklace consisting of roughly cubic glass beads on wire links similar to those found in the necklace noted above. The surviving beads consist of fifteen of blue glass, and five made up of layers of different colours: blue, white, red, white, and blue in sequence and vertically pierced. The beaded links were interspersed with flat scroll-shaped links, now represented by four examples in varying states of preservation. One part only of the fastener, namely the hook, has survived. Length of hook 21.2mm, length of scroll-shaped link *c* 10.5mm, bead lengths *c* 4–5mm, cross-sections *c* 3–3.5mm square. (CA 451, G IV 61, phase IV, early to mid-4th century)

Sections of surviving necklace include: two groups of three-beaded links with scroll-shaped link in centre 93mm; terminal hook with beaded links in the following sequence: two blue, one multi-coloured, one blue, one multi-coloured, three blue, length 70mm (illustrated); in conjunction with three blue-beaded links with one scroll link, length 37mm; two multi-coloured beaded links with scroll-shaped link in the centre, length 34mm; one multi-coloured beaded link with scroll-shaped link, length 30.5mm; with three unconnected beaded links.

With the missing ring-shaped section of the fastener and possibly one or two links now lost, the necklace must have originally been at least 300mm or more in length. Guido (1978, 96, fig 37, no 7) has dated the small square-sectioned beads (long or cube-shaped) in translucent blue and other colours to the late 3rd to late 4th century.

Beads similar to these, in layers of blue, white, and red, were found in a grave deposit at Butt Road, Colchester and dated 2nd century to *c* AD 320 (Crummy 1983, 34, fig 36, no 1415). The most complete parallel for the necklace, however, is that found at Gestingthorpe, Essex. It has plain green and plain blue beads as well as multi-coloured ones as here, and the same flat scroll links. It was dated by Guido to the 3rd or more probably the 4th century (in Draper 1985, 68, fig 31, no 346).

37 Elongated hexagonal plaque or fitting, possibly a link from a necklace. Pierced at the narrow ends and decorated with a row of three S-shaped punch marks across the central section. Dimensions 23.2mm × 7.1mm, thickness 0.7mm. (CA 464, G IV 12, phase V, later 4th century)

Pins and needles

39 Pin with spherical head, a little damaged and bent. Diam head 3.5mm, ht 40mm. (CA 11, A I 2, unphased)

Type 3 pin which Crummy (1983, 29, fig 28) suggests was 'current throughout the Roman period'. One example from Winterton Roman Villa was dated to the 4th century by Stead (1976, 207, fig 106). Compare also the unstratified example from Boxmoor House School (Neal 1974–6, 78, fig 46, no 24).

43 Heavily worn example of pin with a baluster-type head similar to no 42 (CA 233). Max diam head 3.5mm, ht *c* 72mm. (CA 284, E IV 15, phase XIII, after AD 353)

Compare the example from Woodeaton (Kirk 1949, 18, fig 4, no 7) and Boxmoor House School (Neal 1974–6, 78, fig 46, no 22), and the related examples from Warwickshire: Alcester ALC69 60; Coleshill GH 1978, 1001; and Tiddington TR 82 61.

44 Pin with baluster-shaped head with two collars below to divide the head from the shaft, and one above, with a tiny cone as a terminal. The surface is a little eroded in places, otherwise complete. Diam head 3mm, length 99mm. (CA 507, M III 6B, phase II, late 2nd to early 3rd century on)

Compare the example from Braughing (Potter & Trow 1988, 61, fig 25, no 44). It is similar to Crummy's Type 2 pin which she dates to the early 2nd to 3rd century AD (1983, 30, no 511, fig 31). A related example from Wadham House, Dorchester, Dorset was found in a context dated *c* AD 150–70 (Draper & Chaplin 1982, 24, fig 12, no 1).

45 Similar to the pin above, but with two tiny collars at either end of the central baluster-shaped moulding, and a tiny cone-shaped terminal. Tip and much of shaft lost. Diam head *c* 2.5mm, ht 47.5mm. (CA 120, AA II 89, phase III, 3rd century)

One example from Woodeaton had a suggested date of second half of the 2nd century AD (Kirk 1949, 18, no 41, pl IIA, no 9); another piece from Nettleton was found in a 3rd-century context (Wedlake 1982, 216, fig 93, no 2). Compare also the pin from Coleshill GH 1979 588 and the related example from Tiddington TD 81 482.

46 Pin with the head decorated with a panel of very light cross-hatching delimited above and below by a firmly incised line. The terminal of the head is a small neat cone. Complete. Diam head *c* 1mm, ht 114.3mm. (CA 14, A V 11, phase VI, late 3rd to early 4th century)

Compare the example from Hemel Hempstead (Neal 1974–6, 114, fig 63, no 3); and the example from Tiddington M737, and the related M689; M693; and from Alcester ALC 1972 2.

47 As above, in two adjoining fragments, tip and lower part of shaft lost. Ht 39.5mm. (CA 92, AA III 11, phase VIII, early to mid-4th century)

48 Pin with slight drum-shaped head, decorated with fine cross-hatching bounded on either side by a fine narrow collar. In two adjoining pieces, rather corroded on the lower section. Diam head 3.2mm, ht *c* 88mm. (CA 377, D I 128, phase II, later 2nd to early 3rd century?)

Compare the related piece from Hunsbury, Northants (Fell 1936, 62, no 2 (e), fig 3, no 5); also Tiddington TD 81 230.

49 Pin with irregular subspherical head. The upper half is decorated with closely packed hatching; the lower half, of slightly smaller diameter, is undecorated, and separated from the shaft by a small crisply defined collar. The tip and much of the shaft is lost. Max diam head 77mm, ht 44.2mm. (CA 84, C V I, unphased)

Compare the related example from Nettleton, Wilts, said to have been found in a 1st- to 2nd-century context (Wedlake 1982, 216, no 16, fig 93); also the unpublished piece from Black Wong, Thistleton, Rutland THZ 284, and perhaps two other pieces from Tiddington M625 and M734 which may be related. An identical example was found during excavations at Mill Street, Caerleon during the mid-1980s (SF 82/086 281).

Mirrors

72 Internal fragment of a hand mirror disc, the surface is finished on both sides. One side is plain, the other turned with three concentric circles. The piece probably comes from near the centre of the original disc. Measuring 15.5mm × 9.4mm, thickness 0.9mm, original diam at least 65mm and probably greater. (CA 394, D I 174, phase I, 1st century to Antonine)

The delicacy of the fragment suggests that the piece probably belonged to the Group G series of hand mirrors (Lloyd-Morgan 1981, 36–43), which are turning up in increasing numbers in Britain though the main concentration and area of production appears to be centred in the Lower Rhineland. Several examples have recently been noted from excavations in Carlisle, one of which, from Castle Street, 1982, SF no 277, came from a context dated to the Flavian/Trajanic period. Another unpublished fragment from Allens Yard, Towcester, Northants, 1984, is said to have come from a 1st-century AD ditch, which confirms the general dating of the group to Flavian times suggested by previous finds from Britain and the Continent.

Toilet implements

76 Scoop with suspension loop produced by drawing out the upper part of the implement into a wire, looping it back upon itself and winding the remainder in *c* nine turns firmly round the top of the shaft, which is rectangular in cross-section. Damaged, and part of the scoop is lost. Length 70mm. (CA 305, D I 19, phase VI, mid- to late 4th century)

Probably from a toilet set with a matching nail cleaner and tweezers, as in the example from Holt, Denbighshire (Grimes 1930, 128, fig 56, no 19). Compare also the piece from Baldock, Herts (Stead & Rigby 1986, 130, fig 56, no 276); and from the Baths at Caerleon from a context thought to be probably Antonine in date (Zienkiewicz 1986, 183, no 139, fig 60).

77 Scoop of sheet metal formerly part of a toilet set and still retaining part of a wire loop. There appear to be some slight traces of decoration on the shaft. Length 52mm, length of wire loop 14mm. (CA 466, G V 1, unphased)

Compare the examples from Baldock, Herts (Stead & Rigby 1986, 130, fig 56, nos 265, 266, 268); from Puckeridge-Braughing, Herts (Potter & Trow 1988, 61, fig 25, no 29).

78 Scoop, similar to the previous example but with a decorative profile, imitating a collar, just below the suspension ring. A little worn in places. Length 52.1mm. (CA 226, H II 2, unphased)

81 Tweezers, complete and undecorated, with part of an iron rod still held in the upper section, suggesting that they were part of a toilet set. Length 59mm, width 6.5mm. (CA 54, B I 3, phase II, Antonine to 3rd century)

82 Tweezers, complete and undecorated, expanding in width towards the ends. Length 55mm. (CA 461, G V 1, unphased)

Compare similar examples from Skeleton Green, Herts (Partridge 1981, 272, fig 107, no 14); and Lion Walk, Colchester (Crummy 1983, 59, no 1877, fig 63, dated roughly AD 100–350).

83 Tweezers, decorated with a single incised line as border down each side, now in three adjoining pieces but virtually complete. Length 42.8mm, width *c* 4mm. (CA 391, F I 23, phase XII, after AD 353)

Compare the identical examples from Gadebridge Park, Herts (Neal 1974, 140, fig 62, nos 181, 182); *Vindolanda* (Bidwell 1985, 126, fig 42, no 63); and Skeleton Green (Partridge 1981, 105, fig 54, no 11).

85 Small ring with pair of tweezers and nail cleaner attached. The tweezers are decorated with an incised linear border at the edge, as 83 (CA 391) above, but with the addition of an incised saltire just below the head. Tweezers: length 62mm in two pieces but complete. The decoration is similar to that on the tweezers from Tiddington, Warwicks TD 81 380; M592. Nail cleaner: length 57.4mm. Compare 95 (CA 298) listed below. Suspension ring: diam 12.6mm × 10mm, cross-setting *c* 2mm. (CA 322, G I 89, phase IV, early to mid-4th century)

Compare the set on a ring from Butt Road, Colchester, with a late 3rd- to 4th-century date suggested (Crummy 1983, 62–3, fig 67, no 1945).

86 Nail cleaner, the shaft decorated with a panel of incised cross-hatching, and with a bone disc-shaped bead at the head, part of which is now missing. The points of the forked section are broken. Length 41mm, diam head 8.5mm. (CA 69, AA III 10, phase VI, early to mid-4th century or later)

Compare the examples from Woodeaton, Oxon (Kirk 1949, 25, no 1, fig 6, no 5); Cirencester (Wacher & McWhirr 1982, 103, fig 30, no 71); and Nettleton, Wilts (Wedlake 1982, 219, fig 94, nos 8, 11; also no 7 said to have come from the 3rd- to 4th- century levels); and Alcester ALC 72 2 10.

90 Nail cleaner with bone bead terminal; rather crudely cut, the shaft is bent and encrusted. Probably related to nos 87–9. Length 48mm, diam head 6mm × 6.5mm. (CA 401, G IA 63, phase V, later 4th century)

Compare with the similarly poorly preserved piece from Bleachfield Street, Alcester 1976–7 671.

91 Nail cleaner, complete, with domed subspherical head and two well-defined collars beneath. Below this is a small panel decorated with cross-hatching and beneath it a simple moulded double collar. The shaft is rectangular in cross-section, flaring gently out towards the forked end. Length 48mm. (CA 502, F U/S, unphased)

Compare the more elaborately decorated example from Nettleton, Wilts, which was with other pieces from a general context dated 3rd–4th century (Wedlake 1982, 219, fig 94, no 4).

92 Nail cleaner with crude drum-shaped knob terminal and square cross-sectioned shaft, becoming rectangular towards the bifurcation. A little bent and with some surface damage. Length 67mm. (CA 443, J I 11, phase VIII, 3rd century?)

Probably a crude version of the nail cleaners with disc-shaped bone terminals, as 86 etc above.

93 Nail cleaner, cast with loop for attachment, now broken, and below it a baluster-shaped moulding with square cross-section, framed by three fine collars on either side. A little bent. Length 61mm. (CA 107, AA II 13A)

Compare the cruder example from Balkerne Lane, Colchester, from a context dated *c* AD 250–300 (Crummy 1983, 58, fig 62, no 1875).

94 Nail cleaner with suspension loop cast in one piece. Below the loop are two collars decorated with light, closely incised cross-hatching; the rest of the shaft is plain. The tips of the forked end are damaged. Length 52.5mm. (CA 390, F I 21, phase XII, after AD 353)

An example from the Roman theatre at *Verulamium* was said to have come from 'late 4th-century brown earth' (Kenyon 1934, 259, fig 12, no 17); another from Neatham, Hants came from a context dated late 3rd to 4th century (Millett & Graham 1986, 105, no 53, fig 71). Compare also the slightly smaller piece from Tiddington, Warwicks, TD 81 853.

95 Nail cleaner made of heavy sheet metal with no trace of decoration. Length 77mm. (CA 298, D I T/S, unphased)

Compare the damaged example from Balkerne Lane, Colchester from a context dated *c* AD 60/61 to *c* 75/80 (Crummy 1983, Type 1a, 57–8, fig 62, no 1869) and an unpublished piece from Piddington Villa, Northants, 1985 498.

96 Nail cleaner of heavy sheet metal, waisted between the suspension loop and the main body. Decorated with three dot-and-circle patterns on one side just below the loop. Complete. Length 66.5mm. (CA 109, AA III 39, unphased)

Compare the damaged example from Lion Walk, Colchester site C, from a context dated *c* AD 44–49/55 (Crummy 1983, Type 1B, 58, fig 62, no 1871). Dot-and-circle patterns are also found decorating an unpublished nail cleaner from Thistleton Black Wong, Rutland (THZ 2951 BZ 92 400).

98 Nail cleaner, with upper section bent over to form a suspension loop. The lower section widens out slightly and is decorated with grooves, the bifurcation is virtually all lost. Length 45mm, width 3.5mm. (CA 472, E V 18, phase VI, early 3rd century?)

Compare a similar piece with linear decoration from Camerton, said to come from a 1st-century AD layer (Wedlake 1958, 259, fig 59, no 3T); and a longer, more elegantly proportioned example on a chatelaine from Colchester (Crummy 1983, 62, fig 67, no 1945 from a modern context).

Medical implements

104 Ligula, decorated with a closely engraved spiral line just above the spoon section for *c* 5mm; complete. Length 113mm. (CA 441, E II 32, phase IV, Hadrianic–Antonine)

A similar piece from *Verulamium* came from a layer dated AD 270–80 (Frere 1972, 124, fig 35, no 70); and there were other pieces from Baldock, Herts (Stead & Rigby 1986, 130, fig 56, nos 242, 243); and Puckeridge-Braughing, Herts (Potter & Trow 1988, 61, fig 24, no 15).

105 Medical instrument with probe at one end and spoon-shaped spatula at the other, rather encrusted. Length *c* 150mm. (CA 349, G I 89, phase IV, early to mid-4th century)

Compare the example from a 2nd-century context at Cirencester (McWhirr 1986, 230, fig 152, no 6); and a similar piece from a doctor's grave at Cologne dated to the second half of the 1st century AD (Künzl 1983, 98–9, Abb 78, the first item on the left of the plate); and another now in the Landesmuseum, Trier (Künzl 1984, 174, Taf 22, no K3).

106 Handle of medical instrument, with remains of an elongated spoon-shaped spatula, with a decorative S-shaped spiral twist. Length *c* 105mm. (CA 135, B IA 7, unphased)

Compare the complete example from Puckeridge-Braughing, Herts (Potter & Trow 1988, 61, fig 24, no 9); two now in the Landesmuseum, Trier from a doctor's grave (Künzl 1984, 155, Taf 5, nos A3b, A3c); and an incomplete piece from Lion Walk, Colchester, from a context dated AD 100–350 (Crummy 1983, 60, no 1917, fig 64).

107 Shaft of implement with S-shaped spiral twist to grip, tapering towards one end. Length 44.6mm. (CA 151, C VIA 15, unphased)

Compare the shaft of 106 (CA 135) above. Alternatively the fragment might have been part of the handle of a spoon.

108 Elongated spoon-shaped spatula from a toilet or medical implement. Length 45.2mm. (CA 319, E II 9, phase XIII, after AD 353)

Compare a similar fragment from Great Dunmow, Essex (Wickenden 1988, 43, fig 34, no 1).

109 Grip of a medical implement, possibly the needle used for cataract operations. The shaft is octagonal in cross-section with one end decorated with a series of sharply defined collars and mouldings, the other has only a single incised collar. In two adjoining pieces. Length 80.7mm. (CA 95, AA III 29, phase IV, later 3rd century on)

Compare the shafts of the implements illustrated and discussed by Feugère, Künzl & Weisser (1988, esp fig 1, 13, 14, 17, 27).

Spoons

114 Spoon with a small circular bowl and tapering handle, in two adjoining pieces, the surface a little chipped and corroded in places, otherwise complete. Length 103.5mm, diam bowl 22.1mm. (CA 367, G I 162, unphased)

Strong (1966, 155, fig 32) dates this form of spoon to the 1st century AD, which can be confirmed by finds from recent excavations, such as the damaged piece from Skeleton Green, Herts, from a context dated mid-Augustan to early Tiberian *c* 10 BC to AD 20 (Partridge 1981, 107, fig 55, no 23); and another from Balkerne Lane, Colchester, found in a context dated *c* AD 50/55–75/80 (Crummy 1983, 69, no 2008, fig 73). Compare also the spoons from Tiddington, Warwicks, no M23; M37 and M666.

115 Fragment of a spoon consisting of part of a circular bowl with adjoining handle and part of the 'rat tail'; heavily encrusted but undoubtedly a 1st-century piece as above. Present length 25mm. (CA 24, A X 5, unphased)

118 Spoon with crude fiddle-shaped bowl and offset handle. The bowl, which is bent out of shape, still bears traces of tinning; the handle is incomplete and is in six adjoining pieces. Length *c* 85mm, max width bowl 22.5mm. (CA 405, G III 1, unphased)

Strong (1966, 177–8, fig 36c) noted that the spoon with offset handle and fiddle-shaped bowl came in during the 2nd and 3rd centuries AD. There are three comparable examples from Balkerne Lane, Colchester 1973–6 of which only one comes from a usefully dated context (Crummy 1983, 69, fig no 73, no 2016, *c* AD 250–300; no 2018 consists of only the bowl: no 2019 again consists of the bowl alone). Compare also the related examples from Alcester ALC 72 3, ALC 73 31 and the more highly decorated fragments from Tiddington M61 and M598. Three incomplete examples were also found during excavations by L P Wenham at Malton, Yorks, 1968–9.

119 Incomplete bowl of spoon, undecorated, perhaps medieval. Present length 24mm, max width 28.6mm. (CA 10, A XI 2, unphased)

Vessels

120 Flat-bottomed bowl with straight sides and a slight, horizontally projecting rim. Undecorated and well used, with approximately a quarter of the side replaced with a patch, with traces of the rivets at the edge of the base and sides, and with further traces of patching under the rim. Opposite the repair and under the lip of the bowl there are two rivet-holes and the probable site of a crude handle escutcheon. The matching handle would have been in the area now repaired, and may have been lost at the time the original damage was caused. Diam base *c* 181mm, ht bowl *c* 33–8mm, max diam across top *c* 199mm. (CA 174, D I 6, phase VI, mid- to late 4th century)

Den Boesterd has dated these 'basins with vertical wall and horizontal rim' to the late 1st to 2nd century AD. One of the examples, no 194 with diam 287mm, is illustrated showing the drop handles with escutcheons *in situ* (1956, 57, nos 194, 195, pl VIII, no 194). Note also the related example from the collection of Mrs P H Onderwater of Oosterbeck (den Boesterd 1967, 119, fig 2, no 6).

121 Fragment of rim of vessel, probably a bowl, with outwardly turned lip. Some traces of tinning or silvering can be identified. Date uncertain. Length 45.4mm, thickness of wall 1.5mm, present depth *c* 15mm, original diam ?*c* 320mm. (CA 492, G V U/S)

122 Cast vessel escutcheon, leaf-shaped, but with lower end lost. The surface is poorly preserved and cracked giving the false impression of incised decoration. Date uncertain. Present ht 53.5mm, max width 16mm. (CA 139, C III 3A, unphased)

123 Vessel escutcheon of roughly diamond-shaped heavy sheet metal with the edges turned slightly back. Traces of lead solder are still *in situ* on the reverse. A little damaged in places round the edge. Ht 53.7mm, max width 30.1mm, thickness *c* 1.2mm or more. (CA 534, M IV 6, unphased)

Compare the related diamond-shaped escutcheon with suspension ring attached in the collections at Vienne, no provenance or date given (Boucher 1971, 160, no 334 with pl, ht 40mm).

124 Fitting, probably escutcheon of heavy bronze vessel. The tip is lost as is the integral loop for the suspension ring or other fitting. Rather encrusted; no trace of solder surviving inside the concave reverse side. Present length 48mm, depth *c* 10mm, max width 28.6mm. (CA 244, D I 40, phase V, early to mid-4th century?)

Figural and miscellaneous domestic items

125 Foot of a small item of domestic furniture or small stand in the form of a right human foot with sandal or light boot. The upper section is socketed but now broken. Ht 35.3mm, length of foot *c* 18mm. (CA 19, U/S, unphased)

Note the virtually identical foot with lower part of leg now in the Grosvenor Museum, Chester acc no 558.R.1967, ht 35mm and unpublished. There is also a more recent find of another identical piece from excavations at the Riding School Field site, Caerleon SF 79/131/1226 1157, length 33mm. A cast foot with sandal and tang just above the ankle for attachment was found at Dover and has a suggested date of *c* AD 210–70 (Philp 1981, 149, fig 31, no 70). Two stylized feet with sandals survive on the mid-1st century AD folding stool or *sella* from a burial at Nijmegen found in 1907 (Zadoks-Josephus Jitta *et al* 1973, 83–4, no 143 with pl). Two other examples of feet from furniture in the shape of besandaled human feet, with sockets for attachment at the ankle, are also in the Nijmegen collections (*ibid*, 84, 85, no 144, 145 with pls).

Literacy/communication

128 Drop-shaped seal box lid with inlaid enamel decoration which now appears as dark red, yellow, and a transparent white to pale green colour. The enamel in the outer cell, echoing the drop shape of the lid, has alternating panels of the yellow and white enamel. The innermost ring-shaped cell contains yellow enamel and is partially surrounded by an inverted A-shaped cell containing dark red enamel. The hinge section has been lost, otherwise complete. Length 43mm, depth of lid *c* 4mm, max width 21.8mm. (CA 158, A XVI 17, unphased)

Compare the complete example from *Segontium* found under the cellar floor in the *praetorium* and dated by Wheeler (1930, 141, fig 61, no 18) to 'not later than *c* AD 230'; another from Lion Walk, Colchester came from a context dated late Roman or later (Crummy 1983, 104, no 2523, fig 106). A further example comes from Brancaster, Norfolk (Hinchcliffe & Sparey Green *et al* 1985, 213, fig 90, no 60), with a near-identical unpublished piece coming from Bleachfield Street, Alcester, 1976–7, 217.

129 Base of a drop-shaped seal box, pierced by three holes; the tip is lost. Length 40.5mm, depth 4.6mm, max width 22.7mm. (CA 380, G IV 1A, unphased)

Military

131 ?Unfinished loop of a cuirass hook from a *lorica segmentata*? With remains of a nail-hole in the expanded flattened section. Length *c* 81mm, cross-section *c* 2.0mm × 2.8mm. (CA 311, E IV 23, phase III, Neronian–Trajanic)

Compare the more complete example from Longthorpe (Frere & St Joseph 1974, 50, fig 26, no 31), and from Ffrith, Clwyd (Blockley 1989, 149, fig 5, no 8).

132 Lower section of legionary apron mount, consisting of a hemispherical terminal knob with a curved section rising above the intermediate moulded section. A V-shaped tongue behind is bent into the hollow channel and would have firmly gripped the lower part of the leather strap. Present length 22.5mm, depth 7.6mm, width 11.8mm. (CA 192, C VIA 89, phase II, late 2nd century)

Compare the complete examples from Longthorpe (Frere & St Joseph 1974, 54, no 47, 49, fig 28).

133 ?Military plaque or fitting with remains of a rivet *in situ* behind the stylized palmette terminal. The piece is incomplete, being broken across a nail-hole. Length 29.8mm, thickness *c* 2mm, max width 11.4mm. (CA 333, J I 1, unphased)

134 Drop-shaped pendant or military fitting, the upper ?looped section is lost. Decorated on one side with an engraved medial line, corroded on back. Present length 28mm, thickness *c* 1.1mm, max width 8.6mm. (CA 395, D I T/S, unphased)

135 Half a crudely made buckle plate with remains of a rivet made of rolled sheet metal still *in situ* in one of the two rivet-holes. The buckle, loop, pin, and swivel are lost. Possibly from a *lorica segmentata*. Length 29.8mm, max width 14.2mm. (CA 23, AA II 1, unphased)

136 Half a buckle plate, which appears to belong with the previous item. Length 31.5mm, max width 14.4mm. (CA 33, A XI 19, unphased)

137 Tube, tapering towards each end, heavily corroded. Length 48.2mm. (CA 300, G IA 13, phase VII+, late 4th century on)

Probably a military tube or bead. Compare the examples from the fortress at Birrens, four of which were dated Antonine I (*c* AD 142–55), the other two being unstratified (Robertson 1975, 110, no 18, fig 30, no 5; 110, nos 20–2, fig 30, no 7; 116, no 87, fig 37, no 10, 11); with others from Chester (Newstead 1924, 81, pl VII, no 10); and Woodeaton (Kirk 1949, 28, no 14, fig 7, no 5).

Horse furniture

139 Strap junction or fitting consisting of an openwork plaque with symmetrical scroll decoration, with traces of 'tinning' still *in situ* on the central portion. Attached to an undecorated rectangular back-plate by two hollow dome-headed rivets passing through the centre of the solid circular terminals, and by a slightly larger rivet passing through the central disc-shaped section. Max dimensions upper plaque 88.1mm × 16.3mm, max dimensions lower plaque 87mm × 10mm, diam head of largest rivet 12.7mm, diam head of smaller rivets 9.0mm, 9.8mm, max overall ht of fitting 12mm. (CA 442, D I 214, phase VIII, late 4th century)

This may be related to strap junctions such as the piece from Middlebie, Dumfriesshire, where a repeated openwork design conceals two strap bars, one at either end (MacGregor 1976, vol 2, no 33). The presence of the three rivets on the Alcester piece suggests that the fitting may have been used to strengthen a narrow strap at a vulnerable point or, more likely, to decorate the harness in a prominent place such as the cheek strap. A fitting which may be related is the damaged flat rectangular loop with an elaborately enamelled panel on the outer face, found recently at Hanbury Street, Droitwich, Worcs. A military association seems perhaps more likely than a native, civilian origin. Note also the virtually identical no 140, CA 358.

141 Fragment of a 'platform' terret with circular cross-section loop (141a). The oval platform is decorated with hollow cells in the form of bud-shaped motifs on either side of a solid disc. On either side of the platform, on the ring, are further lentoid cells. No traces of enamelling have survived. Length 42.3mm, cross-section loop *c* 6.3mm × 7.4mm. (CA 275, D I 48, phase VI, mid- to late 4th century)

For decorated platform terrets, all with panels of enamelled decoration, see MacGregor (1976, vol 1, fig 1, no 3, 4, 6 from Saham Toney, Norfolk with enamelling on the ring adjacent to the platform; also 45–6 for discussion with map 9 and listings on 67–9; vol 2, compare the following examples, no 2 Balmuidy, Lanarkshire; no 65 Birrens, Dumfriesshire; no 66 Birrens; no 68, 69 Fremington Hagg, Yorks; no 70 Great Chesters, or Benwell, Northumberland; no 71 High Rochester, Northumberland; no 72 Middlebie, Dumfriesshire; no 74 Traprain Law, East Lothian).

A further corroded fragment (141b) may or may not belong with the above, and consists of part of a ring, roughly circular in cross-section, with iron and copper alloy corrosion products covering a larger area inside the curve of the ring.

142 'Dropped bar' terret ring, consisting of a circular ring with a roughly oval cross-section now a little bent out of shape, with a smaller rectangular loop with subrectangular cross-section attached below. Complete, undecorated and rather corroded. External diam of ring 28.2mm × 33mm, cross-section of ring *c* 7.3mm × 3.5mm, present ht 37mm. (CA 432, G IA 90, phase IV, early to mid-4th century)

Compare the examples of this type discussed and listed by MacGregor (1976, vol 1, 41–2 with check list and distribution map no 5, 60–2; vol 2, no 59 from Muircleugh, Berwickshire and the related no 100 from Templeborough, Yorkshire). Another example was found in a robber trench during excavations at *Verulamium* (Frere 1972, 130, fig 40, no 126).

143 Central link of a straight bar snaffle, or from a three-link bridle bit. The ring terminals are broken through extreme wear. Length 100.3mm, depth *c* 19mm, max thickness 10.8mm. (CA 225, G II 2, unphased)

Compare the related copper alloy examples from Place Fell, Westmoreland (MacGregor 1976, vol 2, no 8; Palk 1984, no SB 10, fig C 45, who suggests a mid- to late 1st-century date on p 82); Rise, Holderness, Yorks (MacGregor 1976, vol 2, no 10; Palk 1984, 52–3, no SB 11, fig C 46) and an unprovenanced piece now in the Fitzwilliam Museum, Cambridge (Palk 1984, 56, no SB 21, fig C 50).

144 Hollow ring, with roughly circular cross-section, incomplete, no decoration visible. External diam *c* 42.5mm, cross-section *c* 12mm × 16mm. (CA 143, A XVI 10, unphased)

146 Lunular-shaped pin or fitting with the points of the crescent up. The shaft is rectangular in cross-section. Max width crescent 68.6mm, max ht crescent 64.7mm, total ht 130.7mm, max cross-section shaft 6.5mm × 2.9mm. (CA 490, L XII 10, unphased)

Compare the smaller examples of lunulate pins from the Netherlands (Zadoks-Josephus Jitta & Witteveen 1977, 188, pl 35, no 51 from the Hunerberg, Nijmegen 1884; no 54 from Nijmegen pre 1921). The shaft is too large for it to have been used as a personal ornament, though it may have been slotted into a larger item, perhaps the apex of a domestic shrine, or attached to a cart or carriage as an ornament and an apotropaic amulet.

Studs and nails

147 Stud with flat circular head and notched edge, and a square cross-sectioned shaft. The head is divided with three concentric rings, giving a central circular field which would have been inlaid with enamel, and three surrounding ring-shaped fields, the outer two of which still retain traces of millefiore enamel. Diam 35.2mm, ht 19.5mm. (CA 491, L XII 10, unphased)

A near-identical piece from an Antonine I context (*c* AD 142–55) was found during excavations at the fort of Birrens (Robertson 1975, 110, no 37; fig 31, no 3). Related pieces are reported from South Shields (Allason-Jones & Miket 1984, 92, no 3.4 — damaged; and the near identical no 3.5, p 94 with figs). A similar piece from Gestingthorpe with only two concentric rings of millefiore around the central field was dated later 2nd to early 3rd century AD and it was suggested that studs of this type were used to decorate horse trappings, perhaps as bridle decoration (Draper 1985, 27, 29, fig 9, no 14).

148 Domed, lentoid-shaped stud, with slightly damaged square cross-sectioned pin. Probably military in origin and use. Head 25.8mm × 12.2mm, ht *c* 12mm. (CA 253, D I T/S, unphased)

Compare the example from Brancaster (Hinchcliffe & Sparey-Green *et al* 1985, 211, no 46, fig 89).

149 Hollow-headed stud filled with lead solder and iron pin. The stud is of sheet metal in the form of a stylized lion mask, of which about two-thirds survive. Diam *c* 26.5mm, ht *c* 11mm. (CA 168, A XVIIB 1, unphased)

Compare the light-weight copper alloy studs from burial 3 of cemetery A at Skeleton Green, Herts, dated to the Antonine period. These were used at this site and elsewhere to attach and decorate the lock plate for the modest-sized casket which had been reused to hold the ashes from the cremation (Partridge 1981, 312–13, fig 117, also 315–16 and table XLVI, 320–1 with discussion). A similar unpublished example was found at the excavation of the Roman villa at Piddington, Northants 1981 149; and a closer parallel comes from Doncaster DQ 5 171. The type is not restricted to Britain as witnessed by the range of lion head plaques and fittings in the Landesmuseum, Trier, which includes five small lion head studs related to this one (Menzel 1966, 63–7, especially nos 154–8; 66–7, Abb nos 19–23 respectively).

151 Stud with conical head and slight flange to edge, with lead filler inside and traces of original iron pin *in situ*. Diam head 22.2mm, ht *c* 7mm. (CA 454, G IV 61, phase IV, early to mid-4th century)

152 Hollow dome-headed stud, filled with lead solder, now decayed and cracked, with possible trace of iron pin at centre. Diam head *c* 36mm, ht 13.7mm. (CA 127, AA I 74, unphased)

167 Nail with solid subspherical head, tip of shaft bent. Diam head *c* 8.3mm, ht *c* 30.5mm. (CA 535, M III 3, phase IV, Roman/post-Roman)

183 Crudely shaped tack or nail head? Square with rectangular cross-section. Cross-section head 3.3mm × 6.5mm, ht 17.7mm. (CA 12, A IX 5, unphased)

Plaques and bindings

191 Decorative strip or appliqué with an irregular line of repoussé dots as a border to the longer sides, and remains of a nail-hole for attachment at either end. A little bent out of shape. *c* 38.6mm × 13.5mm, thickness 0.6mm. (CA 286, E II 9, phase XIII, after AD 353)

Compare the similar pieces from Woodeaton, Oxon (Kirk 1949, 43, pl VIA, no 4), and Nor'nour (Dudley 1967, 22, fig 9, no 29), and from Coleshill, Warwicks GH 1979 215 fragments (b) and (c).

192 Strip with linear repoussé decoration including two lines of heavy repoussé beading on raised panels as borders, with a narrow outer raised line at the edge. A little damaged and with traces of solder at the back. Length 36.4mm, width 25.1mm. (CA 60, AA III 11, phase VIII, early to mid-4th century)

The presence of the solder suggests that the strip was attached to some larger metal object, possibly the rim of a bronze vessel, or some item of military use. The most obvious candidate in this latter instance would be a helmet, with the strip used as edging round the skull section, perhaps as a brow band.

193 Plaque or binding slightly narrowing towards one end, and with two incised parallel lines acting as border decoration to the longer sides. Possibly some trace of solder at the wider end. Length 48.5mm, thickness *c* 0.7mm, max width 33mm. (CA 102, AA II 12, unphased)

194 Strip with longitudinal repoussé decoration. Length *c* 31.5mm, present width 7.9mm. (CA 337, F III +, unphased)

195 Subrectangular plaque or fitting of sheet metal with angular cross-section and concave sides. One end lost, slightly earth-encrusted. Length 31.2mm, depth 2.6mm, max width 15.5mm. (CA 456, D II 29, unphased)

Probably the handle plate of a knife.

Miscellaneous fittings

218 Collar with moulded decoration, made from rolled strip. Length of strip *c* 20mm, max thickness *c* 1.5mm, ht *c* 17mm. (CA 531, M III 17, phase I, late 2nd to early 3rd century)

Compare the closely related example from Coleshill GM 1979 113.

219 Collar similar to the above, with lightly moulded borders. Length of strip *c* 18.5mm, max thickness 1–1.5mm, ht *c* 14mm. (CA 493, F I T/S, unphased)

220 Fragment or fitting with moulded decoration of variable thickness. 32.3mm × 15.2mm, max thickness 3.2mm. (CA 203, H I 1, unphased)

224 Roughly trapezoidal fitting with nail-hole towards one end. Original date and function uncertain. Length 27.6mm, max width 19.5mm. (CA 306, E I 40, phase XIII, after AD 353)

225 Hook-shaped fitting, the flat head originally pierced with a hole for suspension or attachment. The lower 'hook' section with triangular outline is unfinished in appearance. Overall length *c* 49mm. (CA 421, D I 206, phase VI, mid- to late 4th century?)

228 Fragment of disc with central hole used as ?washer or ?keyhole plate. Diam *c* 50mm, thickness 0.9mm, present size 36.0mm × 18.5mm. (CA 182, E U/S)

Compare the lock plate dated mid-2nd century from South Shields in Miket (1983, 111, fig 70, no 42).

Discussion

One of the interesting aspects of the Birch Abbey finds has been the wide range of bracelet types. As can be seen from cemetery finds such as the well-known collection from the 4th-century burials at Lankhills, Winchester, some women had up to ten or more examples in different styles and materials (Clarke 1979, grave 143, fig 77, fourteen pieces in bone and copper alloy; grave 337, fig 91, ten pieces in shale, bone, and copper alloy). It is perhaps surprising that despite evidence for bone bracelets from other domestic sites in Alcester, none were found during this excavation. Other than fibulae, which are discussed elsewhere, most of the personal ornaments are of 3rd- or 4th-century date. The pins, especially the ones which are most simple in style, would have been almost universal and would have remained in use and production for as long as elaborately dressed hair was felt to be fashionable. The find of further 1st-century AD mirror fragments to supplement the pieces from the Bleachfield Street excavations 1975–6, nos 450, 650, does suggest that there always were families able to purchase these little luxuries. Care for the person is also emphasized by the finds of tweezers, scoops, and nail cleaners. Several of these modest implements are well paralleled by other finds from Alcester and elsewhere in the region.

To some extent the table ware used in the kitchen and dining room would be local pottery supplemented by finer wares including samian. So it is particularly useful to have a small 1st-century bronze bowl, CA 174, surviving as a reminder of the complete dining and drinking services in copper alloy and silver that were a sign of wealth and the civilized way to enjoy life, even in the furthest provinces of the Empire. It is interesting to note that a slightly larger and better-preserved vessel, no M 51, was found during early excavations at Tiddington. Vessels any larger than these two pieces would presumably have been cut up for scrap and the metal recycled once they had become worn out and broken beyond repair.

As has been seen from other collections of finds made in and around Alcester, there are tantalizing fragments of military hardware, one of the more interesting being the piece of scale armour CA 106. These fragments of equipment can only suggest the presence of soldiers, but not the length of time they spent within the Roman town. Similarly, finds of seal boxes and writing equipment cannot be taken as a sign of general literacy, but it does indicate that there were some people with basic skills, and perhaps more, in accounting and record keeping of the sort necessary to keep a small business going.

The finds from this excavation follow similar patterns to those discovered in earlier excavations. It reveals a small community partly self-sufficient within the region for its daily needs, with some relatively more prosperous families who were at different times able to buy in exotic goods. Although there appears to be, on this site at least, a certain weighting towards items made during the later years of the Empire, there is enough material present to indicate activity at all periods even though this might have varied in intensity over the years.

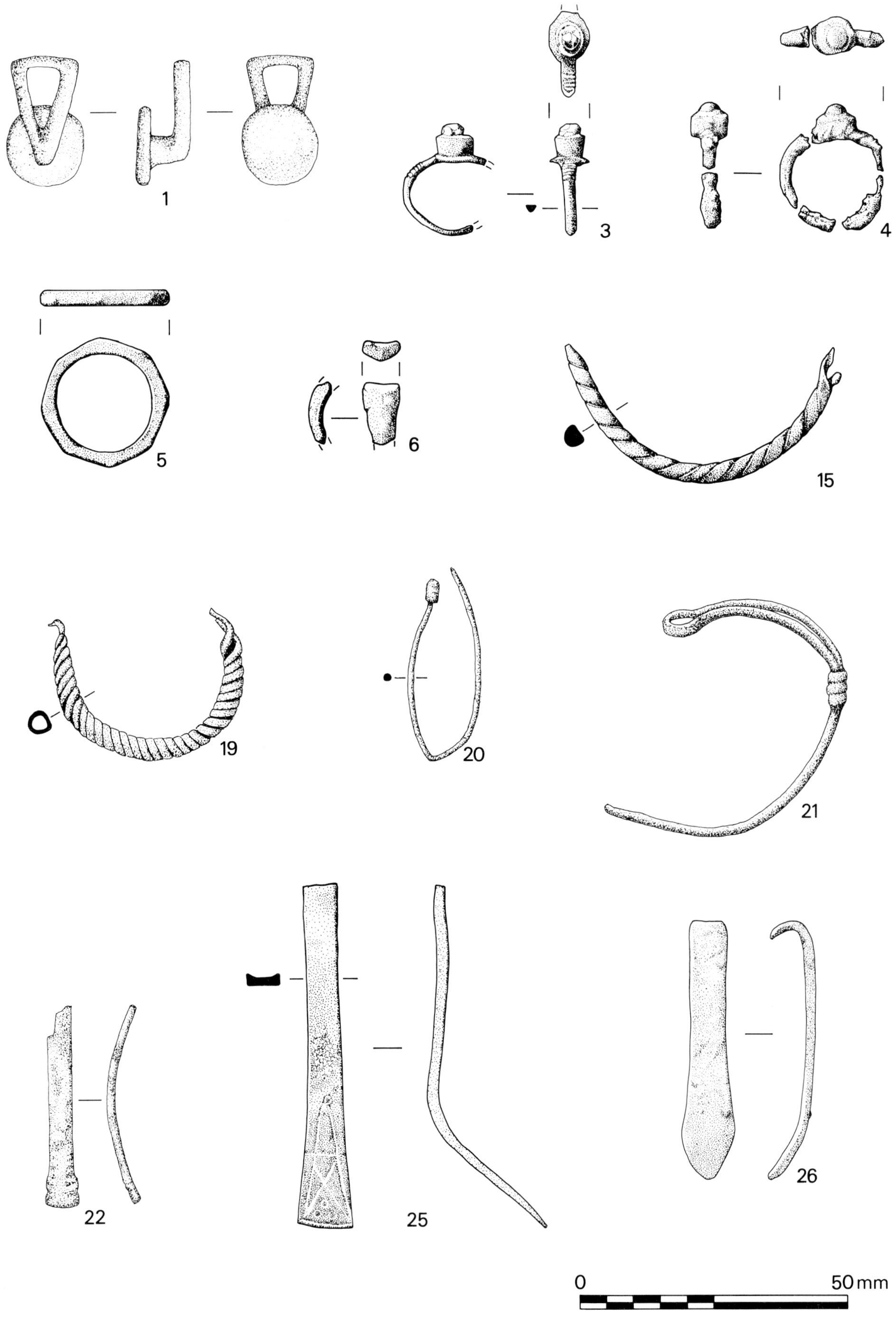

Figure 82 Copper alloy (except brooches), nos 1–26

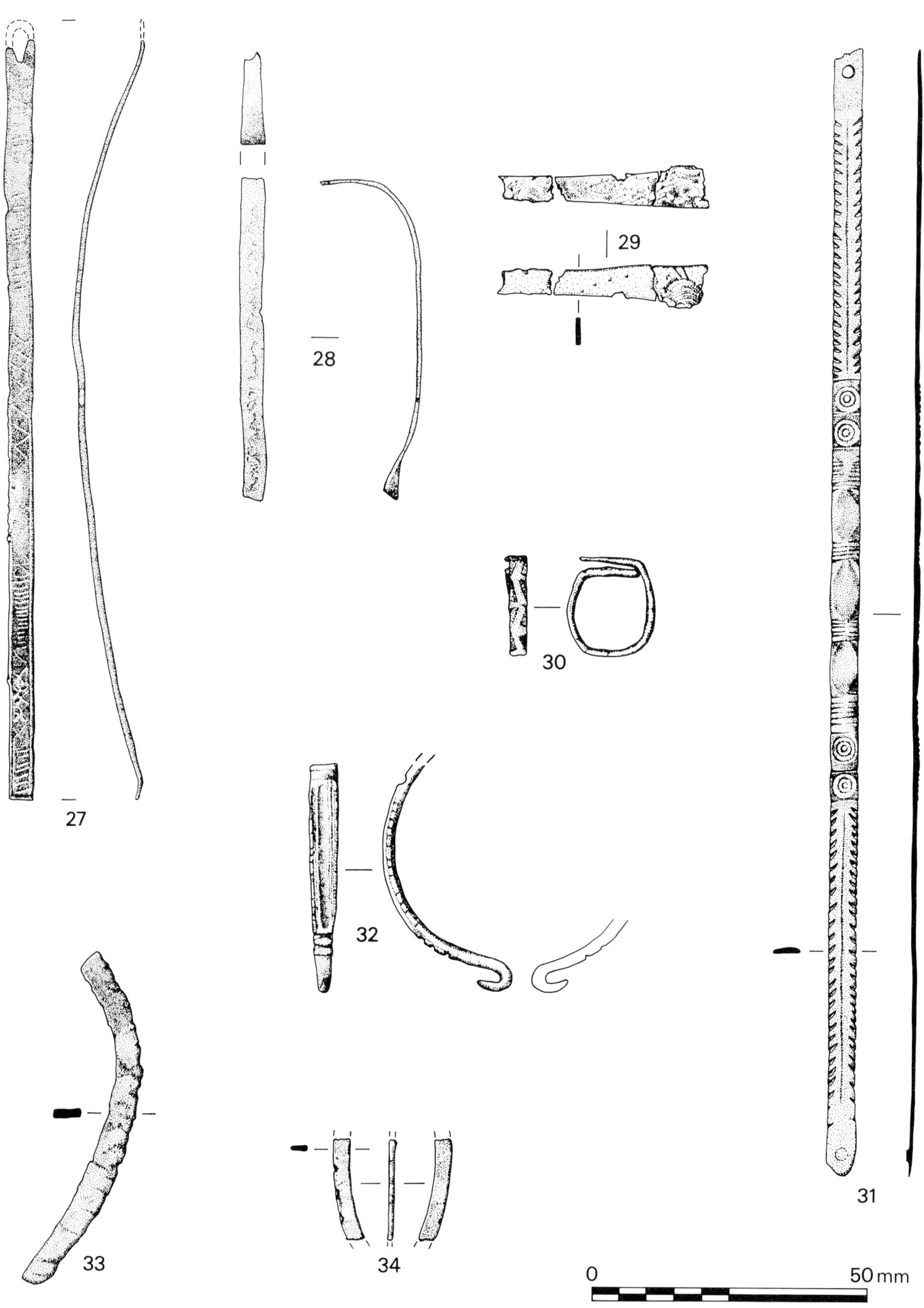

Figure 83 Copper alloy (except brooches), nos 27–34

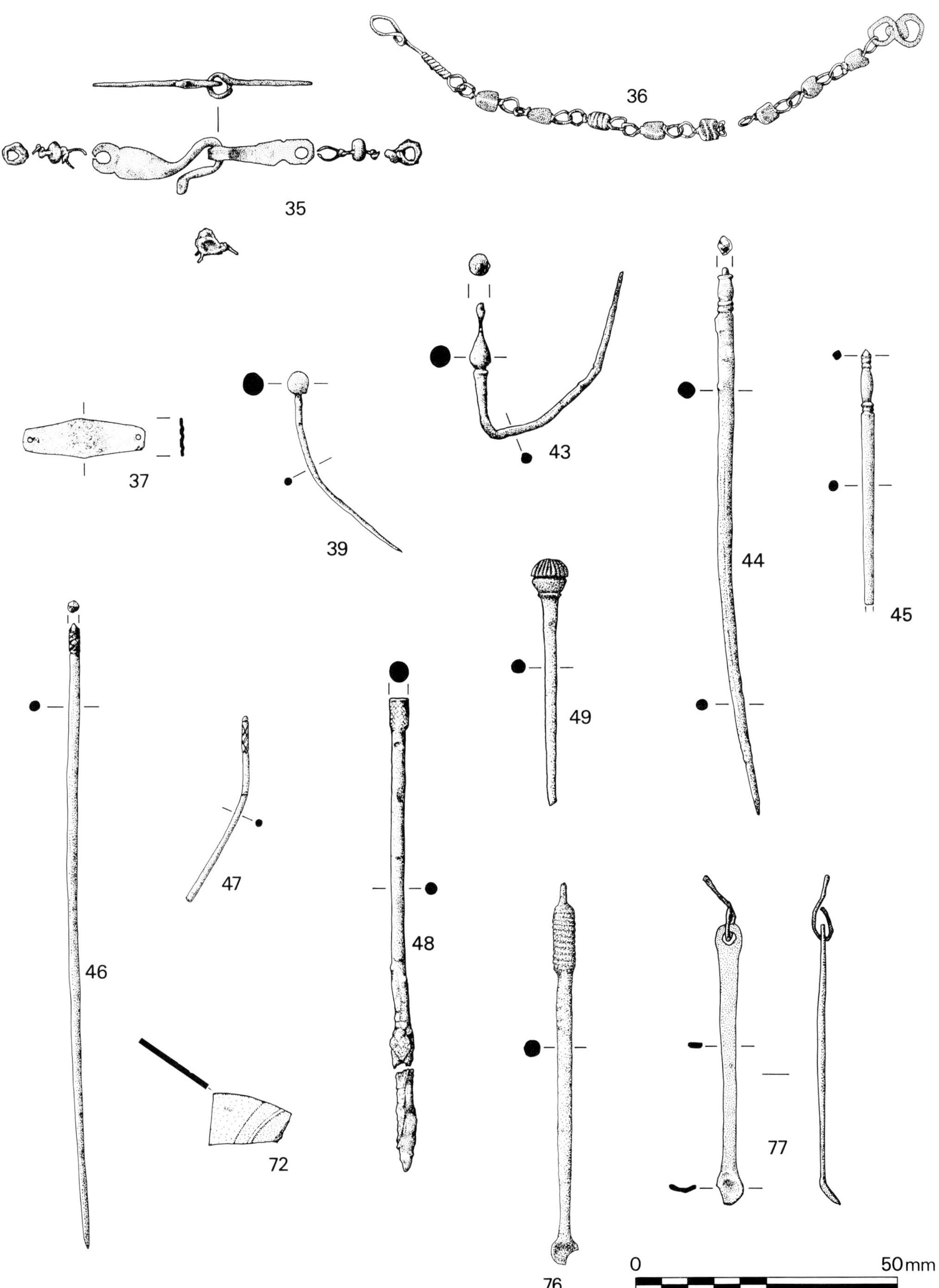

Figure 84 Copper alloy (except brooches), nos 35–77

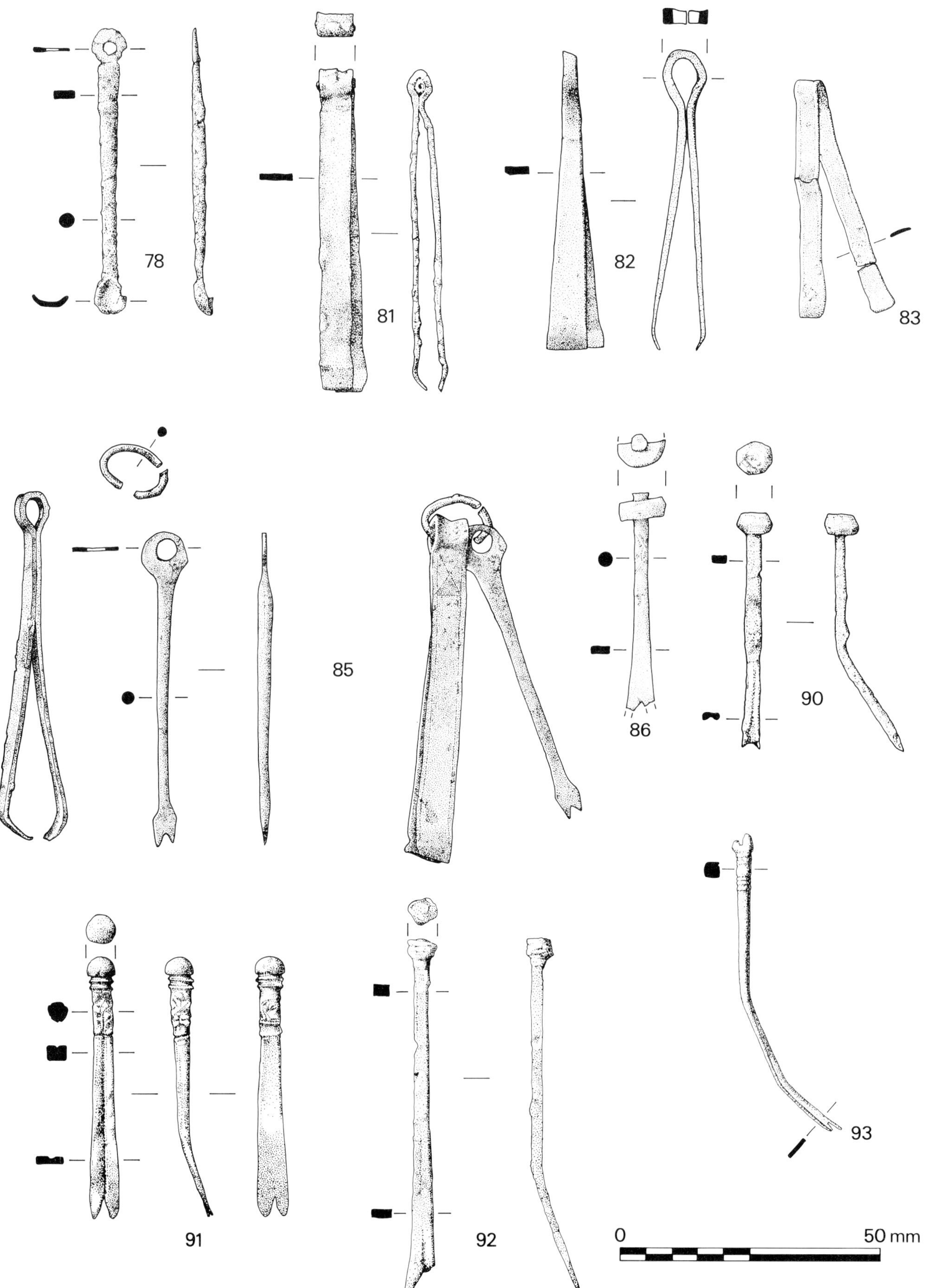

Figure 85 Copper alloy (except brooches), nos 78–93

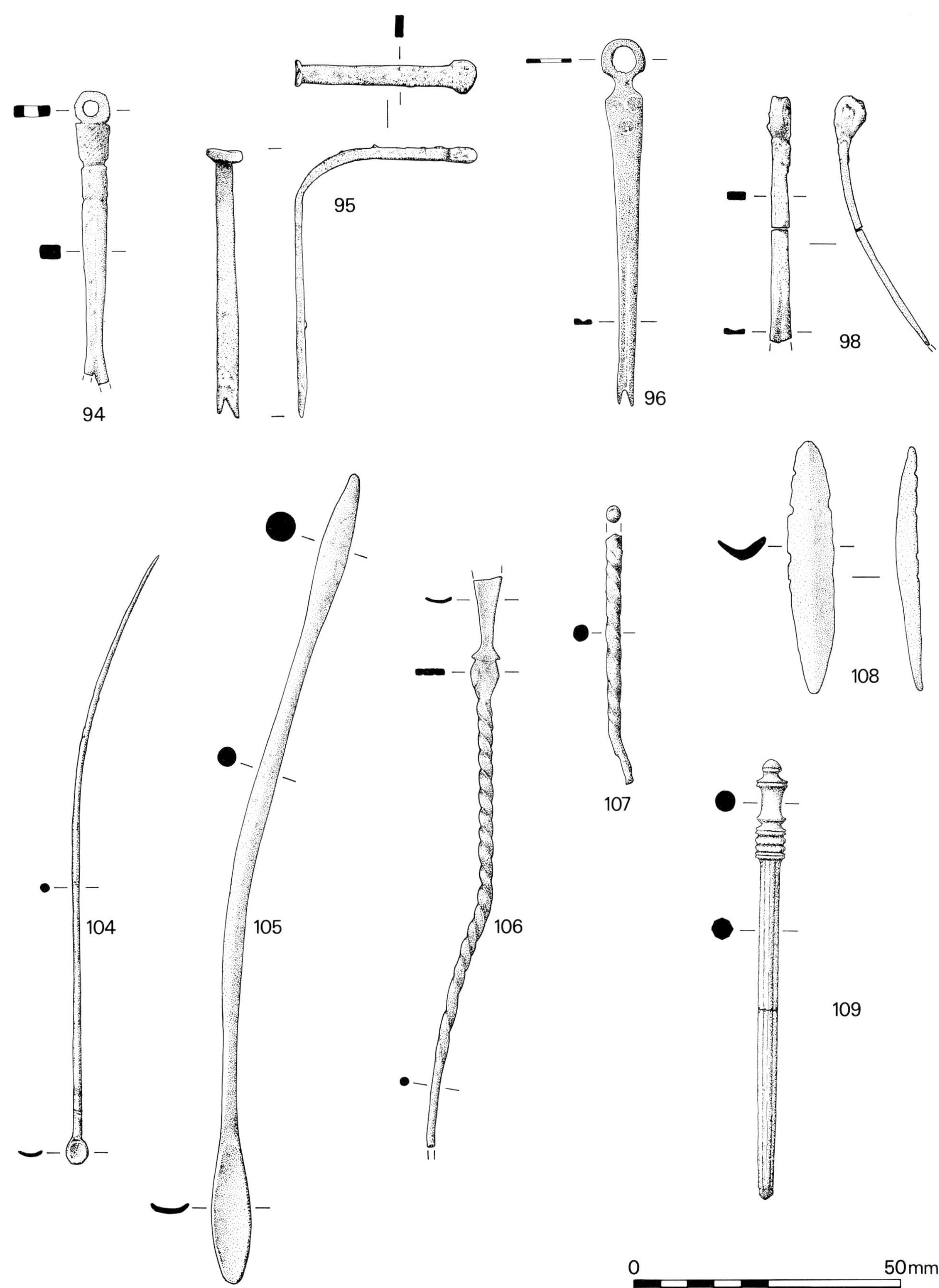

Figure 86 Copper alloy (except brooches), nos 94–109

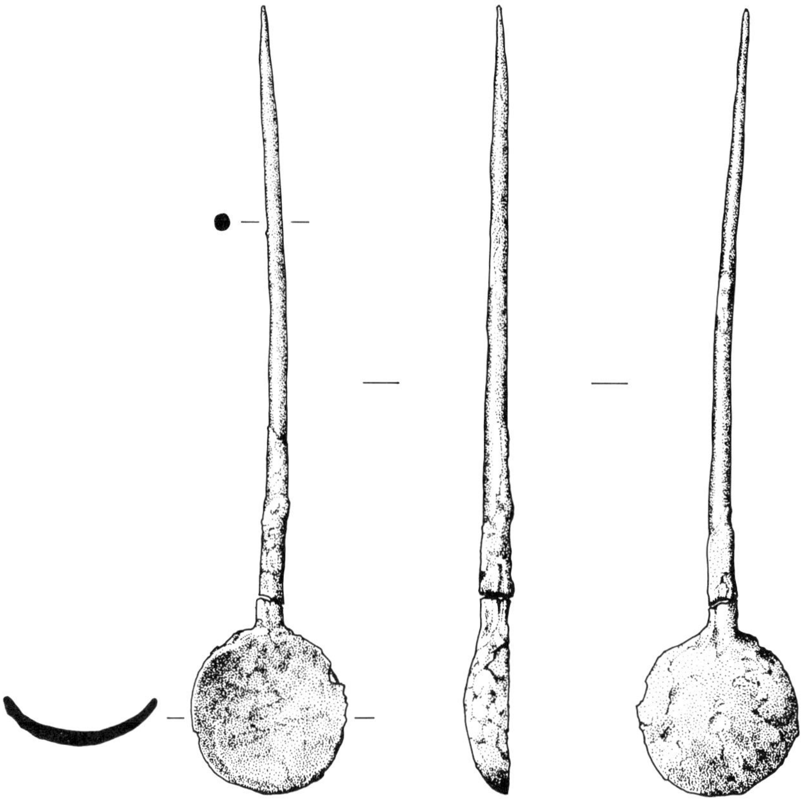

114

115

119

118

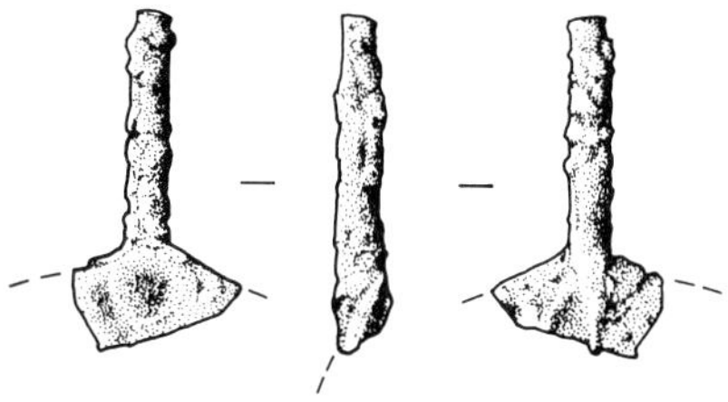

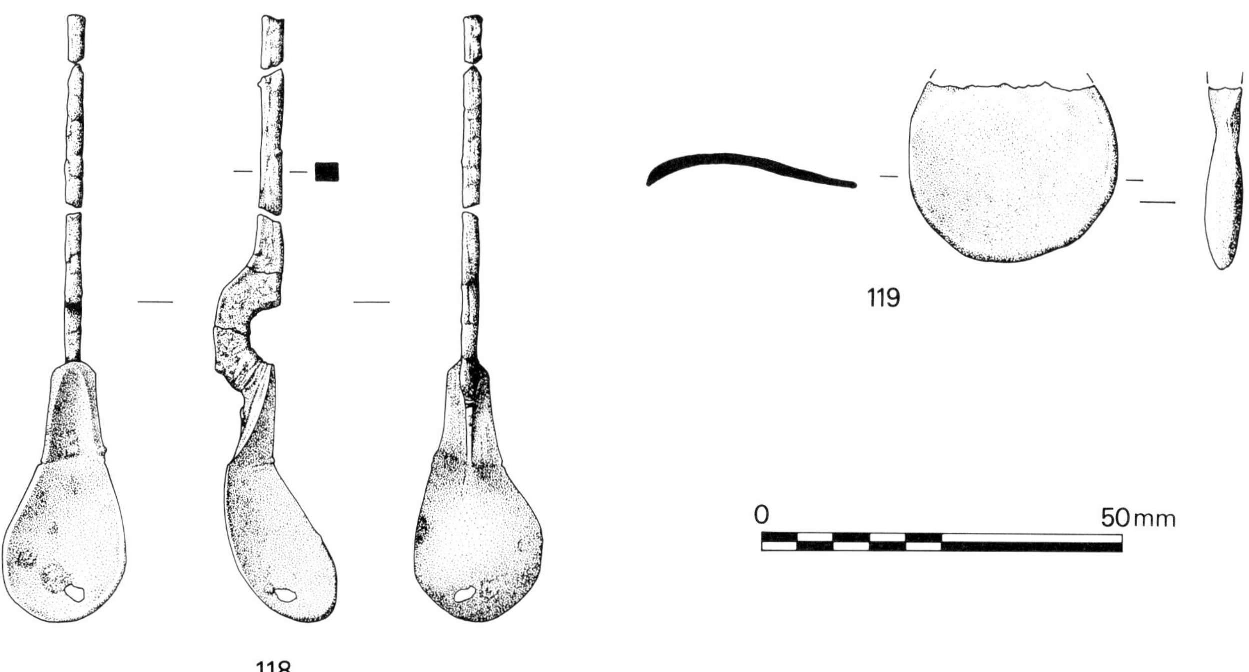

Figure 87 Copper alloy (except brooches), nos 114–19

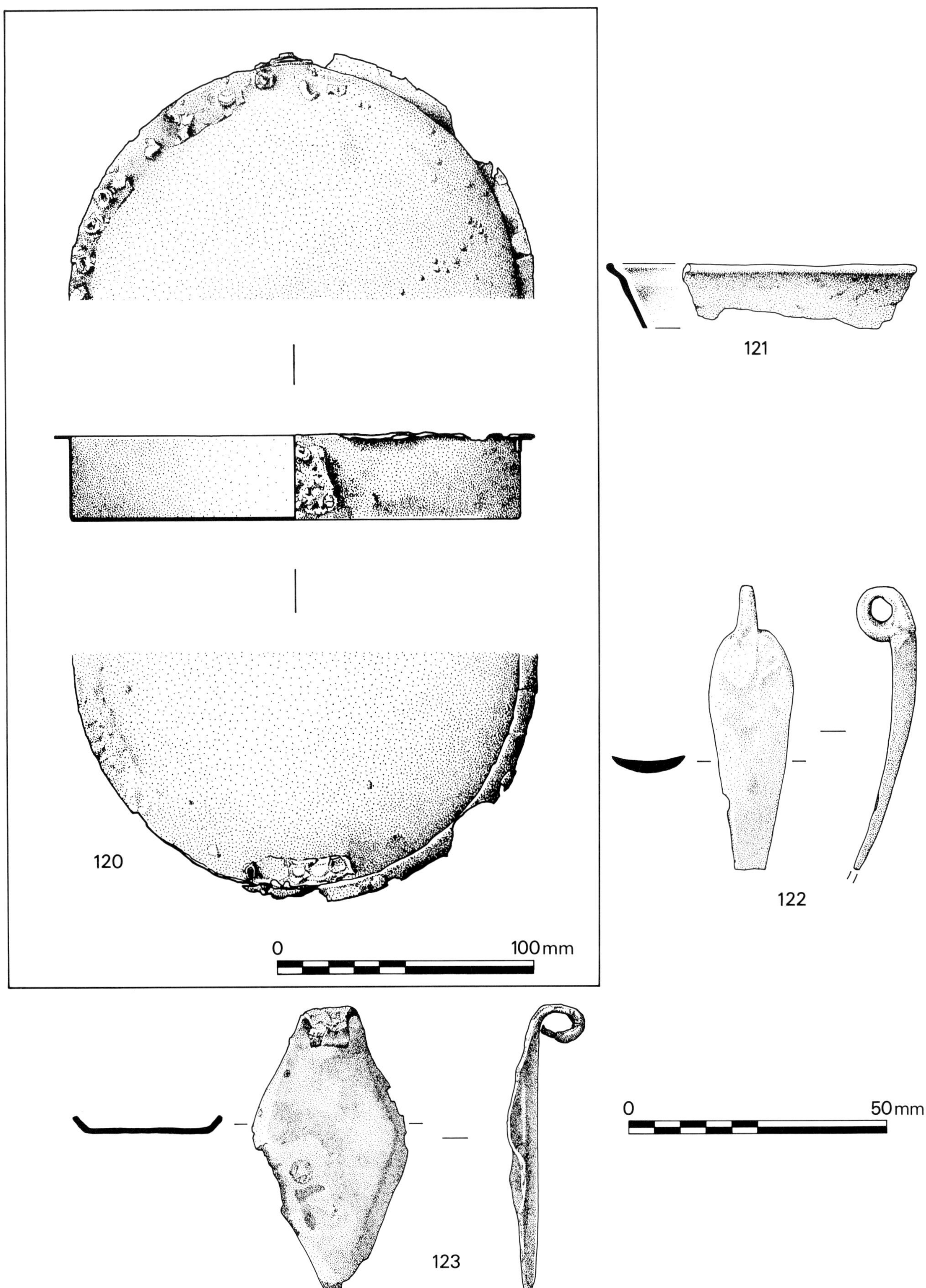

Figure 88 Copper alloy (except brooches), nos 120–3

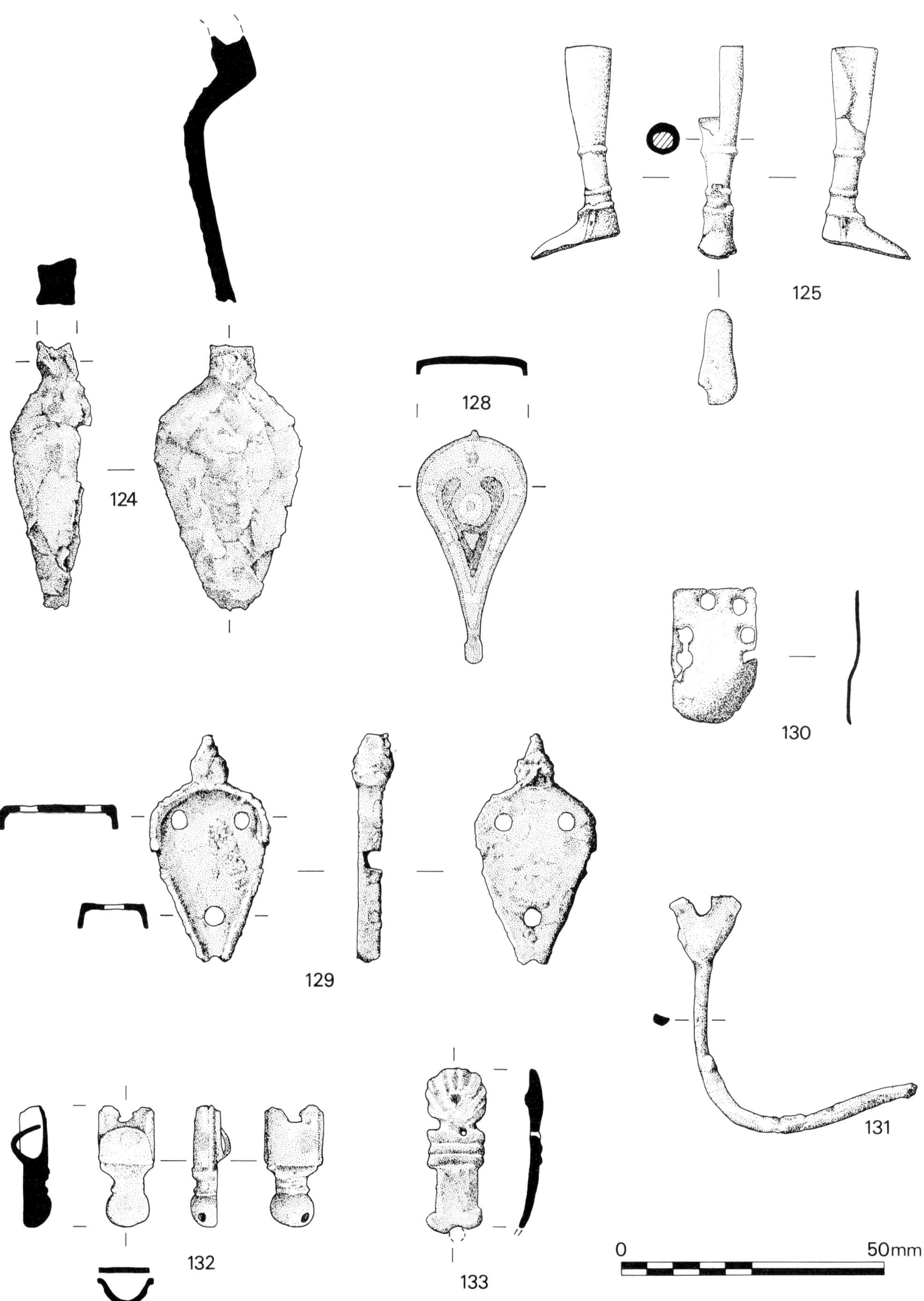

Figure 89 Copper alloy (except brooches), nos 124–33

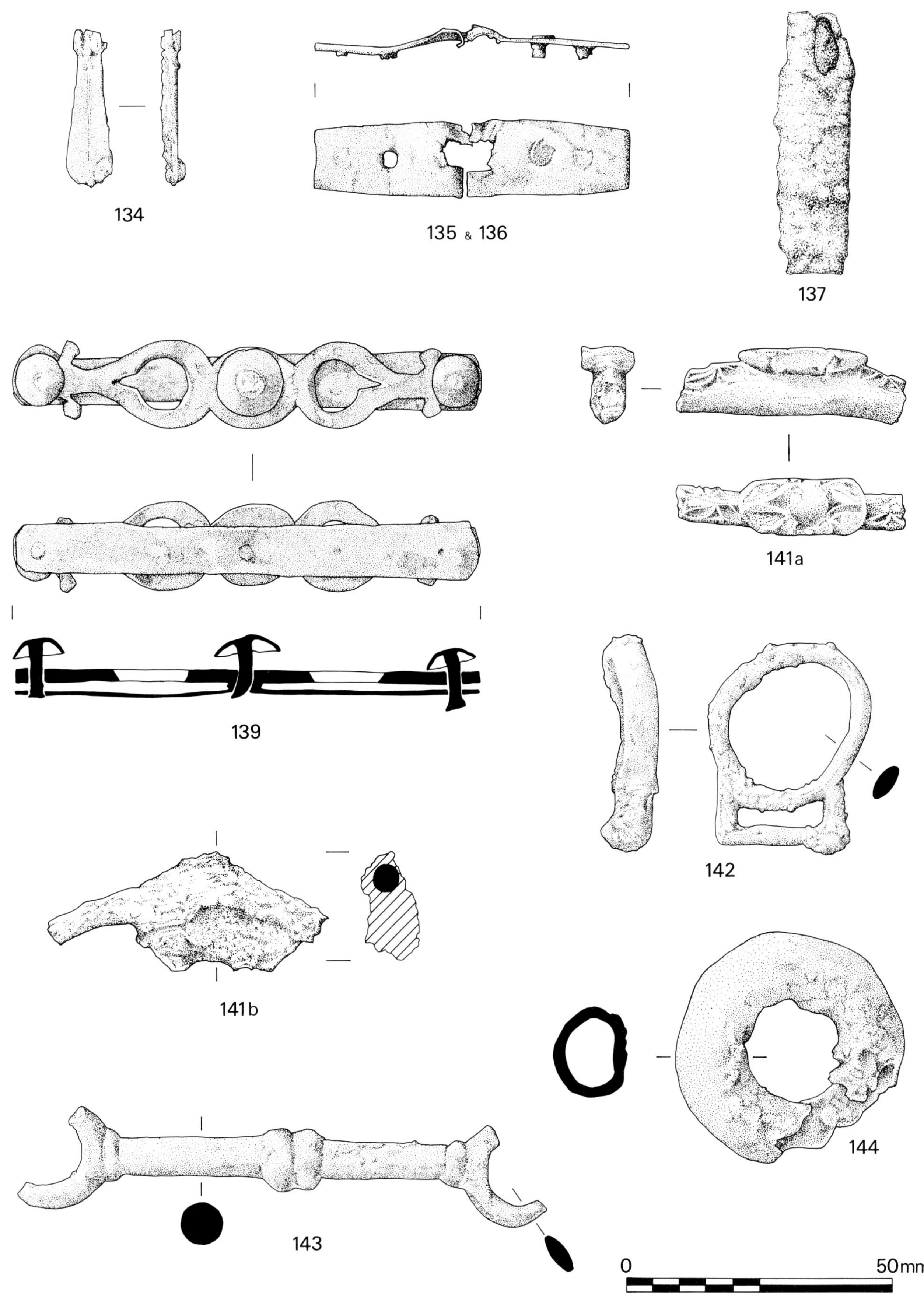

Figure 90 Copper alloy (except brooches), nos 134–44

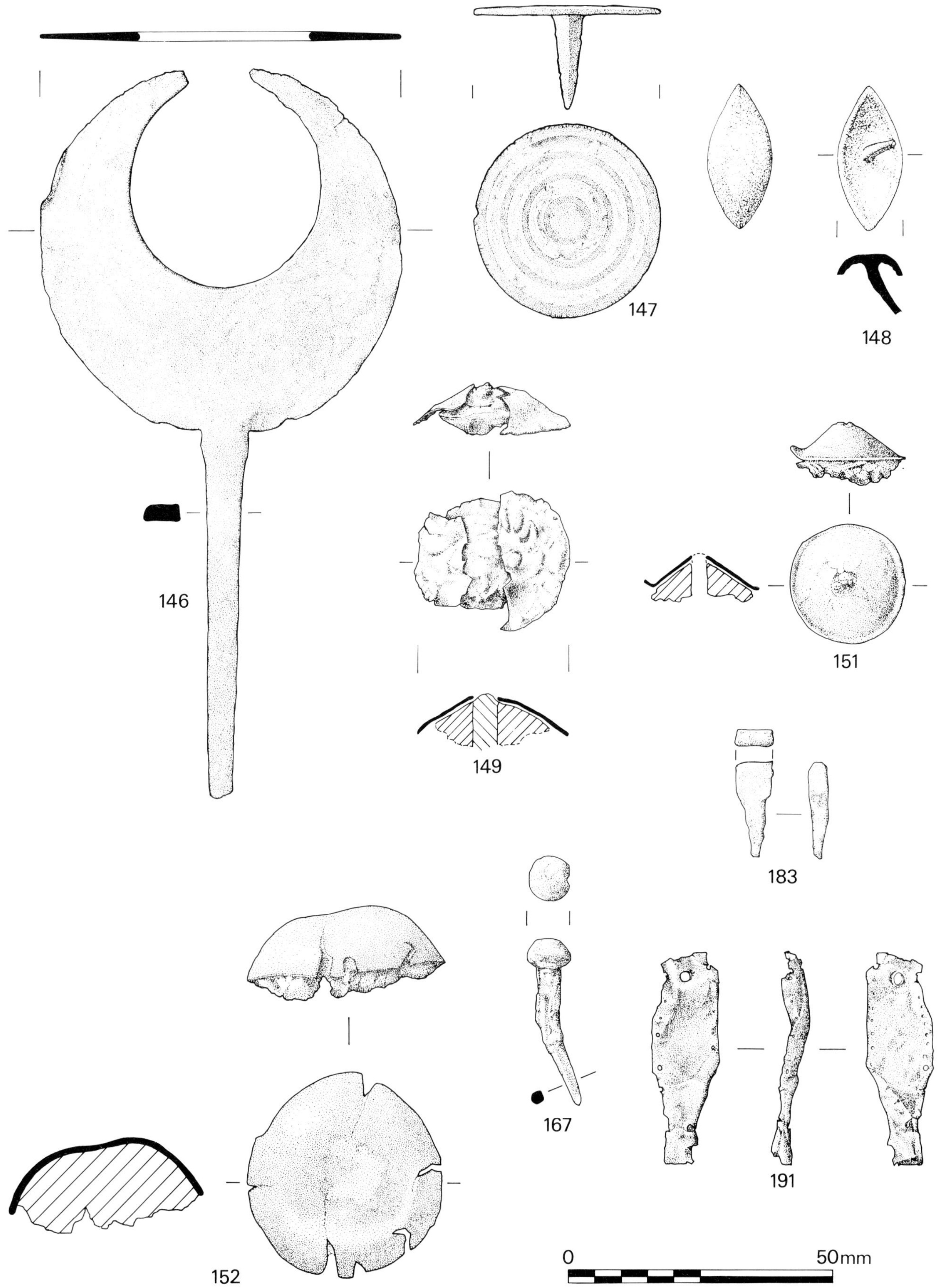

Figure 91 Copper alloy (except brooches), nos 146–91

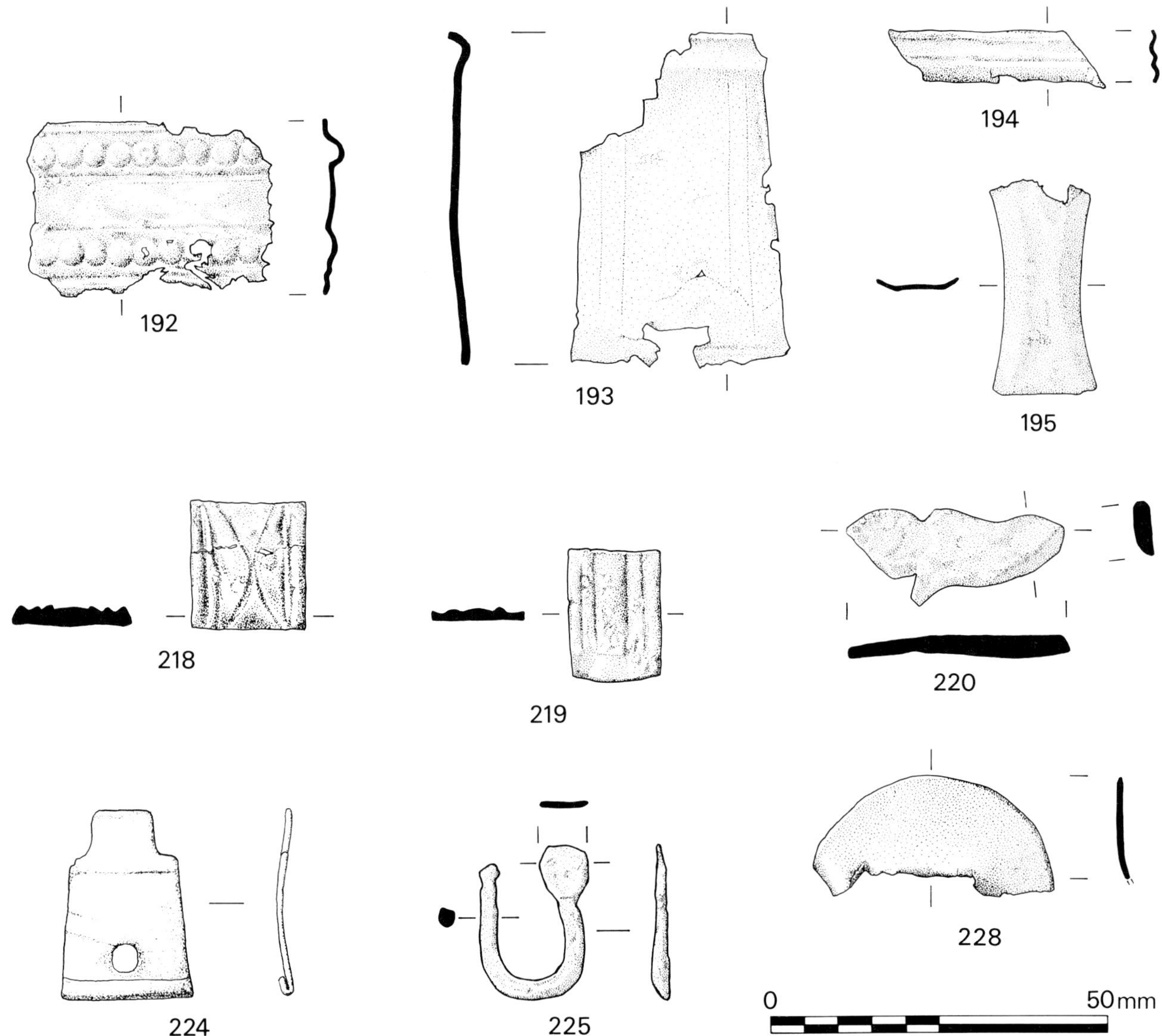

Figure 92 Copper alloy (except brooches), nos 192–228

Iron objects

Quita Mould

Introduction

[M4:A4] This report comprises a discussion of the Roman ironwork accompanied by a catalogue of the illustrated material and a separate catalogue in microfiche of all the Roman or possibly Roman material found during the excavations. Some post-Roman material appears in the catalogue but details of most of the post-Roman material can be found in the archive. The catalogues are arranged by function. Individual objects mentioned in the text are followed by their catalogue number within brackets, those objects with published illustrations are preceded by an asterisk *.

Over 550 iron objects were examined, see table 11. In addition 2065 timber nails were found, details of which are summarized in the full catalogue. Approximately 10% of the objects recovered were found to be of post-Roman date and, although described in the full catalogue, receive little further comment here.

About half of the contexts identified during the excavations remain unphased. Objects of known Roman type occurred in recognized Roman deposits, unphased contexts, topsoil and unstratified, and it is likely that a high proportion of those objects lacking diagnostic features which occur in non-Roman deposits also derive from the Roman occupation.

The ironwork from the Birch Abbey excavations comprised the usual components to be found in a civilian occupation assemblage, having a variety of structural fittings and domestic equipment to be expected at a settlement. In addition, a range of tools was found reflecting the variety of crafts required to serve the needs of the local community.

Table 11
Roman and possibly Roman iron objects

Category	Object and quantity
Weaponry	spearhead 1; sheath binding 1; bell-shaped stud 1
Tools, metal	set/chisel 1; punch 3; file 2; rake 1; tongs handle 1; fire-shovel 1
Tools, wood	gouge 1; chisel, paring 3; chisel/wedge 1; bradawl 1
Tools, leather	punch, circular 1; awl 10
Tools, plaster	modelling tool 1; trowel 1
Tools, stone	gouge 2
Tools, textile	needle 3
Agricultural	oxgoad 1; blade, hooked 1; hoe/pitchfork tine 1; turf-cutter 1
Miscellaneous	?peel 1; ratchet 1; socketed point 2; socket, nailed 1
Ferrules	conical 6; collar 5
Transport	(harness) snaffle bit 2; hipposandal 3; (cart fittings) linchpin 2; spiked collar 1
Jewellery	finger-ring 1
Dress fittings	shoe cleat 2; hobnail 176
Writing equipment	stylus 16
Locking mechanism	locks 1; keys 14
Blades	shears 1; cleaver 1; razor 1; knife 7
Domestic equipment	fire dog 1; candlestick 1; candleholder 1; ladle 1; bucket 1; handle, stem/strip 4; handle, spirally twisted 3; handle, ring 2; handle, drop 1
Structural fittings	hinge 1; hinge staple 7; wall-hook 1; ring-headed pin 4; split spiked-loop 11; joiner's dog 13; cramp 3; cramp, 3-tined 2; staple, U-shaped 6; staple, T-shaped 1; stud head 3; nail 2019
Miscellaneous	chain fragment 2; chain links 3; ring 11; hook 3; angle-bracket 2; nailed binding fragment 15; sheet, nailed fragment 3; sheet fragment 8; strap fragment 15; strip fragment 38; stem 1; wire fragment 3; hooked terminal 3; pierced shank 3; bar fragment 4; object fragment 10; fragment unidentifiable 28

Catalogue of illustrated objects (figs 93–7)

Weaponry

Spearhead

1 Open, nailed, round-sectioned socket and plano-convex sectioned, leaf-shaped blade tapering to a pointed tip, now broken, bent at a right-angle to the socket. Flaking. Length 160mm, blade length 70mm, width 36mm, socket diam 25mm. (FE 308, G III 1, unphased)

Bell-shaped stud

2 Large bell-shaped stud head with central boss, shouldered before the shank which tapers to a pointed tip. Shank length 73mm, head diam 35mm. (FE 403, M III 6B, phase II, late 2nd to early 3rd century on)

Sheath binding

3 Rectangular-shaped, looped binding of rectangular section, possibly a sheath binding. Length 45mm, width 11mm. (FE 291, D I 126A, phase II, later 2nd to early 3rd century?)

Tools

Metalworking

See also miscellaneous implements (no 41).

Set/chisel

4 Heavy set/chisel with square head narrowing into a round-sectioned neck and expanding into a wide-splayed blade. Length 158mm, head length 48mm, blade width 84mm. (FE 160, D I 2, phase VIII, late 4th century)

Punches

6 Round-sectioned punch tapering to a pointed tip from a flat, slightly burred head. Length 101mm, max diam 14mm. (FE 187B, D I 2A, phase VIII, late 4th century)
7 Small domed head expanding from the neck to a distinct shoulder before tapering to a long, square-sectioned, pointed tip. Length 98mm, head diam 12mm, shoulder width 13mm. (FE 278, F I 5, phase XIII, after AD 353)

File

9 Fine rectangular-sectioned stem tapering to a pointed tip at each end with a series of fine teeth across two faces. Length 86mm, max width 5mm. (FE 323, D IV 3, unphased)

?Rake

10 Rectangular-shaped blade of flat section with the beginnings of a centrally placed handle or tang. Possibly a small ash rake or scraper. Length 40mm, width 70mm. (FE 210A, D I 34, phase VI, mid- to late 4th century?)

?Tongs handle

11 Round-sectioned stem with hooked terminal with flattened tongue-like end. Possibly the handle from a small pair of tongs. Length 142mm, diam 5mm, hook length 45mm. (FE 254, D I 87, phase V, early to mid-4th century?)

Fire shovel

12 Large ovate blade with broken handle. Original record states the implement was tanged, but this is not borne out by surviving illustration (see also strap fragments 172 below). Not seen. Length 380mm, blade width 150mm, tang length 150mm. (FE 202, D I 5, phase VI?, mid- to late 4th century?)

Carpenter's tools

Gouge

13 Fragment of socketed gouge with broken socket. Length 100mm, blade width 20mm, socket width 30mm. (FE 213, D I 40, phase V, early to mid-4th century?)

Paring chisels

15 Rectangular-sectioned stem with a large shoulder tapering in thickness to a long, narrow, broken blade. Length 141mm, max width 19mm, blade width 10mm. (FE 258, H II 74, phase II, Antonine to 3rd century)
16 Rectangular-sectioned stem with flat head, flattening and expanding into a flaring, straight-ended blade. Length 164mm, blade length 82mm, width 22mm. (FE 260, H II 6A, phase III, Antonine to 3rd century on)

Chisel/wedge

17 Thick wedge-sectioned blade with a straight, bevelled edge and a short, broken, centrally placed tang. Possibly a short, wide-bladed mortise chisel or small wedge. Length 75mm, width 35mm, tang length 20mm. (FE 242, H III 1, unphased)

Bradawl

18 Slender, rectangular-sectioned, chisel-ended stem with pointed tang separated by a slightly expanded shoulder. Length 196mm, max width 13mm, edge width 6mm. (FE 377, G V 100, phase VI, late 4th century)

Mason's tools

Gouge

20 Square-sectioned stem with flat head and narrow gouge blade of U-shaped section. Length 95mm, blade length 60mm, width 9mm. (FE 259, H II 6A, phase III, Antonine to 3rd century on)

Leatherworking

Circular punch

21 Round-sectioned stem with a flat head and a long U-shaped gouge blade with penannular cutting face. Length 126mm; gouge blade 59mm, width 6mm; head diam 16mm. (FE 253, D I 87, phase V, early to mid-4th century?)

Awls

23 Fine square-sectioned awl tapering from a slightly thickened central shoulder to a pointed tip at each end. Length 102mm, max width 7mm. (FE 67, B I 3, phase II, Antonine to 3rd century)
25 As 23 above. Length 148mm, max width 7mm. (FE 185, D I 17, phase V, early to mid-4th century?)
27 Long round-sectioned stem with a bent tip, expanding to a distinct shoulder before tapering to a short pointed tip. Length 129mm, max diam 6mm. (FE 277, D I 135, phase VI, mid- to late 4th century?)
30 Small bent awl with square-sectioned tang and round-sectioned point separated by an expanded shoulder. Length 98mm, max width 6mm. (FE 193, G I 24, phase IX+, late 4th century)
31 Rectangular-sectioned stem tapering to a pointed tip at one end and a gently pointed tip at the other. Length 127mm, max width 8mm. (FE 401, M III 13, phase III, mid-4th century)

Plasterworking

Trowel

32 Long centrally-placed, rectangular-sectioned tang and flat, broken blade. The slightly cranked tang suggests this is a spatulate blade rather than a knife; there is no distinct back or edge visible. Possibly a trowel of Manning's type IV (1976, 27, no 71 and fig 5). Length 126mm, blade length 50mm, width 27mm. (FE 337, E VII 1, unphased)

Modelling tool

33 Thick round-sectioned stem flattening at each end into a straight-ended, flat, slightly flaring blade. Stem decorated by a series of three transverse mouldings with three bands of non-ferrous metal inlay. Manning type 3 (1985, 32, fig 7.3). Length 116mm, blade length 25mm, width 13mm. (FE 285C, G I 89, phase IV, early to mid-4th century)

Agricultural tools

Oxgoad

37 Double spirally twisted ferrule with a pointed tine. Length 34mm, diam 15mm, tine length 19mm. (FE 105, AA III 9, unphased)

Hooked blade

38 Small crescentic blade curving into a blunt tip and a straight, square-sectioned tang. In radiograph the back and edge are indistinguishable. Length 105mm, blade length 70mm, width 30mm. (FE 317, D II 24, unphased)

Tine

39 Heavy round-sectioned stem with curving profile tapering from a broken end to a bluntly pointed tip. Possibly a tine from a forked hoe or pitchfork. Length 170mm, diam 18mm. (FE 310, F I 41, phase XII, after AD 353)

Turf-cutter

40 Large, crescentic, flat-sectioned blade with open socket formed by folding the side wings inward. The nailed socket is broken. Length 136mm, blade length 160mm, width 60mm. (FE 376, G V 88, unphased)

Miscellaneous implements

?Baker's peel

41 Rectangular-sectioned strap handle and long stem spirally twisted in opposing directions expanding to a slight shoulder before the flat circular ring head with rectangular finial. Length 700mm, head diam 105mm. (FE 353, F I 5, phase XIII, after AD 353)

Transport

Cart fittings

Linchpin

56 Spatulate-headed linchpin with turned over loop and rectangular-sectioned shank. Manning type 2b (1985, 74, and fig 20). Length 161mm, head width 40mm. (FE 374, D II 14, unphased)

Spiked collar

58 Spiked collar of rectangular section, the tapering arms ending in clenched tips in opposing planes. Width 78mm, strap width 22mm, arm length 138mm. (FE 324, G IA 90, phase IV, early to mid-4th century)

Hipposandal

62 Hipposandal with pierced sole, heel hook, and side wings joining to form a front loop. Manning type 2 (1985, 65, and fig 16,2). Flaking. Length 160mm, sole width 70mm, max width 135mm. (FE 16, A XI 2, unphased)

Writing equipment

Styli

75 Wedge-sectioned eraser with upper stem decorated by a transverse moulding, broken before the point. Manning type 4 (1985, 85). Flaking. Length 93mm, diam 5mm, eraser width 7mm. (FE 46, A X 11, unphased)
77 Wedge-sectioned eraser and round-sectioned stem expanding to a slight shoulder above the point. Manning type 2. Encrusted, flaking. Length 133mm, diam 6mm, eraser width 7mm. (FE 126, AA IIIA 15, phase III, later 3rd century)
79 Waisted eraser and stem expanding to a distinct shoulder before the pointed tip. The shoulder is decorated with a transverse moulding. Manning type 4. Flaking. Length 116mm, diam 5mm, eraser width 8mm. (FE 340, D II 29, unphased)
82 Broken, waisted eraser, shouldered stem and point. The shoulder is decorated with a series of transverse mouldings with an inlaid non-ferrous band. Manning type 4. Length 136mm, diam 7mm. (FE 192, G I 14, phase IX, late 4th century)

Keys

93 Long rectangular-sectioned strip handle with rolled loop terminal and broken bit at right-angles to the handle. Flaking. Length 146mm, handle width 10mm. (FE 119A, AA II 51, phase VI, early to mid-4th century)
96 Rectangular-sectioned strap handle with a ring terminal, looped stem ends in a two-toothed bit. Length 150mm, bit length 22mm. (FE 289A, G IA 59, phase VII+, late 4th century)
100 Round-sectioned stem tapering from a shoulder to a pointed pivot. The rectangular bit with a slit in each edge is set to one side of the stem. Length 68mm, diam 20mm, bit length 13mm. (FE 270, D I 128, phase II, 2nd century)

Blades

Shears

106 Triangular blade with straight back and edge meeting at a pointed tip, now missing. The rectangular-sectioned tang set on line with the back flattens and expands into the beginnings of the spring. The shoulder of the blade is decorated with a series of notches. Flaking. Length 148mm, blade length 83mm, width 19mm, spring width 24mm. (FE 298, D I 173, phase II, later 2nd to early 3rd century)

Cleaver

107 Large blade with straight back and convex edge rising to meet the back at a rounded tip. The large round-sectioned socket is on line with the back and has minerally preserved organic remains present from the haft within. A triangular hole is present in one side of the socket, so that it appears like an open socket with a closed collar terminal. Manning type 2a (1985, 122 and fig 30). Length 330mm, blade length 221mm, width 105mm. (FE 188, D II 2, phase IX, late 4th century)

Razor

108 Slender blade with straight back and edge, the back dropping to meet the edge in a gently pointed tip; solid round-sectioned handle with a small ring terminal. Manning type 4 (1985, 110, and fig 28). Fractured, flaking. Length 132mm, blade length 85mm, width 12mm. (FE 159, D I 1, unphased)

Knives

Blades with a centrally placed tang

109 Narrow blade with straight back and edge, broken before the tip, and centrally placed tang. Back and edge cannot be distinguished in radiograph. Length 106mm, blade length 68mm, width 19mm. (FE 212, D I 23, phase VIII, late 4th century)
110 Small wide blade with straight back and slightly convex edge, broken before the tip, and with a centrally placed tang. Flaking. Length 97mm, blade length 73mm, width 30mm. (FE 256, G IV 1A, unphased)

Domestic equipment

Fire dog

116 Long rectangular-sectioned strap with a pair of down-turning strap legs at either end. Centre of the strap is pierced by a long oval hole where the strap is distinctly thickened in section. Length 353mm, width 25mm, leg length 63mm, width 28mm. (FE 143, A XVI 14, unphased)

Candlestick

117 Tripod candlestick with round-sectioned socket, long stem and remains of three round-sectioned legs. Ht 127mm, socket diam 22mm, surviving leg span 62mm. (FE 235, D I 71, phase V, early to mid-4th century?)

Candleholder

118 Round-sectioned socket and clenched rectangular-sectioned shank tapering to a pointed tip. Length 83/62mm, diam 17mm. (FE 269, D I 87B, phase V, early to mid-4th century)

Discussion

Weaponry

A single spearhead (*1) was found unstratified. The head being now bent at right-angles to the socket gives the object the appearance of being an ash rake or similar implement but the leaf-shape of the blade makes this interpretation less likely. A small rectangular collar (*3) found in a later 2nd- to early 3rd-century deposit in a well may be a sheath binding.

Of particular interest is the bell-shaped stud (*2) found in a layer (M III 6B) dating from the late 2nd century onward, which lay on top of what has tentatively been identified as the first defensive rampart of the town. This is the only bell-shaped stud of iron known to the author, although copper alloy examples are fairly common finds on Roman excavations. Having a long pointed shank, the Birch Abbey stud falls into type 1 of Allason-Jones' two categories (1985, 95), although at 73mm the shank is rather longer than is usual for the type. The majority of type 1 studs have been found in military contexts but examples from civilian sites such as Shakenoak and Newport, Isle of Wight, are known (*ibid*, 100).

The various suggestions as to the original use of such bell-shaped studs have been comprehensively summarized by Allason-Jones (1985) in her recent article. This example having been found on its own, as have so many of the type 1 studs, lends weight to the suggestion that they were used as dagger pommels like the example from *Carnuntum* found *in situ* (*ibid*, pl II). The Alcester stud may have been detached from its dagger when deposited, but it is puzzling that no part of an accompanying blade has been found with a type 1 stud where preservation of the blade might have been expected (within the 3rd-century cremation burial 59 (1967) at Brougham in Cumbria for example). It would seem that these studs may have had other uses as yet unknown.

Craft tools

An interesting collection of tools was found. As the Roman origin of several tools from unphased contexts or topsoil is doubtful, these objects are only briefly mentioned in the text.

Metalworking

Evidence for metalworking was found in site D in phases V and VI dating to the 4th century, where hearths occurred in a rectangular structure DC surrounded by pits containing metalworking waste.

A broken ash rake (*10) and a handle (*11), possibly broken from a small pair of tongs, both implements used by the smith, were found in pits containing metalworking debris. The hooked terminal of the handle (*11) can be paralleled on tongs from London (Manning 1985, 6 A10 and pl 2). The hook would serve to hold a link to keep the handles and thereby the jaws of the tongs closed, allowing the smith both to hold the object being worked and to strike it at the same time. A number of other objects, most notably a leatherworking punch (*21), an awl (26), a socketed gouge (*13), a candleholder (*118), and a ratchet (44), along with various small structural fittings and strip fragments, were also found associated with metalworking waste in the pits. Presumably they had been scattered around the area of the smithing hearths, possibly originally intended for reforging, when the working areas were cleared and the debris deposited in the pits.

A utensil (*12) with an ovate blade was found lying on burnt clay (D I 5) at the mouth of the flue of a metalworking hearth (D I 3), whilst to the west of the hearth other iron objects (FE 165) were noted, being set in a layer of charcoal and burnt bone (D I 6/9). None of these objects has been seen by the author but a surviving illustration of the implement (*12) suggests it is a fire-shovel. One might expect the head to be dished in the manner of the fire-shovels found at the Carrawburgh Mithraeum (Manning 1976, 39 and fig 23, 149) and Fishbourne (Manning 1972, 164 and fig 60, 6). However, the illustration shows encrustation on the object and it may be that any dishing is masked. The implement was originally recorded as being tanged but this is not borne out in the illustration and lengths of strap found in the same context bearing the same small find number suggest that the object had a long strap handle originally.

Another implement (*41), somewhat similar, is unusual being reminiscent of a baker's peel but differing in that the normally flat, solid head is pierced to produce a large ring head. Its long, spirally twisted stem suggests it was also associated with the hearth, possibly used to move a small vessel which fitted the central circular hole (64mm diam) in and out of the hot embers. If this were the case it may have had an industrial rather than a domestic function. It was found in a ditch presumably of late 4th-century date in site F. However, the deposit lay immediately below topsoil and it may be a post-medieval intrusion as the condition of the metal would suggest.

Metalworking tools including a set or heavy chisel (*4), punches (5, *6), and files (8, *9), identified as being used for metalworking because of the close spacing of the teeth, were all recovered from site D. A small punch (*7), probably used to make holes in hot metal, was found in ditch fill in site F. Two fullers (FE 154, FE 268), and a punch (FE 172) with a notched end possibly used as a swage, occurred in topsoil (areas D, J, and E respectively) and appear to be modern tools.

Woodworking

A broken socketed gouge (*13 mentioned above), and paring chisels (*15, *16) from site H, were carpenter's tools. The claw hammer (FE 186) appears to be modern although Roman examples are known from Pompeii and Novaesium-Neuss (Gaitzsch 1980, Taf 16, 84 and Taf 53, 269). It was found in a deposit (E IV 2) which contained only Roman material but was not well sealed. A small wedge-shaped tool with a central tang (*17) found in topsoil can be paralleled by examples from a ditch of the early fort at Newstead (Curle 1911, pl 59, 1 and 66, 9). The Alcester example has a bevelled edge which suggests it was used for working wood. A tanged, chisel-ended tool (*18) found in a late 4th-century deposit may be a long bradawl or possibly a fine rake tine (see agricultural implements below).

Stoneworking

Two narrow-bladed gouges (19, *20) were found with semi-circular-shaped cutting faces suggesting they were mason's tools. One (19) was found in site AA, where a possible shoemaker's workshop has been identified, and as it was similar to the circular punch below, these gouges may also have been leatherworking tools.

Leatherworking

A similar implement (*21) was found in an early to mid-4th-century pit, as mentioned above. The narrow gouge blade has an almost circular cutting edge indicating it was used to punch circular holes from leather. Several examples are known from Britain (Manning 1985, 42 E32, 33 and comparanda).

A relatively large number of awls (10) was found during the excavations, varying in length and section (for example *23, *25, *27, *30, *31). A quantity of leather off-cuts was found in pit F associated with the large timber building AA suggesting that shoemaking was carried out in the vicinity. A single awl (22) and a small gouge (19, see above) were found in this area; the other awls were distributed across the area of excavations, three being recovered from deposits of 4th-century date in site D (*25, 26, *27).

It is possible that the fine, socketed points (42, 43) and broken needle fragments (34, 35, 36) were also associated with leatherworking.

Modelling tools

A double spatulate-ended modelling tool of Manning's type 3 (1985, 32 and fig 7, 3) with a decorated handle (*33) found in an early to mid-4th-century layer, and a broken blade from a small trowel (*32) of Manning's type IV (1976, 27, 71, and fig 5), found in topsoil, were probably used to work wet plaster.

Agricultural implements

Evidence of agricultural activity is relatively poor. A small hooked blade (*38) is likely to have been used for cutting vegetation whether for reaping, pruning, or gathering foliage to feed stock. The small, socketed, crescentic blade is probably a turf-cutter (*40), whilst a fragment of thick, curved stem (*39) may be broken from a forked hoe or a pitchfork tine. A single oxgoad (*37), indicating traction ploughing, was found. Although the possibility of it being a pen nib cannot be ruled out, it would have been a rather unwieldy implement for the purpose.

Transport

Two spatulate-headed linchpins (*56, 57) of Manning's type 2b (1985, 74, and fig 20) were found. There was a spiked collar (*58) which may also be a cart fitting, although its occurrence in a foundation trench dated to the 4th century makes it more likely to be a structural fitting. A broken bit link (60) came from a late 2nd-century layer.

Three hipposandals (*62, 63, 64) of Manning's type 2 (1985, 65 and fig 16) were found. The five horseshoe fragments and the oxshoe are post-Roman. One horseshoe fragment (68) was recovered from a context sealed by deposits which appeared to be Roman (D II 14).

Blades

A triangular blade from a pair of shears (*106) was found in a later 2nd- to early 3rd-century pit. The shoulder of the blade was decorated by a series of notches more usually seen on examples of medieval date. Shears were used as we use scissors today and being general-purpose tools may have been used in textile working as were the needle fragments mentioned above. A cleaver (*107) of Manning's type 2a (1985, 120–2 and fig 30) used for butchering meat was found in D II 2, a late 4th-century context; bone evidence in pit C II 21 also indicated butchery. A narrow blade with a solid handle (*108) of Manning's type 4 (1985, 110 and fig 28) is of a type thought to belong to the earlier Roman period, going out of use during the 2nd century. Its distinctive shape suggests a specific use, probably as a razor. A knife (*115) from a 4th-century layer is unusual in having a copper alloy handle. The remaining seven Roman knife blades represent a selection of commonly found domestic knives (eg *109, *110).

Domestic equipment

The range of domestic implements included a tripod candlestick (*117) and a socketed candleholder (*118) from 4th-century deposits, fragments from a ladle (119), bucket fittings (120), and a selection of keys (eg *93, *96) and handles. It is worth noting that the pivot terminal of a lever-lock key (*100), used to work a sophisticated locking mechanism, was found in a cobble surface dated to the 2nd to early 3rd century (D I 128).

A fire dog (*116) was found with charcoal and burnt clay, associated with pottery of 2nd- and 3rd-century date, in a slot showing traces of heavy burning.

Writing equipment

Sixteen styli were found, ranging from plain examples (eg *77, 84, 85, 87) to those with stems decorated with transverse mouldings and inlaid bands of non-ferrous metal of a contrasting colour (*75, *79, *82, 88). Four of the styli (*82, 83, 84, 85) were recovered from 4th-century contexts in area G I, apparently coming from outside the main building of the area (in G IV).

Personal items

A broken finger-ring (70) and a possible penannular bracelet (71) were the only items of jewellery, whilst two small cleats (72, 73) and hobnails from footwear were the only dress fittings recovered.

Structural fittings

The range of structural fittings was comparable with that found on the majority of Roman excavations. The usual range of timber nail types was found, including Manning's types 1a, 1b, 2, 3, and 4 (1985, 134–7 and fig 32). As is usually the case the vast majority, some 92.5%, were of type 1b, occurring in a wide range of sizes reflecting the various general uses to which they had been put.

Iron from burials

Iron objects were found in seven burials from the Birch Abbey excavations.

All the nails recovered from burials were of Manning's type 1b. Minerally preserved wood remains found on eight nails from the mid- to late 4th-century female burial HB 47 indicate that the coffin boards were 40–44mm (1½–1¾in) thick. The eight nails were originally recorded as 120mm in length and had been driven horizontally into the coffin boards, with the lid and base board being some 280mm apart. Minerally preserved wood remains from five nails from HB 65 suggest the coffin boards were thinner, 11–25mm (½–1in) in thickness.

A small quantity of hobnails from nailed footwear were found in the area of the feet in three burials (HB 11, 27, 65). In the male burial HB 11, which contained a minimum of six hobnails below the feet, staining of the surrounding soil was also noted. HB 65, dated to the late 4th century, contained nineteen hobnails located below the heels.

Table 12 Iron objects from burials

Burial	Area	Nails	Hobnails	Object
HB 11	A V 4	2	6	–
HB 13	B III 8	1	–	–
HB 27	A III 101	?	?	–
HB 38	A XVII 2	4	–	–
HB 43	F IA 2	4	–	nailed bindings (205)
HB 47	D I 120	12	–	–
HB 65	G V 6A	21	19	–

(? indicates presence recorded but object/s not seen by the author).

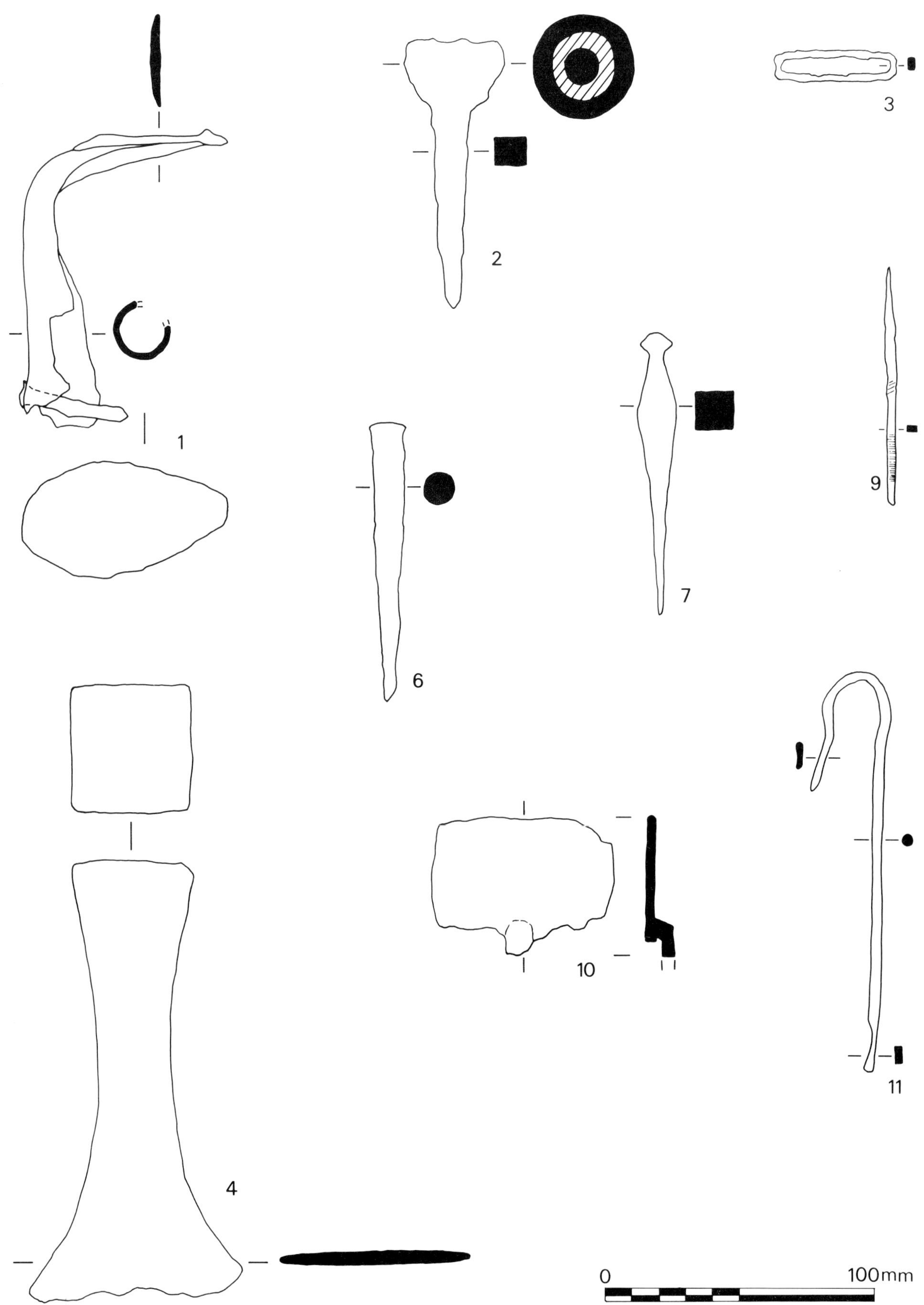

Figure 93 Iron objects, nos 1–11

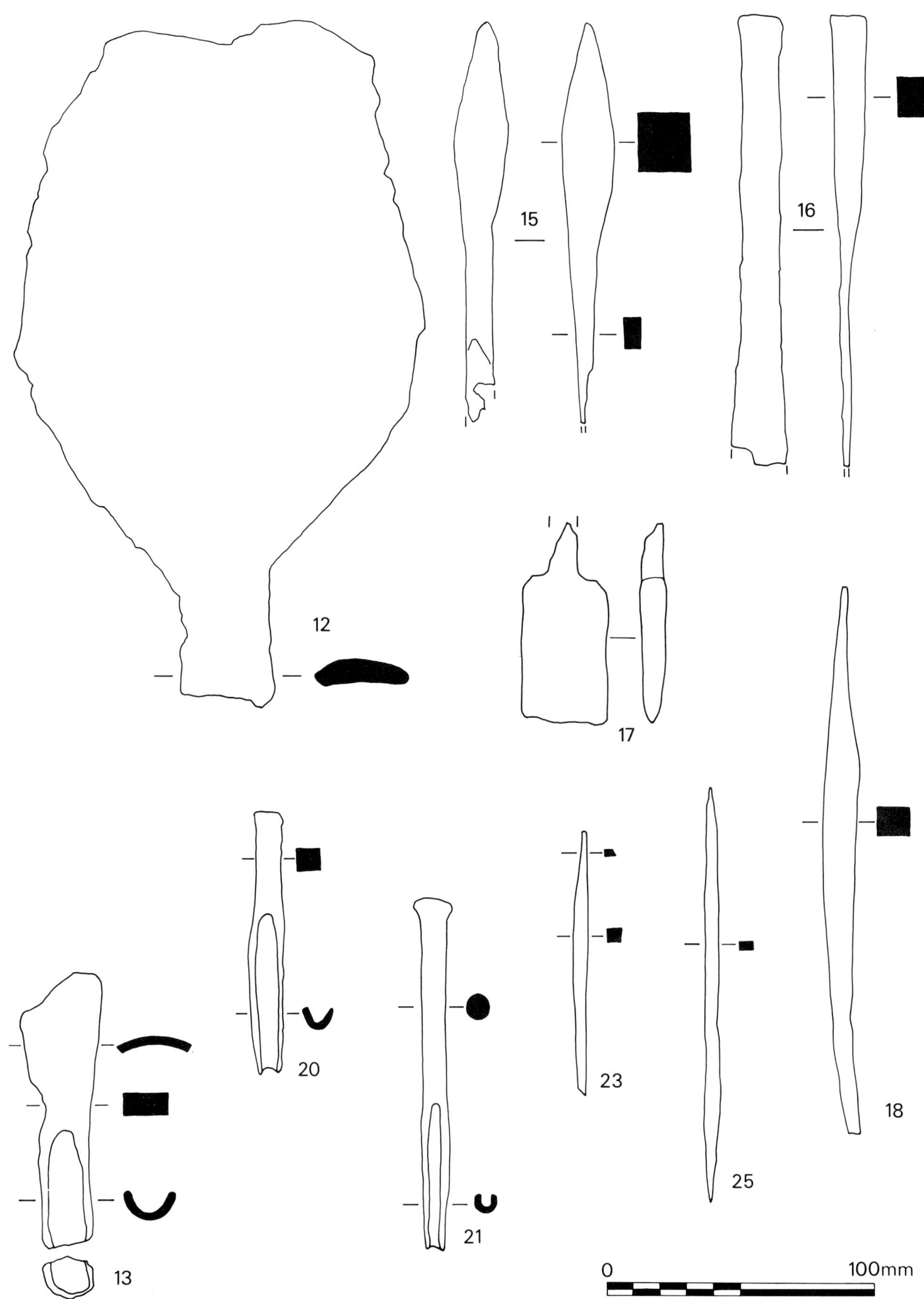

Figure 94 Iron objects, nos 12–25

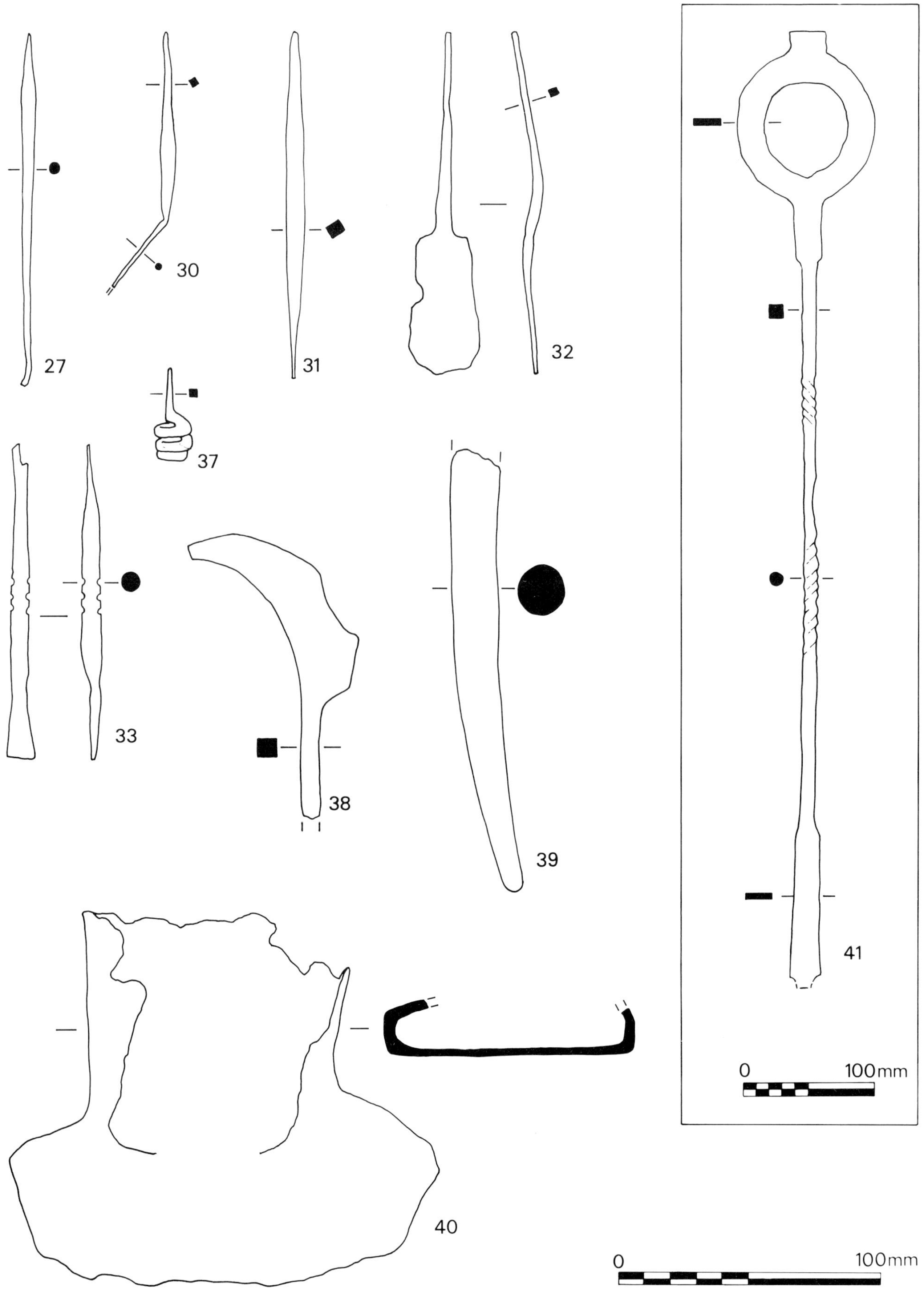

Figure 95 Iron objects, nos 27–41

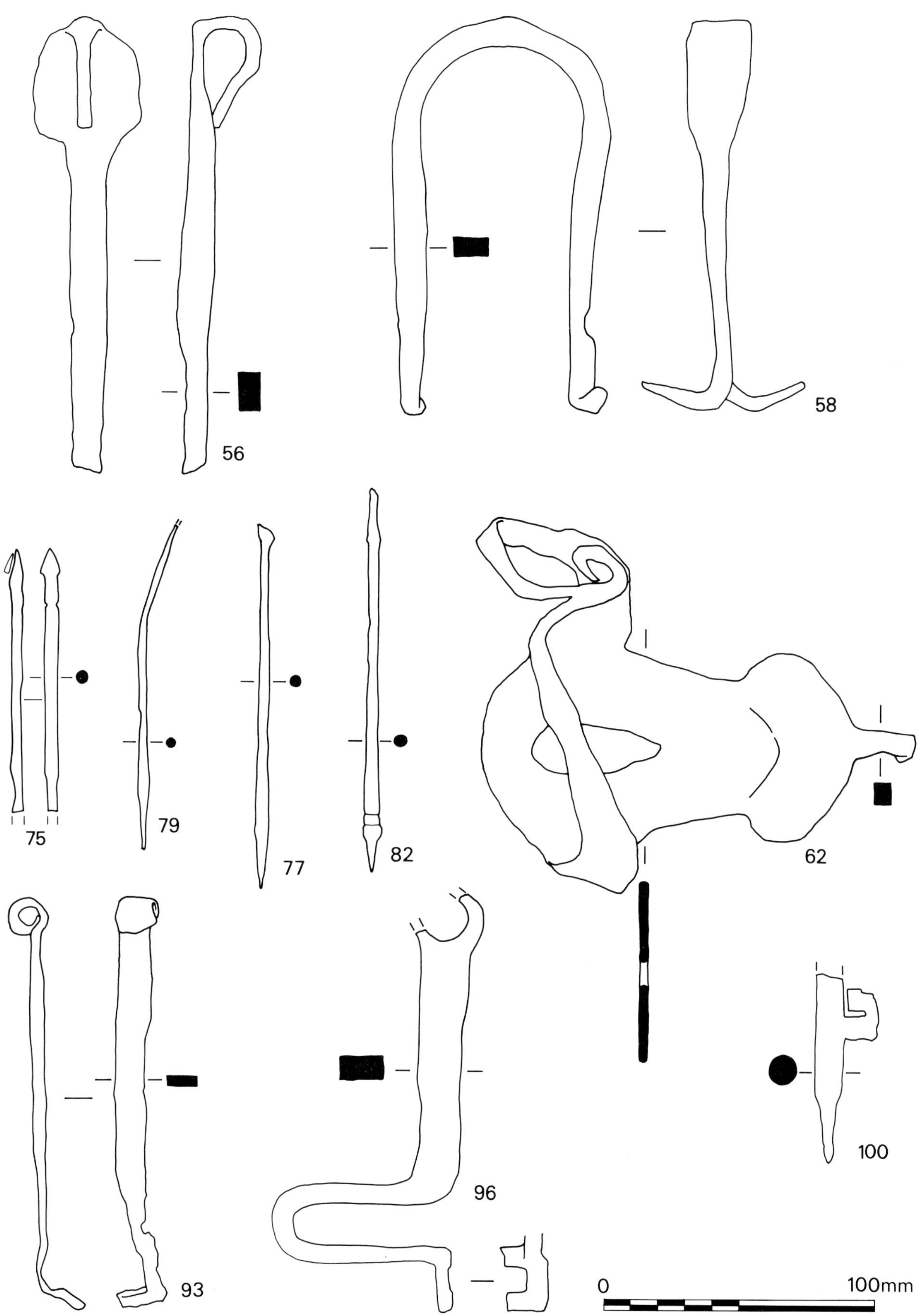

Figure 96 Iron objects, nos 56–100

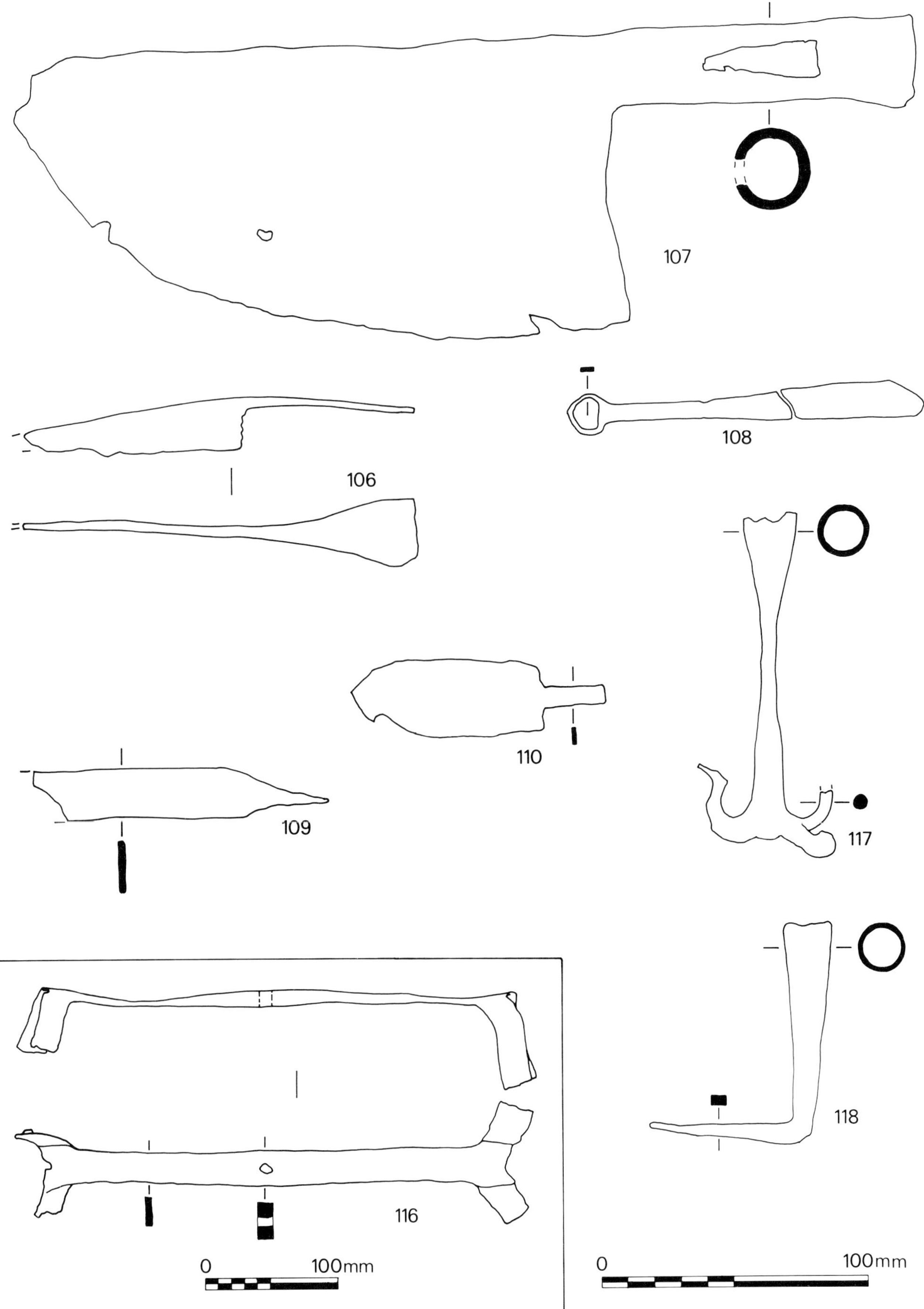

Figure 97 Iron objects, nos 106–18

Iron slag

Gerry McDonnell

[M4:C12] A total of 27.5kg of iron working slag samples was recovered from the site. There was no evidence of iron smelting. The main concentrations of slag were in trench D I, associated with phases V and VI. It is probable that the hearths in structures DC and DCA were smiths' forges.

Crucible fragments

Justine Bayley

A total of five crucible fragments was examined and their surfaces analysed qualitatively by energy dispersive X-ray fluorescence (XRF). The metals detected are listed in the table 13 (in order of XRF signal strength; those in brackets only gave weak signals). The fragments all showed some signs of vitrification, either of the crucible itself or of the added extra outer layer (EOL) of less refractory clay. The vitrification did not penetrate deeply into the crucibles, showing them to be well suited to their function.

At least two different types of crucible are represented by the sherds. One is a beaker form with a pedestal base which is common throughout Roman Britain (Bayley 1988, fig 5, 4); dated examples belong mainly to the late 1st or 2nd century and include those from Colchester (Bayley 1984a) and Baldock (Stead & Rigby 1986, fig 63, 410). An added extra outer layer in less refractory clay is a common feature of this type of crucible. As the two body sherds also have this feature they are likely to be from crucibles of the same general form as the base (SL 30, fig 98, no 1), though there is no suggestion that they are parts of the same vessel. SL 30 is from a late 4th-century pit, and has a rather narrower base relative to its overall size than is common for crucibles of this type. It could thus be seen as a transitional form, falling between the broad-base beakers and the conical-based crucibles (see below) which might explain the late date of the context in which it was found. The body sherds are either unstratified or unphased.

Table 13 X-ray fluorescence analysis of crucible fragments

Site reference	Sherd type	Metals detected
P 3 (A I 4E)	rim	Zn (Cu Pb)
ST 5 (A X 5)	base	Cu Zn (Pb)
SL 28/P 16 (B III 4)	body + EOL	Zn Cu
SL 27 (B IV 1)	body + EOL	Zn Cu Pb Sn
SL 30 (G I 24A)	base + EOL	Cu Pb Sn (Zn)

Key: Cu = copper, Zn = zinc, Pb = lead, Sn = tin

The second base (ST 5, fig 98, no 2) is conical (cf Bayley 1988, fig 5, 5) which is normally a later Roman crucible form though the example here is from an unphased context. The rim (P 3, fig 98, no 3), which is from an early to mid-4th-century context, may be from another vessel of this form though its internal rim diameter (40–50mm) is considerably less than the maximum diameter of the vessel which is unusual in conical-based crucibles. Published examples include those from Gestingthorpe (Draper 1985, fig 38, 434–5) and Sewingshields (Bayley 1984b, fig 20, 1).

Because each metal has a different pattern of chemical behaviour, the amounts of them that remain on the crucibles are not in the same proportions as in the metal that was being melted. The relative amounts are further altered by corrosion during burial and, on top of all this, the XRF signals detected are not in direct proportion to the amount of each metal present. It can be seen then that the analytical results, as presented in table 13, do not give a good indication of the nature of the alloys that were being melted. They can, however, be interpreted in the light of experience and this leads to the suggestion that two of the beaker form crucibles (SL 27 and 30) were used to melt bronzes (copper-tin alloys) or gunmetals (copper-tin-zinc alloys), with or without added lead. The other three sherds (SL 28, P 3, and ST 5) are from crucibles that may possibly have been used to melt brasses (copper-zinc alloys).

Lead objects

Quita Mould

[M4:D1] Eight Roman or possibly Roman objects of lead, and a small quantity of waste and scrap were found at the Birch Abbey excavations. The details are summarized in tables 14 and 15. The most significant items are illustrated in figs 99–100 and summarily described below whilst the full catalogue can be found in microfiche. Descriptions of post-Roman objects can be found in the site archive. All of the three pewter objects are likely to be post-Roman.

Catalogue of illustrated objects (figs 99–100)

1 Open lamp. Shallow, circular bowl of thick sheet with small lip, hammer marks present on the interior. Diam 97mm, ht 20mm. (OM 36, D II 20, unphased)

2 Weight. Circular, centrally pierced weight with flat upper and lower face. Sides decorated with a series of transverse mouldings. Diam 23mm, ht 11mm, weight 24.21g. (OM 22, D I 100, phase II, later 2nd to early 3rd century?)

3 ?Weight. Conical, centrally pierced object with flat base and concave sides. Diam 30mm, ht 30mm, weight 85.06g. (OM 31, G IV 17, phase VI, late 4th century)

5 Cramp. Pottery cramp comprising two parallel strips joined by a shank at each end. Length 47mm, shank length 6mm, max width 10mm. (OM 38, D II 29A, unphased)

Table 14 Lead objects

Object	Quantity
Open lamp	1
?Weight	2
Caulking	1
Cramp	1
Stem	1
Disc	1
?Lid	1

Table 15 Lead scrap and waste

Scrap and waste	Quantity (g)
Sheet	261.78
Sheet, offcut	353.45
Molten waste	317.42
Total	932.65

Discussion

A shallow, circular bowl with a small lip (no 1) was found in a context (D II 20) which, although containing only Roman material, was not well sealed. It is likely to be an open lamp. The wick would have rested in the lip with one end trailing in the fat or oil. An open lamp is vulnerable to spillage and the choice of lead for its construction would have the advantage of making it particularly stable and difficult to knock over. Lead lamp holders are known from Roman contexts (cf examples from Newstead: Curle 1911, pl 79, 3, 4, 9), being similar in shape and thickness to the more commonly found iron examples. Open lamps are less commonly recognized; however, a rudely shaped open lamp in stone was found in the *Praetentura* (*ibid*, pl 79, 1) at Newstead.

A circular, centrally pierced object (no 2) was found in a pit in a later 2nd- to early 3rd-century deposit (D I 100). It is likely to be an *uncia* weight, although weighing slightly less, lead being easily oxidized and an unreliable material to use as a weight (Kisch 1965, 81, 221). As the object is centrally pierced, it could have been used as a spindle whorl. A conical object (no 3), also centrally pierced, weighing just under three *unciae*, was found in a possible hearth (G IV 17) in building GE dating to the late 4th century. It is not of a shape commonly used for Roman weights (*ibid*, 92) and may possibly have been a decorative finial rather than a weight.

A cramp (no 5) used to mend broken pottery was found in a large pit to the west edge of street C (D II 29A) containing a remarkable group of samian vessels and coarse pottery sherds.

The majority of the lead, just under a kilogram in weight, was scrap and waste deriving from lead fittings from buildings, found principally in topsoil or unstratified. The offcuts produced when cutting sheet to size were discarded during the installation or repair of sheet lead flashings or other fittings. The broken sheet fragments probably resulted from their subsequent decay or demolition. The small amount of solidified molten waste found is likely to come from demolition debris.

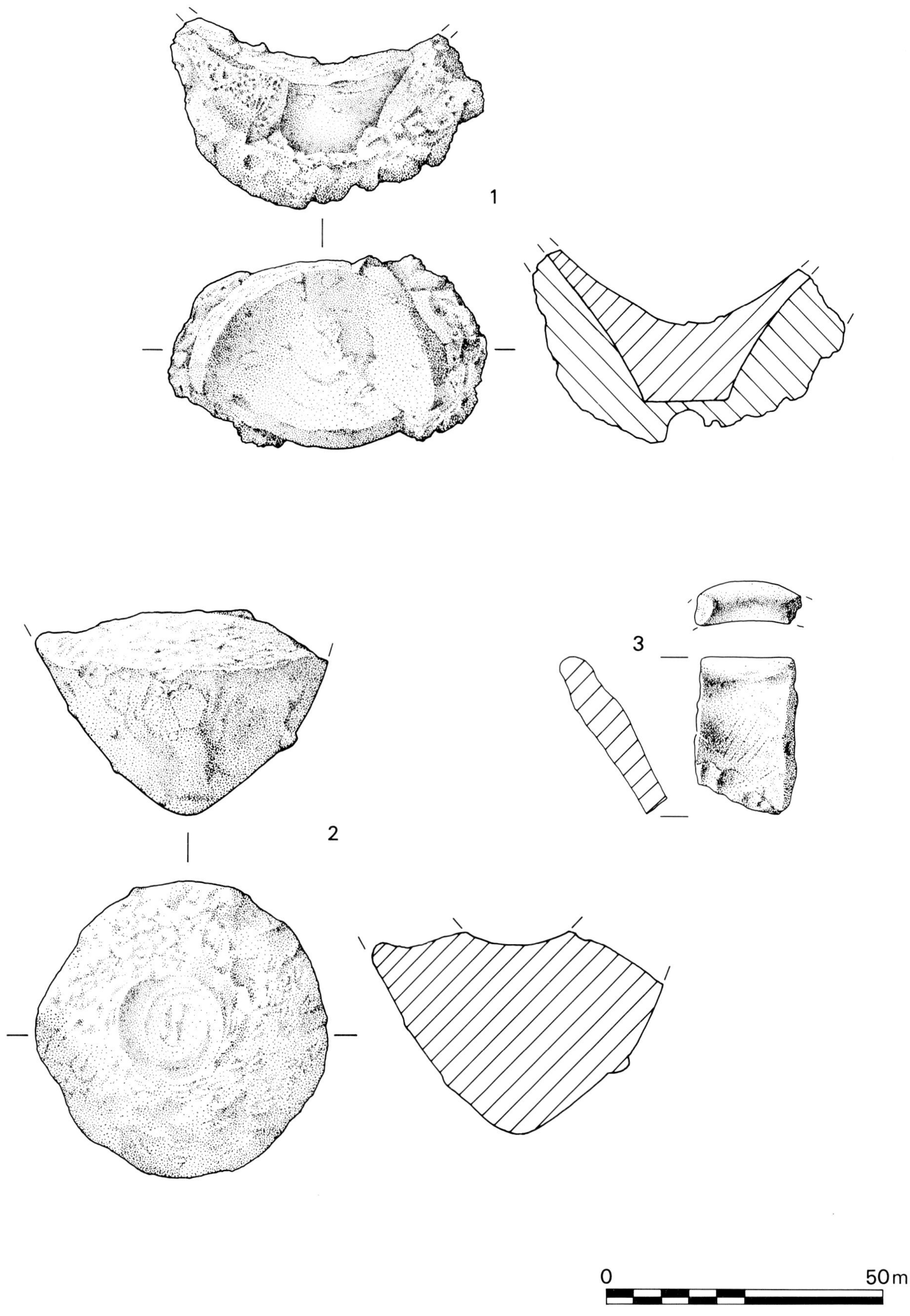

Figure 98 Crucibles

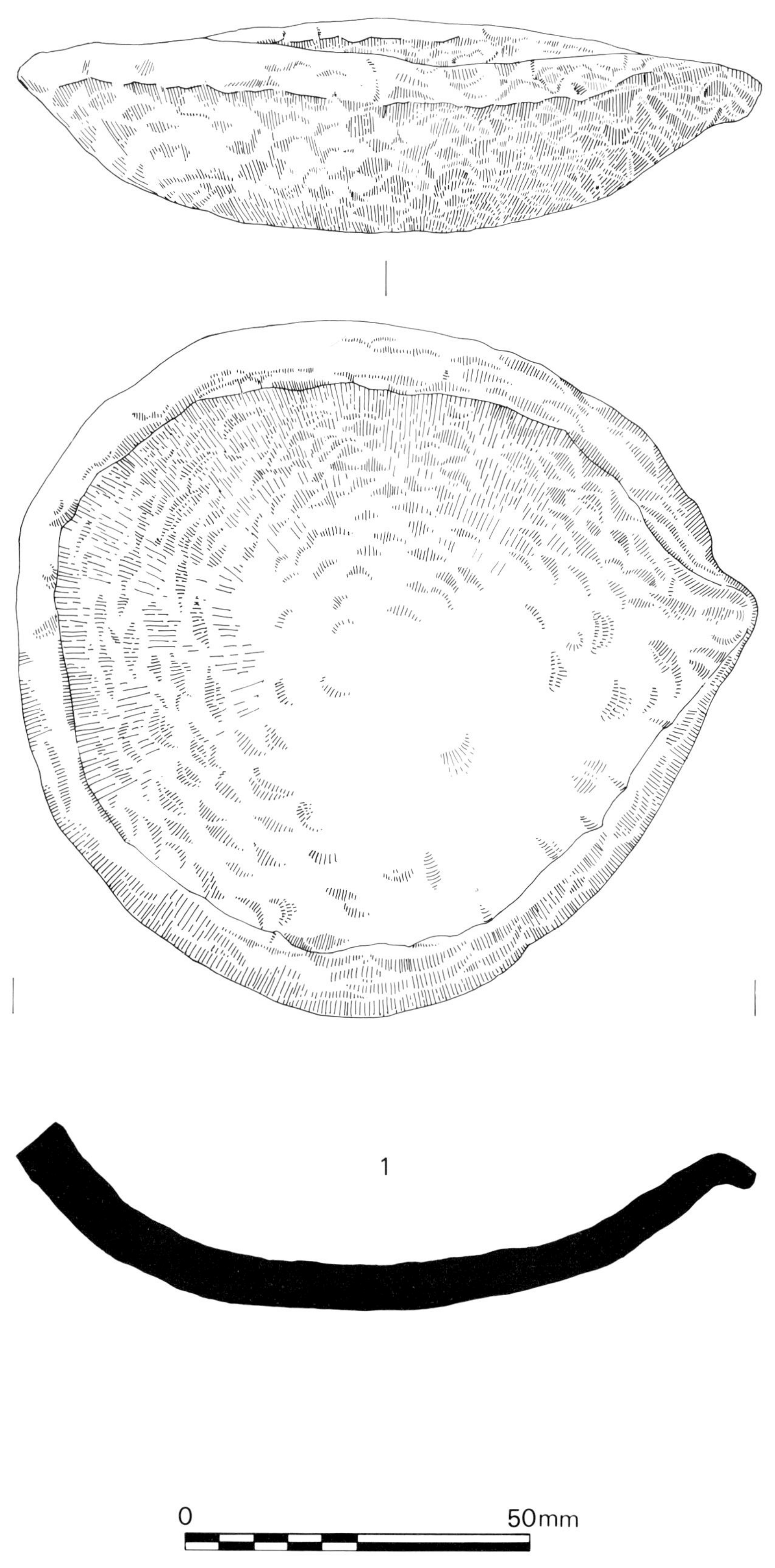

Figure 99 Lead object, no 1

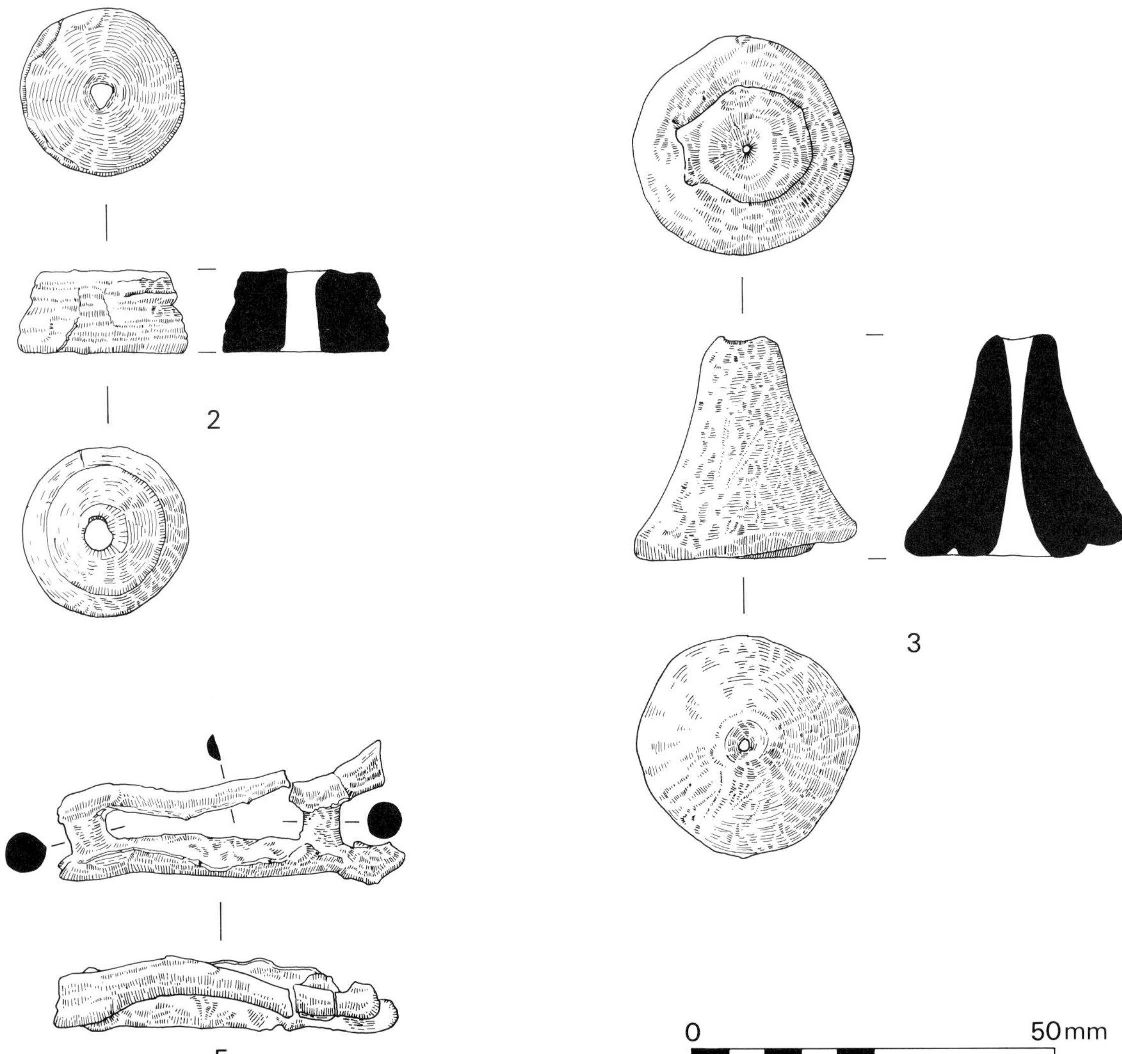

Figure 100 Lead objects, nos 2–5

Bone and bone products

Animal bone

At the time of the excavation W T W Potts visited the site and took samples of animal bone from several pits, a total of just under 4000 items. Cattle bones formed the greater part (70%) of the identified fragments; sheep or goat were next most numerous with 25%; while pig, horse, dog, deer, cat, and birds formed the remainder. Oysters were also present. The bones were not retained. In view of the selective nature of the sampling and the summary and potentially misleading nature of the data, further details are not published here.

Worked bone

G Lloyd-Morgan

See also microfiche [M4:D4].

Catalogue of illustrated objects (figs 101–2)

Bead

1 Biconical bead, turned and decorated with incised lines grouped at either end, leaving the wider central area unornamented. Length 19.1mm, max diam 6.8mm. (BO 67, D II 24, unphased)

Compare the larger cylindrical jet bead which has been turned to give the suggestion of segments grouped at each end with a wider plain band in the centre, found at Butt Road, Colchester 1976–9 from a context dated *c* AD 320–450 (Crummy 1983, 34, no 1370, fig 36). Note also the biconical glass beads with banded decoration dated by Guido (1978, 98, fig 37, no 15) to the 3rd and 4th centuries onwards, which could also be related.

Pins and needles

2 Incomplete pin with low conical head, tip and lower part of shaft lost. Length 42.7mm, max diam at head 6.1mm. (BO 8B, AA I 2, unphased)

Crummy type 1 pin dated *c* AD 70–200/250 (Crummy 1979, 159–60, fig 1, no 1). Four examples are reported from Dover in a context dated to *c* AD 190/200–208. Compare also the examples from Warwickshire, including Alcester, Bleachfield Street 1976–7 no 362, 475; ALC 72 45; and Tiddington TD 81 784.

5 As above, complete and with straight sides. Length *c* 65mm, max diam shaft *c* 6mm. (BO 48, G II 3, phase V, later 4th century)

6 Probably a type 1 pin with a rough, angular cross-section, head crudely finished into a conoid. Length 106.2mm, max cross-section 3.2mm × 5mm. (BO 97, G II 12, phase V, later 4th century)

7 Crude version of a type 1 pin, tip and lower part of the shaft missing. Present length 52.6mm, max diam shaft *c* 4mm. (BO 117, AA II 2, unphased)

8 Complete pin, with flat head and slight bevelling around the edge. Probably Crummy type 1. Length 92.8mm, max diam shaft 7.2–7.7mm. (BO 8A, AA I 2, unphased)

Compare the similar, roughly shaped head of Tiddington M731.

12 Pin with slight, conical head and two incised grooves beneath to suggest a collar. Tip and lower part of shaft lost. Length 68.2mm, max diam shaft 3.1–3.6mm. (BO 23, AA II 16, phase V, later 3rd century on)

Crummy type 2 pin dated *c* AD 50–200/250 (Crummy 1979, 160, fig 1, no 2). Compare the examples from Rosemary Lane, Canterbury, with the second example coming from a late 2nd-century pit (Bennett *et al* 1982, 181, fig 94, nos 81, 87, discussion p 41); also the examples from Alcester, Bleachfield Street 1976–7, nos 397, 522, 524; ALC 1969 77; and Tiddington TD 81 805 and the related M715, M716, M721.

13 As above, in two adjoining pieces but complete. Length 102.7mm, max diam shaft 3.5mm. (BO 24, AA II 2, unphased)

14 As above, but more crudely made with a roughly ovoid cross-section. Tip and lower part of shaft lost. Present length 62mm, max cross-section 2.5mm × 3.2mm. (BO 25, AA I 30, phase VI, later 3rd to early 4th century)

19 As above but with one well-defined and two slightly incised grooves beneath the tiny subspherical head, giving the effect of two collars. The tip and lower part of the shaft are lost. Present length 58.2mm max diam shaft 3.3mm. (BO 63, D I 112, phase IV, late 3rd century)

Note also a fragment of shaft which may belong to this pin. Length 20.7mm.

20 As above but with conical head and four grooves below it giving an effect of three collars. The tip and lower part of the shaft are lost. Length 42.6mm, max diam shaft 3.7mm. (BO 34, A XVI 17, unphased)

21 Possibly a crude version of a type 2 pin. The upper part of the shaft and angular head are decorated with heavy hatching. The well-defined collar in between has been left undecorated. The tip and much of the shaft are lost. Present length 47.7mm, max diam head 5.3mm. (BO 51, G I 24, phase IX+, late 4th century)

22 Pin with subspherical head; the tip and part of the shaft are lost. Present length 70.7mm, diam head 12.7–13.7mm. (BO 1, A XI 2, unphased)

Crummy type 3 pin dated to *c* 200 — late 4th/early 5th century (Crummy 1979, 161, fig 1, no 3). An example from Wadham House, Dorchester, Dorset came from a context dated early 4th century (Draper & Chaplin 1982, 24, fig 12, no 5); another from *Verulamium* from a context dated AD 275–300 (Frere 1984, 73, fig 31, no 276). The type is well represented at Alcester with nineteen pieces from Bleachfield Street 1976–7; ALC 1969 13; ALC 1972 46; and Tiddington with six pieces from earlier excavations with TD 80 5 and TD 81 880.

28 As above but with ovoid/flattened subspherical head, complete. Length 52.8mm, diam head 6.3–7.4mm. (BO 28, C VI 4, phase IX, mid-4th century on)

30 As above, complete. Length 93.9mm, diam head 8.0–8.3mm. (BO 42, D I 29, phase IV, late 3rd century?)

35 As above; complete though the tip may have been broken and resharpened. Length 77.5mm, diam head 4.0–4.6mm. (BO 93, G V 100, phase VI, late 4th century)

37 Possibly a variant of Crummy type 3, with the head a small subspherical shape separated by a deep groove from the shaft. Complete. Length 116.2mm, max diam shaft 4.8–5.2mm. (BO 91, G V 5, phase VI, late 4th century)

38 Similar to no 37 above but incomplete, the tip and most of the shaft has been lost and the remaining section has been split in half, only one piece of which has survived. Present length 15.8mm, max diam shaft 4.4mm. (BO 84, E V 9, phase XIII, after AD 353)

39 Pin with ovoid head and a well-defined collar flaring out below. The tip and part of the shaft are lost. Present length 73.7mm, max diam head 4.3–4.7mm. (BO 18, A XIV 2, unphased)

Crummy type 5 pin dated *c* AD 250 — late 4th/early 5th century. Compare the similar examples from Gestingthorpe, Essex (Draper 1985, 68, fig 32, nos 366–9); and another from *Verulamium* from a context dated AD 300–70 (Frere 1984, 71, fig 30, no 270). Other examples have been found at Bleachfield Street, Alcester 1976 17, 52, 73, 139, 177, 185, 372.

41 Type 5 pin with a tiny conical head and four well-defined collars beneath it. Complete. Length 87.2mm, max diam head 5.7mm. (BO 78, G IV 23, phase VI, late 4th century)

42 Upper section only of a pin with cylindrical head, decorated with two incised grooves. The tip and most of the shaft is lost. Present length 30mm, diam head *c* 7mm. (BO 5, A V 4, phase VIII, early to mid-4th century)

A pin of Crummy type 6, dated AD 200 — late 4th/early 5th century (Crummy 1979, 162, fig 1, no 8). Compare the related example from Winterton dated 3rd or 4th century (Stead 1976, 207, fig 107, no 86); and from Nettleton (Wedlake 1982, 201, fig 82, no 26); also the slightly damaged piece from Bleachfield Street, Alcester 1976–7 184.

43 Upper section only of a pin, the head having a subrectangular cross-section and a cone-shaped terminal. Between this and the lower collar the mid-section of the head is decorated with two crudely incised spirals. Present length 29.3mm, max cross-section of head 5.5mm × 7.1mm. (BO 40, D I 2, phase VIII, late 4th century)

This may be a variant of a type 6 pin. Compare the pin from Old Winteringham dated 3rd or 4th century (Stead 1976, 207, fig 106, no 68); and a similar piece from Wroxeter (Bushe-Fox 1914, 22, pl X, fig 2, 6th from left); and the better-finished, related example from Alcester ALC 72 46.

44 Complete pin with large conical head with eight irregularly spaced incised lines running from base to tip. Length 107.3mm, diam head *c* 6mm. (BO 96, L III 10, phase IV, late Roman/modern)

A related unpublished piece was found during excavations at Doncaster SF no DT/KK 81.

45 Conical head of ?pin; broken off, and slightly trimmed at edge. Length 31.3mm, max diam 8mm. (BO 31, C VIA 14, phase IX, mid-4th century on)

52 Needle, crudely finished with a roughly conical-shaped head, pierced with a narrow circular eye near the upper end of the shaft at approximately its greatest diam. Tip a little damaged? Length 68.4mm, max diam shaft 4mm. (BO 38, A XXIIA 4, unphased)

Compare the similar pieces from South Shields (Allason-Jones & Miket 1984, 67, nos 2.275, 2.277, 2.281, 2.282, with figs); also the example from Alcester ALC 69 88.

54 Upper portion of bone needle or implement with roughly oval eyelet within the expanded head. Present length 40mm. (BO 100, K I 26, medieval)

55 Needle or bodkin, tip lost. Most of the shaft has a circular cross-section which flattens out to a rectangular cross-section in the upper part, where it is pierced by a rectangular eye. Length 112.2mm. (BO 56, D I 36, phase VI, mid- to late 4th century?)

One example from Colchester was found in a pit in Balkerne Lane dated *c* AD 150 to *c* 250 (Crummy 1983, 67, no 1982, fig 70). Other examples are reported from South Shields (Allason-Jones & Miket 1984, 65, nos 2.268, 2.269, and figs; compare also 67, nos 2.270, 2.271, 2.272, with figs) and from Alcester ALC 72 42.

58 Needle or bodkin, with angular cross-section, and subrectangular eyelet. The tip and lower part of the shaft are lost. Present length 80.5mm, max cross-section shaft 6.6mm × 3.4mm. (BO 98, K I 26, unphased)

Textile manufacture

76 Triangular bone weaving tablet, broken across one hole with the loss of most of one corner, made from a fragment of animal scapula with irregular cross-section, undecorated. Present size 46.3mm × 35.3mm, original ht *c* 43mm, thickness *c* 1.8–3.6mm. (BO 72, F I 5, phase XIII, after AD 353)

The use of sets of weaving tablets for making braid and, in conjunction with a loom, to make a firm border or edging to lengths of cloth is discussed by Wild (1970a, 73–4, table O) who lists the finds then known from Roman Britain and the Rhineland (Wild's fig 63 is a triangular tablet from London). A number of further pieces have been found in Britain. One damaged example from Lion Walk, Colchester was dated *c* AD 150–400 (Crummy 1983, 67–8, fig 72, no 2006), a piece slightly smaller than ours from *Verulamium* was in a context dated AD 360–70 (Frere 1972, 150, fig 55, no 204), and two others from Caerleon were found in the drain of the Legionary Baths in the upper sediment level dated to *c* AD 160–230 (Zienkiewicz 1986, 207, nos 12, 13, fig 73).

Spoons

77 Spoon with most of the circular bowl missing, and the end of the handle lost. The handle continues into the bowl as a 'rat tail'. Present length 86mm, present width bowl 23.3mm, original diam *c* 25mm or more. (BO 10, AA II 8, unphased)

This form of spoon is dated to the 1st century AD when it is made in silver or copper alloy (Strong 1966, 155, fig 32), and it seems highly likely that this skeuomorph in worked bone should also have a similar date, perhaps extending into the early 2nd century. Compare the examples in copper alloy from Birch Abbey nos 114–17. Spoons of this type are not uncommon. Four pieces were reported from *Verulamium* coming from a wide range of dated contexts (Frere 1984, 73, fig 31, no 282 from context dated AD 80–120; no 283 from context dated AD 270–310. Two other pieces were listed but not illustrated and came from contexts dated AD 180–220; and AD 145–50). Another piece from Neatham, Hants came from a layer dated late 2nd to early 3rd century (Millett & Graham 1986, 127, fig 86, no 435).

78 Circular bowl of spoon, as above. Most of the handle, which ended in a 'rat-tail' on the bowl, is now lost. Diam bowl 26.3–27.5mm, depth 8.4mm. (BO 77, D I 110, unphased)

Knives

79 Clasp knife, the clasp carved in the form of a pig's trotter. Perfect but for a couple of small chips. Much of the original triangular-shaped iron blade has been lost, leaving only the central section. The iron collar and swivel are still *in situ* on the clasp but the metal is rather corroded. Overall length handle 77.1mm, max depth 13.2mm, 18.2mm. (BO 82, D II 28, unphased)

An exact parallel to this, also in bone but without the blade, was reported by von Mercklin as being in the Allard Pierson Museum, Amsterdam, and formerly in the Scheurleer collection no 3424, length 71mm, width 15mm. He also notes two other similar pieces. One was from Trier in the collection of the Trier Landesmuseum. The other, in the Römische Germanisches Zentral Museum in Mainz, was said to be from Cologne (von Mercklin 1940, 343, pl XXXVI, also note 26). Other clasp knives with bone handles carved in the form of animals have been reported from Britain, such as the tiger gnawing its ?prey, found at Wroxeter in 1913 (Bushe-Fox 1914, 22, pl X, fig 1); and the unpublished greyhound-like dog's head with ears pinned back, on a handle found during excavations at Wanborough, Wilts, in 1970. It is also interesting to note an earlier discovery in Warwickshire during excavations at Tiddington of another representational handle — this time the bone clasp was in the form of a stylized scabbard (Fieldhouse *et al* 1931, 36, no 11, with new find no M50).

80 Incomplete upper section of a calcified bone knife handle, incised with crude cross-hatching in bands and panels. Present length 38.8mm, max surviving cross-section 14.4mm. (BO 85, G IA 83, phase IV, early to mid-4th century)

Compare the more complete example from Gestingthorpe (Draper 1985, 71, no 392, fig 33), and the elegant piece decorated with two bands of cross-hatching, from a late rubble deposit at the south gate of Silchester (Fulford 1984, 115, fig 38, no 5). A similar fragment to this with simple hatched decoration was reported from Tiddington, Warwicks TD 80 1125.

81 Club-shaped bone knife handle, just over half of which survives. Originally it had an oval cross-section. The blade and tang are lost. Date uncertain, post-Roman? Length 74mm, max cross-section at base *c* 30 × 15mm. (BO 52, H II 39, unphased)

Furniture fittings and decoration

82 Undecorated bone hinge fitting, damaged and blackened by fire. Length 28.7mm, max diam *c* 21mm. (BO 69, D I 138, unphased)

The function of these short cylindrical fittings as hinges for boxes and smaller chests is described in Frere (1972, 149–50, figs 53, 54). Of the several examples illustrated no 188 came from a context dated AD 150–155/160, no 190 from a context dated AD 145–50. A further example from *Verulamium* is undated (Frere 1984, 69, fig 29, no 254). Another example, from London, was found in a context dated not later than AD 125 (Jones 1980, 95, fig 54, no 491).

83 Decorated bone plaque used for furniture inlay with, originally, a series of dot and three turned concentric circles along the central horizontal axis, framed on both sides with the smaller dot and two turned concentric circles, of which only two complete examples survive, with the trace of a third. The positions of two nail-holes are noticeable at the break on the lower edge. Present length 40.5mm, present width 16mm, thickness 2.2mm. (BO 13, AA I 1, unphased)

Compare the similarly decorated plaques from *Verulamium* (Frere 1972, 150, fig 54, no 193); and from Cirencester (McWhirr 1986, 114, no 236, fig 84). A group of surviving inlays from a small casket was found at Droitwich, Worcs from a context dated prior to the destruction of the site during the late 3rd century AD (Barfield 1977).

84 Small bone plaque or fitting with remains of two adjacent nail- or peg-holes at one end, and the remains of a ?light graffito on the outer face. Length 33.3mm, max width 11mm, depth *c* 0.2mm. (BO 41, E I 1, unphased)

Gaming counters

85 Counter, one side plain, the other plain but slightly dished in the centre. Diam *c* 19.5mm, depth 2mm. (BO 89, D II 29A, unphased)

One piece from Canterbury came from a context dated AD 270–90 (Frere *et al* 1982, 124, fig 62, no 41); another from Gestingthorpe was found in the same context as a belt plaque dated to the 2nd or 3rd century (Draper 1985, 71, fig 33, no 395). Examples from Warwickshire include those from excavations at Alcester, Bleachfield Street 1976–7, 181, 353, and 392; Coleshill 1979 Area A 435; and no M940 from early excavations at Tiddington.

86 Counter, a little irregular in outline, one side plain and with a slightly bevelled edge with, in the centre, the graffito 'VI'. The other side is turned with four concentric circles. Diam 19.5mm, depth 3.8mm. (BO 73, F III 3, unphased)

Compare the example from Balkerne Lane, Colchester 1975 also with 'VI' inscribed on the undecorated side (Hassall & Tomlin 1978, 478, no 35); and the counter no M640 from Tiddington with 'X' on the reverse.

89 Counter, turned with five concentric circles on one side. Diam *c* 23.5mm, depth 3.1mm. (BO 16, AA III 10, phase VI, late 3rd to early 4th century)

90 As above but turned with six concentric circles on one side. Diam *c* 20.3–20.9mm, depth 4.4mm. (BO 26, AA I 76, phase VI, late 3rd to early 4th century)

Horse furniture

91 Bone cheekpiece with circular cross-section tapering towards the ends, and with a centrally cut hole of rectangular cross-section; slightly damaged, undecorated. Length 117.8mm, max cross-section *c* 23mm, cross-section hole *c* 23.0mm × 6.5mm. (BO 64, G I 90, unphased)

An undecorated example with a suggested date *c* AD 160 comes from Wroxeter, with a second, decorated piece of the same date (Atkinson 1942, 231, nos 3, and 4, pl 62A, nos 2 and 1 respectively). A decorated example from the Roman Fort at Ilkley, Yorks was said to have come from the Antonine destruction layer (Hartley 1966, 69, fig 15, no 4). Another piece from a Claudio–Neronian context was reported from the Roman fort at Longthorpe, Cambs (Dannell & Wild 1987, 95, fig 25, no 96).

Discussion

As might be expected, the small finds of worked bones are mainly of a domestic nature, and can be classed under the general headings of personal ornaments, household, recreation, and transport, and for the most part they follow the general pattern of goods found on many civilian sites. The pins account for the greatest proportion of items, with further fragmentary shafts and broken tips. As with the finds from Bleachfield Street, Alcester 1975–6, the simple forms of Crummy's types 1–3 predominate, type 3 with its spherical head being the most common from both sites. It is particularly unfortunate that the bone bead (no 1) is unphased, as few well-stratified and dated examples have been reported from Britain.

The bone spoons 77 and 78 with circular bowls are not uncommon finds, and can be compared with four, roughly contemporary copper alloy examples nos 114–17, from the same site. Bone grips for tanged knives of all sizes are represented by only one poorly preserved piece, no 80, though a few more examples might have been anticipated. However the clasp knife, 79, is a significant addition to the bone assemblage from Alcester. Although two other clasp knives were found during early excavations at Tiddington, Warwicks, M49, M50, the Birch Abbey example far outclasses them. A pig's trotter may not be the most elegant choice of motif to use as a handle, but the shape fits snugly into the hand and the realism of the carving is a delight. Two continental parallels are known. Presumably it was made in a larger town or city where such craftsmanship would find a ready market. Fixtures and fittings for chests and smaller boxes, used for storage and transport of personal and domestic goods, are represented. More mundane items such as needles used for making and mending were found, though copper alloy or iron needles would have been more appropriate for use with finer materials. Weaving tablets are not frequently found; presumably a certain number were made of wood, and broken pieces would soon be jettisoned. The patterning on braids that can be achieved with a set of triangular tablets is more limited than when a set of square tablets is used. It could be suggested that the Birch Abbey tablet, 76, was used with other triangular pieces mainly for making a firm selvedge and starting border for lengths of cloth.

Curiously enough no dice have been found at Birch Abbey, though several examples have been found elsewhere at Alcester. Six gaming counters were turned up, nicely complementing the three pieces from Bleachfield Street.

Finally, a bone cheek piece in relatively good condition — with other items in copper alloy, including two terrets and a bit — bears witness to the use of the horse.

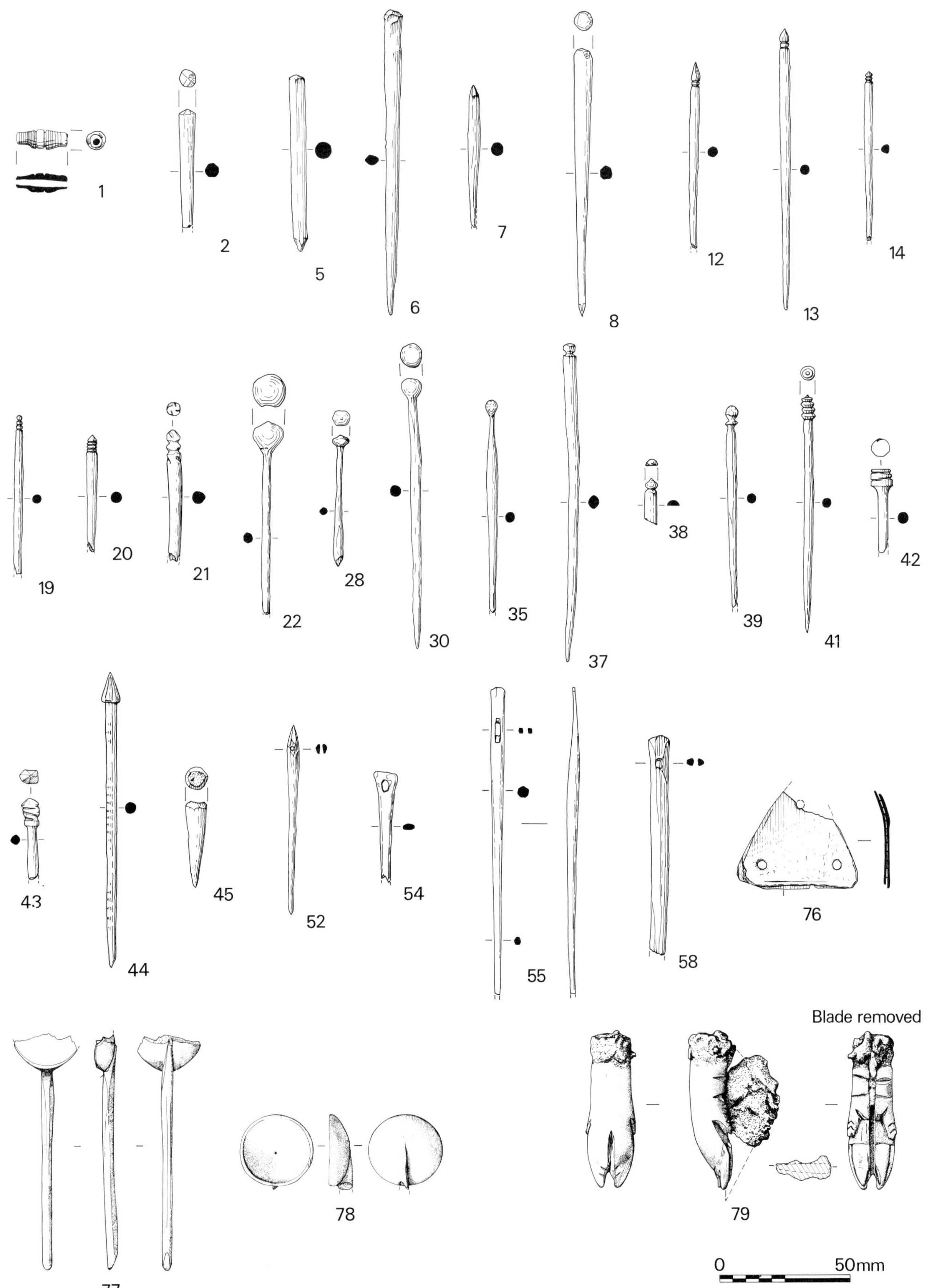

Figure 101 Worked bone, nos 1–79

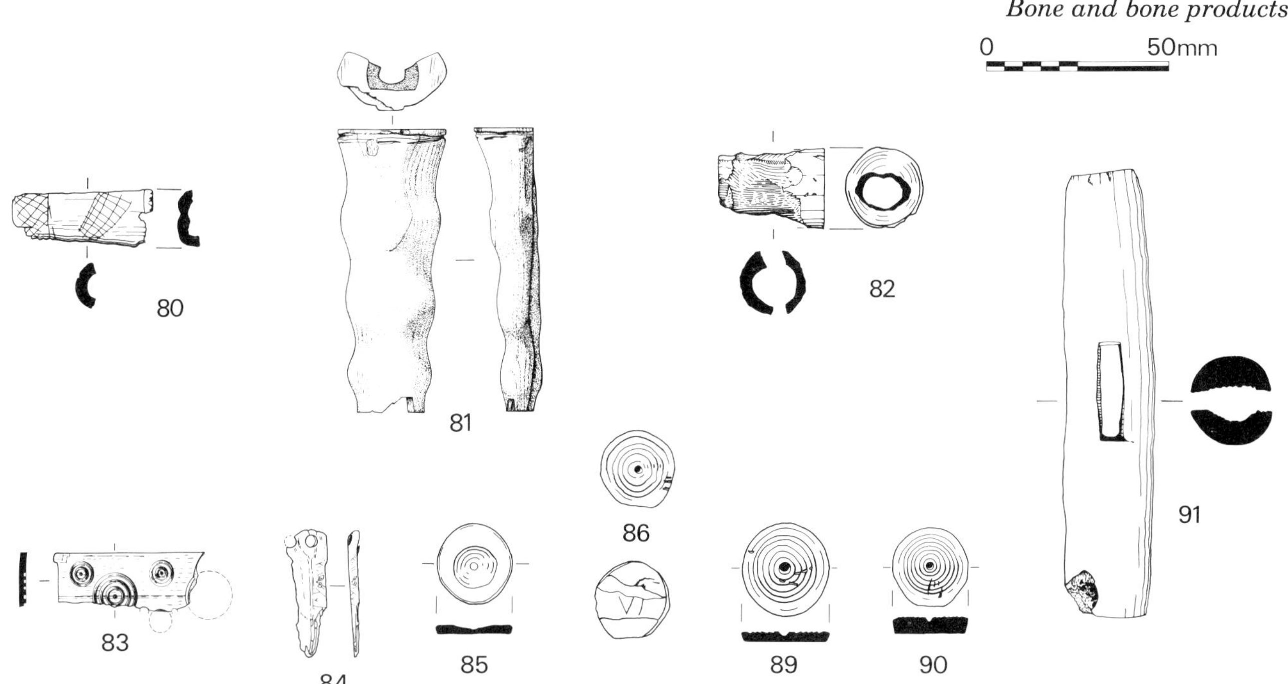

Figure 102 Worked bone, nos 80–91

Human skeletal remains

C B Denston

Introduction

[M4:E3] The material consisted of remains of adult and non-adult individuals. There were 31 adult inhumations, 24 non-adult inhumations, and one cremation. The preservation of the adult remains varied from grave to grave. In some cases individuals were represented by a single fragment or a few fragments of a bone; in others there were skeletons with fragmentary skulls and postcranial bones. There were few fairly well-preserved skeletons. The non-adults fared the same, though two-thirds of the burials were represented by skull and postcranial bones.

Measurements of the skull and long bones were taken according to the techniques of Buxton & Morant (1933), Morant (1936), and Mukherjee *et al* (1955). The statures of the adult individuals were computed employing the regression formulae of Trotter & Gleser (1952), with the maximum length measurements of all the long bones of a skeleton utilized where possible. As many data as possible have been recorded on record sheets and are available for study at the Department of Physical Anthropology, University of Cambridge where the skeletons are also stored. This report was written in the late 1960s.

Sex and age at death

Thirty adults were studied (a further adult skeleton, HB 6a, was omitted from the original study group). Of these, sixteen were possible males, eleven were females, and in the remaining three cases the sex was indeterminable. Those that could be aged with a certain amount of assurance were the following ages: 20–30 years, four persons; 30–45 years, nine persons; 40–50 years, two persons; 50–60 years, one person; two aged.

The non-adults were well represented and numbered 24. Of these, seven were possibly foetal; twelve in the range from birth to 18 months; one, 9–12 years; one, 13–14 years.

Osteometric variability

Worthwhile measurements were recorded from nine crania and ten mandibles associated with the crania. Of these, eight were male skulls, and two female. The cephalic indices of the male ranged from 70.0mm to 78.1mm, with a mean of 75.1mm. The mean cephalic index compares well with the 74.4mm (Belgae), 75.6mm (Dobunni), and 75.7mm (Brigantes) of the Romano-British period (Goodman & Morant 1940). The mean also compares very well with the male Romans from Great Casterton — 75.0mm (Denston 1970).

The reconstructed stature of four females ranged from 1.543m (5ft 0¾in) to 1.613m (5ft 3½in) with a mean of 1.562m (5ft 1½in). The stature for the males ranged from 1.619m (5ft 3¾in) to 1.803m (5ft 11in), with a mean of 1.714m (5ft 7½in). The mean stature for the males is 6mm (¼in) shorter than that for the males at Great Casterton — 1.720m (5ft 7¾in), and 38mm (1½in) in excess of the 1.676m (5ft 6in) of males from Maiden Castle (Trevor 1954). The mean of 1.562m (5ft 1½in) for the females is 32mm (1¼in) more than the 1.530m (5ft 0¼in) for the combined

Iron Age and Romano-British females, also from Maiden Castle. For platymeria, six out of six female femora came within the index, and six out of eleven male femora. For platycenemia, no female tibiae came within the index, and two out of ten male tibae.

Oral health

Periodontal infection, as judged from alveolar recession, affected ten out of thirteen individuals: two to a slight degree, seven to a medium degree. Slight enamel hypoplasia was present in nine dentitions out of twelve, with one to a medium degree. Ante-mortem tooth loss was not uncommon and loss occurred of incisors, canines, premolars, and more frequently, the molar teeth. Ante-mortem tooth loss occurred in ten out of thirteen dentitions. Abscesses were relatively common and were present in nine out of thirteen dentitions, and dental decay in seven out of fourteen dentitions. The frequencies were: caries 20/220, 9.9%; ante-mortem tooth loss 66/349, 18.9%; abscesses 34/283, 12.0%. The abscess rate was higher than that of the adult Romans from Great Casterton, with a lower incident rate for caries and ante-mortem tooth loss. The Alcester observations were inferior in numbers though.

Evidence of disease and injury

Bones, possibly representing fifteen individuals, displayed varying degrees of arthritis, osteoarthritis being dominant. Osteoarthritis affected the vertebral column to a slight degree of seven individuals, to a medium degree in four individuals, and extensively in two individuals. It was also evident in nine groups of postcranial remains, with eburnation occurring in three of these individuals. Trauma had occurred in various bones of thirteen individuals, nasal bones, clavicles, ribs, fibulae, an ulna, a radius, a talus, a tibia, and metatarsal bones. Perhaps worthy of note was a stress fracture, or hairline fracture, of a metatarsal bone, displaying a callus round the healed joint; also a fibula that had been fractured in two places. The ratio for osteoarthritis was two females to twelve males. The ratio for trauma was three females to ten males. The left tibia of one male, HB 11, was 26mm longer than the right, and bowed, and considerably swollen in the upper third of the shaft. It is possible that there had been a fracture of this portion of the shaft, or osteitis deformans. A possible tumour was evident of the ilium of the right innominate of one female, HB 47. Evidence was also present in the form of a lesion in the medial articular condyle of the left tibia for a case of osteochondritis dissecans, in male HB 17. Perhaps the most significant, or most interesting aspect of the pathology, was displayed in the male skeleton HB 6. Extensive osteoarthritis occurred throughout the skeleton, with eburnation caused by bone rubbing on bone of the acetabulum, and head of the left femur. Extensive osteoarthritis had occurred of the calcanae and talae of the feet, with also two lumber vertebrae ankylosed. Three thoracic vertebrae, possibly the lower three, were also completely ankylosed, with the body portion of the middle one in a state of complete collapse: this is indicative of tuberculosis. The collapse of this lower thoracic vertebra must have produced a hump-back condition for this individual: angular kyphosis. Another interesting feature was that a female, HB 47, had six lumbar vertebrae instead of the usual five.

Cremation

The single cremation contained the remains of an adult human male, and parts of a sheep/goat and a bird.

Ecology

Botanical remains

A J Gouldwell

[M4:G12] Five samples associated with the medieval corn dryer in trench C IIIA were examined. Coal, wood charcoal of *Quercus* sp and *Populus / Salix*, and seeds/fruits of wheat, oats, fat hen, bird's foot trefoil, and common vetch were identified. The small quantities present were inadequate to support archaeobotanical reconstruction.

Insect remains from pit F and their environmental implications

P J Osborne

The insect fauna discussed here was extracted from material collected in 1964/5 from a pit also containing waterlogged leather (pit F, AA II 87, phase III, 3rd century). It was first described in 1971 (Osborne 1971) and is re-presented here, partly for the sake of completeness but also because, in the twenty years which have elapsed since the first publication, many similar deposits have been examined, contributing something to the interpretation of what was at the time a pioneer investigation. The opportunity is also taken of updating the nomenclature which in the earlier paper followed that of Kloet & Hincks (1945) and is now amended to that of Lucht (1987). Although the opportunity to reinterpret the earlier findings in the light of later evidence is welcomed, it was gratifying to note that although the interpretation can be extended, the conclusions remain substantially the same.

The matrix from which the insect remains were recovered was an organic mud whose most conspicuous constituents were offcuts of leather, bones, and fragments of pottery. The material was washed down in the now familiar way with warm water. A thick, greasy scum which appeared on the surface, together with a soupy smell, were attributed to the wealth of animal matter contained. Many pieces of insect cuticle were present, often in remarkably good condition, from which members of table 16 were identified. As mentioned above, the classification of the beetles follows that of Lucht (1987) and so may appear in places to differ from the 1971 list. This, however, is due to taxonomic revision, not to a change of mind about identification.

Implications of the insect fauna

A number of lifestyles are represented by the species appearing in table 16, but predominating over all the rest by a very large margin, in terms of species but more particularly in terms of individuals, are those whose chosen habitat is decaying organic refuse. Thus, the majority of those species of which more than one individual was recovered belonged to this group. The organic matter suggested was fairly specific in some instances. For example the members of the genus *Aphodius* are almost always found in the dung of grazing animals whilst *Sphaeridium bipustulatum*, and the species of *Cercyon* and *Oxytelus*, are most frequently but not exclusively found in this pabulum. On the other hand many members of the genus *Monotoma* seem to have a predilection for heaps of grass cuttings. Many of the more abundant species, however, do not seem too particular about the nature of the refuse. The most numerous beetle found, *Anthicus floralis*, the little earwig *Labia minor*, the histerid *Acritus nigricornis*, the various lathridiids, and the mycetophagid *Typhaea stercorea*, are all found in situations resembling compost heaps or haystack bottoms while the many numerous staphylinids occur wherever prey, in the form of small arthropods, usually dipterous larvae, is abundant. Despite the presence of many bones, no beetles attracted to carrion or to dried bones were found, except perhaps the histerid *Atholus bimaculatus*. This species is also predatory, often on dipterous maggots which are common in carrion, but it may also be found in dung.

The occurrence of so many insects which live amongst accumulated vegetable refuse, together with the presence of many bones and fragments of leather, suggest that the pit was an excavation used for the disposal of a wide spectrum of rubbish.

In addition to the fauna which actually lived in the pit a number of species appear to have been introduced into this rather circumscribed environment with commodities destined for disposal. A beetle which was clearly very common at Alcester was the notorious Furniture Beetle, *Anobium punctatum*. This species is not known as British until the Bronze Age, since when it has become all too common throughout the country. It is not suggested that it did not live here before this time but that it was probably a very minor element in the fauna. The usual habitat of this species is dead, dry seasoned wood which is not of frequent occurrence in nature, being found, as a rule, when a tree has died but remains standing. When man started to provide this habitat with timber structures or artefacts designed to last a number of years the beetle rapidly assumed pest status and has retained it to the present day. When heavy infestations of this insect occur many specimens, having accomplished their tasks of mating and laying eggs, are to be found dead on the floor and it is suggested that those recorded here could have been

Table 16 Insect remains from pit F

Faunal list	Nos of individ-uals
Dermaptera	
Labiidae	
Labia minor (L)	10
Hemiptera	
Cimicidae	
Cimex sp	1
Coleoptera	
Carabidae	
Trechus quadristriatus (Schr) or *obtusus* Er	1
Bembidion lampros (Hbst)	1
Bembidion unicolor Chaud or *guttula* (F)	5
Harpalus (subg *Ophonus*) sp	1
Pterostichus vernalis (Pz)	1
Agonum marginatum (L)	1
Dromius quadriguttatus (L)	1
Syntomus foveatus (Fourcr)	1
Hydraenidae	
Ochthebius minimus (F)	1
Helophorus spp	10
Hydrophilidae	
Sphaeridium bipustulatum F	14
Cercyon spp	311
Cryptopleurum minutum (F)	14
Cryptopleurum crenatum (Pz)	2
Histeridae	
Acritus nigricornis (Hoffm)	33
Atholus bimaculatus (L)	21
Histerid sp (larval heads probably of *Atholus bimaculatus*)	30
Liodidae	
Amphicyllus globus (F)	1
Scydmaenidae	
Scydmaenus tarsatus Mull	3
Orthoperidae	
Sericoderus lateralis (Gyll)	3
Ptiliidae	
Acrotrichis sp (p?)	7
Staphylinidae	
Omalium rivulare (Pk)	2
Xylodromus concinnus (Marsh)	12
Lesteva longelytrata (Goeze)	2
Trogophloeus spp	51
Oxytelus sculptus Grav	52
Oxytelus rugosus (F)	13
Oxytelus sculpturatus Grav	1
Platystethus arenarius (Fourcr)	62
Platystethus cornutus (Grav)	13
Platystethus capito Heer	1
Platystethus nitens (Sahlb)	7
Stenus spp	5
Stilicus orbiculatus (Payk)	1
Lithocharis orchraceus (Grav)	12
Leptacinus sulcifrons (Steph)	86
Leptacinus batychrus (Gyll)	16
Phacophallus parumpunctatus (Gyll)	32
Xantholinus linearis (Ol) or *longiventris* Heer 3	
Philonthus spp	59
Tachyporus hypnorum (F)	3
Tachinus laticollis Grav	1
Leucoparyphus silphoides (L)	10
Falagria sulcata (Payk)	9
Aleochara moesta Grav	8
Pselaphidae	
Tychus niger (Payk)	1
Cantharidae	
Rhagonycha fulva (Scop)	1
Malachiidae	
Malachius marginellus Ol	5
Buprestidae	
Trachys troglodytes Gyll	1
Nitidulidae	
Cateretes rufilabris (Lat)	1
Meligethes sp	2
Cucujidae	
Monotoma spinicollis Aubé	13
Monotoma picipes Hbst	88
Monotoma bicolor Villa	1
Monotoma longicollis (Gyll)	21
Oryzaephilus surinamensis (L)	20
Pediacus dermestoides (F)	1
Cryptophagidae	
Cryptophagus sp (p?)	28
Atomaria sp (p?)	13
Lathridiidae	
Enicmus minutus (L)	9
Enicmus sp	2
Corticaria group	24
Mycetophagidae	
Typhaea stercorea (L)	33
Colydiidae	
Endophloeus markovitchianus (Pill et Mitt)	1
Cerylon histeroides (F)	1
Lyctidae	
Lyctus fuscus (L)	13
Anobiidae	
Stegobium paniceum (L)	4
Anobium punctatum (Geer)	83
Ptinidae	
Ptinus spp	10
Anthicidae	
Anthicus bifasciatus (Rossi)	7
Anthicus floralis (L)	220
Tenebrionidae	
Palorus subdepressus (Woll)	1

Faunal list	Nos of individuals
Tenebrio obscurus F	1
Scarabaeidae	
Trox scaber (L)	2
Onthophagus sp	1
Oxyomus sylvestris (Scop)	2
Aphodius spp	61
Cerambycidae	
Hesperophanes fasciculatus Fald	13
Chrysomelidae	
Hydrothassa aucta (F)	1
Phyllotreta nemorum (L)	1
Haltica sp	1
Chaetocnema concinna (Marsh)	2
Chaetocnema sp	1
Bruchidae	
gen et sp indet	1
Scolytidae	
Scolytus rugulosus (Mull)	1
Scolytus intricatus (Ratz)	1
Curculionidae	
Apion carduorum Kirby	1
Apion subulatum Kirby	1
Apion nigritarse Kirby	1
Apion spp	17
Phyllobius sp	1
Sitona sp	5
Hypera sp (p?)	2
Sitophilus granarius (L)	2
Baris sp	1
Micrelus ericae (Gyll)	1
Ceutorhynchus sp	1
Diptera	
Sphaeroceridae	
Sphaerocerus sp nr *pusilla* Fln	
Muscidae	
Probably either *Orthellia* or *Dasyphora*	

swept up and thrown into the pit with leather scraps from the timber floor of the leather-working factory postulated by Mahany.

A group of beetles well represented here are those whose habitat is man's stored food products. Most of these, *Oryzaephilus surinamensis*, *Palorus subdepressus*, and *Sitophilus granarius*, are attached to whole grain or prepared cereal products. When first reported (Osborne 1971) it was a matter for speculation whether their occurrence was a unique event and that they had been reintroduced later by modern commerce, as had been thought prior to their discovery at Alcester, or whether they had survived in this country since Roman times. It is now well established from many records that the latter is the case and that it is fairly certain that it was Roman commercial traffic which distributed these pests about the world. It is uncertain how they got into the refuse pit, however. The answer which seemed obvious in 1971 was that a contemporary housewife, finding her stock of cereal was weevily, threw it away into the refuse pit. This group of species has appeared in so many sites since their first discovery that, although this may have happened occasionally, it seems unlikely to have been the only route by which the beetles reached the refuse pits and cess pits in which they have so often been found. A simple experiment (Osborne 1983) showed, however, that recognizable remains of these insects could survive the passage through the human alimentary tract and thus enter the matrix in faecal material, in many cases apparently the most obvious route. At Alcester either way might have been the one taken but the possibility that human sewage may have been amongst the pit's contents cannot be ruled out. The other stored-product pest recorded was *Stegobium paniceum*, the so-called Drugstore Beetle. This differs from the other species in being capable of living in a much wider range of products and is noteworthy as having apparently been able to arrive on the British scene well before the more restricted grain pests, as it has been recorded from the Bronze Age site at Wilsford, Wilts (Osborne 1989).

A yet more exotic species to be found at Alcester was the cerambycid *Hesperophanes fasciculatus*. Fragments, curiously all elytra, of at least thirteen individuals of this beetle were recovered and, having defied the author's attempts to identify them beyond family level, were submitted to Mr E A J Duffey of the Commonwealth Institute of Entomology who named them as the Mediterranean species *Hesperophanes fasciculatus*. The larvae of this insect live in the wood of many different species of tree and the beetle appears to be most abundant in Greece and neighbouring countries. Members of the family Cerambycidae are frequently transported about in the larval state when the timber in which they were living has been made into some sort of movable artefact. Adult beetles subsequently appear, often after a protracted larval existence, in a quite alien locality. This misfortune is well known to happen to *Hesperophanes* and would be the most likely reason for the appearance of the beetle at Alcester in Roman times, having been imported from somewhere further south in, perhaps, a piece of furniture.

Most of the remainder of the fauna seems to have come into the pit from outside, either under its own power or in discarded refuse. Thus the Carabidae are mobile predators and probably the arrival of most of the specimens recovered was adventitious.

With the plant-eating Chrysomelidae and Curculionidae it is possible that at least some went into the pit with plant remains which had been used as animal fodder, floor covering, or for some other domestic purpose. On the other hand the very diversity of the plants which would have to be represented, each by only a single beetle, is more suggestive of simply accidental occurrences. However they got in, if they were living in the vicinity of the site they suggest a landscape of open arable or meadow land with such plants as thistles, various

Papilionaceae and Ranunculaceae, although there are too few of these phytophages to allow firm conclusions to be drawn.

Although no species were found which live on the foliage of trees, a small number were present whose habitat is dead wood. Of these the majority are normally found under the bark of rotten logs but they are so few in number that all could have been brought to the site in a single piece of wood. The two species of *Scolytus* also live under bark but often on living trees. Both fly readily, however, and each was represented by only one individual so that, again, a chance introduction seems probable.

One more insect found is particularly worthy of notice. There is a single pronotum of a bug of the family Cimicidae which is indistinguishable from the pronotum of that especially unpleasant pest, the Bed Bug, *Cimex lectularius*. Unfortunately it is also very similar to the pronotum of the Pigeon Bug so it is not possible to be absolutely certain that the Romans were afflicted with Bed Bugs, but it seems highly probable.

Conclusions

Pit F was almost certainly a place for the disposal of rubbish. This rubbish seems to have been an amalgam of floor sweepings from the leather workshop, bones, domestic refuse, animal dung, and possibly human sewage, supporting an indigenous population of beetles and fly maggots. This fauna was augmented from time to time by insects already installed in material before it became refuse or which were living locally and got in by chance. Though evidence is very meagre, what there is suggests that the countryside in the vicinity was mostly open meadowland. All the species named are still found living in Britain today so that there is no evidence for a climate differing from that of the present. The only exception to this was the longhorn beetle *Hesperophanes fasciculatus* whose presence can be accounted for far more simply as a man-assisted immigrant than by postulating a suitable climatic regime.

Building materials

Daub

Rowan Ferguson

The bulk of the extant daub came from site D I phase VI and probably related to structure DC or its predecessor DB. The impressions found in the daub can be explained by the technique of wattle and daub infill described by Brunskill (1978, 58–9). This consists of a framework of vertical and horizontal timbers which was filled in with upright staves across which pliable withies were interwoven. The impressions of timbers are all incomplete but suggest that they were at least 45mm wide. There were two impressions of staves which had been neatly cut to sharp points. The impressions of withies were most numerous and these were generally about 25–30mm in diameter although there were two smaller examples (*c* 7mm and *c* 16mm) from site D I. Some of the larger pieces of daub show that the withies were tightly packed with each row often almost touching the next.

Where the complete thickness of the daub panels could be measured they fell into two groups *c* 27–30mm thick and *c* 40mm thick. There were also some incomplete pieces which were over 50mm thick.

Contexts containing daub

Area A Unphased: A XVIIB 11
Area C Unphased: C V 4
Area D Later 2nd to early 3rd century?, phase II: D I 109; late 3rd century?, phase IV: D I 58, D I 94; early to mid-4th century?, phase V: D I 46, D I 98; mid- to late 4th century?, phase VI: D I 19, D I 47, D I 48, D I 49, D I 91; late 4th century, phase VIII: D I 24, D I 25; unphased: D I 122
Area G Late 4th century, phase VII+: G IA 51, G IA 51A; unphased: G I 23

Decorated wall plaster

Joan Liversidge and Stephen Cracknell

[M5:A3] This description of the decorated wall plaster was written by JL shortly after the completion of the excavations; the discussion was added by SC. The plaster itself is now lost. Details of the contexts from which wall plaster was recovered can be found in the microfiche.

Site C

A small group of painted fragments from site C provided evidence for decoration with a plain yellow ground which sometimes bore traces of a black line. The shape of a single piece of red with a white line 50mm wide suggests that it came from a window opening. Two fragments were painted to imitate marble wall veneers with either grey stippling on a red ground or large black and small red splashes on pink.

Site D

The very fragmentary remains of painted plaster from this site suggest that one room at least had white walls with panelled decoration. The rectangular panels were outlined by fine yellow or dark red lines with beaded corners, set in a framework of yellow, edged with black or red lines. One scrap may show the remains of a black curvilinear design next to green, bordered by a white line 5mm wide, possibly painted on a red ground. Another piece has traces of a black pattern on red. Narrow white lines on a purple ground sometimes meet at an acute angle and so may belong to a geometric motif. Light brown stripes and lines sometimes edged with red, or white lines on a brown ground, also occur. Several examples were found imitating marble, stippled in red or grey on a pink ground, or black on white.

Site G

The material from IA suggests at least one room with yellow walls. It was divided up into either rectangles for the dado or panels from further up the wall by a red stripe 15mm wide, edged by white lines 10mm in width. Solid red rectangles with beaded corners on yellow may also have occurred. Fine red or black lines, 2mm wide, found associated with a border of black (10mm wide), grey (23mm wide), and white (10mm) also probably belong to panelling. Other colour combinations of stripes on the yellow ground included pink and two shades of red, or red and white. Rose lines, 8mm wide, meet in a right-angle on a white ground, and plain red plaster also occurs.

More yellow from G IV probably comes from the same type of decoration as G IA. Pieces of a plain reddish-brown ground were found, sometimes with a red stripe (18mm wide) edged with white. White painted walls must also have existed in this area with panels framed with wide bands and lines of varying width in deep pink, and fine lines of green. Convex fragments with traces of red or deep pink may come from a window opening. A single scrap shows signs of white stripping on a pink ground.

From G V came plain red, yellow, and white, with a variety of combinations of lines and stripes of varying width including green, black, and white; yellow, white, and red; and red or pink on white. Several pieces show a fine white line and a purple strip 18mm wide dividing an area of reddish-brown from white. The only evidence for more enterprising designs is one scrap which may have formed part of a purple curvilinear motif on white, and another with slightly curved dark red lines 2–5mm wide painted over a band of yellow, grey-green, and ?white, with an occasional black blob. Pink and red stippling on white also occurred.

On the whole the decorative schemes seem to have been simple, but they are very fragmentary and the occasional scrap with traces of a pattern may indicate that more enterprising designs have failed to survive.

Discussion

The earliest plaster from a C VI/VIA phased context came from phase VII, from east of street B. It may have derived from structure CEA, or less probably from CWA, CWB, or CWC. The later plaster, from two phase IX contexts, came from layers associated with the demolition of the phase VIII structure CEB. The plaster from CIIIA must relate to some other building in the vicinity.

All the plaster from site D came from trench I. Although there were some examples from a phase I ditch, the majority belonged to phase IV or later. It was derived from structure DB which was built in phase IV.

Some plaster on site G came from trenches I, IA, and II, but mostly it came from trenches IV and V. Apart from a single occurrence in a beam slot which might be ascribed to phase I, the plaster from phased contexts all came from phase IV or later and derived from structure GC and its successor GE.

Tile

Rowan Ferguson

Buildings in Alcester are known to have been roofed with both hexagonal limestone tiles and fired clay *tegulae* and *imbrices*. Limestone tiles have generally been seen as a late development (McWhirr 1981, 112). Most of the tile was discarded on site but the following 'type sherds' were retained.

Two incomplete stone tiles were found from G IA 20 (phase X, late 4th century) and A XVIIB 2 (unphased) — see stone report nos 17–18. Three examples of *tegulae* (also incomplete) were retained. One of these occurred in A VIIB 2 with the limestone tile, the other two were from D I 2 and 6.

A fragment of a stamped tile has also been found in F V 14A (unphased) (fig 103). The stamp reading

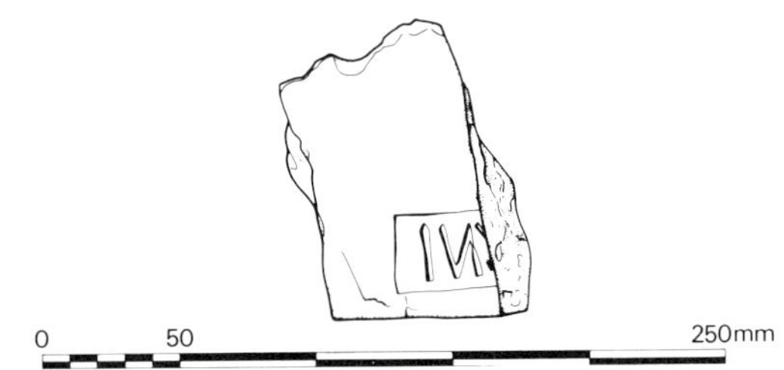

Figure 103 Stamped tile

NI[seems to be related to a stamp reading]ERNI[from the flood barrier site dug in 1973. There is no evidence for this stamp outside Alcester and it was presumably that of a local manufacturer.

As well as the *in situ* hypocaust on site L, three pieces of hypocaust tile with combed decoration were found in site F: two from F I 5 (phase XIII, after AD 353) and one from F IV 14 (phase XIII, after AD 353). There are other scattered finds of hypocaust tile from the town and there is no other evidence to suggest that any of the buildings on sites F or the adjacent E, J, and P were heated in this way.

Tesserae

Jeremy Evans

Eight white limestone *tesserae* were recovered from the excavations, all from topsoil, one from site AA, one from site B, four from site L, and two unprovenanced. They vary in size from 10–28mm × 13–29mm, with thicknesses ranging from 6 to 31mm.

Wood

V Snetterton-Lewis

[M5:A7] A list of the provenances of the wood samples is in the microfiche. The majority are from pit and ditch fills rather than merely the wells. Most, unsurprisingly, are from sites A, AA, B, and C which are lower-lying.

Only one group survived to be studied in 1989, W32, from well fill D I 229 (phase II, later 2nd to early 3rd century?). It consists of fragments of wood probably from larger pieces and three fragments of roughly circular section (*c* 20mm in diameter), perhaps from a wattle fence.

Other finds

Coal

A H V Smith

[M5:A9] Reflectance measurements were made on five coal samples from sites D I and C VI and one was also examined for spores. The coal probably all came from one coalfield, with the Warwickshire coalfield considered the most likely source.

Intaglios

Martin Henig

The intaglios are illustrated in plate 2.

1 Silver finger-ring with wide hoop. Small cornelian intaglio in bezel. External width of ring 20mm; depth 18mm; distance across bezel 12.5mm. Form: Henig 1974 and 1978, type V, which is characteristic of the second half of the 2nd century.

The intaglio, which is oval with a flat upper face measuring 8mm × 6mm, depicts a hare in profile to the left (or to the right in impression).

Previous publication: Henig 1974 and 1978, no 622. Comparanda: Krug 1980, nos 419, 420 (cornelians); Henig 1978, no App 178 (glass in a 3rd-century bronze ring from Chester). Hares were frequently coursed by hounds, see for example Henig 1974 and 1978 no 624. (OM 37, D II 40, unphased).

2 Cornelian intaglio, oval with a flat upper face, form F1, 12.5mm × 10.5mm × 2.5mm. The subject is the god Mercury standing to the front and facing right; in his left hand there is a purse and in his right a caduceus; he has a cloak over his right arm (reversed in impression). Ground line.

Previous publication: Henig 1974 and 1978, no 40. For comparanda see Henig 1974, no 38, and list. The type is exceedingly common. For the style of the engraving, see especially Zienkiewicz 1986, 130, no 9 (amethyst from a drain deposit at Caerleon dated *c* AD 85–100). (ST 129, F II U/S, unphased).

3 Nicolo intaglio (light blue on brownish tinted chalcedony), oval with a flat upper face bevelled around the edges, form F4, 12.5mm × 11mm × 2.5mm. The theme is a war galley proceeding over the sea to the right (reversed in impression). Three shields and three spears symbolize marines; below the ship, the sea is indicated by means of short wheel-cuts.

Previous publication: Henig 1974 and 1978, no 534. For other warships see Henig 1974 and 1978, no 533 (nicolo from *Verulamium*) and especially no 535 (jasper from London); Guiraud 1988, no 552 (glass from Arles) and no 533 (white stone from Alesia) are especially close.

The gem is probably of 1st-century date. (ST 157, F I 126, phase II, 1st century).

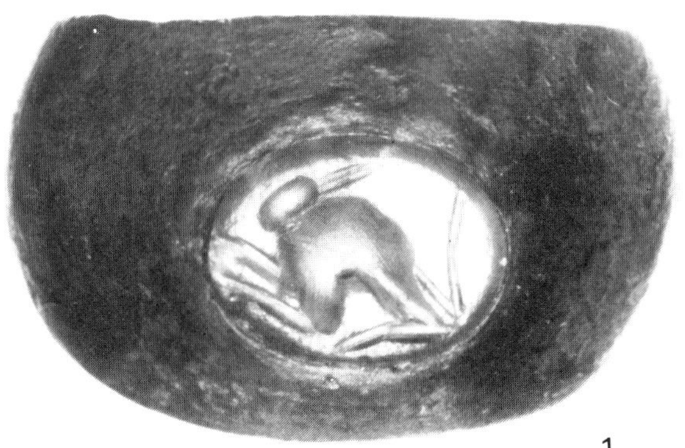

1

2

3

Plate 2 Intaglios (4× natural size)

Glass

Jennifer Price and Sally Cottam

[M5:A13] The Birch Abbey excavations produced more than 512 fragments of Roman glass, from at least 42 vessels. Although the group was not large, a wide range of table wares and household wares was recognized. Only two fragments of window glass were identified. The state of preservation of the vessels varied considerably, with many represented by only one fragment. Four vessels however, nos 9, 10, 11, and 25 (figs 104–5), which came from three pits, were substantially complete. Iridescent and other weathering was visible on virtually all of the fragments.

There were some discrepancies between the group of fragments seen by Dorothy Charlesworth before 1981 and that received by us in 1990. We have not seen the eleven beads, two gaming counters and one ring inlay listed in Charlesworth's notes, and vessel fragments recorded by her are also missing.

A large proportion of the group, nearly a tenth of the total number of fragments, was severely melted. Where identifiable, these melted pieces came from 1st–2nd-century blue/green bottles. Much of the melted glass was residual, from the late 4th-century pit D I 25, associated with a variety of other waste material including metalworking debris.

Catalogue of illustrated items (figs 104–5)

Abbreviations

PH	Present height
RD	Rim diameter
BD	Base diameter
WT	Wall thickness
BT	Base thickness
Dim	Dimensions
Ht	Height
Diam	Diameter

All measurements are in millimetres.

Pillar moulded bowls

Blue-green

1 Rim and body fragment. Rim edge mostly missing. Upper part of one rib, with tooling mark on top edge. Exterior lightly wheel-polished above rib. Interior wheel-polished. Iridescent surfaces. PH: 42mm. WT: 5mm. (GL 167, G I 58, phase IX, late 4th century)

Blown vessels

Coloured

8 Four body fragments, two joining from wall and lower body of cylindrical bowl. Yellow. Vertical side with rounded carination and wide lower body tapering in. Light irregular scratches on interior surfaces. Patchy iridescence. PH: 52mm. BD: *c* 160mm. (GL422, C XII 7; GL 428, C XII 1; GL 429 C XII 7, unphased)
Also
a) Very many small fragments. Yellow. (GL 218, D I 173, phase II, later 2nd to early 3rd century)

9 Over 175 fragments and many chips, rim, neck, handle, body, and base of conical jug. Yellow/green. Rim turned out, up and in and flattened. Narrow cylindrical neck. Slight constriction at junction with straight side expanding out. Lower body tapering in to open, pushed-in base ring. Base slightly concave. Angular ribbon handle with central rib, applied to upper body and attached below rim, with claw attachment and central pinched trail running down body. Patchy iridescent surface. Occasional bubbles. Ht: 290mm. RD: 33mm. BD: 74mm. Neck length: 92mm. WT: 1.5mm. (GL 423, D II 29A, unphased)

10 Thirty-four fragments, mostly joined in two pieces: rim, neck, handle, body, and base of short-necked conical jug. Yellow/green. Uneven rim bent out, up and in and flattened. Narrow cylindrical neck. Slight constriction at base of neck. Slightly convex curved body, expanding out to rounded carination. Lower body tapering in. Open pushed-in base ring, slightly concave base. Curved ribbon handle with edge ribs applied to upper body and attached below rim. Patchy clouded and iridescent surfaces. Strain cracks. Small bubbles. Ht: 152mm. RD: 21mm. BD: 64mm. Max diam: 105mm. Neck length: 22mm. (D II 28; GL 223, D II 60, unphased)
Also
a) Shoulder fragment. Yellow/green. (GL 44, AA I 18, phase VII, late 3rd to early 4th century)
b) Cylindrical neck fragment. Yellow/green. (GL 58, C I 16, unphased)
c) Body fragment. Trace of neck. Pale yellow/green. (GL389, G V 2, unphased)

Colourless

11 Nine joined fragments of carinated cup. Curved rim, edge cracked off and wheel polished. Almost vertical side expanding out to angular carination. Straight lower body tapering in. Separately blown foot, edges missing. Two wheel-cut lines on rim, one on upper body, one on lower body. Clouded surface with patches of iridescence. Occasional medium bubbles. PH: 102mm. RD: 93mm. WT: 1–2mm. (GL 416, D II 29A, unphased)

14 Rim fragment, cylindrical cup. Vertical rim, edge cracked off and ground. Horizontal narrow abraded band on upper body. Patchy clouded surfaces. PH: 21mm. WT: 1.5mm. (GL 137, D I 25, phase VIII, late 4th century)

Blue / green

Cups and bowls

16 Rim fragment. Vertical rim, edge fire-rounded, side distorted by heat. Small elongated bubbles parallel to rim. PH: 12mm. WT: 2mm. (GL 32, AA I 12, unphased)

17 Base fragment, cup or bowl. Tubular pushed-in base ring, concave base. Broken edge of body carefully smoothed. Wear on base ring. Iridescent surfaces. Tiny bubbles. PH: 6mm. BD: 80mm. WT: 1mm. (GL 431, L V 1, unphased)

Jugs and jars

18 Rim fragment from spout of jug. Folded rim turned in and flattened. Yellow streak through rim. Elongated bubbles parallel to edge. Dim: 7mm × 20mm. WT: 1.5mm. (GL 68, AA II 285, unphased)

19 Base fragment of jar or jug. Lower body tapering in, open pushed-in base ring. Distorted by heat. Edge worn. Iridescent outer surface. PH 20mm. WT: 4mm. (GL 379 D I 176, unphased)

Flasks and unguent bottles

20 Two joining neck and body fragments, ?tubular unguent bottle. Narrow cylindrical neck. Slight constriction at junction of neck and body, straight upper body. Elongated bubbles. PH: 25mm. Neck diam: *c* 15mm. (GL 92, AA II 78, phase II, late 2nd to early 3rd century)

Blue / green bottles

Rims, necks, shoulders, and handles

22 Three rim, neck, and handle fragments, joining. Rim bent out, up and in and flattened. Cylindrical neck. Upper edge of angular reeded handle with folded upper attachment joining neck below rim. Elongated bubbles. PH: 56mm. Handle width: 45mm. Neck diam: 36mm. (GL 129, D II 1; GL188 D I T/S, unphased)

Square bottles

25 Nineteen fragments, nearly complete square bottle. Rim bent out, up, in, and flattened. Cylindrical neck with slight tooling marks at base. Angular reeded handle applied to shoulder, attached to neck below rim. Horizontal shoulder, straight sides. Horizontal marks below shoulder on all sides indicating height of mould and central indents above base. Concave base with L-shaped corner mouldings surrounding moulded letters SAI. Patchy iridescent surface and cloudy streaks. Bubbly. Ht: 230mm. RD: 58mm. Body ht: 191mm. BD: 117mm × 114mm. (D II 29A, unphased: from pit group, mostly mid-2nd century)
26 Two fragments, lower body and base edge. Square bottle. Base design, part of circular moulding close to edge. Weathered surfaces. Medium bubbles. PH: 63mm. BT at edge: 5mm. (GL 150, D I 34, phase VI, mid- to late 4th century?)

Hexagonal bottles

28 Two base fragments, joining. Hexagonal bottle. Slightly concave base, thickening towards centre. One edge visible. Base design: three concentric circles with central dot. Patchy iridescence. Occasional bubbles. Diam of outer circle: 120mm. BT at edge: 3.5mm. (D II 29A, unphased)

Prismatic bottles

30 Base fragment. Bottle. Trace of edge. Base design: two concentric circular mouldings. Slightly melted. Dim: 21mm × 15mm. BT: 4.5mm. (GL 56, A III 9, unphased)
31 Base fragment. Bottle. Base design: circular moulding, with trace of further moulding. No visible weathering. Small bubbles. Dim: 26mm × 10mm. BT: 6.5mm. (GL 23, A X 8, unphased)

Late Roman glass

34 Rim fragment, cup? Blue/green. Everted rim, edge fire-rounded. Cylindrical upper body. Fine lines parallel to rim on both surfaces, ?lightly ground. Iridescent surfaces. Bubbly. PH: 10mm. WT: 1mm. (GL 165, D I 71, phase V, early to mid-4th century?)
36 Lower body and base fragment, of cup? Pale yellow/green. Convex body, trace of decoration. Concave base. Iridescent surfaces. PH: 21mm. WT: 1mm. (GL 190, G I 105, phase IV, early to mid-4th century)

Discussion

The assemblage can be divided into four broad date categories, which will be discussed sequentially. The earliest group consists of nine fragments from vessels typical of the 1st century. Six of these are from blue/green pillar moulded bowls (Isings 1957, form 3), representing at least five vessels. Blue/green pillar moulded bowls are frequently found on 1st-century sites in Roman Britain. Strongly coloured and polychrome pillar moulded bowls were never very common and became rare after the Neronian period, while blue/green examples continued to be used in considerable numbers in the Flavian period. Nos 2 and 6 are possibly from the same bowl, as both come from the context D I 173. The fragments are all from well-moulded and polished bowls, with prominent ribs. Nos 2–5 all have abraded bands, wheel-cut lines or a combination of both on the inside surface of the body. No 1, from the rim of a vessel, is lightly wheel-polished on the exterior surface above the rib. The base fragment, no 6, comes from a bowl with ribs extending the full length of side and base. The seventh fragment of 1st-century date comes from a peacock-blue cast vessel. Although it is not possible to recognize its form, it is probably of pre-Flavian manufacture, strongly coloured vessels becoming less common after this period.

Two joining pieces come from the neck and upper body of a blue/green tubular unguent bottle (no 20), a type usually occurring in 1st-century contexts (*ibid*, form 8). There are similar vessels in blue/green glass amongst the large number of unguent bottles in the Neronian assemblage found at Kingsholm (Price & Cool 1985, 44).

The second group of vessels dates from the late 1st century to the late 2nd century. This group, with over 493 fragments, constitutes by far the largest section of the assemblage, outweighing the total number of fragments from the other date bands by a ratio of nearly 30 to 1. It also contains the pit groups mentioned above, from which numerous fragments and four nearly complete vessels were excavated.

Of particular interest is pit fill D II 29A, which contained at least six glass vessels, in association with a large number of complete samian bowls dated to *c* AD 150–60. Three — a carinated cup, a conical jug, and a square bottle (nos 9, 11, and 25) — were nearly complete. The base of a hexagonal bottle (no 28), several fragments from this or other prismatic bottles, and small pieces from two unidentified colourless vessels (not catalogued), were also found in this pit. One of the colourless vessels was indented. The colourless carinated drinking cup (no 11) belongs to a group of biconical cups with wheel-cut lines quite common in early to mid-2nd-century contexts in the western provinces. Similar vessels have been found at *Verulamium* (Charlesworth 1972, 207, nos 43–4, fig 77 and Charlesworth 1984, 155, fig 63.45), Hardnott (Charlesworth 1959, 37–8, fig 3), Exeter (Charlesworth 1979, 224, fig 70.9), and elsewhere. At Felmongers, Harlow, a pit group was found containing at least 30 vessels, including three or more biconical cups, a conical jug, three square bottles, and one hexagonal bottle, in association with samian dated to AD 160–70 (Price 1987). Cup no 8 from Harlow, although slightly smaller than the Alcester cup, and in greenish/colourless glass, is almost identical in form, showing two wheel-cut lines below the rim, one on the upper body and one on the lower body, and a separately blown foot. Two other cups (nos 9–10) in the Harlow pit, although more fragmentary, are also closely comparable with the Alcester cup.

The conical jug (no 9), in yellow/green glass, with a long narrow neck, an angular handle with a pinched trail, and an open pushed-in base ring, belongs to a group of strongly coloured conical and globular jugs found in Britain, the Rhineland, and central and northern France (Isings 1957, form 55). Although these jugs are common in the 1st century and early 2nd century, they have also been uncovered in several later contexts. An example was found in a drain deposit at Housesteads, a context postdating AD 128 (Charlesworth 1971, 35–7, fig 9), and others came from pits at Felmongers, Harlow (associated with samian dated to *c* AD 160–70) and most significantly at Park St, Towcester (four jugs associated with samian dated *c* AD 155–65; Price 1980, 66, fig 15). The discovery of the Alcester jug provides another example from a mid-2nd-century context,

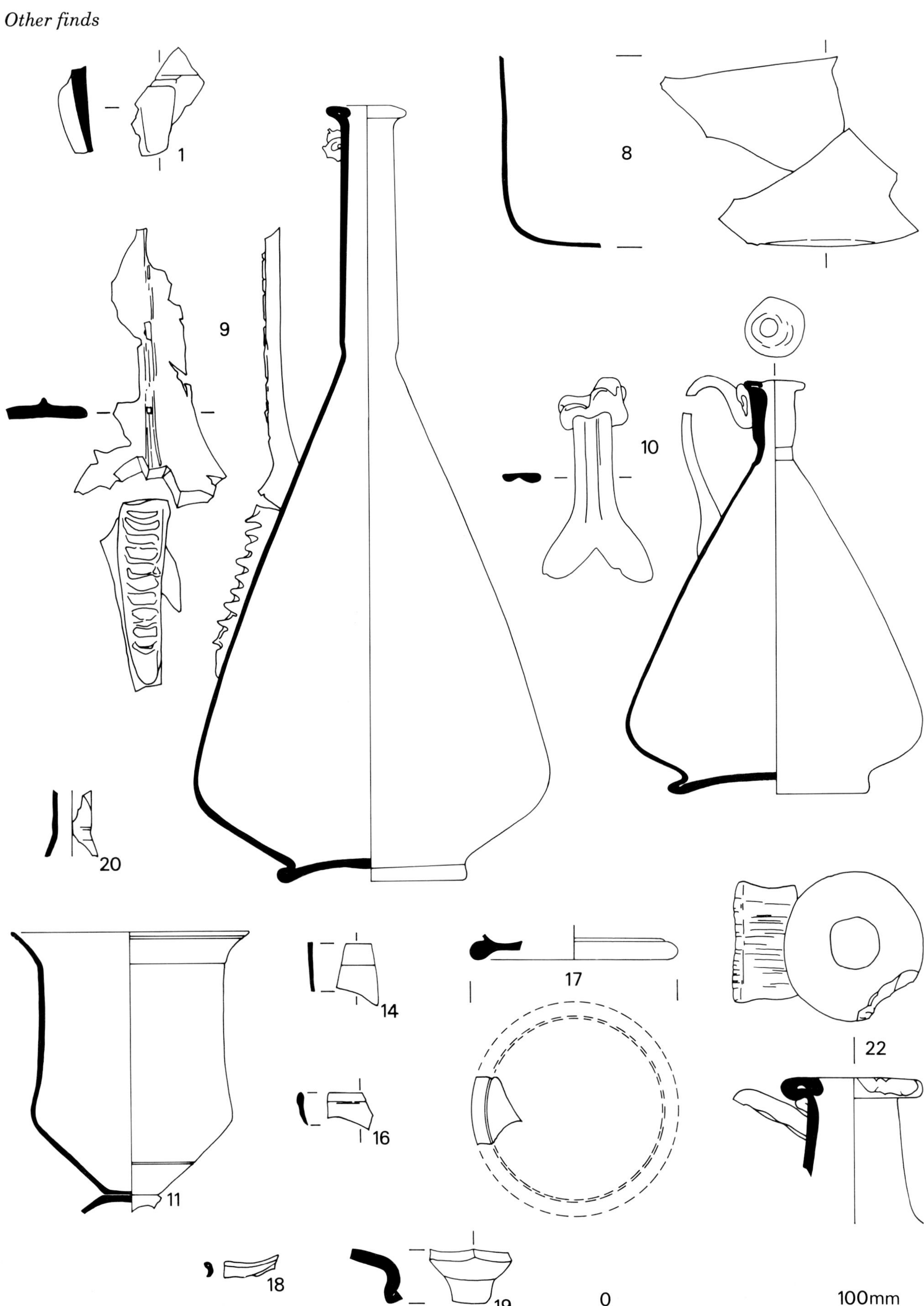

Figure 104 Glass vessels, nos 1–24

Figure 105 Glass vessels, nos 25–36

adding weight to the suggestion that production of this form in yellow/green and yellow/brown glass continued after other strongly coloured vessels had gone out of production. The pit group from Towcester, although much larger, shows particularly close parallels with that from Alcester. Two of the four jugs in the Towcester group (nos 7 and 9) are nearly identical in form to the Alcester jug, no 7 being yellow/green with a yellow/brown handle and no 9 being yellow/brown. In addition there are two, or possibly three examples of wheel-cut colourless drinking cups in the group. The greatest similarity between the two pit groups occurs in the blue/green square bottles, which are both nearly complete. Although the dimensions of the two vessels as recorded are slightly different, both show identical base designs, with four L-shaped corner pieces and the letters SAI across the centre. The Alcester example (Wright 1967, 207, no 24) also shows the trace of an erased letter in the mould, possibly an I, beneath the A, at the centre of the base. Two other bases with comparable designs are known, from *Verulamium* and Colchester (unpublished). In addition, a much smaller one with \I between L-shaped corner pieces comes from Usk, and SAI (retrograde) is known from the fort at Cramond on the Antonine Wall (unpublished).

Also found in pit fill D II 29A were several blue/green bottle fragments including the base of a hexagonal bottle with a base design of three concentric rings and central pellet. The presence of a hexagonal bottle in this pit provides a valuable indicator of this bottle form continuing in use until the middle of the 2nd century. Another base from a hexagonal bottle was found at Alcester in 1926, with a moulded base inscription SABIILO (Wright 1952, 106, no 17). The dates of production of both square and hexagonal bottles are discussed further below.

Two other jugs were found in the excavations. No 10, an almost complete yellow/green conical jug of unusual form, came from two further pits on site D II. The lower section of the vessel, with an open, pushed-in base, was found in pit D II 60, associated with pottery dating from the mid-2nd to the mid-3rd century. The upper body, neck, and handle of the vessel, which joins the lower section, was found in the nearby pit D II 28. Parallels for this jug are difficult to find. The body and base are closely comparable with the Isings form 55 jugs discussed above, and a broadly similar date has been presumed for this form. The very short neck and curved handle, however, are quite different. A similar neck and handle fragment, which is slightly larger and bluish/green in colour, was recorded in a Period 3 context (*c* AD 100–270) at Fishbourne (Harden & Price 1971, 361, fig 142, 93). The last jug, mentioned in Dorothy Charlesworth's notes but now missing, was found in B I 3, and appears to have been blue/green in colour, with a body and base similar to no 9 from pit fill D II 29A, discussed above.

Much of the remaining glass from this period comes from residual deposits. The fragments suggest a very wide range of forms including at least three more early to mid-2nd-century colourless wheel-cut cups (nos 12, 13, 15), similar to no 11 from pit fill D II 29A, discussed above.

Four fragments (no 8) come from the lower body of a carinated bowl in yellow glass. Similar blown vessels with tubular rims are quite common finds on 1st- and early 2nd-century sites in Roman Britain. A dark blue vessel was found at Long Melford, Suffolk, with Neronian samian (Avent & Howlett 1980, 246, fig 41), and four bowls, one in yellow/brown glass, were found in the pit at Felmongers, Harlow, dated to *c* AD 160–70.

Another blue/green fragment, from the tubular base of a cup or bowl, shows evidence of careful reworking of the broken upper edge of the base for some secondary purpose. A fragment from the rim of a blue/green spouted jug (no 18) was also found. This form of jug has an infolded rim which is drawn in to form a pouring spout. A colourless example with an applied trail was found at Caerleon (Allen 1986, 108–9, fig 42, 57) in a deposit dating from the late 2nd to 3rd century. Another spouted jug in green glass from a burial at Skeleton Green (Charlesworth 1981, 271, B.XXXV, fig 106, 12) is dated to the 2nd–3rd century, and this date is also likely for the Alcester fragment.

Fragments from three possible blue/green flasks or unguent bottles were found, one with unmarvered trailed decoration, but these are too small for precise identification. This section also contained a base fragment from a blue/green jar (no 19), as well as a blue/green body fragment with a shallow vertical rib which may have come from a jug or jar.

Bottle fragments form over 30% of the assemblage, a proportion quite usual on sites occupied during the 1st and 2nd centuries. All the fragments recovered were blue/green with the exception of one colourless body fragment. Discounting those found in pit fill D II 29A, a minimum of seven bottles is represented. One is cylindrical, one is hexagonal, one is colourless prismatic, and the remainder are blue/green prismatic. However, when the volume of fragments is taken into consideration, the true number of bottles represented must be much greater.

Cylindrical bottles (Isings 1957, form 51) are common in later 1st-century contexts but seem to go out of use after the Trajanic period. Square bottles (*ibid*, form 50), however, were produced in large numbers from the later 1st century until at least the end of the 2nd century. Hexagonal bottles are not recognized as commonly as other types. They occur in 1st- and early 2nd-century contexts, but have been noted less frequently after this time. Apart from those pieces found in pit fill D II 29A, only small fragments of prismatic bottles were found. Parts of designs of concentric circles were visible on five of the base fragments.

Only one fragment, no 14, from a colourless vessel with a cracked-off rim and a horizontal abraded band, can be assigned to the 3rd century. This is likely to come from a more or less cylindrical cup, with a thickened concave base, and is a form which has not often received attention in Romano-British glass assemblages. An intact specimen is known from the 3rd-century cemetery at Brougham (Cumbria) and another was found at the General Accident site, York (both unpublished).

Nine fragments dating from the 4th century were recognized. These included a blue/green fragment with a fire-rounded rim from a type of cup usually made in pale green bubbly glass in the mid- to later 4th century. Similarly formed rims are present on four beakers in pale green glass from Burgh Castle (Harden 1983, 86–8, fig 37, nos 85, 87–9). At the Alchester road site, Towcester, fragments from pale green and yellowish-green vessels with fire-rounded rims were found in mid-4th-century contexts (Price & Cool 1983, 117, 122, fig 47, nos 40–4). No 36 came from the convex lower body of a small yellow/green cup, showing a trace of applied decoration. A grave dated *c* AD 330–50 at Lankhills, Winchester, produced a comparable vessel in pale green glass (Harden 1979, 211–13, fig 27, 62). Several fragments from vessels with abraded bands in addition to applied trails were also found at the Alchester road site, Towcester (Price & Cool 1983, 116–17, 120, nos 19–22, 24, and 25). With only a small fragment surviving, it is not possible to determine the exact details of the decoration on this example. No 37 was a small pale green fragment from an applied pad base, showing a central pontil mark. All the fragments of 4th-century glass were very bubbly.

Finally, two fragments of cast matt/glossy window panes were identified. This type of window glass was in use from the 1st to 3rd centuries and very common in Roman Britain (Harden 1974).

Leather

J H Thornton

This report was written in the late 1960s.

Catalogue (fig 106)

1 (L4, A XV 9, unphased) A quantity of leather-cutting scrap with the characteristic angles and curves formed between adjacent sections of the shoe.

(a) A fragment of cutting scrap from the edge of the skin showing the typical back line of a moccasin which has been cut from it (Thornton 1973, fig 6). Width across curved part 50mm.

(b) A fragment of cutting scrap with an apparently deliberately curved edge. It is not clear whether this is actually part of a shoe section or the 'marrying-in' cutting scrap from one. The purpose of a small slot penetrating the section is not known. Length 102mm, ht 60mm.

(c) A very small composite fragment resembling in its curvature and composition the lasting margin of an upper folded over the edge of a shoe bottom. This resemblance, however, may be quite fortuitous and the specimen may not even be leather. Not illustrated.

(d) Fragments of material of a woody nature, some with leather adhering. It is just possible that they may belong to a wooden shoe sole or patten since these were worn in Romano-British times. Not illustrated.

The remainder of the scrap consists mainly of very small fragments and includes some pieces of thong.

2 (L3, AA II 87, phase III, 3rd century) A large quantity of cutting scrap with the usual angles and curves, probably both upper and bottom leather; also some shoe fragments and pieces of thong.

(a) An offcut from the top of a decorated quarter (see 6b below) showing four re-entrant cuts where tie-loops and/or decorative three-lobed bosses were cut. Goat or sheep skin. Length *c* 120mm.

(b) A fragment from near the edge of the skin with three re-entrant semicircular cuts similar to 6a below. Length 55mm.

(c)Two oval pieces, 40mm × 24mm and 32mm × 21mm; the larger (illustrated) one has a lobed end. These may be the cutting scrap from decorative 'windows' or tie-loops in the shoe upper (Charlesworth & Thornton 1973, fig 2, shoe no 2, a and b).

(d) A piece of cutting scrap with a concave edge showing two 'starts' or overcuts. It also has impressions of what may be the shoemaker's guide lines as seen in a specimen in the Museum of London (Thornton 1973, fig 6, left). Length 60mm.

(e) Repair heel seat piece with remains *in situ* of the thonging used to attach it to the original sole which had worn away at the back. It still shows a slight moulding where it was pulled up round the edges of the seat. Possibly left foot. Length 80mm, width 54mm.

(f) Fragment of sole edge. Not illustrated.

3 (L2, AA III 93, phase V, later 3rd century on) Small fragments, the largest *c* 31mm × 23mm, of what may be charred leather, possibly from a shoe sole but with no really identifiable features. Not illustrated.

4 (L1, B III 9, unphased) A few fragments of shoe sole with large nail-holes; otherwise no identifiable features. Not illustrated.

5 (L5, C I 72, phase III, 3rd century) Pieces of leather-cutting scrap of various shapes. The straight and curved edges show where the required sections, probably shoe uppers, were cut from. One L-shaped piece has an overcut where the shoemaker's knife went too far. Not illustrated.

6 (L6, C I 73, phase III, 3rd century) A small quantity of cut leather fragments including pieces of thong used possibly for uniting shoe bottom components, some triangular cutting scrap, and unusual quarter offcuts (a) and (b).

(a) This quarter offcut, length 57mm, width 17mm, has two semicircular re-entrant cuts which may be the result of cutting the instep tie loops commonly found on Romano-British shoes (Charlesworth & Thornton 1973, fig 5, shoe no 5).

(b) One of the triangular fragments has one three-lobed re-entrant cut and the remains of another similar one; it is probably the waste made in cutting an ornamental quarter which had the corresponding three-lobed decoration (Charlesworth & Thornton 1973, fig 3, shoe no 3, a and b). The smallness of the lobes suggests that a punch must have been used to make them.

7 (L7, C VI 109, phase I, late 1st–2nd century) Fragmentary remains of a right-foot nailed shoe bottom unit. The individual sections are themselves delaminated so that it is not certain how many there are but there appear to be three — insole, middlesole, and sole. Nail-holes remain and there are impressions of the nail-heads on the grain surface of the sole (the surface next to the ground when used), and there are also some impressions of the turned-over nail-points on the insole surface (see Thornton 1973, 3–4 and fig 2 for a description of Romano-British nailing). The fragment is now in three parts and it is not completely certain how these fitted together but a suggested reconstruction is shown. The nailed method of shoe construction and a multi-layer bottom is typically Romano-British. Length *c* 160mm, width (across fore-part) 66mm.

Jet and shale

Jeremy Evans

Twelve pieces of jet and shale were recovered from the excavations, of which ten were available for study (two jet fragments from A XVIIA 1, unphased are missing).

Jet (fig 107)

1 A fragment of the tip of a pin shaft. Length 35mm, min diam 2mm, max diam 6mm. Not illustrated. (J 1, A IX 21, unphased)

2 Badly broken, faceted, pin head. These polyhedral jet pins were one of the commonest jet pin types (cf Lawson 1975, no 65). Cf Crummy's (1979) type 4 pins, dated to after AD 250, although she suggests jet examples may start earlier. Diam *c* 14mm, surviving ht *c* 13mm. (J 8, G IA 5, phase VI, late 4th century)

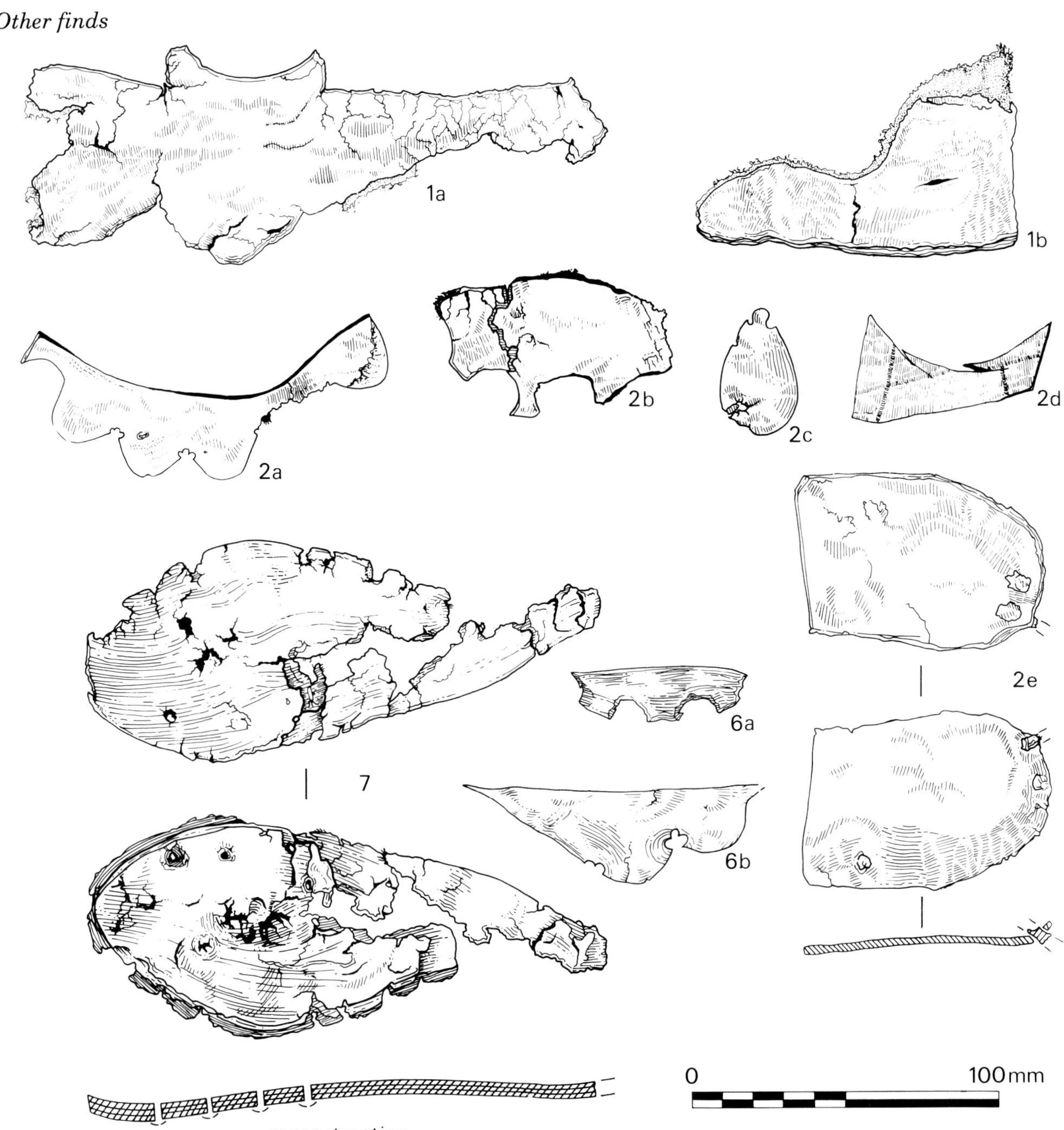

Figure 106 Leather

Shale (fig 107)

Unfortunately all the shale objects have dried out since excavation, without conservation, and measurements may not, therefore, be truly representative.

3 Shale bracelet, lathe-turned with an internal ridge where the core has been detached. This latter action was clearly done by turning to each side of the ridge and then by drilling or piercing round these grooves with a large number of fine holes *c* 1mm in diameter. The external diameter is decorated with three cordons defined by four turned grooves, all of which have been laterally notched at *c* 1.5mm intervals. Cf Lawson 1975, no 41b for the profile. Internal diam 60mm, width 8mm. (J 6, A XVIIA 4, unphased)

4 Fragment of a plain shale bracelet with a D-shaped section, cf Lawson 1975, no 18c. It has a slight internal ridge where it has been cut off from the core and not fully smoothed off. Internal diam 70mm, width 7mm, thickness 5.5mm. Not illustrated. (J 2, AA II 2, unphased)

5 Fragment of a plain shale bracelet of oval section, cf Lawson 1975, no 23d. Internal diam 65mm, width 7.5mm, thickness 5.5mm. Not illustrated. (J 3, AA III 7, phase IX, mid-4th century)

6 Fragment of a plain shale bracelet of thin, subrectangular section, cf Lawson 1975, no 28b. Internal diam 70mm, width 3.5mm, thickness 6mm. (J 9, D I 24, phase VIII, late 4th century)

7 Fragment of a shale bangle of oval section decorated with two turned grooves, cf Lawson 1975, no 42b for section. Internal diam 90mm, width 16mm, thickness 11mm. (J 10, D I 173, phase II, later 2nd to early 3rd century?)

8 Fragment of a plain shale bracelet of D-shaped section, cf Lawson 1975, no 18c. Internal diam 55mm, width 9mm, thickness 5mm. Not illustrated. (J 7, D II 1, unphased)

9 Fragment of a plain shale bracelet of D-shaped section, cf Lawson 1975, no 18c. Internal diam 70mm, width 10.5mm, thickness 6.5mm. Not illustrated. (J 4, C III 59, unphased)

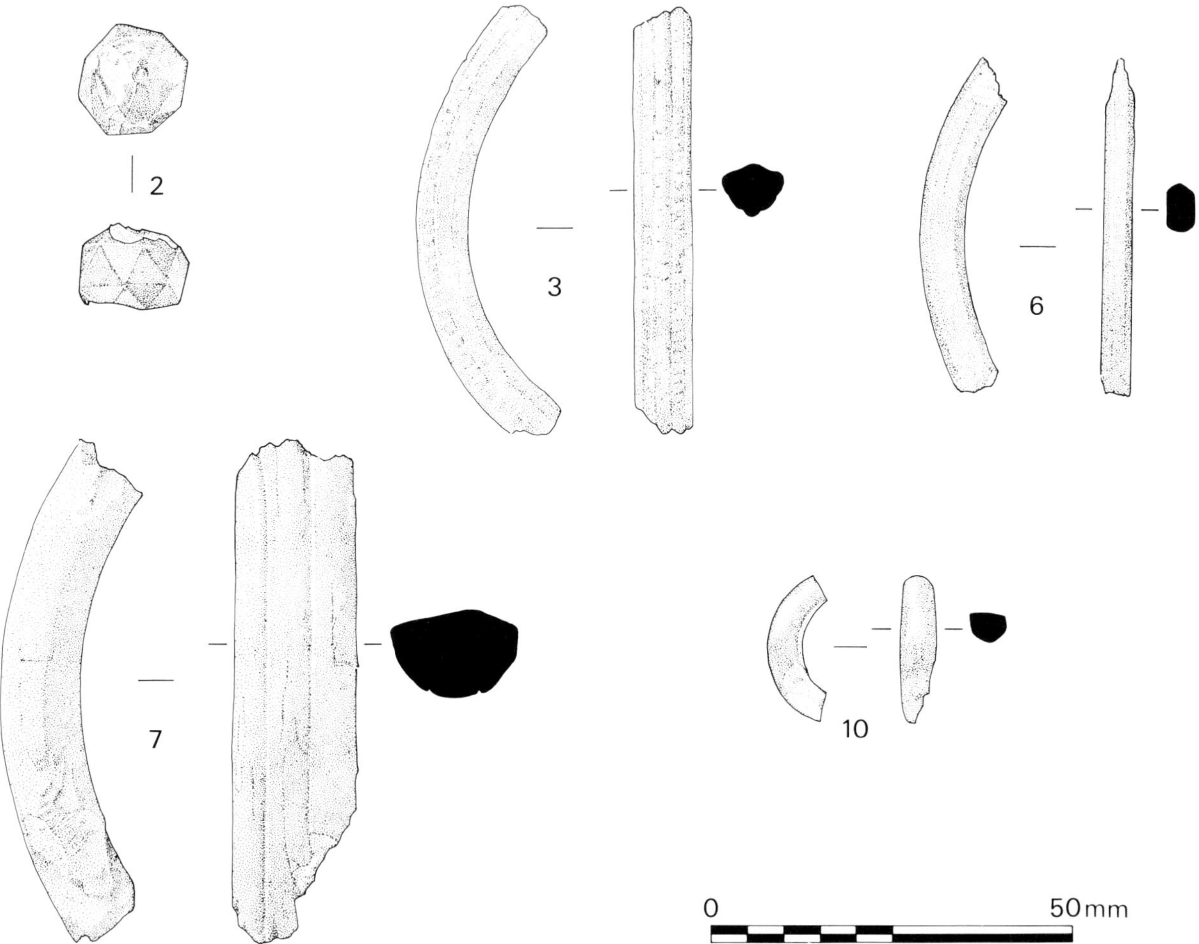

Figure 107 Jet and shale

10 Fragment of a shale ring with D-shaped section, perhaps a finger-ring, but rather thick, alternatively a hair-ring or dress fastener (Lawson 1975, 256). Cf Lawson 1975, nos 59–60 for two other plain rings in jet. Internal diam *c* 14mm, width 4.5mm, thickness 4mm. (J 5, C IIIA 33, unphased)

The sizes of the shale bracelets are generally similar to those from Silchester (Lawson 1975, fig 3) although fewer seem to be decorated, two in eight compared with about half of the Silchester ones.

Worked stone and quernstones

Jeremy Evans with contributions by John Crossling

Catalogue of illustrated stone items (figs 108–18)

Microfiche [M5:B11]

Inscribed stone

1 Constaninian milestone. A rectangular-sectioned column of oolitic limestone bearing the inscription ... FL VAL/CONSTANTINO/PIO/FELICI/INVICT[O]/AVG. (JRS LVI, 220, no 10). Ht 700mm, width 335mm, depth 90mm. Geology: limestone, L3. (ST174, G IV 1A, phase VI, late 4th century)

2 The corner of a moulded panel in oolitic limestone. It is quite heavily abraded post-breakage but the heavy marking on the panel, which should have been protected by the moulding, tends to suggest a deliberate destruction of the inscription which it may have carried. The panel is well prepared with the back being quite well finished and its edges chamfered to form the moulding. Max surviving length 310mm, max surviving width 270mm, thickness of panel 55mm, depth of panel below moulding 37mm. Geology: limestone, L2. (ST115, C IIIA 13, unphased)

Altars

3 A small altar in oolitic limestone — like the inscription panel, no 2 above. It has well-smoothed sides and front with no trace of an inscription but the back is roughly pecked and not well finished. The double moulding around the top is similarly only roughed-out at the back, which was obviously not meant to be viewed. There are three crudely cut parallel grooves in the top for libations, possibly by a different hand given the care of the other work. The bottom of the altar was chamfered and well smoothed but the base was not well finished, suggesting it was designed to be earthfast against a wall. Ht 300mm, width of panel 155mm, width of side panels 127mm. Geology: limestone, L2. (ST77, B IA 15, phase IV, mid- to late 4th century)

4 A small altar in sandstone. Like ST77 this came from the primary silting of a well. It is rectangular in section with well-cut and smoothed surfaces and no trace of an inscription. The base is poorly finished and convex so that it does not stand vertically, but at an angle of around 82°. The mason would appear to have had it in this position when carving it since the mouldings on the two sides are not remotely symmetrical when it is set vertically, but much more so when it is set at this angle. Both sides have a double moulding at the top, the surface of which is pecked and rather uneven. In the centre of the top is an oval moulding *c* 103mm × 90mm, *c* 20mm high in which there is an oval depression *c* 58mm × 49mm and *c* 11mm deep with a pecked base for libations. The base of the shaft is stepped out with a square moulding *c* 15mm × 15mm on the right, and 10mm × 15mm on the left, to a base 220mm wide and 120mm broad. Given the uneven nature of the base, the altar was presumably designed to be earthfast, otherwise it would easily overbalance. Ht 310mm, width of base 220mm, width of shaft 157mm. Geology: sandstone, S2. (ST 78, B IA 15, phase IV, mid- to 4th century)

Other carved stonework

5 A squared block of yellow oolitic limestone with vertical pecked sides and a well-smoothed flat base. The smooth flat upper surface bears two concentric circular grooves, respectively *c* 9mm and 10mm wide, 5mm and 6mm deep, and *c* 60mm and 140mm in diam. The well-smoothed base, particularly in contrast to the sides, suggests the stone was prepared to be set up on a flat surface, probably for casting vessels in pewter or working sheet bronze. Max surviving length 140mm, width 220mm, thickness 75mm. Geology: limestone, L3. (ST 137, D I 126, phase II, later 2nd to early 3rd century?)
6 A roughly triangular block of sandstone, broken at the edges, but probably substantially complete. It has a rectangular, slightly concave slot cut into the upper surface. It would seem to be a metalworking mould, presumably for casting bronze or another non-ferrous metal into ingots. It came from a pit which contained other material associated with metalworking. Depth of slot 7mm, width of slot 34mm, surviving length of slot 140mm, length 170mm, width 125mm, thickness 59mm. Geology: sandstone, S2. (ST 106, D I 47, phase VI, mid- to late 4th century?)
7 About a quarter of the base of a stone tank or trough, probably ovoid in shape, in yellow limestone. The base is fairly flat and has been comparatively well finished with fairly coarse pecking, as has the exterior wall. The interior is very rough and uneven and is poorly finished. Max surviving length 375mm, max surviving ht 145mm, thickness of centre of base *c* 50mm. Geology: limestone, L3. (ST 173, D II 67, unphased)
8 A rectangular tank in oolitic limestone. The surfaces are still fairly irregular. The exterior sides have faint vertical tooling lines whilst the interior ones are pecked. Max ht 220mm, max length 570mm, depth of tank 145mm, thickness of base 750mm, max thickness of side 85mm. Geology: limestone, L3. (ST 33, A II 30, unphased)

Other stone objects

9 A roughly ovoid, irregularly shaped piece of limestone. Burnt. Pierced with a drilled hole 12mm in diam. Perhaps a small loomweight or net weight. Length 51mm, width 44mm, thickness 19mm, weight 0.06kg. Geology: limestone. (ST 95, D I 1A, unphased)
10 A broken subrectangular block of limestone. It is roughly shaped apart from the face which seems to have been fashioned into a crude stamp consisting of an ovoid ridge within a subrectangular border, to act as a producer's mark for some soft commodity (butter/ointment, etc). Possibly post-Roman. Maximum surviving length 5mm, width 40mm, thickness 22mm, weight 0.086kg. Geology: limestone. (ST 139, F I topsoil)
16 Irregular, diamond-shaped stone roof tile, with a single nail-hole in the top corner drilled from both sides. Max length 280mm, max width 270mm, max thickness 18mm, weight 2.30kg. Geology: sandstone, S4. (ST 93, C VI 24, phase VII, early to mid-4th century)
29 Stone block with socket for timber upright, perhaps from a door frame or verandah. Missing. (ST 164, C VIA 50, phase VIII, 4th century)

Whetstones and hones

41 An ovoid-shaped whetstone, which fits very well in the left hand. The soft siltstone retains a large number of knife strokes on the upper surface, with fewer on the reverse. Length 126mm, width 58mm, thickness 21mm. Geology: siltstone, SI1. (ST 105, D I 71, phase V, early to mid-4th century?)
42 A subcircular wedge-shaped whetstone, roughly shaped and worn smooth from use on both faces. Length 155mm, width 110mm, thickness 34–15mm. Geology: sandstone, S7. (ST 79, C IIIA 11–13, unphased)
45 Hone with circular section. Missing. (ST 89, A XVIIB 1, unphased)
46 Hone fragment with subrectangular section. Missing. (ST 104, D I 36, phase VI, mid- to late 4th century)
47 Hone fragment with square section. Missing. (ST 134, G I 137, phase IV, early to mid-4th century)
48 Circular-sectioned hone fragment. Missing. (ST 167, K IV 1, unphased)

Grinding stones and mortars

49 Square ashlar sandstone block with well-finished sides but unfinished base, the upper surface of which has been used as a large palette, resulting in a smooth concave surface up to 18mm deeper than its edges. It is described here as a palette since the motion used on it was clearly circular, as opposed to the back and forward motion of a saddle quern. Perhaps used for grinding medicines, condiments, or food like a *mortarium*. Length 240mm, width max 185mm, weight 6kg+, ht 96mm. Geology: sandstone, S2. (ST 144, D IV 2, unphased)
50 About half of a subsquare sandstone mortar: the end and half of two sides remain. The sides have been finished and smoothed, but the base is irregular and unfinished. Max surviving ht 130mm, max surviving length 110mm, width 160mm, weight 1.90kg, diam of mortar *c* 110mm, maximum surviving depth of mortar 90mm. Geology: sandstone, S2. (ST 26, B I 6, unphased)
51 A bun-shaped circular stone of some height. The upper grinding surface is smooth, heavily worn, and quite concave; the side and flat base are both fairly roughly shaped. There is no evidence of a feed pipe in the piece, suggesting it was a palette/grinding stone rather than a quern. Weight *c* 6kg, diam 290mm, stone ht 107mm, grinding surface angle *c* 13°. Geology: conglomerate, C1. (ST 158, G IA 8, phase IX/X, late 4th century)
52 Three fragments comprising *c* 25% of the circumference of the grinding surface of a mortar. The grinding surface is strongly concave and worn very smooth with no trace of preparation and there is a flat, pecked area around it, 45–65mm wide. The vertical side is pecked and fairly roughly finished. The base is rough and unfinished. There is an example of a similar mortar from *Tripontium* (unpublished in the Warwickshire Museum). Weight 4.10kg, diam *c* 300mm, stone thickness 70mm+, grinding surface angle *c* 30°. Geology: sandstone, S1. (ST 120, A XIV 29, unphased, late 2nd to late 3rd century)
55 About 95% of the lower stone of a rotary quern, probably of Romano-British domestic type (it may well pair with no 56). It is a bi-convex disc with a spindle-hole 27mm in diameter and 32mm deep (which does not penetrate the base). The grinding surface was pecked and has heavy wear especially around the spindle-hole. It has near-vertical, well-shaped sides and an irregular, rough base. Weight *c* 11kg, diam 340mm, stone ht 105mm, grinding surface angle *c* 9°. Geology: conglomerate, C1. (ST 42, A XIV 29, unphased, late 2nd to late 3rd century)
56 A fragment comprising *c* 15% of the upper stone of a rotary quern of Romano-British domestic type. It has a grinding surface with no evidence of preparation and showing some wear except for a band smoothed for around 17mm around the feed pipe, perhaps cut to improve grain flow to the grinding surface. The side is sloped inward a little and is pecked and well finished; the upper surface is well finished. The feed pipe is of slightly elliptical shape with a diameter of around 75mm and a length of 45mm. The handle was secured in a square cut rectangular slot in the upper surface *c* 30mm square and 72mm long. The stone thins towards the feed pipe from 65mm at the circumference to 45mm. Weight 3.80kg, diam 350mm, stone thickness 65–45mm, grinding surface angle *c* 7°+. Geology: conglomerate, C1. (ST 117, A XIV 29, unphased, late 2nd to late 3rd century)
57 A complete lower stone in two pieces, probably from a beehive or Romano-British domestic-type quern. It has a grinding surface worn smooth in large areas, but not in others, and prepared by pecking. The unusual form is that of a convex disc with a concave and unusually well-finished base which is roughly pecked. The angle of the grinding surface varies from 7° on one side to 2° on the other. This and the wear tend to suggest that it was used in an oscillating rather than a rotary manner. The spindle-hole is 18mm in diam and 14mm deep and does not penetrate the base. The side is vertical and pecked. Weight *c* 13kg, diam 345mm, stone ht 95mm, grinding surface angle *c* 2–7°. Geology: millstone grit, M2. (ST 121, A XIV 29, unphased, late 2nd to late 3rd century)

58 About 80% of a millstone in nine fragments. It has a concentrically grooved surface (grooves *c* 25mm apart, 10mm wide and 8mm deep) worn heavily on one side especially, and least worn towards the feed pipe. The vertical sides are pecked and the upper surface is flat and roughly pecked with a collar 45mm wide and 10mm high running around the circumference. The feed pipe is 90mm in diameter, *c* 65mm long, and has two wedge-shaped slots running off from it, into which the mechanism for turning the stone would have fitted. It must have been driven by animal or water power and is in all probability from a watermill. Weight *c* 85kg, diam 650mm, stone ht 145mm, grinding surface angle *c* 6°. Geology: millstone grit, M1. (ST 41, A XIV 29, unphased, late 2nd to late 3rd century)
59 About 25% from the upper stone of a rotary quernstone. It is probably of early Roman date. The side is vertical, pecked, and well shaped, and the upper surface is dished with a slight hopper and pecked and smoothed. The feed pipe is around 60mm in diam and the grinding surface is pecked. There is a wedge-shaped handle slot cut into the upper surface, 85mm long, 8mm deep and from 55 to 16mm wide. Weight *c* 3.5kg, diam 340mm, stone ht 100mm, grinding surface angle >5°. Geology: millstone grit, M2. (ST 40, A XIV 29, unphased, late 2nd to late 3rd century)
60 Base stone of a rotary quern with non-penetrating spindle-hole and angled grinding surface, probably of Romano-British domestic type. Missing. (ST 39, A XIV 29, unphased)
61 About 40% of the upper stone of a Romano-British domestic type with angled grinding surface and stone thinning towards the feed pipe. There is a slight 'hopper' around the elliptical feed pipe *c* 7mm deep. Grinding surface worn smooth. Upper surface and side well pecked. Weight 3.20kg, diam 350mm, stone ht 52mm, grinding surface angle indeterminable. Geology: C1. (ST 118, A XIV 29, unphased)
65 Upper stone of a rotary quernstone of Romano-British domestic type. It has quite a steeply angled grinding surface flattening towards the circumference. The steeply angled centre of the stone is concentrically grooved with a band of radial grooves around the circumference. The feed-pipe would appear to be circular. Missing. (ST 156, A XVIIB 10, unphased)
66 Three joining fragments comprising around 25% of an upper stone of a rotary quern of Romano-British domestic type (or possibly a millstone, see 'Discussion' below, pp 245–7). The grinding surface is worn and concentrically grooved near the centre. The side is vertical, pecked, and partly smoothed, and the upper surface is fairly flat and roughly pecked. The feed pipe is 90mm in diam and 60mm long. From its edge, cut into the grinding surface, is a rectangular slot 72mm long, 13mm deep and 30mm wide, presumably for bedding an iron rynd. Weight 7.85kg, diam 500mm, stone thickness 70mm, grinding surface angle 11°. Geology: millstone grit, M2. (ST 159, A XVIIB 14, unphased)
69 A small fragment (*c* 9% of the circumference) of a flat, lower(?) millstone with a radially grooved and quite well-worn grinding surface. The grooves are *c* 10mm wide, *c* 10mm apart, and now *c* 5mm deep. The outer 30mm of the grinding surface is *c* 10mm higher, suggesting that the upper stone was *c* 80mm less in diam. The side is vertical and roughly dressed unlike the base. Weight 5.00kg, diam *c* 550+mm, stone ht 95mm, grinding surface angle flat(?). Geology: millstone grit, M2. (ST 122, B IA 14, phase IV, mid- to late 4th century)
71 About 20% of the circumference of an upper stone of a thick 'rotary quern' of Romano-British domestic type (or possibly a millstone, see 'Discussion' below, pp 245–7). It has a very smooth, worn grinding surface with no visible signs of preparation. The grinding surface has the unusual feature of a rectangular cut slot 45mm wide, 25mm deep, and at least 40mm long extending radially from the edge of the feed pipe which must have been used as a bedding for an iron rynd. The grinding surface is laterally concave strongly suggesting that it must have been used like a beehive quern with oscillating motions rather than as a rotary quern. The side is well pecked and the upper surface very roughly treated. There is a handle slot 17mm deep and 75mm long cut into the upper surface. Weight 5.05kg, diam *c* 480mm, stone thickness 85mm, angle of grinding surface *c* 11°. Geology: sandstone, S5. (ST 13, B IV 4, unphased)
72 A fragment from the upper stone of a rotary quern of Romano-British domestic type. The grinding surface is prepared with radial grooves *c* 10mm apart, *c* 4mm wide, and *c* 2mm deep or cut in harps. The side is slightly insloping, pecked, and well finished, and the upper surface, parallel to the grinding surface, is poorly finished and pecked, with a collar 50mm wide and 10mm high around the feed pipe. Wright (pers comm) suggests 3rd–4th century parallels in Derbyshire and Yorkshire. Weight 3.80kg, stone diam *c* 500mm, stone thickness 63mm, grinding surface angle *c* 4°. Geology: conglomerate, C2. (ST 25, C I 3, unphased)
74 A segment from the upper stone of a rotary quern of Romano-British domestic type. It has a slightly worn, well-pecked grinding surface and a vertical, pecked, and partly smoothed side. The upper surface is elaborately moulded and fully smoothed. The feed pipe is 50mm in diam and 45mm long. It seems a most unusual piece: there are no decorated querns in the collection of over 180 from the Stanwick Villa site, Northants. Wright (pers comm) cites a similar stone from Winster, Derbys in millstone grit and a number of decorated stones from the rest of the county. Weight 3.65kg, diam 500mm, stone thickness (max) 45mm, grinding surface angle 11°. Geology: conglomerate, C2. (ST 27, C IV 1, unphased)
75 A fragment representing less than 10% of the circumference of the upper stone of another unusual rotary quernstone of Romano-British domestic type with moulded decoration. The grinding surface is reasonably worn and was prepared by pecking. The well-moulded side has a groove around it dividing it into two unequal cordons and is fully smoothed. This could partly be for the attachment of a handle through use of an iron loop around the circumference, but it is probably just a decorative feature. The upper surface has an elaborate moulded decoration. Wright (pers comm) cites a good parallel to this in millstone grit from Aldwarke, Derbys (unpublished). Weight 1.75kg, diam *c* 400mm, stone thickness 55–40mm, grinding surface angle *c* 4°. Geology: conglomerate, C1. (ST 101, D I 49, phase VI, mid- to late 4th century?)
77 Fragment (*c* 12%) from the circumference of an upper stone of a rotary quern of Romano-British domestic type. It has a reasonably worn grinding surface with no evidence of preparation. The side is vertical and quite well finished. The upper surface is moderately well finished and is parallel to the grinding surface. The spindle-hole is of elliptical shape to help secure the handle and has a minimum diam of 64mm. Weight *c* 4kg, diam 420mm, stone thickness 65mm, angle of grinding surface 11°. Geology: conglomerate, C1. (ST 103, D I 49, phase VI, mid- to late 4th century?)
78 A fragment from the circumference of an upper stone of a rotary quern of Romano-British domestic type or a millstone. The grinding surface, which is a little worn, is concentrically grooved. The grooves are *c* 10mm apart, 7mm wide, and 4mm deep. The side is vertical and roughly pecked and the upper surface is roughly pecked except on the collar around the circumference. The collar is *c* 65mm wide and 10mm high and has been smoothed. This, the low grinding angle, and the concentric grooving on the grinding surface tend to suggest that this was a millstone. Weight 1.90kg, diam *c* 550mm, stone thickness 45mm, grinding surface angle 3°. Geology: millstone grit, M1. (ST 123, D I 92, phase VI, mid- to late 4th century)
79 A fragment from the circumference of an upper stone of a rotary quernstone, probably a millstone given its large diam *c* 0.65m and thickness *c* 0.09m. The upper surface of the stone is pecked and has a collar around the circumference. The grinding surface would appear to have been concentrically grooved. Missing. (ST 131, D I 101, phase VI, mid- to late 4th century?)
86 Around 35% of the circumference of an upper stone of a rotary quern of Romano-British domestic type. It has a well-worn grinding surface, especially towards the circumference, with no trace of preparation. The vertical side is well finished and smoothed as is the upper surface. The feed pipe is 80mm in diam and 65mm long. The stone thins towards the feed pipe. There is a square-sectioned slot for bedding the handle cut into the upper surface. It is 25mm square and extends 75mm from the circumference. Cf Curwen 1937, fig 15. Weight 4.25kg, diam 330mm, stone thickness 75–65mm, grinding surface angle 12°. Geology: conglomerate, C1. (ST 143, J II 8, phase VIII, 3rd century?)
88 About 25% of the upper stone of a rotary quern of Romano-British domestic type. The grinding surface is finely pecked and shows some wear. The vertical side and upper surface are well shaped and finely pecked. There is a slight hopper around the feed pipe, the diam of which is 65mm and its depth 20mm. The 'hopper' is *c* 100mm in diam and 5mm deep. The stone thins towards the feed pipe. Weight 1.55kg, diam 320mm, stone ht 55mm, stone thickness 45–35mm, grinding surface angle 13°. Geology: sandstone, S6. (ST 172, K XIV 8, unphased)

Figure 108 Worked stone, nos 1–4

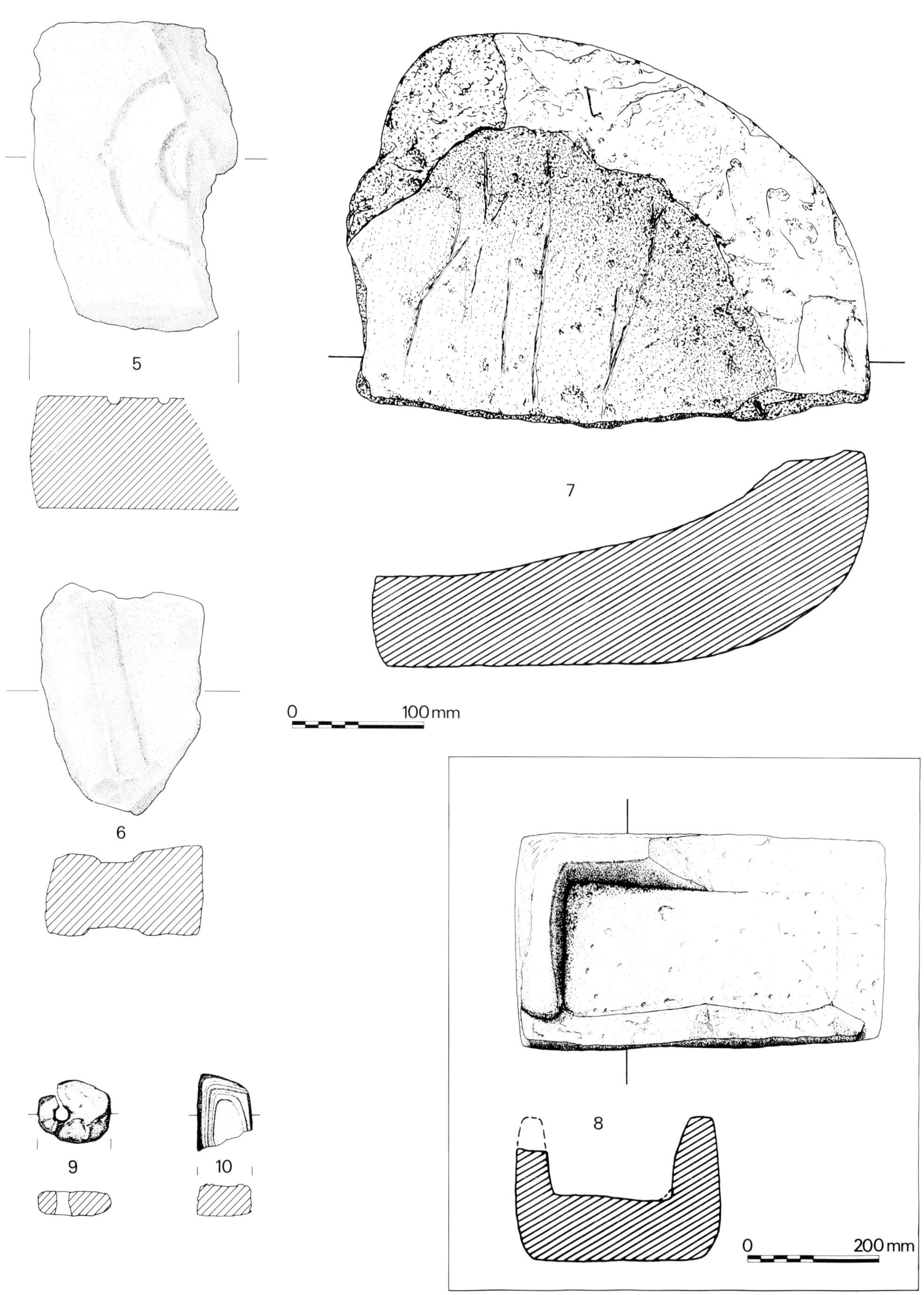

Figure 109 Worked stone, nos 5–10

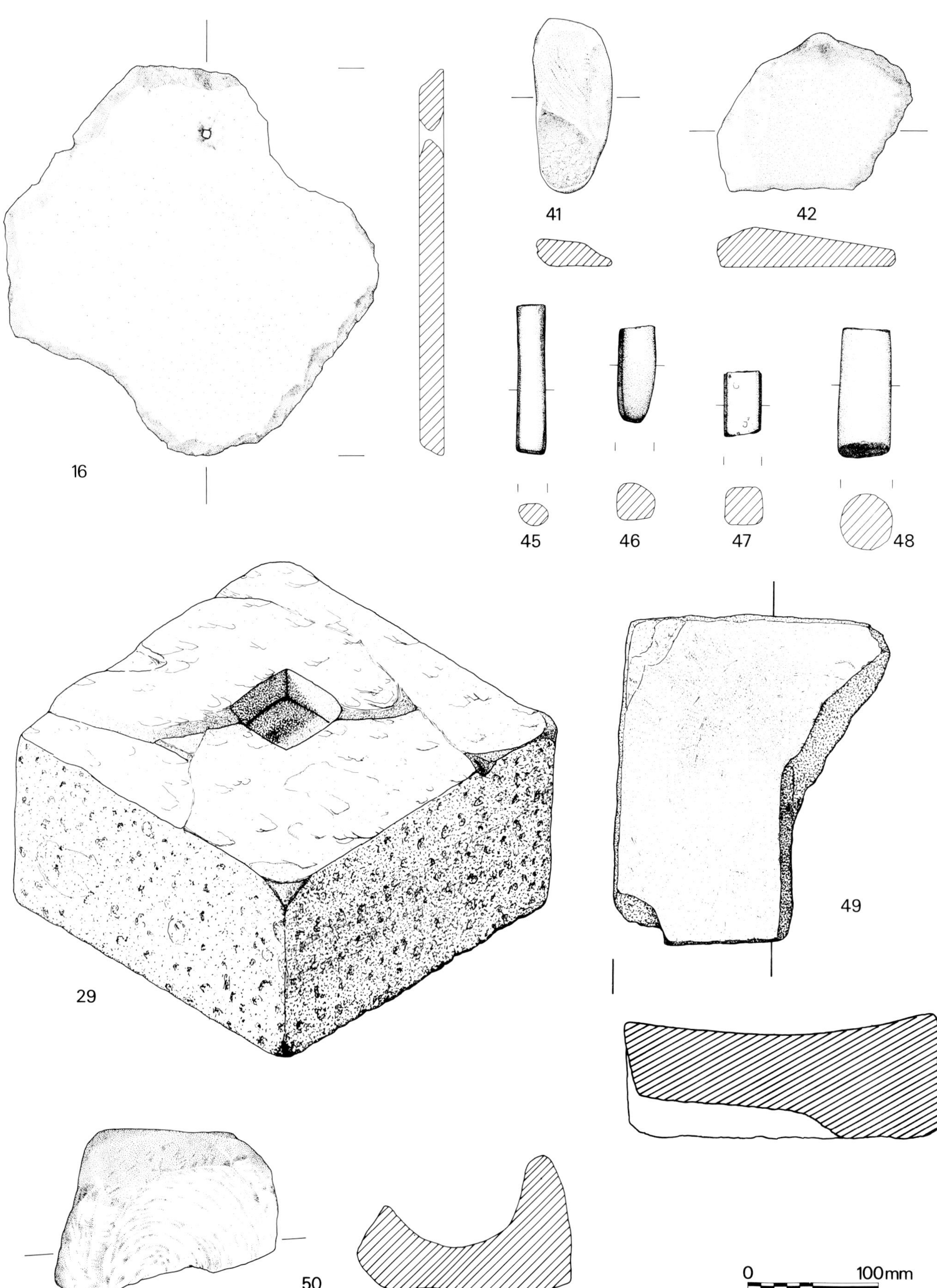

Figure 110 Worked stone, nos 16–50

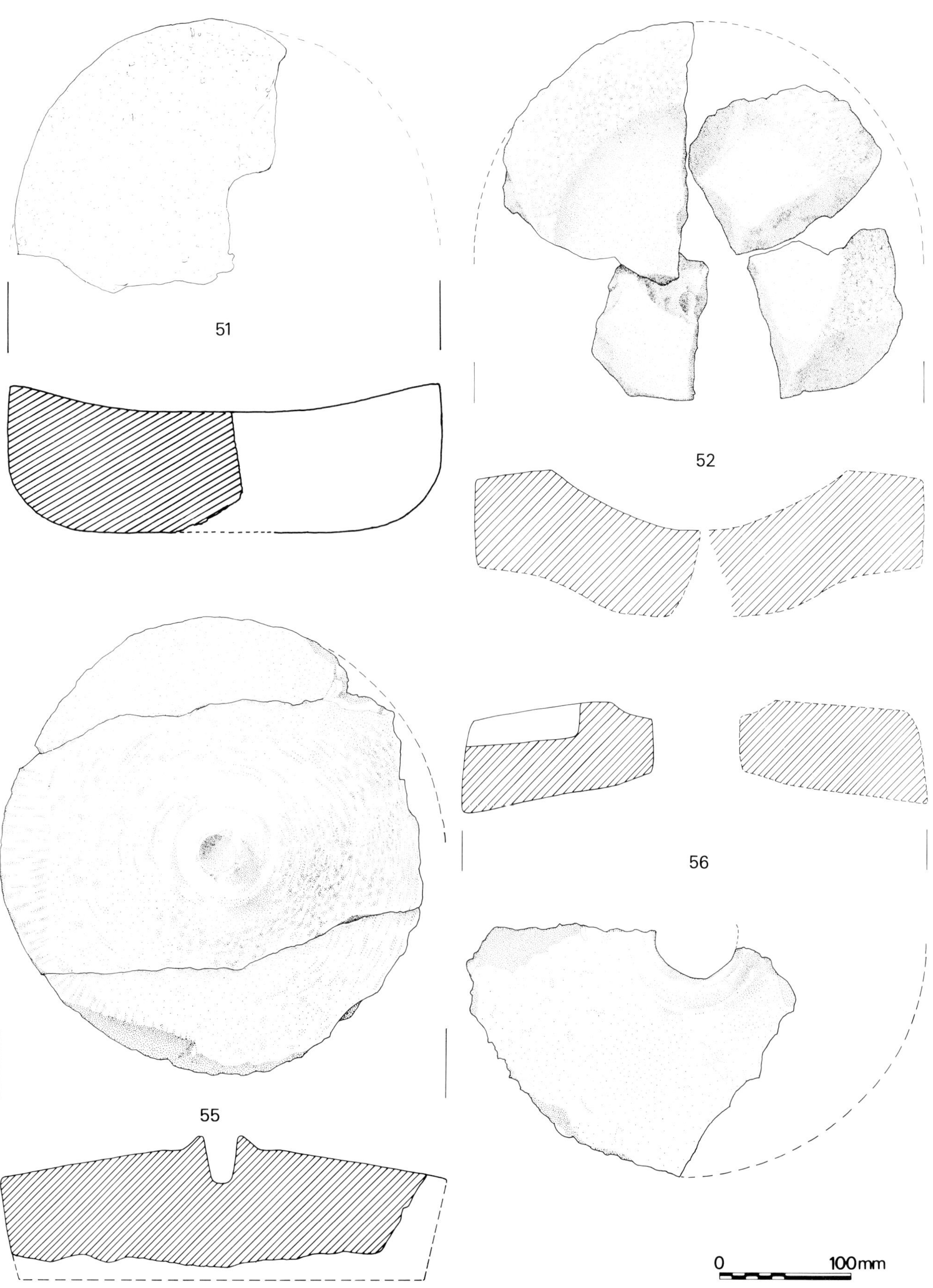

Figure 111 Worked stone, nos 51–6

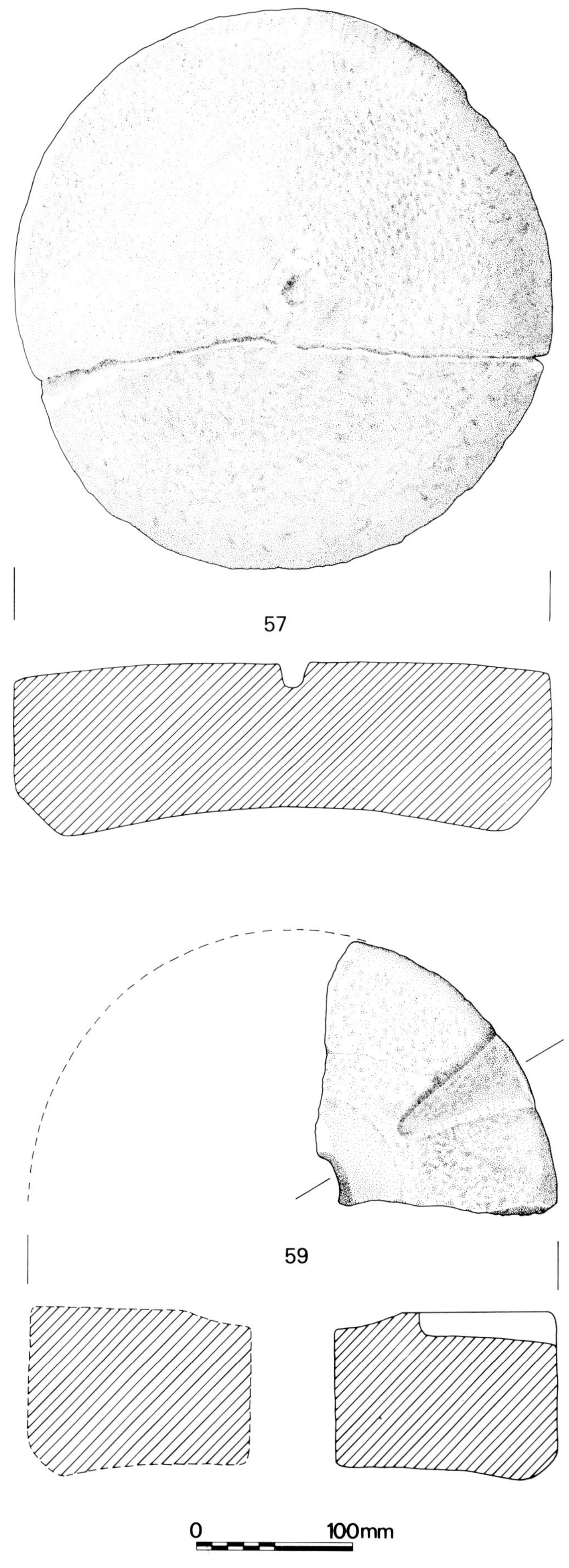

Figure 112 Worked stone, nos 57 and 59

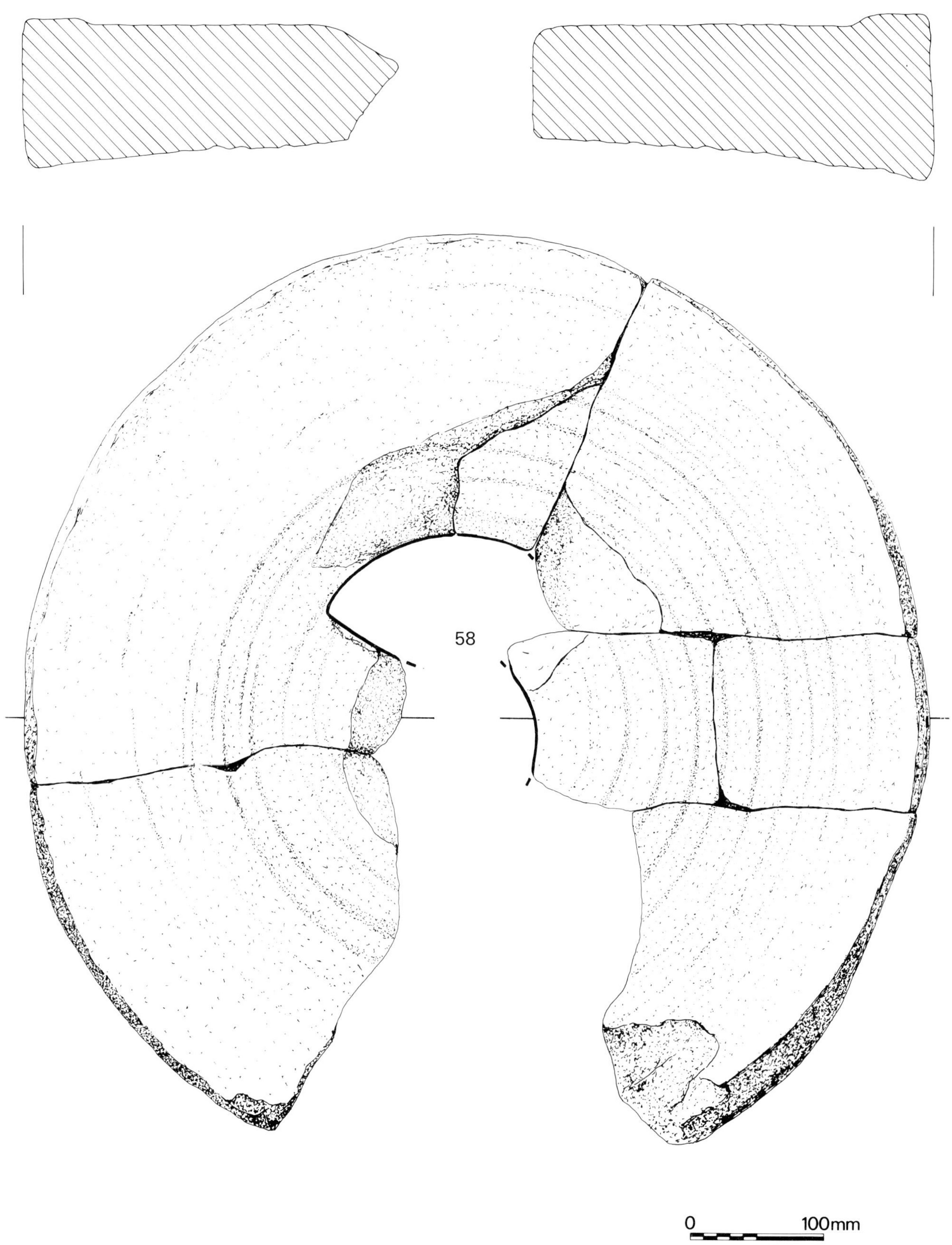

Figure 113 Worked stone, no 58

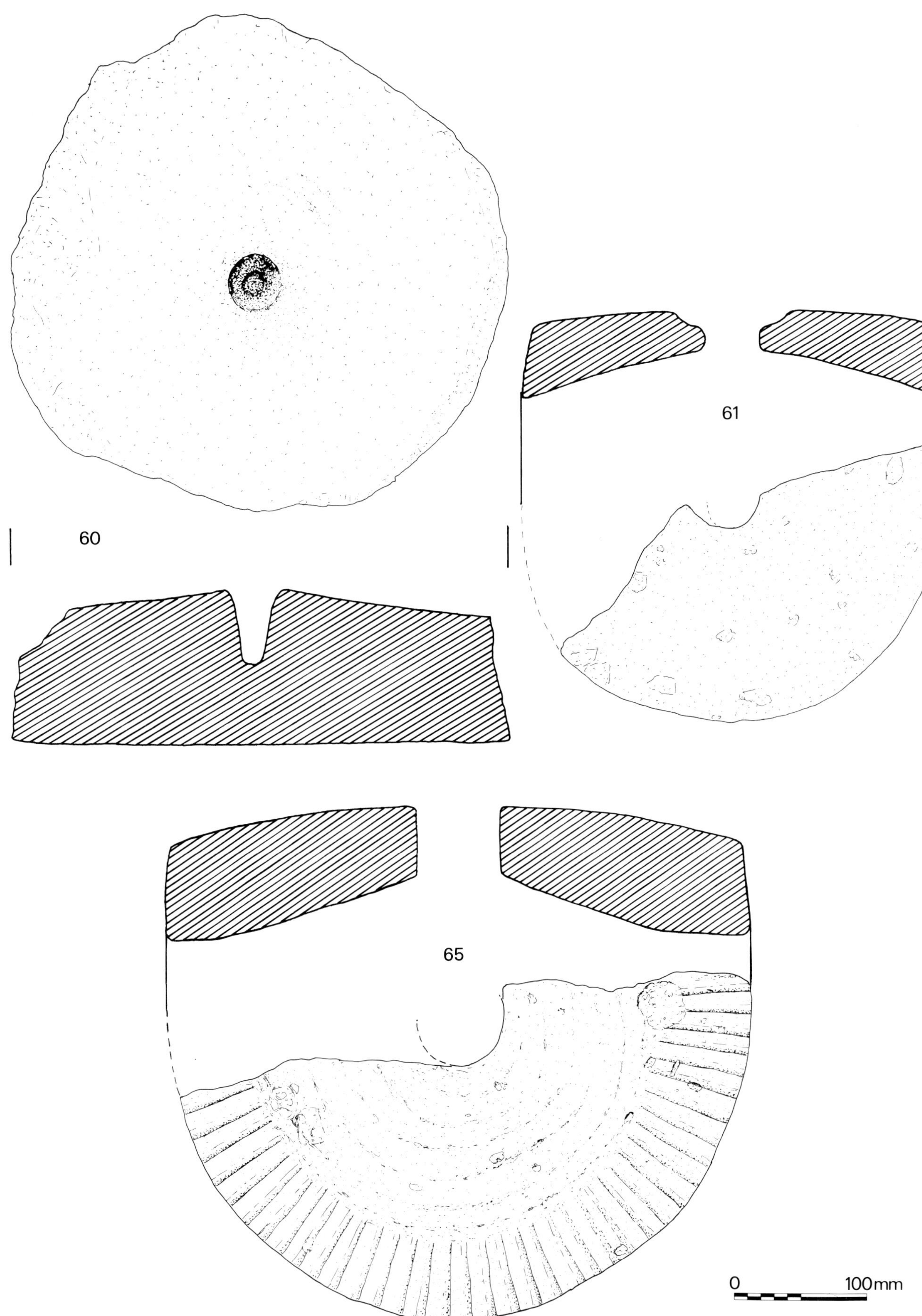

Figure 114 Worked stone, nos 60–5

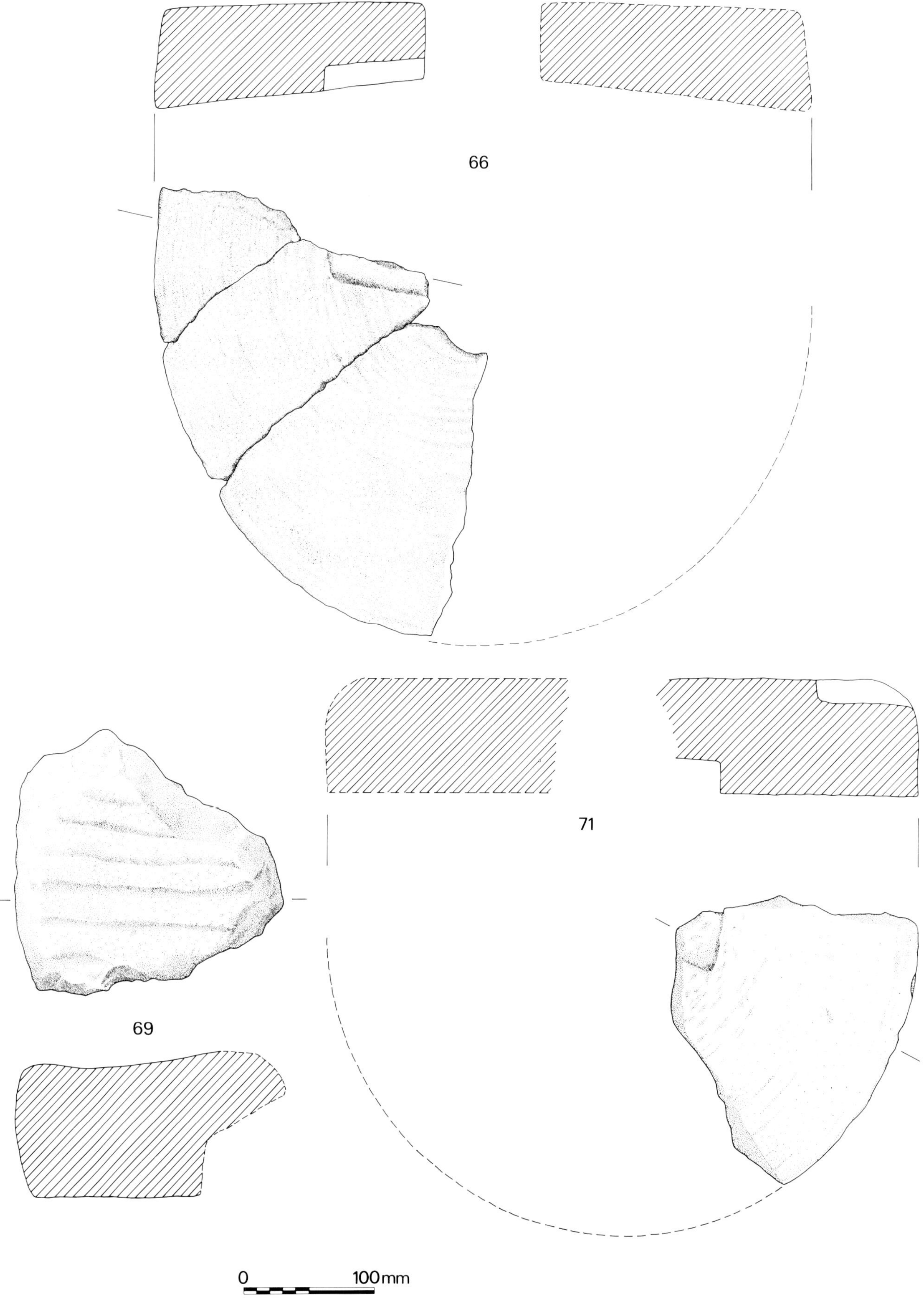

Figure 115 Worked stone, nos 66–71

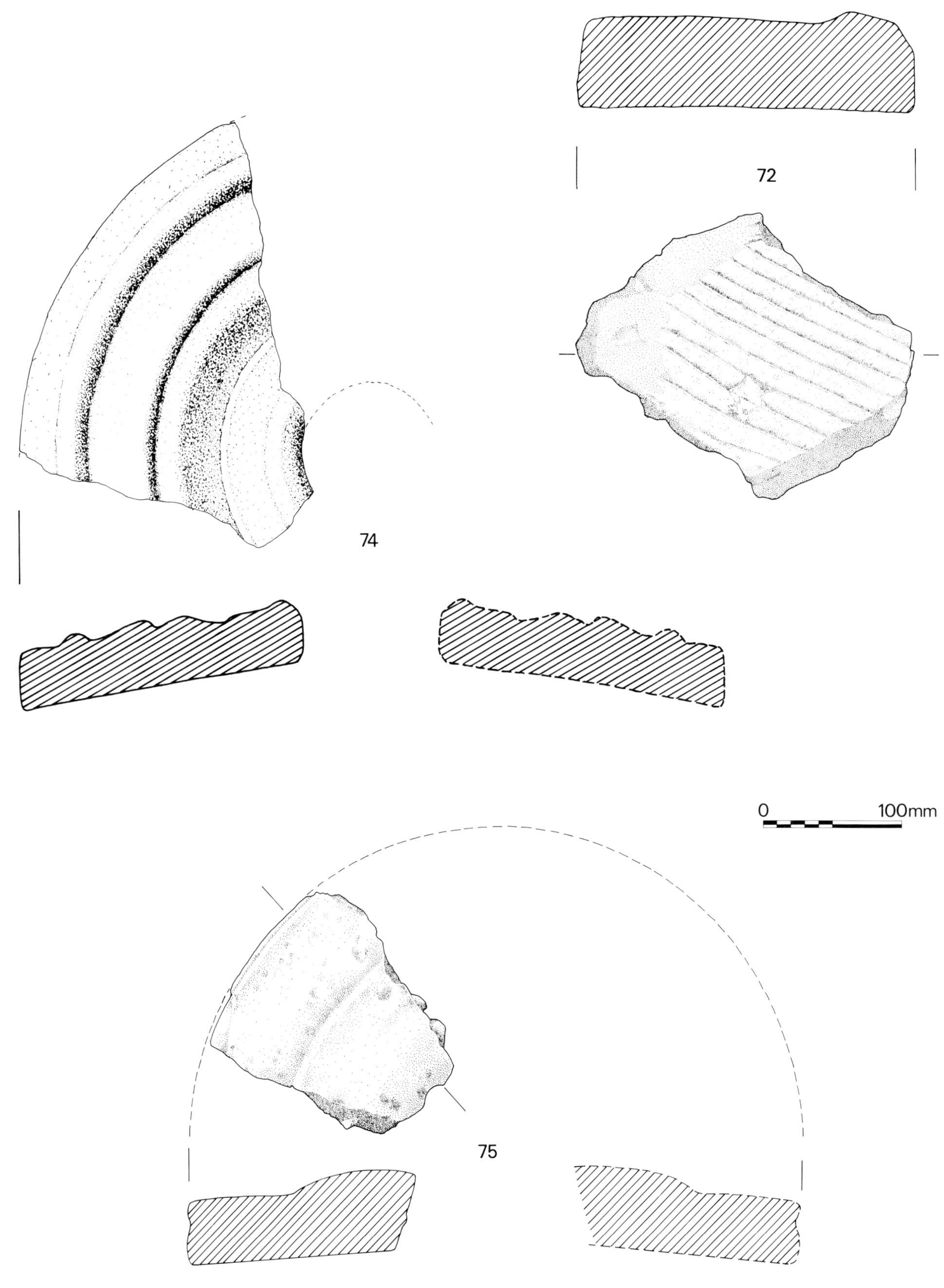

Figure 116 Worked stone, nos 72–5

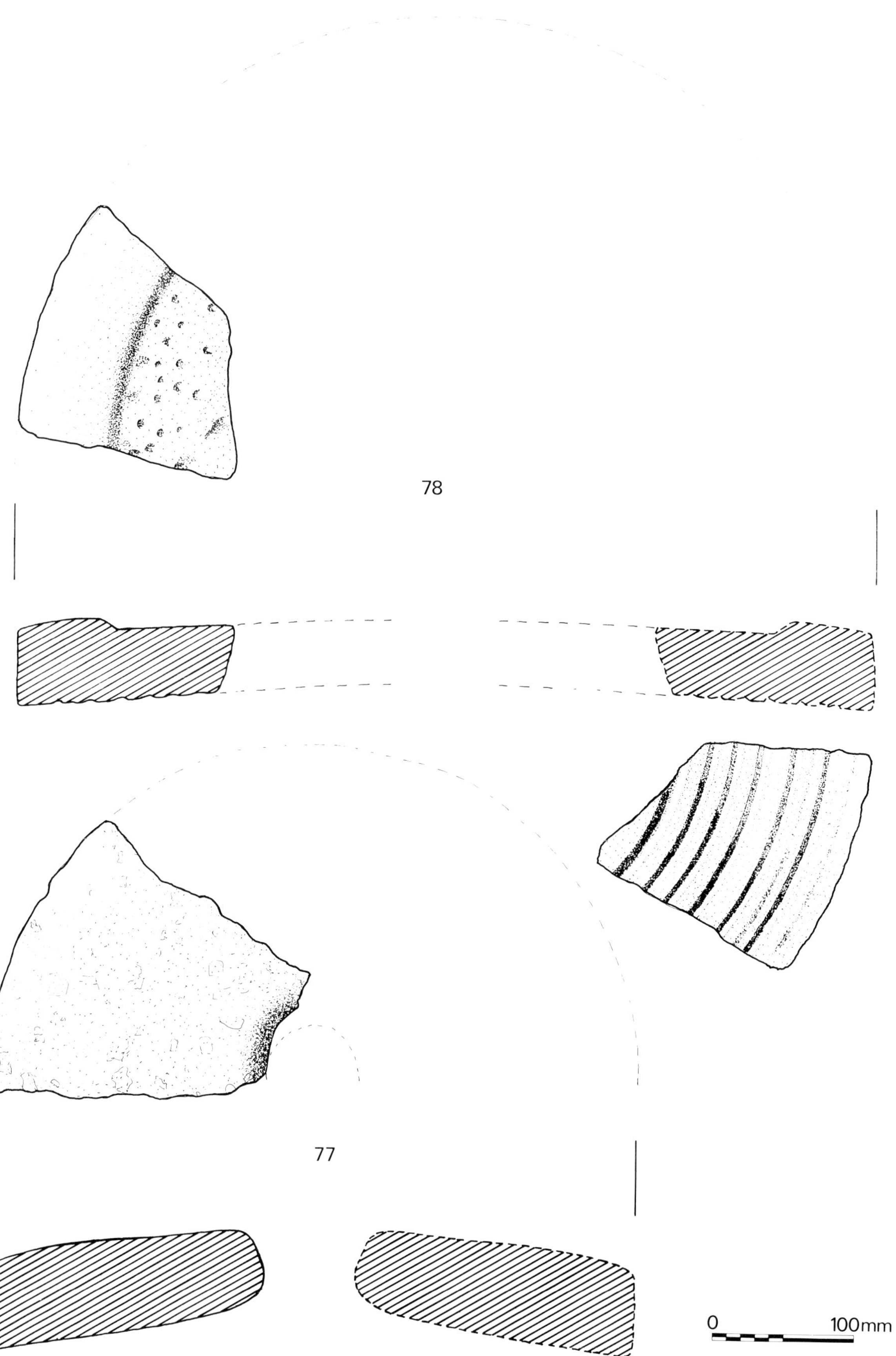

Figure 117 Worked stone, nos 77–8

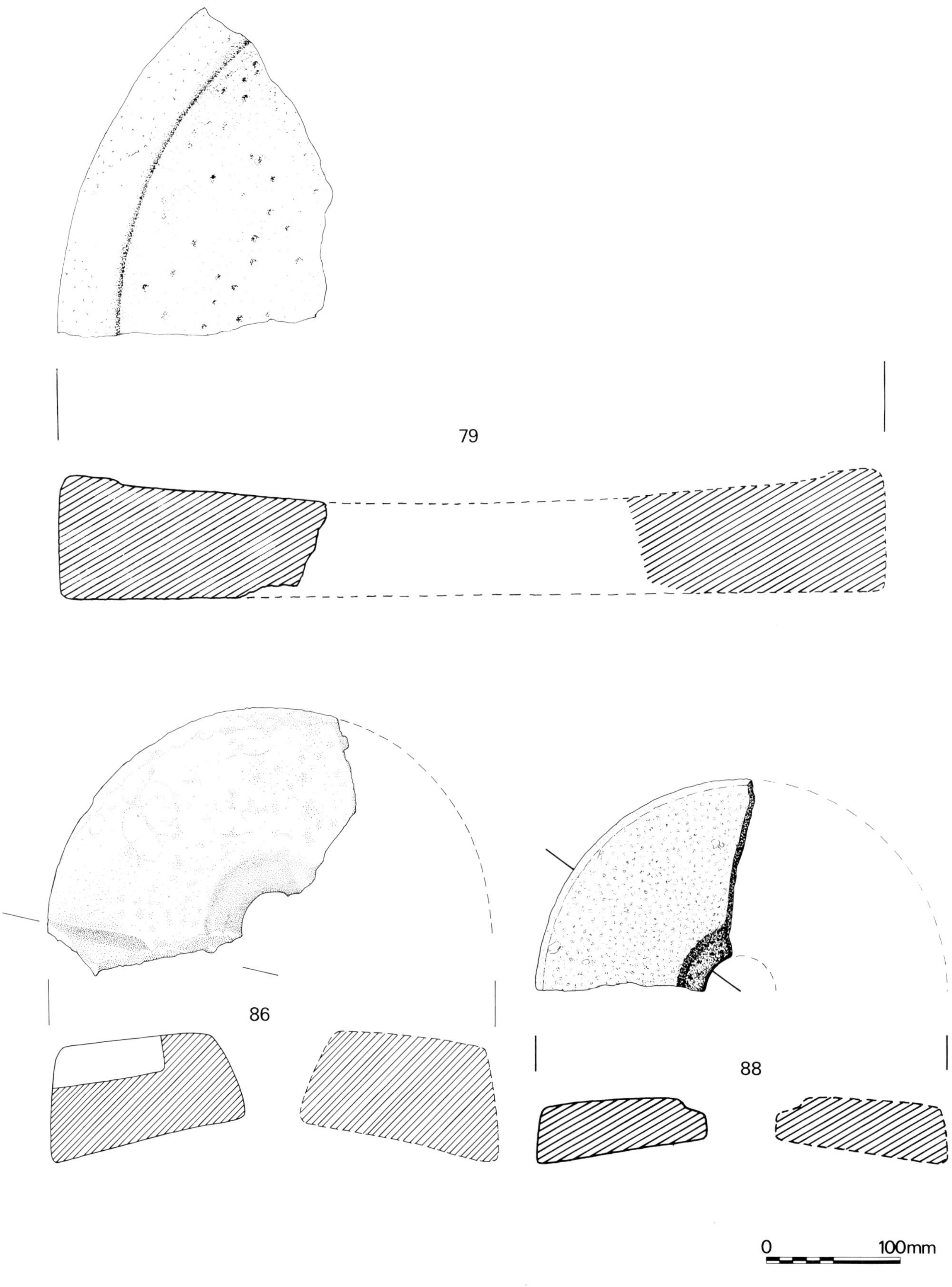

Figure 118 Worked stone, nos 79–88

Discussion

Worked stone

The worked stone includes a rectangular-sectioned milestone of Constantine I (no 1) together with the corner of a moulded inscription (?) panel (no 2), both in oolitic limestone which seems to have been generally used for fine stonework at Alcester. There is another Constantinian milestone in the area from *Tripontium* (Webster 1962).

There are no other architectural fragments from these excavations, reflecting the general lack of stone buildings (although there is a fine oolitic limestone column-base, reused as an altar from Hughes' excavations). The two small altars (nos 3 and 4) may have been ritually disposed of in a well-shaft, but bear no inscription, which suggests either that one had been painted on or, perhaps, that they were unused. The latter possibility is emphasized by the very poor manufacture of no 4, which does not stand vertically. If this is the case, then the unused stones may just have been dumped in the well backfill. A hint to the contrary is given by the crudely cut grooves in the top of no 3, which, if they are secondary, imply the altar was used before disposal. A similar altar, reused amongst paving, was found at Haymes near Cheltenham (Rawes 1986, 89 and fig 15g) also without an inscription, perhaps strengthening the suggestion of a painted one on the Alcester examples.

Two carved stones (nos 5 and 6) suggest an association with metalworking. No 6 has a longitudinally concave rectangular slot cut into it which would appear to be an ingot mould for a non-ferrous metal, presumably a copper alloy. It is from a pit (D I 47) associated with metalworking debris from the smithy (structure DC), suggesting that non-ferrous metal working was also practised there. No 5 is a rather unusual mould of two concentric circles cut into a block of oolitic limestone. If it is a mould, then it can only have been for cold-working sheet bronze or for casting pewter since limestone would not withstand the temperatures of molten copper alloy etc. It cannot be easily interpreted as being used for casting a vessel as such, but it might well be appropriate for casting an elaborate double foot-ring base.

Other stonework includes several limestone roof tiles, all from 4th-century contexts and one in sandstone. There are a few fragments of tufa scattered across the site, suggesting a bath building with a barrel-vaulted roof in the vicinity: perhaps they are from the stone structures excavated by Hughes and Tomlinson.

The hones and whetstones break down into two basic categories, as at Stanwick Villa, Northants (pers examination), of rectangular- or circular-sectioned rods about 100–150mm in length, and a larger and more irregularly shaped collection, hand-sized and fitting comfortably in the hand. Presumably there is a functional differentiation between these two groups, perhaps with the former group being used for sharpening knives and the latter for various other, larger tools.

Other minor stone small finds seem fairly usual, apart from the possible stamp (no 10), if it is Roman.

There are four mortars/grinding stones in the collection. No 50 is a true mortar, whilst the other three are more like stone *mortaria* or large palettes (nos 49, 51, and 52). Stone mortars are not uncommon on military sites in the north and there are several from the Roman fort at Binchester, Co Durham, but the large stonework collection from Stanwick Villa, Northants does not include any to date. The *mortarium*/palette form of nos 49, 51, and 52 would seem to be a regional feature and there is an almost complete (unpublished) example in the Warwickshire Museum from *Tripontium*.

Quernstones

The distribution of the quernstones is shown on fig 119. There are three clear concentrations of material in trenches A XIV, A XVIIB, and G I–IV, and a lesser one in D I. The concentration in trenches G I–IV is in fact illusory, comprising nos 80–5, all fragments of lava quernstone and all probably originating from a single quernstone. (Note: these were originally classified as slag on site, hence the SL numbers.) The concentration in A XVIIB seems to derive from a collection of stone used as bedding for a clay-capped platform (context A XVIIB 10) and the querns are more probably a result of stone collecting for this purpose than *in situ* activity. Similarly, the two stones from trench C IIIA were reused in the walls of the medieval 'corn dryer', and most of the other querns from the site come from posthole packing, well backfills, or rubble layers.

The remarkable concentration from A XIV 29, however, is rather different, in that it represents a dump of quernstones in and sealed by a clay layer, which seals the backfill of 'ditch' A and precedes the first metalled road. The group includes stones representing most of a millstone (no 58) probably from a watermill given its considerable thickness and weight. (Its thickness of 145mm can be compared with a millstone of 900mm in diameter and 60mm in thickness from Stanwick Villa which is almost certainly from an animal-powered mill.) The presence of a watermill would explain the curiously meandering course of 'ditch' A, which is embanked on its downhill side (ie away from the settlement) and can have little defensive purpose and seems rather southerly to mark the extent of the settlement in the 3rd century. Were 'ditch' A interpreted as a mill-race, fed from the Spittle Brook and running into the Alne, then its meandering course nearly along the contour line and its embankment on its downhill side would be explained, whilst the group of piles in trench AA III might represent the foundations of the mill itself. However, it would appear that the course of 'ditch' A does not follow the modern contours very well and it might well not have been capable of serving as a continuous watercourse.

There does not seem to be any inconsistency between the large collection of quernstones from A XIV 29 and their being a dump from a demolished mill. The rotary querns might have been used for

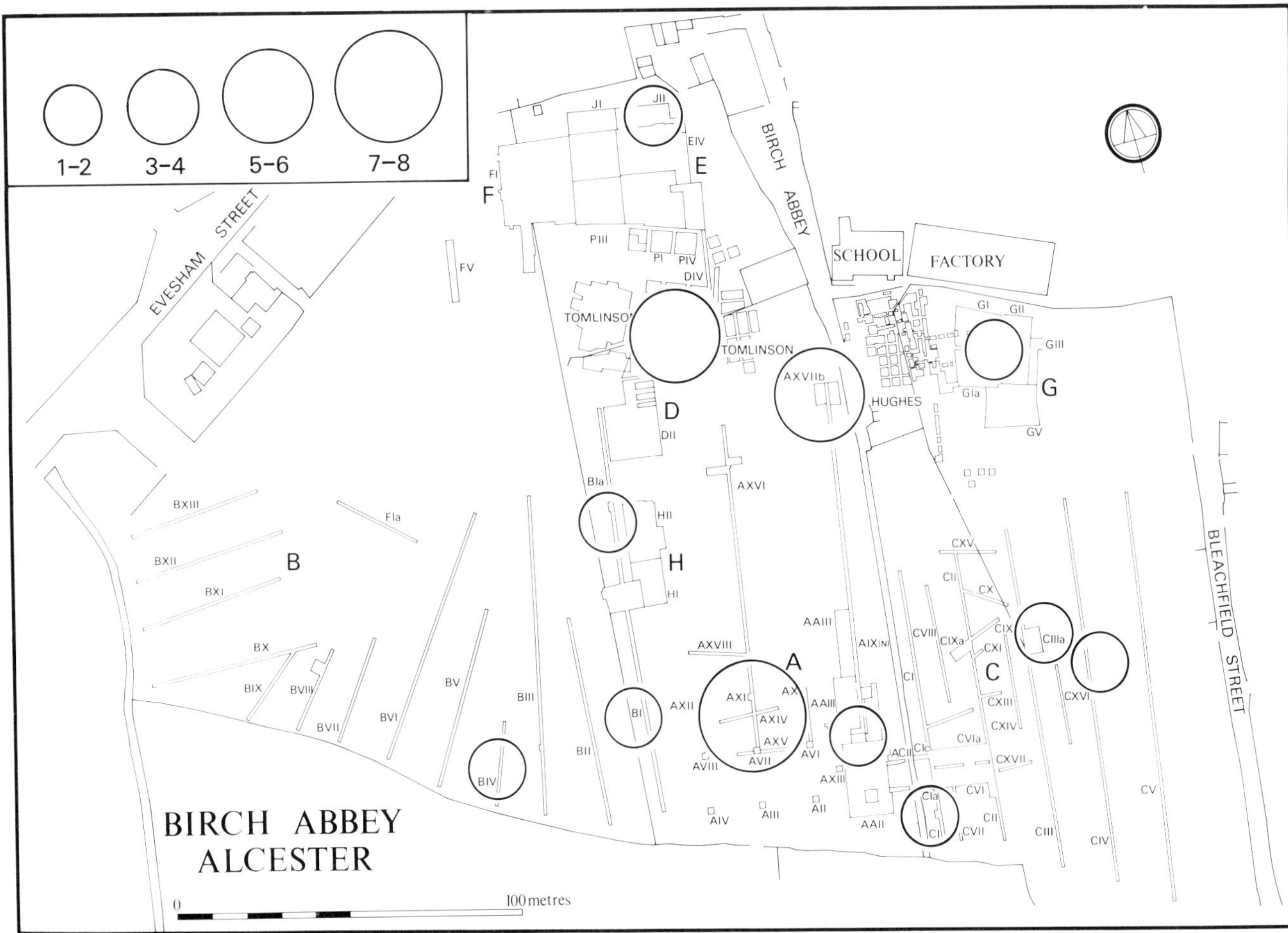

Figure 119 Distribution of quernstones

producing finer meals, or for producing small quantities, or for testing samples of grain prior to milling (Spain 1984). Spain (*ibid*, note 68) cites examples of associated quernstones at the mills at Haltwhistle Burn, Ickham, and the Athenian Agora. The mill, if such it was, represented by the piles (Part 1, fig 16, trenches AA I and AA III) must have been of the usual undershot type, like other Romano-British examples (*ibid*). Wright (pers comm) kindly comments that 'the material from A XIV 29 has only the one millstone, the other stones are mostly of small diameter and apparently early style (non-penetrating spindle-holes in lower stones appear to be an early feature, as do smaller sizes). It is an interesting group and would seem to represent debris from a specialized milling facility of some description.'

There are a number of other possible millstones from the site. No 79 with its large diameter and collar around the circumference might be another water millstone fragment. No 78, of millstone grit, with a concentrically grooved grinding surface, low grinding surface angle and large diameter, is also likely to be a millstone. Nos 72 and 87, probably from the Forest of Dean conglomerate, both have diameters suggestive of millstones given that their grinding surfaces are cut in harps and no 72 has a very flat grinding surface. Nos 66 and 71 clearly started life as millstones given their rectangular rynd bridges cut into the grinding surface for an underdriven mechanism. As Wright (pers comm) kindly points out, the handle slot on the top of no 71 and the uneven wear suggest that this was later reused as an oscillating rotary quern. There seems to be a number of underdriven quernstones in the area with two similar Old Red Sandstone ones from Tiddington (Palmer pers comm). There is also an upper stone from *Tripontium* (unpublished) of this general type with two opposed triangular slots cut into the grinding surface. There is one lower millstone fragment, no 69, in millstone grit with a radially grooved surface. All told there seems to be a considerable concentration of millstones from the site.

Typologically the earliest stone is no 59, which with its fairly flat grinding surface, a relatively small circumference, and a reasonable height appears to be related to the Wessex types (Curwen 1937). The height/diameter ratio of this stone stands out when compared with that of other quernstones in the collection. It is from A XIV 29, a 3rd-century group, associated with other fairly early types. The collection of base stones, some five as opposed to eighteen upper stones, seems to be fairly typical (Wright pers comm), probably because upper stones were more fragile.

The proportion of base stones with spindle-holes which do not penetrate the stone is in contrast to Tiddington (Palmer in prep) where all but one of the stones are penetrated, perhaps suggesting a rather earlier chronological range for the Alcester material.

The highly decorated stones (nos 74 and 75) are a further unusual feature of the quernstone assemblage, and would appear to be another part of the regional tradition since, whilst there are no highly decorated ones from Tiddington, there are two with small cordons and there is also a highly decorated one from Wasperton (Palmer pers comm), and another heavily cordoned fragment from *Tripontium* (unpublished). This type of highly decorated quern is absent from large collections in the north (Wright forthcoming) and from the east Midlands (Stanwick Villa, pers examination; King 1986) although Wright (pers comm) points to a concentration of them in Derbyshire. The elaborate moulded decoration on these stones suggests a high degree of skill amongst their craftsmen and it is tempting to wonder if they were also involved in the production of sculptured stonework.

The vast majority of grinding surfaces (where their method of preparation can be determined) were pecked. Four stones (nos 58, 66, 73, and 78) have concentric grooves (58 is the water(?) millstone, nos 66 and 78 are probably millstones, whilst the fragment 73 is in millstone grit and could be), three have radial grooves around the edge of the stone (nos 54, 65, and lower millstone fragment no 69), and two are cut in harps (nos 72 and 87) both probably millstones.

Rectangular cut handle slots are only found on four stones (nos 56, 59, 71, and 86) cut into the top of the stone. The general lack of handle slots is no doubt in part due to their being attached to the bridge in the top of the feed pipe (cf Curwen 1941, figs 24a–27 and plate III) and at least three feed pipes are clearly non-circular to provide a better attachment for central handles.

Three stones (nos 72, 87, and 88) have slight collars and very shallow hoppers around the feed pipe.

It is notable that not a single definite beehive quern was recovered from the site, whilst no 59 would seem to suggest that at the time of the Roman conquest the local quernstone tradition may have been similar to the Wessex type.

Geology and typology

The sources of the stone used for sculptured stonework at Alcester would seem to have been oolitic limestone from the Inferior Oolite Series, perhaps from nearby to the south-east, and limestone from the Jurassic Oolitic Limestones, perhaps from the Oxfordshire oolite limestone.

Roofing stone would also, generally, seem to have been from local limestone, although tufa, necessary for vaulting hypocausts, seems to have been brought in from further afield as a specialist material.

Both stones associated with metalworking (nos 5 and 6) would seem to be from sources near the town — the Inferior Oolite, and Arden stone from central Warwickshire — and were presumably prepared locally.

Unfortunately little can be said of the origins of the hones and whetstones, although the number of different sources of sandstone represented might well suggest that they travelled some distance, and their low weight would not be a restraint on this as it would be for larger stone objects.

The stone mortars/palettes occur in sandstone and conglomerate (groups S1, S2, and C1) with the true mortar in group S2. The latter group may have a Warwickshire source, whilst C1 is probably from the Forest of Dean and S1 might be related to this source. This suggests that the production of this type of mortar/palette was a fairly widespread feature in the west Midlands.

Turning to the quernstones, the majority, eleven quernstones, fell into the conglomerate group C1. The two in group C2 of conglomerates were respectively probably and possibly from the Forest of Dean. The second largest grouping was of three stones in millstone grit, group M1, and four in group M2, together, perhaps, with one stone in sandstone, group S5, possibly of carboniferous millstone grit. Two northern sources are possible, with the source of M2 probably being Derbyshire. The remaining three stones were in two different sandstones and a breccia (groups S3, S6, and O1).

In contrast to the building stone the sources of the quernstones were clearly more distant and must represent stone types best suited to this function rather than just the nearest available source of stone which could be used, which would be the local sandstones. It is interesting that the prime sources drawn upon are to the north and the Severn Valley with no evidence of material from the east. The use of the Severn Valley area seems to reflect the flow of other materials into the area, especially pottery (Severn Valley wares and Black-Burnished 1).

Briggs (1988), however, offers a cautionary warning against assuming that the millstone grit querns were actually transported from source areas of this stone, rather than the opportunistic use of local millstone grit boulders of glacial origin, which would have been available in both Northamptonshire and Warwickshire (*ibid*, fig 16.1). If his arguments are accepted, then the quernstones would show the major flow of the stone *trade* coming up the Severn from the Forest of Dean.

Some features of typology do seem to be related to the geological source of the quernstones. All the grinding surfaces in the group of three stones in M1 are concentrically grooved with all, perhaps, being millstones. However, only one (no 66) of the four from the second millstone grit group (M2) seems to have been so treated; it is also probably a millstone.

Both of the elaborately decorated stones (nos 74 and 75) are in conglomerate and may be from the Forest of Dean. Underdriven millstones with cut rynd bridges occur in sandstone (no 71, group S5) and in the ?Derbyshire millstone grit (no 66, group M2). It seems quite likely that the source of stones in millstone grit M1 was a single workshop, given the typological similarities of the stones. It is of note that all the millstone grit querns from Tiddington had concentrically grooved surfaces, perhaps suggesting that they also relate to this source (Palmer pers comm). The sources in the Forest of Dean probably represent a number of different workshops given the typological diversity of the products, and would seem to include a workshop producing highly decorated stones.

Comparison with the sources of stone found in the east Midlands (King 1986, fig 8 and map 4) shows that there were major differences in the sources of the Alcester assemblage. There are no puddingstone or Greensand querns, the sources of which are in the east Midlands. Also, there is a very low proportion of lava querns, which probably reflects the high cost of land transport for products imported on the east coast. Millstone grit querns seem to be similarly represented in the east and the west Midlands but the predominant source at Alcester — the Forest of Dean — is only weakly represented in the north of King's study area, no doubt representing high land-transport costs.

Discussion *Stephen Cracknell*

This section centres on the finds and the economic and social aspects of the sites — detailed analysis of the building types and site layout can be found in Part 1 although there are a few further comments here. In common with the rest of the report, it does not include any extensive notes on the excavations directed by Tomlinson and Hughes, which were also in the southern extramural area. The discussion does, however, include site L, which strictly belongs to the northern part of the extramural area, but which is included here for convenience. Further discussion of sites K and M, which investigated the town's defences, has been reserved for the forthcoming volume on the defended area (Cracknell forthcoming).

The Roman town at its maximum extent covered an area of about 30ha (72 acres), with the ?late 2nd-century defences enclosing 8.1ha (later expanded to 9.3ha). It was situated at a crossroads and river crossing; there was no formal street grid. The town was already large before the defensive circuit was built on what appears to have been a largely undeveloped area away from the main focus of the original settlement. The result was that the extensive 'pre-mural' settlement, which included Birch Abbey, was turned into an extensive extramural settlement. The ratio of extramural area to defended area was one of the highest in Britain, perhaps only matched at Water Newton with its extensive industrial suburbs (see Esmonde Cleary 1987) and at Chesterton-on-Fosse (D Adams pers comm, following geophysical survey). Unlike the situation in the larger *civitas* capitals, most of the town was always outside the walls — the extramural settlement was integral to the town as a whole, not an insignificant appendage.

The Birch Abbey sites extended over an area of 5.7ha in the southern part of the extramural area. Of this, the open area excavations covered some 4400sq m and the trial trenches an additional 1600sq m, a sample of just over 10%. (Hughes' and Tomlinson's excavations covered a further 1000sq m.) The site L trenches totalled 130sq m spread over an area of 6800sq m (a 2% sample). However, the rate of archaeological recovery will have been higher than this, with significantly more than 10% of the well-preserved structures being investigated. Indeed, 90% of the area was 10m or less from the nearest archaeological trench.

In the 1st century the Birch Abbey site was on the periphery of the emerging town, with enclosure systems stretching across sites A, B, C, D, and H. To its north there are clear signs of activity from an early date — at No 6 Birch Abbey (Cracknell 1985, 27), at 1–5 Bleachfield Street (Booth forthcoming (d)), and at Baromix (Taylor 1969; 1972). Some of it may have been military but this has not yet been proven.

At Birch Abbey, building activity was initially restricted to the street A frontages which remained the most intensively developed areas, eventually acquiring well-appointed buildings of varied design and function in the late Roman period (including, in particular, Tomlinson's and Hughes' stone buildings). Elsewhere development was slower. By the late 2nd century the central part of the site was being used for quarrying and dumping and a boundary ditch or mill leet was dug to the south. By the end of the 3rd century the ditch had been abandoned and buildings were being constructed beyond its former line.

There is limited evidence that the countryside in the vicinity of site AA at the southern edge of the town was mostly open meadow land (on the basis of the beetles found in pit F). Pollen samples from other sites in the town (eg Gateway Supermarket, Cracknell forthcoming) indicate an open landscape by this time. There would have been meadows on the river margins with cereal crops growing on the higher land beyond.

Artefact deposition and survival

The survival of artefacts and structures will have been affected by ploughing but there was no evidence for significant post-Roman occupation which might have caused more extensive damage. The main Birch Abbey sites lie on a gentle slope, dropping from north to south, with the varying depths of topsoil indicating plough deposition. On site E, at the top of the slope there was somewhat less than 0.3m of overburden; sites D and G were covered by 0.5m; site AA by 0.7m; and the lower parts of site B by up to 1m of deposits. Despite this evidence for considerable plough deposition on the lower parts of the site, the long sequence of mid- to late 4th-century structures on sites E and F suggests that any corresponding plough erosion has not had a significant effect on the preservation of the deposits at the top of the slope. Site L, which was on level ground, was covered by about 0.4m of soil.

As machines were used to strip the sites, few of the artefacts in the upper part of the topsoil — those most likely to have been moved significant distances by the plough — will have been recovered. The finds from the lower topsoil which comprise the majority of the unstratified finds reported here are unlikely to have moved far from their original point of deposition.

The factors affecting deposition are more complex: the details have been discussed in Part 1 but it is worth making some general points here about the extent and nature of the deposits. Table 17 gives the depths of stratigraphy on each site, ignoring the lower parts of any features which were cut into the subsoil. In addition to these stratified deposits significant pit groups were present on sites AA, D, G, and H. Sites C, E, F, J, and P, on the other hand, had relatively few artefact-rich deposits: site C was bisected by street C and had few occupation layers; sites E, F, J, and P were dominated by structural features (eg postholes and beam slots) and again bisected by street C and had few occupation deposits.

Apart from the possibility of levelling before the laying of the gravel surfaces on sites E, F, J, and P, none of the sites showed evidence of truncation during the Roman period. However, it should be noted that most of the finds were 1st or 2nd century in date although most of the structures were later. Much of the 3rd- and particularly 4th-century rubbish must have been deposited off-site.

On the basis of the nature of the deposits, then, more finds would be expected on sites G, D, and AA than on sites C, E, F, J, and P and this is indeed the case.

Wood and leather fragments were recovered from some of the lower-lying pit and ditch fills on sites A, AA, B, and C with significant preserved remains in pit F (AA II 87), which contained leather scraps and insect remains. Several other samples were collected by the excavator and sent for study but these deteriorated and could not be analysed when the time came.

Bones are generally reasonably well preserved in Alcester. The human bones are the subject of a detailed report; a limited sample of animal bones from various features was studied on site and a short summary is printed here.

Table 17 Dimensions of stratified deposits in area excavations

Site	Approx. thickness (m)	Area (sq m)
AA north	0.7	214
AA south	0.7	260
BI	?	81
C	0.4	199
D	0.4	635
E	0.4	925
F	0.4*	700
G	0.5	600
H	?	250
J	0.4*	270
L	0.5	130
P	0.4*	135

* there are no appropriate sections for sites F, J, and P but the depth of stratigraphy was similar to that on site E.

Economic and social activity

On some areas of the Birch Abbey site unusual structures and artefact assemblages point to specialized economic or social activities and much of the discussion below relates to industrial and commercial structures and assemblages. This is not because the Birch Abbey area was an industrial suburb but simply because this is what stands out in the archaeological record. There are many other undifferentiated structures which may have been entirely domestic in character although they are much more likely to have combined the functions of house, shop, workshop, and warehouse. These structures are no less significant — merely less noticeable.

Many could have had agricultural functions but no farms have been certainly identified although there are plenty of examples of large plots and some structures with associated drains which might have been suitable for housing cattle (see eg site G I). The classic farmhouse complex of house, byre, and barn was not present. Only a few specialized agricultural implements have been identified but many more have a wide range of possible functions including agricultural ones. However, it is noticeable that no drying kilns were found. Alcester is on the periphery of the main distribution of drying kilns (Morris 1979, 185–6) so this may not be significant despite their presence at nearby Roman Tiddington (Palmer 1983).

There was limited evidence of religious observances on sites B, D, and F. Burials were more widespread, with examples on all sites except site C although there were no formal cemeteries.

The discussion below is concentrated on the non-ceramic assemblages as the limitations of the coarse pottery data make detailed analysis of them unhelpful.

Sites AA and C (Part 1, pp 25–59, figs 14–41)

Site AA was initially characterized by ditches, part of the enclosure system extending as far as site D, with the earliest activity on the site dated to the late 1st century AD. Ditch A, the 'boundary ditch' or 'mill leet', is dated to the late 2nd century. The first, and indeed only substantial building on the site, structure AA, was a complex structure of probably more than one build, dating to the 3rd century (phase III). Very few non-ceramic finds can be attributed to this phase and if it were not for pit F, the 'Leather Pit,', there would be nothing to suggest what activities had been carried on there. The pit contained waterlogged leather shoe scraps presumably from a nearby workshop, most likely structure AA. It is salutary to note that there was no concentration of leatherworking tools on site AA (though one was found in AA I 17, dating to phase VI) which would have identified a leather workshop in the absence of the waterlogged deposits. The pit also contained a longhorn beetle, a native of the Mediterranean, perhaps imported in a piece of furniture.

Phases V and VI on sites AA and C saw the building of three timber structures CWA, CWB, and CWC. The non-ceramic finds from these phases consisted of one brooch (cat no 12), four bone pins (cat nos 12, 14, and 61), two sawn antlers and one sawn scapula (cat nos 92, 94), leather scraps (cat no 3), three riveted sherds, a pottery counter, and assorted iron and copper alloy objects. The only specialized metal object was the leatherworking awl mentioned above. The sawn bone came from the postholes of structure CWC (phase VI), and as the other bone objects were largely from AA I and AA III, these finds do not necessarily represent intensive specialized activity.

There were few non-ceramic finds from site C east and none which indicate specialized activity.

Site A trial trenches

The trial trenches on site A contained a wide variety of artefact types with particular concentrations in trenches A XI and A XIV in the south, and in A XVII, A XVIIA, and A XVIIB in the north. The northern concentration of artefacts may partly reflect the proximity of the trenches to the street A frontage, where there are likely to have been buildings.

Both of the concentrations are particularly notable for the evidence of milling in the form of quern stones. The querns in A XVII, A XVIIA, and A XVIIB had been reused as a foundation for a platform and thus do not reflect milling *in situ*, but the southern concentration is more significant. It has already been noted (Part 1, p 170) that ditch A may have been a mill leet and the heavy millstone (cat no 58) and other querns from A XIV 29 add weight to this interpretation. It has not proved possible to identify any structures associated with these querns although some timber 'piles' were present. (See also discussion of activities on site D for further evidence of milling.)

Site C trial trenches

The trial trenches on site C produced no significant groupings of finds apart from a concentration in trenches C III and C IIIA where a larger area was opened up in connection with the excavation of a medieval drying kiln. The one noticeable feature was the absence of human burials which were a regular feature of sites A and B to the west and of site G to the north (although there is no suggestion that any of these areas were formal cemeteries).

Site D (Part 1, pp 60–84, figs 42–62)

The earliest features on this site were not urban in character, being part of a series of enclosures stretching across sites A, B, H, and D (Part 1, fig 45). The only structure associated with the enclosures was DA on site D I although others could have lain outside the excavated areas. The enclosures date from the 1st century through to the early Antonine period.

Site D I on the corner of streets A and C had a chequered history. The earliest structure (or structures) identified on the site was building DA, dating to before the middle of the 2nd century (phase I). It is just possible that the pit D II 29A was related although the consideration that the pit was on the opposite side of street C and dated mid-2nd century must count against this.

Building DA may have been the source of the many glass fragments found in the 4th-century phases but the glass could have originated in other structures beyond the edge of D I. Most of the glass was dated to the 2nd century so that it is unlikely that it was in use in the 4th-century structures (unless it can be regarded as heirlooms). Much of it was found on D I in phase V/VI pits which also contained metalworking debris and most of the rest came from phase VIII layers dating to the late 4th century. However, production of glass from raw materials or glass vessels from cullet can be ruled out despite some of the glass being melted. The methods are quite distinct and no glass wasters were found; the introduction of hot slag into the pits may well have melted any glass already deposited in them.

After building DA fell into disuse there was a long break before the site was reoccupied in the late 3rd century (phase IV) by a well-furnished domestic structure, DB, more in keeping with the other houses on this side of street A. The painted plaster found in phase IV–VI contexts presumably derives from this structure rather than from the later smithy.

The smithy itself (structures DC and DCA) was in use in the 4th century, during phases V and VI. The building was simply built, with at least one end open. The burnt daub found in phase VI contexts probably came from the smithy rather than from some conflagration of structure DB. The use of open walls is paralleled in building D at Manchester, one of several structures associated with a smithing and smelting area (Jones 1974, 57–61, 67, 148). Manchester is one of the few places where the presence of smithing is authenticated by metallurgical analysis, with bowl-shaped hearths being the common form.

Iron blooms are likely to have been imported from Worcester where extensive evidence of iron smelting has been identified, presumably using a now worked-out ore source (G McDonnell pers comm). Most of the iron slag from site D I came from pits dating to phase V or VI, particularly from the pit complexes D I 40, D I 87A–D (phase V) directly to the south of structure DC and from another two pits, D I 34 and D I 36 (phase VI) 10m east of the structure. The last two pits lay close to a bowl-shaped hearth, D I 30, and may have contained debris derived from its use. Another pit, D I 47, in the north end of structure DC, contained ashy material. The finds from these features and the (relatively few) finds associated with the hearths themselves are worth describing in detail as the assemblage seems characteristic of what might be expected at a smithy. In all, there are seventeen catalogued iron objects (excluding nails) from site D I, phases V and VI. Considering the clear evidence for iron-working, this is not an excessive total either when compared with the site D I total of

34 objects or when compared with Birch Abbey as a whole. It must be noted, however, that at Manchester there was nothing about the artefacts which would have identified the smithing in the absence of the hearths and slag (Jones 1974).

There were, naturally, finds directly associated with iron-working — an iron fire shovel (cat no 12, (FE 202) from one of the hearths, D I 5, see Part 1, fig 51), an iron rake (cat no 10), a tongs handle (cat no 11), two stone hones (cat nos 40, 41), coal, and slag. The iron objects FE 165 identified in Part 1, fig 51 cannot now be located.

There were also items which might be interpreted as stock-in-trade, other workers' equipment brought in for repair, the traces of ancillary activities, or just general rubbish. Iron items included a pierced shank (cat no 179), strip fragments (cat no 189), a ratchet fragment (cat no 44), hob nails (cat no 74), a cramp (cat no 148), staples (cat no 149), a stud head (cat no 153), a joiner's dog (cat no 142), a candle holder (cat no 118), and a spirally twisted handle (cat no 125). Leatherworking was represented by an iron awl (cat no 26) and a circular punch (cat no 21); there were bone pins (cat no 31) and needles; and items of copper alloy (see below). There were a few fragments of glass. Incidental finds were three coins (a 1st/2nd-century coin (cat no 426) from D I 36, a pit; and two coins (cat nos 107, 125) dating to 268–70 and 270–3 from D I 47, also a pit) and a finger-ring with a cornelian intaglio (cat no 1). These incidental finds are a reminder that, although iron smithing was archaeologically the best-preserved activity, it was not the only activity.

This is further demonstrated by the indications of copper alloy working with some items coming from the pits which contained iron slag, showing that the two metalworking activities were contemporaneous. At the side of one of the hearths was a heavily repaired dish (cat no 120, CA 174, see Part 1, fig 51). There was a possible stone mould (cat no 6) from one of the pits, D I 47. The fragments of copper alloy included a bracelet (cat no 23), sheet metal (cat nos 213–14), wire (cat no 351), and a vessel escutcheon (cat no 124). There was originally a crucible from D I 47 but the whereabouts of this are now unknown. As with the iron objects and iron-working, the number of copper alloy objects and brooches from phases associated with copper alloy working was not disproportionately large: less than one-third of the objects and one-third of the scrap and fragments from site D I were attributed to phases V and VI. (There was also evidence for copper alloy working on site G: see below.)

The variety of activities represented is further emphasized by a concentration of quern stones in the north-west corner of the trench (five found in three contexts: D I 49 (three examples — cat nos 75–7), D I 92 (cat no 78), and D I 101 (cat no 79)) in contexts attributed to phase VI but not strongly associated with the smithy.

Apart from the enclosures, the earliest significant feature on site D II was a roadside pit D II 29/29A (Part 1, fig 58). It contained a finds assemblage which was partly contemporary with the end of the life of structure DA on site D I and partly of a later date.

The lowest layers of the pit were not particularly rich in finds but the earliest secondary fill, D II 29A, contained a remarkable group of 69 mostly complete, unworn samian vessels dating to AD 150–60 and at least six unworn glass vessels including a carinated cup (cat no 11), a conical jug (cat no 9), and a square bottle (cat no 25), again all virtually complete. There are close parallels for the glassware: dated AD 160–70 at Harlow (Price 1987) and AD 155–65 at Towcester (Price 1980). A Dressel 20 *amphora* (with *tituli picti* and graffiti) from the pit was also dated to the mid- to late 2nd century. Much of the coarse pottery was of the same date (see 'Pottery pit groups' microfiche M2:A1) but the layer contained clearly later Black-Burnished 1 dishes (eg fig M8, no 13) as well. Other finds were a bone gaming counter (cat no 85), a pottery cramp made of lead (cat no 5), the skeleton of a dog, oyster shells, and nails.

The main fill of the pit, D II 29, included pottery, a copper alloy bracelet fragment (cat no 24), a copper alloy plaque (cat no 195), and an iron stylus (cat no 79).

The samian, glassware, and *amphora* are clearly a contemporary group. The duplication of unworn samian and glass types suggests a trader's stock (the *amphora* did not appear greatly worn, but it is much more difficult to be definitive about its condition; the condition of the coarse pottery is uncertain). Several pottery shops are known from the Roman world (Rhodes 1989; note that the references to 'Alchester' in this article should read 'Alcester'). In Britain shops often concentrated on samian but frequently sold other items alongside; fine pottery wares and glass were commonplace but provisions such as figs, barley, lentils, and coriander might also be included in the goods on offer (*ibid*, 53–5). It should be noted that some of the vessels at Alcester were incomplete, implying that they, at least, were broken before being thrown into the pit. The presence of other pottery, introduced at a later date, might be explained if the pit had been roofed over in the intervening period. But there is still the problem of the lack of a building in the immediate vicinity. There is nothing resembling a building on site D II at this time (phases I–II); the structures in trench D I were on the other side of the road.

The pit group as a whole bears a superficial resemblance to the Towcester group (Lambrick 1980, 45) but its origins are different. At Towcester, pit F 176 contained seven complete or nearly complete glass vessels, seventeen samian pots, all more-or-less complete, and fragments of other vessels including coarse wares. The samian stamps were from a variety of dates and the glassware seemed to be pairs of vessels leading the excavator to interpret the assemblage as part of a set of 2nd-century table ware.

One other find of note on trench D II was a jar which was inscribed 'Epon[ae]' after firing, and which presumably contained an offering to the goddess (graffiti cat no 37).

Sites E, F, J, and P (Part 1, pp 85–106, figs 63–79)

Sites E, F, J, and P together made up a large area in the angle of streets A and C, with several unusual structures. Of these sites, site J was too small and too peripheral to contribute much to the study of the economy and the whereabouts of the site P finds, from Ullin Place's excavations, is not known so that most of the discussion here relates to sites E and F.

In the mid-1st century, phases I and II, the area was occupied by a trackway, slots, and postholes. There was one outstanding find, a nicolo intaglio (site F, cat no 3). (A second intaglio also from site F was unstratified.)

Phases III and IV were marked by the digging of a quadrilateral enclosure on the west side of street C and the construction of two successive round houses on the other side. The only category of finds with significant representation at this time is brooches, with five of the 24 examples from sites E and F assigned to these phases. Three of these were trumpet brooches with an overall *floruit* of AD 75–150/75, providing much of the dating evidence. Although a second quadrilateral structure was built on site F in phase XI in the last half of the 4th century, both the difference in date and the lack of any structural continuity suggest that it was simply the restrictions of site layout — bounded on two sides by roads — which occasioned the similarity of the structures. However, the possibility of a link is discussed further below.

Phases V–VIII, dating to the late 2nd and through the 3rd century, were dominated by a series of rectilinear buildings and smaller 'booths', mostly aligned parallel to, or at right-angles to, street C. Building EC, dating to phase V (late 2nd century) is the only structure on the Birch Abbey site which conforms to the classic 'strip' plan. Even so, its narrow façade was to the north, not onto any known street.

Although it can be argued that structure EC and the booths ED–EJ might have been connected with the postulated market area to the north of the Birch Abbey sites, there is nothing in the non-ceramic finds to confirm (or refute) this. If an increased coin loss in the area of a market might be expected in the increasingly monetarized economy, there is no evidence of this, with most of the coins from the site dating to phase XIII (see below). However, this is not a strong argument and there are only moderate numbers of coins from the 'market areas' to the north — eight from No 6 Birch Abbey (Cracknell 1985, M2:A11); nineteen from No 34 Evesham Street (Cracknell 1985, M2:D8); and only a few from Baromix 1972 (J Evans pers comm).

There is no evidence for the function of the post-built phase VII–VIII structures EK–EM.

The complexity and variety of interpretations which are possible for the phase IX–XII structures combined with the rarity of finds makes it impossible to assign roles to them with any certainty. The provision of stone for the walls — a relatively uncommon feature at Alcester — seems to rule out use as a farmyard.

In one interpretation of the phase XI structure there are ranges of buildings 5m wide, partly supported on the stone enclosure wall, on three sides of the courtyard. This has a passing resemblance to the 1st-century Romano-Celtic *temenos* at Hayling Island (Downey *et al* 1980) although it is rather smaller. However, at Alcester there was no central shrine and, importantly, no huge collection of ritual objects like that at Hayling. (Only one object from site F has apparent religious implications — the unstratified intaglio depicting Mercury.) Taking everything into account the case for religious usage is rather weak.

Nevertheless, the overall paucity of pits and pottery from site F suggests that, looking at the Roman period as a whole — a rather dangerous occupation — non-domestic use dominated the site.

Similar arguments could be applied to the quadrilateral enclosure of phase III, although in this case there is no reason to consider the double palisade as a covered lean-to structure.

In contrast to the situation in phases IX–XII, in phase XIII there were considerably more finds. This is despite the fact that the only features of the site were the post alignments or insubstantial roadside 'shops' FG and PA at the side of street A and the patchy cobble surfaces which were spread over much of the area. Most of the finds were not specific to any particular activity. The copper alloy included, for example, a ring (cat no 14), two pins (cat nos 43, 53), a spatula (cat no 108), a nail (cat no 165), and a fitting (cat no 224). Three pieces of hypocaust tile were found on site F in phase XIII contexts (F I 5, F IV 14) but there is no evidence to suggest that any of the buildings in the vicinity were heated in this way.

A single context, a ditch, F I 5, was responsible for many of the finds. This ditch, stratigraphically just under the topsoil, was aligned north-east to south-west (Part 1, fig 63), conspicuously at variance to the other alignments on the site and suggesting the possibility of a late replanning of the site layout. The two coins from it have a *terminus post quem* of AD 353. In fact, most of the coins from sites E, F, J, and P were mid-4th century in date. Nineteen of the 29 coins ascribed to particular phases came from phase XIII contexts. The coins were randomly distributed about sites E and F and do not seem to represent a dispersed hoard; nor were they connected to the 'shops'.

Site H and the adjacent trenches B I and B IA (Part 1, pp 107–14, figs 80–4)

Phase I on sites H, B I, and B IA was represented by enclosure gullies, part of the much larger system of conjoined enclosures already mentioned. In phase II, dating to the Antonine period through to the early 3rd century, several pits were dug. These were probably originally quarry pits for sand and gravel, later being backfilled with earth and rubbish. Most contained moderate quantities of finds but apart from pit B I 10, particularly one of its fills B I 3, none were exceptional. Fill B I 3 was mainly notable for the quantity of coarse pottery, with over 105 vessels represented (see 'Pottery pit groups' in microfiche M2:A1). Although there were samian vessels and glass fragments, there was nothing comparable to the quality and quantity of vessels in the near-contemporary D II 29A, which lay further to the north on the same side of the trackway.

The first building on the site, HA, was assigned to phase III. There were no finds to indicate a special purpose for this building. Outside it was a well, B IA 3, which continued in use for some time. It was periodically cleaned out and fell into disrepair in the 4th century. The lowest fills of the well, B IA 15, included 4th-century coarse pottery, a coin of Valentinian (cat no 397), a possible stone weight (cat no 13), a quern (cat no 69), animal bones, tiles, and two uninscribed stone altars (cat nos 3, 4) — one of the few indications of religious activity at Birch Abbey. Although this deposit could be regarded as a religious dedication or alternatively an example of iconoclasm, most of the assemblage is unexceptional and it may be that it merely represents rubbish disposal.

Site B trial trenches (Part 1, fig 85)

The trial trenches (excluding B I and B IA) on site B were twice as extensive as those on site A, yet far fewer artefacts were recovered, despite the presence of ditch A which would have been a suitable repository for rubbish after it went out of use. This is partly because they were machine trenches, quickly cleaned up and not excavated by hand below this level, as some of the site A ones were. The main feature of site B was the human burials. At Birch Abbey as a whole there were 56 burials scattered over all the sites with the exception of site C. All except one were inhumations indicating that they are likely to belong to the second half of the Roman period and are contemporary with the main building phases.

Apart from the 1964–6 excavations there have been several other excavations in the south-west corner of the Roman town but none very large. Watching briefs at 2 Newport Drive (Part 1, fig 3, no 75), 22 Hadrian's Walk (no 62), and 28 Hadrian's Walk (no 72) were all negative. However, a cemetery is known from the area to the west and north (no 7) and it is likely that there was some ribbon development along Ryknild Street. There were stone structures at Acorn House, Evesham Street (no 56; Cracknell 1985, 53–7). The presence of the burials and the low density of occupation shows that site B was peripheral to the town.

Site G (Part 1, pp 115–35, figs 86–100)

Site G contained not only unparalleled structures in the form of the timber-and-stone buildings GC (phase IV) and GE (phases VI–IX), but also a unique artefact assemblage.

A total of 27 examples of graffiti were found on storage jars deposited on site G. Altogether the Birch Abbey sites only produced 45 vessels with graffiti so that this figure from one site must indicate that it was the focus of a particular activity, with the graffiti being inscribed there. The presence of 'personal' graffiti as well as tally marks suggests the need to differentiate either the ownership or the contents of the jars.

The earliest examples of graffiti were on six sherds dating to phase IV, of which five came from demolition deposits assigned to the start of the phase, before building GC was constructed. These could be associated with the 2nd/3rd-century buildings GA and GB; and it should be noted that most of the sherds are of 1st- or 2nd-century date. A larger group, however, was found in the burnt phase V deposits deriving from the demolition of structure GC in the late 4th century — including nine sherds which were recovered from a single context (G IA 63).

The graffiti were on storage jars. Indeed, site G contained a very high proportion of storage jars compared with the other Birch Abbey sites, indicating a storage function at some stage in the life of the site. It is notable that about ten *amphorae* were recovered, mostly from site G I, and mostly dating to phase IV or later.

However, there is a chronological problem. The storage jars were mostly of 1st- or 2nd-century date and the three *amphorae* which were available for study by Williams were all early Roman types. Yet most of the sherds were found in 4th-century contexts. Unless they had an extraordinary life span, they should be residual and not associated with building GC. It is possible that the *amphorae* and storage jars relate to an earlier store or that this was a long-term function of the site.

Although this function may partly account for the high incidence of *non-personal* graffiti there, storage jars are not normally disproportionately given graffiti (see 'Graffiti', p 124). Effectively, there are two independent traits, both of which mark out the site as unusual: the presence of storage vessels and the presence of graffiti.

As well as the semi-literate graffiti, there were two other groups of artefacts indicating that site G was a particular 'focus' for literacy. Six of the sixteen iron styli and one of the two seal boxes were found on the site. The styli belonged to phase IV onwards and their use could have been associated with structures GC and GE. The seal box came from the lower topsoil.

Although the graffiti *could* have been made with the styli, they could equally have been made with any sharp tool and there is no reason to suppose that such carefully made implements would have been used for this purpose. It is noticeable, though unsurprising, that most of these discarded 'artefacts' — graffiti, styli, and seal boxes — came from outside the main buildings on the site. The contrast between the location of the storage jars with graffiti — largely found in demolition deposits — and the location of the styli — found in a variety of contexts — suggests different deposition processes were at work confirming that the styli were not directly associated with the storage jars. The presence of burnt soils and clays in the phase V demolition deposits could indicate that building GC burnt down; if the chronological problems could be surmounted, it could be argued that the storage jars may have been caught up in the conflagration although they do not show signs of burning. The styli, on the other hand, seem to have been lost on a casual basis.

Coins are well represented on site G — showing trade of the stored goods perhaps, although this kind of argument does not seem to hold elsewhere on Birch Abbey. There are also bone pins and needles with over one-quarter of the Birch Abbey total of 74 examples spread fairly evenly from phase IV to IX. Whilst this may represent some specialist activity, it could merely reflect the chance survival of domestic artefacts.

Small-scale copper alloy working seems to have occurred at two distinct times on site G — just as it occurred sporadically elsewhere on the Birch Abbey sites. A crucible and a waste lump were found in a phase IX pit (G I 24, 24A), and there were eleven pieces of casting waste from phase V (cat no 355), with a small amount elsewhere.

Stone artefacts were also well represented on site G with nine items plus six fragments of a quern.

First-century coins and brooches (see 'Chronology', below) indicate an early focus of activity on site G or more probably to its north (not to the south as the trenches there failed to reveal early activity). Unfortunately no corresponding structures were identified. Despite this and the residuality apparent in the pottery assemblage there is no doubt that the main activity on the site dates to the end rather than to the beginning of the Roman period. The structural continuity between GC and GE shows that they cannot have been separated by many years, and the presence of a Constantinian milestone in the foundations of GE shows that it was built no earlier than AD 337, the end of Constantine's reign.

Structures GC and GE themselves were made of stone and timber, including multiple timbers in some of the postholes (Part 1, p 116). The walls were plastered and painted. The multiple timber posts appear to be contemporary, presumably substituting for unavailable larger-diameter posts although there was no general scarcity of good-sized building wood locally: it was only a few years later that Alcester's town wall was heavily underpinned by large, freshly cut timbers.

In summary, the site had a specialized storage function, may have been involved in trade, and was a 'focus' of literacy although it is uncertain which buildings were associated with which activities. Buildings GC and GE were well-appointed, mid- to late-4th-century structures.

Site L (Part 1, pp 136–40, figs 102–4)

No large areas were opened up on site L and in that respect the paucity of finds is to be expected. The only notable artefacts were two styli (cat no 88 in L III, cat no 90 in L I). The most significant structure on this site was a building with a hypocaust in L VIII. *Tesserae* and *opus signinum* indicate a substantial structure, perhaps similar in status to those excavated by Tomlinson and Hughes on the south side of street A.

Chronology

The dating evidence for the Birch Abbey sites is given in tables M1 and M8. Table M8 lists the datable finds which were recovered from 'phased' contexts. (About 2,600 of the 4,400 contexts were assigned to a particular phase.) This table excludes Roman coarse pottery (for which see table M1) but includes samian, *mortaria*, and *amphorae*. Using the table, full details of the individual objects can be discovered in the finds catalogues under the relevant catalogue number. There are three exceptions to this: glass fragments, 'other' samian, and unillustrated *mortaria*. Many of the glass fragments are not individually numbered in the catalogue but can be found by referring to their small finds number (GL . . .). The 'other' samian was not examined in detail by Brian Hartley *et al* when they looked at the 'latest vessels in the contexts concerned and/or any pieces of intrinsic interest'. However, this 'other' samian was scanned and dated and this information is included in the table; the information about this part of the samian assemblage is not amplified elsewhere. Again, where unillustrated *mortaria* might provide dates for a particular phase, this information was included in the table.

Table M1, covering Roman coarse pottery, has a wider remit and was compiled in a different way. It is essentially a list of which pottery types were found in which context but it also includes the relevant illustration numbers (figs 1–43), the date of the illustrated examples drawn from parallels elsewhere, and the phase (if any) to which the context has been assigned. Most of this table was compiled by Lee and Lindquist in the early 1980s and it was originally used as a tool for dating the structural phases of the sites. However, the dates of the illustrated vessels were revised by Evans in 1991. No attempt has been made to undertake a more comprehensive revision of the pottery dates.

The dating evidence will be discussed below, looking at each type of material in turn, but some general points must be made here. First, the stratigraphic integrity of some of the coins is in doubt. It appears that the prisoners from Winson Green prison who worked on the site did not report all coin finds immediately and may have subsequently replaced some coins in different contexts (*see* 'Coins', pp 157–61). However, the assemblage as a whole is clearly not biased as it is similar to the assemblages from other Alcester sites (compare figs 72–4).

A second factor affecting most sites is the high degree of residuality, with many 1st- and 2nd-century finds on sites which are dominated by 3rd- and 4th-century structures. On sites with significant residuality and relatively small quantities of finds which are likely to be contemporary with any particular phase, it is necessarily a matter of judgement where to draw the line between residuality and intrusion. If a few more finds were designated intrusive the date of the phase would become significantly earlier; if a few more were residual the phase would become later. Some of the Birch Abbey structures are well dated — for example phase XIII on sites E and F produced fourteen coins dating to the middle of the 4th century — but elsewhere, particularly on site AA, the dating evidence is much weaker. By and large the balance between intrusion and residuality has been weighted to minimize the amount of intrusive material so that the phase dates, whilst being the most plausible date, lie towards the end of the possible range.

Coarse pottery

The use of pottery for dating has been discussed in some detail on a site by site basis in Part 1 and also by Evans above. In terms of overall dates, much of the illustrated Black-Burnished 1 is Hadrianic or Antonine and most of the reduced wares, which form a substantial proportion of the corpus, should date to before AD 200. In fact, the evidence of Gas House Lane, Alcester suggests that reduced wares virtually ceased to be used after the end of the 2nd century (excepting shell-tempered wares) (Evans in Cracknell forthcoming). The majority of the oxidized wares are Severn Valley products which are generally commoner in Alcester in the 3rd and 4th centuries than earlier, though at Birch Abbey, once again, the 1st- and 2nd-century types are over-represented. Samian declined on the Birch Abbey site after *c* AD 170. Nene Valley products were poorly represented, even before AD 240 when Oxfordshire potters began to sell fine wares to the town. After this date the Oxfordshire potters became the predominant suppliers of colour-coated wares. Shell-tempered ware occurs in Alcester in the 3rd century, with wheel-made products appearing after the mid-4th century.

The wheel-made shell-tempered wares are concentrated on sites F and G; late Oxfordshire types (AD 270 on) are concentrated on sites AA and G; Black-Burnished 1 flanged bowls are concentrated on sites G, A, and AA; and the only sites with more than a single late Nene Valley type are AA, F, and G. This pattern agrees reasonably well with the structural evidence. There are several late structures on both sites F and G, none on B, E, H, and J, and only small or uncertain structures on C and D (although more late pottery might have been expected in the late pits on D II). Structure AA on site AA should have fallen out of use by the 4th century but there are several later phases of pits and ditches to account for the late pottery there.

Other finds

On the Birch Abbey sites *fibulae*, coins, samian, and *mortaria* are particularly important for dating. In addition, some of the copper alloy and glass objects are also well dated.

The *fibulae* almost all date to the first two centuries AD; few are dated as 3rd century and none 4th century, a reflection of the general decline in their use throughout the country (there are, for example, relatively few brooches at the later Roman Lankhills cemetery at Winchester (Clarke 1979)). There were no crossbow-type *fibulae* at Birch Abbey, although this is unsurprising; indeed, as far as I am aware, only one crossbow brooch has been found in Alcester (at 1–5 Bleachfield Street, Booth forthcoming (d))

The vast majority of the 38 datable brooches found in contexts which have been ascribed to a phase were 'residual'. Perhaps it would be more appropriate to regard at least some of these as heirlooms. Amongst the few which were found in contemporary situations, five were from site D. There is no apparent reason for this concentration on site D — they all predate the 4th-century metalworking phases on that site.

At the other end of the Roman time scale is a group of iron brooches, leading Mackreth to conclude that there was a pre-Roman site in the very near neighbourhood of the excavations. It has to be said that there is no other evidence for this at present. However, four of the nine iron brooches were found on site G and, coupled with the presence of other early brooches on this site, this tends to confirm the suggestion (Part 1, p 165) that the early focus of the town was nearby.

The 415 identified Roman coins from the excavations represent about one-quarter of the total found in the town. As with the brooches, the coin loss pattern with its relatively strong early peak (compare figs 72 and 74) suggests an early inception to the site which is not reflected in the structural evidence. The coins taken on their own might indicate a mid-Neronian start to the site. The presence of the five Dobunnic coins is not taken by Casey and Brickstock to represent a pre-Roman settlement. Nevertheless, the coins do place Alcester securely in the *civitas* of the Dobunni. A further three Dobunnic coins are known at present from the town and only one non-Dobunnic 'Iron Age' coin — a possible Corieltauvian example with an uncertain findspot. Unfortunately the present location of the coin itself is unknown.

Three of the five Dobunnic coins were found on site G (which can be compared with four out of nine early iron brooches found there). Even though these figures need to be set against a background of a high level of finds recovery from all phases of site G, they are still exceptional. Nevertheless, when the comparison is broadened to include all Flavian and pre-Flavian coins (cat nos 1–36), the dominance of site G decreases.

The samian pottery suggests occupation of the town in the early 60s. The samian list has a much stronger Central Gaulish than Southern Gaulish peak which shows that deposition was taking place in the 2nd century much more than in the 1st century. This pattern is borne out by the structures, with many more datable to the 2nd century than earlier although there was still little building compared with in subsequent centuries.

The decline of the samian supply is something of a problem. The decline dates from about AD 170, well before the supply of samian to Alcester ceased. (There are, for example, sizeable later groups at Gas House Lane (Cracknell forthcoming).) There were also plenty of structures on the sites with DA, EB, EC, HA, and GA possibly dating to the late 2nd century. So samian should have been in use at Birch Abbey. As there is no reason to believe that the survival of late 2nd-century deposits was any poorer than the survival of earlier deposits, the samian must have been deposited elsewhere.

Any depositional factors which might affect the samian should also affect the coin lists, pottery, and other finds. In so far as it goes, the coin list shows the normal late 2nd-century pattern for sites with continuous occupation (ie a late 2nd-century decline in coin numbers) but this is hardly conclusive evidence. The other groups of finds are not very useful as depositional indicators, so the reason for the premature decline in samian remains unknown.

Some types of glass are reasonably easy to date. Of the 42 or more vessels identified, seven can be dated to the 1st century whilst virtually all of the rest are described as late 1st to late 2nd century. As this coincides with the peak of samian usage it is clearly not the case that glassware was substituted for samian when supplies of the latter dried up. Once again a large proportion of the assemblage must be regarded as residual. The dating of the 1st-century glass is not sufficiently precise to throw light on the date of the origins of the site.

Of the 50 copper alloy objects with dated parallels, 17 can be compared with 1st-century objects, 17 with 2nd-century, 27 with 3rd-century, and 21 with 4th-century objects (some have parallels stretching over more than one century). This is a remarkably even spread through the Roman era when compared with some of the other artefact types although some of this may be due to the wide date bands. Nevertheless the dates do, for once, reflect the use of the site throughout the Roman period. There is no significant concentration of objects on any particular site although it is worth noting that four of the five mirrors — all 1st century — were found on sites AA and C.

Site development and structure

The initial Roman presence at Alcester was in a fort on the ridge well to the south of the town and the origins of the town proper may well lie in a second fort just to the north of Birch Abbey. However, only nine copper alloy objects and three iron objects from Birch Abbey have or may have military links. They were distributed over the whole area with no particular concentrations and were not necessarily early in date.

The supposed presence of the fort would not guarantee the development of a town — just as the presence of garrisons on Hadrian's Wall and in Wales did not always result in urbanization — and economic factors were also important. Alcester's apparent economic assets were the good-quality farming land in the district and its location at a crossroads and river crossing. On the other hand, its situation on the periphery of the Romanized 'lowland' zone may have acted as a brake on development.

There is no evidence for late Iron Age occupation in the immediate area, although agricultural use of the land is likely. Burnham (1986) makes a useful distinction between the origins of small towns in north-west Britain (for present purposes north and west of the Fosse Way) — where, on his figures, military origins seem to predominate — and those to the south-east where the existence of Iron Age settlement was more significant. In either case, the location of the site in relation to the road network was important for the subsequent development of the town. Whilst applying such generalizations to individual sites is not always appropriate, Alcester's origins group it with those towns to the north and west, again emphasizing that the town lay on the margins of 'truly' Romanized Britain.

At first sight the structure of Roman Alcester seems peculiar, being centred not at the crossroads but to one side of it but, although the road network was of obvious importance in the Romano-British infrastructure, towns were not necessarily located exactly at the nodal points. Several towns lie off the main road network — for example Alchester and Godmanchester — and had only minor suburban settlement on the roads (see Esmonde Cleary 1987, 173–4 for a discussion). So the sites which would be regarded as prime sites for development now — because of their position at crossroads or on a main street — do not seem to have been necessarily so important in the Roman world. The early growth presumably originated around the second fort and this partly accounts for the morphology of Roman Alcester and the ability of street A, the main Droitwich- Stratford through route, to attract the most prestigious buildings in the extramural area. It may be that development was most intensive here simply because it started earlier.

Occupation at Birch Abbey continued until at least the end of the 4th century. On site F there are three phases of building which belong to after AD 353 and on site G phases VI to X date to after AD 337; there are also several 4th-century phases on site D. It is probable that some of these phases stretched into the 5th century and the sub-Roman period although there are no diagnostic artefacts or structures.

The intensity of occupation varied over the centuries. The majority of finds from the Birch Abbey sites date to before AD 200, although most of the excavated structures were later in date. This must be largely a reflection of changing patterns of rubbish disposal. None the less, it is possible that the Birch Abbey area was more intensively occupied in the 1st and 2nd centuries than is apparent from the list of dated structures. Cill beams may not have left any archaeological traces under the palimpsest of later occupation and there may have been ephemeral structures in the areas which could only be trenched.

Initially the focus of occupation would have been partly to the north of the main Birch Abbey sites, for

Table 18 Phase starts by date

Date	Site A/C	B/H	D	E,F,J,P	G	Total
50–99	1	1	1	3		6
100–49		2		1		3
150–99	1		2	1	1	5
200–49				2	1	3
250–99	5	1	1	3	1	11
300–49	2		1		1	4
350–			4	3	6	13

example at Baromix, which might include the site of the fort (Taylor 1969; 1972), and at 64 Bleachfield St (Cracknell & Ferguson 1985)) with Birch Abbey used for dumping, but later it moved south.

There may have been a diminution in the intensity of occupation early in the 3rd century — exemplified by the relatively low count of Black-Burnished 1 and the lack of East Gaulish samian — and such a temporary decline would be in keeping with what was probably the rapid development of the newly defended area in the bend of the river to the north. However, other indicators such as the coin list do not confirm this and there seems to be no real longer-term slackening of the pace of building development. Tables 18 and 19, looking at the number of phases of activity and the number of buildings erected in 50-year periods, do not mark out the 3rd century as a period of significant decline.

As Burnham points out (1987, 184–5), the imposition of a defensive circuit on a small town does not normally seem to have resulted in a significant contraction of the extramural area before the 4th century, and this seems to have been the case at Alcester. The continued development of the Birch Abbey area demonstrates that after the initial danger passed away security was not a great consideration. (The defences had clearly been built with security in mind as they surrounded an easily defensible, but largely undeveloped area.) The strength of urban life in Alcester in the 4th century contrasts with nearby Tiddington where occupation ceased in at least one part of the central area in the 3rd century (Palmer 1983).

The variety of building forms at Birch Abbey reflects that of Roman small towns in general (Burnham & Wacher 1990, *passim*). In contrast to many small towns, however, Birch Abbey does not seem to have been dominated by one type: the strip building set end-on to the street frontage. It is sometimes argued that the presence of strip buildings reflects pressure on space and the consequent cost of properties on the frontages but Roman small towns often have underdeveloped frontages and this argument is not convincing. It may be that strip buildings are a cultural phenomenon rather than an economic one and that the lack of them in Alcester is a local cultural trait. It is possible, nevertheless, that the most intensive urban development occurred in the largely unexplored defended area and that it is there that the strip buildings will be found.

Economic and cultural connections

Roman Alcester was roughly equidistant from the three *civitas* capitals of Leicester, Cirencester, and Wroxeter but economically it was more strongly connected to Cirencester than to the two other towns.

Most of the copper alloy objects have widely dispersed parallels both in Britain and abroad but amongst the pins, nail cleaners, and tweezers there appears to be an emerging group of items with Warwickshire/Gloucestershire and to a lesser extent Oxfordshire/Wiltshire/Northamptonshire associations. The pins (cat nos 46–9) and nail cleaners (cat nos 86–9, 94) are characterized by cross-hatched decoration. In addition, a set of tweezers with a nail cleaner attached (cat no 85) may be related to this group. Many of the brooches find parallels in the Severn Valley and its eastern catchment area. The worked stone originated from several sources but stone mortars, palettes, and querns show connections with the Forest of Dean and probably Derbyshire. There is no evidence of material from the east although the relative paucity of useful stone deposits may have had some effect on this. The coal on the site probably originated in the north Warwickshire coalfield despite the availability of Forest of Dean deposits.

As Evans shows in his discussion of the coarse pottery, Alcester lies within the Severn Valley pottery distribution area, in contrast to Tiddington, some 12km to the east where Severn Valley ware accounts for less than 7% of the coarse wares. The presence of Malvernian ware also demonstrates a connection with the west but this pottery was never economically important. It is also significant that the site was receiving little pottery from the Nene Valley further to the east in contrast to the amount coming in from the Oxfordshire kilns.

At first sight the connection of the brooches, some copper alloy, the Severn Valley ware, and some stone with the Severn Valley might be taken to reflect the cultural continuum demonstrated by the five Dobunnic coins from the site, but at present the case for this is unproven. As the northern Dobunni and the Severn catchment area seem to have been virtually coterminous, it may be constraints of water transport which engendered these apparent groupings.

Mortaria initially reached Alcester from *Verulamium* and perhaps from North-East Gaul but for most of the Roman period the main suppliers were Mancetter and Oxfordshire. Once again the Nene Valley was not well represented.

Worcester was a major iron smelting centre and much of the raw iron must have come from there although this connection is not visible in the archaeological record as iron tools are much the same throughout Roman Britain. Equally, the source of archaeologically invisible salt at Droitwich must have been important for Alcester.

Table 19 Building starts by date

Date	Site: A/C	B/H	D	E, F, J, P	G	Large buildings	All buildings
50–99			**DA**	**EA**		2	2
100–49				**EB**		1	1
150–99		**HA**		**EC**	GA	2	3
200–49	**AA**			ED–EJ, **EK**, **EL**, FA, FB		3	12
250–99	CEA, CWA		**DB**	**EM**, FC, **FD**	GB	4	7
300–49	CEB, CWB, CWC		**DC**		**GC**, GD	2	6
350–			**DD**, DE, DF	**FE**, **FF**, FG, PA	**GE**, GF, **GH**, GJ	5	11

Note: large structures in **bold**

Looking further afield, there is little to connect Alcester with the Marches and Wales, presumably because of the relatively low level of Romanization there.

Alcester was one of the westernmost Romano-British small towns with only Worcester, Droitwich, and Kenchester to its west. It lay just beyond the edge of the dense concentration of (known) villas associated with the Jurassic ridge (Jones & Mattingly 1990, 21, map 6:39) and was thus on the periphery of 'Romanized' Britain. As such it will not have been typical of small towns in the heartland of the province (*ibid*, 151, map 5:9 for an analysis of acculturation as measured by the density of villas and settlements). Alcester, it is beginning to emerge, was not necessarily typical of its genre.

The excavation of a Romano-British 'small town' on the scale of the 1964–6 project is unlikely ever to occur again. There are relatively few sites where the stratigraphy is so extensive, and where it does exist there is now a presumption that the remains will be preserved *in situ* and neither developed nor excavated (Department of the Environment 1990). The project revealed a comprehensive picture of the development of the southern one-fifth of Roman Alcester's built-up area including a wealth of structural and other details, showing what can emerge from such an approach if the resources are available.

Bibliography

Ainsworth, C J & Ratcliffe-Densham, H B A, 1974 Spectroscopy and a Roman cremation from Sompting, Sussex, *Britannia*, **5**, 310–16

Allan, J P, 1984 *Medieval and post-medieval finds from Exeter 1971–1980*, Exeter Archaeol Reports **3**

Allason-Jones, L, 1985 Bell-shaped studs?, in M C C Bishop (ed) *The production and distribution of Roman military equipment, BAR Int Ser* **S275**, 95–108, Oxford

Allason-Jones, L & Mckay, B, 1985 *Coventina's Well. A shrine on Hadrian's Wall*, Trustees of the Clayton Collection, Chesters Museum

Allason-Jones, L & Miket, R, 1984 *The catalogue of small finds from South Shields Roman fort*, Soc Antiquaries Newcastle-upon-Tyne Monogr ser **2**

Allen, D, 1972 The fibula of CRICIRV, *Germania*, **50**, 122–32

—— 1986 The glass vessels, in J D Zienkiewicz (ed) *The legionary Fortress baths at Caerleon, II. The finds*, Cardiff, 98–116

Anderson, A C, 1980 *A guide to Roman fine wares*, Vorda Research Series 1, Heyworth, Wilts

Atkinson, D, 1914 A hoard of samian ware from Pompeii, *J Roman Stud*, **4**, 27–64

—— 1942 *Report on excavations at Wroxeter (the Roman city of* Viroconium*) in the county of Salop 1923–1927*, Oxford

Avent, R & Howlett, T, 1980 Excavations at Roman Long Melford, 1970–1972, *Proc Suffolk Inst Archaeol Hist*, **34**, 229–49

Barfield, L, 1977 Roman bone inlay from Bays Meadow, Droitwich, *Antiq J*, **57** (2), 332–3

Barton, I M, 1958 Further excavations at Pennocrucium near Stretton Bridge, 1953–4, *Trans Birmingham Warwickshire Archaeol Soc*, **74**, 1956 (1958), 6–9

Bayley, J, 1984a Some technological finds from Lion Walk and Balkerne Lane, in P Crummy (ed) *Excavations at Lion Walk, Balkerne Lane and Middleborough, Colchester, England*, Colchester Archaeol Rep 3, 214–15

—— 1984b Technological finds from Sewingshields, in D Haigh & M J D Savage Sewingshields, *Archaeol Aeliana*, 5 ser, **12**, 33–147

—— 1988 Non-ferrous metalworking — continuity and change, in E A Slater and J O Tate (eds) *Science and Archaeology, Glasgow 1987, BAR* **196**, 193–208

Beijerinck, W, 1947 *Zadenatlas der Nederlandsche Flora*, Wageningen

Bell, A & Evans, J, forthcoming The pottery from the CEU excavations, in P R Wilson *Excavations at Catterick 1956–88*, HBMCE monogr, chapter 8

Bennett, P, Frere, S S & Stow, S, 1982 *The archaeology of Canterbury vol I: Excavations at Canterbury Castle*, Maidstone

Berggren, G, 1981 *Atlas of seeds and small fruits of north-west European plant species*, vol 3, Stockholm

Bidwell, P T, 1985 *The Roman fort of Vindolanda at Chesterholm, Northumberland*, HBMCE Archaeol Rep 1

Bird, J, Graham, A H, Sheldon H & Townend P, 1978 *Southwark excavations 1972–1974*, London

Bird, J & Marsh, G, 1978 Samian ware, in J Bird, A H Graham, H Sheldon & P Townsend *Southwark excavations 1972–74*, London

Birley, E, 1958 A catalogue and survey of the metal-work from Traprain Law, *Proc Soc Antiq Scot*, **89**, 118–226

Blalock, H M, 1972 *Social statistics*, 2 edn

Blockley, K, 1989 Excavations on the Romano-British settlement at Ffrith, Clwyd 1967–8, *J Flintshire Hist Soc*, **32**, 135–65

Bonsor, G E, 1931 *The archaeological expedition along the Guadalquivir, 1889–1901*, New York

Boon, G C, 1962 Remarks on Roman Usk, *The Monmouthshire Antiquary*, **1 (ii)**, 28–33

—— 1969 Belgic and Roman Silchester: The excavations of 1954–8, with an excursus on the early history of *Calleva*, *Archaeologia*, **102**, 1–81

Boon, G C & Hassall, M, 1982 *Report on the excavations at Usk l965-l976: the coins, inscriptions and graffiti*, Cardiff

Booth, P M, 1980 *Roman Alcester*, Warwick

—— 1983 Excavations at 64 Bleachfield Street, Alcester, Warwickshire, 1981, *Trans Birmingham Warwickshire Archaeol Soc*, **93**, 1983 (1989), 9–32

—— 1988 Roman pottery in Warwickshire — production and demand, *J Roman Pottery Stud*, **1**, 22–41

—— forthcoming (a) The Iron Age, Roman and Anglo-Saxon pottery, in N J Palmer *Tiddington Roman Settlement*

—— forthcoming (b) The Roman pottery, in G Crawford *et al*, *Excavations at Wasperton*

—— forthcoming (c) The Roman pottery, in Report on excavations at Coleshill, Warwicks

—— forthcoming (d) Excavations at 1–5 Bleachfield Street, Alcester, CBA

Boucher, S, 1971 *Inventaire des collections publiques Françaises, 17, Vienne, Bronzes Antiques*, Paris

Brailsford, J W, 1962 *Hod Hill, vol 1. Antiquities from Hod Hill in the Durden collection*, London

Branigan, K & Fowler, P J, 1976 *The Roman West Country*, Trowbridge

Brassington, M, 1980 Derby Racecourse kiln excavations 1972–3, *Antiq J*, **40**, 41–61

Brewer, R J, 1986 The bronze brooches, in J D Zinkiewiecz, *The legionary fortress baths at Caerleon II. The finds*, 168–172, National Museum of Wales and Cadw, Cardiff

Brickstock, R J, 1987 *Copies of the FEL TEMP REPARATIO coinage in Britain: their chronology and archaeological significance*, *BAR* **176**

Briggs, S, 1988 The lithology, origin and dispersal of some quernstones from Yorkshire in J Price & P R Wilson (eds) *Recent Research in Roman Yorkshire*, *BAR* **193**, 289–312

British Museum, 1958 *Guide to the antiquities of Roman Britain*, London

Brodribb, A C C, Hands, A R & Walker, D R, 1968 *Excavations at Shakenoak Farm, near Wilcote, Oxfordshire, Part I: Sites A and D*, Oxford

—— 1971 *Excavations at Shakenoak Farm, near Wilcote, Oxfordshire, II: sites B and H*, Oxford

—— 1973 *Excavations at Shakenoak Farm, near Wilcote, Oxfordshire, Part IV: Site C*, Oxford

—— 1978 *Excavations at Shakenoak Farm, near Wilcote, Oxfordshire, Part V: Sites K and E*, Oxford

Brunskill, R W, 1978 *Illustrated handbook of vernacular architecture*, London

Buckland, P, 1978 A first-century shield from Doncaster, Yorkshire, *Britannia*, **9**, 247–69

Buckland, P C & Magilton, J R, 1986 *The archaeology of Doncaster, 1, the Roman civil settlement*, *BAR* **148**

Burnham, B, 1986 The origins of Romano-British small towns, *Oxford J Archaeol*, **5**, 185–203

—— 1987 The morphology of Romano-British 'small towns', *Archaeol J*, **144**, 156–90

Burnham, B & Wacher, J, 1990 *The 'small towns' of Roman Britain*, London

Bushe-Fox, J P, 1913 *Excavations on the site of the Roman town at Wroxeter, Shropshire, 1912*, Res Rep Comm Soc Antiq London **1**

—— 1914 *Second report on the excavations of the Roman town at Wroxeter, Shropshire, 1913*, Res Rep Comm Soc Antiq London **2**

—— 1916 *Third report on the excavations on the site of the Roman town at Wroxeter, Shropshire, 1914*, Res Rep Comm Soc Antiq London **4**

—— 1932 *Third report on the excavations on the site of the Roman fort at Richborough, Kent*, Res Rep Comm Soc Antiq London **10**

—— 1949 *Fourth report on the excavations of the Roman fort at Richborough, Kent*, Res Rep Comm Soc Antiq London **16**

Buxton, L H D & Morant, G M, 1933 The essential craniological technique, part 1. Definitions of points and planes, *J Royal Anthropological Inst*, **63**, 19–47

Cadbury, D A, Hawkes, J G & Readett, R C, 1971 *A computer-mapped flora. A study of the county of Warwickshire*, London

Callender, M H, 1965 *Roman Amphorae*, London

Cameron, H & Lucas, J, 1967 *Tripontium*, first interim report, *Trans Birmingham Warwickshire Archaeol Soc*, **83**, 1967 (1969), 130–79

—— 1973 *Tripontium* second interim report, *Trans Birmingham and Warwickshire Archaeol Soc*, **85**, 93–144

Campion, G F, 1938 Roman relics found at Broxtowe, *The Thornton Society of Nottinghamshire, excavation section*, **3**, 6–18

Carson, R A G, 1971 Sequence marks on the coinage of Carausius and Allectus, in R A G Carson (ed) *Mints, dies and currency*, London, 57–65

—— 1987 Carausius et fratres sui . . . again, in *Mélanges de numismatique offerts à Pierre Bastien*, Wettern, 145–9

Casey, P J, 1977 Carausius and Allectus — rulers in Gaul?, *Britannia*, **8**, 283–303

—— 1986 *Understanding ancient coins*, London

—— 1989 Coin evidence and the end of Roman Wales, *Archaeol J*, **146**, 320-30

Charlesworth, D, 1959 Roman glass in the Tullie House Museum, *Trans Cumberland Westmorland Antiq Archaeol Soc*, ser 2, **59**, 32–40

—— 1971 A group of vessels from the Commandant's House, Housesteads, *J Glass Stud*, **13**, 34–7

—— 1972 The glass, in S S Frere *Verulamium excavations, Volume I*, Res Rep Comm Soc Antiq London **28**, 203–7

—— 1973 The Aesica hoard, *Archaeol Aeliana*, 5 ser, **1**, 225–34

—— 1979 Glass, in P T Bidwell *The legionary bath-house and basilica and forum at Exeter*, Exeter, 222–31

—— 1981 The glass, and glass from the burials, in C Partridge *Skeleton Green, a late Iron Age and Romano-British site, Britannia Monogr Ser* **2**, 119–271

—— 1984 The glass, in S S Frere *Verulamium excavations, Volume III*, Oxford Univ Comm for Archaeol, Monogr 1, 145–73

Charlesworth, D & Thornton, J H, 1973 Leather from *Mediobogdum*, the Roman fort of Hardknott, *Britannia*, **4**, 141–52

Christison, D, 1901 Account of the excavation of the Roman station of Camelon, near Falkirk Stirlingshire, undertaken by the Society in 1900, *Proc Soc Antiq Scotland*, **35**, 329–417

CIL Corpus Inscriptionum Latinarum (1863–)

Clarke, G, 1979 *Pre-Roman and Roman Winchester: part II The Roman cemetery at Lankhills*, Winchester Stud **3**

Clifford, E M, 1961 *Bagendon: a Belgic oppidum, a record of the excavations of 1954–56*, Cambridge

Collingwood, R G, 1930 Romano-Celtic art in Northumbria, *Archaeologia*, **80**, 37–58

—— 1931 Roman objects from Stanwix, *Trans Cumberland Westmorland Antiq Archaeol Soc*, n ser, **31**, 69–80

Cotton, M A, 1947 Excavations at Silchester 1938–9, *Archaeologia*, **92**, 121–67

Cox, J C, 1891 Some further finds in Deepdale Cavern, Buxton, *J Derbyshire Archaeol Natural History Soc*, **13**, 194–9

Cracknell, S, 1985 Roman Alcester: recent archaeological excavations, *Trans Birmingham Warwickshire Archaeol Soc*, **94**, 1–62

—— forthcoming *Roman Alcester: the defences and defended area, CBA Res Rep*

Cracknell, S & Ferguson, R, 1985 The Builder's Yard site, Bleachfield Street, Alcester, 1987: salvage recording, *Trans Birmingham Warwickshire Archaeol Soc*, **94**, 1985–6 (1990), 126–32

Cracknell, S & Jones, M, 1985 Medieval kiln debris from School Road, Alcester, *Trans Birmingham Warwickshire Archaeol Soc*, **94**, 1985 (1989), 107–22

Crummy, N, 1979 A chronology of Romano-British bone pins, *Britannia* **10**, 157–63

—— 1983 *The Roman small finds from excavations in Colchester 1971–9*, Colchester Archaeol Rep **2**

—— 1988 *The post-Roman small finds from excavations in Colchester 1971–85*, Colchester Archaeol Rep **5**

Cunliffe, B, 1971 *Excavations at Fishbourne, 1961–69, volume II, the finds*, Res Rep Comm Soc Antiq London **27**

—— 1974 *Iron Age communities of Britain*, London

Curle, A O, 1915 Account of the excavations on Traprain Law in the parish of Prestonkirk, county of Haddinton, in 1914, *Proc Soc Antiq Scotland*, **49**, 139–202

Curle, J, 1911 *A Roman frontier post and its people: the fort of Newstead in the parish of Melrose*, Glasgow

Curwen, E C, 1937 Querns, *Antiquity*, **11**, 133–51

—— 1941 More about querns, *Antiquity*, **15**, 15–32

Daniels, C M, 1959 The Roman bath house at Red House, Beaufort, near Corbridge, *Archaeol Aeliana*, 4 ser, **37**, 85–176

Dannell, G B, 1971 The samian pottery, in B Cunliffe *Excavations at Fishbourne, 1961–69, volume II, the finds*, Res Rep Comm Soc Antiq London **27**, 200–318

Dannell, G B & Hartley, B R, 1974 The samian pottery, in C J Ainsworth and W B A Ratcliffe-Densham, Spectoscopy and a Roman cremation from Sompting, Sussex, *Britannia*, **5**, 312–15

Dannell, G B & Wild, J P, 1987 *Longthorpe II. The military works-depot: an episode in landscape history, Britannia Monogr Ser* **8**, London

Darling, M J, 1977 Pottery from early military sites in western Britain, in J Dore & K Greene (eds) *Roman pottery studies in Britain and beyond, BAR Supplementary Ser* **30**, 57–100

den Boesterd, M H P, 1956 *Description of the collections in the Rijksmuseum G K Kam at Nijmegen. V: The bronze vessels*, Nijmegen

—— 1967 Roman bronze vessels from rivers, *Berichten van de Rijksdienst voor het Oudheidkundig Bodemonderzoek* 17, 115–20

Déchelette, J, 1904 *Les vases céramiques ornés de la Gaule romaine*, Paris

Denston, C B, 1970 The human skeletal remains from Great Casterton, unpublished

de Groot, J, 1960 Masclus von la Graufesenque, *Germania*, **38 (5, 15)**, 55–65

Department of the Environment 1990 *Planning policy guidance 16: archaeology and planning*, HMSO

Dickinson, B, forthcoming The site 46 samian ware, in P R Wilson *Excavations at Catterick 1956–88*, HBMCE monogr

Dool, J *et al*, 1985 Roman Derby: excavations, 1968–1983, *J Derbyshire Archaeol Soc*, **105**, 1–345

Dore, J & Greene K, eds 1977 *Roman pottery studies in Britain and beyond, BAR Supplementary Ser* **30**

Down, A, 1978 *Chichester Excavations, III*, Chichester

Down, A & Rule, M, 1971 *Chichester excavations, vol I*, Chichester

Downey, R, King, A & Soffe, G, 1980 The Hayling Island temple and religious connections across the Channel, in W Rodwell (ed) *Temples, churches, and religion: recent research in Roman Britain, BAR* **77**, 289–301

Draper, J, 1985 *Excavations by Mr H P Cooper on the Roman site at Hill Farm, Gestingthorpe, Essex*, East Anglian Archaeol Rep 25

Draper, J & Chaplin, C, 1982 *Dorchester excavations, vol I*, Dorset Natural History and Archaeol Soc Monogr ser 2

Dressel, H, 1978 *Saggi Sull Instrumentum Domesticum*, Perugia

Droop, J P & Newstead, R, 1931 Excavations in the Deanery Field, Chester 1928. II: The Finds, *Liverpool Annals of Archaeology Anthropology*, **18**, 113–47

Dudley, D, 1967 Excavations on Nor'nour in the Isles of Scilly 1962–6, *Archaeol J*, **124**, 1–64

Esmonde Cleary, S, 1987 *Extra-mural areas of Romano-British towns, BAR* **169**

Evans, E, Dowdell, G & Thomas, H J, 1985 A third-century maritime establishment at Cold Knap, Barry, South Glamorgan, *Britannia*, **16**, 57–125

Evans, J, 1987 Graffiti and the evidence of literacy and pottery use in Roman Britain, *Archaeol J*, **144**, 191–204

—— 1990 From Roman Britain to the Celtic West, *Oxford J Archaeol*, **9 (1)**, 91–104

—— forthcoming The pottery from Chew Down and Worberry Gate, in D Batchelor, Report on excavations at Chew Down and Worberry Gate, Somerset

—— in prep The Roman pottery from Gas House Lane, in S Cracknell, Roman Alcester: defences and defended area, *CBA Res Rep*

Exner, K, 1939 Die provinzialrömischen Emailfibeln der Rheinlande, *Bericht des Römische-Germanische Kommission*, **29**, 33–121

Farrar, R A H, 1977 A Romano-British Black-Burnished ware industry at Ower in the Isle of Purbeck, Dorset, in J Dore & K Greene (eds) *Roman pottery studies in Britain and beyond, BAR Supplementary Ser* **30**, 199–228

Fell, C I, 1936 The Hunsbury Hillfort, Northants. A new survey of the material, *Archaeol J*, **93 (1)**, 57–100

Ferguson, R, 1985 Roman pottery, in S Cracknell, Roman Alcester: recent archaeological excavations, *Trans Birmingham Warwickshire Archaeol Soc*, **94**, 1985–6 (1990), 16–22

—— forthcoming (a) The Roman pottery from the Gateway supermarket site, in S Cracknell, Roman Alcester: defences and defended area, *CBA Res Rep*

—— forthcoming (b) The Roman pottery, in P Booth, Report on excavations at 1–5 Bleachfield Street, Alcester, CBA

Feugère, M, 1985 *Les Fibules en Gaule Méridionale de la conquête à la fin du Ve siècle après J C*, Revue Archéologique de Narbonnaise Supplément 12

Feugère, M, Künzl, E & Weisser, U, 1988 *Les Aiguilles a Cataracte de Montballet (Saône-et-Loire)*, Société des Amis des Arts et des Sciences de Tournus 87

Fieldhouse, W J, May, T & Wellstood, F C, 1931 *A Romano-British industrial settlement near Tiddington, Stratford-on-Avon*, Birmingham

Fischer, U, 1966 Zu den Fibeln Almgren 101, *Jahrschrift für mitteldeutsche Vergeschicte*, **50**, 229–62

France, N E & Gobel, B M, 1985 *The Romano-British temple at Harlow*, Gloucester

Frere, S S, 1962 Excavations at Dorchester-on-Thames 1962, *Archaeol J*, **119**, 114–49

—— 1972 *Verulamium excavations, Volume I*, Res Rep Comm Soc Antiq London **28**

—— 1983a Roman Britain in 1982, I. Sites explored, *Britannia*, **14**, 280–335

—— 1983b *Verulamium excavations, Volume II*, Res Rep Comm Soc Antiq London **41**

—— 1984 *Verulamium excavations, Volume III*, Oxford Univ Comm for Archaeol Monogr 1

Frere, S S & St Joseph, J K, 1974 The Roman fortress at Longthorpe, *Britannia*, **5**, 1–129

Frere, S S & Stow, S, 1983 *Excavations in the St George's Street and Burgate Street Areas*, Archaeology of Canterbury 7

Frere, S S, Stow, S & Bennett, P, 1982 *The Archaeology of Canterbury, vol 2. Excavations on the Roman and medieval defences of Canterbury*, Maidstone

Friendship-Taylor, R M, 1979 The excavation of the Belgic and Romano-British settlement at Quinton, Northamptonshire, Site 'B', 1973–7, *J Northampton Museums and Art Gallery*, **13**, 2–176

Fulford, M G, 1975 *New Forest Roman pottery*, *BAR* **17**

—— 1984 *Silchester defences 1974–80*, *Britannia Monogr Ser* **5**

Funari, P P A (in press) *The typological transformations of the Dressel 20 amphora: a semiotic approach*, *BAR*

Gaitzsch, W, 1980 *Eiserne römische Werkzeuge. Studien zur römischen Werkzeugkunde in Italien und nordlichen Provinzen des Imperium Romanum*, 2 vols, *BAR Int Ser* **78**

Gardner, W & Savory, H N, 1964 *Dinorben, a hillfort occupied in early Iron Age and Roman times*, Cardiff

Gillam, J P, 1970 *Types of Roman coarse pottery vessels in Northern Britain*, Newcastle-upon Tyne, 3 edn

—— 1976 Coarse fumed ware in north Britain and beyond, *Glasgow Archaeol J*, **4**, 57–80

Going, C, 1992 Economic 'long waves' in the Roman period? *Oxford J Archaeol*, **11**, 93–117

Goodburn, R, 1978 Roman Britain in 1977, I. Sites Explored, *Britannia*, **9**, 403–72

—— 1979 Roman Britain in 1978, I. Sites Explored, *Britannia*, **10**, 268–338

Goodman, C N & Morant, G M, 1940 The human remains of the Iron Age and other periods from Maiden Castle, Dorset, *Biometrika*, **21 (II and IV)**

Gould, J, 1964 Excavations at Wall (Staffordshire), 1961–3 on the site of the early Roman Forts and of the late Roman defences, *Trans Lichfield S Staffordshire Archaeol Historical Soc*, **5**, 1–50

—— 1967 Excavations at Wall, Staffs, 1964–6, on the site of the Roman Forts, *Trans Lichfield S Staffordshire Archaeol Historical Soc*, **8**, 1–40

Green, S & Young, C J, 1985 The Roman pottery, in B Cunliffe and P Davenport *The temple of Sulis Minerva at Bath, Vol 1 (1) The site*, Oxford Univ Comm for Archaeol Monogr 7, 143–60

Greene, K, 1978 Imported fine wares in Britain to AD 250: a guide to identification, in P Arthur & G Marsh (eds) *Early fine wares in Roman Britain*, *BAR* **57**, 15–30

Grimes, W F, 1930 *Holt, Denbighshire: The works-depôt of the Twentieth Legion at Castle Lyons*, Y Cymmrodor 41, London

Guido, M, 1978 *The glass beads of the Prehistoric and Roman periods in Britain and Ireland*, Res Rep Comm Soc Antiq London **35**

Guiraud, H, 1988 *Initailles et camées de l'époque romaine en Gaule*, suppl to *Gallia*, **48**

Hamp, E P, 1975 Social gradience in British spoken Latin, *Britannia*, **6**, 150–62

Hanson, W S, Daniels, C M, Dore, J N & Gillam, J P, 1979 The Agricolan supply base at Red House, Corbridge, *Archaeol Aeliana*, 5 ser, **7**, 1–88

Harden, D B, 1974 Window glass from the Romano-British bath-house at Garden Hill, Hartfield, Sussex, *Antiq J*, **47**, 280–1

—— 1979 Glass vessels, in G Clarke (ed) *Pre-Roman and Roman Winchester, Part II — The Roman cemetery at Lankhills*, 209–20, Oxford

—— 1983 The glass hoard, in *Burgh Castle, excavations by Charles Green 1958–1961*, East Anglia Archaeol 20, 78–89

Harden, D B & Price, J, 1971 The glass, in B W Cunliffe *Excavations at Fishbourne, 1961–1969, Vol II, the finds*, Res Rep Comm Soc Antiq London **27**, 317–74

Hartley, B R, 1954 Heronbridge excavations: bronze worker's hearth, *J Chester Archaeol Soc*, **41**, 1–14

—— 1961a The samian ware, in K A Steer, Excavations at Mumrills Roman fort 1958–60, *Proc Soc Antiq Scot*, **94**, 100–10

—— 1961b Samian pottery, in G Webster, An excavation on the Roman site at Little Chester, Derby, *Derbyshire Archaeol J*, **81**, 95–104

—— 1966 The Roman fort at Ilkley, excavation of 1962, *Proc Leeds Philosophical and Literary Soc*, Literary and Historical section **12 (2)**, 23–72

—— 1971 The samian ware, in A C C Brodribb, A R Hands & D R Walker *Excavations at Shakenoak Farm, near Wilcote, Oxfordshire, II: sites B and H*, Oxford, 59–70

—— 1972a Samian in A Fox & W Ravenhill, The Roman fort at Nanstallon, Cornwall, *Britannia*, **3**, 100–2

—— 1972b The Roman occupations of Scotland: the evidence of samian ware, *Britannia*, **3**, 1–55

—— 1972c Samian ware, in S S Frere *Verulamium excavations, Volume I*, Res Rep Comm Soc Antiq London **28**, 216–62

—— 1983 Samian ware, in G Webster & L Smith, The examination of a Romano-British rural establishment at Barnsley Park, Gloucestershire, 1961–79, *Trans Bristol Gloucestershire Archaeol Soc*, **101**, 169–74

—— 1984 Samian ware: C unusual forms, in S S Frere *Verulamium excavations, Volume III*, Oxford Univ Comm for Archaeol Monogr 1, 197–9

Hartley, K F, 1967 *Mortaria* from Mancetter, 1964, in C Mahany, Excavations at Manduessedum 1964, *Trans Birmingham Warwickshire Archaeol Soc*, **84**, 1967 (1970), 28–34

—— 1972 The *mortarium* stamps, in S S Frere *Verulamium exavations, Volume I*, Res Rep Comm Soc Antiq London **28**, 371–81

—— 1977 Two major potteries producing *mortaria* in the first century AD, in J Dore & K Greene (eds) *Roman pottery studies in Britain and beyond, BAR Int Ser* **S30**, 5–17

—— 1981a The *mortaria*, in B Philp *The excavation of the Roman forts of the Classis Britannica at Dover, 1970–1977*, Dover, 203–7

—— 1981b Painted fine wares made in the raetian workshops near Wilderspool, Cheshire, in A C & A S Anderson (eds) *Roman pottery research in Britain and north-west Europe, BAR Int Ser* **S123**, 471–9

—— 1984 The *mortarium* stamps, in S S Frere *Verulamium excavations, Volume III*, Oxford Comm for Archaeol Monogr 1, 280–91

—— 1985 The *mortaria*, in L F Pitts & J K St Joseph *Inchtuthil, the Roman legionary fortress excavations 1952–65, Britannia Monogr Ser* **6**, 330–3

—— 1989 *Mortarium* fabrics, in P T Marney *Roman and Belgic pottery from excavations in Milton Keynes 1972–82*, Buckinghamshire Archaeol Soc Monogr Ser 2, 132–3

Hartley, K F & Webster, P V, 1973 The Romano-British pottery kilns near Wilderspool, *Archaeol J*, **130**, 77–103

Haselgrove, C C, 1987 *Iron Age coinage in South East England; the archaeological context*, Oxford

—— forthcoming The coins, in H Hurst (ed) *Excavations at Kingsholm, Gloucester*

Hassall, M & Rhodes, J, 1974 Excavations at New Market Hall, Gloucester, *Trans Bristol Gloucestershire Archaeol Soc*, **93**, 15–100

Hassall, M W C & Tomlin, R S O, 1978 Roman Britain in 1977, *Britannia*, **9**, 403–85

Hattatt, R, 1985 *Iron Age and Roman brooches, a second selection of brooches from the author's collection*, Oxford

Hawkes, C F C, 1927 Excavations at Alchester, 1926, *Antiq J*, **7**, 147–84

—— 1961 The western 3rd C culture and the Belgic Dobunni, in E M Clifford *Bagendon: a Belgic oppidum, a record of the excavations of 1954–56*, 43–73, Cambridge

Hawkes, C F C & Hull, M R, 1947 *Camulodunum, first report on the excavations at Colchester, 1930–1939*, Res Rep Comm Soc Antiq London **14**

Hemsley, R, 1959 A Romano-British pottery kiln at *Manduessedum*, *Trans Birmingham Warwickshire Archaeol Soc*, **77**, 1959 (1961) 5–17

Henig, M, 1974 *A corpus of Roman engraved gemstones from British sites, BAR* **8**, 1 edn

—— 1978 *A corpus of Roman engraved gemstones from British sites, BAR* **8**, 2 edn

Hermet, F, 1934 *La Graufesenque (Condatomago)*, Paris

Hinchcliffe, J & Sparey Green, C *et al*, 1985 *Excavations at Brancaster 1974 and 1977*, East Anglian Archaeol 23

Hobley, B, 1966 A Neronian–Vespasianic military site at 'The Lunt', Baginton, Warwickshire, *Trans Birmingham Warwickshire Archaeol Soc*, **83**, 1966 (1969), 65–129

—— 1973 Excavations at 'The Lunt' Roman military site, Baginton, Warwickshire, 1968–71, second interim report, *Trans Birmingham Warwickshire Archaeol Soc*, **85**, 7–92

Hodgson, J M, 1976 *Soil survey field handbook*, Soil survey technical monogr 5, Harpenden

Holbrook, N & Bidwell, P T, 1991 *Roman finds from Exeter*, Exeter Archaeol Rep **4**

Howe, M D, Perrin, J R & Mackreth, D F, 1980 *Roman pottery from the Nene Valley: a guide*, Peterborough City Museum Occas Paper 2

Hughes, H V, 1961 A Romano-British kiln site at Perry Barr, Birmingham, *Trans Birmingham Warwickshire Archaeol Soc*, **77**, 34–107

Hull, M R, 1958 *Roman Colchester*, Res Rep Comm Soc Antiq London **20**

—— 1967 The Nor'Nour brooches, in D Dudley, Excavations on Nor'nour in the Isles of Scilly 1962–6, *Archaeol J*, **124**, 28–64

Hume, A, 1863 *Ancient Neols; or, some account of the antiquities found near Dove Point, on the sea-coast of Cheshire*, London

Hurst, H R, 1985 *Kingsolm*, Gloucester archaeol rep **1**

Isings, C, 1957 *Roman glass from dated finds*, Groningen

Jacobs, J, 1913 Sigillatafunde aus einem römischen Keller zu Bregenz, *Jahrbuch für Altertumskunde*, **6**, 172–84

Jarrett, M G & Wrathmell, S, 1981 *Whitton: an Iron Age and Roman farmstead in South Glamorgan*, Cardiff

Jones, D M, 1980 *Excavations at Billingsgate Buildings 'Triangle', Lower Thames Street 1974,* London Middlesex Archaeol Soc Special Pap 4

Jones, G D B, 1974 *Roman Manchester*

Jones, G D B & Mattingly, D, 1990 *An atlas of Roman Britain*, Oxford

Karnitsch, P, 1955 *Die verzierte Sigillata von Lauriacum (Lorch-Enns)*, Linz

— 1959 *Die Reliefsigillata von Ovilava*, Linz

Keeley, J, 1986 The coarse pottery, in A McWhirr *Cirencester excavations III, Houses in Roman Cirencester*, Cirencester, 158–89

Kelly, J H, 1958 Excavations at Reynard's Cave, Dovedale, 1959, *J Derbyshire Archaeol Natural History Soc*, **78**, 1958 (1960), 117–23

Kenward, H K, 1974 Methods for palaeo-entomology on site and in the laboratory, *Science and Archaeology*, **13**, 16–24

Kenyon, K M, 1934 The Roman theatre at *Verulamium*, St Albans, *Archaeologia*, **84**, 213–61

—— 1948 *Excavations at the Jewry Wall site, Leicester*, Res Rep Comm Soc Antiq London **15**

King, D, 1986 Petrology, dating and distribution of querns and millstones. The results of research in Bedfordshire, Buckinghamshire and Middlesex, *Institute Archaeol Bull*, **23**, 65–126

Kirk, J R, 1949 Bronzes from Woodeaton, Oxon, *Oxoniensia*, **14**, 1–45

Kisch, B, 1965 *Scales and weights: a historical outline*, Yale University, USA

Kloet, G S & Hincks, W D, 1945 *A checklist of British insects*, Stockport

Knorr, R, 1912a *Die Terra-Sigillata-Gefässe von Aislingen*, Dillingen

—— 1912b *Südgallische Terra-Sigillata-Gefässe von Rottweil*, Stuttgart

—— 1919 *Töpfer und Fabriken verzierter Terra-Sigillata des ersten Jahrhunderts*, Stuttgart

—— 1952 *Terra-Sigillata-Gefässe des ersten Jahrhunderts mit Töpfernamen*, Stuttgart

Krug, A, 1980 Antike Gemmen im Römisch-Germanischen Museum Köln, *Bericht der Römisch-Germanischen Kommission*, **61**, 151–260

Künzl, E, 1983 *Medizinische Instrumente aus Sepulkralfunden der römischen Kaiserzeit*, Kunst und Altertum am Rhein, 115, Bonn, Cologne

—— 1984 Medizinische Instrumente der Römerzeit aus Trier und Umgebung in Rheinischen Landesmuseum, Trier, *Trierer Zeitschrift*, **47**, 153–237

Lambrick, G, 1980 Excavations at Park Street, Towcester, *Northamptonshire Archaeol*, **15**, 35–118

Laubenheimer, F, 1985 *La Production des Amphores en Gaul Narbonaise*, Paris

Lawson, A J, 1975 Shale and jet objects from Silchester, *Archaeologia* **105**, 241–76

Leach, P, 1982 *Ilchester, volume 1, excavations 1974–5*, Bristol

Leech, R, 1982 *Excavations at Catsgore 1970–1973. A Romano-British Village*, Western Archaeol Trust Excavation Monogr 2

—— 1986 The excavation of a Romano-Celtic temple and a later cemetery on Lamyatt Beacon, Somerset, *Britannia*, **17**, 259–328

Leeds, E T, 1911 A Romano-Celtic brooch of the second century, from Hook Norton, Oxfordshire, *Proc Soc Antiq London*, 2 ser, **23** (2), 406–7

Livens, R, 1976 A Don Terret from Anglesey with a discussion of the type, in George C Boon & J M Lewis (eds) *Welsh antiquity. Essays mainly on Prehistoric topics presented to H N Savory upon his retirement as Keeper of Archaeology*, 149–162, National Museum of Wales, Cardiff

Liversidge, J, 1968 *Britain in the Roman Empire*, London

Lloyd-Morgan, G, 1981 *Description of the collections in the Rijksmuseum G M Kam at Nijmegen. IX: The Mirrors*, Nijmegen

Loeschcke, S, 1919 *Lampen aus Vindonissa*, Zürich

Lucht, W H, 1987 *Die Kafer Mitteleuropas*, Katalog, Goeke & Evers, Krefeld

Macdonald, J & Curle A O, 1929 The Roman fort at Mumrills, near Falkirk, *Proc Soc Antiq Scot*, **63**, 396–575

MacGregor, M, 1976 *Early Celtic art in north Britain. A study of decorative metalwork from the third century BC to the third century AD*, Leicester

Mackreth, D F, 1963 Two brooches from Alcester, *Trans Birmingham Warwickshire Archaeol Soc*, **81**, 1963 (1966), 140–1

Mackreth, D F, 1993 Brooches from the vicinity of Osmanthorpe, in M C Bishop and P W M Freeman, Recent work at Osmanthorpe, Nottinghamshire, *Britannia*, **24**, 160–189

—— 1978 The Roman brooches, in A Down *Chichester Excavations, III*, Chichester, 277–87

—— 1982 Two brooches from Stonea, Cambs, and Bicester, Oxon, and the origin of the Aesica Brooch, *Britannia*, **13**, 310–15

—— 1985 Brooches from Roman Derby, in J Dool *et al* Roman Derby: excavations, 1968–1983, *J Derbyshire Archaeol Soc*, **105**, 281–99

—— 1988 Excavation of an Iron Age and Roman enclosure at Werrington, Cambridgeshire, *Britannia*, **19**, 59–151

—— forthcoming (a) The Beckford brooches, in forthcoming report on excavations

—— forthcoming (b) The Wroxeter brooches, in G Webster, forthcoming Wroxeter military fascicule

—— forthcoming (c) The Kingsholm Coppice Corner brooches, in P Garrod & M Atkin, forthcoming report on site

—— forthcoming (d) The brooches from Stonea in R P J Jackson & T W Potter, forthcoming report on site

—— forthcoming (e) The brooches from sites 433 and 434, in J Wacher & P R Wilson (eds) *Excavations at Catterick 1956–88*, HMBCE monogr

McWhirr, A, 1981 *Roman Gloucestershire*, Gloucester

—— 1986 *Cirencester excavations III: Houses in Roman Cirencester*, Cirencester

McWhirr, A, Viner, L & Wells, C, 1982 *Cirencester excavations II Romano-British cemeteries at Cirencester*, Cirencester

Mahany, C, 1970 Excavations at *Manduessedum* 1964, *Trans Birmingham Warwickshire Archaeol Soc*, **84**, 18–44

Manning, W H, 1972 The iron objects, in S S Frere *Verulamium excavations Volume I*, Res Rep Comm Soc Antiq London **28**, 163–95.

—— 1976 *Catalogue of Romano-British ironwork in the Museum of Antiquities Newcastle Upon Tyne*, Newcastle-upon-Tyne

Manning, W H, 1985 *Catalogue of Romano-British iron tools, fittings and weapons in the British Museum*, London

Marney, P T, 1989 *Roman and Belgic pottery from excavations in Milton Keynes 1972–1982*, Buckinghamshire Archaeol Soc Monogr **2**

Marsh, G, 1978 Early second-century fine wares in the London area, in P Arthur & G Marsh (eds) *Early fine wares in Roman Britain, BAR* **57**, 119–223

—— 1981 London's samian supply and its relationship to the development of the Gallic samian industry, in A C Anderson & A S Anderson (eds) *Roman pottery research in Britain and North West Europe, BAR Int Ser* **123**, 173–238

Martin-Kilcher, S, 1983 Les amphores romaines a huile de Betique (Dressel 20 et 23) d'Augst (*Colonia Augusta Rauricorum*) et Kaiseraugst (*Castrum Rauracense*). Un rapport preliminary, in J M Blazquez & J Remesal (eds) *Produccion Y Comercio Del Aceite En La Antiguedad, Il Congresso*, 337–47, Madrid

Mattingly, D J, 1988 Oil for export? A comparison of Libyan, Spanish and Tunisian olive-oil production in the Roman empire, *J Roman Archaeol*, **1**, 33–56

May, T & Hope, L E, 1917 *Catalogue of the Roman pottery in the museum 'Tullie House', Carlisle*, Kendal

Meikle, R D, 1984 *Willows and poplars of Great Britain and Ireland.* Botanical Soc Brit Isles Handbook 4, Botanical Society of the British Isles, London

Menzel, H, 1966 *Die römischen Bronzen aus Deutschland vol II: Trier*, Mainz am Rhein

Miket, R, 1983 *The Roman fort at South Shields. Excavation of the defences 1977–1981*, Tyne and Wear County Council Museums, Newcastle

Millett, M, 1983 *A comparative study of some contemporaneous pottery assemblages from Roman Britain*, unpublished D Phil thesis, University of Oxford

—— 1990 *The Romanization of Britain*, Cambridge

Millett, M & Graham, D, 1986 *Excavations on the Romano-British small town at Neatham, Hampshire 1969–1979, Hampshire Field Club Monogr* **3**

Mitchelson, N, 1964 Roman Malton: the civilian settlement. Excavations in Orchard Field 1949–1952, *Yorkshire Archaeol J*, **41 (2)**, 209–61

Morant, G M, 1936 A biometric study of the human mandible. *Biometrika*, **28, 84 and 122**

Morris, P, 1979 *Agricultural buildings in Roman Britain, BAR* **70**

Mukherjee, R, Rao, C R & Trevor, J C, 1955 *The ancient inhabitants of Jebel Moya*, Occas Publ Cambridge University Museum Archaeol Ethnology **3**

Munsell Color, 1988 *Munsell Soil Color Charts*, Baltimore, Maryland

Neal, D S, 1974 *The excavation of the Roman villa in Gadebridge Park, Hemel Hempstead, 1963–8*, Res Rep Comm Soc Antiq London **31**

—— 1974–6 Northchurch, Boxmoor, Hemel Hempstead Station: the excavations of three Roman buildings in the Bulbourne Valley, *Hertfordshire Archaeol*, **4**, 1–135

Newstead, R, 1924 Report on the excavations on the site of the Roman Camp at the Deanery Field, Chester, *Liverpool Annals Archaeol Anthropology*, **11**, 59–86

Niblett, R, 1985 *Sheepen: an early Roman industrial site of Camulodunum, CBA Res Rep* **57**

Num Chron Numismatic Chronicle

O & P 1920 See Oswald & Davies-Price 1920

Osborne, P J, 1971 An insect fauna from the Roman site at Alcester, Warwickshire, *Britannia*, **2**, 156–65

—— 1983 An insect fauna from a modern cess pit and its comparison with probable cess pit assemblages from archaeological sites, *J Archaeol Sci*, **10**, 453–63

—— 1989 Insects, in P Ashbee, M Bell & E Proudfoot (eds) *Wilsord Shaft; excavations 1960–2*, HBMCE Archaeol Rep 11, 96–9 and microfiche

Oswald, F, 1937 *Index of figure-types on terra sigillata (samian ware)*, Liverpool

Oswald, F & Davies Price, T, 1920 *An introduction to the study of terra sigillata*, London

Palk, N A, 1984 *Iron Age bridle bits from Britain*, University of Edinburgh Dept Archaeol Occas Paper 10

Palmer, N, 1980 A beaker burial and medieval tenement in the Hamel, Oxford, *Oxoniensia*, **45**, 124–225

—— 1983 Tiddington Roman settlement: second interim report, *West Midlands Archaeol News Sheet*, **26**, 37–47

—— in prep *Tiddington Roman Settlement*

Partridge, C, 1981 *Skeleton Green: a late Iron Age and Romano-British Site, Britannia Monogr Ser* **2**

Peacock, D P S, 1967 The heavy mineral analysis of pottery, a preliminary report, *Archaeometry*, **10**, 97–100

—— 1968a Romano-British pottery production in the Malvern district of Worcestershire, *Trans Worcestershire Archaeol Soc*, **1**, 15–28

—— 1968b A petrological study of certain Iron Age pottery from Western England, *Proc Prehis Soc*, **34**, 414–27

—— 1969 A contribution to the study of Glastonbury ware from South West Britain, *Antiq J*, **49**, 41–61

—— 1971 Petrology of the coarse pottery, in B Cuncliffe *Excavations at Fishbourne, 1961–69, volume II, the finds*, Res Rep Comm Soc Antiq London **27**, 255–9

—— 1978 The Rhine and the problem of Gaulish wine in Roman Britain, in J du Plat Taylor & H Cleere (eds) *Roman Shipping and Trade: Britain and the Rhine Provinces, CBA Res Rep* **24**, 49–51

Peacock, D P S & Williams, D F, 1986 *Amphorae and the Roman economy*, London

Philp, B J, 1981 *The excavation of the Roman forts of the Classis Britannica at Dover 1970–1977*, Kent Monogr Ser 3

Pieksma, E J, 1982 *A petrological study of Dressel 20 amphora*, unpublished MSc thesis, University of Southampton

Platt, C & Coleman-Smith, R, 1975 *Excavations in medieval Southampton 1953–1965, vol II: the small finds*, Leicester

Plouviez, J, 1976 The pottery, in S E West & J Plouviez *The Romano-British site at Icklingham*, East Anglian Archaeol 3, 85–102

Ponsich, M, 1974 *Implantation Rurale Antique sur le Bas-Guadalquivir*, **1**, Madrid

—— 1979 *Implantation Rurale Antique sur le Bas-Guadalquivir*, **2**, Paris

Potter, T W, 1977 The Biglands milefortlet and the Cumberland coast defences, *Britannia*, **8**, 149–83

—— 1979 *Romans in North-West England, excavations at the Roman forts of Ravenglass, Watercrook and Browness-on-Solway*, Cumberland and Westmorland Antiquarian Archaeol Soc Res Ser 1

—— 1981 The Roman occupation of the central Fenland, *Britannia* **12**, 79–133

Potter, T W & Trow, S W, 1988 Puckeridge-Braughing, Herts: the Ermine Street excavations 1971–72, *Hertfordshire Archaeol*, **10**, 1–191

Price, J, 1980 The Roman glass, in G Lambrick, Excavations in Park Street, Towcester, 1963–8, *Northamptonshire Archaeol*, **15**, 35–118

—— 1987 Glass from Felmongers, Harlow in Essex. A dated deposit of vessel glass found in an Antonine pit, *Annales du 10e Congres de l'Association Internationale pour l'Histoire du Verre*, 185–206

Price, J & Cool, H E M, 1983 Glass from the excavations of 1974–76, in A E Brown & C Woodfield Excavations at Towcester, Northamptonshire: The Alchester Road Suburb, *Northamptonshire Archaeol*, **18**, 115–24

—— 1985 Glass, in H R Hurst *Kingsholm*, Gloucester Archaeol Rep **1**, 41–54

Pulinger, J & Young, C J, 1981 Obelisk kilns, Harston, *Proc Cambridge Antiq Soc*, **71**, 1–24

Rae, A & Rae, V, 1974 The Roman fort at Cramond, Edinburgh, excavations 1954–1966, *Britannia*, **5**, 163–224

Rankov, N B, 1982 Roman Britain 1981, I. Sites explored, *Britannia*, **13**, 328–95

Ratkai, S, 1987 The medieval pottery, in S Cracknell, Bridge End, Warwick: archaeological excavation of a medieval street frontage, *Trans Birmingham Warwickshire Archaeol Soc*, **95**, 33–58

—— forthcoming (a) Medieval pottery, in S Cracknell, 'Bard's Walk', Wood Street, Stratford-upon-Avon: medieval structures excavated in 1989, *Trans Birmingham Warwickshire Archaeol Soc*

—— forthcoming (b) see Ratkai, S, 1987

—— forthcoming (c) Medieval pottery, in S Cracknell, Roman Alcester: excavations of the defences, 1986

—— forthcoming (d) Medieval pottery, in P Booth, Excavations at 1–5 Bleachfield Street, Alcester, CBA

Ravetz, A, 1964 The 4th-century inflation and Romano-British coin finds, *Numis Chron*, 7 ser, **4**, 201–31

Rawes, B, 1972 Roman pottery kilns at Gloucester, *Trans Bristol Gloucestershire Archaeol Soc*, **91**, 1972 (1973), 18–59

—— 1980 The Romano-British site at Wycomb, Andoversford, excavations 1969–1970, *Trans Bristol Gloucestershire Archaeol Soc*, **98**, 1980 (1981), 11–55

—— 1981 The Romano-British Site at Brockworth, Glos, *Britannia* **12**, 45–77

—— 1982 Gloucester Severn Valley ware, *Trans Bristol Gloucestershire Archaeol Soc*, **100**, 1982 (1983), 33–46

—— 1986 The Romano-British settlement at Haymes, Cleeve Hill, near Cheltenham, *Trans Bristol Gloucestershire Archaeol Soc*, **104**, 1986 (1987), 61–93

Redknap, M, 1985 Twelfth- and thirteenth-century Coventry wares with special reference to a waster group from the Cannon Park estate, Coventry, *Medieval Ceramics*, **9**, 65–77

Renfrew, J R, 1973 *Palaeoethnobotany. The Prehistoric food plants of the Near East and Europe*, New York and London

Rhodes, M, 1989 Roman pottery lost *en route* from the kiln to the user — a gazetteer, *J Roman Pottery Stud*, **2**, 44–58

Richmond, I A, 1949 Excavations at the Roman fort of Newstead, 1947, *Proc Soc Antiq Scotland*, **84**, 1949–50 (1952), 1–38

—— 1968 *Hod Hill, volume 2, excavations carried out between 1951 and 1958 for the Trustees of the British Museum*, London

Ricken, H, 1948 *Die Bilderschüsseln der römischen Töpfer von Rheinzabern*, Tafelband, Speyer

Ricken, H & Fischer, C, 1963 *Die Bilderschüsseln der römischen Töpfer von Rheinzabern*, Textband, Bonn

Rigby, V, 1982 The coarse pottery, in J Wacher & A McWhirr *Cirencester excavations I, Early Roman occupation at Cirencester*, Cirencester, 153–200

Riha, E, 1979 *Die römischen Fibeln aus Augst und Kaiseraugst*, Forschungen in Augst 3, Augst

Rivet, A L F, 1958 *Town and country in Roman Britain*, London

Robertson, A S, 1975 *Birrens (Blatobulgium)*, Edinburgh

Robinson, H R, 1975 *The armour of Imperial Rome*, London

Rodriguez-Almeida, E, 1979 Monte Testaccio: i mercatores dell'olio della Betica, *Mélanges de École Française de Rome*, **91**, 874–975

—— 1986 *Il Monte Testaccio*, Rome

Roger, O, 1913 Bildertypen von Augsburger Sigillaten, *Zeitschrift des Historischen Vereins für Schwaben und Neuburg*, **39**, Taf 1, 1, 26–70

Rogers, G B, 1974 *Poteries sigillées de la Gaule centrale*, suppl to Gallia, **28**

Rogerson, A, 1977 *Excavations at Scole 1973*, East Anglian Archaeol **5**, 97–224

S & S 1958 See Stanfield & Simpson 1958

Sanders, J, 1973 *Late Roman shell-gritted ware in Southern Britain*, unpublished BA dissertation, London Institute of Archaeology

—— 1979 The Roman pottery, in G Lambrick & M Robinson *Iron Age and Roman settlements at Farmoor, Oxfordshire, CBA Res Rep* **32**, 46–54

Saunders, C & Havercroft, A, 1977 A kiln of the potter Oastrius and related excavations at Little Munden Farm, Bricket Wood, *Hertfordshire Archaeol*, **5**, 109–56

Schweingruber, F H, 1982 *Mikroskopische Holzanatomie / Anatomie microscopique du bois / Microscopic wood anatomy*, Teufen, Switzerland, 2 edn

Scott, K, 1981 Mancetter village; a first century fort, *Trans Birmingham Warwickshire Archaeol Soc*, **91**, 1981 (1984), 1–24

Sellwood, L, 1984 Tribal boundaries as viewed from the perspective of numistic evidence, in B Cunliffe & D Miles (eds) *Aspects of the Iron Age in central southern England*, Oxford Univ Comm for Archaeol Monogr 2

Shiel, N, 1977 *The episode of Carausius and Allectus*, *BAR* **40**

—— 1978 Carausius et fratres sui, *Brit Numis J*, 7–11

Simon, H G, 1976 Terra Sigillata: Bilderschüsseln und Töpferstempel auf glatten Ware, in Das Kastell Munningen im Nordlinger Ries (Dietwulf Baatz) *Saalburg Jahrbuch*, **33**, 37–53

Simpson, G, 1957 Metallic black slip vases from Central Gaul with applied and moulded decoration, *Antiq J*, **37 (1 & 2)**, 29–42

—— 1965 A rare sherd from Ashfurlong, *Wolverton & District Archaeological Society Newsletter*, **9**, 7

Spain, G R, 1984 Romano-British water mills, *Archaeol Cantiana*, **100**, 1984 (1985), 101–28

Spence Bate, C, 1866 On the discovery of a Romano-British cemetery near Plymouth, *Archaeologia*, **40**, 500–9

Stanfield, J A & Simpson, G, 1958 *Central Gaulish potters*, London

Stead, I M, 1976 *Excavations at Winterton Roman villa, and other Roman sites in north Lincolnshire, 1958–1967*, Department of the Environment Archaeol Rep **9**

Stead, I M & Rigby, V, 1986 *Baldock. The excavation of a Roman and pre-Roman settlement 1968–72, Britannia Monogr Ser* **7**

—— 1989 *Verulamium: the King Harry Lane site*, HBMCE Archaeol Rep 12

Streeten, A D F, 1979 Appendices I–II, in D J Freke, The excavation of a 16th-century pottery kiln at Lower Peacock, Hartfield, East Sussex, 1977, *Post-Medieval Archaeol*, **13**, 114–20

Strong, D E, 1966 *Greek and Roman gold and silver plate*, London

Swan, V G, 1984 *The pottery kilns of Roman Britain*, Royal Commission Historic Monuments Suppl Ser 5

Symmonds, R, 1990 The problems of roughcast beakers and related colour-coated wares, *J Roman Pottery Stud*, **3**, 1–17

Taylor, S, 1969 Interim report on Roman Alcester, *W Midlands Archaeol News Sheet*, **12**, 16, 21–2, and 33

—— 1972 Interim report on Roman Alcester, *W Midlands Archaeol News Sheet*, **15**, 14

Terrisse, J R, 1968 *Les céramiques sigillées gallo-romaines des Martres-de-Veyre (Puy-de-Dôme)*, suppl to *Gallia*, **19**

Thompson, F H, 1958 A Romano-British pottery kiln at North Hykeham, Lincolnshire, *Antiq J*, **38**, 15–51

—— 1963 Two Romano-British Trumpet brooches with silver inlay, *Antiq J*, **43**, 289–90

Thornton, J H, 1973 Excavated shoes to 1600, *Trans Museums Assistants Group*, **12**, 2–13

Tomber, R, 1980 *The petrology of Severn Valley ware; kilns and selected distributions*, unpublished MSc thesis, University of Southampton

Trevor, J C, 1954 [unpublished — recalculated from Goodman & Morant 1940]

Trotter, M & Gleser, G C, 1952 Estimation of stature from long bones of American Whites and Negros, *Amer J Physical Anthropology*, new ser, **10**, 463–514

Trow, S D, 1988 Excavations at Ditches hillfort, North Cerney, Gloucestershire, 1982–3, *Trans Bristol Gloucestershire Archaeol Society*, **106**, 19–85

Vince, A, 1977 The medieval and post-medieval ceramic industry of the Malvern region: the study of ware and its distribution, in D P S Peacock *Pottery and early commerce: characterisation and trade in Roman and later ceramics*, London

von Mercklin, E, 1940 Römische Klappermessergriffe, *Festscrift Viktoru Hoffilleru*, 339–52, Zagreb

Wacher, J, 1971 Yorkshire towns in the fourth century, in R M Butler (ed) *Soldier and civilian in Roman Yorkshire*, Leicester

Wacher, J & McWhirr, A, 1982 *Cirencester excavations I. Early Roman occupation at Cirencester*, Cirencester

Walke, N & Walke, I, 1968 Reliefsigillata von Gauting, *Bericht der römisch-germanischen Kommission*, 46–7

Wallace, C & Webster, P, 1989 Jugs and lids in Black Burnished Ware, *J Roman Pottery Stud*, **2**, 88–91

Ward, S, 1990 *Excavations at Chester, the lesser medieval religious houses: sites investigated 1964–83*, Grosvenor Museum Archaeol excavation and survey rep 6, Chester

Webster, G, 1958 The Roman military advance under Ostorius Scapula, *Archaeol J*, **115**, 49–98

—— 1960 The discovery of a Roman fort at Waddon Hill, Stoke Abbott, 1959, *Proc Dorset Natural History Archaeol Soc*, **82**, 88–108

—— 1962 The Caves Inn milestone, *Trans Birmingham Warwickshire Archaeol Soc*, **80**, 1962 (1965), 82–3

—— 1963 Roman finds from Red Hill, near Oakengates, *Trans Shropshire Archaeol Soc*, **57 (2)**, 132–3

—— 1969 *Romano-British coarse pottery; a student's guide, CBA Res Rep* **6**

—— 1970 The military situations in Britain between AD 43 and 71, *Britannia*, **1**, 179–97

—— 1971 A hoard of Roman military equipment from Fremington Hagg, in R M Butler (ed) *Soldier and civilian in Roman Yorkshire*, Leicester, 107–26

—— 1981 Final report on the excavations of the Roman fort at Waddon Hill, Stoke Abbott, 1963–69, *Proc Dorset Natural History Archaeol Soc*, **101**, 51–90

Webster, G & Daniels, C, 1970 A street section at Wroxeter in 1966, *Trans Shropshire Archaeol Soc*, **59**, 15–23

Webster, G & Dudley, D, 1973 *The Roman conquest of Britain, AD 43–57*, London

Webster, P V, 1976 Severn Valley ware: a preliminary study *Trans Bristol Gloucestershire Archaeol Soc*, **94**, 1976 (1977), 18–46

—— 1993 Coarse pottery, in P J Casey, J L Davies & J Evans *Excavations at Segontium (Caernarfon) Roman fort, 1975–79, CBA Res Rep* **90**, 250–308

Webster, P V & Hartley, K F, 1973 The Romano-British pottery kilns near Wilderspool, *Archaeol J*, **130**, 77–103

Webster, T B L, 1969 *Monuments illustrating New Comedy*, London

Wedlake, W J, 1958 *Excavations at Camerton, Somerset*, privately printed, Camerton Excavation Club

—— 1982 *The excavation of the shrine of Apollo at Nettleton, Wiltshire 1956–1971*, Res Rep Comm Soc Antiq London **40**
Wheeler, R E M, 1923 *Segontium and the Roman occupation of Wales*, Y Cymmrodor, **33**, London
—— 1930 *London in Roman times*, London Museum Catalogues 3, London
—— 1943 *Maiden Castle, Dorset*, Res Rep Comm Soc Antiq London **12**
Wheeler, R E M & Wheeler, T V, 1928 The Roman amphitheatre at Caerleon, Monmouthshire, *Archaeologia*, **78**, 111–218
—— 1936 *Verulamium, a Belgic and two Roman cities*, Res Rep Comm Soc Antiq London **11**
Wickenden, N P, 1988 *Excavations at Great Dunmow, Essex: a Romano-British small town in the Trinovantian civitas*, East Anglian Archaeol 41
Wild, J P, 1970a *Textile Manufacture in the northern Roman provinces*, Cambridge
—— 1970b Button and loop fasteners in the Roman provinces, *Britannia*, **1**, 137–55
Williams, A, 1947 Canterbury Excavations in 1945, *Archaeol Cantiana*, **40**, 68–100
Williams, D F, 1979 The heavy mineral separation of ancient ceramics by centrifugation: a preliminary report, *Archaeometry*, **21**, 177–82
Williams, D F & Peacock, D P S, 1983 The importation of olive-oil into Roman Britain, in J M Blazquez & J Remesal (eds) *Produccion Y Comercio Del Aceite En La Antiguedad, Il Congresso*, Madrid, 263–80
Wilson, D R, 1973 Roman Britain in 1972, I. Sites explored, *Britannia*, **4**, 271–323
—— 1974 Roman Britain in 1974, I. Sites explored, *Britannia*, **5**, 397–460
Wright, E, forthcoming Quern report, in J Wacher & P R Wilson *Excavations at Catterick 1956–88*, HBMCE monogr
Wright, R P, 1952 The inscriptions, in Roman Britain in 1951, *J Roman Stud*, **42**, 86–109
—— 1966 Inscription no 52, *J Roman Stud*, **56**, 224
—— 1967 The inscriptions in Roman Britain in 1966, *J Roman Stud*, **56**, 174–210
Wright, T, 1872 *Uriconium: an historical account of the ancient Roman City and of the excavations made upon its site at Wroxeter in Shropshire*, London
Young, C J, 1977 *Oxfordshire Roman pottery*, *BAR* **43**
—— 1980 The late Roman fine wares, in B Rawes The Romano-British site at Wycomb, Andoversford, excavations 1969–1970, *Trans Bristol Gloucestershire Archaeol Soc*, **98** 1980 (1981), 41–6
Ypey, J, 1976–7 Mondharpen, *Antiek*, **11**, 209–31
Zadoks-Josephus Jitta, A N, Peters, W J T & Witteveen, A M, 1973 *Description of the collections in the Rijksmuseum G M Kam at Nijmegen. VII: the figural bronzes*, Nijmegen
Zadoks-Josephus Jitta, A N & Witteveen, A M, 1977 Roman bronze lunulae from the Netherlands, *Oudheidkundige Mededelingen uit het Rijksmuseum van Oudheden te Leiden*, **58**, 167–95
Zevi, F, 1966 Appunti sulle anfore romane, *Archaeolgia Classica*, **17**, 208–47
Zienkiewicz J D, 1986 *The legionary fortress baths at Caerleon II. The finds*, National Museum of Wales and Cadw, Cardiff

Index *by Lesley Adkins*

Main page references are given in bold. Entries which are shown in italics are page numbers on which figures and tables occur. As most of this report refers to Roman finds, there is no separate entry for Roman or Romano-British. The microfiche has not been indexed: full references to the microfiche are given throughout the text. References to Part 1 refer to the index in the accompanying volume

Table of Contents

Table of Contents

Table of Contents